European Yearbook of International Economic Law

Volume 11

The European Yearbook of International Economic Law (EYIEL) is a Springer-publication in the field of International Economic Law (IEL), a field increasingly emancipating itself from Public International Law scholarship and evolving into a fully-fledged academic discipline in its own right. With the yearbook, editors and publisher make a significant contribution to the development of this "new" discipline and provide an international source of reference of the highest possible quality.

The EYIEL covers all areas of IEL, in particular WTO Law, External Trade Law of major trading countries, important Regional Economic Integration agreements, International Competition Law, International Investment Regulation, International Monetary Law, International Intellectual Property Protection and International Tax Law. The yearbook consists of four major parts: (1) Part one brings together topical articles dealing with current legal problems in the different areas of IEL as described above, (2) part two provides analytical reports on the development of regional economic integration around the globe, (3) part three covers the developments inside the major international institutions engaged with IEL (WTO, IMF, Worldbank, G8 etc.), and (4) part four contains book reviews and documentation.

EYIEL publishes articles following a substantive review by the editors and external experts as appropriate.

The editors have published extensively in the field of IEL and European Law alike. They are supported by an international Advisory Board consisting of established scholars of the highest reputation.

More information about this series at http://www.springer.com/series/8165

Marc Bungenberg • Markus Krajewski •
Christian J. Tams • Jörg Philipp Terhechte •
Andreas R. Ziegler

Editors

European Yearbook of International Economic Law 2020

 Springer

Editors
Marc Bungenberg
Faculty of Law
Saarland University
Saarbrücken, Germany

Markus Krajewski
Faculty of Law
University of Erlangen-Nuremberg
Erlangen, Germany

Christian J. Tams
School of Law
University of Glasgow
Glasgow, UK

Jörg Philipp Terhechte
Competition and Regulation Institute
Leuphana University of Lüneburg
Lüneburg, Germany

Andreas R. Ziegler
Faculty of Law and Criminal Sciences
University of Lausanne
Lausanne, Switzerland

ISSN 2364-8392   ISSN 2364-8406   (electronic)
European Yearbook of International Economic Law
ISBN 978-3-030-59070-3   ISBN 978-3-030-59071-0   (eBook)
https://doi.org/10.1007/978-3-030-59071-0

This Springer imprint is published by the registered company Springer Nature Switzerland AG.
The registered company address is: Gewerbestrasse 11, 6330 Cham, Switzerland

Editorial

The European Yearbook of International Economic Law (EYIEL) celebrates its tenth anniversary in challenging times. COVID-19 and the political, economic and social consequences of the pandemic have significant effects on everyone—editing a yearbook is no difference. However, when the editors discussed the focus of Volume 11 of the EYIEL in the summer of 2019, no one could have anticipated what the following months would bring: Lockdowns, home schooling, work from home, digital teaching, online conferences and meetings—not to mention personal challenges in private and family lives. All this has affected not only the editors and the publisher, but more importantly also our authors. As a consequence, this Volume—which is the 2020 Volume—only appears in the spring of 2021. We take some comfort in the fact that many chapters of this Volume benefitted from the "online first" option which allows the publication of the electronic version of a chapter on Springer's website as soon as the chapter is finalised. Nevertheless, a yearbook should be more than the sum of its online chapters. We are, therefore, happy to present the Volume 11 of the EYIEL *as a book,* and a carefully curated one: a comprehensive collection of different chapters speaking to various aspects of a general theme.

The general theme of Volume 11 of the EYIEL addressed in Part I of the yearbook focuses on **rights and obligations of business entities under international economic law**. Businesses are the predominant actors in international trade, investment and financial exchanges. The editors thought that focusing on the role of businesses in international economic law, their rights and duties and the challenges they face in contemporary international law would be a suitable general topic for the EYIEL. Despite its current importance with regard to new laws on human rights due diligence of companies, the topic is not a new one: Transnational corporations have been the subject of debates in international law since the 1960s, and this year's general theme can, therefore, be considered an international economic law "classic".

One of the pioneers of this field is *Peter Muchlinski* who graciously accepted the editors' invitation to contribute the opening essay. Since the first edition of his seminal treatise "Multinational Enterprises and the Law" in 1995, he has been a staunch observer and a well-known expert commentator on corporations in international economic law. He reminds us that corporations are not just bearers of rights and duties under international law, but that they also significantly contribute to its creation. It seems, therefore, fitting that his distinguished essay assesses the changing nature of corporate influence on the making of international economic law. He shows that economic globalisation has increasingly empowered multinational enterprises (MNEs) as participants in the development of international economic law. While MNEs have traditionally influenced international economic law through lobbying and consultations, these traditional systems of influence have been complemented, and in some areas replaced, by multi-stakeholder initiatives (MSIs). In these initiatives, the participants, including MNEs, have a direct capacity to create new regulatory norms independently of states and international organisations. *Muchlinski* examines these MSIs through a series of illustrative examples taken from the field of corporate social responsibility and considers the implications of these developments for norm creation, and for effective and legitimate governance as well as future challenges posed to MSIs given the uncertain future of global economic regulation amid the rise of assertive economic nationalism.

Following the distinguished essay, the first two contributions address the field of business and **human rights** as one of the most controversial and current areas of duties of business actors. *Ondrej Svoboda* takes a look at the system of the Organisation for Economic Co-operation and Development (OECD) National Contact Points (NCPs) tasked with the implementation of the OECD Guidelines for Multinational Enterprises twenty years after the system was established and ten years after the last update of the OECD Guidelines. As the number and visibility of cases submitted to NCPs is increasing along with their ability to make a difference, their achievements call for close scrutiny and reflection. *Svoboda* also considers possible revisions that could keep the Guidelines and the NCP system at the forefront of international business and human rights standards and to address emerging challenges such as climate change.

Moving from the international arena to the domestic level, *Giesela Rühl* comments on the envisaged German Supply Chain Act from a choice of law and comparative legal perspective. Aiming at the protection of human rights in global supply chains, countries such as the United Kingdom, France and the Netherlands have introduced domestic legislation in this respect. Similar plans are underway in Germany with a proposed Supply Chain Act introducing mandatory human rights due diligence obligations. *Rühl* argues that any such Act will necessarily be limited in both its spatial and in its substantive reach and, therefore, recommends that Germany refrains from passing national legislation—and supports the adoption of a European instrument instead.

The next two chapters focus on the impact of regulations against **corruption** and businesses. *Cecily Rose* looks at the United Nations Convention Against Corruption (UNCAC) from an international economic law perspective. Like other transnational criminal law treaties, the UN Convention against Corruption seeks to ensure that domestic anti-corruption laws are relatively harmonised, and that states cooperate with each other in investigations, prosecutions, and asset recovery. Corruption is seen from a predominantly criminal law perspective. As *Rose* notes, this marks a contrast to the debates of the 1970s, when the problem of corruption was also approached within the framework of international economic law. Yet, efforts to regulate corrupt conduct through both a code of conduct and a treaty failed. When states returned to the issue of corruption in the 1990s, they focused on criminalisation and cooperation. Today, free trade agreements deal with corruption largely by cross reference to this substantial body of transnational criminal law treaties governing corruption.

Even though corruption is typically a bilateral act requiring the cooperation of both the private party and the State, both sides are not usually treated in the same way by international tribunals. In most cases, bribery—the act committed by the private actor—results in far more severe consequences than the behaviour of the respondent State. *Aloysius Llamzon* questions this approach on the basis of the law on state responsibility. Under the International Law Commission Articles on State Responsibility (ILC Articles), it is no excuse for a State to say that its public officials were acting in excess of authority or contrary to instructions—under Article 7, *ultra vires* acts of public officials are always attributable to the State. Based on this, *Llamzon* argues that when treaty and customary international law on the consequences of corruption are carefully considered, no specific rule of treaty or customary international law exists that can justify the implicit exemption of States from the consequences of accepting bribery. He claims that a system that seeks to hold accountable both parties to a corrupt transaction—viz. the private investor and the State—would be a more durable way to enhance arbitration as a tool for preventing corruption in foreign investment.

This approach leads seamlessly to the subsequent section on **international investment law**. *Barnali Choudhury* argues that issues of human rights must be given greater consideration in international investment treaties. Businesses are being asked to give greater attention to human rights matters in almost every area apart from international investment treaties. To ensure international investment law aligns with progress in other areas of the law, international investment law must provide a role for human rights. According to *Choudhury,* this can be achieved *inter alia* through independent provisions on human rights, investor obligations, and carveouts. Such an approach would be specifically important in light of the fact that COVID-19 highlighted the pre-existing weaknesses in the social structure that leave vulnerable members of society at risk, reinforcing the importance of states being able to protect their nationals' human rights.

Taking a different angle, *Patricia Wiater* assesses the rights of action of business entities in regional economic systems. She reminds us that direct and state-independent rights of action of private business entities are still exceptional in international economic law and are limited to a small number of regional economic systems. Based on the examples of the European Union (EU), the European Economic Area (EEA), the East African Community (EAC), the Southern African Development Community (SADC), the Economic Community of West African States (ECOWAS) and the Caribbean Community (CARICOM), *Wiater* examines the *status quo* of the procedural empowerment of business entities under regional integration frameworks. She shows that both the contracting states and the regional economic courts engaged in interpreting individual rights of action attribute different functions to the role of business entities as litigants: They include the effectiveness of law enforcement in the integration process by means of court proceedings and the guarantee of freedom from burdensome interventions in the legal or economic positions of a company.

International security law is typically not understood as part of international economic law. Yet, two subfields of security law nevertheless have a significant impact on business entities. *Katerina Galai* illustrates this by assessing the current regulation of private military companies (PMCs). These entities dispose of vast resources and perform various security functions from strategy and logistics to civilian detention and combat training. Although PMCs are regulated by the industry internationally and guided by performance standards, the effectiveness of PMC regulation is often questioned. *Galai,* therefore, examines the full landscape of PMC regulation, discussing rule-making and standard-setting, as well as enforcement and the capacity to establish accountability for misconduct. Identifying particular challenges posed by PMCs and limitations of different bodies of law that attempt to regulate them, she proposes adjustments that would limit the possibility of impunity.

Dual-use export controls are probably among the better-known intersections between international economic law and international security. *Machiko Kanetake* looks at these measures and recent challenges to the multilateral regime regulating them. International standard-setting in the field of export control has been shaped by the presence of non-binding yet effective multilateral regimes. A central element is the Wassenaar Arrangement concerning export controls for conventional arms as well as for dual-use goods and technologies. However, multilateralism in the context of dual-use export control has been subject to various political and normative challenges as numerous attempts to circumvent the Wassenaar Arrangement based exclusively on national security narratives indicate. The multilateral regime has also been fundamentally challenged by human rights narratives. *Kanetake* sheds light on these dual challenges through the analysis of export controls over digital and other so-called emerging technologies.

Part II of the EYIEL addresses **current challenges, development and events** in European and international economic law. *Gijs Berends* assesses the European Parliament and its Role in EU Trade Policy after the May 2019 elections, looking at the formal and informal powers of the European Parliament for the instruments of EU trade policy and asking whether the new legislature is likely to change trade policy in the coming five years.

Another development that has attracted a lot of political and scholarly attention in recent years is the WTO crisis. *Jelena Bäumler* traces developments inside as well as outside the WTO with a view to assessing the magnitude of the crisis. She argues that while certain developments inside the WTO must be considered with developments taking place outside of the WTO to understand the crisis.

Elisabeth Bürgi Bonanomi and *Theresa Tribaldos* ask what can be learned from the European Free Trade Area (EFTA)-Indonesian Agreement for EU/EFTA-

Mercado Común del Sur (Mercosur) agreements regarding process and production methods (PPM)-based trade measures to promote sustainable farming systems. They suggest that the primary concern regarding PPMs is not whether, but *how* these can be designed to avoid impinging on fundamental principles of international economic law, and make some recommendations for the optimal design of nuanced, sustainability-oriented trade rules.

Looking at other aspects of inter-regional integration, *Alberto do Amaral Junior* and *Marina Martins Martes* analyse the Mercosur-EU Free Trade Agreement (FTA) and its obligation to implement the Paris Agreement on Climate Change. Adopting a Brazilian perspective, they argue that a breach of environmental obligations would have serious political effects on the implementation of the FTA as a whole.

As in previous years, the final section of the Yearbook—Part III—comments on **current scholarship** in international economic law, with a significant focus on recent works on international investment law: *Andreas Kulick* reviews Rodrigo Polanco's "The Return of the Home State to Investor-State Disputes" (CUP 2019). *Joanna Dingwall* takes a look at "Maritime Disputes and International Law—Disputed Waters and Seabed Resources in Asia and Europe" by Constantinos Yiallourides (Routledge 2019). Martin Jarrett's "Contributory Fault and Investor Misconduct in Investment Arbitration" (CUP 2019) is reviewed by *Markus P. Beham*. *Julian Scheu* reflects on "State Responsibility, Climate Change and Human Rights under International Law" (Hart 2019) by Margaretha Wewerinke-Singh while *Silvia Steininger* assesses Prabhash Ranjan's "India and Bilateral Investment Treaties—Refusal, Acceptance, Backlash" (OUP 2019). Last but not least, our co-editor Christian J. Tams comments on "The ICSID Convention, Regulations and Rules: A Practical Commentary" (Elgar 2019) by Julien Fouret, Rémy Gerbay and Gloria M. Alvarez.

While COVID19 has prevented a proper celebration of the Yearbook's tenth anniversary (e.g. with a symposium or academic event), the editors have decided to mark the occasion by enlarging the editorial board. We are extremely happy and proud to announce that three outstanding and well-known experts will join the editorial board in 2021 and increase the diversity of themes and perspectives on international economic law represented on it: *Christina Binder* (Bundeswehr University Munich) will bring her expertise on international human rights law, rights of indigenous peoples and investment law to the yearbook. *Giesela Rühl* (Humboldt University of Berlin), a leading scholar in European and international private and civil procedural law as well as of comparative law and economic analysis of law, will help us broaden the focus of the yearbook to cover matters of private international economic law. With her profound knowledge in international trade law, environmental law and sustainable development, *Jelena Bäumler* (Leuphana University Lüneburg) will ensure that the yearbook will not lose sight of the broader context in which international economic law is situated and the challenges it faces with regard to global sustainable governance. With these three wonderful colleagues on board, we are very confident that EYIEL's second decade will be as fruitful and stimulating as the first. Once again: Welcome Christina, Giesela and Jelena!

The Editors

Saarbrücken, Germany   Marc Bungenberg
Erlangen, Germany   Markus Krajewski
Glasgow, UK   Christian J. Tams
Lüneburg, Germany   Jörg Philipp Terhechte
Lausanne, Switzerland   Andreas R. Ziegler
April 2021

Contents

Part I
Rights and Obligations of Business Entities under International Economic Law

The Changing Nature of Corporate Influence in the Making of International Economic Law: Towards "Multistakeholderism"

Peter Muchlinski

Contents

Abstract This contribution considers the influence of multinational enterprises (MNEs) in the development of international economic law (IEL) and the institutional contexts in which this is exercised. Economic globalisation has increasingly empowered MNEs as participants in the development of IEL. Greater corporate power has arisen from increasingly market-based state and intergovernmental organisation (IGO) policies, the expertise and technical knowledge possessed by firms and the concurrent development of transnational commercial and technical networks requiring new forms of regulation to operate successfully. MNEs have traditionally influenced IEL through lobbying and consultations before IGOs, within certain procedural boundaries based on the multilateral, state-focused, nature of IGOs. In more recent years, traditional IGO-based systems of influence have been complemented, and in some areas replaced, by multi-stakeholder initiatives (MSIs). Their core characteristic is the involvement of "stakeholders", global actors who have a "stake" in an issue, who come together to work out a collaborative solution to issues of mutual concern. In MSIs the participants, including MNEs, have a direct capacity to create new regulatory norms independently of states and IGOs. MSIs will be examined through a series of illustrative examples taken from the field of corporate social responsibility. The implications of these developments for norm creation, and for effective and legitimate governance, will be considered. The contribution will end by briefly discussing the future challenges posed to MSIs

P. Muchlinski (✉)
The School of Law, SOAS, University of London, London, UK
e-mail: pm29@soas.ac.uk

© Springer Nature Switzerland AG 2021
M. Bungenberg et al. (eds.), *European Yearbook of International Economic Law 2020*,
European Yearbook of International Economic Law (2022) 11: 3–30,
https://doi.org/10.1007/8165_2020_52, Published online: 29 January 2021

3

given the uncertain future of global economic regulation amid the rise of assertive economic nationalism.

1   Introduction

This contribution asks how multinational enterprises impact on the content of international economic law. International non-state actors, including MNEs, have always been influential in the development of international law.[1] In recent decades, the process of economic globalisation has facilitated corporate trade and investment, in line with the liberal market policies that have dominated since the early 1980s, benefitting MNEs through enhanced market access and business opportunities.[2] It has also increasingly empowered MNEs, and business interests more generally, as participants in the development of standards and norms in IEL, given the expertise and technical knowledge possessed by firms and the development of transnational commercial and technical networks requiring new forms of regulation to operate successfully.[3] In recent years the liberal model of IEL has been challenged on the basis of calls for greater corporate social responsibility and accountability.[4] Perhaps paradoxically, as calls for greater corporate accountability have grown, so has corporate involvement in the norm creating process.

By way of introduction, Sect. 2 considers how economic globalisation has changed the regulatory model of IEL and how this has affected the nature, and institutional context, of corporate influence and power. MNEs have traditionally influenced IEL norms through lobbying and consultations before intergovernmental organisations, within certain procedural boundaries based on their multilateral, state-focused, nature. Examples of such arrangements, and their resulting problems, will be discussed in Sect. 3. In more recent years, traditional IGO-based systems of influence have been complemented, and in some areas replaced, by multi-stakeholder initiatives. These range from informal "round-tables" to sophisticated international organisations such as the International Standards Organisation (ISO) which performs regulatory functions outside the multilateral framework of IGOs. The core characteristic of MSIs is the involvement of "stakeholders", global actors who have a "stake" in an issue, who come together to work out a collaborative

---

[1]See generally the contributions in Noortmann and Ryngaert (2010). See also Noortmann et al. (2015) and Ryngaert (2016). See also Arato (2015), who suggests that corporate actors make IEL through the conclusion of investment contracts which acquire the force of law through investor-state dispute settlement (ISDS) conducted before arbitral tribunals, and Stephan (2011), who discusses the impact of private non-state actors in the development of international law.

[2]See further Muchlinski (2011, 2012).

[3]See Pauwelyn et al. (2012), pp. 501–505.

[4]See Muchlinski (2011) and (2012).

solution to issues of mutual concern.[5] MSIs will be examined through a series of illustrative examples, taken from the field of corporate social responsibility, in Sect. 4. The implications of these developments for IEL norm creation and for effective and legitimate governance will be considered. The contribution will end with Sect. 5 briefly discussing the future challenges posed to MSIs given the uncertain future of global economic regulation amid the recent rise of assertive economic nationalism.

2 The Liberal Model of International Economic Law and Its Regulation

IEL rests on liberal economic foundations.[6] Initially this was a form of "embedded liberalism".[7] The reconstruction of the post-World War II economy involved the partial abandonment of free trade through a managed multilateral international economic system where market forces would be subjected to state intervention aimed at achieving social goals such as full employment, resulting in tolerance for national policies favouring such objectives. It relied heavily on US leadership, which encouraged continued trade negotiations under the General Agreement on Tariffs and Trade (GATT) and coordination of financial policies through the World Bank and the International Monetary Fund (IMF) to protect national balance-of-payments and stability. This system was increasingly fraught with problems leading to the ending of the US dollar's convertibility into gold in 1971 and the rise of non-tariff barriers to trade.[8]

By the 1970s critical voices advocated the revival of liberal market policies, both at the domestic and international levels, leading to a major shift in thinking, especially in the US and UK, towards what has come to be called "neoliberalism".[9] "Neoliberalism" is a very wide term and its recent overuse has limited its explanatory power. However, it serves as a useful shorthand for certain policies associated with

---

[5]See Gleckmann (2018), Preface para. xiii. See also Raymond and Denardis (2015), p. 574, who assert, "multistakeholderism entails two or more classes of actors engaged in a common governance enterprise concerning issues they regard as public in nature and characterized by polyarchic authority relations constituted by procedural rules." Polyarchy, "entails situations where authority is distributed among a number of actors" Raymond and Denardis (2015), p. 580.

[6]This section draws upon Muchlinski (2021), ch. 3 sec. 3(b).

[7]See Ruggie (1982, 1992) and Wilkinson (2000).

[8]See Kollen Ghizoni S, Nixon Ends Convertibility of US Dollars to Gold and Announces Wage/Price Controls, Federal Reserve History, August 1971, https://www.federalreservehistory.org/essays/gold_convertibility_ends?view=print (last accessed 21 August 2020); Ray (1987).

[9]See further Slobodian (2018), Harvey (2007) and Eagleton-Price (2016); Metcalfe S, Neoliberalism: the idea that swallowed the world, The Guardian, 17 August 2017 https://www.theguardian.com/news/2017/aug/18/neoliberalism-the-idea-that-changed-the-world (last accessed 21 August 2020). For a perspective doubting the value of the term see Venugopal (2015). For a useful introduction to "neo-classical" or "neo-liberal" theories of international economic organisation see Sally (1998).

liberalised markets. Promoted by corporate influence, "neoliberalism" has been legitimated by appeals to freedom, competitiveness, efficiency and individual fulfilment through consumerism as a form of discursive power shaping the boundaries of regulatory discourse since the 1980s.[10]

"Neoliberalism" promotes an increasingly integrated global economy, where barriers to trade and investment fall, and where the state is reinvented as the "market-state" a source of facilitative rules creating an economic space in which integrated, efficient global production chains emerge.[11] It assumes that the market allocates resources most efficiently, requiring a facilitative regulatory order leading to an "open" international economy overseen by global rules, promulgated by IGOs which constrain state rights to regulate in ways that undermine global market freedom.[12]

The MNE is an important "medium for integrating and organising resource utilisation on a global scale".[13] It integrates different national economies, with different comparative advantages in skills, labour, raw materials and know-how, through the international division of labour within the enterprise and through the global production and supply chains that MNEs establish. Crucial to this is a world economy in which MNEs are free to set up affiliates whenever and wherever they wish, to engage in uninhibited intra-firm trade, and trade with third parties.

The shift from "embedded liberalism" to "neoliberalism" involves a shift in regulatory models. The regime of IEL created after World War II was a "public law" model of regulation.[14] At the domestic level states developed rules facilitating the incorporation of businesses and the control of their operations. At the international level rules evolved to regulate state powers in the economic sphere and, thereby, to achieve a degree of harmonisation between domestic systems in areas that affect international trade and investment.

In a "public law" model of regulation, corporations, as private law actors, lack legal personality in international law and so cannot directly create international legal obligations, though, on a functional basis, they may be the beneficiaries of rights and holders of obligations under specific treaty regimes.[15] Such regimes may be the outcome of corporate influence, but this is not necessarily the case. For example, while some argue that international investment law is a form of direct MNE-based lawmaking,[16] it is better seen as a state-sponsored system of protection from the

---

[10] See Fuchs (2007), ch. 6.

[11] "Market-state" denotes a state that outsources public functions to private providers, uses public–private partnerships to deliver public services and infrastructure, privatises public enterprises, and liberalises and deregulates markets and firms. See further Crouch (2004) and Crouch (2011).

[12] See further Slobodian (2018).

[13] See Hood and Young (1979), p. 327.

[14] See Cata Backer (2008).

[15] See Muchlinski P, Corporations in International Law, Max Planck Encyclopaedia of International Law, last updated June 2014, https://opil.ouplaw.com/view/10.1093/law:epil/9780199231690/law-9780199231690-e1513 (last accessed 21 August 2020), para. 6–9.

[16] See Arato (2015).

costs of regulatory compliance for foreign investors and, in more recent agreements, market-access facilitation inspired by the rise of the open-market model of international economic governance.[17] Equally, the establishment of the International Centre for Settlement of Investment Disputes (ICSID) in 1966 was not the result of corporate lobbying or pressure, but an institutional initiative on the part of the World Bank, as explained in Sect. 3.

The rise of the liberal "market-state" and the shift towards economic globalisation since the 1980s has changed the "public law" model of IEL. As the state cedes functions hitherto reserved for the public sphere to private undertakings, such as the provision of public services and utilities, the power of private firms to shape the regulatory environment increases. Participating firms will negotiate the contractual forms and institutional structures of the resulting public-private partnerships and privatised firms.[18] Corporate power is further enhanced by the possession of technical knowledge and innovative capacity, empowering firms to address specific economic and technological challenges. Furthermore, MNEs in particular have a significant degree of political power. Stephen Wilks is of the opinion that the political power of a corporation is measured according to the possession of sufficient resources, motivation and opportunity to pursue political goals and capacity to participate in the political process. These factors will favour firms with large size and resources, market share and international reach.[19] Small and medium sized enterprises (SMEs), and purely domestic corporations, are unlikely to share such advantages.

The mix of economic opportunities created by the liberal market order, and the possession of technical skills, knowledge and political power have privileged MNEs as influential actors. However, the vacating of regulatory space to non-state actors through the rise of the "market-state", while favouring the most powerful multinational firms, has also empowered social issue oriented non-governmental organisations (NGOs) as alternative voices to MNEs in the construction of transnational political and regulatory discourse.[20] Doris Fuchs notes that corporate resources give an advantage in developing, "the density of messages, establishing scientific evidence and identifying and communicating persuasive arguments" but cannot guarantee the maintenance of business's discursive power in the face of possibly changing societal norms and perceptions of business legitimacy.[21]

The shift towards market-oriented policies has also downgraded the capacity of IGOs to set regulatory standards furthering non-market goals.[22] During the 1980s and early 1990s the United Nations (UN) system initiated a series of high-level

---

[17]See for an historical perspective linking investment protection treaties to "neoliberal" ideas, Slobodian (2018), pp. 136–143.

[18]See further Likosky (2005, 2006).

[19]Wilks (2013), pp. 37–40. See further Fuchs (2007), ch. 3, 6. See also Ruggie (2018).

[20]See further Yaziji and Doh (2009).

[21]Fuchs (2007), p. 154.

[22]See Gleckmann (2018), pp. 30–33 on which this paragraph draws.

conferences on matters highlighted by the rise of globalisation ranging from the role of women, housing, poverty, the environment, population and development. These initiatives produced little change in international public policy as they coincided with the rise of increasing scepticism among market-oriented UN member states over providing public funding for such programmes. In the long-term this encouraged a non-regulatory, voluntary, approach to control of corporate behaviour, and was a significant factor in the development of MSIs.

Corporate actors may affect the development of IEL through indirect and direct means, representing a distinction between the power to influence official lawmakers and the capacity to make laws autonomously, a function hitherto reserved exclusively to states under the "public law" model of regulation. To date indirect means of influencing norm development have come from corporate lobbying and consultations within IGOs, based on rules covering the accreditation of non-state actors to participate in their deliberations. As will be shown in Sect. 3, some IGOs have developed more formal multi-stakeholder approaches to this process, but generally stopping short of giving MNEs, and other non-state actors, rights to vote or otherwise formally endorse new norms. In addition to participation as accredited delegates to IGOs, MNEs, and other non-state actors, have found a new forum for debating and adopting IEL norms by way of MSIs that operate outside traditional IGO structures. These involve a range of objectives from policy-oriented multi-stakeholder groups, standard-setting organisations and project-oriented groups. MSIs will be discussed by reference to examples of each type of group in Sect. 4.

3 Corporate Influence and Lobbying Before Intergovernmental Organisations

Corporate lobbying is well researched at the domestic level, especially in the US context.[23] It is less well understood at the international level. Early literature on MNE-state relations focused on the capacity of MNEs to set themselves outside the territorial control of states but was silent on the impact of MNEs on specific policy outcomes.[24] Early research on corporate lobbying focused on multilateral environmental agreements. The result was more complex than the MNE-state relations

---

[23]This is in part due to the transparency required under the US Lobbying Disclosure Act 1995 as amended (2 U.S.C. §1601, et seq.); see Straus J, The Lobbying Disclosure Act at 20: Analysis and Issues for Congress, Congressional Research Service 7-5700, 1 December 2015, https://fas.org/sgp/crs/misc/R44292.pdf (last accessed 21 August 2020). The UK introduced a similar law in 2014: Transparency of Lobbying, Non-party Campaigning and Trade Union Administration Act 2014 c. 4, http://www.legislation.gov.uk/ukpga/2014/4 (last accessed 21 August 2020). See further OECD, Principles for Transparency and Integrity in Lobbying, https://www.oecd.org/gov/ethics/oecdprinciplesfortransparencyandintegrityinlobbying.htm (last accessed 21 August 2020).

[24]See e.g. Vernon (1973), Strange (1994) and Stopford et al. (1991). For a review of more recent contributions to this debate see Ougaard (2008).

literature suggested. Though corporate actors have significant power, this is coordinated by other interest groups such as environmental NGOs.[25] Corporate lobbying has also been studied in trade policy with a focus on influence over industry specific outcomes such as the protection of sectors vulnerable to international competition and liberalising sectors for firms enjoying a competitive advantage therein.[26] In recent years lobbying coalitions of firms joined through global production chains led by producer and/or retailer MNEs have pressed for the adoption of preferential trade agreements.[27] More recent research has shown the importance of individual firm characteristics as a variable in predicting the degree of trade lobbying that a firm may undertake, the size and international engagement of the firm being decisive factors in their promotion of trade and investment liberalisation.[28] This finding is confirmed in relation to corporate lobbying over foreign policy where, again, the largest and most multinational firms are the main source of lobbying expenditures for promoting market opening policies.[29]

On investment rules, MNEs are most likely to lobby for investment protection and intellectual property protection provisions in international economic agreements.[30] They are among the major proponents of bilateral investment treaties (BITs) and of supranational dispute settlement bodies such as ICSID.[31] However, this should be seen in a historical context. The founding of ICSID was not a result of corporate lobbying, but of the work of World Bank officials in the 1960s, who designed the ICSID Convention in the absence of any generally articulated desire on the part of international business for international investor-state arbitration.[32] Since then, broader factors have contributed to the popularity of investor-state dispute settlement (ISDS) before ICSID, and other arbitral bodies, including increased FDI flows and a larger number of BITs now in existence, creating more opportunities for treaty related disputes, coupled with the "demonstration effect" caused by large, successful, claims, creating increased demand for ISDS. This is reinforced by a

---

[25] See e.g. Rowlands (2001) and Falkner (2003).

[26] Robert-Nicoud F and Baldwin R, Entry and Asymmetric Lobbying: Why Governments Pick Losers, CEP Discussion Paper No. 791, May 2007, http://eprints.lse.ac.uk/19726/1/Entry_and_ Asymmetric_Lobbying_Why_Governments_Pick_Losers.pdf (last accessed 21 August 2020).

[27] Manger (2012).

[28] Kim and Osgood (2019).

[29] Kim I and Miller H, Multinational Corporations and their Influence Through Lobbying on Foreign Policy, Brookings Institution, 2 December 2019, https://www.brookings.edu/wp-content/ uploads/2019/12/Kim_Milner_manuscript.pdf (last accessed 21 August 2020).

[30] Ibid, p. 6.

[31] Ibid.

[32] See further St John (2018), ch. 4–5, who notes at pp. 111–117 that World Bank officials had a choice of foreign investment promotion policies between a multilateral code, international investment insurance and a dispute settlement body. They dismissed a multilateral code as carrying too much political risk. Developing countries would believe it was biased against them while developed countries would see any compromise code as too weak. Dispute settlement was preferred mainly on the grounds of lower cost and ease of implementation as compared to investment insurance.

constituency of professional interests, led by major transnational law firms, that profit from ISDS and whose staff act as principal counsel, and often as arbitrators, in ISDS cases.[33] Accordingly, the rise in investor-state arbitration is not an inevitable consequence of the ICSID Convention, though it is facilitated through it, but of these other factors many of which would have been unforeseeable to the drafters, but which have come together in the early twenty-first century to promote ISDS.

Corporate lobbying at the international level lacks organised legal regulation, as compared to the domestic level.[34] It is, nonetheless, a significant factor in international rule making. Corporate input into international regulatory policy choices is desirable as corporations will have substantive knowledge and expertise relevant to the solution of international policy issues. Corporate actors are encouraged to offer advice and consultation to IGOs on a regular basis.[35] On the other hand, corporate contributions pose a number of potential dangers including the risk of undue influence, regulatory capture and other forms of subverting the regulatory process in the name of profit.[36] As Durkee concludes,

> [p]erhaps as a result of that essential ambivalence, there is no consistent regulatory response to business lobbying across international institutions, either within or outside of the UN.[37]

Representatives of special interests usually enter the deliberations of IGOs through a system of NGO accreditation. The UN Economic and Social Council (ECOSOC) system is the most established one.[38] This covers a number of UN specialised agencies dealing with economic and social issues. The accreditation system allows NGOs, meeting the criteria for accreditation, to attend meetings as observers, offer their views both orally and in writing, organise side events, and to network and lobby. However, NGOs have no votes over resolutions or other policy decisions. Accreditation is limited to NGOs whose principal source of income is from membership subscriptions, thus excluding individual corporations.[39] Business interests have used overt forms of representation, for example through accredited trade associations, and covert forms of representation, through front organisations purporting to be grass roots NGOs but acting on behalf of business interests.[40] This has led to some challenging situations.

---

[33]See St John (2018), p. 22 and ch. 8; and see further van Harten (2007).

[34]On which see further Durkee (2018).

[35]Ibid., p. 1750.

[36]Ibid.

[37]Ibid.

[38]See ECOSOC, Introduction to ECOSOC Consultative Status, http://csonet.org/index.php?menu=30 (last accessed 21 August 2020) and ECOSOC, Res. 1996/31, 24 July 1996, http://csonet.org/content/documents/199631.pdf (last accessed 21 August 2020). See further United Nations, Working with ECOSOC: an NGOs Guide to Consultative Status, 2018, http://csonet.org/index.php?menu=134 (last accessed 21 August 2020).

[39]ECOSOC, Res. 1996/31, 24 July 1996, http://csonet.org/content/documents/199631.pdf (last accessed 21 August 2020), para 13.

[40]Durkee (2018), pp. 1766–1774.

For example, the World Health Organisation (WHO) revised its rules for engagement with non-state actors in 2016 following its experience with tobacco association infiltration.[41] Tobacco firms, including Philip Morris and British American Tobacco, took over the International Tobacco Growers Association, a body representing tobacco farmers in developing countries, to further their campaign against WHO tobacco control activities.[42] In light of this experience, the revised WHO Framework of Engagement with Non-State Actors (the Framework) stresses the need for openness and transparency when a non-state actor seeks accreditation.[43] The Framework also makes a distinction between "private sector entities" and other NGOs, the former being defined as

> commercial enterprises, that is to say businesses that are intended to make a profit for their owners. The term also refers to entities that represent, or are governed or controlled by, private sector entities. This group includes (but is not limited to) business associations representing commercial enterprises, entities not "at arm's length" from their commercial sponsors, and partially or fully State-owned commercial enterprises acting like private sector entities.[44]

The WHO will undertake a due diligence analysis of such a body to avoid conflicts of interest that could undermine its policy functions.[45] In addition, paragraph 44 of the Framework asserts that, "WHO does not engage with the tobacco industry or non-State actors that work to further the interests of the tobacco industry. WHO also does not engage with the arms industry." The WHO response to tobacco industry interference is a special case. Other IGOs have followed different routes.

For example, the International Labour Organisation (ILO) explicitly includes business representatives within its "tripartite" decision-making structure alongside government and trade union representatives. The ILO has adopted International Labour Conventions involving a consensus between governmental, labour and business representatives.[46] By contrast the Food and Agriculture Organisation (FAO) expressly excludes private sector food producers from its definition of civil

---

[41]WHO, Framework of Engagement with Non-State Actors, WHA69.10 Agenda item 11.3, 28 May 2016, https://apps.who.int/gb/ebwha/pdf_files/wha69/a69_r10-en.pdf (last accessed 21 August 2020); Durkee (2018), pp. 1806–1809.

[42]See, for the various methods used to undermine the WHO initiatives during the 1990s, Committee of Experts on Tobacco Industry, Tobacco Company Strategies to Undermine Tobacco Control Activities at the World Health Organisation, July 2000, https://perma.cc/9WKS-5N3X (last accessed 21 August 2020).

[43]WHO, Framework of Engagement with Non-State Actors, 28 May 2016, https://apps.who.int/gb/ebwha/pdf_files/wha69/a69_r10-en.pdf (last accessed 21 August 2020), para. 37–43.

[44]Ibid para. 10.

[45]Ibid para. 13.

[46]By Article 3(1) of the ILO Constitution, Member States are entitled to send four representatives: two governmental representatives and, by agreement, one each from the most representative employers and trade union organisations in the country. See further ILO, Rules of the Game: A brief introduction to International Labour Standards, 2014 http://www.ilo.org/wcmsp5/groups/public/%2D%2D-ed_norm/%2D%2D-normes/documents/publication/wcms_318141.pdf (last accessed 21 August 2020), pp. 14–20; Servais (2017), ch. 3; Hepple (2005), ch. 2.

society organisations (CSOs) entitled to accreditation. Such bodies are to be included in the FAOs private sector partnership strategy unless, on a case-by-case basis, they can be included in the non-profit definition of a CSO.[47] The IMF engages in informal consultations with private sector entities without a formal accreditation or procedural mechanism, while the UN Commission on International Trade Law (UNCITRAL), with its focus on the development of harmonised international trade law standards, has traditionally included business representatives within its discussions.[48]

The UN Conference on Trade and Development (UNCTAD) encourages CSO participation through observer status which is given at the prerogative of the member states under an autonomous UNCTAD procedure.[49] Current CSOs enjoying observer status range widely and include development related bodies, chambers of commerce, trade unions, and specialised professional associations in specific sectors such as trade, sustainable development, transport, banking, insurance, environment and commodities.[50] CSOs are granted status in two different categories depending on their areas of work. General observer status is reserved for organisations possessing expertise allowing participation in the public meetings of all the inter-governmental bodies of UNCTAD. Special observer status is granted to organisa-tions which have a special area of competence. Their representatives are entitled to participate in UNCTAD public meetings on specific matters within their compe-tence. There are currently 241 CSOs participating in the activities of UNCTAD.[51]

The World Trade Organisation (WTO) has made efforts over the years to accommodate NGOs, including trade representatives, within its deliberations. The legal basis for the WTO's rules for engagement with NGOs is Article V (2) of the Marrakesh Agreement Establishing the WTO:

---

[47] See FAO, Strategy for Partnerships with Civil Society Organisations, 2013, http://www.fao.org/3/a-i3443e.pdf (last accessed 21 August 2020), pp. 3 and 8. See also FAO, Strategy for Partnerships with the Private Sector, 2013, http://www.fao.org/3/a-i3444e.pdf (last accessed 23 August 2020), which introduces a risk assessment strategy to avoid potential conflicts of interest with private sector partners.

[48] For detailed discussion see Durkee (2018), pp. 1812–1817. See further IMF, Civil Society and the IMF, https://www.imf.org/en/About/Partners/civil-society (last accessed 21 August 2020). In 2007 France criticised the informal working methods of UNCITRAL see UNCITRAL, France's Obser-vations on UNCITRAL's working methods, UN Doc. A/CN.9/635, 24 May 2007, https://undocs.org/en/A/CN.9/635 (last accessed 21 August 2020).

[49] UNCTAD, UNCTAD and Civil Society, https://unctad.org/en/Pages/About%20UNCTAD/UNCTAD%20And%20Civil%20Society/UNCTAD-And-Civil-Society.aspx (last accessed 21 August 2020). The procedure is governed by rule 77 of the rules of procedure of the Trade and Development Board, and its Decisions 43 (VII) and 507 (EX–53).

[50] UNCTAD, Organisations with Observer Status, https://unctad.org/en/Pages/About%20UNCTAD/UNCTAD%20And%20Civil%20Society/NGOs-IGOs-with-observer-status.aspx (last accessed 21 August 2020).

[51] See UNCTAD, List of non-governmental organizations participating in the activities of UNCTAD, UN Doc. TD/B/NGO/LIST/26, 16 December 2019, https://unctad.org/meetings/en/SessionalDocuments/tdngolistd26_en.pdf (last accessed 21 August 2020).

The General Council may make appropriate arrangements for consultations and cooperation with non-governmental organizations concerned with matters related to those of the WTO.[52]

This leaves non-state actor participation in the hands of the members. Only in recent years has a basic system of accreditation been established.[53] Previously, NGOs had to register for specific WTO meetings, giving rise to criticism that there was no way of granting permanent accreditation. The WTO responded by allowing Geneva-based NGOs to request a WTO-NGO badge, valid for 1 year giving,

access to the WTO building and facilitates participation in events that are public or dedicated to NGOs, such as WTO Secretariat briefings.[54]

Each application is considered on an individual basis without guaranteed authorisation. No distinction is made between non-business and business-NGOs. Apart from attending specific meetings, there are two principal methods for NGOs to have an input: participation in the annual WTO Public Forum and the submission of position papers, making non-business and business NGO involvement rather limited. That said, is there significant corporate lobbying behind the scenes?

It is clear that business interests were significantly involved in the Uruguay Round negotiations which led to the creation of the WTO. New agreements in services (General Agreement on Trade in Services; GATS), trade related intellectual property measures (Agreement on Trade-Related Aspects of Intellectual Property Rights; TRIPS) and trade related investment measures (Agreement on Trade-Related Investment Measures; TRIMS) were all influenced by organised industry sector lobbies working through their respective nation states and the EU.[55] Also significant is the use of the WTO dispute settlement mechanism by member states to further national corporate interests. For example, in the *Bananas* case, the US, and other Central and Latin American members, argued that market access into the EU by vertically integrated US MNEs, which produced bananas in these Central and Latin American countries for worldwide export, was impeded by a discriminatory scheme of preferential treatment for European based banana distributors introduced in 1993.[56] Corporate interests lobbied their respective governments for support. Three firms, Geest, Fyffes and Jamaica Producers, allied with the Caribbean Banana

---

[52]WTO, Marrakesh Agreement Establishing the WTO, https://www.wto.org/english/docs_e/legal_e/04-wto_e.htm (last accessed 21 August 2020).

[53]On the development of WTO engagement with NGOs see Perez-Esteve M, WTO rules and practices for transparency and engagement with civil society organizations, Staff Working Paper ERSD-2012-14, 18 September 2012, https://www.wto.org/english/res_e/reser_e/ersd201214_e.pdf (last accessed 21 August 2020).

[54]WTO, NGOs and the WTO, https://www.wto.org/english/forums_e/ngo_e/ngo_e.htm#:~:text=NGOs%20can%20be%20accredited%20to,of%20discussions%20between%20WTO%20members (last accessed 21 August 2020).

[55]See further Hoad (2002), Gad (2003) and De Bièvre et al. (2016).

[56]See Appellate Body Report, *European Communities – Regime for the Importation Distribution and Sale of Bananas*, WT/DS27/AB/R, adopted 25 September 1997, https://www.wto.org/english/tratop_e/dispu_e/cases_e/ds27_e.htm (last accessed 21 August 2020).

Exporters Association (CBEA) and its London lobbying office to protect the EU regime. Producers of Latin American "dollar" bananas, Dole Foods, Chiquita and Del Monte, lobbied actively against the proposed 1993 EU regime. Chiquita was the major force behind the US Trade Representative's decision to bring the WTO case. Importers of dollar bananas lobbied and litigated against the 1993 regime in German courts and in the EU. Caribbean producers used the CBEA to lobby in favour of preferences and inclusion of Banana Protocols in the Lomé Convention.[57] The case dragged on for years and was eventually settled in 2012.[58] More recently tobacco corporations used their political influence to encourage a complaint by Ukraine, Honduras, the Dominican Republic, Cuba and Indonesia against Australia's plain packaging rules at the WTO.[59] However, the WTO Panel rejected the claims and this was upheld by the Appellate Body.[60] Such limited successes and the recent eclipsing of the WTO by the US, with the effective incapacitation of the WTO Appellate Body,[61] suggests that this forum may have lost much of the attraction that it had for corporate interests when, over the last two decades, it was a new and vibrant institutional champion of the liberal international economic order.

The arrangements discussed above have grown on an organisation-specific basis to meet the need for business, and non-business, NGO input that is both relevant and supportive of the IGO's programme. These procedures have not protected IGO decision and norm making from the risk of capture or subversion by corporate interests, as the WHO case illustrates, nor have all IGOs sought to control such influence. While most arrangements fall short of a direct role for businesses in rule making, the arrangements at UNCITRAL come close to this due to the nature of its mandate.

A major concern is whether detailed accreditation rules, placing the burden of approval on the IGO, are effective in ensuring useful and accountable business participation.[62] They may encourage the use of "fronting" organisations and covert

---

[57] See Hoekman and Kostecki (2009), p. 160.

[58] Appellate Body Report, *European Communities – Regime for the Importation Distribution and Sale of Bananas*, WT/DS27/AB/R, adopted 25 September 1997, https://www.wto.org/english/tratop_e/dispu_e/cases_e/ds27_e.htm (last accessed 21 August 2020).

[59] Curran and Eckhardt (2017).

[60] Appellate Body Report, *Australia – Certain Measures Concerning Trademarks, Geographical Indications and Other Plain Packaging Requirements Applicable to Tobacco Products and Packaging*, WT/DS435/27 WT/DS441/28, adopted 29 June 2020, https://www.wto.org/english/tratop_e/dispu_e/cases_e/ds435_e.htm#bkmk435abr (last accessed 21 August 2020).

[61] See Walker A, Trade disputes settlement system facing crisis, BBC News, 8 December 2019, https://www.bbc.co.uk/news/business-50681431 (last accessed 21 August 2020). See further Pauwelyn (2019). See also Office of the United States Trade Representative, 2020 Trade Policy Agenda and 2019 Annual Report of the President of the United States on the Trade Agreements Program, 2019, https://ustr.gov/sites/default/files/2020_Trade_Policy_Agenda_and_2019_Annual_Report.pdf (last accessed 21 August 2020), especially pp. 13–14. For a Chinese critique of the US position see Guohua (2019).

[62] See Durkee (2018), pp. 1823–1825.

lobbying of officials and governments.[63] Equally, existing structures perpetuate the idea that business-oriented, and other, NGOs are merely consultants for whom full voting rights are unnecessary. As noted in the previous section, this proposition may no longer fit with the reality of economic power exercised by MNEs, or social influence exercised by non-business NGOs, both of which operate in the regulatory gap left by the "market-state", and the resulting retreat of IGOs from interventionist economic regulation.[64] One response to this regulatory gap has been the development of MSI's.

4 Multi-Stakeholder Initiatives

Such arrangements originate in the development of international environmental standards.[65] The UN Conference on Environment and Development (UNCED) Secretariat, led by Maurice Strong, was keen to involve a range of stakeholder groups, including business and industry.[66] A new post of corporate adviser to UNCED was created, filled by Stefan Schmidtheiny of the World Business Council for Sustainable Development (WBCSD).[67] The resulting *Rio Declaration (Agenda 21)* – to date the most influential repository of MNE responsibilities in the international environmental field[68] – contained an approach to sustainable development that reflected closely the concerns of the WBCSD.[69] The emphasis is on the application of "green" technology to environmental issues and upon co-operation between business and governments in the realisation of sustainable development goals.

More recently, the Sustainable Development Goals (SDGs) programme of the UN emphasises the role of both business and non-business stakeholders in developing policy responses.[70] UN Resolution 70/1 *Transforming our world: the 2030 Agenda for Sustainable Development*, which lays down the SGDs, acknowledges,

---

[63]Durkee (2018), pp. 1823–1825, and see further Durkee (2017).

[64]On which see further Gleckmann (2018), ch. 1.

[65]See Rowlands (2001); Dodds et al. (2019).

[66]The UNCED recognised nine "Major Groups" representing the main currents of stakeholder interest in UN activities related to sustainable development. There were: women, children and youth, indigenous peoples, NGOs, local authorities, workers and trade unions, business and industry and the scientific and technical community and farmers: Strandenaes (2019), pp. 15–16. For the history of stakeholder engagement prior to the UNCED and subsequently up to the UN Sustainable Development Goals see Dodds et al. (2019) ch. 3.

[67]See Gleckman (1995), pp. 95–97.

[68]UNCED, Agenda 21: Programme of Action for Sustainable Development, 3 to 14 June 1992, https://sustainabledevelopment.un.org/content/documents/Agenda21.pdf   (last   accessed 21 August 2020).

[69]See Gleckman (1995), pp. 95–97; Rowlands (2001), p. 144; Ford (2004), pp. 310–312.

[70]See UN Sustainable Development Goals Knowledge Platform, https://sustainabledevelopment.un.org/?menu=1300 (last accessed 21 August 2020) and Dodds (2019), pp. 88–93.

"the role of the diverse private sector, ranging from micro-enterprises to cooperatives to multinationals, and that of civil society organizations and philanthropic organizations in the implementation of the new Agenda."[71] The SDGs elaborate on the role of business and industry through public-private partnerships and on the need for corporate social responsibility.[72]

These two examples illustrate how multi-stakeholder interests have entered multilateral institutions. However, these are not fully developed MSIs. According to Harris Gleckman, there is a significant conceptual distinction between multi-stakeholder governance and multi-constituency consultations.[73] The latter take place within the boundaries of an IGO, or a nation-state, and act as a means for the organisation, or government, to take account of various constituency positions before coming to a normative decision. Multi-stakeholder governance, by contrast, creates autonomous bodies which work on a global, regional or local problem, independent of IGOs or governments, and come to normative conclusions that carry their own internal authority. The confusion arises, according to Gleckman, because the UN system mistakenly borrowed the language of multistakeholderism from corporate and administrative management concepts applicable to businesses and administrative offices but not to IGOs, which act more like parliaments and congresses coming to decisions after hearing constituents.[74]

The development of true MSIs in international economic regulation begins with Internet governance.[75] The Internet Corporation for Assigned Names and Numbers (ICANN) is a key example. Established in 1998, ICANN, "grew out of a U.S. Government commitment to transfer the policy and technical management of the [Domain Name System] DNS to a non-profit corporation based in the U.S. with global participation."[76] ICANN's governance model is described as, a "multistakeholder model":

> This decentralized governance model places individuals, industry, non-commercial interests and government on an equal level. Unlike more traditional, top-down governance models, where governments make policy decisions, the multistakeholder approach used by ICANN allows for community-based consensus-driven policy-making. The idea is that Internet governance should mimic the structure of the Internet itself – borderless and open to all.[77]

---

[71]UN GA, Transforming our world: the 2030 Agenda for Sustainable Development, UN Doc. A / RES/70/1, 21 October 2015, https://sustainabledevelopment.un.org/post2015/transformingourworld (last accessed 21 August 2020), para. 41.

[72]UN Sustainable Development Goals Knowledge Platform, Stakeholder Engagement: Business and Industry, https://sustainabledevelopment.un.org/majorgroups/businessandindustry (last accessed 21 August 2020). On multi-stakeholder partnerships in the UN system in the field of sustainable development see further the contributions in Dodds (2019).

[73]See Gleckmann (2018), pp. 12–13.

[74]Gleckmann (2018), pp. 12–13.

[75]See further Raymond and Denardis (2015). See also Antonova (2008).

[76]ICANN, ICANN History Project", https://www.icann.org/history (last accessed 21 August 2020).

[77]ICANN, Beginners Guide to Participating in ICANN, 2013, https://www.icann.org/resources/pages/beginners-guides-2012-03-06-en (last accessed 21 August 2020), p. 2.

In practice ICANN has faced many challenges in attaining genuine multi-stakeholder participation, the most recent being its transformation into a genuinely global arrangement free of US governmental influence, when, in 2017, the US Department of Commerce ended its stewardship functions in ICANN.[78]

MSIs have had a significant influence on recent developments relating to corporate responsibility and the observance of human rights.[79] These arrangements range in function from: policy-oriented multi-stakeholder groups, standard-setting organisations and project-oriented groups.[80] One leading example of each type of arrangement will be discussed and its contribution assessed.

At the level of policy-making, the Kimberley Process Certification Scheme (KPCS) was established in 2003 as a multilateral trade regime to prevent the flow of "conflict diamonds" defined as "rough diamonds used by rebel movements or their allies to finance conflict aimed at undermining legitimate governments" specifically responding to then contemporary conflicts in Liberia, Sierra Leone, and the Democratic Republic of Congo.[81] The KPCS arose from negotiations between a coalition of countries in Southern Africa, the international diamond industry including De Beers, the world's largest diamond mining company, and human rights NGOs. The scheme now has 55 member countries and is backed by UN resolutions.[82] The KPCS allows states to implement safeguards on shipments of rough diamonds and certify them as "conflict free" under national laws.[83] The KPCS Core Document makes industry self-regulation the basis of certification:

> Participants understand that a voluntary system of industry self-regulation, as referred to in the Preamble of this Document, will provide for a system of warranties underpinned through verification by independent auditors of individual companies and supported by internal penalties set by industry, which will help to facilitate the full traceability of rough diamond transactions by government authorities.[84]

The scheme has been successful in reducing trade in conflict diamonds but has significant design weaknesses, highlighted when the issue of human rights violations in the diamond mining industry in Zimbabwe arose at the end of the last decade.

---

[78]For analysis of the difficulties surrounding multistakeholderism in ICANN see Radu (2019), ch. 4. See also ICANN, History: 6 January, 2017 Last Formal Agreement with U.S. Government Ends, https://www.icann.org/en/history/icann-usg (last accessed 21 August 2020).

[79]See Jerbi (2012) and Tamo (2016).

[80]See generally Gleckmann (2018), pp. 16–25.

[81]See for background Holmes (2007), Wexler (2010) and Howard (2016).

[82]See Kimberley Process, List of Participants – 2020 Status, https://www.kimberleyprocess.com/en/2020-kp-participants-list (last accessed 21 August 2020). See, most recently, UN GA, The role of diamonds in fuelling conflict: breaking the link between the illicit transaction of rough diamonds and armed conflict as a contribution to prevention and settlement of conflicts, UN Doc. A/74/L.39, 6 February 2020, https://undocs.org/en/A/74/L.39 (last accessed 23 August 2020).

[83]Kimberley Process, What is the Kimberley Process?, https://www.kimberleyprocess.com/en/what-kp (last accessed 21 August 2020).

[84]Kimberley Process Certification Scheme, Section IV, https://www.kimberleyprocess.com/en/kpcs-core-document (last accessed 21 August 2020).

While the KPCS initially sought a ban on diamond exports from Zimbabwe in 2009, Zimbabwe was reinstated in 2011 after assurances were given that the government would seek to control abuses. Diamonds extracted in Zimbabwe were not "conflict diamonds" as they were not used to finance civil war but as a source of profit for Zimbabwean officials and miners. This raised the question whether such a narrow subject-matter definition could act as an effective tool against more general human rights abuses in the diamond mining industry.[85] The decision on Zimbabwe, coupled with failure to control the trade in conflict diamonds from Côte d'Ivoire, and unwillingness to take serious action in the face of blatant breaches of the rules over a number of years by Venezuela, led Global Witness, one of the strongest NGO supporters of the KPCS, to withdraw from the organisation in 2011.[86] Global Witness now pursues a campaign to encourage diamond firms to apply human rights due diligence to identify and remedy human rights risks in their global supply chains.[87]

Notwithstanding its shortcomings, the Kimberley Process is a significant example of law-making through MSIs. Diamond miners and NGOs were active in drawing up the content of the KPCS Core Document, acting as more than mere consultants or lobbyists. Furthermore, they play an important policing role as the system depends as much on NGO monitoring and corporate compliance with certification as it does on member state regulation.[88] Although the KPCS is based on an informal international instrument, it is arguable that this has now been elevated to a binding normative level through national implementation laws, UN backing and a general sense that this process should be observed.[89] If the weaknesses of the KPCS are properly addressed then significant progress could yet be made in the elimination of human rights abuses in the global diamond mining industry.[90] Notably, the World Diamond Council, the representative body for diamond trade, has itself advocated reforms including a widening of the definition of "conflict diamonds" to cover all forms of systemic violence, including those carried out by state and private security forces.[91]

---

[85] See Cullen (2013), pp. 77–78.

[86] Global Witness, Global Witness leaves Kimberley Process, calls on diamond trade to be held accountable, 2 December 2011, https://www.globalwitness.org/en/archive/global-witness-leaves-kimberley-process-calls-diamond-trade-be-held-accountable/ (last accessed 21 August 2020). See further Cullen (2013), pp. 70–77; Winetroub (2013).

[87] See Global Witness, Campaigns: Conflict Diamonds, https://www.globalwitness.org/en/campaigns/conflict-diamonds/#more (last accessed 21 August 2020).

[88] See further, on the role of private business actors in supporting the implementation and enforcement of international law, Butler (2020).

[89] See Ezeudu (2014).

[90] See further Winetroub (2013) for a detailed analysis of possible reforms.

[91] See World Diamond Council, Kimberley Process must grasp historic opportunity to correct its limitations, WDC President to tell special UN General Assembly meeting in New York, 28 February 2019, https://www.kimberleyprocess.com/en/press-release-kp-must-grasp-historic-opportunity-correct-its-limitations-wdc-president-tell-special (last accessed 21 August 2020) and World Diamond

A leading example for international business standard-setting by MSIs is the International Standards Association (ISO). The ISO has produced international product and process standards in many areas.[92] It is a hybrid private-public regulatory regime. The private dimension comes from the 164 participating national standard setting bodies all having strong local industry membership.[93] The public dimension arises from the adoption of ISO standards as benchmarks for national laws and IGO standards and norms.[94] The ISO asserts that standard setting is a multi-stakeholder process as the Technical Committees that draw up standards are,

> made up of experts from the relevant industry, but also from consumer associations, academia, NGOs and government.[95]

In practice, industry sets the agenda over what standards should be drawn up, dominates the negotiation and adoption process either directly, through industry representatives, or indirectly, through government representatives, and it is companies that ultimately implement ISO standards mostly on the basis of voluntary compliance.[96] This is unsurprising given that the technical nature of much of the standard setting is likely to be of interest mainly to the industry sectors involved. This changed when, in the 1990s, ISO adopted the ISO 14000 Environmental Management Standard and, more recently, in 2010, the ISO 26000 Social Responsibility Standard. The shift towards corporate environmental and social responsibility created a need for wider inputs.

The ISO 14000 negotiations were criticised for not achieving effective stakeholder involvement.[97] By contrast, the adoption of ISO 26000 reveals a much more inclusive and public system of stakeholder consultation.[98] This followed recommendations made by a multi-stakeholder advisory group established to ensure a process

---

Council, WDC to continue advocating for the strengthening of the scope of Kimberley Process, 22 November 2019, https://www.kimberleyprocess.com/en/press-release-world-diamond-council-following-kimberley-process-plenary-meeting-new-delhi-india (last accessed 21 August 2020).

[92] See ISO, Standards, https://www.iso.org/standards.html (last accessed 21 August 2020).

[93] See ISO, About US: Members, https://www.iso.org/members.html (last accessed 21 August 2020).

[94] See Clapp (2004). But see Fontanelli (2011) who argues that ISO and Codex Alimentarius Commission standards are not transformed into hard law by the WTO TBS and SPS Agreements but are used as factual benchmarks in determining whether a Member's domestic measures infringe their terms.

[95] See ISO, Key Principles in ISO Standard Development, https://www.iso.org/developing-standards.html (last accessed 21 August 2020). There are currently 328 Technical Committees: ISO, List of Technical Committees, https://www.iso.org/technical-committees.html (last accessed 21 August 2020).

[96] See Fontanelli (2011), pp. 903–904.

[97] See ISO, The ISO 14000 Family Environmental Management, https://www.iso.org/iso-14001-environmental-management.html (last accessed 21 August 2020). On how business interests were promoted over other interests, including those of developing countries, in the ISO 14000 standard setting process see Clapp (2004) and Mikulich (2003).

[98] See Webb (2015) on which this paragraph draws.

capable of reflecting the diversity of interests associated with social responsibility. The working group membership consisted of 450 experts and 210 observers from 99 ISO member countries and another 42 liaison organisations. Kernaghan Webb describes the working group as,

> organised into six categories: government (including inter-governmental members), industry, labour, consumers, non-governmental organisations, and an 'other' category that included representatives of standards developers, consultants, and academics. In addition, the process was designed to ensure balanced participation from developed and developing countries, through a twinning of leadership (one developed and developing country leader) and through use of a trust fund to ensure the participation of persons who might otherwise not be able to participate.[99]

The negotiation process also involved other international bodies and IGOs with an interest in social responsibility, making ISO 26000 a significant repository of concepts found across several specialised social responsibility bodies.[100] ISO 26000 was developed through a two-level deliberative consensus process. First, the standard was agreed to by consensus of the 450 working group members. Secondly it had to be approved by at least two thirds of the ISO voting membership. It passed with 93% of the vote.[101]

Accordingly, ISO 26000 may be seen as a strong instrument based on genuine multi-stakeholder consensus, giving it a high degree of legitimacy. That said several legitimacy barriers exist. In particular major human rights NGOs did not take part. Furthermore, it is only available for a fee though this may not stop governmental authorities or corporate actors using it.[102] Finally, to a significant extent, ISO 26000 has been eclipsed by the UN Guiding Principles on Business and Human Rights (UNGPS), though it has applied the due diligence concept found there.[103]

The legal impact of ISO standards ultimately depends on whether they are transformed into binding laws through domestic or international regulations. For example, the WTO Agreement on Technical Barriers to Trade (TBT Agreement) recognises ISO standards as international standards to be followed by members in their trade policies. However, members following more stringent standards may be challenged for introducing barriers to trade incompatible with international standards recognised by the TBT Agreement.[104] This does not amount to a formal adoption of ISO standards as "law" within the WTO system. Rather, ISO standards are used as factual benchmarks in determining whether a Member's domestic measures infringe their terms and may act as a *de facto* "ceiling" to permissible regulation and not as a

---

[99]Webb (2015), p. 475.

[100]Webb (2015), pp. 477–480.

[101]Webb (2015), p. 476.

[102]Webb (2015), pp. 481–483 on which the ensuing text draws.

[103]UN, Guiding Principles on Business and Human Rights, 2011, https://www.ohchr.org/documents/publications/guidingprinciplesbusinesshr_en.pdf (last accessed 21 August 2020).

[104]See Clapp (2004).

"floor" which was their original conception.[105] Equally at the domestic law level ISO standards contain no obligation to transform them into binding legal norms. On the other hand, ISO 26000 can be used informally as evidence of an international consensus, an emerging international social responsibility "custom", which may influence the development of standards and be used in litigation as guidance on appropriate corporate behaviour in the context of a legal claim.[106]

The Accord on Fire and Building Safety in Bangladesh of 15 May 2013 offers an example of a project-specific MSI.[107] It was created in the aftermath of the Rana Plaza building collapse that led to more than 1,100 deaths and over 2000 injuries.[108] The Accord is administered by the Bangladesh Accord Foundation incorporated in the Netherlands in October 2013. It is,

> a legally-binding agreement between global brands & retailers and **IndustriALL Global Union** and **UNI Global Union** and eight of their Bangladeshi affiliated unions to work towards a safe and healthy garment and textile industry in Bangladesh.[109]

The Accord was renewed for a further 3 years in 2018.[110] It introduces an independent inspection programme supported by brands in which workers and trade unions are involved;[111] public disclosure of all factories, inspection reports and corrective action plans;[112] a commitment by signatory brands to ensure sufficient funds for remediation and to maintain sourcing relationships capped at €300,000 per company per year of the Accord;[113] democratically elected health and safety committees in all factories to identify and act on health and safety risks;[114] and worker empowerment through an extensive training programme, complaints mechanism and right to refuse unsafe work.[115]

The Accord creates a private enforcement regime imposing binding contractual obligations on sub-contractors, sanctioned by termination of the business relationship between the brand and the sub-contractor where the latter fails to observe

---

[105]See Fontanelli (2011).

[106]See further Webb (2015), pp. 483–500.

[107]This study is taken from Muchlinski (2021), ch. 13.

[108]Bangladesh Accord Foundation, Accord on Fire and Building Safety in Bangladesh, 13 May 2013, https://admin.bangladeshaccord.org/wp-content/uploads/2018/08/2013-Accord.pdf (last accessed 21 August 2020).

[109]Bangladesh Accord Foundation, About the Accord, http://bangladeshaccord.org/about/ (last accessed 21 August 2020). For the full list of brand and trade union signatories see http://bangladeshaccord.org/signatories/ (last accessed 21 August 2020).

[110]Text available at 2018 Accord on Fire and Building Safety in Bangladesh: May 2018, 21 June 2017, https://admin.bangladeshaccord.org/wp-content/uploads/2018/08/2018-Accord.pdf (last accessed). All references are to the 2018 Bangladesh Accord Revision.

[111]Ibid para. 4–6.

[112]Ibid para. 7–10.

[113]Ibid para. 19.

[114]Ibid para. 12a.

[115]Ibid para. 11, 13 and 10.

adequate health and safety for its workers.[116] Compliance is supported by various incentives built into supply contracts.[117] Terminated suppliers are listed on the website of the Bangladesh Accord Foundation.[118] Though an obvious sanction, in practice it may lead to job losses and a resulting worsening of local worker conditions. The naming and shaming of sub-contractors, coupled with long-term remediation of shortcomings in labour practices, may be all that can be reasonably done.[119]

The impact of the Accord on worker rights has been positive in terms of quantifiable matters such as improved health and safety measures, more light or better ventilation. However, some unintended consequences include the cutting of working hours and the ending of overtime resulting in a loss of income for already precarious workers.[120] Improved working conditions may also lead to job displacement in sub-contractor firms that can only afford to make improvements required by retailers through more automation.[121] Although the Accord requires a financial contribution from brand members this is small. Furthermore, the "top-down" nature of such arrangements may offer limited results. Unless self-regulatory regimes pay serious attention to what workers on the ground actually need and want the formal meeting of code targets will mean little.[122]

When the Accord expires in 2021, its work will be handed over to a national regulatory body, supported by the ILO, and be carried forward from that point. If the Steering Committee determines that no such body is ready, the Accord shall be extended for another 12 months. Should such a body be ready to take up the work before the ending date, the Accord Steering Committee may decide to terminate the effort as appropriate to the overall goals of the programme.[123]

The three examples offered have been picked as they are well known. Many other case-studies could be cited.[124] They all share the same formal commitment to multi-stakeholder engagement for ensuring legitimate and consensual corporate responsibility norm creation. Equally, each initiative has highlighted certain legitimacy problems, notwithstanding their undoubted progress. Thus, the Kimberley Process shows that the initial definition of the subject matter to be covered may restrict effective engagement with the underlying issues, allowing corporate participants too

---

[116]Ibid para. 16.

[117]Ibid para. 17.

[118]See "152 Ineligible Suppliers" at Bangladesh Accord Foundation, https://bangladeshaccord.org/factories (last accessed 21 August 2020).

[119]Rawling (2015), p. 672.

[120]See Sinkovics et al. (2016).

[121]Ibid.

[122]Ibid p. 644 and see further Rawling (2015), p. 670; Selwyn (2013).

[123]2018 Bangladesh Accord Revision, Introduction para. 2.

[124]See further the case studies in Jerbi (2012) who examines, in addition to the Kimberley Process, the Voluntary Principles on Security and Human Rights, the Extractive Industries Transparency Initiative, and the role of multi-stakeholder arrangements in operationalizing the UNGPs.

much leeway. Examples of diamonds being produced in the context of human rights violations undermines their marketing as romantic objects, a major reason why corporate interests are themselves calling for reform.[125] As for the ISO, the process adopting ISO 26000 was a pragmatic response towards non-business stakeholder engagement to ensure the legitimacy of the new standard. However, it did not persuade the major human rights NGOs to take part. They decided to prioritise the UNGPs as a focus for stakeholder input. This may be in part a financial decision based on limited resources but may also reflect preferences of forum choice.[126] Simply put, the UN carries more legitimacy as a forum for normative development in human rights and corporate responsibility than the ISO, with its long tradition of narrow, technically and managerially focused, standard setting. Finally, while the Bangladesh Accord offers an example of what can be done by a strongly motivated MSI to supplement inadequate local health and safety regulation with a private contract-based regime, its ultimate dependence on Bangladeshi regulatory co-operation and the risk of that petering out with no clear replacement may make this a temporary and, ultimately, failed initiative.

More generally, MSIs, need to take heed of a number of design and procedure questions to ensure their effective and legitimate operation. Detailed analysis has been done elsewhere.[127] However, a brief summary of the main concerns offers a useful conclusion to this section. These revolve around how the "stakeholders" are identified and admitted to the arrangement; how power imbalances between various stakeholders are dealt with; and how transparency and accountability is to be achieved.

Choice of stakeholders is central to the effectiveness and legitimacy of the arrangement, as shown by ISO 26000. However, selection can be random and dominated by the "convener" of the MSI.[128] The convener is the main mover and broker of the group, often a powerful and influential stakeholder.[129] As such they may frame membership of the group in their own interests and downgrade, or ignore, other relevant stakeholders.[130] Indeed, it has been argued that a major disadvantage

---

[125]See e.g. De Beers, Why De Beers, https://www.debeers.co.uk/en-gb/why-de-beers.html (last accessed 21 August 2020).

[126]Webb (2015), pp. 481–482.

[127]See Gleckmann (2018), especially ch. 4 and 5; Buxton N et al., Multistakeholderism: a critical look, Workshop Report, The Transnational Institute, 10 September 2019, https://www.tni.org/files/publication-downloads/multistakeholderism-workshop-report-tni.pdf (last accessed 23 August 2020); Schleifer (2019) and Biekart and Fowler (2018).

[128]See Gleckmann (2018), pp. 65–71.

[129]See on corporate influence over MSIs, Buxton N et al., Multistakeholderism: a critical look, Workshop Report, The Transnational Institute, 10 September 2019, https://www.tni.org/files/publication-downloads/multistakeholderism-workshop-report-tni.pdf (last accessed 23 August 2020).

[130]See further Schleifer (2019) comparing the differing levels of stakeholder engagement and business control in the Roundtable on Sustainable Biomaterials, the Roundtable on Responsible Soy, and Bonsucro, formerly known as the Better Sugarcane Initiative.

of corporate responsibility MSIs is capture by corporate interests to ensure low standards.[131] To avoid this, certain safeguards need to be built into selection and decision-making procedures.

Safeguards include, in particular, mechanisms for ensuring that relevant stakeholders are aware of the MSI's existence, and its potential impact on their concerns, requiring clear terms of reference and their effective communication. These mechanisms need to accept that many relevant stakeholders form diverse groups making full representation in the MSI difficult. A simple statement that "all relevant stakeholders" are included is insufficient. The MSI must have a flexible, continuously evolving, approach to membership and the hearing of representations.[132] In addition, well-funded NGOs from the Global North will have more resources than those from the Global South, leaving a potential gap in representation of stakeholders from affected communities and requiring active support for their inclusion.[133]

Turning to power imbalances, due to more limited resources, non-profit NGOs and other representatives of "grass roots" interests will have less power relative to large businesses.[134] While such bodies can highlight, and suggest remedies for, harmful corporate behaviour, they may be unable to counter corporate priorities in the MSI because of their more limited ability to attend meetings and carry out other relevant functions. This is further exacerbated by the capacity of a "convener" corporate interest to invite only those NGOs that show a degree to willingness to compromise over normative developments, excluding more "radical" voices.[135] Often the only sanction an NGO has when it is dissatisfied with the work of an MSI is to leave, as Global Witness did from the Kimberley Process, leaving more "compliant" NGOs in place. It tests the assumptions of voluntarism and cooperation that underlie the MSI approach.[136] To be effective the MSI must ensure that the more powerful actors are prepared to give up some of their power advantages and accept coequal participation from all relevant stakeholders in return for the advantages of greater normative legitimacy. This requires the observance of basic democratic practices in decision-making and internal dispute resolution mechanisms to be in place.[137] This also raises the question of how the MSI will be financed to ensure that

---

[131] See McKeon (2017).

[132] Gleckmann (2018), pp. 87–89.

[133] See further MSI Integrity and the Duke Human Rights Centre at the Kenan Institute for Ethics, The New Regulators? Assessing the landscape of multi-stakeholder initiatives, June 2017, http://www.msi-integrity.org/dev/wp-content/uploads/2017/05/The-New-Regulators-MSI-Database-Report.pdf (last accessed 21 August 2020).

[134] See Molina-Gallart (2014) discussing such imbalances in NGO-corporate partnerships.

[135] See Buxton N et al., Multistakeholderism: a critical look, Workshop Report, The Transnational Institute, 10 September 2019, https://www.tni.org/files/publication-downloads/multistakeholderism-workshop-report-tni.pdf (last accessed 23 August 2020), p. 10.

[136] Gleckmann (2018), pp. 90–92.

[137] See further Gleckmann (2018), pp. 121–124.

effective participation is not undermined by a lack of resources among certain stakeholders.[138]

Finally, the question of transparency and accountability of the MSI towards the public needs to be addressed. In practice few MSIs publish detailed budgets or highlight conflicts of interests among participating stakeholders.[139] If MSIs fail to be transparent and accountable about their sources of funding, expenditure, decision-making and composition they risk becoming perceived as illegitimate. In the absence of external regulatory control, MSIs have a strong responsibility to ensure they follow basic democratic practices on transparency and accountability.[140]

Some progress has been made by MSIs themselves. For example, the International Social and Environmental Accreditation and Labelling (ISEAL) Alliance was formed to ensure credible and legitimate standard setting by environmental sustainability MSIs. The ISEAL Credibility Principles stress the need for standard-setters to observe principles of good institutional governance including balanced representation, impartiality, transparency, accessibility, truthfulness in the use of standards and the application of sound revenue models and organisational management strategies.[141] The ISEAL standards offer a useful template for other MSIs to follow.

A further example of procedural standard setting comes from the Institute for Multi-Stakeholder Initiative Integrity (MSI Integrity). This is a non-profit organisation, "dedicated to understanding the human rights impact and value of voluntary MSIs that address business and human rights."[142] This body has developed an MSI Evaluation Tool to help MSIs assess whether their membership and procedures adhere to good governance practices.[143] As with the ISEAL Credibility Principles the MSI Evaluation Tool stresses the need to

(a) address any power imbalances or adversarial relationships that may disadvantage stakeholders with fewer resources, such as global south or local representatives, or civil society or affected community participants; (b) ensure it has sufficient resources to operate effectively; and, (c) establish decision-making processes that are efficient, inclusive, and capable of

---

[138]On financing see further Gleckmann (2018), pp. 129–131 stressing also the need for financial transparency in relation to the operating and programme budgets of the MSI.

[139]Gleckmann (2018), p. 98.

[140]See further Gleckmann (2018), pp.125–129.

[141]ISEAL, ISEAL Credibility Principles, June 2013, https://www.isealalliance.org/credible-sustainability-standards/iseal-credibility-principles (last accessed 21 August 2020) on which this paragraph draws. ISEAL is currently undertaking a revision of this instrument: https://www.isealalliance.org/credibility-principles-consultation (last accessed 21 August 2020).

[142]See MSI Integrity, Our Mission and Vision, http://www.msi-integrity.org/test-home/mission-principles/ (last accessed 21 August 2020).

[143]MSI Integrity, MSI Evaluation Tool, http://www.msi-integrity.org/evaluations/msi-evaluation-tool-2/ (last accessed 21 August 2020). See also MSI Integrity, The Essential Elements of MSI Design, 2017, http://www.msi-integrity.org/wp-content/uploads/2017/11/Essential_Elements_2017.pdf (last accessed 21 August 2020).

overcoming internal disputes. Finally, to the extent that transnational standard-setting MSIs operate as governance tools, they must also be transparent and accountable.[144]

The Evaluation Tool fleshes these principles out into a detailed check-list of the minimum requirements to meet these goals.

Such initiatives remain voluntary and may be ignored with legal impunity. There remains a strong case for giving such standards legal strength. If MSIs are here to stay as an institutional form of privatised norm creation in IEL then their proper functioning can, and should, come under better regulatory control. Regulation is required of their members as individual legal entities, whether private for-profit corporations, trade unions, non-profit NGOs or community groups subject, respectively, to corporate, labour and voluntary organisation laws. It seems incongruous not to demand a similar level of legal accountability of the MSI in which they participate. States have an important role to play here, one that may have been conveniently ignored under the banner of "deregulating business". How this is to be done requires further examination of the legal nature of MSIs as organisations and the role of contract and statute in giving legal force, and regulatory control, to their operational practices.[145]

5   Concluding Remarks: The Future of Multi-Stakeholder Initiatives

This contribution has charted the shift in corporate influence over the content of IEL from the multilateral regulatory order, dominated by governments and IGOs, in which corporate actors exert informal influence as consultants and lobbyists but are denied a place as active lawmakers, to the increasing use of MSIs as a means of filling regulatory gaps created by technological change and the retreat of the "market-state", and IGOs, from direct regulation, resulting in enhanced corporate power and influence coordinated by its counterweight in CSOs and other NGOs.

The focus has been on MSIs in the corporate responsibility field, given its prominence as a forum in which such arrangements have been used. MSI governance remains a relatively hit and miss process, with much depending on the capacity and integrity of the individual body. Some attempts have been made to systematise good governance practices in MSIs through the ISEAL Alliance and MSI Integrity. However, what may be needed is greater involvement by traditional lawmakers in the regulation of governance in MSIs to ensure proper legal accountability and, in the interim, the incorporation of good governance standards into contracts binding on MSI members.

---

[144]MSI Integrity, The Essential Elements of MSI Design, 2017, http://www.msi-integrity.org/wp-content/uploads/2017/11/Essential_Elements_2017.pdf (last accessed 21 August 2020), p. 6.
[145]See further Webb (2015).

The previous discussion assumes a commitment towards open and democratic approaches to securing corporate responsibility in IEL. The future may not follow this path. The rise of China as a superpower, and the rise of authoritarian nationalism elsewhere, may signal a possible move towards an alternative "authoritarian" model of international law, that emphasises state sovereignty and negotiations based on power relations, in which the state is seen increasingly as the only legitimate stakeholder.[146] Additionally, the rise of economic nationalism and protectionism, as promoted by the Trump administration in the US, suggests a reduction in concern over corporate responsibility. That said, the pro-business Trump administration has not objected to corporate-led MSIs.[147]

The future role of MSIs may be one of state-sanctioned corporate domination leading to increasingly less intrusive, optional, standards of corporate responsibility.[148] Corporations from authoritarian states, like China, that wish to expand globally, will require a degree of social legitimacy. Corporate dominated MSIs could offer this while also working in the interests of corporations from democracies by minimising corporate exposure to mandatory responsibility standards, offering "soft" alternatives based on voluntary corporate disclosure and reporting and the absence of strong liability rules.[149] If so, then MSIs could find themselves not at the forefront of a normative corporate responsibility revolution but as active participants in the very opposite – the progressive deregulation of corporate responsibility. It is to be hoped that current developments in national mandatory social responsibility and corporate human rights due diligence requirements offer the vision of a better alternative model.[150] However, this remains at an early stage and may itself become restricted through corporate influence and governmental reluctance to weaken ties with business. Much remains open to question in this uncertain environment.

---

[146]On which see further Ginsburg (2020) and Buxton N et al., Multistakeholderism: a critical look, Workshop Report, The Transnational Institute, 10 September 2019, https://www.tni.org/files/publication-downloads/multistakeholderism-workshop-report-tni.pdf (last accessed 23 August 2020), p. 13.

[147]See Buxton N et al., Multistakeholderism: a critical look, Workshop Report, The Transnational Institute, 10 September 2019, https://www.tni.org/files/publication-downloads/multistakeholderism-workshop-report-tni.pdf (last accessed 23 August 2020), p. 13.

[148]See Johns et al. (2019).

[149]Buxton N et al., Multistakeholderism: a critical look, Workshop Report, The Transnational Institute, 10 September 2019, https://www.tni.org/files/publication-downloads/multistakeholderism-workshop-report-tni.pdf (last accessed 23 August 2020), p. 13.

[150]On which see Muchlinski (2021), ch. 14 and Business and Human Rights Resource Centre, Mandatory Due Diligence, https://www.business-humanrights.org/en/mandatory-due-diligence (last accessed 23 August 2020).

References

Antonova S (2008) Powerscape of internet governance – how was global multistakeholderism invented in ICANN? VDM Verlag, Saarbrücken

Arato J (2015) Corporations as lawmakers. Harv Int Law J 56(2):229–295

Biekart K, Fowler A (2018) Ownership dynamics in local multi-stakeholder initiatives. Third World Q 39(9):1692–1710

Butler J (2020) The corporate keepers of international law. Am J Int Law 114(2):189–220

Cata Backer L (2008) Multinational corporations as objects and sources of transnational regulation. ILSA J Int Comp Law 14(2):499–523

Clapp J (2004) The privatization of global environmental governance: ISO 14000 and the developing world. In: Levy D, Newell P (eds) The business of global environmental governance. MIT Press, Cambridge, pp 223–248

Crouch C (2004) Post-democracy. Polity Press, Cambridge

Crouch C (2011) The strange non-death of neoliberalism. Polity Press, Cambridge

Cullen H (2013) Is there future for the Kimberley process certification scheme for conflict diamonds? Macquarie Law J 12:61–80

Curran L, Eckhardt J (2017) Smoke screen? The globalization of production, transnational lobbying and the international political economy of plain tobacco packaging. Rev Int Polit Econ 24 (1):87–118

De Bièvre D, Poletti A, Hanegraaff M, Beyers J (2016) International institutions and interest mobilization: the WTO and lobbying in EU and US trade policy. J World Trade 50(2):289–312

Dodds F et al (2019) Stakeholder democracy: represented democracy in a time of fear. Routledge, Abingdon

Durkee M (2017) Astroturf activism. Stanford Law Rev 69:201–268

Durkee M (2018) International lobbying law. Yale Law J 127:1742–1826

Eagleton-Price M (2016) Neoliberalism: the key concepts. Routledge, London

Ezeudu M (2014) From soft law process to hard law obligations: the Kimberley process and contemporary international legislative process. Eur J Law Reform 16(1):104–132

Falkner R (2003) Private environmental governance and international relations: exploring the links. Global Environ Politics 3(2):72–87

Fontanelli F (2011) ISO and codex standards and international trade law: what gets said is not what's heard. Int Comp Law Q 60(4):895–932

Ford L (2004) Challenging global environmental governance of toxics: social movement agency and global civil society. In: Levy D, Newell P (eds) The business of global environmental governance. MIT Press, Cambridge, pp 305–328

Fuchs D (2007) Business power in global governance. Lynne Rienner Publishers, Boulder

Gad M (2003) Impact of multinational enterprises on multilateral rule making: the pharmaceutical industry and the TRIPS Uruguay round negotiations. Law Bus Rev Am 9(4):667–698

Ginsburg T (2020) Authoritarian international law? Am J Int Law 114(2):221–260

Gleckman H (1995) Transnational corporations' strategic responses to 'sustainable development. In: Bergesen H, Parmann G, Thommessen Ø (eds) Green globe yearbook. Oxford University Press, Oxford, pp 93–106

Gleckmann H (2018) Multistakeholder governance and democracy: a global challenge. Routledge, Abingdon

Guohua Y (2019) The causes of the crisis confronting the WTO appellate body. J WTO China 9 (4):102–126

Harvey D (2007) A brief history of neoliberalism. Oxford University Press, Oxford

Hepple B (2005) Labour laws and global trade. Hart Publishing, Oxford

Hoad D (2002) The World Trade Organisation, corporate interests and global opposition: Seattle and after. Geography 87(2):148–154

Hoekman B, Kostecki M (2009) Political economy of the world trading system: WTO and beyond. Oxford University Press, Oxford

Holmes J (2007) The Kimberley process: evidence of change in international law. Brigham Young Univ Int Law ManagReview 3(2):213–232

Hood N, Young S (1979) The economics of multinational enterprise. Longman, London

Howard A (2016) Blood diamonds: the successes and failures of the Kimberley process certification scheme in Angola, Sierra Leone and Zimbabwe. Wash Univ Global Stud Law Rev 15 (1):137–160

Jerbi S (2012) Assessing the roles of multi-stakeholder initiatives in advancing the business and human rights agenda. Int Rev Red Cross 94(887):1027–1046

Johns L, Pelc K, Wellhausen R (2019) How a retreat from global economic governance may empower business interests. J Polit 81(2):731–738

Kim I, Osgood I (2019) Firms in trade and trade politics. Annu Rev Polit Sci 22:399–417

Likosky M (2005) Privatising development: transnational law, infrastructure and human rights. Martinus Nijhoff Publishers, Leiden

Likosky M (2006) Law, infrastructure and human rights. Cambridge University Press, Cambridge

Manger M (2012) Vertical trade specialization and the formation of North-South PTAs. World Polit 64(4):622–658

McKeon N (2017) Are equity and sustainability a likely outcome when foxes and chickens share the same coop? Critiquing the concept of multistakeholder governance of food security. Globalizations 14(3):379–398

Mikulich C (2003) ISO 14000-14001, the developing world's perspective. Tulane Environ Law J 17(1):117–162

Molina-Gallart N (2014) Strange bedfellows? NGO–corporate relations in international development: an NGO perspective. Development studies research. Open Access J 1(1):42–53

Muchlinski P (2011) The changing face of transnational business governance: private corporate law liability and accountability of transnational groups in a post-financial crisis world. Indiana J Global Legal Stud 18(2):665–705

Muchlinski P (2012) Multinational enterprises and international economic law: contesting regulatory agendas over the last twenty years. Jpn Yearb Int Econ Law 21:53–92

Muchlinski P (2021) Multinational enterprises and the law. Oxford University Press, Oxford

Noortmann M, Ryngaert C (2010) Non-state actor dynamics in international law: from law-takers to law-makers. Ashgate Publishing, Farnham

Noortmann M, Reinisch A, Ryngaert C (2015) Non-state actors in international law. Hart Publishing, Oxford

Ougaard M (2008) Review essay: private institutions and business power in global governance. Glob Gov 14(3):387–403

Pauwelyn J (2019) WTO dispute settlement post 2019: what to expect? J Int Econ Law 22 (3):297–321

Pauwelyn J, Wessel R, Wouters J (2012) Informal international lawmaking: an assessment and template to keep it both effective and accountable. In: Pauwelyn J, Wessel R, Wouters J (eds) Informal international lawmaking. Oxford University Press, Oxford, pp 500–537

Radu R (2019) Negotiating internet governance. Oxford University Press, Oxford

Rawling M (2015) Legislative regulation of global value chains to protect workers: a preliminary assessment. Econ Labour Relat Rev 26(4):660–677

Ray E (1987) Changing patterns of protectionism: the fall in tariffs and the rise in non-tariff barriers symposium: the political economy of international trade law and policy. Northwest J Int Law Bus 8:285–327

Raymond M, DeNardis L (2015) Multistakeholderism: anatomy of an inchoate global institution. Int Theory 7(3):572–616

Rowlands I (2001) Transnational corporations and global environmental politics. In: Josselin D, Wallace W (eds) Non-state actors in world politics. Palgrave Macmillan, London, pp 133–149

Ruggie J (1982) International regimes, transactions, and change: embedded liberalism in the postwar economic order. Int Organ 36(2):379–415

Ruggie J (1992) Multilateralism: the anatomy of an institution. Int Organ 46(3):561–598

Ruggie J (2018) Multinationals as global institution: power, authority and relative autonomy. Regulat Govern 12(3):317–333

Ryngaert C (2016) Non-state actors: carving out a space in a state-centred international legal system. Netherlands Int Law Rev 63:183–195

Sally R (1998) Classical liberalism and international economic order. Routledge, London

Schleifer P (2019) Varieties of multi-stakeholder governance: selecting legitimation strategies in transnational sustainability politics. Globalizations 16(1):50–66

Selwyn B (2013) Social upgrading and labour in global production networks: a critique and an alternative conception. Compet Chang 17(1):75–90

Servais JM (2017) International labour law. Kluwer Law International, The Hague

Sinkovics N, Ferdous Hoque S, Sinkovics R (2016) Rana Plaza collapse aftermath: are CSR compliance and auditing pressures effective? Account Auditing Accountability J 29(4):617–649

Slobodian Q (2018) Globalists: the end of empire and the birth of neoliberalism. Harvard University Press, Cambridge

St John T (2018) The rise of investor-state arbitration: politics, law and unintended consequences. Oxford University Press, Oxford

Stephan P (2011) Privatizing international law. Va Law Rev 97(7):1573–1664

Stopford J, Strange S, Henley J (1991) Rival states, rival firms. Cambridge University Press, Cambridge

Strandenaes J (2019) Stakeholder democracy – re-engaging the peoples of the world. In: Dodds F et al (eds) Stakeholder democracy: represented democracy in a time of fear. Routledge, Abingdon, pp 7–21

Strange S (1994) States and markets. Continuum, London

Tamo A (2016) New thinking on transnational corporations and human rights: towards a multi-stakeholder approach. Netherlands Q Human Rights 34(2):147–173

Van Harten G (2007) Investment treaty arbitration and public law. Oxford University Press, Oxford

Venugopal R (2015) Neoliberalism as concept. Econ Soc 44(2):165–187

Vernon R (1973) Sovereignty at bay. Pelican, Harmondsworth

Webb K (2015) ISO 26000 social responsibility standard as 'proto law' and a new form of global custom: positioning ISO 26000 in the emerging transnational regulatory governance rule instrument architecture. Transnational Legal Theory 6(2):466–500

Wexler L (2010) Regulating resource curses: institutional design and evolution of the blood diamond regime. Cardozo Law Rev 31(5):1717–1780

Wilkinson R (2000) Multilateralism and the World Trade Organization. Routledge, London

Wilks S (2013) The political power of the business corporation. Edward Elgar, Cheltenham

Winetroub A (2013) A diamond scheme is forever lost: the Kimberley process's deteriorating tripartite structure and its consequences for the scheme's survival. Indiana J Global Legal Stud 20(2):1425–1444

Yaziji M, Doh J (2009) NGOs and corporations: conflict and collaboration. Cambridge University Press, Cambridge

Peter Muchlinski is Emeritus Professor of International Commercial Law at the School of Law, the School of Oriental and African Studies, University of London. He is the author of *Multinational Enterprises and the Law* (Oxford University Press, 2nd ed., 2007, third edition forthcoming 2021). He specialises in the regulation of multinational enterprises, international investment law and business and human rights.

Coming of Age: The System of OECD National Contact Points for Responsible Business Conduct in Its 20 Years

Ondřej Svoboda

Contents

Abstract The Organisation for Economic Co-operation and Development (OECD) Guidelines for Multinational Enterprises are one of the most recognised international instruments within the universe of responsible business conduct (RBC) and business and human rights (BHR). To fully understand their role, and to critically discuss their implications and country practice, it is necessary to address a network of account- ability mechanisms which ensure that corporate actors are socially responsible and respect human rights – National Contact Points (NCPs). NCPs are tasked with the implementation of the OECD Guidelines through promotional activities and by helping resolve 'specific instances' of alleged non-observance of the Guidelines. The number and visibility of cases submitted to NCPs is increasing along their ability to make a difference. The 20th anniversary of the NCPs as a grievance

This article was supported by the Charles University, project UNCE – Human Rights Research Centre, UNCE/HUM/011. The opinions expressed in this article do not represent an official position of the Secretariat of the National Contact Point of the Czech Republic and are just and only the author's. I am especially grateful to Baxter Roberts, Jan Kunstýř and Ludmila Hyklová for their valuable comments.

O. Svoboda (✉)
Faculty of Law, Charles University, Prague, Czech Republic

© Springer Nature Switzerland AG 2021   31
M. Bungenberg et al. (eds.), *European Yearbook of International Economic Law 2020*,
European Yearbook of International Economic Law (2022) 11: 31–54,
https://doi.org/10.1007/8165_2020_53, Published online: 19 November 2020

mechanism (2020), and the tenth anniversary of the last update of the Guidelines (2021), is an appropriate juncture to reflect on the achievements so far. It is also a time to consider possible revisions that may enhance the ability of the Guidelines and the NCP system to remain at the forefront of international RBC standards and are fit to address emerging challenges such as climate change.

1 Introduction

The awareness of broader environmental and societal issues is steadily increasing with younger generations. Survey results published in 2017 indicate that 76% of millennials regarded business as a force for positive social impact and change.[1] At the same time, many feel that large businesses are not fulfilling their potential to alleviate society's challenges. Millennials also have a heightened sense of global responsibility and driving demand for sustainable investments.[2] As younger generations accumulate wealth and become a larger subset of economic actors, firms shift strategies to adopt to the growing awareness of these new socially-responsible investors. The increasing recognition of the impact that businesses have on the protection of the entire spectrum of internationally recognised human rights – civil and political rights, as well as economic, social and cultural rights – raises new challenges. A number of international instruments have been developed to establish norms for responsible business conduct (RBC) and several others are currently under consideration.

Since its adoption in 1976, the Organisation for Economic Co-operation and Development (OECD) Guidelines for Multinational Enterprises (hereafter Guidelines) are the most comprehensive international instrument on RBC. They provide guidance for RBC in a broad spectrum of areas on which businesses have an impact, such as labour, environment, human rights, consumer protection, competition, taxation, transparency and technology. The specific chapters are in many instances closely linked to non-OECD multilateral instruments as well as to OECD instruments, e.g. the OECD Convention on Combating Bribery.

With the endorsement of the United Nations Guiding Principles for Business and Human Rights (UNGPs) by the Human Rights Council in 2011,[3] corporate human rights due diligence was fully integrated into the Guidelines.[4] Completed with a

---

[1]Deloitte (2017), p. 7.

[2]Ernst & Young (2017). See also Ruggie and Middleton (2019), pp. 144–150.

[3]UN Human Rights Council (2011).

[4]UN General Assembly (2018), para 20.

human rights chapter,[5] the updated Guidelines from 2011 have become consistent with the UN Protect, Respect and Remedy Framework. The new full-fledged chapter on human rights implies that while states have the duty to protect human rights, enterprises should respect human rights, which means in practice that they should address adverse human rights impacts arising from their business models. With this development, the Guidelines made a shift in paradigm by broadening their focus from investors' and economic perspectives to the people whose rights might be infringed.[6]

The Guidelines, endorsed by all 48 adhering governments, are unique in two aspects. First and foremost, they are the first international instrument to integrate respect for human rights as a corporate responsibility. But perhaps just as importantly, they establish a network of accountability mechanisms to ensure that corporate actors are socially responsible and respect human rights – National Contact Points for Responsible Business Conduct (NCPs). The substance of this paper focusses on this feature of the Guidelines. All governments adhering to the OECD Declaration on International Investment and Multinational Enterprises are required to establish an NCP. The network of NCPs still represents the only government-backed multi-stakeholder grievance mechanism that addresses issues related to adverse impacts linked to companies' operations across global supply chains.

NCPs are tasked with implementation of the Guidelines through promotional activities and by helping to resolve 'specific instances' (or, in other words, cases) of alleged non-observance of the Guidelines. The number and visibility of the cases submitted to NCPs are increasing as well as their ability to make a difference. Between 2000 and 2015, 366 specific instances were filed with NCPs. Today, the total number of cases filed is over 500 and in the years since the 2011 revision of the Guidelines, cases with a human rights element have accounted for over 50% of all cases received. They cover cases in more than 90 countries, including emerging economies such as China, India, Indonesia, and in developing countries such as Cameroon, the Democratic Republic of Congo and Papua New Guinea.[7] Some of these cases have attracted broad public attention in developed as well developing economies. Another evidence of the uniqueness of the NCP system is the fact that NCPs are hybrid institutions, which are state-based but have certain exterritorial powers, and are non-judicial."[8] Considering this development, it is no surprise that the emerging "jurisprudence" from NCP cases is becoming a field of academic and broader public study and analysis.[9]

---

[5]The Guidelines further includes chapters on employment and industrial relations, environment, information disclosure, anticorruption, consumer interests, science and technology, competition, and taxation.

[6]Kaufmann (2018), p. 30.

[7]The OECD maintains a record of specific instances handled by the NCPs through an online database, see https://mneguidelines.oecd.org/database/ (last accessed 20 May 2020).

[8]Buhmann (2019), p. 42.

[9]See e.g. Buhmann (2018), pp. 390–410.

At the same time, NCPs are increasingly confronted with complex cases, frequently spanning multiple jurisdictions and involving numerous business relationships. This is largely due to the rise of so-called global value chains (GVCs) as a means of carrying out international production, trade and investment, whereby different stages of the production process are located across different countries. Institutionally, NCPs are of different shapes and sizes. As result, the NCP landscape is highly fragmented. Some NCPs have neither the resources nor the capacity to carry out entrusted functions, nor the necessary support from its host government in terms of finance or personnel. This situation leads to particular challenges regarding coordination when a complaint relates to different NCPs. Evidently, coordination in cases where more NCPs are involved could be improved. However, this raises the related question of a level playing field in terms of equivalence among NCPs.[10] The serious concern that different structures, roles and powers of NCPs create an uneven playing filed is frequently echoed and undermines the legitimacy of the system as a whole.[11]

Regarding outcomes from cases submitted to an NCP, the recent analysis shows that the majority of the concluded or withdrawn cases did not result in a mutually-agreed settlement or other agreement between the disputing parties. According to some commentators, even the 2011 revision of the Guidelines did not make a significant difference in human rights terms:

> There has been little change both in the very small number of cases initiated using this process and in their outcomes, meaning that companies are as likely and as able as ever to disregard or disengage with the process or its recommendations; and after a brief period of enthusiasm, the number of cases lodged with NCPs appear to be at a historic low point.[12]

Given the unique nature of the NCP mechanism, it is clear that they have strengths as well as weaknesses. Despite an increasing number of successful outcomes and achievements,[13] its critics highlight a widespread lack of remedies for victims under the NCP system and call for a reform of the current rules.[14] Uneven

---

[10]Kaufmann (2018), pp. 31–33. Functional equivalence means that regardless of how a NCP is structured, all NCPs must operate in accordance with a set of criteria. „Building functional equivalence"is also one of four pillars of the OECD Action Plan to Strengthen National Contact Points for Responsible Business Conduct 2019–2021.

[11]Sanchez (2015), p. 118.

[12]Khoury and Whyte (2019), pp. 368–369, 376.

[13]E.g. Dutch NCP (2017a) Final statement: Former employees of Bralima vs. Bralima and Heineken, https://www.oecdguidelines.nl/documents/publication/2017/08/18/final-statement-notification-bralima-vs-heineken (last accessed 20 May 2020); French NCP (2017) Final statement: Natixis-Natixis Global Asset Manager and Unite Here, https://www.tresor.economie.gouv.fr/Articles/422bdea0-4e4a-4bf4-8e44-c8a471316fe4/files/06015fda-82da-4d1d-a0ce-358ced22aca8 (last accessed 20 May 2020); Swiss NCP (2018) Final statement: Specific instance regarding Fédération Internationale de Football Association (FIFA) and Building and Wood Workers' International (BWI), https://www.seco.admin.ch/seco/en/home/Aussenwirtschaftspolitik_Wirtschaftliche_Zusammenarbeit/Wirtschaftsbeziehungen/NKP/Statements_zu_konkreten_Faellen.html (last accessed 20 May 2020).

[14]OECD Watch (2019).

performance handling of specific instances, including parallel proceedings or delays raise challenges for the legitimacy and effectivity of the system.[15] The year 2020 marks the 20th anniversary of this system's existence.[16]

This contribution critically analyses procedural as well as substantive issues in order to look to the future of this mechanism on RBC and offer a perspective towards the next generation of NCPs. It examines the OECD instruments and reports as well on the regulation and practice of several NCPs.

This paper is divided into five sections. Following this introduction, the second section deals with the effort to improve the current state of the NCP system in addressing issues relating to the functioning and performance of NCPs – through peer reviews and cooperation among NCPs. The third section explores how states support indirect enforcement powers of NCPs' statements in practice and how they build policy coherence at the same time. The fourth section underscores new challenges faced by NCPs, specifically climate change. The final section reflects on the role of NCPs over the coming decade.

2 Enhancing the Effectiveness of the OECD Guidelines and Fostering the Functioning of NCPs

NCPs constitute a distinctive feature of the Guidelines and provide a strong mechanism to support their implementation and ensure accountability. The NCPs are also referenced as an example of a state-based grievance mechanism in the UN Guiding Principles on Business and Human Rights.[17] To fulfil their role to further the effectiveness of the Guidelines,[18] NCPs must operate in accordance with the principles of visibility, accessibility, transparency and accountability in order to promote functional equivalence.[19] Adherents thus should provide sufficient resources for their NCPs to ensure proper functioning.[20] However, the procedural handling of specific instances is frequently debated and criticised because of the divergent

---

[15]OECD (2016), p. 27.

[16]It was the 2000 review of the Guidelines that is considered to be instrumental in establishing the system of NCPs by providing clear procedural guidance on their functioning.

[17]NCPs are referenced in the Commentary to Guiding Principle 25 which reads "As part of their duty to protect against business-related human rights abuse, States must take appropriate steps to ensure, through judicial, administrative, legislative or other appropriate means, that when such abuses occur within their territory and/or jurisdiction those affected have access to effective remedy."

[18]OECD Council (2011), Section I, para 1.

[19]OECD (2011), Sections A-D.

[20]Adhering countries committed themselves to "make available human and financial resources to their National Contact Points so that they can effectively fulfil their responsibilities, taking into account internal budget priorities and practices."OECD Council (2011), Section I, para 4.

approach and capacity of respective NCPs.[21] This challenge is well documented. OECD Secretary-General Angel Gurría recognised recently that "the NCP landscape is not even" and that "[s]ome countries are clearly not doing enough."[22] To improve the situation and help in implementation of the Guidelines, the OECD has focused to enhance the effectiveness of the NCP system through peer reviews and improved cooperation.

2.1 Peer-Review

Peer reviews are a tool used across the OECD and other international organisations to assess implementation of government policies.[23] In the case of NCPs, they are in principle voluntary. However, pressure is building on adherents to take this more seriously as it will be shown below. In recognition of their importance, the G7 Leaders Declaration in June 2015 committed the G7 governments to "strengthening mechanisms for providing access to remedies including the National Contact Points". In order to do this, the G7 governments committed to ensuring that their own NCPs are effective and that they "lead by example".[24] In addition, at the June 2017 OECD Ministerial Council Meeting, members' governments committed "to having fully functioning and adequately resourced National Contact Points, and to undertake a peer learning, capacity building exercise or a peer review by 2021, with a view to having all countries peer reviewed by 2023."[25] Peer reviews were a central component of the first Action Plan to strengthen National Contact Points (2016–2018), and continue being central under the second Action Plan (2019–2021).[26]

Governments have sought to increase the effectiveness of peer reviews by asking the OECD to play a facilitating role. In the 2011 update of the Guidelines, a new provision was added to Section II of the Procedural Guidance inviting the Investment Committee to facilitate voluntary peer evaluations: "In discharging its responsibilities, the Committee will be assisted by the OECD Secretariat, which, under the overall guidance of the Investment Committee, and subject to the Organisation's Programme of Work and Budget, will [. . .] facilitate peer learning activities, including voluntary peer evaluations, as well as capacity building and training, in particular, for NCPs of new adhering countries, on the implementation procedures of the

---

[21]Davarnejad (2011), p. 363; Robinson (2014), pp. 72–73; Svoboda (2018), p. 63.

[22]Gurría (2018) Opening remarks at the OECD Global Forum on Responsible Business Conduct, https://mneguidelines.oecd.org/global-forum-on-rbc-2018-opening-remarks.htm (last accessed 24 January 2020).

[23]OECD (2003).

[24]G7 (2015).

[25]OECD Ministerial Council (2017), para. 17.3.

[26]OECD (2019d).

Guidelines such as promotion and the facilitation of conciliation and mediation."[27] The Commentary on the Implementation Procedures further encourages NCPs "to engage in horizontal, thematic peer reviews and voluntary NCP peer evaluations".[28]

In terms of procedures, the NCP peer-review process usually starts with a preparatory phase. This includes the composition and preparation of the peer review team. Peer review teams are normally kept small, composed of two to four reviewers form different NCPs. Other NCPs can participate as observers. The criteria for a selection are an expression of interest, experience and geographical balance. Peer review teams also always involve a member of the OECD Secretariat. The OECD Secretariat assists with an analysis of documents relating to the structure and functioning of the NCP and collects responses to questionnaires from the NCP under review, as well as key stakeholders from business, trade unions and civil society organisations.

An on-site visit usually follows, which normally takes place over 2–3 days. During the on-site visit, the peer review team conducts interviews and other consultations with members of the NCP and relevant government agencies, as well as stakeholders from business, trade unions, and civil society organisations. Inputs of stakeholders are very important in demonstrating how an NCP functions in practice. They respond to questions from the peer review team about their current/past relationship to the NCP. As the objective of the peer review is to better understand the practical functioning of the NCP, stakeholders are asked to focus on providing information relevant to the performance of the NCP, rather than general information about RBC issues.

In practice, the main purpose of peer reviews of NCPs is to assess whether and how the NCP fulfils its mandates to promote the Guidelines and to contribute to the resolution of issues that arise relating to implementation of the Guidelines in specific instances. Peer reviews also consider how the NCP fulfils the core criteria for functional equivalence of NCPs – visibility, accessibility, transparency, and accountability – and how it handles specific instances in a manner that is impartial, predictable, equitable and compatible with the principles and standards of the Guidelines. The peer review aims to identify the strengths and weaknesses of the NCP, provide peer-learning input for the benefit of the NCP under review and the wider NCP community and, where necessary, provide recommendations for improvement.

Peer reviews are thus instrumental in achieving three goals: (1) alignment with core criteria for the NCP as set out in the Guidelines; (2) mapping of the NCP's strengths and providing recommendations and identifying opportunities for improvement; and (3) serving as a learning tool for other governments in the NCP network. In addition, they can be used to strengthen the NCP position vis-à-vis other ministries. Close collaboration with an international organisation (in this case, the OECD) may enhance the status of NCPs within some government administrations.

---

[27]OECD (2011), Section II, para 5(c).
[28]OECD (2011), para 19.

The findings of the peer review also have a broader value by contributing to the strengthening of the NCP system as a whole through sharing lessons learned and good practices with the broader NCP community. They are shared with other NCPs and with stakeholders, and thereby help not only the government of the reviewed NCP but also other governments to learn from the findings of the review, and to maintain the transparency of the process. To fulfil this aim, NCP Peer reviews reports with a timetable for next peer reviews are in principle publicly accessible.[29]

At the end of the peer-review process, the OECD issues a report with recommendations. Follow-up of NCP recommendations is also important. For this reason, the report itself is normally made public, including the recommendations, in the hope that local stakeholders can play a role in holding the NCP accountable for addressing the recommendations. Several NCPs publish reports on their efforts to implement these recommendations.[30] Particularly for trade unions and NGOs, follow-up and implementation are a critical part of a peer review. Some commentators have observed that "there are many recommendations that NCPs have only partially implemented or have chosen not to act upon at all [. . .] which ultimately undermines the effectiveness of the peer review process for delivering needed improvements to the NCP system."[31]

2.2 Cooperation Among NCPs

While NCPs have a long-standing practice of cooperating and exchanging information, there is an increasing pressure given by the complex business environment on fostering their collaboration. NCPs meet bi-annually at the OECD to share experiences and discuss ways in which the NCP system can be strengthened. NCPs are also encouraged to consult with each other in handling specific instances. Some situations require more formal assistance request in this respect, for example, to determine which NCPs should act as the "lead NCP" and handle a specific instance related to operations by an enterprise with business relations in several countries and where

---

[29]See http://www.oecd.org/daf/inv/mne/ncppeerreviews.htm (last accessed 21 May 2020).

[30]See e.g. French NCP (2019) Report on implementation of recommendations, https://mneguidelines.oecd.org/France-NCP-follow-up-report-implementation-of-recommendations-from-peer-review-English.pdf (last accessed 20 May 2020); German NCP (2019) Report on implementation of recommendations, https://www.bmwi.de/Redaktion/DE/Downloads/M-O/oecd-peer-review-of-the-german-ncp.pdf?__blob=publicationFile&v=4 (last accessed 20 May 2020).

[31]Accountability Counsel, ICAR, OECD Watch (2018) Advancing and Strengthening the OECD National Contact Point Peer Review Process, https://www.accountabilitycounsel.org/wp-content/uploads/2018/06/ncp-peer-review-research-report_final.pdf (last accessed 2 January 2020), pp. 10–14.

cases involve impacts in several jurisdictions. The OECD's guidance notes for NCPs recognises the importance of these types of cooperation.[32]

The logic of cooperation in dealing with specific instances is established in a decision of the OECD Council that requires NCPs to co-operate where needed, on any matter related to the Guidelines relevant to their activities.[33] The Procedural Guidance of the Guidelines provides a broad direction for NCPs to handle a specific instance, as follows: "Generally, issues will be dealt with by the NCP of the country in which the issues have arisen."[34] In cases where issues arise from an enterprise's activity in several adhering countries, NCPs are asked to consult with the NCP(s) of the other country/countries concerned and coordinate on who should lead the specific instance.

The OECD Secretariat has acknowledged, however, that since the 2011 revision of the Guidelines it may be more difficult in some cases to identify a lead NCP in light of different expectations regarding RBC across business relationships and supply chains and not simply in a company's direct operations.[35] These types of multi-jurisdictional specific instances pose a variety of challenges for NCPs. Fact-finding and building relationships with parties given language barriers in some cases can pose different levels of difficulty. Some tasks that may in many cases be straight-forward, such as assigning an external third-party mediator to handle a case, may become extremely difficult when it must be done on behalf of several NCPs. It should come as a no surprise that the majority of the procedural rules developed by NCPs to handle specific instances have started to reflect this need to cooperate within the NCP network.[36]

In multi-jurisdictional specific instances, an analysis of which NCP will take the lead needs to take into account where the emphasis of the complaint falls and the degree each NCP and/or country is linked to the impact (causing, contributing or directly linked). The guiding maxim for NCP coordination in handling such cases is to take actions "to further the effectiveness of the Guidelines". But this exercise always involves a degree of judgment. Solutions are not often black and white but practical options may arise. For instance, a specific instance was notified by a group of NGOs regarding the activities of Pohang Iron and Steel Enterprise (POSCO) India operating in India, and two of its investors, the Dutch Pension Fund ABP and its pension administrator APG, and the Norwegian Bank Investment Management (NBIM) in 2012. The notified Norwegian, Dutch, and Korean NCPs agreed that

---

[32]OECD (2019a).

[33]OECD Council (2011), para I.2: "National Contact Points in different countries shall co-operate if such need arises, on any matter related to the Guidelines relevant to their activities. As a general procedure, discussions at the national level should be initiated before contacts with other National Contact Points are undertaken."

[34]OECD (2011), para 23.

[35]OECD (2016), p. 55.

[36]Twenty three NCPs out of the 36 NCP which have published rules of procedure or terms of reference for handling of specific instances include provisions describing coordination with other NCPs.

each NCP should handle the notification against the enterprise registered in their respective country. Consequently, the Norwegian NCP assessed the alleged breach by NBIM, the Dutch NCP assessed the alleged breach by ABP and APG, and the Korean NCP assessed the alleged breach by POSCO.[37] As such each NCP handled the case with respect to the issues raised involving the enterprise's human rights impact and the due diligence from their jurisdiction.

Cooperation also involves level playing field concerns. Trade union representatives at the OECD (TUAC) have usefully summarised these concerns by noting that "in a small number of countries there is quite simply no NCP to cooperate with, because either the NCP does not exist, or it is not functioning."[38] In other countries, however, the NCPs are well-resourced, have a strong institutional status within their own government administration and have developed experience in dealing with specific instances. This mismatch between some NCPs is indeed a complex issue concerning the functioning of the whole NCP system. It can even lead to situations where a NCP from a different state "overtakes" the specific instance which primarily falls within a different jurisdiction. A question of how to cooperate in such cases between different NCPs thus will still much depend on the particularities of the given specific instance as well as on the recommendation of OECD bodies such as the Investment Committee and Working Party on Responsible Business Conduct (WPRBC) and on the willingness of respective NCPs or their government to collaborate.

3 Exploring Indirect Enforcement Powers and Building Policy Coherence

Despite the efforts of NCPs and the growing case examples in this area, the ability to enforce actions or recommendations from NCPs remains questionable. A uniform, binding approach in the area of business and human rights is lacking regardless of several past attempts. Some initiatives in this respect remain pending, including the development of the Hague Rules on Business and Human Rights Arbitration and an ongoing UN discussion on a legally binding instrument on business activities and human rights. However, as it stands today, neither states nor businesses nor other stakeholders are able to enforce the Guidelines through legal instruments.[39] One of a major weakness of the NCP system is thus a lack of enforcement powers to ensure corporate compliance with human rights standards.

---

[37]Norwegian NCP (2013) Final statement: Complaint from Lok Shakti Abhiyan, Korean Transnational Corporations Watch, Fair Green and Global Alliance and Forum for Environment and Development v. POSCO (South Korea), ABP/APG and NBIM (Netherlands), https://www.responsiblebusiness.no/files/2015/11/nbim_final-1.pdf (last accessed 20 May 2020), pp. 5–8.

[38]OECD (2019a), p. 26.

[39]Wetzel (2016), p. 115.

By its nature, proceedings before the NCP are based on goodwill of both parties which is required for successful mediation or good services provided by a NCP. NCPs cannot impose sanctions, award compensation or compel parties to participate in dispute-resolution proceedings. Ultimately, the NCPs are dependent on the cooperation of the parties to a specific issue.[40] In addition, NCPs can only make recommendations to the parties, since their subsequent implementation is merely voluntary. The issue of an effective remedy became even a subject to the scrutiny of the UN High Commissioner for Human Rights under the Accountability and Remedy Project. The UN High Commissioner found room for improvement, e.g. in case of the Korean, Mexican and Brazilian NCPs.[41] Despite the described 'softness' of the mechanism, NCP statements published at the end of a process become important sources of information on corporates' behaviour. They can serve 'the court of public opinion'. Condemnation of the company or its rejection to engage may cause serious reputational damage and indirectly related loss of market share or attractiveness for investors.[42]

More governments have started to employ a wider range of tools at their disposal in order to address societal responsibilities, including when supporting or partnering with businesses. Behaviour of companies may play a role in the context of public procurement, trade diplomacy, export credits, or subsidies for the private sector, among other areas. In a similar vein, the Council of Europe identified the same policy areas as follows:

> Those member states which have implemented the OECD Guidelines should ensure the effectiveness of their National Contact Points (NCPs) established under these guidelines, in particular by [. . .] considering whether to make public the recommendations of NCPs; and ensuring that such recommendations are taken into account by governmental authorities in their decisions on public procurement, export credits or investment guarantees.[43]

3.1 Public Procurement

Integration of human rights into public procurement law, policy and practice is an critical prerequisite to achieving RBC, inter alia via the promotion of human rights due diligence by government suppliers.[44] When RBC considerations are part of the procurement process as a prerequisite to participating in bidding processes it incentivises companies to conduct human rights-based due diligence as well as to

---

[40]Khoury and Whyte (2019), p. 371.

[41]UN High Commissioner for Human Rights (2016), para 70(g); UN High Commissioner for Human Rights (2017a), para 108(u); UN High Commissioner for Human Rights (2017b), para 76.

[42]Panayotis (2005), p. 257; Svoboda (2018), pp. 58–62.

[43]Council of Europe (2016), para 53.

[44]O'Brien and Martin-Ortega (2019), p. 233.

submit themselves to monitoring, assessment of performance, and corrective action for violations.

This emerging trend of conditioning public procurement processes on RBC due diligence is especially visible in the EU. Under the revised EU Procurement Directives, a procurement tender has to take into account a wider range of environmental, social and economic issues.[45] Furthermore, the Directive foresees the mandatory exclusion of economic operators convicted by final judgment of child labour and other forms of trafficking while this is not limited to the tendering phase, but rather reinforced by an obligation to terminate any contracts awarded to companies subsequently convicted of those offences.[46] NCPs statements could be similarly incorporated. To support this approach, the Council of the EU recently considered what support could be provided to public authorities covered by the revised EU Procurement Directives, through tools and guidance for the implementation of the Guidelines (and the UN Guiding Principles and the ILO Tripartite Declaration).[47] The EU is thus considering the introduction of a link with the NCP mechanism and public procurement within the EU.[48]

3.2 Export Credits and Trade Support

Some states have already committed to imposing trade and investment related sanctions for businesses refusing to participate in the NCP process. In case of granting export credits, human rights risks are particularly high where export granting agencies (ECAs) finance or insure large-scale projects such as industrial, extractive (e.g. oil, mining), infrastructure (e.g. roads, airports) or energy projects (e.g. dams, power plants).[49] In 1998, the ECAs of OECD member states agreed for the first time to set joint standards which were finally laid down in the 2003 Recommendation on Common Approaches on Environment and Officially Supported Export Credits (Common Approaches).[50] After several revisions, the Common Approaches have remained ECAs' key guidance document for environmental and social impact assessments, including adverse project-related human rights impacts, until this date.[51]

With regards to the compliance with the Guidelines, an important change is an option of taking an assessment of companies' behaviour in NCP specific instance procedure into account in granting export credits. Accordingly, a review of projects

---

[45]European Union (2014), para 97.

[46]European Union (2014), Art. 57(1)(f) and Art. 73(b). See also Sanchez-Graells (2019), p. 102.

[47]EU Foreign Affairs Council (2016), para.11.

[48]OECD (2017d), p. 3.

[49]Linder (2019), p. 77.

[50]OECD Council (2016).

[51]Linder (2019), p. 80.

applying for granting should consider any statements or reports made publicly available by their NCPs at the conclusion of a specific instance.[52] For instance, the UK Export Finance (UKEF) committed itself to "consider any reports made publicly available by the UK National Contact Point (NCP) in respect of the human rights record of a company when considering a project for export credit."[53] Such integration of findings can be a strong incentive for exporters as well as a guidance how to use NCPs' conclusions in practice.

Trade diplomacy is another policy area which has recently provided fertile soil to integrate RBC standards and NCPs. Trade missions and trade advocacy support are typical governmental services to business to support their trade and investment efforts abroad.[54] Canada could be considered a frontrunner in this regard. Canada's corporate social responsibility (CSR) strategy states: "Companies will also face withdrawal of TCS [the Canadian Trade Commissioner Service] and other Government of Canada advocacy support abroad for non-participation in the dialogue facilitation processes of Canada's NCP and Office of the Extractive Sector CSR Counsellor."[55]

This Canadian strategy has already been deployed in practice in a specific instance commenced in January 2014. In response to the China Gold International Resources' refusal to engage in the process before the Canadian NCP, the NCP decided to impose sanctions on the company. The penalties included the withdrawal of services of the Trade Commissioner concerning support of China Gold International Resources abroad.[56] This was the first specific instance resulting in the withdrawal of government-based trade advocacy support from a company for its failure to participate in the specific instance procedure.

Canada has also taken a lead in creating an independent ombudsperson for Responsible Enterprise as well as a multi-stakeholder Advisory Body. The ombudsperson is mandated to review allegations of human rights abuses arising from the operations of Canadian companies abroad, initially focusing on the mining, oil and gas, and garment sectors and then expanding to other sectors. The government expects that the ombudsperson will be guided in his role by the Guidelines and will refer cases to the Canadian NCP, where appropriate, and where parties are in

---

[52]OECD Council (2016), para 16.

[53]HM Government (2016) Good Business: UK National Action Plan on Business and Human Rights, https://www.gov.uk/government/publications/bhr-action-plan (last accessed 20 May 2020), para 17(ii).

[54]OECD (2017a), p. 3; UN Human Rights Council (2018).

[55]Government of Canada (2014) Doing Business the Canadian Way: A Strategy to Advance Corporate Social Responsibility in Canada's Extractive Sector Abroad, https://www.international.gc.ca/trade-agreements-accords-commerciaux/topics-domaines/other-autre/csr-strat-rse.aspx?lang=eng (last accessed 20 May 2020), p. 12.

[56]Canadian NCP (2015) Final Statement on the Request for Review regarding the Operations of China Gold International Resources Corp. Ltd., at the Copper Polymetallic Mine at the Gyama Valley, Tibet Autonomous Region, https://www.international.gc.ca/trade-agreements-accords-commerciaux/ncp-pcn/statement-gyama-valley.aspx?lang=eng (last accessed 20 May 2020).

agreement.[57] The Canadian NCP and RBC element will likely influence the government's trade policy even more as both new institutions are located at the Ministry of International Trade Diversification.

The EU has echoed the potential significance of this RBC dimension in trade diplomacy tools. In June 2016, the European Council encouraged "EU Institutions and Member States to address their responsibilities [..] when supporting or partnering with businesses (e.g. through export credit, trade promotion, or subsidies for the private sector)."[58] Similar steps from other governments or NCPs have been rather exceptional until now. However, similar initiatives are likely to arise in the future.

3.3   Investment Protection

States may also wish to incorporate the NCPs into their investment treaties. Ongoing reform of international investment law provides states with an opportunity to align international instruments with their human rights obligations and in turn achieve greater policy coherence. A number of new model investment treaties enhance RBC, CSR, consumer protection, and environmental and labour standards, as well as human rights.[59] Academics and governments have conceived various ways to integrate the Guidelines and other international instruments into investment treaties, which then brings RBC into the normative framework for these preferential rules that apply to certain foreign investors. Some commentators have suggested that counterclaims in investor-state dispute settlement cases under investment treaties may be a way of achieving a more binding form of observance of the Guidelines.[60] Others have suggested that investment treaty makers may also consider conditioning access to treaty benefits on RBC compliance, drawing analogies from other policy approaches discussed above.

Still, there are other ways of interaction between the NCPs and investment treaties. States may consider a direct connection to the NCP system. For instance, investment tribunals may be invited or directed to take NCP statements and reports on specific investor's conduct into account. Such step could constitute a strong incentive for stakeholders to make use of NCP services, including trade unions, the civil society and indigenous people adversely affected by business operations of an

---

[57]Government of Canada (2019) Minister Carr announces appointment of first Canadian Ombudsperson for Responsible Enterprise, https://www.canada.ca/en/global-affairs/news/2019/04/minister-carr-announces-appointment-of-first-canadian-ombudsperson-for-responsible-enterprise.html (last accessed 2 March 2020).

[58]EU Foreign Affairs Council (2016), para 11.

[59]E.g. Brazilian Model CFIA (2015); India Model BIT (2015); Colombia Model BIT (2017); Dutch Model BIT (2018); Belgium-Luxembourg Economic Union Model BIT (2019). For further background reading, see generally Gaukrodger (2019), pp. 86–102.

[60]Schill (2018), p. 71.

investor. This may subsequently contribute to ensuring a better balance between corporate rights and responsibilities and more generally the legitimacy of investment agreements.[61] Among others, the European Commission is currently reflecting on potential linkages between the NCP network and investment agreements. In response to concerns raised over equal protection for investors, communities and workers alike during the parliamentary debate on the Investment Protection Agreement between the EU and its Member States and Vietnam, a representative of the Commission stated that the OECD grievance mechanism, signed by all Member States, provided for additional guidelines on human rights for multinationals.[62]

In sum, the various tools at the disposal of governments are increasingly seen as levers for achieving economic, social, and environmental policy goals to compensate for the weak enforcement power of NCPs. This development creates ramifications even beyond particular cases. The growing body of NCPs' statements continues "to contribute, incrementally, to institutionalisation of transnational systems of multinational regulation; systems that will have legal effect whether or not this is law as classically understood."[63]

4 Future Challenge: Climate Change

The tenth anniversary of the last update of the Guidelines in 2021 will be a timely opportunity to assess the current scope of the Guidelines, in light of emerging issues of relevance to the implementation of RBC. Today, climate change is considered by many as a serious threat to human rights globally. This looming challenge draws growing attention of the public as well policymakers and business. Governments and international organisations increasingly take into account environmental concerns in their policies. The Paris Agreement and the European Union's Green Deal are probably the most prominent examples of this global trend.[64] Business bears an important responsibility to address this issue because it produces a very large portion of carbon emissions. Correspondingly, the public expects more action by business to prevent detrimental activities to the environment and demands climate-friendly products and services.

Without any doubt, climate change is thus likely one of the most serious concerns to consider in terms of interlinkages and overlaps which encourage further

---

[61]For more on building a new regulatory agenda of multinational corporations and the rebalancing of international economic law see Muchlinski (2016), pp. 405–414.

[62]European Parliament (2019).

[63]Backer (2009), p. 305.

[64]The Paris Agreement is the first international climate change agreement to expressly refer to human rights. Specifically, the Preamble acknowledges "that climate change is a common concern of humankind, Parties should, when taking action to address climate change, respect, promote and consider their respective obligations on human rights [. . .]".

exploration. But what is the role of the Guidelines and NCPs in this field and how do they respond to this pressing issue?

The Guidelines include a chapter dedicated to environment (Chapter VI). It provides a set of recommendations for enterprises to raise their environmental performance and help maximise their contribution to environmental protection through improved internal management and better planning. The chapter on human rights is also relevant to environmental impacts, which are often linked to human rights impacts.[65] The Guidelines urge companies to contribute to sustainable development while preventing negative impact on people and society at large. Regarding climate change, the 2011 update further specifies that enterprises should "reduce greenhouse gas emissions" and "[be] efficient in their consumption of energy and natural resources."[66] In this way, the Guidelines not only require business to reduce their carbon emissions, but also set targets to improve their environmental performance, consistent with national and international commitments. Subsequently, NCPs can hold companies accountable for climate and human rights issues.

As the OECD developed several industry-specific guidance, future work – building on the previous efforts – could be further expanded to provide similar recommendations in the area of climate, biodiversity, waste, etc.[67] For instance, the recently adopted OECD Due Diligence Guidance for Responsible Business Conduct, reflects the expectation that companies carry out risk-based due diligence, also applicable to environmental impacts, in the environment-related examples.[68] The sectoral due diligence guidance instruments address environmental impacts as well. The OECD Due Diligence Guidance for Responsible Supply Chains in the Garment and Footwear Sector includes modules on hazardous chemicals, water and greenhouse gas emissions.[69] The OECD-FAO Guidance for Responsible Agricultural Supply Chains covers protecting watersheds, and maintaining biodiversity and sustainable management of natural resources, and promoting good agricultural practices to improve soil fertility, avoid soil erosion, and minimize greenhouse gas emissions.[70] A further stream of work could be developed on the basis of the OECD Paper on Responsible Business Conduct for Institutional Investors. Additional guidance focused on the role of due diligence for climate risk management by institutional investors would provide a coherent framework for responding to emerging expectations on climate reporting and due diligence.

---

[65]UN Forum on Business and Human Rights (2019).

[66]Guidelines, Chapter VI, subsection 6(b). See also discussion in Riddell (2016), pp. 56–58.

[67]Action by business to address climate change has been discussed in various editions of the Global Forums on RBC (2017, 2019), as well as in the 2019 sectoral Forums on garment and footwear; and minerals.

[68]OECD (2018).

[69]OECD (2017b), modules 8–10.

[70]OECD (2017c) OECD-FAO Guidance for Responsible Agricultural Supply Chains.

Furthermore, the OECD organised two sessions on RBC during the recent Conference of the Parties (COP25) in Madrid. This included a joint session with the Office of the High Commissioner for Human Rights (OHCHR) on "The business and human rights dimension of climate change: addressing access to remedy."[71] The panel highlighted the continued relevance of the Guidelines to the nexus between human rights and climate-related risks and impacts for business, as well as the role of the NCPs in handling grievances. This view is supported by the emerging NCP case law.

Environmental impacts are regularly the focus of specific instances submitted to NCPs. As of the end 2019, approximately 20% of submitted specific instances related to environmental impacts. Global trends in climate litigation and legislation requiring more stringent supply chains, due diligence and reporting put pressure on companies to take action and align their business with climate goals.

The issue is now even more topical as first specific instances concerning climate change arise. The Dutch NCP received a submission by a group of four NGOs complaining of ING Bank's disclosure policy on its clients' carbon emissions and the publication of a target limit for such emissions in accordance with the Paris Climate Agreement. Complainants asked the NCP to examine ING's climate policy and to urge ING to align its climate and other policies with the Guidelines.[72] Indeed, neither the Paris Agreement nor climate change are explicitly covered in the Guidelines. At the same time, there is currently no internationally agreed guidance or standard on what is expected from financial institutions in terms of climate-change specific due diligence and the related disclosure. Though, the Dutch NCP determined that the specific instance merits further consideration, offered its good offices to the parties and issued its final statement accepted by both parties in April 2019. The final conclusions included the ING's intention to reach intermediary targets in line with the Paris Agreement, consideration of the feasibility of developing a joint roadmap on intermediate targets setting and disclosure and finally, a joint call on the Dutch government to request the International Energy Agency to develop two 1.5° C scenarios, one with and without the use of Carbon Capture and Storage.[73]

Looking into the details of the case, despite the legally non-binding language providing ING with a certain leeway, the company shifted from its uncompromising position at the beginning of mediation. Initially approached by the NCP, ING replied that "[d]ue to the lack of information on the emissions of our clients around the world and the lack of an international methodology to determine the impact of such

---

[71]OECD (2019b, c).

[72]Dutch NCP (2017b) Initial assessment: Notification Oxfam Novib, Greenpeace, BankTrack, Friends of the Earth Netherlands (Milieudefensie) vs ING, https://www.oecdguidelines.nl/notifications/documents/publication/2017/11/14/publication-dutch-ncp-initial-assessment-filed-by-4-ngos-vs.-ing-bank (last accessed 20 May 2020), pp. 1–2.

[73]Dutch NCP (2019) Final Statement: Oxfam Novib, Greenpeace Netherlands, BankTrack and Friends of the Earth Netherlands (Milieudefensie) versus ING, https://www.oecdguidelines.nl/latest/news/2019/04/19/final-statement-dutch-ncp-specific-instance-4-ngos-versus-ing-bank (last accessed 20 May 2020), p. 6.

emissions in a climate scenario, it is impossible for ING to satisfy the complainants' request in this regard," adding "there is no internationally operating bank in the world that could do otherwise." The bank also refused the NGOs' request to establish and pursue a target to lower indirect emissions in line with efforts to limit global warming to 1.5°C. According to the bank, "[t]his request does not align with the 2°C scenario currently adhered to by the international community."[74] Comparing this stance with the final outcomes, there is clearly a progress made on the behalf of ING. To see if the accepted recommendations will materialise in practice, it was agreed that a follow-up evaluation by the NCP on the outcomes will be conducted in the second quarter of 2020.[75]

On a general note, a NCP for the first time has taken a clear position on climate goals while a big financial institution agreed to bring its portfolio in line with the Paris Agreement. The specific instance is thus of particular relevance to understand the expectations on business to mitigate and address impacts on climate. The statement reaffirms the application of the "cause, contribute, directly linked" language of the Guidelines to business responsibility to address climate impacts and draws attention to the specific recommendations of the Guidelines which frame this responsibility.

Following this ground-breaking specific instance, new cases relating to climate change emerge rapidly. In November 2019, a group of NGOs filed a complaint with the Slovenian and UK NCPs alleging that the UK-based company Ascent Resources violated the Guidelines in applying for a permit to expand a fracking operation in a natural gas field in Slovenia. The complainants argued that the company was failing to take adequate steps to consider and address the potential environmental impacts of fracking, including its contribution to the threat of runaway climate change.[76] In December 2019, ClientEarth submitted a complaint of over 100 pages to the UK NCP against the oil and gas company BP which allegedly misled the public with its claims of commitment to a low carbon future.[77] The latest case has been initiated in January 2020 before the Australian NCP by Friends of the Earth. The complaint claims that ANZ Banking Group, Australia's' largest financier of fossil fuel

[74]Dutch NCP (2017b) Initial assessment: Notification Oxfam Novib, Greenpeace, BankTrack, Friends of the Earth Netherlands (Milieudefensie) vs ING, https://www.oecdguidelines.nl/notifications/documents/publication/2017/11/14/publication-dutch-ncp-initial-assessment-filed-by-4-ngos-vs.-ing-bank (last accessed 20 May 2020), p. 3.

[75]Dutch NCP (2019) Final Statement: Oxfam Novib, Greenpeace Netherlands, BankTrack and Friends of the Earth Netherlands (Milieudefensie) versus ING, https://www.oecdguidelines.nl/latest/news/2019/04/19/final-statement-dutch-ncp-specific-instance-4-ngos-versus-ing-bank (last accessed 20 May 2020), pp. 6–7.

[76]Climate Change Litigation Databases (2019) Specific instance under the OECD Guidelines for Multinational Enterprises submitted to the Slovenian and UK National Contact Point for the OECD Guidelines, http://climatecasechart.com/non-us-case/specific-instance-under-the-oecd-guidelines-for-multinational-enterprises-submitted-to-the-slovenian-and-uk-national-contact-point-for-the-oecd-guidelines/ (last accessed 22 February 2020).

[77]ClientEarth (2019) Our OECD complaint against BP explained, https://www.clientearth.org/our-oecd-complaint-against-bp-explained/ (last accessed 14 February 2020).

industries, has failed to meaningfully adhere to the Paris Agreement reduction targets across its lending portfolio and to disclose the full extent of it is lending emissions.[78] Consequently, there is a growing number of cases being brought in several countries to "ensure greater transparency of climate risks and a rapid transition away from fossil fuels to renewable energy."[79]

5 Conclusion

The 20th anniversary of the NCPs as a grievance mechanism (2020), and the tenth anniversary of the last update of the Guidelines (2021) provide timely opportunities for adherents to reflect on the achievements and potential new approaches to address emerging policy concerns. To commemorate the 20th anniversary of the NCP system, this contribution offered a reflection on the main achievements and challenges while situating NCPs in the wider context of grievance mechanism. It is also an opportunity to highlight the impact of successful cases and reflect the increasing diversity of cases being brought to NCPs.

The reinforcement of implementation procedures through clearer and more predictable rules for the handling of complaints by NCPs was among the main declared objectives of the 2011 revision.[80] Still, 6 years later, Roel Nieuwenkamp, a former Chair of the OECD WPRBC, stated: "My conclusion on the effectiveness of NCPs as a non-judicial grievance mechanism on business & human rights is that the glass is half full, but we must take active steps to fill it to the brim. Functioning NCPs which currently have strong track records with respect to outcomes in cases can serve as mentors to those lagging behind."[81]

To improve the situation, the adhering governments, NCPs and the OECD are implementing a number of steps together. Regarding peer reviews and cooperation within the NCP network, it is clear that they are crucial elements to foster NCPs' functional equivalence and thus the effectiveness of the Guidelines. Under the current framework of the Guidelines they provide tools to support convergence among the fundamentally different positions of NCPs and their roles and powers regarding individual complaints. As of January 2020, 17 peer reviews have been

---

[78]Friends of the Earth Australia (2020) Bushfire survivors launch claim against ANZ under international law for financing climate change, 20 January 2020, https://www.foe.org.au/bushfire_survivors_launch_claim_against_anz (last accessed 1 March 2020).

[79]Greenpeace (2017) NGOs v. ING, A press release: ING Bank on the hook for not reporting climate pollution, https://www.greenpeace.org/international/press-release/11850/ing-bank-on-the-hook-for-not-reporting-climate-pollution/ (last accessed 19 February 2020).

[80]Schekulin (2011), p. 2.

[81]Nieuwenkamp (2017) Outcomes from OECD National Contact Point cases: More remedy than you may think!. The Netherlands at International Organisations Blog, https://www.permanentrepresentations.nl/latest/news/2017/12/5/blog%2D%2D-outcomes-from-oecd-national-contact-point-cases-more-remedy-than-you-may-think (last accessed 4 March 2020).

completed, 3 are ongoing and an additional 12 are committed for the period 2020–2023 while the remaining 16 adherents have not been scheduled yet.[82] The development underscores the increasing adhering governments' will to improve and build upon the NCP system.

At the same time, NCPs' findings on compliance with the Guidelines are more frequently incorporated into state's various sanctioning mechanisms to bridge the enforcement gap. The important development is that non-compliance with NCPs' recommendation or just unwillingness to take part in proceedings before an NCP may lead to a withdrawal of various types of public support, such as export credits or participation in trade missions or public procurement. In addition, there are voices calling on exploring clauses in investment agreements which would stipulate that only those investors that can demonstrate compliance with the Guidelines would be eligible for protection under such agreements.[83]

Another test for the effectiveness of the Guidelines and the NCP network relates to emerging areas or increasingly acute challenges, such as addressing business' impacts on the environment, in particular related to climate, biodiversity, waste and plastics, as well as digitalisation and artificial intelligence. A recent statement by the Dutch NCP highlighted that a company's business plan should be consistent with relevant national policies and international environmental commitments such as the Paris Agreement. This case has already inspired other stakeholders to draw business attention to their responsibility to address climate impacts under the Guidelines.

To conclude, there is clearly a demand for policy coherence and maximising the potential of the NCP mechanism from both states and stakeholders and that synergy can work in both ways. The BHR/RBC landscape of which NCPs are an influential part will offer new opportunities to engage and promote the values of the Guidelines. At the same time, the increased role for NCPs in policy coherence is envisaged by numerous National Action Plans on business and human rights under the UNGPs.[84] Still, in its twentieth year, the NCP system must commit to continuously adapt in order to succeed in the face of new challenges.

References

Accountability Counsel, ICAR, OECD Watch (2018) Advancing and strengthening the OECD national contact point peer review process, https://www.accountabilitycounsel.org/wp-content/uploads/2018/06/ncp-peer-review-research-report_final.pdf. Last accessed 2 Jan 2020

---

[82]OECD (2020), p. 44.

[83]Nieuwenkamp and Sinivuori (2015), p. 2.

[84]The UNGPs refer to the NCPs in the Commentary to Guiding Principle 25, where they are listed among State-based grievance mechanisms. NCPs are included in several National action plans on business and human rights, for instance of Belgium. Chile, the Czech Republic, Denmark, Finland, France, Germany, Ireland, Italy, Luxembourg, Poland, South Korea, Spain, Switzerland or the United States.

Backer LC (2009) Rights and accountability in development (raid) v. das air and global witness v. Afrimex - small steps towards an autonomous transnational legal system for the regulation of multinational corporations. Melb J Int Law 10(1):258–307

Buhmann K (2018) Analysing OECD national contact point statements for guidance on human rights due diligence: method, findings and outlook. Nordic J Human Rights 36(4):390–410

Buhmann K (2019) National Contact Points under OECD's Gudelines for multinational enterprises: institutional diversity affecting assessments of delivery of access to remedy. In: Enneking L, Giesen I, Schaap AJ, Ryngaert C, Kristen F, Roorda L (eds) Accountability, international business operations and the law. Routledge, London, pp 38–59

Canadian NCP (2015) Final statement on the request for review regarding the operations of China Gold International Resources Corp. Ltd., at the Copper Polymetallic Mine at the Gyama Valley, Tibet Autonomous Region, https://www.international.gc.ca/trade-agreements-accords-commerciaux/ncp-pcn/statement-gyama-valley.aspx?lang=eng. Last accessed 20 May 2020

ClientEarth (2019) Our OECD complaint against BP explained, https://www.clientearth.org/our-oecd-complaint-against-bp-explained/. Last accessed 14 Feb 2020

Climate Change Litigation Databases (2019) Specific instance under the OECD Guidelines for Multinational Enterprises submitted to the Slovenian and UK National Contact Point for the OECD Guidelines, http://climatecasechart.com/non-us-case/specific-instance-under-the-oecd-guidelines-for-multinational-enterprises-submitted-to-the-slovenian-and-uk-national-contact-point-for-the-oecd-guidelines/. Last accessed 22 Feb 2020

Council of Europe (2016) Recommendation CM/Rec(2016)3 of the Committee of Ministers to member states adopted on 2 March 2016

Davarnejad L (2011) In the shadow of soft law: the handling of corporate social responsibility disputes under the OECD guidelines for multinational enterprises. J Disput Resolut 2:351–385

Deloitte (2017) Millennial survey

Dutch NCP (2017a) Final statement: Former employees of Bralima vs. Bralima and Heineken, https://www.oecdguidelines.nl/documents/publication/2017/08/18/final-statement-notification-bralima-vs-heineken. Last accessed 20 May 2020

Dutch NCP (2017b) Initial assessment: Notification Oxfam Novib, Greenpeace, BankTrack, Friends of the Earth Netherlands (Milieudefensie) vs ING, https://www.oecdguidelines.nl/notifications/documents/publication/2017/11/14/publication-dutch-ncp-initial-assessment-filed-by-4-ngos-vs.-ing-bank. Last accessed 20 May 2020

Dutch NCP (2019) Final Statement: Oxfam Novib, Greenpeace Netherlands, BankTrack and Friends of the Earth Netherlands (Milieudefensie) versus ING, https://www.oecdguidelines.nl/latest/news/2019/04/19/final-statement-dutch-ncp-specific-instance-4-ngos-versus-ing-bank. Last accessed 20 May 2020

Ernst & Young (2017) Sustainable investing: the millennial investor

EU Foreign Affairs Council (2016) Council conclusion on business & human rights. 10254/16

European Parliament (2019) Committee on International Trade's Meeting of Tuesday 3 December 2019

European Union (2014) Directive 2014/24/EU of the European Parliament and of the Council of 26 February 2014 on public procurement and repealing Directive 2004/18/EC, OJ L 94 L 94/65

French NCP (2017) Final statement: Natixis-Natixis Global Asset Manager and Unite Here, https://www.tresor.economie.gouv.fr/Articles/422bdea0-4e4a-4bf4-8e44-c8a471316fe4/files/06015fda-82da-4d1d-a0ce-358ced22aca8. Last accessed 20 May 2020

French NCP (2019) Report on implementation of recommendations, https://mneguidelines.oecd.org/France-NCP-follow-up-report-implementation-of-recommendations-from-peer-review-English.pdf. Last accessed 20 May 2020

Friends of the Earth Australia (2020) Bushfire survivors launch claim against ANZ under international law for financing climate change, 20 January 2020, https://www.foe.org.au/bushfire_survivors_launch_claim_against_anz. Last accessed 1 March 2020

G7 (2015) Leaders' Declaration: G7 Summit on 7–8 June 2015

Gaukrodger D (2019) Business responsibilities and investment treaties: consultation paper by the OECD Secretariat

German NCP (2019) Report on implementation of recommendations, https://www.bmwi.de/Redaktion/DE/Downloads/M-O/oecd-peer-review-of-the-german-ncp.pdf?__blob=publicationFile&v=4. Last accessed 20 May 2020

Government of Canada (2014) Doing business the Canadian way: a strategy to advance corporate social responsibility in Canada's Extractive Sector Abroad, https://www.international.gc.ca/trade-agreements-accords-commerciaux/topics-domaines/other-autre/csr-strat-rse.aspx?lang=eng. Last accessed 20 May 2020

Government of Canada (2019) Minister Carr announces appointment of first Canadian Ombudsperson for Responsible Enterprise, https://www.canada.ca/en/global-affairs/news/2019/04/minister-carr-announces-appointment-of-first-canadian-ombudsperson-for-responsible-enterprise.html. Last accessed 2 March 2020

Greenpeace (2017) NGOs v. ING, A press release: ING Bank on the hook for not reporting climate pollution, https://www.greenpeace.org/international/press-release/11850/ing-bank-on-the-hook-for-not-reporting-climate-pollution/. Last accessed 19 Feb 2020

Gurría A (2018) Opening remarks at the OECD Global forum on responsible business conduct, https://mneguidelines.oecd.org/global-forum-on-rbc-2018-opening-remarks.htm. Last accessed 24 Jan 2020

HM Government (2016) Good Business: UK National Action Plan on Business and Human Rights, https://www.gov.uk/government/publications/bhr-action-plan. Last accessed 20 May 2020

Kaufmann C (2018) OECD MNE guidelines quo vadis? Making responsible business conduct work for better lives. In: OECD (ed) OECD guidelines for multinational enterprises: a glass half full. OECD Publishing, Paris, pp 29–36

Khoury S, Whyte D (2019) Sideling corporate rights violations: the failure of the OECD's regulatory consensus. J Human Rights 18(4):363–381

Linder L (2019) Human rights, export credits and development cooperation: accountability for bilateral agencies. Edward Elgar, Cheltenham

Muchlinski P (2016) Regulating multinational enterprises. In: Bungenberg M, Herrmann C, Krajewski M, Terhechte JP (eds) European yearbook of international economic law 2016. Springer, Heidelberg, pp 391–422

Nieuwenkamp R (2017) Outcomes from OECD National Contact Point cases: More remedy than you may think!. The Netherlands at International Organisations Blog, https://www.permanentrepresentations.nl/latest/news/2017/12/5/blog%2D%2D-outcomes-from-oecd-national-contact-point-cases-more-remedy-than-you-may-think. Last accessed 4 March 2020

Nieuwenkamp R, Sinivuori K (2015) The road to responsible investment treaties. Columb FDI Perspect 134:1–3

Norwegian NCP (2013) Final statement: Complaint from Lok Shakti Abhiyan, Korean Transnational Corporations Watch, Fair Green and Global Alliance and Forum for Environment and Development v. POSCO (South Korea), ABP/APG and NBIM (Netherlands), https://www.responsiblebusiness.no/files/2015/11/nbim_final-1.pdf. Last accessed 20 May 2020

O'Brien CM, Martin-Ortega O (2019) Public procurement and human rights: towards legal and policy coherence in pursuit of sustainable market economies. In: Martin-Ortega O, O'Brien CM (eds) Public procurement and human rights: opportunities, risks and dilemmas for the state as buyer. Edward Elgar, Cheltenham, pp 225–235

OECD (2003) Peer review: an OECD tool for co-operation and change

OECD (2011) OECD guidelines for multinational enterprises

OECD (2016) Implementing the OECD guidelines for multinational enterprises: the national contact points from 2000 to 2015

OECD (2017a) Responsible business conduct and economic diplomacy tools

OECD (2017b) OECD due diligence guidance for responsible supply chains in the garment and footwear sector

OECD (2017c) OECD-FAO guidance for responsible agricultural supply chains

OECD (2017d) Responsible business conduct in government procurement practices

OECD (2018) OECD due diligence guidance for responsible business conduct

OECD (2019a) Guide for national contact points on coordination when handling specific instances

OECD (2019b) The business and human rights dimension of climate change: addressing access to remedy: concept note

OECD (2019c) Global climate action and responsible business conduct: what does it mean for business to act responsibly in the face of a climate emergency?: Background Note

OECD (2019d) Action plan to strengthen national contact points for responsible business conduct (2019–2021)

OECD (2020) Annual report on the OECD guidelines for multinational enterprises 2019

OECD Council (2011) Amendment of the Decision of the Council on the OECD Guidelines for Multinational Enterprises. OECD/LEGAL/0307

OECD Council (2016) Recommendation of the Council on common approaches for officially supported export credits and environmental and social due diligence. OECD/LEGAL/0393

OECD Ministerial Council (2017) Making globalisation work: better lives for all

OECD Watch (2019) The state of remedy under the OECD guidelines: understanding NCP cases concluded in 2018 through the lens of remedy

Panayotis PM (2005) La mise en œuvre des Principes directeurs de l'OCDE à l'intention des entreprises multinationales: Réflexions sur le nouveau mandat des Points de contact nationaux, International Law. Forum Du Droit Int 7(4):251–260

Riddell A (2016) Human rights responsibility of private corporations for climate change? The state as a catalyst for compliance. In: Quirico O, Boumghar M (eds) Climate change and human rights: an international and comparative law. Routledge, Abingdon, pp 53–68

Robinson S (2014) International obligations, states responsibility and judicial review under the OECD guidelines for multinational enterprises regime. Utrecht J Int Eur Law 30(78):68–81

Ruggie JG, Middleton EK (2019) Money, Millennials and human rights: sustaining 'sustainable investing'. Global Pol 10(1):144–150

Sanchez O (2015) The roles and powers of the OECD National Contact Points Regarding Complains on an alleged breach of the OECD guidelines for multinational enterprises by a transnational corporation. Nordic J Int Law 84(1):89–126

Sanchez-Graells A (2019) Public procurement and 'core' human rights: a sketch of the European Union legal framework. In: Martin-Ortega O, O'Brien CM (eds) Public procurement and human rights: opportunities, risks and dilemmas for the state as buyer. Edward Elgar, Cheltenham, pp 96–114

Schekulin M (2011) Shaping global business conduct: the 2011 update of the OECD guidelines for multinational enterprises. Columb FDI Perspect 47:1–3

Schill SW (2018) The OECD guidelines for multinational enterprises and international investment agreements: converging universes. In: Bonucci N, Kessedjian C (eds) 40 ans des lignes directrices de l'OCDE pour les entreprises mulinationales/40 Years of the OECD Guidelines for Multinational Enterprises. Pedone, Paris, pp 63–78

Svoboda O (2018) The OECD guidelines for multinational enterprises and the increasing relevance of the system of National Contact Points. In: Šturma P, Mozetic VA (eds) Business and human rights. rw&w Science & New Media, Waldkirchen, pp 52–63

Swiss NCP (2018) Final statement: Specific instance regarding Fédération Internationale de Football Association (FIFA) and Building and Wood Workers' International (BWI), https://www.seco.admin.ch/seco/en/home/Aussenwirtschaftspolitik_Wirtschaftliche_Zusammenarbeit/Wirtschaftsbeziehungen/NKP/Statements_zu_konkreten_Faellen.html. Last accessed 20 May 2020

UN Forum on Business and Human Rights (2019) Addressing environmental harms – the business and human rights connection session

UN General Assembly (2018) Working Group on the issue of human rights and transnational corporations and other business enterprises: Note by the Secretary-General. A/73/163

UN High Commissioner for Human Rights (2016) Report of the Working Group on the issue of human rights and transnational corporations and other business enterprises on its mission to Brazil. A/HRC/32/45/Add.1

UN High Commissioner for Human Rights (2017a) Report of the Working Group on the issue of human rights and transnational corporations and other business enterprises on its mission to Mexico. A/HRC/35/32/Add.2

UN High Commissioner for Human Rights (2017b) Report of the Working Group on the issue of human rights and transnational corporations and other business enterprises on its visit to the Republic of Korea. A/HRC/35/32/Add.1

UN Human Rights Council (2011) Report of the Special Representative of the Secretary General on the issue of human rights and transnational corporations and other business enterprises, John Ruggie. A/HRC/17/31

UN Human Rights Council (2018) Report of the Working Group on the issue of human rights and transnational corporations and other business enterprises. A/HRC/38/48

Wetzel JR (2016) Human rights in transnational business: translating human rights obligations into compliance procedures. Springer, Basel

Ondřej Svoboda serves as a legal advisor at the Unit of International Law of the Ministry of Industry and Trade of the Czech Republic where he provides complex expertise in investment and trade law issues and legal counsel supporting the Czech position in conducting the EU Common Commercial Policy. Furthermore, he acts as a Deputy Head of the Secretariat of the Czech National Contact Point for the OECD Guidelines for Multinational Enterprises and lectures public international law and international economic law at the Faculty of Law of the Charles University.

Towards a German Supply Chain Act?
Comments from a Choice of Law
and a Comparative Perspective

Giesela Rühl

Contents

Abstract The protection of human rights in global supply chains has become one of the most hotly debated issues in public and private (international) law. In a number of countries, including the United Kingdom, France and the Netherlands, these debates have led to the introduction of domestic human rights legislation. In other countries reform plans are under way. In Germany, for example, the federal government recently announced plans to adopt a German Supply Chain Act, which, if passed as suggested, will introduce both mandatory human rights due diligence obligations and mandatory corporate liability provisions. The following article takes this announcement as an opportunity to look at the idea of a German Supply Chain Act from both a choice of law and from a comparative perspective. It argues that that any such Act will necessarily be limited in both its spatial and in its substantive reach and, therefore, recommends that Germany refrains from passing national legislation—and supports the adoption of a European instrument instead.

G. Rühl (✉)
Humboldt-University of Berlin, Berlin, Germany
e-mail: giesela.ruehl@hu-berlin.de

© Springer Nature Switzerland AG 2020
M. Bungenberg et al. (eds.), *European Yearbook of International Economic Law 2020*,
European Yearbook of International Economic Law (2022) 11: 55–82,
https://doi.org/10.1007/8165_2020_61, Published online: 29 December 2020

1 Introduction

Over the past decades the internationalization of commerce has given rise to global supply chains that link production sites in the Global South with companies and consumers in the Global North. If things go well, these supply chains are beneficial for all parties involved: In the Global North, companies profit from low production costs and consumers from lower prices. In the Global South, jobs are created that are the motor for economic development and progress. Unfortunately, however, reality is often very different. Since human rights are not always sufficiently protected around the world it happens too often that companies and consumers in the Global North unduly benefit from unbearable living and working conditions in the Global South. Catastrophes such as the collapse of the Rana Plaza factory building in Bangladesh[1] or the fire at the Ali Enterprises factory in Pakistan[2] have, therefore, inspired a discussion about whether companies from the Global North can be held liable for damages resulting from human rights violations committed by their foreign subsidiaries, suppliers or contractual partners in the Global South?

Under most national laws, including German law this question is currently answered in the negative. The reason is simple: Parent and buyer companies are legally independent of their foreign subsidiaries and suppliers.[3] Therefore, they are under no general obligation to make sure that their foreign subsidiaries or suppliers comply with human rights (legal entity principle).[4] However, at least with regard to German law the legal situation could change soon: In July 2020 the Federal German government, represented by Federal Minister for Economic Cooperation and Development, Gerd Müller, and the Federal Minister of Labour and Social Affairs, Hubertus Heil, announced plans to adopt a German Supply Chain Act. Arguing that only few—too few—German companies were voluntarily paying attention to human rights in their supply chains both Ministers claimed that it was necessary to introduce both mandatory human rights due diligence obligations and mandatory corporate liability provisions.

Of course, it remains to be seen whether the idea of a German Supply Chain Act will eventually be realized. Suffice it to say that the announcement of the two Ministers has not only met with enthusiastic approval. In fact, a number of voices, including the Federal Minister for Economic Affairs, Peter Altmaier, have raised concerns and expressed scepticism. However, no matter what the chances of realization are, there is no denying the fact that the idea to protect human rights in global supply chains through mandatory human rights due diligence obligations has gained

---

[1]See https://www.business-humanrights.org/de and https://www.ecchr.eu.

[2]See https://www.business-humanrights.org/de and https://www.ecchr.eu.

[3]See, for example, Dowling (2020), pp. 219 ff.; Palombo (2019), pp. 267 ff.; Wagner (2016), pp. 757 ff.

[4]In many countries, however, it is discussed whether and how the legal entity principle may be overcome to better protect human rights in global supply chains. See, for example Dowling (2020), pp. 228 ff; Weller and Thomale (2017), pp. 509 ff.

popularity over the past years. In fact, a number of countries, including France, the Netherlands, the United Kingdom, and Switzerland have adopted—or are contemplating to adopt—legislation that requires companies to protect human rights in their supply chains.[5] In addition, the European Commissioner for Justice, *Didier Reynders*, announced plans to prepare a human rights due diligence instrument in April 2020 and promised to present a first draft in early 2021.[6] And, finally, a Working Group set up by the United Nations Human Rights Committee in 2014[7] is working on a binding Business and Human Rights Treaty.[8]

In the light of the above, the following article sheds light on the idea of a German Supply Chain Act. It looks at the project from both a choice of law and from a comparative perspective (infra Sects. 3 and 4)—and argues that any national legislation will necessarily be limited in both its spatial and in its substantive reach. It, therefore, recommends that the German legislature refrains from passing national legislation—and supports the adoption of a European instrument instead. Before going into the details, however, a few words relating to the background of the proposed German Supply Chain Act are in order (infra Sect. 2).

2 Background: The UN Guiding Principles for Business and Human Rights

Like most of the above-mentioned—national or international—law reform projects the idea of a German Supply Chain Act goes back to the UN Guiding Principles for Business and Human Rights, the so-called Ruggie Principles. Adopted in 2011, the Guiding Principles set out in great detail what measures companies should take to identify, prevent and mitigate human rights violations and how they should react if

---

[5]See for an overview of existing and planned legislation British Institute of International and Comparative Law et al. (2020), Final Report, pp. 192 ff. and Part III (Country Reports), Littenberg and Binder (2019); Marx et al. (2019), pp. 132 f.

[6]See the press release available at https://ec.europa.eu/commission/presscorner/detail/en/mex_20_323.

[7]Human Rights Council, Elaboration of an international legally binding instrument on transnational corporations and other business enterprises with respect to human rights, A/HRC/26/L.22/Rev. 1 (20. Juni 2014), abrufbar unter https://documents-dds-ny.un.org/doc/UNDOC/LTD/G14/058/99/PDF/G1405899.pdf?OpenElement. See De Schutter (2015), pp. 41 ff.

[8]Since its inception the Working Group has published three drafts, the most recent in August 2020. Second Revised Draft of 6 August 2020 "Legally Binding Instrument to Regulate, in International Human Rights Law, the Activities of Transnational Corporations and Other Business Enterprises", available at https://www.ohchr.org/Documents/HRBodies/HRCouncil/WGTransCorp/Session6/OEIGWG_Chair-Rapporteur_second_revised_draft_LBI_on_TNCs_and_OBEs_with_respect_to_Human_Rights.pdf. Previous drafts date from 2018 and 2019 and are available at https://www.ohchr.org/Documents/HRBodies/HRCouncil/WGTransCorp/Session3/DraftLBI.pdf and https://www.ohchr.org/Documents/HRBodies/HRCouncil/WGTransCorp/OEIGWG_RevisedDraft_LBI.pdf.

human rights violation occur.[9] However, since the Guiding Principles do not create new international law obligations[10] they are only effective if and to the extent that they are voluntarily transposed by states into their domestic law. But to this day this has not yet happened. Rather, most states implement the Guiding Principles by means of so-called National Action Plans.[11] And these National Actions Plans—including the German one of 2016[12]—refrain from imposing any mandatory human rights to diligence obligations on companies. However, in contrast to most other National Action Plans the German National Action Plan—and the coalition agreement entered into by the two parties that currently form the Federal German Government[13]—stipulates that a mandatory legal regime will be implemented if less than 50% of all companies voluntarily comply with the Guiding Principles by 2020.[14]

To find out whether legislative action was needed, the German Government, therefore, initiated a monitoring process and asked companies whether and how they dealt with human rights in their supply chains. The rather sobering, but fairly unsurprising result: In 2020, only 13–17% of German companies, and hence much less than 50%, can be considered to be compliant.[15] The above-mentioned two Ministers, therefore, decided to move forward with the idea of a German Supply Chain Act (*Lieferkettengesetz*) the details of which have not yet been released. However, there is an unofficial draft that has been circulating since the beginning of 2019[16] and a draft White Paper (*Eckpunktepapier*) of 2020 that is currently

---

[9]UN Guiding Principles for Business and Human Rights, pp. 13 ff., Principles No 11-24.

[10]UN Guiding Principles for Business and Human Rights, p. 1 ("Nothing in these Guiding Principles should be read as creating new international law obligations . . .").

[11]See for an overview the list available at https://www.ohchr.org/EN/Issues/Business/Pages/NationalActionPlans.aspx.

[12]National Action Plan for Business and Human Rights. Implementation of the UN Guiding Principles on Business and Human Rights 2016–2020, English version available at https://www.auswaertiges-amt.de/blob/610714/fb740510e8c2fa83dc507afad0b2d7ad/nap-wirtschaft-menschenrechte-engl-data.pdf.

[13]Ein neuer Aufbruch für Europa. Eine neue Dynamik für Deutschland. Ein neuer Zusammenhalt für unser Land—Koalitionsvertrag zwischen CDU, CSU und SPD, 19. Legislaturperiode (2018), p. 156, para. 7382 ff.

[14]National Action Plan for Business and Human Rights (note 12), p. 10.

[15]Monitoring of the status of implementation of the human rights due diligence obligations of enterprises set out in the National Action Plan for Business and Human Rights 2016–2020, Final Report (2020), p. 5, English version available at https://www.auswaertiges-amt.de/blob/2417212/9c8158fe4c737426fa4d7217436accc7/201013-nap-monitoring-abschlussbericht-data.pdf.

[16]Gestaltungsmöglichkeiten eines Mantelgesetzes zur nachhaltigen Gestaltung globaler Wertschöpfungsketten und zur Änderung wirtschaftsrechtlicher Vorschriften (Nachhaltige Wertschöpfungskettengesetz—NaWKG) einschließlich eines Stammgesetzes zur Regelung menschenrechtlicher und umweltbezogener Sorgfaltspflichten in globalen Wertschöpfungsketten (Sorgfaltspflichtengesetz—SorgfaltspflichtenG), Draft of 1 February 2019 (on file with the author). See for a first appraisal Weller and Nasse (2020), pp. 120 ff.

(internally) discussed by the Federal Government.[17] Based on a proposal prepared by various non-governmental organizations[18] both the draft and the White Paper suggest to establish broad human rights due diligence obligations across the entire supply chain and to allow victims to sue German companies for damages in case of violations. The remainder of this article will take this draft as well as the White Papier as a baseline to discuss the potential spatial and substantive reach of a future German Supply Chain Act.

3 Spatial Reach: The (Important) Role of Private International Law

Starting point for any discussion about the spatial reach of a potential German Supply Chain Act is the fact that it will—by definition—regulate international cases. More specifically, it will regulate the conduct and, as the case may be, the tortious liability of German companies vis-à-vis third parties located in foreign countries. The applicability of the private law provision of the Act will, therefore, depend on the rules of private international law, more specifically the rules of the Rome II Regulation on the law applicable to non-contractual obligations.[19,20]

It should be noted, however, that claims for human rights violations cannot only be based on tort law, but also on company law, namely when a European company is directly held liable for torts committed by a foreign subsidiary (piercing the corporate veil). These cases, however, are outside the scope of the envisioned German Supply Chain Act and, hence, will not be discussed in the following. Suffice it to say that according to the relevant private international law provisions of the Member States these claims are governed by the law of the (administrative or statutory) seat of the foreign subsidiary.[21]

---

[17]Entwurf für Eckpunkte eines Bundesgesetzes über die Stärkung der unternehmerischen Sorgfaltspflichten zur Vermeidung von Menschenrechtsverletzungen in globalen Wertschöpfungsketten (Sorgfaltspflichtengesetz), Draft of 10 March 2020 (on file with the author).

[18]Klinger et al. (2016).

[19]Regulation (EC) No. 864/2007 of the European Parliament and the Council of 11 July 2007 on the law applicable to non-contractual obligations ("Rome II") OJ 2007 L 199/40.

[20]Weller and Nasse (2020), pp. 131 ff. See also Mansel (2018), pp. 454 ff. Wagner (2016), pp. 739 ff.; Weller and Thomale (2017), pp. 523 f. A detailed discussion of characterization matters is offered by Wendelstein (2019), pp. 124 ff.

[21]See—with regard to German private international law—Mansel (2018), pp. 452 f.

3.1 The Rome II Regulation

According to Articles 1 and 2, the Rome II Regulation determines the law applicable to all non-contractual obligations arising out of tort. It applies to all "situations involving a conflict of laws" and does not require that a case has a connection to the EU or one of its Member States.[22] In fact, since the Regulation enjoys universal application it also applies to situations that have (only) connections to non-Member States. With regard to supply chains cases—which will more often than not involve damage that occurs in countries outside Europe—the applicable tort law—and, hence, the spatial reach of the German Supply Action—will usually depend on the provisions of the Rome II Regulation.[23] Nonetheless, it deserves to be mentioned that the Rome II Regulation will not apply if the damage in question arises out of an event that occurred before 11 January 2009.[24] And it will also not apply if the non-contractual obligation in question is excluded from the Regulation's scope by virtue of its Article 1(2). In both cases court will have to resort to national choice law rules to determine the applicable tort law. However, with regard to the cases that will most likely be covered by a future German Supply Chain Act these exceptions are unlikely to materialize.

3.2 In Theory: Free Party Choice of Law

On the basis of the Rome II Regulation the easiest way to ensure application of the envisioned German Supply Chain Act is Article 14. According to this provision the parties to a non-contractual relationship may choose the applicable law (a) by an express or implied agreement entered into after the event giving rise to the damage occurred or, (b) where all the parties are pursuing a commercial activity, also by an agreement freely negotiated before the event giving rise to the damage occurred. However, since the parties to a tortious relationship often have conflicting interests, Article 14 is unlikely to play a major role in international human rights cases.[25] The applicable law will, therefore, usually have to be determined with the help of the remaining choice of law rules of the Rome II Regulation, which—in classic

---

[22]See, for example, Dickinson (2017), p. 1564.

[23]Enneking (2017), p. 49, note 33; Halfmeier (2015), p. 490, para 1 ff.; Kessedijan (2018), pp. 148 f.; Rühl (2020a), p. 97; Symeonides (2008), p. 174; Van den Eeckhout (2012), p. 188; Van den Eeckhout (2017), p. 49.

[24]Case C-412/10, Homawoo, ECLI:EU:C:2011:747, para. 37; Dickinson (2017), p. 1563.

[25]Enneking (2017), p. 52; Kessedijan (2018), p. 149. In a similar vein Habersack and Ehrl (2019), pp. 189 f.; Thomale and Hübner (2017), p. 392 pointing to "reasons rooted in game theory and behavioural economics". An implicit (partial) choice of German law was discussed—and rejected by both the Court of First Instance and the Court of Appeal in the KiK case. See LG Dortmund, Judgment of 10 January 2019, ECLI:DE:LGDO:2019:0110.7O95.15.00, para. 42; OLG Hamm, Decision of 21 May 2019, ECLI:DE:OLGHAM:2019:0521.9U44.19.00, para. 16 ff.

European manner—primarily strive for legal certainty and predictability while leaving little room for judicial discretion.[26] In the context of human rights actions resort will usually be had to the general choice of law rule of Article 4 Rome II Regulation or the special choice of law rule for environmental damage of Article 7 Rome II Regulation.

3.3 In Practice: Law of the Place of Injury

According to the general choice of law rule of Article 4(1) Rome II Regulation, claims arising out of tort are governed by the law of the country in which the damage occurs. Despite the somewhat unclear wording there is broad agreement that this means that the provision calls for application of the law of the place of injury (*lex loci damni*).[27] In the typical supply chain case that the German legislature tries to cover with the German Supply Chain Act this place will usually to be located where the impaired legal interest—life, health, property—was first violated. Damage claims for human rights violations will, therefore, usually be governed by the law of the production country in the Global South and, thus, foreign law,[28] not German law.

3.4 In Environmental Damage Cases: Victim's Right to Choose

German law, however, may apply if Article 4(1) Rome II Regulation is superseded by Article 7 Rome II Regulation.[29] The provision applies to environmental damage as well as to personal injury and damage sustained by persons or property as a result of such damage and gives the injured party the right to seek compensation on the basis of either the place of injury and or the law of the place in which the event giving rise to the damage occurred (place of action). If the place of injury is located abroad while the place of action is to be located in Germany, the injured party can, therefore, choose to claim compensation in accordance with German law including a future German Supply Chain Act.

---

[26]Recital 6. See for a critical appraisal Symeonides (2008), pp. 179 ff.

[27]See, for example, Dickinson (2017), p. 1567; von Hein (2015a), p. 497, para. 5 and pp. 503 ff., para. 13 ff.; Symeonides (2008), p. 179.

[28]Enneking (2008), p. 300; Enneking (2009), p. 928; Enneking (2017), p. 50; Halfmeier (2018), p. 41; Kessedijan (2018), p. 149; Van Calster (2014), p. 130; Lehmann and Eichel (2019), p. 96; Rühl (2020a), pp. 97 f.; Van den Eeckhout (2012), pp. 189 f.; Van den Eeckhout (2017), pp. 50 f.; Wagner (2016), p. 744.

[29]See for a detailed discussion Enneking (2008), pp. 302 ff.; Enneking (2009), pp. 928 f.; Enneking (2017), pp. 52 ff.; Hartmann (2018), pp. 300 f.; Lehmann and Eichel (2019), pp. 93 ff.; Mansel (2018), pp. 459 ff.; Otero Carcá-Castrillón (2011), pp. 565 ff.; Wagner (2016), pp. 743 f.

As so often, however, the devil is in the detail. And this is because it is unclear where the place of action is to be located in typical supply chain cases. In particular, it is unclear whether it is possible to locate it at the seat of the—German—parent or buyer company. In the literature a number of voices assume this to be the case if relevant decisions are made at the seat or if the parent or buyer company violates environmental organization, monitoring or control obligations that it has to fulfil at its seat.[30] Others, in contrast, argue that actions or omissions at the seat should always be excluded as irrelevant preparatory acts.[31] They claim that the place of action is only at the place where the actual cause of the environmental damage—for example the emitting plant—is to be located.[32] This place will, of course, often—and especially in the cases of interest here—be identical with the place of injury. It is therefore unclear whether Article 7 Rome II Regulation can actually pave the way to application of a German Supply Chain Act. But even if it does—which in the end remains for the CJEU to decide—only environmental damage cases will be covered.

3.5   Roads to Domestic Law?

The above analysis shows that according to Articles 4 and 7 of the Rome II Regulation the private law provisions of a German Supply Chain Act would—if at all—be applied in the case of environmental damage and only at the choice of the injured party. It goes without saying that such a spatially limited scope of application would call the effectiveness of the entire project into question. This is why a number of proposals have been made to ensure application of German law in other ways. The most prominent resort to Article 4(3), Article 17 or Article 16 Rome II Regulation.

3.5.1   Manifestly More Closely Connected?

According to Article 4(3) of the Rome II Regulation a law other than the law of the place of injury may apply, if the tort in question is manifestly more closely connected with some other place. With regard to supply chain cases it has been argued that the provision can be used to apply the law of the parent or buyer company in the Global North.[33] However, this would require that the human rights violation as such is

---

[30]Demeyere (2015), pp. 388 f.; Enneking (2008), pp. 302 f.; Enneking (2009), p. 928; Enneking (2017), p. 53; Habersack and Ehrl (2019), pp. 188 f.; Kessedijan (2018), p. 149; Otero Carc-á-Castrillón (2011), pp. 571 f.; Van den Eeckhout (2012), p. 191; Van den Eeckhout (2017), p. 53. In a similar vein Van Calster (2014), p. 131; Hartmann (2018), pp. 300 f.; Mansel (2018), pp. 462 f.

[31]Wagner (2016), pp. 744 f.

[32]Generally von Hein (2015b), p. 615, para. 18.

[33]Thomale and Hübner (2017), pp. 391 f.; Weller and Thomale (2017), p. 524. In a similar vein Heinen (2018), pp. 93 and 94; Van den Eeckhout (2012), pp. 190 f.; Van den Eeckhout (2017), p. 52 and—with regard to the French *Loi de vigilance*—Hoffberger (2017), p. 482.

manifestly more closely connected to that law than to the law where the human rights violation actually took place. In the cases of interest here, in which a foreign subsidiary or a foreign supplier always stands between the parent or customer company and the injured party, it is hard to see that this requirement will ever be met.[34] And it is probably for this reason that authors who wish to rely on Article 4 (3) Rome II Regulation do not even claim that human rights violations are manifestly more closely connected with the law of the parent or buyer company. Rather, they argue that Article 4(3) Rome II Regulation should be applied to protect the victims.[35] More specifically, they maintain that application of the law of the place of injury had to be corrected "teleologically" and Article 4(3) Rome II Regulation to be interpreted "praeter regulationem"[36] so as to allow the victim to choose the law of the parent or buyer company.[37]

This reading of Article 4(3) Rome II Regulation, however, comes with problems. For one, the wording of Article 4(3) Rome II Regulation does neither refer to the interests of the victims nor does it allow victims to unilaterally choose the applicable law. And for another, the history of the provision quite clear shows that the European legislature—very consciously—decided to limit the injured party's right to choose the applicable law to environmental damage.[38] In addition, a proposal of the European Parliament to use Article 4(3) Rome II Regulation to protect the legitimate expectations of the parties and to take into account the consequences associated with the application of foreign law[39] did not meet with approval.[40] Application of Article 4(3) Rome II Regulation in supply chain cases is, therefore, not an option and rightly rejected by the majority in the literature.[41]

---

[34]Enneking (2008), pp. 300 f.; Enneking (2017), pp. 51 f.; Habersack and Ehrl (2019), p. 185; Halfmeier (2018), p. 42; Stürner (2014), pp. 370 f.; Stürner (2015), p. 851; Van Calster (2014), p. 130; Van Dam (2011), p. 231. In a similar vein LG Dortmund, 10 January 2019, Az. 7–O 95/15, ECLI:DE:LGDO:2019:0110.7O95.15.00, para. 43; OLG Hamm, 21 May 2019, Az. 9 U 44/19, ECLI:DE:OLGHAM:2019:0521.9U44.19.00, para. 25.

[35]Thomale and Hübner (2017), pp. 391 f.; Weller and Thomale (2017), p. 524.

[36]Weller and Thomale (2017), p. 525.

[37]Thomale and Hübner (2017), pp. 391 f.; Weller and Thomale (2017), p. 524.

[38]Mansel (2018), pp. 457 f.; Wendelstein (2019), pp. 141 ff. In a similar vein Habersack and Ehrl (2019), pp. 184 f.

[39]European Parliament legislative resolution on the proposal for a regulation of the European Parliament and of the Council on the law applicable to non-contractual obligations ("Rome II"), COM(2003)0427—C5-0338/2003—2003/0168(COD) of 6 July 005, P6_TA(2005)0284. See for a detailed discussion von Hein (2008a), pp. 560 ff.; von Hein (2008b), pp. 1685 f.; von Hein (2009) p. 18.

[40]See for a detailed discussion Enneking (2017), pp. 51 f.; Fulli-Lemaire (2019), p. 251; Halfmeier (2018), p. 42; Mansel (2018), pp. 455 ff.; Pförtner (2018), pp. 324 f.; Stürner (2015), pp. 850 f.; Van den Eeckhout (2012), pp. 190 f.; Wagner (2016), pp. 740 f; Weller et al. (2016), pp. 393 f.; Wendelstein (2019), pp. 141 ff.

[41]Habersack and Ehrl (2019), p. 185; Halfmeier (2018), p. 41; Garcimartín Alférez (2007), p. I-84 and p. 566; Mansel (2018), p. 456; Pförtner (2018), pp. 324 f.; Rühl (2020a), pp. 101 ff.; Stone (2015), p. 303; Stürner (2015), p. 850. In a similar vein Enneking (2008), pp. 301 f., Enneking (2017), pp. 51 f. and—with regard to the French *Loi de vigilance*—Palombo (2019), p. 280.

3.5.2 Rules of Safety and Conduct?

A second proposal to ensure application of a German Supply Chain Act makes use of Article 17 Rome II Regulation. According to this provision account shall be taken of the rules of safety and conduct which were in force at the place and time of the event giving rise to the liability. And some authors claim that human rights due diligence obligations as well as liability rules to be found in the law of the parent or buyer company could be considered as rules of safety and conduct.[42] However, application of Article 17 Rome II Regulation in supply chain cases turns out to be equally problematic as application of Article 4(3) Rome II Regulation. Leaving aside the above-mentioned problem of determining where the place of action is to be located in the cases of interest here, Article 17 Rome II Regulation does not result in application of the law of the place of action, but merely requires courts to take account of the rules of safety and conduct of that place.[43] In addition, there is broad agreement that Article 17 Rome II Regulation can neither be used to undermine the fundamental decision of the European legislature to call for application of the law at the place of injury.[44] Nor can the provision be used to establish liability that does not exist under that law.[45] Rather, its role is limited to ensure that tortfeasors may trust that an action that is permitted at the place of action will not give rise to liability under the otherwise applicable law.[46]

3.5.3 Overriding Mandatory Provisions?

In the light of the above, the only possible road to application of domestic law in supply chain cases seems to be Article 16 Rome II Regulation. The provision allows application of domestic law if it is overriding mandatory in nature. Under the condition that a German Supply Chain Act meets this requirement it may, therefore, be applied irrespective of the otherwise applicable law. But will the provisions of the German Supply Chain qualify as overriding mandatory provisions? The details depend on the specificities of the Act which are as of yet unknown. However, the

---

[42]See, for example, Enneking (2009), p. 930; Grabosch (2013), pp. 88 ff.; Van den Eeckhout (2012), pp. 179 and 191; Van den Eeckhout (2017), p. 53. Equally—with regard to the French *Loi de vigilance*—d'Avout (2017), p. 2062.

[43]Enneking (2017), p. 59; Rühl (2020a), p. 103; von Hein (2015d), p. 743, para. 3.

[44]Enneking (2017), p. 59; Halfmeier (2018), pp. 42 f.; Pförtner (2018), pp. 326 f.; Rühl (2020a), p. 103; Mansel (2018), pp. 465 ff.; Wagner (2016), pp. 742 f.; Wendelstein (2019), pp. 143 f. See also Van Hoek (2008), p. 166.

[45]Enneking (2017), p. 59; Halfmeier (2018), pp. 42 f.; Pförtner (2018), pp. 326 f.; Rühl (2020a), p. 103; Mansel (2018), pp. 465 ff.; Wagner (2016), pp. 742 f.; Wendelstein (2019), pp. 143 f. See also Van Hoek (2008), p. 166.

[46]Enneking (2017), p. 59; Halfmeier (2018), pp. 42 f.; Pförtner (2018), pp. 326 f.; Rühl (2020a), p. 103; Mansel (2018), pp. 465 ff.; Wagner (2016), pp. 742 f.; Wendelstein (2019), pp. 143 f.; von Hein (2015d), p. 742, para. 2. See also Van Hoek (2008), p. 166.

unofficial draft Supply Chain Act of 2019 expressly states in § 15 that the provisions of the Act are to be regarded as overriding mandatory in nature.[47] And the draft White Papier of 2020 which is the basis for the current (internal) discussions confirms this position.[48] It is, therefore, to be expected, that any future version of the Supply Chain Act will contain a provision that corresponds to § 15 of the 2019 draft. This finding, however, raises at least two questions.

Who Determines Whether a Provision is Overriding Mandatory in Nature?
The first question is whether the German—or any other national—legislature can simply declare that national provisions are overriding mandatory in the meaning of Article 16 Rome II Regulation. Doubts are in order because Article 16 Rome II Regulation is a European—and not a domestic—provision and as such not at the disposal of the German—or any other national—legislature. In fact, it is not even for the German legislature—but for national courts and eventually the CJEU—to interpret Article 16 Rome II Regulation and to decide what requirements need to be met before a provision of domestic law can be considered to be overriding mandatory in nature.

In the end, however, the road that the German legislature will most likely choose will lead to success and, hence, to application of the German Supply Chain Act. And this is because the notion of overriding mandatory provision employed in Article 16 Rome II Regulation should—in light of Recital 7[49]—be interpreted in accordance with the definition to be found in Article 9(1) of the Rome I Regulation.[50,51] According to this definition provisions are overriding mandatory in nature if they are "regarded as crucial by a country for safeguarding its public interests". As a consequence, it is essentially for national legislatures to decide whether a provision of domestic law should be overriding mandatory in nature. And according to the case law of the CJEU Member States have broad discretion to do so.[52] Should the German legislature eventually decide to expressly classify the provisions of the German Supply Chain Act as overriding mandatory provisions, there is, hence, no reason to be believe that this would not be accepted for the purposes of Article 16 Rome II Regulation. In fact, according to the CJEU the only limits that Member States are facing when elevating national provisions to the status of overriding mandatory provisions derive from their obligations under primary and secondary

---

[47]§ 15 reads: "In the context of non-contractual liability claims, the obligations under §§ 4 to 10 govern the due diligence requirements to be observed, without regard to the law applicable to the non-contractual obligation under private international law."

[48]Entwurf für Eckpunkte eines Sorgfaltspflichtengesetz (note 17), p. 4, at 3. b).

[49]Recital 7 calls for consistent interpretation of the Rome I and II Regulations.

[50]Regulation (EC) No. 593/2008 of the European Parliament and of the Council on the law applicable too contractual obligations (Rome I), OJ L 177/6.

[51]Case C-149/18 Da Silva Martins, ECLI:EU:C:2019:84, para. 27 ff.

[52]Case C-184/12 Unamar, ECLI:EU:C:2013:663, para. 41 ff.; CJEU, case C-149/18, Da Silva Martins, ECLI:EU:C:2019:84, para. 30 f.

European Union law.[53] Provisions of national law may, therefore, not be considered to be overriding mandatory in nature if this results in a breach of European Union law. With regard to a German Supply Chain Act, however, it is hard to see how this could be the case.

Who Is Bound to Apply Overriding Mandatory Provisions?
The second question raised by the application of Article 16 Rome II Regulation relates to the reach of a German Supply Chain Act when its provisions are classified as overriding mandatory provisions. There is, of course, no doubt that German courts will be bound to apply the German Supply Chain Act. In proceedings before German courts, German companies will, therefore, not be able to avoid liability arguing that they were under no human rights due diligence obligations under the applicable foreign law. But what about other courts? Will courts in other states, notably courts in other EU Member States will be bound to apply the German Supply Chain Act?

The answer depends on the—highly controversial—question of whether and to what extent courts in other Member States must apply—or at least take into account—foreign overriding mandatory provisions, notably the overriding mandatory provisions of other EU Member States. Article 16 Rome II Regulation does not provide an answer because no agreement could be reached during the legislative procedure.[54] Some voices in the literature, therefore, claim that courts in other EU Members States must not apply or take into account foreign overriding mandatory provisions.[55] Others argue that the Rome II Regulation does not take a stance, but leaves the decision whether to apply or consider foreign overriding mandatory provisions to each country.[56] The latter view is supported by the *Nikiforidis* judgment of the CJEU,[57] in which the Court held—with a view to Article 9(3) Rome I Regulation—that Member States did not have to apply overriding mandatory provisions of other EU Member States, but that Article 9(3) Rome I Regulation did not prohibit such mandatory provisions from being taken into account "as matters of fact" within the framework of the actually applicable law.[58] It follows that a German Supply Chain Act will indeed be applicable under the Rome II Regulation if its provisions are classified as overriding mandatory rules. However, application will only be guaranteed before German, but not before other courts.

---

[53]Case C-184/12 Unamar, ECLI:EU:C:2013:663, para. 46.

[54]See for details Arif (2011), p. 117; von Hein (2015c), pp. 734 ff., para. 11.

[55]See, for example, Arif (2011), p. 117; Mankowski (2019), pp. 418 f., para. 562; Wagner (2008), p. 15.

[56]See, for example, Garcimartín Alférez (2007), p. I-90; Leible and Lehmann (2007), p. 726; von Hein (2015c), p. 740, para. 21.

[57]Case C-135/15 Nikiforidis, ECLI:EU:C:2016:774.

[58]Ibid para. 55.

4 Substantive Reach: The (Invaluable) Role of Comparative Law

The German Supply Chain Act will, if adopted, not be the first law that seeks to improve the protection of human rights in global supply chains. As indicated at the beginning of this article, a number of domestic legislatures but also the European legislature have recently enacted laws that pursue similar objectives. It is, therefore, obvious to ask whether there is anything that the German legislature can learn from these laws.[59]

4.1 Human Rights Due Diligence Legislation

Existing human rights legislation can largely be grouped into three different categories depending on the reach of the obligations established: A first category merely imposes human rights-related reporting obligations on companies. Examples include the EU Non-Financial Reporting Directive of 2014[60] and the UK Modern Slavery Act of 2015.[61] A second category of laws establishes genuine human rights due diligence obligations and, hence, does not only require companies to disclose human rights related information, but mandates a certain human rights relevant behaviour. Prominent examples are the 2018 EU Conflict Minerals Regulation[62] and the 2019 Dutch Child Labour Due Diligence Act.[63] A last category of law reform projects, finally, does not only establish human rights due diligence obligations, but also sanctions their violation with claims for damages by the victims. So far the only law that belongs into this category is the 2017 French Law on the supervisory obligations

---

[59]See for an overview British Institute of International and Comparative Law et al. (2020), Final Report, pp. 192. ff. and Part III (Country Reports); Littenberg and Binder (2019); Marx et al. (2019), pp. 132 f. (Annex 2).

[60]Directive 2014/95/EU of the European Parliament and of the Council of 22 October 2014 amending Directive 2013/34/EU as regards disclosure of non-financial and diversity information by certain large undertakings and groups, OJ 2014 L 330/1.

[61]Modern Slavery Act 2015, ch. 30.

[62]Regulation (EU) 2017/821 of the European Parliament and of the Council of 17 May 2017 laying down supply chain due diligence obligations for Union importers of tin, tantalum and tungsten, their ores, and gold originating from conflict-affected and high-risk areas, OJ 2017 L 330/1. See Fleischer and Hahn (2018), p. 400; Habersack and Ehrl (2019), pp. 178 f.

[63]Wet van 24 oktober 2019 houdende de invoering van een zorgplicht ter voorkoming van de levering van goederen en diensten die met behulp van kinderarbeid tot stand zijn gekomen, Staatsblad 2019, 401. An unofficial English translation is available at https://www.ropesgray.com/en/newsroom/alerts/2019/06/Dutch-Child-Labor-Due-Diligence-Act-Approved-by-Senate-Implications-for-Global-Companies.

of parent companies and contracting companies, the so-called *Loi de vigilance*.[64] It is also the law that is usually cited as a role model for a German Supply Chain Act. The following comparative observations will, therefore, focus on the French *Loi de vigilance* and ask if it holds any lessons for Germany.

Before going into the details, however, it deserves to be mentioned that, in addition to Germany, plans to adopt legislation belonging to the third category of human rights legislation were also contemplated in Switzerland for a long time. In fact, after years of discussion[65] Switzerland held a popular vote on a proposal submitted by the Swiss Responsible Business Initiative (*Konzernverantwortungsinitiative*) on 29 November 2020.[66] If adopted, the Swiss Constitution would have been amended to include broad human rights due diligence obligations as well as rather strict liability rules.[67] However, the proposal was narrowly rejected[68] so that now a counter proposal by the Swiss Parliament will become law.[69] This counter-proposal, however, does not go as far as the proposal by the Swiss Responsible Business Initiative.[70] In particular, it is limited to disclosure obligations on the one hand and narrow, sector-specific human rights due diligence obligations. In addition, it does not contain any liability rules.

4.2   In Particular: The French Loi de Vigilance

In April 2013, more than 1000 people were killed in the collapse of the 8-story Rana Plaza factory building in Bangladesh.[71] The catastrophe caused horror around the globe. But the outrage was particularly great in Europe since, in the ruins, labels and documents were found that linked major European textile retailers to the catastrophe.

---

[64]Loi No. 399/2017 du 23 mars 2017 relative au devoir de vigilance des sociétés mères et des entreprises donneuses d'ordre, JO du 28 mars 2017.

[65]See for a very good overview the information and documents prepared by the Swiss Federal Agency of Justice (Bundesamt für Justiz), available at https://www.bj.admin.ch/bj/de/home/wirtschaft/gesetzgebung/konzernverantwortungsinitiative.html.

[66]See the press release of the Swiss Government of 1 July 2020, available at https://www.admin.ch/gov/de/start/dokumentation/medienmitteilungen/bundesrat.msg-id-79692.html.

[67]See for a (more) detailed discussion of the proposal Bueno (2020), pp. 239 ff.; Bohrer (2018), pp. 195 ff.; Handschin (2017), pp. 1000 ff.; Kaufmann (2016), pp. 45 ff.; Palombo (2019), pp. 277 f.; Werro (2019), pp. 166 ff.

[68]See the preliminary results available at https://www.bk.admin.ch/ch/d/pore/va/20201129/index.html.

[69]See also the press release of the Swiss Parliament of 9 June 2020, available at https://www.parlament.ch/de/services/news/Seiten/2020/20200609090519598194158159041_bsd048.aspx.

[70]A concise comparison of the original proposal submitted by the Responsible Business Initiative and the counter-proposal of the Swiss Parliament is available at https://www.bj.admin.ch/bj/de/home/wirtschaft/gesetzgebung/konzernverantwortungsinitiative.html.

[71]More detailed information available at https://www.business-humanrights.org/de und https://www.ecchr.eu.

In France this gave rise to a debate about the protection of human rights in global supply chains that eventually—after a long and controversial legislative process[72]—led to the adoption of the *Loi de vigilance* on 23 March 2017.

4.2.1 Remarkable Design

The *Loi de vigilance* consists, in essence, of two provisions inserted into the French Commercial Code (Articles L. 225-102-4 and L. 225-102-5 CCom).[73] They require French companies to draw up, publish and implement a vigilance plan (*plan de vigilance*), which must include reasonable vigilance measures aimed at identifying and preventing violations of human rights and fundamental freedoms, serious bodily injury, environmental damage or health risks. In addition, they provide for a number of sanctions if the monitoring plan is not—or not properly—drawn up, published or implemented. For at least three reasons all this is truly remarkable.

First, the *Loi de vigilance* establishes genuine human rights due diligence obligations, which means that the companies covered must actually do something to protect human rights (Article L. 225-102-4 I para. 3 CCom). Unlike, for example, the European Non-Financial Reporting Directive and the UK Modern Slavery Act, the *Loi de vigilance* is, thus, not limited to pure reporting or disclosure obligations. And unlike, for example, the European Conflict Minerals Regulation and the Dutch Child Labour Act it is not limited to the protection of certain human rights but covers human rights and the environment across the board.

Second, the *Loi de vigilance* extends these human rights due diligence obligations to third parties (Article L. 225-102-4 I para. 3 CCom). Companies covered by the new law, therefore, do not only have to protect human rights themselves. They must also ensure that controlled companies (*sociétés directement ou indirectement controllées*), subcontractors (*sous-traitants*) and suppliers (*fournisseurs*) do the same. The *Loi de vigilance*, thus, effectively overcomes the legal entity principle that is the main reason why companies currently cannot be held accountable for human rights violations committed by their foreign subsidiaries, suppliers or contracting partners.

Third, compliance with the human rights due diligence obligation is monitored and violations are sanctioned. In particular, the vigilance plan can be submitted to judicial review upon request of any party with a legitimate interest, notably non-governmental organizations (Article L. 225-102-4 II para. 1 CCom). In addition—and most strikingly—potential victims can claim damages in accordance with and under the conditions of Articles 1240 and 1241 of the French Civil Code (Article L. 225-102-5 CCom).

---

[72]See for details Petitjean (2019) as well as Conseil général de l'économie (2020), pp. 12 ff.

[73]The full French text is available at www.legifrance.gouv.fr. An unofficial English translated can be found at https://corporatejustice.org/documents/publications/ngo-translation-french-corporate-duty-of-vigilance-law.pdf.

4.2.2 Limited Reach

In light of the above, there is no denying the fact, that the *Loi de vigilance* is a revolutionary law. However, all that glitters is not gold. Ground-breaking as the new French law may be, it does not go as far as is often assumed. In fact, it is substantially limited in at least three ways.

Limited Territorial Scope of Application
The first limitation relates to the territorial scope of the *Loi de vigilance*: As a French law, it only applies if French law is applicable by virtue of the rules of private international law. And just as the Rome II Regulation will usually not lead to application of the German Supply Chain Act cases it will usually not lead to application of the French *Loi de vigilance*.[74] To make sure that the *Loi de vigilance* is not void of any meaning, the majority in the literature, therefore, proceeds as the German legislature intends to proceed and classifies its provisions as overriding mandatory provisions in the meaning of Article 16 Rome II Regulation.[75] However, while the German legislature will most likely expressly declare that the provisions of the German Supply Act are overriding mandatory in nature, there is no such provision in the *Loi de vigilance*. The French Parliament even rejected a proposal to expressly classify the provisions of the *Loi de vigilance* as overriding mandatory in nature.[76] Some authors, therefore, doubt that Article 16 Rome II Regulation can be used to ensure application of the *Loi de vigilance*.[77] A closer look, however, reveals that the French Parliament rejected the inclusion of an express statement because it assumed that it was clear from the spirit and the wording of the law that it would apply irrespective of the otherwise applicable law.[78] The *Loi de vigilance* can, therefore, be applied with the help of Article 16 Rome II Regulation. However, this also means that application will essentially be limited to French courts.

---

[74]Rühl (2020b), pp. 1420 f.; Mansel (2018), p. 445; Nasse (2019), pp. 798 f. See, however, d'Avout (2017), p. 2061 who argues that only the liability rule of Article L. 225-102-5 CCom can be classified as tortious, while he assumes that the obligation to establish, publish and implement a vigilance plan embodied in Article 225-102-4 CCom belongs to company law.

[75]Kessedijan (2018), p. 151; Mansel (2018), pp. 445 and 454; Nasse (2019), pp. 799 f.; Nordhues (2019), pp. 317 f.; Palombo (2019), p. 280; Pataut (2017), p. 838. In a similar vein—with regard to the draft of 2015—Boskovic (2016), p. 387.

[76]Assemblée nationale XIVe législature, Session ordinaire de 2014–2015, Première séance du lundi 30 mars 2015, Discussion to Amendment No. 18, available at http://www.assemblee-nationale.fr/14/cri/2014-2015/20150193.asp#P490680.

[77]Barsan (2017), p. 432; Danis-Fatôme and Viney (2017), p. 1618; Parance and Groulx (2018), pp. 47 f.; Spitzer (2019), pp. 106 f.; Weller and Pato (2018), p. 414.

[78]See the rapporteur's answer to Amendment No. 18: "... ils sont satisfaits car ce qu'ils proposent est inclus non seulement dans l'esprit mais dans le texte de la proposition de loi."

Limited Personal Scope of Application

The second limitation that the *Loi de vigilance* is facing relates to its personal scope.[79] In fact, companies must meet a total of three criteria to be bound by the new French law: First, they must have their registered office (*siège social*) in France.[80] Second, they must be organized in a certain corporate form, namely in the form of a public company (*société anonyme*), a partnership limited by shares (*société en commandite par actions*) or a European public company (*société européenne*).[81] And, third, they must—in two consecutive financial years and alone or together with their subsidiaries—employ (1) more than 5000 employees in France or (2) more than 10,000 employees worldwide. Certainly, one does not need to be a polymath to realize that the number of companies that are actually bound by the *Loi de vigilance* must be small. And while it is not known how small the number is,[82] estimates assume that it cannot exceed 300.[83] This is in line with the results of a recent study which, after analyzing publicly available data, concluded that only 237 companies have to comply with the requirements of the new French law.[84]

Limited Rights and Obligations

The third limitation, finally, relates to the rights and obligations created by the *Loi de vigilance*. These also do not go as far as usually assumed.[85] To begin with, the *Loi de vigilance* does not require companies to avoid all human rights violations, but only those that are deemed to be serious (*atteintes graves*). In addition, the human rights due diligence obligation does not extend to all companies in the supply chain. In fact, according to Article L. 225-102-4 I para. 3 CCom only companies with whom an established commercial relationship (*relation commerciale établie*) exists have to be covered by the vigilance plan. And while there is some confusion about what exactly an established commercial relationship is,[86] there can be no doubt that the requirement is meant as limitation. Finally, the *Loi de vigilance* does not make it easy for

---

[79]See for a detailed discussion Brabant and Savourey (2017a), pp. 1 ff.; Rühl (2020b), pp. 1418 ff.

[80]That the *Loi de vigilance* only covers companies with registered seat does not follow from the wording of Article L. 225-102-4 I CCom, but was confirmed immediately after adoption of the law through the French Constitutional Council. See Conseil constitutionnel, Décision no 2017-750 DC du 23 mars 2017, para. 3, available at https://www.conseil-constitutionnel.fr/decision/2017/2017750DC.htm.

[81]According to the predominant, although not uncontested, view, the *Loi de vigilance* also covers simplified public companies (*societés par actions simplifies*). See Daoud and Sfoggia (2019), p. 96; Hannoun (2017), p. 811. See also—with regard to the draft of 2015—Périn (2015), pp. 218.

[82]Conseil général de l'économie (2020), pp. 18 ff. See also the detailed study by CCFD-Terre Solidaire and Sherpa (2019).

[83]Fleischer and Danninger (2017), p. 2850: 150 companies; Brabant and Savourey (2017a), pp. 1 f: 150 to 200 companies; Renaud et al. (2019), p. 7: 300 companies.

[84]CCFD-Terre Solidaire and Sherpa (2019), p. 10.

[85]Rühl (2020b), pp. 1422 ff.

[86]See for a detailed discussion Daoud and Sfoggia (2019), pp. 97 f.; Jazottes (2018), pp. 28 ff.; Nasse (2019), pp. 793 f.

victims to claim damages for human rights violations. In particular, there is no provision that would reverse or ease the burden of proof. Victims must, therefore, prove all requirements that for a claim for damages, including the misconduct of the company (*faute*) and causality (*lien the causalité*) between misconduct and damage. In particular, they must demonstrate and prove in case of doubt that the vigilance plan was insufficiently drawn up or implemented and that damage has therefore occurred. In view of the complexity of supply chains, this will more often than not be a difficult task.[87]

5 Conclusion: Limited Effectiveness of National Law in Times of Globalisation

The above considerations show that the German legislature is in good company when it tries to protect human rights in supply chains with the help of national law. However, the above considerations also show that any German law will run into at least two problems. To begin with, its spatial reach will be limited. In fact, since its provisions will only be applicable as overriding mandatory provisions in the meaning of Article 16 Rome II Regulation it will only be applied by German courts. And since the Rome II Regulation is of European origin, only the European legislature could ensure a wider spatial reach of national human rights legislation. In fact, only the European legislature could take up proposals to amend either Article 4(3) Rome II Regulation or to include a new choice of law provision for human rights violations that would allow the victims to choose the law of the parent or buyer company.[88] However, while such a provision would be convenient for victims *ex post* it would result in legal uncertainty for all companies that try to find out *ex ante* what their obligations are. The deterrence function of tort law would, thus, be severely impaired.[89] But even if one assumes that a new choice of law rule is the way forward, its adoption would take some time. At least for the foreseeable future the spatial reach of any German human rights legislation—and, in fact, the spatial reach of any national human rights legislation—will, therefore, remain limited.

In addition, a German Supply Chain Act will also most likely be limited in its substantive reach. To be sure, nobody knows what exactly the Act will look like. However, the *Loi de vigilance* as well as first reactions in Germany tell us that a German Supply Chain Act will not sail through the German Parliament without any resistance. In fact, the *Loi de vigilance* was not limited as described above because

---

[87]Brabant and Savourey (2017b), p. 3; Hannoun (2017), p. 816; Métais and Valette (2019), p. 52; Rühl (2020b), pp. 1428 ff. In a similar vein—with regard to the draft of 2015—Périn (2015), pp. 218 and 224.

[88]See, for example, Enneking (2017), p. 65; Kessedijan (2018), pp. 149 f.; Marx et al. (2019), pp. 114 f.; Van den Eeckhout (2012), p. 194; Van den Eeckhout (2017), pp. 57 f.

[89]See for a detailed discussion Rühl (2011), pp. 655 f. (with further references).

the French legislature did not recognize that this would impair the effectiveness of the new law. Rather, it was limited because more far-reaching proposals were rejected out of concerns that they would put French companies at a disadvantage compared to companies from other countries.[90] And there is no reason to believe that any attempts to make a German Supply Chain Act a more effective law would not run into the same problems as in France. Indeed, the German Minister of Commerce, Peter Altmaier, has already announced that a German Supply Chain Act, if ever adopted, will be "business friendly" meaning that—as a in France—only a small number of—larger—companies will be covered.[91] And according to media reports the draft White Papier, which is currently discussed in the Federal Government, has already been washed-down upon his request. It is therefore more than likely that a German Supply Chain Act will be—just as the *Loi de vigilance*—a compromise and as such of limited use.[92]

Now, one could, of course, argue that this view is too pessimistic and that one should just try harder to pass a meaningful piece of legislation.[93] But even if it were possible to bring a strict Supply Chain Act through the German Parliament chances are that little would be achieved. In fact, one will have to doubt quite fundamentally that in a globalized world the human rights situation in the countries of the Global South can actually be improved with the help of national law.[94] The reason is simple: compliance with human rights due diligence obligations in global supply chains is costly.[95] And most companies will—quite rationally—try to avoid or at least reduce these costs.[96] Some will, therefore, move their headquarters to countries where they do not have to comply with human rights due diligence obligations. Others will withdraw from particularly problematic countries and relocate their production to countries where human rights due diligence obligations can be more easily fulfilled. Again others will strive for greater automation of production processes which will be the more attractive the more expensive the use of human labour becomes. And

---

[90]See for a detailed presentation of the legislative history Petitjean (2019).

[91]See, for example, https://www.tagesschau.de/wirtschaft/lieferkettengesetz-streit-ueber-eckpunkte-101.html.

[92]Rühl (2020b), pp. 1430 f. See also the study on the practical application of the *Loi de vigilance* Renaud et al. (2019) as well as the official report of the Conseil général de l'économie (2020).

[93]See, for example, Nordhues (2019), pp. 319 ff.

[94]Rühl (2020a), pp. 123 ff.; Rühl (2020b), pp. 1431 f; Equally skeptical Bueno (2020), p. 244 (with regard to Swiss law); Wagner (2016), p. 781; Sykes (2012), p. 2197 (with regard to the Alien Tort Claims Act). See also Geistfeld (2019), pp. 142 ff., 144 f. who generally doubts that liability claims of the victims can set incentive to protect human rights and who, therefore, suggests to allow consumers in the Global North to sue companies for damages if they fail to comply with human rights relation information obligations.

[95]See for a detailed empirical analysis of the costs that various types of regulation might incur British Institute of International and Comparative Law et al. (2020), Final Report, pp. 290 ff., especially 401 ff. as well as Synthesis Report, pp. 65 ff.

[96]Rühl (2020a), pp. 123 ff.; Sykes (2012), pp. 2196 f. ("tools for strategic response"). See for an empirical analyses of current due diligence (market) practice British Institute of International and Comparative Law et al. (2020), Final Report, pp. 44 ff. and Synthesis Report, pp. 14 ff.

companies which cannot or do not want to do any of this, will adapt their organizational structures to ensure that their liability risk is as low as possible. For example, they will try to avoid any impression of economic power or control over individual suppliers or subsidiaries and simply comply with their obligations through the use of forms, codes of conduct, contractual agreements.[97] It is obvious that all this will hardly improve the human rights situation on the ground.

The same, however, holds true if companies—or at least a substantial number of them—make serious efforts to protect human rights in their supply chains. For one, companies may not be able to monitor their foreign subsidiaries and suppliers and exert the kind of influence on their behaviour necessary to actually change things for the better.[98] And for another, not all companies operating in global competitive markets can simply shoulder the costs that are necessarily associated with the protection of human rights.[99] Many will, therefore, (have to) pass on at least part of the additional costs to their customers through the price of the products they sell. And if customers are not prepared to pay this higher price[100] because there are cheaper alternatives, there is a risk that companies that take their human rights due diligence seriously will be forced out of the market.[101] In the worst case scenario, only companies that do not have to worry about human rights in their supply chains will be left behind.[102]

6 Outlook: Towards a European Supply Chain Instrument!

So what should Germany do? The answer is obvious: I think that in the interest of effective protection of human rights and the environment in global supply chains, the German government should not proceed with the idea of a German Supply Chain

---

[97]Note that the use of contractual clauses and codes of conduct is already the most frequently used due diligence action which companies undertake to prevent, mitigate or remedy adverse human rights and environmental impacts in their supply chains. See British Institute of International and Comparative Law et al. (2020), Final Report, p. 152 and Synthesis Report, p. 15.

[98]Rühl (2020a), pp. 124 f.; For more on this problem see Sykes (2012), pp. 2185 f., 2198 ff. ("monitoring capacity").

[99]Rühl (2020a), pp. 125 f.; Sykes (2012), pp. 2164 f.; Wagner (2016), pp. 780 f.

[100]See for a detailed analyses of consumers' willingness to pay for better protection of human rights in global supply chains Geistfeld (2019), pp. 146 ff. See also the studies and experiments by Bartling et al. (2015), pp. 219 ff. Kimeldorf et al. (2006), pp. 24 ff.

[101]Rühl (2020a), p. 125; Wagner (2016), pp. 780 f. Geistfeld (2019), p. 143; Weller et al. (2016), p. 418. See also—with regard to claims based on the Alien Tort Claims Act—Sykes (2012), pp. 2193 ff. 2202.

[102]On this point Sykes (2012), pp. 2195 f. who notes that the Canadian company Talisman Energy was replaced by a Chinese company—after Talisman Energy had decided to withdraw from Sudan out of fear to be suit in den US on the basis of the Alien Tort Claims Act. See, however, Stiglitz (2011), pp. 10 ff., who considers these fears to be exaggerated and without empirical basis. Equally sceptical Keitner (2012), pp. 2214, 2215 f.

Act but support the plans of *Didier Reynders* to adopt a European instrument instead.[103] Such a European instrument would, in essence, come with three major advantages when compared to a national instrument:[104] First, it would be applicable in the entire European Union, namely directly if adopted as regulation and indirectly if adopted as directive.[105] Therefore, it would, second, create equal conditions for all European companies and, thus, avoid distortions of competition at least within Europe.[106] And, third, a European Supply Chain Act would set standards which—due to the size of the European single market—could actually lead to an improvement of the human rights situation in the countries of the Global South.[107]

What is more important, however, is: Works to adopt a European instrument are already under way. One can, therefore, not argue that calling for a common European approach would effectively mean to postpone or even shelf the issue for good. In fact, the idea of a European instrument is not only on the agenda of the European Commission, but also of the European Parliament. In 2016 and 2017, for example, it adopted two resolutions endorsing an informal Green Card initiative of eight national parliaments[108] to better protect human rights in global value chains.[109] In addition a cross-party group of Members of the European Parliament[110] presented a shadow action plan to implement the UN's guiding principles for business and human rights in the EU in 2019.[111] And most recently, in September 2020 the JURI

---

[103]Rühl (2020a), pp. 125 f. See for a detailed discussion of regulatory options at EU level British Institute of International and Comparative Law et al. (2020), Final Report, pp. 239 ff. and Synthesis Report, pp. 42 ff.

[104]See for an empirical analysis of the potential effects of regulation at EU level British Institute of International and Comparative Law et al. (2020), Final Report, pp. 142 ff. and Synthesis Report, pp. 19 f.

[105]If adopted as regulation the provisions of a European instrument will apply as uniform international law that make the determination of the applicable law obsolete. If adopted as directive its national implementing provisions will qualify as overriding mandatory provision in the meaning of Article 16 Rome II Regulation in all Member States.

[106]See generally on the effect of a European instrument on competition empirical analysis of British Institute of International and Comparative Law et al. (2020), Final Report, pp. 438 ff. as well as Synthesis Report, pp. 67 f.

[107]In a similar vein British Institute of International and Comparative Law et al. (2020), Final Report, pp. 549 and 558 and Synthesis Report, pp. 70 f.

[108]See http://corporatejustice.org/news/132-members-of-8-european-parliaments-support-duty-of-care-legislation-for-eu-corporations. See also the response of the European Commission in its Annual Report on Relations between the European Commission and National Parliaments, COM (2017) 601 final, p. 10.

[109]Resolution of the European Parliament of 25 October 2016 on corporate liability for serious human rights abuses in third countries (2015/2315(INI)), P8_TA(2016)0405; Resolution of the European Parliament of 12 September 2017 on the impact of international trade and the EU's trade policies on global value chains (2016/2301(INI)), P8_TA (2017)0330.

[110]For more information on the group see https://responsiblebusinessconduct.eu.

[111]Shadow EU Action Plan on the Implementation of the UN Guiding Principles on Business and Human Rights within the EU, available at https://responsiblebusinessconduct.eu/wp/wp-content/uploads/2019/03/SHADOW-EU-Action-Plan-on-Business-and-Human-Rights.pdf.

Committee of the European Parliament published a draft report on corporate due diligence and corporate accountability that includes a fully-fletched proposal for a Corporate Due Diligence and Corporate Accountability Directive.[112] Against this background, there is reason to hope that a European instrument can be adopted in either 2021 or 2022. To simultaneously push the idea of a national German Supply Chain Act does not seem to make much sense.

However, having said that it should be emphasized that a European instrument, quite naturally, will not be a self-fulfilling prophecy. It will not automatically lead to better protection of human rights around the world. Rather it must be borne in mind that the realities of a globalised and competitively organised do not only set limits to national law, but also to European law—limits that create the danger that a lot of money and energy will be invested in measures that do not help people in the countries of the Global South. There is, hence, a need to examine more carefully what the conditions of a regulatory regime are that can actually make a difference on the ground. To this end it will most likely be of the essence to extend a European instrument to all companies that sell their goods in the European single market. Unlike the French *Loi de vigilance*, which only addresses French companies, all companies offering their goods in the European Union—including companies from third countries—would therefore have to be included in the scope of application of a European instrument. In addition, accompanying measures such as import restrictions or certification systems would have to ensure that only products that meet European standards are actually sold in Europe. And finally, it should not be forgotten that even a European human rights due diligence instrument cannot replace effective protection of human rights by the countries of the Global South themselves. All efforts to impose human rights due diligence obligations on companies must therefore be complemented by measures that bring these countries on board. Together with a European human rights due diligence instrument these measures will then hopefully pave the way for a human rights-compliant organisation of global supply chains.

References

Arif Y (2011) Overriding mandatory provisions and administrative authorisations according to the Rome II Regulation. Eur Leg Forum 11(3-4):113–122

Barsan I (2017) Corporate accountability: non-financial disclosure and liability – a French perspective. Eur Company Financ Law Rev 14(3):399–434

Bartling B, Weber RA, Yao L (2015) Do markets erode social responsibility? Q J Econ 130 (2):219–266

Bohrer A (2018) Die Haftung schweizerischer Unternehmen für Menschenrechtsverletzungen im Ausland? Überlegungen zur "Konzern-Initiative". In: Fleischer H et al (eds) Corporate social responsibility. Mohr Siebeck, Tübingen, pp 195–212

---

[112]JURI Committee of the European Parliament, Draft Report with recommendations to the Commission on corporate due diligence and corporate accountability (2020/2129(INL)).

Boskovic O (2016) Brèves remarques sur le devoir de vigilance et le droit international privé. Recueil Dalloz 2016:385–387

Brabant S, Savourey E (2017a) Scope of the law corporate duty of vigilance. Companies subject to the vigilance obligations. Revue Internationale de la Compliance et de l'Éthique des Affaires, Étude 92:1–8. http://www.bhrinlaw.org/frenchcorporatedutylaw_articles.pdf

Brabant S, Savourey E (2017b) A closer look at the penalites faced by companies. Revue Internationale de la Compliance et de l'Éthique des Affaires, Commentaires: 1–5. http://www.bhrinlaw.org/frenchcorporatedutylaw_articles.pdf

British Institute of International and Comparative Law et al (2020) Study on due diligence requirements through the supply chains. https://op.europa.eu/en/publication-detail/-/publication/8ba0a8fd-4c83-11ea-b8b7-01aa75ed71a1/language-en

Bueno N (2020) The Swiss popular initiative on responsible business. From responsibility to liability. In: Enneking L, Giesen I, Schaap AJ et al (eds) Accountability, international business operations, and the law. Providing justice for corporate human rights violations in global value chains. Routledge, London, pp 239–258

CCFD-Terre Solidaire and Sherpa (2019) Le radar du devoir de vigilance. Identifier les entreprises soumises à la loi. https://plan-vigilance.org/wp-content/uploads/2019/06/2019-06-26-Radar-DDV-16-pages-Web.pdf.

Conseil général de l'économie (2020) Evaluation de la mise en oeuvre de la loi n° 2017-399 du 27 mars 2017 relative au devoir de vigilance des sociétés mères et des entreprises donneuses d'ordre. https://www.economie.gouv.fr/files/files/directions_services/cge/devoirs-vigilances-entreprises.pdf

D'Avout L (2017) Devoir de vigilance des sociétés mères et "entreprise onneuses d'ordre". Recueil Dalloz 2017:2060–2062

Danis-Fatôme A, Viney G (2017) La responsabilité civile dans la loi relative au devoir de vigilance ds sociétés mères et des entreprises donneuses d'ordre. Recueil Dalloz 2017:1610–1618

Daoud D, Sfoggia S (2019) Les entreprises face aux premiers contentieux de la loi sur le devoir de vigilance. Revue des Juristes de Sciences Po No. 16:95–101

De Schutter O (2015) Towards a new treaty on business and human rights. Bus Hum Rights J 1 (1):41–67

Demeyere S (2015) Liability of a mother company for its subsidiary in French, Belgian, and English law. Eur Rev Private Law 23(3):385–413

Dickinson A (2017) Rome II Regulation (non-contractual obligations). In: Basedow J, Rühl G, Ferrari F, de Miguel Asensio P (eds) Encyclopedia of private international law. Edward Elgar, Cheltenham, pp. 1562–1574

Dowling P (2020) Limited liability and separate corporate personality in multinational corporate groups. Conceptual flaws, accountability gaps, and the case for profit-risk liability. In: Enneking L, Giesen I, Schaap AJ et al (eds) Accountability, international business operations, and the law. Providing justice for corporate human rights violations in global value chains. Routledge, London, pp 219–238

Enneking L (2008) The common denominator of the Trafigura case, foreign direct liability cases and the Rome II Regulation. An essay on the consequences of private international law for the feasibility of regulating multinational corporations through tort law. Eur Private Int Law 16 (2):283–311

Enneking L (2009) Crossing the Atlantic? The political and legal feasibility of European Foreign Direct liability cases. George Wash Int Law Rev 40(4):903–938

Enneking L (2017) Judicial remedies: the issue of applicable law. In: Álvarez Rubio JJ, Yiannibas K (eds) Human rights in business. Routledge, London, pp 38–77

Fleischer H, Danninger N (2017) Konzernhaftung für Menschenrechtsverletzungen – Französische und schweizerische Reformen als Regelungsvorbilder für Deutschland. Der Betrieb 70 (48):2849–2857

Fleischer H, Hahn J (2018) Berichtspflichten über menschenrechtliche Standards in der Lieferkette. Eine internationale Bestandsaufnahme. Recht der Internationalen Wirtschaft 64(7):397–405

Fulli-Lemaire S (2019) Grappling with (global supply) chains: transnational human rights litigation in the agribusiness sector. In: Muir Watt H, Bíziková L, Brandão de Oliveira A, Fernández Arroyo DP (eds) Global private international law, adjudication without frontiers. Edward Elgar, Cheltenham, pp 244–254

Garcimartín Alférez F (2007) The Rome II Regulation: on the way towards a European Private International Law Code. Eur Leg Forum 7(3): I-77–I-91

Geistfeld M (2019) The law an economics of tort liability for human rights violations in global supply chains. J Eur Tort Law 10(2):130–165

Grabosch R (2013) Rechtsschutz vor deutschen Zivilgerichten gegen Beeinträchtigung von Menschenrechten durch transnationalen Unternehmen. In: Nikol R, Bernhard T, Schniederjahn N (eds) Transnationale Unternehmen und Nichtegierungsorganisationen im Völkerrecht. Nomos, Baden-Baden, pp 69–100

Habersack M, Ehrl M (2019) Verantwortlichkeit inländischer Unternehmen für Menschenrechtsverletzungen durch ausländische Zulieferer – de lege lata und de lege ferenda. Archiv für die civilistische Praxis 219(2):155–210

Halfmeier A (2015) Article 3 Rome II. In: Calliess GP (ed) Rome regulations, 2nd edn. Kluwer, Alphen aan den Rijn, pp 490–494

Halfmeier A (2018) Zur Rolle des Kollisionsrechts bei der zivilrechtlichen Haftung für Menschenrechtsverletzungen. In: Krajewski M, Oehm F, Saage-Maaß M (eds) Zivil- und strafrechtliche Unternehmensverantwortung für Menschenrechtsverletzungen. Springer, Heidelberg, pp 33–50

Handschin L (2017) Konzernverantwortungsinitiative: Gesellschaftsrechtliche Aspekte. Aktuelle Juristische Praxis 26(8):1000–1004

Hannoun C (2017) Le devoir de vigilance des sociétés mères et entreprises donneuses d'ordre après la loi du 27 mars 2017. Droit social 2017(10):806–818

Hartmann C (2018) Haftung von Unternehmen für Menschenrechtsverletzungen im Ausland aus Sicht des Internationalen Privat- und Zivilverfahrensrechts. In: Krajewski M, Saage-Maaß M (eds) Die Durchsetzung menschenrechtlicher Sorgfaltspflichten von Unternehmen. Baden-Baden, Nomos, pp 281–310

Heinen A (2018) Auf dem Weg zu einem transnationalen Deliktsrecht? – Zur Begründung deliktischer Sorgfalts- und Organisationspflichten in globalen Wertschöpfungsketten. In: Krajewski M, Saage-Maaß M (eds) Die Durchsetzung menschenrechtlicher Sorgfaltspflichten von Unternehmen. Nomos, Baden-Baden, pp 87–124

Hoffberger E (2017) Das französische Gesetz über die menschenrechtliche due diligence von Muttergesellschaften und Auftrag gebenden Unternehmen. Archiv des Völkerrechts 55 (4):465–486

Jazottes G (2018) Sous-traitance et "relation commerciale établie" au sens de l'article L. 442-6 du code de commerce: quelle pertinence pour le plan de vigilance. Revue Lamy Droit des Affaires No. 139(1):28–31

Kaufmann C (2016) Konzernverantwortungsinitiative: Grenzenlose Verantwortlichkeit. Schweizerische Zeitschrift für Wirtschafts- und Finanzmarktrecht 88(1):45–54

Keitner C (2012) Response: optimizing liability for extraterritorial torts: a response to Professor Sykes. Georgetown Law J 100(6):2211–2216

Kessedijan C (2018) Implementing the UN principles on business and human rights in private international law: European perspectives. In: Zamora Cabot FJ, Heckendorn Urscheler L, De Dycker S (eds) Implementing the UN guiding principles on business and human rights: private international law perspectives. Schulthess, Zürich, pp 141–152

Kimeldorf H, Meyer R, Prasad M, Robinson I (2006) Consumers with a conscience: will they pay more? Contexts 5(1):24–29

Klinger R, Krajewski M, Krebs D, Hartmann C (2016) Verankerung menschenrechtlicher Sorgfaltspflichten von Unternehmen im deutschen Recht

Lehmann M, Eichel F (2019) Globaler Klimawandel und Internationales Privatrecht. Zuständigkeit und anzuwendendes Recht für transnationale Klagen wegen klimawandelbedingter

Individualschäden. Rabels Zeitschrift für ausländisches und internationales Privatrecht 83 (1):77–110

Leible S, Lehmann M (2007) Die neue EG-Verordnung über das auf außervertragliche Schuldverhältnisses anzuwendende Recht ("Rom II"). Recht der Internationalen Wirtschaft 53 (10):721–735

Littenberg MR, Binder NV (2019) Corporate social responsibility disclosure and compliance: an overview of selected legislation, guidance and voluntary initiatives. https://www.ropesgray.com/en/newsroom/alerts/2019/10/Corporate-Social-Responsibility-Disclosure-and-Compliance

Mankowski P (2019) Internationales Privatrecht II, 2nd edn. C.H. Beck, Munich

Mansel HP (2018) Internationales Privatecht de lege lata wie de lege ferenda und Menschenrechtsverantwortlichkeit deutscher Unternehmen. Zeitschrift für Unternehmens- und Gesellschaftsrecht 47(2-3):439–478

Marx M, Bright C, Wouters J et al (2019) Access to legal remedies for victims of corporate human rights abuses in third countries. Study for the European Parliament's Sub-Committee on Human Rights

Métais P, Valette E (2019) Le devoir de vigilance et les enjeux en matière de resposabilité civile. Revue Lamy Droit des Affaires No. 153:49–52

Nasse L (2019) Die neue Sorgfaltspflicht zur Menschenrechtsverantwortung für Großunternehmen in Frankreich. Zeitschrift für Europäisches Privatrecht 27(4):774–802

Nordhues S (2019) Die Haftung der Muttergesellschaft und ihres Vorstands für Menschenrechtsverletzungen im Konzern. Nomos, Baden-Baden

Otero Carcá-Castrillón C (2011) International litigation trends in environmental liability: a European Union-United States comparative perspective. J Private Int Law 7(3):551–581

Palombo D (2019) The duty of care of the parent company: a comparison between French Law, UK precedents and the Swiss proposals. Bus Hum Rights J 4(2):264–286

Parance B, Groulx E (2018) Regard croisés sur le devoir de vigilance et le duty of care. Journal de droit international (Clunet) 145(1):21–52

Pataut E (2017) Le devoir de vigilance. Aspects de droit international privé. Droit social 2017 (10):833–839

Périn PL (2015) Devoir de vigilance et responsabilité illimitée des entreprises: qui trop embrasse mal étreint. Revue trimestrielle de droit commercial 2015(2):215–224

Petitjean O (2019) Devoir de vigilance. Une victoire contre l'impunité des multinationals. Editions Charles Léopold Mayer, Paris

Pförtner F (2018) Menschenrechtliche Sorgfaltspflichten für Unternehmen – eine Betrachtung aus kollisionsrechtlicher Perspektive. In: Krajewski M, Saage-Maaß M (eds) Die Durchsetzung menschenrechtlicher Sorgfaltspflichten von Unternehmen. Nomos, Baden-Baden, pp 311–331

Renaud J, Quairel F, Gagnier S et al (2019) The law on duty of vigilance of parent and outsourcing companies. Year 1: Companies must do better

Rühl G (2011) Statut und Effizienz. Ökonomische Grundlagen des Internationalen Privatrechts. Mohr Siebeck, Tübingen

Rühl G (2020a) Unternehmensverantwortung und (Internationales) Privatrecht. In: Reinisch A, Hobe S, Kieninger EM et al (eds) Unternehmensverantwortung und Internationales Recht. C.F. Müller, Heidelberg, pp 89–132

Rühl G (2020b) Die Haftung von Unternehmen für Menschenrechtsverletzungen: Die französische Loi de vigilance als Vorbild für ein deutsches Wertschöpfungskettengesetz? In: Bachmann G, Grundmann S, Mengel A et al (eds) Festschrift für Christine Windbichler. De Gruyter, Berlin, pp 1413–1434

Spitzer M (2019) Human rights, global supply chains, and the role of tort. J Eur Tort Law 10 (2):95–107

Stiglitz JE (2011) Brief as Amicus Curiae in support of petitioners, Mohamad et al v. Palestinian Authority and Palestine Liberation Organization, Kiobel et al v. Royal Dutch Petroleum, United States Supreme Court, Nos. 11-88 and 10-1491. https://www.americanbar.org/content/dam/aba/publications/supreme_court_preview/briefs/10-1491_petitioner_amcu_stiglitz.pdf

Stone P (2015) Choice of law for tort claims. In: Stone P, Farah Y (eds) Research handbook on EU private international law. Edward Elgar, Cheltenham, pp 285–314

Stürner M (2014) Transnationale Menschenrechtsverletzungen im Internationalen Privat- und Verfahrensrecht. Int J Procedural Law 4(2):350–374

Stürner M (2015) Zur Rolle des Kollisionsrechts bei der Durchsetzung von Menschenrechten. In: Hilbig-Lugani K, Jacobs D, Mäsch G et al (eds) Festschrift für Dagmar Coester-Waltjen. Gieseking, Bielefeld, pp 843–854

Sykes AO (2012) Corporate liability for extraterritorial torts under the Alien Tort Statue and beyond: an economic analysis. Georgetown Law J 100(6):2161–2209

Symeonides S (2008) Rome II: a missed opportunity. Am J Comp Law 56(2):173–222

Thomale C, Hübner L (2017) Zivilgerichtliche Durchsetzung völkerrechtlicher Unternehmensverantwortung. JuristenZeitung 72(8):385–397

Van Calster G (2014) The role of private international law in corporate social responsibility. Erasmus Law Rev 8(3):125–144

Van Dam C (2011) Tort law and human rights: brothers in arms. On the role of tort law in the area of business and human rights. J Eur Tort Law 2(3):221–254

Van den Eeckhout V (2012) Corporate human rights violations and private international law. Contemp Readings Law Soc Just 4(2):178–207

Van den Eeckhout V (2017) The private international law dimension of the principles in Europe. In: Zamora Cabot FJ, Heckendorn Urscheler L, De Dycker S (eds) Implementing the UN guiding principles on business and human rights: private international law perspectives. Schulthess, Zürich, pp 37–62

Van Hoek AAH (2008) Transnational corporate social responsibility: some issues with regard to the liability of European corporations for labour law infringements in the countries of establishment of their suppliers. In: Pennings F, Konijn Y, Veldman A (eds) Social responsibility in labour relations: European and comparative perspectives. Kluwer, Alphen aan den Rijn, pp 147–169

von Hein J (2008a) Die Ausweichklausel im europäischen Internationalen Deliktsrecht. In: Baetge D, von Hein J, von Hinden M (eds) Die richtige Ordnung. Festschrift für Jan Kropholler. Mohr Siebeck, Tübingen, pp 553–571

von Hein J (2008b) Something old and something borrowed, but nothing new? Rome II and the European choice-of-law evolution. Tulane Law Rev 82(5):1663–1707

von Hein J (2009) Europäisches Internationales Deliktsrecht nach der Rom II-Verordnung. Zeitschrift für Europäisches Privatrecht 17(1):6–33

von Hein J (2015a) Article 4 Rome II. In: Calliess GP (ed) Rome regulations, 2nd edn. Kluwer, Alphen aan den Rijn, pp 495–534

von Hein J (2015b) Article 7 Rome II. In: Calliess GP (ed) Rome regulations, 2nd edn. Kluwer, Alphen aan den Rijn, pp 603–625

von Hein J (2015c) Article 16 Rome II. In: Calliess GP (ed) Rome regulations, 2nd edn. Kluwer, Alphen aan den Rijn, pp 729–740

von Hein J (2015d) Article 17 Rome II. In: Calliess GP (ed) Rome regulations, 2nd edn. Kluwer, Alphen aan den Rijn, pp 741–759

Wagner G (2008) Die neue Rom II-Verordnung. Praxis des Internationalen Privat- und Verfahrensrechts 28(1):1–17

Wagner G (2016) Haftung für Menschenrechtsverletzungen. Rabels Zeitschrift für ausländisches und internationales Privatrecht 80(4):717–782

Weller MP, Nasse L (2020) Menschenrechtsarbitrage als Gefahrenquelle. Systemkohärenz einer Verkehrspflicht zur Menschenrechtssicherung in Lieferketten. Zeitschrift für Unternehmens- und Gesellschaftsrecht, Sonderheft 22:107–140

Weller M, Pato A (2018) Local parents as 'anchor defendants' in European courts for claims against their foreign subsidiaries in human rights and environmental damages litigation: recent case law and legislative trends. Uniform Law Rev 23:397–413

Weller MP, Thomale C (2017) Menschenrechtsklagen gegen deutsche Unternehmen. Zeitschrift für Unternehmens- und Gesellschaftsrecht 46(4):509–526

Weller MP, Kaller L, Schulz A (2016) Haftung deutscher Unternehmen für Menschenrechtsverletzungen im Ausland. Archiv für die civilistische Praxis 216(3-4):387–420

Wendelstein C (2019) "Menschenrechtliche" Verhaltenspflichten im System des Internationalen Privatrecht. Rabels Zeitschrift für ausländisches und internationales Privatrecht 83(1):111–153

Werro F (2019) The Swiss responsible business initiative and the counter-proposal. J Eur Tort Law 10(2):166–182

Giesela Rühl is a Professor of Private International Law at Humboldt University of Berlin (Germany). She holds both German State Examinations, a Master of Laws from the University of California at Berkeley (USA) as well as a Doctorate and a Post-Doctorate from the University of Hamburg (Germany). She serves on the board of the European Association of Private International Law (EAPIL) and has frequently acted as expert for the JURI Committee of the European Parliament during the past years. Prior to joining Humboldt-University, Giesela was a Professor of Law at the University of Jena (Germany), a Max Weber Fellow at the European University Institute in Florence (Italy), a Senior Research Fellow at the Max Planck Institute for Comparative and International Private Law in Hamburg (Germany) and a Joseph Story Research Fellow at the Harvard Law School in Cambridge (USA). In addition, she held visiting positions at the University of Cambridge, the University of Oxford, the London School of Economics and Political Science (England), the University of Sydney (Australia) and Duke Law School (USA).

An International Economic Law Perspective on the United Nations Convention Against Corruption

Cecily Rose

Contents

Abstract Public international law regulates corruption as a part of transnational criminal law, rather than international economic law. Like other transnational criminal law treaties, the United Nations Convention against Corruption, as well as other regional and international anti-corruption instruments, seek to ensure that domestic anti-corruption laws are relatively harmonized, and that states can cooperate with each other in investigations, prosecutions, and asset recovery. Public international law thus approaches the subject of corruption from a predominantly criminal law perspective, which focuses, in good part, on the criminalization of corrupt conduct by public officials as well as private actors, such as business entities. In the 1970s, however, the problem of corruption was approached by states and other actors partly within the framework of international economic law. Had this approach to the subject of corruption prevailed in the 1970s, then international instruments

The author is grateful for the research assistance of Claire Benn.

C. Rose (✉)
Grotius Centre for International Legal Studies, Leiden Law School, Leiden, The Netherlands
e-mail: c.e.rose@law.leidenuniv.nl

© Springer Nature Switzerland AG 2021   83
M. Bungenberg et al. (eds.), *European Yearbook of International Economic Law 2020*,
European Yearbook of International Economic Law (2022) 11: 83–106,
https://doi.org/10.1007/8165_2021_70, Published online: 10 June 2021

might also detail the measures that business entities should put in place in order to prevent corruption, such as internal compliance programmes. But efforts to regulate corrupt conduct through both a code of conduct and a treaty failed, and the issue of corruption lay dormant at international organizations until the 1990s, when states concluded a spate of ant-corruption treaties that provide for criminalization and cooperation. Today, international economic law, in particular free trade agreements, deal with corruption largely by cross reference to this substantial body of transnational criminal law treaties governing corruption.

1 Introduction

The word corruption commonly brings to mind misconduct by large multinational corporations, such as Siemens or Odebrecht, which have engaged in bribery schemes abroad, for the purpose of securing international business deals. Given that corruption often takes place in the context of foreign direct investment, one might expect it to be regulated under international economic law, perhaps as a part of international trade or investment law. Instead, as a result of historical developments that took place in the 1970s, international law regulates corruption within the framework of transnational criminal law. On the one hand, this is perfectly logical, as acts of corruption have long been criminalized across the globe. Transnational criminal law treaties, such as the United Nations Convention against Corruption (UNCAC), build on this existing foundation of domestic criminal laws by ensuring that domestic anti-corruption laws are relatively harmonized, and that states can cooperate with one another with respect to investigations, prosecutions, and asset recovery.[1] On the other hand, international law's predominantly criminal law approach to corruption means that international law does not regulate, to any significant extent, the measures that business entities should put in place in order to prevent corruption, such as internal compliance programmes.[2] In addition, transnational criminal law arguably underregulates certain areas of the anti-corruption field, such as the process by which the proceeds of corruption are returned from one state to another in a responsible manner that is in keeping with principles of good governance.

This article begins in Sect. 2 by explaining how the regulation of corruption has evolved, from a phenomenon that was discussed within the framework of international economic law in the 1970s, to a phenomenon that is now regulated as part of transnational criminal law.[3] Section 3 then explains that the United Nations

---

[1] United Nations Convention against Corruption (adopted 31 October 2003, entered into force 14 December 2005) 2349 UNTS 41 (UNCAC).

[2] But see OECD, Good Practice Guidance on Internal Controls, Ethics and Compliance (18 February 2010) C(2010)19.

[3] For a more detailed discussion of the history of international anti-corruption law, see Rose (2021).

Convention against Corruption, which was concluded in 2003, regulates corruption primarily from a criminal law perspective, although it includes provisions on the prevention of corruption, including one rather broad provision concerning accounting and auditing standards as preventive measures in the private sector. The focus of this article is on UNCAC because this anti-corruption treaty is the most comprehensive in scope, and the most widely ratified, compared to other international and regional anti-corruption treaties.[4] Finally, Sect. 4 reflects on the current relationship between international anti-corruption law and international trade law, in particular free trade agreements which have begun to incorporate UNCAC provisions.

2 A Historical Perspective on the International Regulation of Corruption

Corporate scandals in the 1970s, all involving American enterprises, gave rise to competing definitions of both the problem of corruption, and the most appropriate international legal solution to it. On the one hand, developing countries pressed for an expansive definition of corruption and a solution grounded in international economic law, in particular a code of conduct for multinational corporations. On the other hand, developed countries pressed for a narrow definition of corruption as bribery and a solution grounded in what we now call transnational criminal law.[5] The first scandal that helped shape the developing world's conception of corruption involved the conduct of the American multinational corporation, International Telephone and Telegraph (ITT) in Chile. The second set of revelations, concerning the misconduct of hundreds of American multinational corporations abroad, came to light in the aftermath of the Watergate scandal in the United States. The following section briefly details these scandals, and describes how they influenced the negotiations in the mid- to late-1970s for what would have been the first international anti-corruption treaty. Ultimately, these negotiations failed because the competing conceptions of both the problem and the solution proved irresolvable amidst the political climate of the 1970s. When the subject of corruption reemerged in

---

[4]See e.g. Inter-American Convention against Corruption (adopted on 29 March 1996, entered into force 6 March 1997) (1996) 35 ILM 724; Convention on the Fight against Corruption involving Officials of the European Communities or Officials of Member States of the European Union (Council of Europe, adopted 26 May 1997, entered into force 28 September 2005) OJ C 195; Convention on Combating Bribery of Foreign Public Officials in International Business Transactions (adopted 21 November 1997, entered into force 15 February 1999) (1998) 37 ILM 1; Council of Europe Criminal Law Convention on Corruption (27 January 1999, entered into force 1 December 2009) CETS No. 173; Council of Europe Civil Law Convention on Corruption (adopted 4 November 1999, entered into force 1 November 2003) CETS No. 174; African Union Convention on Preventing and Combating Corruption (adopted 11 July 2003, entered into force 5 August 2006) (2004) 43 ILM 5.

[5]Boister (2003).

international fora in the 1990s, a narrow conception of corruption and a legal
solution grounded in criminal law distinctly prevailed.

2.1 The Influence of Corporate Scandals on the Framing of Corruption as a Legal Problem

ITT's misconduct in Chile began in the months leading up to the election of Salvador
Allende as president of Chile in 1970.[6] Allende was a Democratic socialist who
promised during his campaign to work towards improving Chile's economic position, in part through the nationalization of certain industries, such as the copper
industry.[7] Allende's plans to expropriate foreign investments in Chile also extended
to service industries, including the national telephone company, which was owned
by a subsidiary of ITT. American companies with investments in Chile were
apprehensive about the prospect of such expropriations, and were opposed to
Allende's election.[8] ITT, however, took active steps to prevent Allende's election
by providing funding to Allende's political opponent prior to the election in
September 1970.[9] ITT also considered participating in the US Central Intelligence
Agency's failed attempt to foment economic chaos in Chile after Allende's election,
with a view towards bringing about a military coup.[10]

After ITT's misconduct came to light in March 1972, due to reporting by an
investigative journalist in the United States, this scandal resonated deeply in Chile,
the United States, and at the United Nations.[11] In April 1972, Allende himself
framed the scandal as one involving the "powerful corruptive influence" of multinational corporations on "public institutions in rich and poor countries alike".[12] He
urged the United Nations Conference on Trade and Development (UNCTAD) to
take up the issue of corporate intervention in the internal affairs of states. Instead, the

---

[6]The election took place on 4 September 1970. The Chilean Congress confirmed Allende's election
on 24 October 1970 and Allende's inauguration was on 3 November 1970.

[7]Garavini (2012), pp. 136–138.

[8]United States Senate, Select Committee to Study Governmental Operations with Respect to
Intelligence Activities, Covert Action in Chile, 1963–1973 (1975), p. 12.

[9]United States Senate, Select Committee to Study Governmental Operations with Respect to
Intelligence Activities, Covert Action in Chile, 1963–1973 (1975), pp. 12–13.

[10]United States Senate, Select Committee to Study Governmental Operations with Respect to
Intelligence Activities, Covert Action in Chile, 1963–1973 (1975), p. 25.

[11]Anderson J, Memos Bare ITT Try for Chile Coup. The Washington Post, 21 March 1972, B13;
Anderson, J, ITT Pledged Millions to Stop Allende. The Washington Post, 22 March 1972, C23;
I.T.T. Is Accused of Having Tried to Influence U.S. Policies. The New York Times, 23 March 1972.

[12]Address Delivered by Mr. Salvador Allende Gossens, President of Chile at the Inaugural
Ceremony on 13 April 1972, Proceedings of the United Nations Conference on Trade and
Development, Third Session, Santiago de Chile, 13 April to 21 May 1971, Volume I, Report and
Annexes (UN 1973), p. 353, para. 62. Hamdani and Ruffing (2015), p. 8; Katzarova (2018).

United Nations Economic and Social Council (ECOSOC) took action, and in 1974 created the United Nations Centre on Transnational Corporations (UNCTC), which worked for years, ultimately unsuccessfully, on a Code of Conduct on Transnational Corporations.[13] Chile's direct contribution to the international regulation of corporate conduct came to an end in 1973, after the overthrow and death of Allende, and the establishment of a corporate-friendly military dictatorship led by Augusto Pinochet. But Chile's expansive framing of the problem of corruption left a legacy that continued to influence negotiations at the United Nations in the latter part of the 1970s.[14] The scandal also prompted years of US Senate hearings on the conduct of American multinational corporations abroad, including that of ITT.[15] The United States' narrow framing of corruption as bribery can be seen as a reaction to Chile's expansive framing, rather than as a proactive response to the next scandal that unfolded in the United States.[16]

Beginning in June 1972, the Watergate scandal in the United States began to unravel, as newspaper reporters covered an attempted burglary of the Democratic National Party headquarters in the Watergate building, in Washington, D.C. Investigative reporting revealed that the burglary was a part of an espionage and sabotage operation being run by President Richard Nixon's reelection campaign, against the Democratic presidential candidates.[17] The scandal mushroomed when further investigations showed that American companies had been using "slush" funds for both illegal campaign contributions in the United States, and also for the payment of bribes to foreign public officials.[18] Due to these revelations, the US Securities and Exchange Commission instituted a voluntary disclosure programme, through which more than 400 American companies ultimately reported having paid bribes totalling more than US$300 million to public officials abroad.[19] The US

---

[13]In 1972, ECOSOC created the Group of Eminent Persons to Study the Impact of Multinational Corporations on Development and on International Relations. ECOSOC Res. 1721 (LIII) The impact of multinational corporations on the development process and on international relations (28 July 1972). In 1974, the Group of Eminent Persons recommended the creation of the CTC. Report of the Group of Eminent Persons to Study the Impact of Multinational Corporations on Development and on International Relations in The Impact of Multinational Corporations on the Development and on International Relations, E/5500/Rev.1, pp. 51–53.

[14]Katzarova (2018), p. 81.

[15]The ITT scandal resulted in the creation of the Senate Subcommittee on Multinational Corporations which was chaired by Frank Church and held hearings between March 1973 and September 1976. The Subcommittee published its findings in seventeen volumes.

[16]Katzarova (2018), p. 77.

[17]See e.g. Bernstein C, Woodward B, FBI Finds Nixon Aides Sabotaged Democrats. The Washington Post, 10 October 1972. See further, Bernstein and Woodward (1974).

[18]United States Senate, The Final Report of the Select Committee on Presidential Campaign Activities (June 1974), pp. 445–447.

[19]United States Senate, Report of the Securities and Exchange Commission on Questionable and Illegal Corporate Payments and Practices, Submitted to the Committee on Banking, Housing and Urban Affairs (May 1976), pp. 6–13; US House of Representatives, Report No 95-640, Unlawful Corporate Payments Act of 1977 (28 September 1977), p. 4.

Senate also held hearings on "the questionable or illegal foreign payments" by American multinational corporations.[20] These hearings led to especially scandalous revelations about the conduct of Lockheed, the largest American defense contractor at the time, which had been engaged in foreign bribery on a massive scale across the globe, including in developed countries such as Italy, Japan, and the Netherlands.[21]

The US Congress responded to this fallout from the Watergate scandal by pursuing both an international treaty, and domestic legislation. In a resolution adopted in November 1975, the US Senate directed the US executive branch to negotiate a treaty within the framework of the General Agreement on Tariffs and Trade (GATT), or another appropriate forum, concerning "questionable or illegal foreign payments".[22] The Senate notably characterized the problem of corruption as rooted in the "policies and practices" of host countries, and thus originating not with American corporations themselves, but in the foreign business cultures in which they were operating. The US executive branch ultimately pursued negotiations not at the GATT, but instead at the United Nations and the Organisation for Economic Cooperation and Development (OECD).[23] At the same time, the US Congress passed domestic legislation, the Foreign Corrupt Practices Act (FCPA) of 1977, which criminalized the bribery of foreign public officials and instituted related accounting and record keeping requirements.[24] The US House of Representatives justified this legislation by reference to concerns about morality, the loss of public confidence in the integrity of the free market system, and the foreign policy implications of such corporate misconduct.[25] Because a UN treaty on corruption did not materialize in the 1970s, the FCPA amounted to a unilateral solution by the United States. American corporations subsequently perceived themselves to be a disadvantage compared to their foreign counterparts, based in countries that did not prohibit the bribery of foreign public officials, and even allowed such payments to be tax deductible as business expenses.

---

[20]The Hearings were held by the Subcommittee on Multinational Corporations of the Senate Foreign Relations Committee, chaired by Senator Frank Church. This was the same Subcommittee that had investigated ITT's activities in Chile 2 years prior. For a detailed account of these hearings see Koehler (2012).

[21]Davis (2019) and Kroeze (2018)

[22]A Resolution to Protect the Ability of the United States to Trade Abroad, Report to Accompany S. Res. 265 (5 November 1975).

[23]The negotiations that took place at the OECD are beyond the scope of this historical summary.

[24]15 U.S.C. ss 78dd-1 to 78dd-3.

[25]US House of Representatives, Report No 95-640, Unlawful Corporate Payments Act of 1977 (28 September 1977), p. 4; Davis (2019), pp. 38–39. Tarullo (2004), p. 673; Pieth (2013), pp. 10–11.

2.2 The Failed Negotiation of a Treaty on Illicit Payments at the United Nations

These scandals helped to shape a political climate in the 1970s that was not conducive to successful treaty negotiations on the issue of corruption within the framework of the United Nations. The scope of the problem was contested by states as soon as the UN General Assembly took up the subject in 1975. The United States put forward a draft General Assembly resolution that conceived of corruption as referring mostly to bribery, and which focused not only on the conduct of bribe givers, i.e. multinational corporations, but also on the conduct of bribe recipients, i.e. public officials in foreign countries.[26] Libya, on the other hand, put forward a resolution that made no reference to bribery, but instead framed corruption as unethical conduct by corporations, and also their home governments (in other words, state sponsorship of corruption by corporations).[27] The General Assembly adopted Resolution 3514, which was sponsored by a group of developing countries.[28] The Resolution struck a compromise of sorts, by condemning "corrupt practices, including bribery, by transnational and other corporations, their intermediaries and others involved, in violation of the laws and regulations of the host countries".[29] The Resolution thus highlighted bribery as a form of corrupt conduct, but also allowed for a broader range of conduct to fall under the umbrella of corrupt conduct. It further tied the issue of corruption to the development of a code of conduct on transnational corporations, which was part of the New International Economic Order (NIEO).[30]

The Ad Hoc Intergovernmental Working Group on Corrupt Practices was created by ECOSOC in August 1976, for the purpose of producing a draft treaty on "illicit payments", a broad term which allowed for an expansive conception of corruption.[31] The draft treaty defined the term "illicit payments" as referring to active and passive bribery[32] as well as "illegal political contributions as defined in national laws and regulations and any payment of royalties and taxes to illegal minority regimes in

---

[26]1975 UN Yearbook, pp. 486–487.

[27]1975 UN Yearbook, pp. 486–487.

[28]The resolution was sponsored by Algeria, Argentina, Benin, Bolivia, Colombia, Costa Rica, Cuba, Democratic Yemen, Ecuador, Egypt, Gabon, Guyana, Iran, Iraq, the Libyan Arab Republic, Madagascar, Nigeria, Pakistan, Peru, Romania, Somalia, the Syrian Arab Republic, Togo, the United Republic of Tanzania, the Upper Volta, Venezuela, and Yugoslavia. 1975 UN Yearbook, p. 487.

[29]UN General Assembly Resolution 3514, para. 1.

[30]UN General Assembly Resolution 3514, preambular paras. 2–3. The General Assembly launched the New International Economic Order in Resolutions 3201, 3202 (1 May 1974). The New International Economic Order emphasized, in part, the need to regulate the activities of transnational corporations in the countries where they operate (i.e. in developing host countries).

[31]1976 UN Yearbook, p. 460; ECOSOC Resolution 2041 (LXI).

[32]Active bribery refers to offering and giving a bribe, whereas passive bribery refers to soliciting or receiving a bribe.

southern Africa in contravention of United Nations resolutions".[33] The inclusion of both active and passive bribery in this definition reflected the focus of the United States, which was concerned with regulating the conduct uncovered by the Watergate scandal. The inclusion of illegal political contributions in this definition reflected the focus of developing countries concerned with the ITT scandal. Meanwhile, the reference to illegal minority regimes in southern Africa reflected the focus of African states on non-compliance by multinational corporations with the economic sanctions that were then in place against Namibia and Southern Rhodesia.[34] In the absence of an agreement about whether to pursue a broad or narrow conception of corruption, the treaty drafts produced by the Working Group tentatively provided for the criminalization of bribery *and/or* illicit payments.[35] In doing so, the drafts satisfied neither developing nor developed countries. In addition to this basic disagreement about what type of conduct to address in the treaty, delegations could not agree on what type of actor should be the focus of the criminalization provision. Several delegations objected to what they perceived as an emphasis on the improper activities of public officials in host countries (i.e. passive bribery), rather than the misconduct of the corporations themselves (i.e. active bribery).[36]

The members of the Working Group disagreed not only about the scope of the treaty, but also about whether a treaty was even the most appropriate way to address the problem (however that problem might be defined). The Working Group itself focused mainly on a criminal law approach to the problem of illicit payments, but it considered other approaches, most significantly a code of conduct.[37] Developing countries represented in the Working Group stressed that the formulation of a code of conduct by the CTC "should be accorded the highest priority", and they eventually made their support for the treaty contingent on the conclusion of a code of conduct.[38] This linkage of the code of conduct to the treaty was fatal for the treaty negotiations. The code of conduct never came to fruition, and in fact negotiations for the code dragged on throughout the 1980s, well past the end of the treaty

---

[33]ECOSOC, Report of the Ad Hoc Intergovernmental Working Group on the Problem of Corrupt Practices on its First, Second, Third and Resumed Third Sessions, E/6006 (5 July 1977); Ad Hoc Intergovernmental Working Group on the Problem of Corrupt Practices, Major Issues to be Considered in the Examination of the Problem of Corrupt Practices, in Particular Bribery, in International Commercial Transactions by Transnational and Other Corporations, Their Intermediaries and Others Involved: Report of the Secretariat, E/AC.64/7 (17 March 1977), para. 19.

[34]See e.g. UN Security Council Resolutions concerning Southern Rhodesia: Resolutions 232 (16 December 1966), 253 (29 May 1968), 277 (18 March 1970), 388 (6 April 1976) (Southern Rhodesia); and UN Security Council Resolution 276 (30 January 1970), concerning Namibia.

[35]ECOSOC, Report of the Ad Hoc Intergovernmental Working Group on the Problem of Corrupt Practices on its First, Second, Third and Resumed Third Sessions, E/6006 (5 July 1977), Art. III.

[36]ECOSOC, Report of the Ad Hoc Intergovernmental Working Group on the Problem of Corrupt Practices on its Fourth, Fifth and Resumed Fifth Sessions, E/1978/115 (7 July 1978), para. 21.

[37]ECOSOC, Report of the Ad Hoc Intergovernmental Working Group on the Problem of Corrupt Practices on its Fourth, Fifth and Resumed Fifth Sessions, E/1978/115 (7 July 1978), pp. 10–11.

[38]ECOSOC, Report of the Ad Hoc Intergovernmental Working Group on the Problem of Corrupt Practices on its Fourth and Fifth Sessions, E/1978/39 (24 April 1978), p. 11.

negotiations in the late 1970s.[39] Although the General Assembly received a nearly complete treaty draft in May 1979, it never took action to convene a diplomatic conference.[40] If states had managed to regulate corporate conduct (including corruption) through a code of conduct, then the subject of corruption would today be governed, at least in part, through international economic law. But attempts to regulate corporate conduct through an international instrument repeatedly faltered, whereas the regulation of corruption through transnational criminal law ultimately succeeded.[41]

2.3 The Reemergence of the Subject of Corruption at International Organizations in the 1990s

During the 1980s, the issue of corruption remained dormant at international organizations, including the United Nations, but also the OECD and the World Bank. But by the early 1990s, with the end of the Cold War and apartheid in southern Africa, global politics had shifted so considerably that successful international negotiations on this issue became possible. By the end of the Cold War, the NIEO had also met its demise, and developing countries were no longer pursuing the regulation of multinational corporations through codes of conduct, as in the 1970s and 1980s. In addition, the US had a special incentive to reinitiate negotiations, as its corporations perceived themselves to be a strategic disadvantage in international business deals, compared to foreign companies that were not subject to foreign bribery laws. In its 1988 amendment of the FCPA, the US Congress once again urged the US executive branch to pursue international negotiations on the subject of corruption.[42] In taking up this issue in the early 1990s, the US executive branch focused on pursuing negotiations through the OECD. These negotiations were ultimately successful, and resulted in the issuance of OECD recommendations on bribery in international business transactions in 1994 and 1997, followed by the conclusion of the OECD Anti-Bribery Convention in 1997.[43]

At the same time, the US instigated negotiations on this subject at the Organization of American States, which culminated in the first anti-corruption treaty in 1996,

---

[39]On the reasons for the failure to negotiate the Code of Conduct see Sauvant (2015), pp. 56–62; Hamdani and Ruffing (2015), Chapter 3.

[40]General Assembly Decision 35/425 (5 December 1980).

[41]See e.g. the failure to negotiate the UN Code of Conduct on Transnational Corporations in the 1980s and the OECD Multilateral Agreement on Investment in the mid to late 1990s.

[42]Pub. L. No. 100-418, 102 Stat. 1415.

[43]OECD, Recommendation on Bribery in International Business Transactions (27 May 1994) C(94) 75/FINAL; OECD Revised Recommendation of the Council on Bribery in International Business Transactions (23 May 1997) C(97)123/FINAL; Convention on Combating Bribery of Foreign Public Officials in International Business Transactions (adopted 21 November 1997, entered into force 15 February 1999) (1998) 37 ILM 1 (OECD Anti-Bribery Convention).

the Inter-American Convention against Corruption.[44] In addition, European members of the OECD further pursued the issue of corruption at the Council of Europe (CoE) and through the European Union (EU), resulting in the 1997 EU Convention against Corruption Involving Public Officials and the 1999 CoE Civil and Criminal Law Conventions on Corruption.[45] The United Nations was comparatively slow to take up the issue of corruption at this stage. UN treaty negotiations on corruption took place in the early 2000s, only after the successful negotiation of a number of regional treaties and the OECD Anti-Bribery Convention. While in the process of negotiating the UN Convention against Transnational Organized Crime (UNTOC), states decided that the issue of corruption merited separate treatment, in another treaty.[46] In 2003, these separate treaty negotiations finally culminated in the UN Convention against Corruption, which is the most comprehensive and widely ratified of the anti-corruption treaties, with 187 states parties as of February 2020.[47] Taken together, this body of treaties embraces a criminal law approach to the regulation of corruption, with the exception of the CoE Civil Law Convention on Corruption. In addition, the legacy of the Watergate scandal endures, as these treaties focus mainly on bribery and related conduct.

3 The Contemporary Transnational Criminal Law Approach to Corruption

The United Nations Convention against Corruption is a transnational criminal law treaty (or "suppression convention"), which like all treaties in this field of public international law, mainly provides for the domestic criminalization of conduct deemed criminal and for international cooperation. Much of UNCAC is therefore devoted to provisions concerning criminalization and enforcement in domestic legal systems, and provisions concerning international cooperation with respect to investigations and prosecutions, namely extradition and mutual legal assistance. In addition, UNCAC contains an unusual chapter on preventive measures, which is

---

[44]Inter-American Convention against Corruption (adopted 29 March 1996, entered into force 6 March 1997) (1996) 35 ILM 724.

[45]Convention on the Fight against Corruption involving Officials of the European Communities or Officials of Member States of the European Union (Council of Europe, adopted 26 May 1997, entered into force 28 September 2005) OJ C 195; Council of Europe Criminal Law Convention on Corruption (adopted 27 January 1999, entered into force 1 December 2009) CETS No 173 (CoE Criminal Law Convention); Council of Europe Civil Law Convention on Corruption (adopted 4 November 1999, entered into force 1 November 2003).

[46]United Nations Convention against Transnational Organized Crime (adopted 15 November 2000, entered into force 29 September 2003) 2225 UNTS 209.

[47]UNODC, Signature and Ratification Status. https://www.unodc.org/unodc/en/corruption/ratification-status.html (last accessed 8 January 2021).

not a standard feature of transnational criminal law treaties.[48] These preventive measures deal with a range of approaches to corruption which are grounded in domestic policies and laws of a non-criminal character.

UNCAC itself does not apply to business enterprises, as the treaty does not directly govern the conduct of public officials or private actors, but instead requires states parties to implement domestic criminalization provisions, and to cooperate with each other in investigating and prosecuting public officials and private actors. But domestic criminalization provisions are potentially of great relevance to the individuals and corporations who run afoul of them, and are subsequently investigated, prosecuted, and perhaps even the subject of requests for international cooperation. Likewise, the chapter on prevention has implications for the private sector, depending on the extent to which states implement these provisions in their domestic laws and policies. This section focuses on UNCAC's criminalization, enforcement, and prevention provisions, in particular those which may have significant ramifications for business entities.

3.1 UNCAC's Criminalization Provisions

The legacy of the 1970s can be seen in UNCAC's criminalization provisions, which focus predominantly on bribery and other similar conduct, and thus reflect the narrow conceptualization of corruption originally put forward by the United States. UNCAC does not define the term corruption, as the drafters could not agree on a definition of this concept and also did not consider it necessary to do so.[49] By omitting a definition of corruption, the drafters avoided the sort of definitional problems that contributed to the failure of treaty negotiations in the 1970s. Instead, the Convention defines a number of criminal acts which fall within the umbrella of "corruption", namely: various types of bribery; embezzlement, misappropriation and other diversion of property; trading in influence; abuse of functions; and illicit enrichment.[50] Compared to other anti-corruption treaties, UNCAC covers the greatest range of possible types of corruption. Yet, the Convention's treatment of the concept of corruption remains narrow when viewed from the perspective of other academic fields,[51] and also from the perspective of developing countries in the 1970s, which wished to include illegal campaign contributions.

The range of corrupt acts covered by UNCAC can be seen as limited insofar as trading in influence and abuse of functions are closely related to (or variants on) bribery. While these represent distinct acts of corruption, they all involve the

---

[48] UNCAC Chapter II.

[49] Spörl (2019), p. 23.

[50] UNCAC Arts. 15–22.

[51] See e.g. the work of economists Rose-Ackerman and Palifka (2016), pp. 8–9 (identifying fraud, conflicts of interest and nepotism as forms of corruption).

exchange of an "undue advantage". Bribery, as defined in UNCAC, concerns the exchange of an undue advantage for the purpose of influencing decision-making.[52] The provisions on bribery address both active and passive bribery, in that they cover the promising, offering or giving of an undue advantage (active bribery), as well as the solicitation or acceptance of an undue advantage (passive bribery).[53] As conceptualized by UNCAC, the bribe giver is always a private actor. In other words, an undue advantage promised by a public official to a private actor does not fall within the scope of UNCAC, or any other anti-corruption treaty, and from an international legal perspective does not qualify as corruption.[54] The recipient of a bribe, according to UNCAC, may be a national public official, a foreign public official, or an official of a public international organization.[55] In addition, private sector bribery is also covered, meaning an undue advantage promised/offered/given, or solicited/accepted from one private actor to another, in order to influence decision-making.[56]

Only some of these bribery provisions are, however, mandatory in character, such that states are required to criminalize the conduct at issue. States parties to UNCAC are required to criminalize the active and passive bribery of national public officials and the active bribery of foreign public officials and officials of public international organizations. But the criminalization of passive bribery of foreign public officials and officials of public international organizations, as well as private sector bribery is not required. Instead, states parties must only consider criminalizing this conduct. Such provisions may be described as obligations of conduct rather than obligations of result, as states parties need not prohibit these forms of bribery, although they must consider doing so (e.g. through debate in a legislative body).

Both trading in influence and abuse of functions are forms of corruption that are designed, in part, to fill gaps that arise because of difficulties involved in proving bribery. In other words, these are both "catch-all" offences that seek to complement the offence of bribery of national public officials. Trading in influence captures situations involving an intermediary who "has real or supposed influence over a public official [and] trades that influence in exchange for an undue advantage from someone seeking that influence".[57] This offence, for example, allows for prosecution even where prosecutors cannot prove a *quid pro quo* between the original instigator and the public official.[58] For trading in influence, prosecutors need only show that

---

[52]Kubiciel (2019).

[53]UNCAC Arts. 15, 16, 21.

[54]For an examination of state sponsored transnational crime from an international law perspective, see Decoeur (2018).

[55]UNCAC Arts. 15, 16.

[56]UNCAC Art. 21.

[57]Llamzon (2019).

[58]Llamzon (2019), pp. 201–203. See Art. 18(a) "The promise offering or giving to a public official or any other person, directly or indirectly of an undue advantage in order that the public official or the person abuse his or her real or supposed influence with a view to obtaining from an administration or public authority of the State party an undue advantage for the original instigator of the act or for any other person".

the original instigator promised or provided funds to the intermediary (i.e. active trading in influence). Furthermore, the offence of abuse of functions is designed to capture situations where prosecutors cannot prove that an exchange actually took place between two or more persons.[59] Instead, abuse of functions concerns the actions and mental state of the public official alone, as prosecutors must prove that a public official violated laws, in the course of his or her official duties, for the purpose of obtaining an undue advantage for himself or a third party. UNCAC does not require the criminalization of trading in influence or abuse of functions, although it does impose an obligation conduct, whereby states must consider doing so.

In contrast with trading in influence and abuse of functions, the offence of embezzlement, misappropriation and other diversion of property covers conduct that is quite distinct from bribery. Such conduct involves a taking of property, rather than an exchange of an undue advantage. UNCAC covers not only embezzlement, misappropriation or other diversion of property by a public official,[60] but also embezzlement by a private actor (i.e. private sector embezzlement).[61] The criminalization of embezzlement, misappropriation, and other diversion of property by a public official is uncontroversial, and states are required to criminalize this conduct. But private sector embezzlement raised concerns during the drafting process, as some delegations objected to addressing purely private sector behaviour.[62] As a result, the provision on private sector embezzlement in UNCAC entails only an obligation of consideration for states parties. Compared to the offences of bribery, trading in influence and abuse of functions, the offence of embezzlement, misappropriation, or other diversion of property by a public official does not involve a private-public *quid pro quo*, and is therefore of little relevance for business entities. But private sector embezzlement is, of course, potentially highly relevant for business entities, among other private sector entities.

---

[59]Rose (2019), p. 210. Article 19 provides "Each State Party shall consider adopting such legislative and other measures as may be necessary to establish as a criminal offence, when committed intentionally, the abuse of functions or position, that is, the performance or failure to perform an act, in violation of laws, by a public official in the discharge of his or her functions, for the purpose of obtaining an undue advantage for himself or herself or for another person or entity".

[60]Article 17 covers embezzlement, misappropriation, or other diversion of property by a public official: "Each State Party shall adopt such legislative and other measures as may be necessary to establish as criminal offences, when committed intentionally, the embezzlement, misappropriation or other diversion by a public official for his or her benefit or for the benefit of another person or entity of any property, public or private funds or securities or any other thing of value entrusted to the public official by virtue of his or her position".

[61]Article 22 covers embezzlement of property in the private sector: "Each State Party shall consider adopting such legislative and other measures as may be necessary to establish as a criminal offence, when committed intentionally in the course of economic, financial or commercial activities, embezzlement by a person who directs or works, in any capacity, in a private sector entity of any property, private funds or securities or any other thing of value entrusted to him or her by virtue of his or her position".

[62]Hess (2019), p. 246.

The offence of illicit enrichment is also of relatively little relevance for business entities as it does not deal with a public-private transaction, but instead focuses on the illicitly obtained wealth of a public official. Illicit enrichment entails the criminalization of "a significant increase in the assets of a public official that he or she cannot reasonably explain in relation to his or her lawful income".[63] This corruption offence is the most controversial of the corruption offences set out in UNCAC, as it involves shifting the burden of proof onto the defendant. Such an offence is useful to prosecutors in situations where other forms of corruption cannot be proven, but the public official's personal wealth far outstrips his or her legal income and cannot be otherwise explained. The offence of illicit enrichment also plays a sort of catch-all function, like trading in influence and abuse of functions, as it allows prosecutors to pursue corruption despite not being able to demonstrate that the wealth at issue represents the proceeds of corruption.

Taken together, this suite of criminalization provisions does not necessarily represent a significant development for corporations, in terms of domestic criminal laws governing their conduct. The only mandatory criminalization provisions that are relevant for the private sector are the offences of active bribery of national public officials and active bribery of foreign public officials and officials of public international organizations. Yet, states parties to UNCAC had, for the most part, already criminalized the bribery of national public officials long before even negotiating UNCAC, although perhaps not in terms identical to those set out in Article 15 of UNCAC.[64] In addition, states parties to the OECD Anti-Bribery Convention had already criminalized the bribery of foreign public officials, as this is the sole focus of this Convention. Although the 44 states parties to the OECD Anti-Bribery Convention represent only a fraction of the 187 states parties to UNCAC, this group of states accounted for 66.96% of world exports in 2017.[65] Thus, the majority of states that are home to multinational corporations operating abroad have already implemented the OECD Anti-Bribery Convention, with the result that UNCAC's provision on the active bribery of foreign public officials only represents a marginal legal development. Finally, trading in influence and abuse of functions are still of relevance for business entities, even though UNCAC does not mandate their criminalization. In practice, nearly all states parties have criminalized abuse of functions, while

---

[63] Art. 19: "Subject to its constitution and the fundamental principles of its legal system, each State Party shall consider adopting such legislative and other measures as may be necessary to establish as a criminal offence, when committed intentionally, illicit enrichment, that is, a significant increase in the assets of a public official that he or she cannot reasonably explain in relation to her or her lawful income".

[64] United Nations Office on Drugs and Crime, State of Implementation of the United Nations Convention against Corruption: Criminalization, Law Enforcement and International Cooperation (2nd ed, 2017), p. 13.

[65] OECD, 2017 Enforcement of the Anti-Bribery Convention (November 2018) Table 1A.

approximately two thirds of states parties have criminalized trading in influence, although often in an incomplete manner.[66]

3.2 UNCAC's Enforcement Provisions

UNCAC's criminalization provisions are accompanied by a series of provisions concerning enforcement, including one provision of potentially great relevance for business entities: Article 26, concerning the liability of legal persons. This provision is designed to ensure that legal as well as natural persons can be held liable for violations of the criminal offences set out in UNCAC, and implemented in domestic laws. Without the capacity to capture the wrongdoing of legal persons, these criminal offences might go unpunished, as economic crimes are commonly committed by complex multinational corporations with decentralized decision-making processes that can make it very difficult to identify responsible individuals.[67] Moreover, even where the identification of responsible individuals is possible, it is still desirable to hold the legal person liable, as well, in order to encourage legal entities to institute corruption prevention mechanisms, such as internal compliance programmes.[68]

To this end, Article 26 requires states parties to UNCAC "to establish the liability of legal persons for participation in the offences established in accordance with this Convention", with the qualifier that this must be done "as may be necessary, consistent with its legal principles".[69] Beyond this basic requirement, however, Article 26 gives states parties discretion to decide whether liability is criminal, civil or administrative in character.[70] But whichever type of liability states parties choose, they must ensure that legal persons are held liable "subject to effective, proportionate and dissuasive criminal or non-criminal sanctions, including monetary sanctions".[71] The possible sanctions can vary widely, and include monetary sanctions and forfeiture, as well as sanctions of an administrative character, such as exclusion from entering public tenders, loss of tax incentives, loss of business licenses, a temporary prohibition on engaging in commercial or other activities,

---

[66]United Nations Office on Drugs and Crime, State of Implementation of the United Nations Convention against Corruption: Criminalization, Law Enforcement and International Cooperation (2nd ed, 2017), pp. 42, 48.

[67]UNODC, State of Implementation of the United Nations Convention against Corruption: Criminalization, Law Enforcement and International Cooperation (2nd ed, 2017), p. 85; Borlini (2019), pp. 274–275.

[68]UNODC, State of Implementation of the United Nations Convention against Corruption: Criminalization, Law Enforcement and International Cooperation (2nd ed, 2017), p. 89.

[69]UNCAC Art. 26(1).

[70]UNCAC Art. 26(2).

[71]UNCAC Art. 26(4).

judicial supervision, or even dissolution of the corporate body.[72] Finally, liability for legal persons must be "without prejudice to the criminal liability of the natural persons who have committed the offences".[73] In other words, the liability of a legal person must not influence the prosecution and conviction of an individual who, for example, directs or works for the entity in question.

Even though states parties to UNCAC are not required to establish criminal liability for legal persons, the first round of country reviews has revealed that more than two thirds of states parties have nevertheless done so.[74] Although criminal liability has traditionally been a feature of common law systems rather than civil law systems, this divide no longer holds true with respect to the liability of legal persons for corruption offences. Even in civil law countries, the laws on the books now trend towards criminal rather than civil or administrative liability for corruption offences committed by legal persons. Many of these laws are relatively recent, however, and have not yet been tested in practice. It is therefore too early to say what impact such laws might have for business entities, as this will depend on the extent to which domestic prosecutors enforce these laws, and how courts impose sanctions.[75] In any event, Article 26 has, at the very least, prompted legislative changes in a significant number of states parties, which could have practical consequences for business entities in the future.

Finally, while UNCAC provides for the liability of legal persons, it also encourages states parties to mitigate the punishment for persons who cooperate with law enforcement authorities.[76] UNCAC requires states parties to encourage persons involved in acts of corruption to supply authorities with information and to help them deprive offenders of the proceeds of crime and recover such proceeds. States are not required to mitigate punishment or provide immunity for persons who provide substantial cooperation, but they must consider providing for such mitigation or immunity.[77]

3.3   UNCAC's Prevention Provisions

UNCAC's chapter on the prevention of corruption primarily focuses on the prevention of corruption in the public sector, while it secondarily addresses the prevention

---

[72]UNODC, State of Implementation of the United Nations Convention against Corruption: Criminalization, Law Enforcement and International Cooperation (2nd ed, 2017), p. 91.

[73]UNCAC Art. 26(3).

[74]UNODC, State of Implementation of the United Nations Convention against Corruption: Criminalization, Law Enforcement and International Cooperation (2nd ed, 2017), p. 87.

[75]UNODC, State of Implementation of the United Nations Convention against Corruption: Criminalization, Law Enforcement and International Cooperation (2nd ed, 2017), pp. 91–92.

[76]UNCAC Art. 37.

[77]UNCAC Arts. 37(2), (3).

of private sector involvement in corruption.[78] The public-sector focus of the prevention chapter is evident in its first provision, Article 5, which emphasizes the importance of good governance in the public sector. States must implement or maintain preventive anti-corruption policies that "reflect the principles of the rule of law, proper management of public affairs and public property, integrity, transparency and accountability".[79] To this end, UNCAC requires states to establish a preventive anti-corruption body (or bodies) to implement anti-corruption policies, among other things.[80] How these broad principles apply in an anti-corruption context is not explained in Article 5, but subsequent provisions provide some clarification. Subsequent prevention provisions deal, for example, with transparent human resources systems in the public sector;[81] codes of conduct for public officials to promote integrity, honesty, and responsibility among public officials;[82] public procurement and the management of public finances in a transparent and accountable manner;[83] and public reporting.[84]

These provisions on prevention are remarkably wide-ranging, as they touch on many different features of good governance, and they can be seen as solutions to wide array of problems in the public sector, going well beyond corruption alone. The provisions also tend to lack specificity, and only some of them are mandatory; many only require states parties to endeavour or consider taking preventive measures. These broad preventive provisions concerning the public sector should be read together with other international instruments, which are largely non-binding, and in some cases provide a great deal of substantive detail.[85] At the time of this writing, it is not yet clear how the UNCAC Review Mechanism will approach the challenges raised by the wide-ranging character of the prevention chapter. The Review Mechanism, which is a treaty body that monitors the implementation of the Convention, is currently in the process of reviewing the implementation of the chapters on prevention and asset recovery, and is yet to produce many country review reports.

Although UNCAC contains only a few provisions concerning the prevention of private sector involvement in corruption, these provisions can nevertheless have important implications for business entities, depending on the extent of domestic implementation. These provisions concern accounting and auditing standards in the private sector (Article 12) and anti-money laundering standards (Articles 14 and 52),

---

[78]UNCAC Chapter II.

[79]UNCAC Art. 5(1).

[80]UNCAC Art. 6(1).

[81]UNCAC Art. 7.

[82]UNCAC Art. 8.

[83]UNCAC Art. 9.

[84]UNCAC Art. 10.

[85]See e.g. OECD, Recommendation of the Council on Public Integrity, OECD/LEGAL/0435 (2017); OECD Guidelines for Managing Conflict of Interests in the Public Sector, OECD/LEGAL/0316 (2003); International Code of Conduct for Public Officials, UN Doc A/RES/51/59 (1997); Council of Europe, Model Code of Conduct for Public Officials, Appendix to Recommendation No. R (2000) 10.

which are relevant not only for banks, but also designated non-financial businesses and professions.[86] Like the prevention provisions concerning the public sector, these provisions concerning the private sector should be read in conjunction with other instruments, such as the Financial Action Task Force's (FATF) Recommendations on money laundering and the financing of terrorism and proliferation.[87]

Article 12 of UNCAC requires states parties to enhance accounting and auditing standards in the private sector, although the precise manner in which states achieve this goal is left to their discretion. Article 12 outlines a number of possibilities, however, including codes of conduct[88] to safeguard the "correct, honourable and proper performance" of business activities and to prevent conflicts of interest; promoting transparency with respect to the identity of persons involved in establishing and managing corporate entities; and ensuring that private enterprises have sufficient accounting and auditing standards in place.[89] Article 12 does not specify which accounting and auditing standards should be used by states parties, but most states use the accounting standards found in the International Financial Reporting Standards (IFRS).[90] The auditing standards found in the International Standards on Auditing (ISA) have been less widely adopted by states, although the World Bank and the International Monetary Fund promote the use of both the ISA and the IFRS.[91] The proper implementation of accounting standards by companies helps to prevent corruption by making it more difficult for companies to make corrupt payments in the first place, and to disguise them after the fact.[92] Apart from their preventive function, accounting and auditing standards that are accompanied by sanctions in case of violation may allow authorities to punish corrupt conduct even where a corruption offence cannot be proven.[93]

States parties are further obliged to institute sanctions for non-compliance with accounting and auditing standards.[94] The use of secret, off-the-books "slush" funds

---

[86]Financial Action Task Force, International Standards on Combating Money Laundering and the Financing of Terrorism and Proliferation: The FATF Recommendations (updated June 2019) (FATF Recommendations) Glossary, p. 115.

[87]Financial Action Task Force, International Standards on Combating Money Laundering and the Financing of Terrorism and Proliferation: The FATF Recommendations (updated June 2019) (FATF Recommendations).

[88]Relevant codes of conduct include: OECD Good Practice Guide on Internal Controls, Ethics and Compliance; OECD Principles on Corporate Governance; International Chamber of Commerce Rules of Conduct and Recommendations to Combat Extortion and Bribery; United Nations Global Compact, Business against Corruption: A Framework for Action; ISO 37001: 2016, Anti-Bribery Management Systems.

[89]UNCAC Art. 12(2).

[90]Hess (2019), p. 129.

[91]The World Bank and the International Monetary Fund encourage the use of such standards through the Report on the Observance of Standards and Codes (ROSC).

[92]Hess (2019), p. 128.

[93]Hess (2019), p. 128

[94]UNCAC Art. 12(3).

must, for example, be prohibited under Article 12.[95] This provision thereby targets, in part, the type of conduct that was uncovered by the Watergate scandal, which revealed the use by American companies of slush funds for both illegal domestic political campaign contributions and for foreign bribery. The 1997 OECD Anti-Bribery Convention also requires its 44 states parties to prohibit such conduct, but Article 12 of UNCAC greatly expands the global reach of this norm.[96] Finally, Article 12 requires states parties to disallow the tax deductibility of expenses that constitute bribes, under Articles 15 and 16 of the Convention.[97] Where appropriate, states must also disallow other expenses incurred in the furtherance of corrupt conduct.[98] In including this provision on tax deductibility, UNCAC mandates a prohibition that the OECD, at present, only urges, rather than requires. Controversy surrounding this issue during the negotiation of the OECD Anti-Bribery Convention prevented its inclusion in the treaty itself, but the OECD Council has since addressed the issue in a number of recommendations.[99]

UNCAC also includes prevention provisions which are designed to prevent money laundering, which can involve not only financial institutions, but also businesses and professions (such as casinos, real estate agents, dealers in precious stones and metals, lawyers and notaries, etc.). Anti-money laundering standards are, however, admittedly of relatively little relevance for many multinational corporations. The term money laundering refers to the process by which the illegal origins of funds are obscured.[100] Public officials seeking to obscure the corrupt origins of funds may, for example, transfer corrupt proceeds to an off-shore bank account under another name, or purchase real estate in another country. UNCAC includes a provision requiring states to criminalize money laundering, but UNCAC is by no means the first treaty to require such criminalization.[101]

In addition, money laundering has been regulated since 1990 by an inter-governmental body, the Financial Action Task Force, which has produced and revised non-binding Recommendations on money laundering, as well as the financing of terrorism and proliferation. Even though these Recommendations have a non-binding character, and were developed by a relatively small group of developed states, they now have nearly universal applicability because their implementation

---

[95]UNCAC Art. 12(3)(a).

[96]OECD Anti-Bribery Convention, Art. 8.

[97]UNCAC Art. 12(4).

[98]UNCAC Art. 12(4).

[99]OECD, Council Recommendation on Tax Measures for Further Combating Bribery of Foreign Public Officials in International Business Transactions (25 May 2009) C(2009)64; OECD, Recommendation of the Council for Further Combating Bribery of Foreign Public Officials in International Business Transactions (26 November 2009, amended on 18 February 2010) C(2009)159/Rev1/FINAL, C(2010)19.

[100]FATF, What is Money Laundering? https://www.fatf-gafi.org/faq/moneylaundering/ (last accessed 8 January 2021).

[101]United Nations Convention against Illicit Traffic in Narcotic Drugs and Psychotropic Substances (adopted 20 December 1988, entered into force 11 November 1990), Art. 3; UNTOC, Art. 6.

and enforcement has been monitored by FATF-Style Regional Bodies, in addition to FATF itself.[102] Because the FATF Recommendations are the most detailed and authoritative normative instrument concerning anti-money laundering measures, UNCAC's comparatively minimalistic anti-money laundering provisions must be read in conjunction with the Recommendations.

Articles 14 and 52 of UNCAC require states parties to institute anti-money laundering regimes, which include requirements for customer identification (as well as beneficial owner identification, where appropriate), record-keeping, and the reporting of suspicious transactions. Customer identification and verification requirements help to deter money laundering by preventing corrupt persons from concealing their identities and the source of their money, through accounts in anonymous or obviously fictitious names.[103] Relatedly, beneficial owner identification requirements help to prevent money laundering by preventing corrupt persons from concealing their identities through the use of corporate vehicles.[104] Record keeping requirements help government authorities to trade and identify the proceeds of corruption when conducting investigations.[105] As a result of such requirements, financial institutions must, for example, retain records obtained through customer due diligence measures, as well as account files and correspondence. Finally, suspicious transaction reporting requirements aim to facilitate the detection of transactions involving the proceeds of corruption by requiring entities to report suspicious transactions to domestic financial intelligence units.[106] The implementation of such measures by states is premised on a risk-based approach, which means that the anti-money laundering measures put in place should be commensurate with the risks for money laundering that have been identified in that country.[107]

4   Reflections on the Relationship Between UNCAC and International Economic Law

By way of a conclusion, this final section reflects on the current state of the relationship between international anti-corruption law and international economic law, and what the current legal architecture leaves to be desired. As detailed in Sect. 2, the regulation of corruption through a code of conduct was very much under discussion in the 1970s and 1980s, but this never came to fruition, as the negotiations

---

[102]Rose (2015), pp. 202–215.

[103]FATF Recommendation 10.

[104]The term beneficial owner refers to a "natural person who ultimately owns or controls a customer and/or the natural person on whose behalf a transaction is being conducted". FATF Recommendations, Glossary, p. 113.

[105]FATF Recommendation 11.

[106]FATF Recommendation 20.

[107]FATF Recommendation 1.

for a Code of Conduct on Transnational Corporations ultimately failed, as did other attempts to regulate corporate conduct through an international instrument.[108] As a result, a relatively narrow criminal law approach to the problem of corruption prevailed, as can be seen in UNCAC and in the vast majority of other anti-corruption treaties. Moreover, like other transnational criminal law treaties, UNCAC focuses on criminalization, enforcement, and international cooperation. Although UNCAC also includes provisions on prevention, which are of some relevance for businesses entities, these provisions lack detail, and can only be fully understood and implemented by states by reference to other instruments, such as non-binding codes of conduct and standards that have been developed by other bodies. UNCAC's prevention provisions thereby have the effect of sketching the legal and policy terrain, while leaving the details to a scattered and diverse set of non-binding instruments.

International economic law, for its part, deals with the problem of corruption by simply referencing or incorporating select provisions of UNCAC, along with other anti-corruption treaties. These cross-references can be seen, for example, in the sub fields of both trade and investment law.[109] This section focuses on trade law, because free trade agreements arguably hold the most potential in terms of the future regulation of corruption from within the framework of international economic law. Free trade agreements demonstrate that the existing body of international anti-corruption law has had some influence on the development of trade law. The Comprehensive and Progressive Agreement for Trans-Pacific Partnership (CPTPP), for example, includes a chapter on transparency and anti-corruption, which requires ratification or accession to UNCAC and incorporates the essence (and in some instances the exact text) of a number of its provisions.[110] In keeping with UNCAC Articles 15 and 16, CPTPP requires states parties to criminalize the active and passive bribery of national public officials and the active bribery of foreign public officials or officials of a public international organization. In addition, CPTPP includes provisions requiring the establishment of liability for legal persons for these bribery offences, the elimination of tax deductions for bribe payments, accounting and auditing standards for the private sector, and protections for reporting persons (i.e. whistle-blowers). Because the anti-corruption provisions set out in the CPTPP merely restate the provisions of UNCAC, the CPTPP does not play

---

[108]See e.g. OECD Multilateral Agreement on Investment.

[109]When allegations of corruption arise in the context of investor-state arbitration proceedings, for example, awards typically cite UNCAC and other anti-corruption treaties to support the proposition that the prohibition on bribery forms part of international public policy. See e.g. World Duty Free Company Limited v. Republic of Kenya, ICSID Case No. ARB/00/7, Award of 4 October 2006; Metal-Tech Limited v. The Republic of Uzbekistan, ICSID Case No. ARB/10/3, Award of 4 October 2013.

[110]Comprehensive and Progressive Agreement for Trans-Pacific Partnership, Chapter 26. After the United States withdrew from the Trans-Pacific Partnership (TPP), the other signatories concluded the Comprehensive and Progressive Agreement for Trans-Pacific Partnership, which incorporates TTP. The current parties are Mexico, Japan, Singapore, New Zealand, Canada, Australia, and Vietnam. See also United States-Mexico-Canada Agreement, Chapter 27.

a role in the development of anti-corruption law. Instead, by including a "mini anti-corruption treaty" within the CPTPP, this trade agreement reiterates and thereby emphasizes the importance of the existing legal obligations that states already bear under UNCAC.

Free trade agreements could, however, go beyond a restatement of select provisions of UNCAC and other anti-corruption treaties, and could instead contribute to the progressive development of areas of the anti-corruption field that have not (yet) been the subject of adequate regulation. Asset recovery, for example, is arguably one of the most important areas of the anti-corruption field that requires further regulation. The term asset recovery refers to the process by which states recover the proceeds of corruption and return them to a foreign jurisdiction. One recent, and high-profile example of asset recovery involves Malaysia and the United States, two states that were involved in the negotiation of the Trans-Pacific Partnership (which never entered into force, but has since been incorporated into the CPTPP).[111] In April 2020, the United States announced that it had repatriated to Malaysia approximately US$300 million in funds stolen from Malaysia's investment development fund, known as 1Malaysia Development Berhad (1MDB).[112] Malaysian government officials have been accused of misappropriating funds from 1MDB and laundering them through financial institutions in the United States, among other foreign jurisdictions. This particular return of assets constitutes one part of a larger international asset recovery effort concerning 1MDB.

UNCAC itself devotes an entire chapter to the issue of asset recovery, with provisions concerning prevention through anti-money laundering measures and international cooperation, in the form of mutual legal assistance.[113] This chapter is widely considered to be the most innovative aspect of UNCAC, as it is the only anti-corruption treaty that specifically and extensively addresses the subject of asset recovery. Yet, the provisions in UNCAC are conservative in character, insofar as they depend on formal and relatively inflexible mutual legal assistance procedures, which tend to function slowly. In addition, UNCAC does not address issues of accountability, transparency, and participation in the context of asset recovery. While these principles feature in the prevention chapter, they do not even appear in the asset recovery chapter.

In recent years, however, there has been growing discontent with respect to manner in which funds are returned to "requesting states" (i.e. states that initiate mutual legal assistance requests with respect to assets). Civil society groups, for example, have highlighted concerns about insufficient or non-existent accountability mechanisms to ensure that funds are not misappropriated again, upon their return to the requesting state.[114] In addition, asset recovery processes are not necessarily

---

[111]Neither Malaysia nor the United States is party to CPTPP at the time of writing.

[112]United States Department of Justice, Press Release, U.S. Repatriates $300 million to Malaysia in Proceeds of Funds Misappropriated from 1Malaysia Development Berhad, 14 April 2020.

[113]UNCAC Chapter V.

[114]See e.g. Civil Society Principles for Accountable Asset Return. https://cifar.eu/what-is-asset-recovery/civil-society-principles-for-accountable-asset-return/ (last accessed 8 January 2021).

carried out in a transparent manner, which would involve publicly available information about the transfer and administration of returned assets. In fact, the memoranda of understanding, which are sometimes concluded between requested and requesting states to govern the return of assets, are often not publicly available. Asset recovery processes have also frequently failed to include stakeholders[115] in decision-making processes and in monitoring processes, to the extent that these exist.

In response to concerns about accountability, transparency, and participation in the context of asset recovery, both civil society organizations and states have developed various principles to govern the responsible return of assets. For example, the state-led Global Forum on Asset Recovery, has developed Principles for Disposition and Transfer of Confiscated Stolen Assets in Corruption Cases, which deal, in broad terms, with accountability, transparency and participation.[116] Given the existing interest, among states and civil society, in increased regulation of asset recovery, free trade agreements could represent a viable mechanism for addressing existing concerns. Beyond just restating provisions already codified in UNCAC, free trade agreements could go further, by stipulating how basic good governance principles apply to the return of assets by one state party, to another. Such rules could govern not only procedural aspects of asset return (accountability, transparency and participation), but also substantive aspects, such as the appropriate uses of returned assets (e.g. as anti-corruption initiatives and development programmes).

These ideas are aspirational, but hopefully not far-fetched, as free trade agreements are already beginning to address corruption. Although international anti-corruption law currently "belongs" to the field of transnational criminal law, rather than international economic law, this picture need not look quite so black and white. International law's predominantly criminal law approach to corruption is a product of history, rather than an inevitable state of affairs. There is potential for international economic law to play a more significant role in developing, rather than just reiterating, international anti-corruption norms.

References

Bernstein C, Woodward B (1974) All the president's men. Simon and Schuster
Boister N (2003) Transnational criminal law? Eur J Int Law 14:953–976
Borlini L (2019) Article 26: Liability of legal persons. In: Rose C, Kubiciel M, Landwehr O (eds) The United Nations Convention against corruption: a commentary. Oxford University Press, pp 274–286
Davis K (2019) Between impunity and imperialism: the regulation of transnational bribery. Oxford University Press

---

[115]Stakeholders in this context refers to individuals, civil society, non-governmental organizations, and community-based organizations. See UNCAC Art. 13.

[116]GFAR Principles for Disposition and Transfer of Confiscated Stolen Assets in Corruption Cases, Principles 4, 10.

Decoeur H (2018) Confronting the shadow state: an international law perspective on state organized crime. Oxford University Press

Garavini G (2012) After empires: European integration, decolonization, & the challenges from the Global South 1957–1986 (Trans: Nybakken R). Oxford University Press

Hamdani K, Ruffing L (2015) United Nations Centre on transnational corporations: corporate conduct and the public interest: with reflections and critical commentary from colleagues, delegates and participants. Routledge

Hess D (2019) Article 22: Embezzlement of property in the private sector. In: Rose C, Kubiciel M, Landwehr O (eds) The United Nations Convention against corruption: a commentary. Oxford University Press, pp 245–50

Katzarova E (2018) The social construction of global construction: from utopia to neoliberalism. Palgrave Macmillan

Koehler M (2012) The story of the foreign corrupt practices act. Ohio State Law J 73:929–1013

Kroeze R (2018) Lockheed (1977) and Flick (1981–1986): Anticorruption as a pragmatic practice in the Netherlands and Germany. In Kroeze R, Vitoria A, Geltner G (eds) Anticorruption in history: from antiquity to the modern era. Oxford University Press, pp 279–291

Kubiciel M (2019) Article 15: Bribery of national public officials. In: Rose C, Kubiciel M, Landwehr O (eds) The United Nations Convention against corruption: a commentary. Oxford University Press, pp 165–174

Llamzon A (2019) Article 18: Trading in influence. In: Rose C, Kubiciel M, Landwehr O (eds) The United Nations Convention against corruption: a commentary. Oxford University Press, pp 192–209

Pieth M (2013) Introduction. In: Pieth M, Low L, Bonucci N (eds) The OECD Convention on bribery: a commentary, 2nd edn. Cambridge University Press, pp 3–56

Rose C (2015) International anti-corruption norms: their creation and influence on domestic legal systems. Oxford University Press

Rose C (2019) Article 19: Abuse of functions. In: Rose C, Kubiciel M, Landwehr O (eds) The United Nations Convention against corruption: a commentary. Oxford University Press, pp 210–218

Rose C (2021, forthcoming) The origins of international anti-corruption law: the failed negotiation of an international agreement on illicit payments. In Boister N, Gless S, Jeßberger F (eds) Histories of transnational criminal law. Oxford University Press

Rose-Ackerman S, Palifka B (2016) Corruption and government: causes, consequences, and reform, 2nd edn. Cambridge University Press

Sauvant K (2015) The negotiations of the United Nations Code of Conduct on transnational corporations. J World Invest Trade 16:11–87

Spörl C (2019) Article 2: Use of terms. In: Rose C, Kubiciel M, Landwehr O (eds) The United Nations Convention against corruption: a commentary. Oxford University Press, pp 21–34

Tarullo D (2004) The limits of institutional design: implementing the OECD Anti-Bribery Convention. Virginia J Int Law 44:665–710

Cecily Rose is an assistant professor of public international law at Leiden Law School. She holds an LL.M. and a PhD from the University of Cambridge, and a J.D. from Columbia Law School. She conducts research in the areas of transnational criminal law and international dispute settlement, and has worked as a consultant in the anti-corruption field for various international organizations. Before joining the faculty at Leiden Law School, Cecily worked as an associate legal officer at the International Court of Justice and the Special Court for Sierra Leone, and in private practice.

State Responsibility for Corruption: A Return to Regular Order

Aloysius P. Llamzon

Contents

Abstract In its paradigmatic form in transnational investment and commerce, corruption is typically a bilateral act requiring the cooperation of both the private party and the State—the so-called "supply" and "demand" sides—and the specific offense committed is bribery. But that symbiotic relationship notwithstanding, both sides are *not* usually treated in the same way by international tribunals. In most cases, bribery results in far more severe consequences upon the claimant corporation than on the respondent State, with the State bearing few if any consequences for the

---

My thanks to Professor Christian Tams and to Judith Crämer for their support and invaluable comments, and to Ms. Genica Endaluz.

A. P. Llamzon (✉)
International Arbitration Group, King & Spalding LLP, Washington, DC, USA

Ateneo de Manila University School of Law, Manila, Philippines
e-mail: allamzon@kslaw.com

© Springer Nature Switzerland AG 2021
M. Bungenberg et al. (eds.), *European Yearbook of International Economic Law 2020*,
European Yearbook of International Economic Law (2022) 11: 107–174,
https://doi.org/10.1007/8165_2021_69, Published online: 12 August 2021

participation of public officials in the bribery that occurred, regardless of whether those acts may (or should) have known to the State.

Why this asymmetric treatment is so requires reflecting on whether a State bears any responsibility for the corruption of its public officials in the first place. This is a foundational issue: the ability of the State to invoke corruption as a complete defense is premised on the idea that a State is not responsible for the corruption its own public officials participated in. Put differently, no matter what the merits of the claimant's claims might be and what breaches the State may have committed, the presence of corruption overrides all other considerations and will cause the dismissal of those claims, often for lack of jurisdiction or inadmissibility. Corruption trumps all other issues.

But that is not how international law ordinarily works: under the ILC Articles on State Responsibility, it is no excuse for a State to say that its public officials were acting in excess of authority or contrary to instructions—under Article 7, *ultra vires* acts of public officials are always attributable to the State. In the absence of any significant case law discussing the ILC Articles within the context of bribery, commentators have begun to fill that *lacuna* with significantly divergent opinions. A significant number maintain that Article 7 applies to corruption as well, and that the public official's participation (or sometimes initiation) of bribery is attributable to the host State. This is so because for the ILC Articles consider what matters to be the *exercise* of State authority, not its propriety.

But if corruption is attributable to the State, what explains the case law's hesitance to assign any consequences to the State? Some eminent scholars answer this question by pointing out that conduct attributable to the State must still meet a second basic element of the ILC Articles: that a breach of an international obligation of that State occurred (Article 2). They view lack of consequences as the product of doctrines specific to international anti-corruption law that affix the consequences of corruption decidedly on the side of the Claimant. These include "legality clauses", transnational public policy, and the unclean hands doctrine and their Latin cognates.

This article contests that view: when treaty and customary international law on the consequences of corruption are carefully considered, no specific rule of treaty or customary international law exists that can justify the implicit exemption of States from the consequences of bribery. Overall, it is hard to say that international law contains a rule requiring that the consequences of bribery or other forms of corruption be borne only by the private party. And just as well: a system that seeks to extract accountability from both the private investor and the State is, in the long run, probably a more durable way to enhance arbitration as a tool for preventing corruption in foreign investment.

1 Introduction: The Centrality of State Responsibility in Corruption Decision-Making

Although imperfect, international arbitration has the ability to hold specific private and public parties to account for violations of both international and national anti-corruption laws to an extent unmatched by any other supra-national mechanism. And in the last few years, it seems that the various public and private actors in the international community have begun to take advantage of that mechanism: the visibility of corruption as an issue in international investment and commercial arbitration has risen in almost parabolic fashion. This ascent in activity should not be surprising: with over $3.6 *trillion*—over 5% of global GDP—estimated as the annual amount lost to corruption globally,[1] corruption in all its forms *must* be occurring far more regularly than is evident in case law and practice. But until recently, the case law was relatively anaemic, with the issue having perhaps its most significant breakout only in 2006 with *World Duty Free v Kenya*. Since then, new cases involving issues of corruption have flourished.[2] For contemporary practitioners, issues involving corruption—including bribery and influence peddling, often coupled with other forms of wrongdoing such as fraud, money laundering, misrepresentation, procurement law violations, and other forms of illegality (all these being the visible manifestations of clandestine corruption)[3]—are increasingly taking on a central role.

---

[1] UN News (2018) The costs of corruption: values, economic development under assault, trillions lost, says Guterres. https://news.un.org/en/story/2018/12/1027971 (last accessed 13 March 2021). ("Every year, trillions of dollars – equivalent to more than five percent of global GDP – are paid in bribes or stolen through corruption, the United Nations reported on the International Day which serves to highlight the pervasive crime, marked this Sunday. [. . .] One trillion dollars are paid in bribes annually, while another 2.6 trillion are stolen; all due to corruption."); Johnson S, (2018) Corruption is costing the global economic $3.6 trillion dollars every year. World Economic Forum, https://www.weforum.org/agenda/2018/12/the-global-economy-loses-3-6-trillion-to-corruption-each-year-says-u-n (last accessed 13 March 2021). ("The annual costs of international corruption amount to a staggering $3.6 trillion in the form of bribes and stolen money, United Nations Secretary-General António Guterres said on International Anti-Corruption Day, December 9.").

[2] As of June 2014, this author found 20 significant investment arbitration cases that alleged corruption in meaningful ways, many of which then led to significant analysis and decisions on various corruption issues (although not nearly all). Llamzon (2014), pp. 102–192 and 305–319. Since then, at least 18 further cases with significant corruption allegations exist, effectively doubling the existing case law on corruption took decades to cumulate within 6 years. Currently, scarcely a day goes by without at least one corruption-related development being reported in daily trade publications on international arbitration—*International Arbitration Reporter* and *Global Arbitration Review* most prominently—as well as related national court setting aside and enforcement proceedings.

[3] *See* Llamzon and Sinclair (2015), p. 468. ("Over the twenty-year span of investment arbitration cases concerning corruption, arbitrators have mostly exhibited reluctance to deal with the issue directly. In some ways, this is understandable, as parties themselves – even those who insinuated or even explicitly invoked corruption at the initial stages of the proceedings – have often stopped short of formally alleging or offering evidence of corruption. Instead, initial insinuations or allegations of

This largely salutary phenomenon is likely to accelerate in the coming years, as some States expand their prosecutorial remit and investigate and punish corporations, private individuals, and public officials (both former and sitting) who engage in corrupt practices extra-territorially.[4] The prosecutions are unlikely to abate, as economists and social scientists continue to place corruption as among the principal issues that affect governance, rule of law, poverty, and sustainable development, and as international lawyers increasingly view anti-corruption not only as a matter of economic law but also as an important human right in itself and in relation to other human rights.[5]

However, one aspect of corruption that continues to be undertheorized and largely undiscussed in the case law is that of State responsibility for corruption.[6] This is a considerable *lacuna* in the international law concerning corruption—whether a State can or should be held responsible for the corruption its public official participated in (or sometimes even initiated) is often an interstitial question for much of corruption decision-making. By definition, bribery—the paradigmatic form of corruption in transnational trade and investment—is committed *bilaterally*: both the employees of the investor as well as public officials of the host State must cooperate for the *quid pro quo* that consummates the offense to occur, affecting public outcomes for private gain. And because the public official was acting in that capacity, the State would, under ordinary rules of State responsibility, be attributable to that State.[7]

But the reality is that in many investment treaties as well as contract-based cases, States bear little to no actual responsibility for those corrupt acts: corruption is considered a complete defense for host States and government entities against an

---

corruption have often given way to defenses based on some of its more visible manifestations, such as fraud or any other serious illegality.") (citations omitted).

[4] A number of cases in international investment arbitration rely on the findings of other jurisdictions—for example prosecutions in the United States under the Foreign Corrupt Practices Act (FCPA) as well in Germany in *Siemens A.G. v. Argentina*; and Canadian and Bangladeshi prosecutorial and judicial actions in *Niko Resources v Bangladesh*. National prosecutors with subpoena and other coercive powers have the ability to conduct exhaustive fact-finding that simply cannot be matched by international arbitral tribunals. *See* Low (2019), pp. 342–345. ("Compared to national investigating authorities, arbitral tribunals possess limited powers to compel the production of evidence and to conduct searches. If national authorities are investigating the matter, the tribunal may consider staying the proceedings until the investigation is complete, on the theory that the investigation may yield relevant evidence that will facilitate the tribunal's task. If not, the tribunal may use its authority to issue orders to a party that it fairly presumes to have relevant evidence (e.g., on the provision of services) in its custody or control, and may take adverse inferences from a failure to produce, in the process of establishing key facts probative of the issue of corruption.").

[5] *See* Peters (2018), p. 1289.

[6] *See* Crawford and Mertenskotter (2016), p. 36. ("In other arbitrations where corruption was at issue, the issue of attribution of corrupt acts to government officials was not discussed.").

[7] *See* Peters (2018), p. 1289. ("To conclude, the fact that an official's behaviour is performed as a quid pro quo in bribery normally does not rule out the attribution of that behaviour to the state. All the more, other types of corrupt conduct by public officials can and should be attributed to the state in accordance with the principles of state responsibility.").

investor's claim. No matter how egregious the wrong that might have been committed against the investor, so long as that investor's employee or agent offered or paid bribes, no recovery is permitted and the consequences of the corrupt act are shifted entirely to the private claimant. Put in other words, the corruption defense effectively acts as a trump over any and all other breaches that might have been committed by the State.[8] That outcome is necessarily premised on the doctrine that a State is *not* responsible for the corruption of its public officials.[9] To lead to that conclusion, one of two things must be true: following the elements of an internationally wrongful act under the International Law Commission's Draft Articles on International Responsibility of States for Internationally Wrongful Acts (ILC Articles), either: (1) the public official's acceptance of a bribe cannot be attributed to the State; or (2) conduct that might be attributable is nonetheless not considered a breach of an international obligation of the State.[10]

This essay discusses these two elements in turn. As no publicly-available international tribunal or court decision has directly analysed the question of State responsibility for corruption, except by way of hint and implication, guidance arises more from scholarly commentary. Professor (now Judge) James Crawford, a towering figure in the law on State responsibility and the Special Rapporteur who helped bring the ILC Articles to a successful conclusion, set out his position on the responsibility of States for corruption in a 2016 article with Paul Mertenskötter.[11] Professor Crawford is sceptical—as this author has been—that bribery committed by a public official would not ultimately be attributable to the State (Sect. 2 below). However, Professor Crawford seems to support the position that a State cannot be held responsible for the corruption of its public officials by focusing on the second element. Finding disagreement with this author's position, Professor Crawford is of the view that a "primary rule" on corruption exists that forestalls certain corrupt conduct by public official from becoming a breach of an international obligation of the State. The question of whether international law exempts States from the *consequences* of corruption notwithstanding what would otherwise be attributable conduct is thus of great importance (Sect. 3). The concluding section then seeks find a way forward that is grounded on the general rules on State responsibility (Sect. 4).

---

[8]Donoghue (2015), p. 761.

[9]As discussed further in Sect. 2.1, both the *Metal-Tech Ltd. v. The Republic of Uzbekistan*, ICSID Case No. ARB/10/3 (04 October 2013) and *Spentex Netherlands, B.V. v. Republic of Uzbekistan*, ICSID Case No. ARB/13/26 (27 December 2016) tribunals have found corruption to be a complete defense, and a finding of corruption in both cases led to dismissal of those cases for lack of jurisdiction. Both tribunals did so with some reluctance given the bilateral nature of bribery, but found scope for balancing the consequences of corruption only as to the costs of the arbitration.

[10]ILC Articles, Article 2 (*"Elements of an internationally wrongful act of a State.* There is an internationally wrongful act of a State when conduct consisting of an action or omission: (a) is attributable to the State under international law; and (b) constitutes a breach of an international obligation of the State.").

[11]Crawford and Mertenskotter (2016), p. 27.

2 Revisiting the "Attribution Asymmetry" in Relation to Corruption Decisionmaking

At its essence, corruption is a bilateral act: bribery, for example, is consummated through an interdependent set of actions and relationships built between investor's employee (or other agent or intermediary) and public official of host State.[12] That interdependence engenders important questions about the role the international law on State responsibility should play when corruption issues are decided upon by investment tribunals.[13] Because bribery cannot succeed without cooperation from both sides of the equation, combating bribery in a meaningful way demands accountability from both sides—the investor as well as the State. If a multinational corporation, for example, would be able to avoid responsibility for corruption by simply saying that its employee was acting outside the company's remit, that would be a very easy defense indeed. Similarly, a host State that can say that any public official engaged in bribery—no matter how powerful and how much in control of all the levers of the State—can never be responsible for corruption will escape the kind of accountability that encourages good governance and the rule of law.

In response, States often contend that they should not be held responsible because they are also the victims of unscrupulous public officials who were never authorized to receive bribes or use their public power to enrich private interests. *World Duty Free v Kenya* is a typical articulation of that argument: the tribunal there acknowledged that it was "a highly disturbing feature in this case that the corrupt recipient of the Claimant's bribe was more than an officer of state but its most senior officer, the Kenyan President, and that it is Kenya which is here advancing as a complete defence to the Claimant's claims the illegalities of its own former President." The tribunal appeared sympathetic to the foreign investor's complaint about "the unfairness of the legal case now advanced by Kenya".[14] Nonetheless, the tribunal permitted corruption as a complete defense, stating that "as regards public policy, the law protects not the litigating parties but the public; or in this case, the mass of tax-payers and other citizens making up one of the poorest countries in the world."[15]

That justification is not fundamentally different than other situations where a State would seek to reject responsibility for violations of international law

---

[12]*See* UN General Assembly, *United Nations Convention Against Corruption*, A/RES/58/4, 58th Session (31 October 2003) Articles 15–16; *Metal-Tech Ltd. v. The Republic of Uzbekistan*, ICSID Case No ARB/10/3, Award, ¶422 (04 October 2013). ("The law is clear – and rightly so – that in such a situation the investor is deprived of protection and, consequently, the host State avoids any potential liability. That does not mean, however, that the State has not participated in creating the situation that leads to the dismissal of the claims. Because of this participation, which is implicit in the very nature of corruption, it appears fair that the Parties share in the costs.").

[13]For a detailed discussion, *see* Llamzon (2013).

[14]*World Duty Free Company Limited v. The Republic of Kenya*, ICSID Case No. ARB/00/7, Award ¶180 (04 October 2006).

[15]*World Duty Free Company Limited v. The Republic of Kenya*, ICSID Case No. ARB/00/7, Award ¶181 (04 October 2006).

committed by its public officials. A State may say that gross human rights violations or breaches of international environmental law cannot engage the responsibility of the State because those public officials who acted did so in an unauthorized manner.[16] In that sense, the State would be able to essentially define itself out of responsibility, having control over the formal scope of its delegated authority as well as its own laws. But the law on State responsibility would not permit such arguments to succeed, in principle: as Judge Higgins noted, "a State will be responsible even for *ultra vires* acts of its servants, that is to say, even when they acted beyond their powers. Indeed, one can go further and say that, if an organ of State, or public servants of States, acted in a way expressly forbidden by the State and which violated international law, the State would still be responsible for that wrongful conduct."[17]

It is not unusual at all for the law on State Responsibility to indict a State for the unlawful acts of its public officials, no matter whether that official was acting within his or her mandate. Under the ILC Articles, it is no excuse for a State to say that its public officials were acting in excess of authority or contrary to instructions:

Article 7. Excess of authority or contravention of instructions

The conduct of an organ of a State or of a person or entity empowered to exercise elements of the governmental authority shall be considered an act of the State under international law if the organ, person or entity acts in that capacity, even if it exceeds its authority or contravenes instructions.[18]

Thus, *ultra vires* acts of public officials remain attributable to the State, as a rule.

2.1 Two Attribution Asymmetries

However, the case law on corruption reveals that the rule articulated in Article 7 of the ILC Articles does not quite apply as envisaged. Two related *"attribution*

---

[16]Another rebuttal to this argument that can be found in *Niko v. Bangladesh*. In response to an argument that a tribunal cannot accept jurisdiction in cases where corruption has tainted the underlying contract because doing so would jeopardize the integrity of the ICSID dispute settlement mechanism, the *Niko* tribunal disagreed, and stated that "such integrity is promoted, and not violated, by the adjudication of disputes submitted to the Centre under a valid consent to arbitrate. [. . .] In so doing, the integrity of the system is protected by the resolution of the contentions made (including allegations of violations of public policy) rather than by avoiding them." *Niko Resources (Bangladesh) Ltd. v. Bangladesh Petroleum Exploration ("Bapex") and Bangladesh Oil Gas and Mineral Corporation ("Petrobangla")*, ICSID Case Nos. ARB/10/11 and ARB/10/18, Decision on Jurisdiction, ¶471 (19 August 2013).

[17]Higgins (1994), p. 150 *citing* Meron T (1957), p. 85.

[18]International Law Commission, *Draft Articles on Responsibility of States for Internationally Wrongful Acts*, UN Doc. A/RES/56/83, 53rd Session of the International Law Commission, Supplement No. 10 (A/56/10) (November 2001) article 7.

asymmetries"[19] that seem to diverge from the rule are at play when assessing whether corrupt acts are attributable to the State:

First, there *is* asymmetry based on the kind of corruption involved: the case law distinguishes between instances where a public official *extorts* or *solicits* a bribe payment and consummated bribery itself. Cases involving allegations by claimants that the State solicited or extorted bribes[20] is a serious problem that international businesses experience with alarming frequency. Leading non-governmental organizations report that foreign investors find themselves routinely on the receiving end of bribe solicitations from host State governments, and that most citizens (57%) in a recent wide-ranging survey think their governments are doing "badly" in fighting corruption.[21] In the investment arbitration context, corrupt solicitations and extortion

---

[19]This "attribution asymmetry" is discussed in greater detail in Llamzon (2014), pp. 238–281.

[20]"Extortion" (sometimes also called "blackmail") is another important type of corruption. Transparency International defines extortion as the "act of utilizing, either directly or indirectly, one's access to a position of power or knowledge to demand unmerited cooperation or compensation as a result of coercive threats." *See* Transparency International. Extortion. https://www.transparency.org/en/corruptionary/extortion (last accessed 13 March 2021).

One can distinguish extortion from bribery by looking into whether the payer receives 'better than fair treatment' or must pay to be treated fairly. Put another way, "extortion" is a situation in which the capacity of the official to withhold a service or benefit otherwise required by law exceeds the capacity of the private party to sustain the loss of that service or benefit. According to Professor Reisman, "[t]he term extortion may be reserved for those situations in which the capacity of the official to withhold a service or benefit otherwise required by law exceeds the capacity of the private party to sustain the loss of that service or benefit." Reisman (1979), p. 38. The difference between solicitation and extortion of bribes is one of degree, the difference being the extent of coercive force used by the public official. The closer the amount of coercive force employed becomes of serious detriment to the enterprise's ability to function and remain a going concern, the more apt the use of "extortion" becomes. Solicitation of bribes by public officials is identified as one of the two principle modalities of transnational bribery under Articles 15(2) and 16(2) of the UN Convention Against Corruption.

[21]Johnson S, (2018) Corruption is costing the global economic $3.6 trillion dollars every year. World Economic Forum, https://www.weforum.org/agenda/2018/12/the-global-economy-loses-3-6-trillion-to-corruption-each-year-says-u-n (last accessed 13 March 2021). ("A 2017 survey from Transparency International, which included responses from 162,136 adults, showed that 25 percent of people worldwide said they had had to pay a bribe to access public services in the past 12 months. Perhaps unsurprisingly, 57 percent of people said their government was doing "badly" at fighting corruption."). *See also* Klaw (2015), p. 62. ("Bribery and extortion remain persistent and disturbing realities in international business and foreign direct investment. In a survey by Transparency International of more than 2700 business executives in twenty-six countries, almost forty percent reported being requested to pay a bribe in the previous year. The percentage of survey respondents reporting bribe solicitation increased to as much as sixty percent when the results were focused solely on high-risk sectors, such as telecommunications and energy, or limited to certain high-risk developing countries. There is also reason to think that such alarmingly high percentages may actually understate the scope of the problem, as available evidence indicates that many people are solicited for payments multiple times per year, often by the same person or segment of government.") (*citing inter alia* Transparency International, Global Corruption Report 2009 (2009); Business Registry for International Bribery and Extortion (BRIBEline) 2010 Brazil Report. TRACE International (2010); Business Registry for International Bribery and Extortion (BRIBEline)

is used as the basis for *investor* claims—*i.e.,* corruption used as a *sword*—about a third of the time, which is considerably less frequent (but still significant) than corruption allegations made by *host States* as a defense against investor claims *i.e.,* corruption used as a *shield.*[22]

Nonetheless, if the public official is the person that sought or initiated the bribe— whether through solicitation or extortion—that conduct seems to be straightfor-wardly attributable to the State. For example, in *EDF Services v Romania,* the former Prime Minister of Romania allegedly sought a \$2.5 million bribe before agreeing to extend the investor's duty-free lease contract. The solicitation of that bribe (perhaps more aptly characterized as extortion) was considered an act that, if proven, would have amounted to a violation of the fair and equitable treatment of the relevant investment treaty.[23] Even if the solicitation was plainly illegal, the fact that the public official was threatening to use public power, a power that official had by dint of his position, would suffice to engage the State's responsibility.

This is consistent with an older body of international case law that recognized corrupt solicitations as engaging State responsibility. In the French-Mexican Claims Commission's *Caire* case,[24] a French citizen, Mr. Caire, ran a boarding house in Mexico where Mexican troops were stationed. A major of the troops staying there, along with two other soldiers, attempted to extort money from Mr. Caire under threat of force. When he refused, the major and a captain of the same brigade arrested and held Caire, and eventually killed him. The Commission considered this conduct to be an official act attributable to the state. Responsibility was justified because the military officers had cloaked themselves in their capacity as State organs, and had used the means available to them by virtue of their position to do so.[25]

Conversely, when a corrupt act is consummated, attribution no longer seems to occur *even in a situation where the public official initiated* the bribe through solicitation or extortion. Returning to the *World Duty Free v. Kenya* case, the investor there freely admitted to paying US\$2 million when Kenya's Head of State, President Daniel Arap Moi, solicited that amount from him (including US \$500,000 paid to the President himself) in order obtain the duty-free airport conces-sions. The tribunal ruled that this was a bribe, invalidated the investment contract, and denied the claimant any form of monetary or non-monetary relief. In so doing, the *World Duty Free* tribunal acknowledged the unfairness of putting the burden of all consequence only upon the investor in a situation where Kenya's Head of State himself initiated the corrupt act:

---

[22] Llamzon (2014), pp. 198–199.

[23] *EDF (Services) Limited. v Romania*, ICSID Case No. ARB/05/13, Award (08 October 2009).

[24] *Estate of Jean-Baptiste Caire (France) v. United Mexican States*, 07 June 1929, *reprinted in* 5 UNRIAA 516 (1952).

[25] *Estate of Jean-Baptiste Caire (France) v. United Mexican States*, 07 June 1929, *reprinted in* 5 UNRIAA 516 (1952). ("lorsque ces organes agissent en dehors de leur compétence, en se couvrant de leur qualité d'organes de l'Etat, et en se servant des moyens mis, à ce titre, à leur disposition").

> It remains nonetheless a highly disturbing feature in this case that the corrupt recipient of the Claimant's bribe was more than an officer of state but its most senior officer, the Kenyan President; and that it is Kenya which is here advancing as a complete defence to the Claimant's claims the illegalities of its own former President. Moreover, on the evidence before this Tribunal, the bribe was apparently solicited by the Kenyan President and not wholly initiated by the Claimant. Although the Kenyan President has now left office and is no longer immune from suit under the Kenyan Constitution, it appears that no attempt has been made by Kenya to prosecute him for corruption or to recover the bribe in civil proceedings. It is not therefore surprising that Mr. Ali feels strongly the unfairness of the legal case now advanced by Kenya, [...].[26]

As to attributability, while the *World Duty Free* tribunal employed national law (*i.e.,* Kenyan and English law) and not international law (which it could have done, as international law forms part of English as well as Kenyan law),[27] the tribunal did make a more general point about attributability that embodies a logic that other cases have employed in the international law context. Ordinarily, the Kenyan President's knowledge of and participation in the corrupt act would be considered as a waiver of the State's right to avoid the concession contract for that reason. However, the tribunal held that "the knowledge of the Kenyan President" was *not* "attributable to Kenya. The President was here acting corruptly, to the detriment of Kenya and in violation of Kenyan law [...]. There is no warrant at English or Kenyan law for attributing knowledge to the state (as the otherwise innocent principal) of a state officer engaged as its agent in bribery."[28] For Dr. Kreindler, this finding from the *World Duty Free* tribunal was a serious error from the perspective of attributability:

> it strains credulity to conclude after the admission of the bribery and the underlying circumstances that the Kenyan head of State was not acting in his official capacity. It seems curious to conclude that he was not acting with apparent authority. And it seems strained to decide that he was not acting manifestly, and not just by 'happenstance', as an organ or agent of the State. Indeed he was the State.[29]

This leads to a *second* observable asymmetry in the case law, one that is based on identity. The attribution of corrupt conduct is different between private and public actors. In international law and in national corporate and civil laws on agency, private corporations are always responsible for the acts of their employees.[30] For

---

[26]*World Duty Free Company Limited v. The Republic of Kenya*, ICSID Case No. ARB/00/7, Award ¶180 (04 October 2006).

[27]Reisman (2000), p. 362 (an ICSID tribunal should apply international law, *inter alia,* where the law of the contracting State party to the dispute calls for the application of international law, including customary international law); Llamzon (2014), pp. 251–252. The *World Duty Free* tribunal's jurisdiction was based on contract, not an investment treaty.

[28]*World Duty Free Company Limited v. The Republic of Kenya*, ICSID Case No. ARB/00/7, Award ¶185 (04 October 2006).

[29]Kreindler (2013), pp. 292–293.

[30]See Kreindler (2013), p. 131. ("On the investor side, [...] there is in fact the accepted principle of attribution of an agent's acts and knowledge to the principal employing him, including under national law, for example: the US Restatement (Third) – Agency §2.04 "Respondeat Superior": the employer is liable for torts committed by employees while acting within their employment. And

host States, however, the case law suggests that the corrupt conduct of public officials are not attributable to the State (barring the first asymmetry above). The water's edge for attributability seems to lie at the point of consummation—if solicitation is met with acceptance in the form of the investor making the bribe payment requested, then it seems that bribery would not be attributable to the State.[31] Starting with *Metal-Tech v Uzbekistan,* a number of tribunals have accepted the idea that the presence of bribery would result in a lack of jurisdiction,[32] which in practice means that a claimant loses the ability to pursue claims against a host State for their breaches of investor protections under the treaty, no matter how plain those breaches might be.

Spentex v Uzbekistan provides an illustrative example. In this "milestone" case where "[f]or the first time, an ICSID tribunal decided that bribery was successfully proven on the basis of an accumulation of major 'red flags'",[33] the corruption allegation in question was a US$6 million payment to a consultant in order to aid the investor with the government tender process concerning the acquisition of a textile manufacturing facility's assets in Uzbekistan. The Tribunal found that "the most compelling explanation of the events surrounding the tender process in June 2006 and the making of the investment is clearly that it involved corrupt activities on the part of the investor and of officials of the Respondent [*i.e., Uzbekistan*]."[34] However, the Tribunal found that Uzbekistan was not cooperative in uncovering the full extent of public official involvement in the corrupt acts: Uzbekistan had alleged that one of Spentex's consultants was associated with the daughter of a high public official and had corruptly influenced the awarding of the contract, but also made clear that the government was not going to do anything about it.[35] In addition, Uzbekistan's expert in the *Spentex* case backed the strategy of non-investigation and non-prosecution of the public official and consultant that sought to use corrupt

---

German Civil Code Sec. 31, German Supreme Court (1991): "knowledge and subjective intent of an agent to commit acts against public policy can be attributed to the legal entity.").

[31] In *World Duty Free v Kenya*, for example, it was alleged that the then-President of Kenya, Daniel Arap-Moi, solicited or extorted a $4 million bribe from the investor. But as the investor then paid the bribe, the solicitation aspect was not considered by the Tribunal. And in its decisionmaking, the State was not held responsible for President Moi's complicity in the bribe. It bears noting, however, that *World Duty Free* was a contract-based dispute that was decided under English law and Kenyan law, as well as transnational public policy. Public international law was not utilized as such, although references to international treaties such as the UN Convention Against Corruption were made.

[32] *Metal-Tech Ltd. v. The Republic of Uzbekistan,* ICSID Case No. ARB/10/3 (04 October 2013). *See also Spentex Netherlands, B.V. v. Republic of Uzbekistan,* ICSID Case No. ARB/13/26 (27 December 2016); Unión Fenosa Gas, S.A. v. Arab Republic of Egypt, ICSID Case No. ARB/14/4 (31 August 2018).

[33] Betz (2017), p. 135.

[34] Betz (2017), p. 134 *citing Spentex Netherlands, B.V. v. Republic of Uzbekistan,* ICSID Case No. ARB/13/26, Award ¶934 (27 December 2016).

[35] Betz (2017), p. 134 *citing Spentex Netherlands, B.V. v. Republic of Uzbekistan,* ICSID Case No. ARB/13/26, Award ¶944 (27 December 2016).

influence "by suggesting the Tribunal should dismiss the Claimant's claims without naming the corrupt officials."[36] The Tribunal expressed real concern with this: "[s]uch an approach would reinforce perverse incentives for respondent States in the context of corruption. It would ask an investment tribunal to dismiss a claimant's claim, while granting impunity to a respondent State both in respect of the alleged corruption and the claimant's investment claims."[37]

The *Spentex* tribunal also acknowledged that corruption always takes two— "those who bribe and those who take bribes"—and that findings of corruption routinely lead to the dismissal of the claimant's claims, punishing only claimants for their conduct "while corrupt host states are left off the hook."[38] The Tribunal expressed disquiet that the claims would have to be dismissed pursuant to the 'legality doctrine' (the parties had agreed "on the legal principle that corrupt practices in the making of an investment are illegal and lead to the dismissal of claims")[39] despite the fact that the "implication of the finding of corruption is that not only the Claimant, but also the Respondent [State], engaged in or condoned illegal activities."[40] Nonetheless, the *Spentex* tribunal found that "for the time being, arbitral tribunals (which apply the law and do not create it) are somewhat helpless to 'sanction' respondent States that have engaged in corruption, since tribunals primarily possess tools to deny remedies to claimants that have engaged in corruption."[41]

Implicit in these statements from the *Spentex* tribunal is its apparent view that corruption ordinarily would be attributable to the host State itself, and that *but for* the 'legality clause' principle, the State would be held responsible for the corruption of its public officials. That implication ties squarely with the idea that State responsibility for corruption follows a different 'primary rule'. This rationale for dissociating a State's responsibility is discussed in Sect. 3 below. For now, however, the rule on attributability itself, as found the ILC Articles, bears further elaboration.

---

[36]Betz (2017), p. 134.

[37]Betz (2017), p. 134 *citing Spentex Netherlands, B.V. v. Republic of Uzbekistan*, ICSID Case No. ARB/13/26, Award ¶940 (27 December 2016).

[38]Betz (2017), p. 134 *citing Spentex Netherlands, B.V. v. Republic of Uzbekistan*, ICSID Case No. ARB/13/26, Award ¶973 (27 December 2016).

[39]*Spentex Netherlands, B.V. v. Republic of Uzbekistan*, ICSID Case No. ARB/13/26, Award ¶969 (27 December 2016).

[40]*Spentex Netherlands, B.V. v. Republic of Uzbekistan*, ICSID Case No. ARB/13/26, Award ¶270 (27 December 2016).

[41]*Spentex Netherlands, B.V. v. Republic of Uzbekistan*, ICSID Case No. ARB/13/26, Award ¶975 (27 December 2016).

2.2 Attribution of Corrupt Conduct Under the Framework of State Responsibility in the ILC Rules

The asymmetries discussed above exemplify the gap on the law on State responsibility for corruption: if a public official initiates acts of bribery against another party, the international responsibility of the State of that corrupting official is engaged. To be more precise, if public officials of a host State solicit or extort bribes from investors, and the other party does *not* pay the bribe, the international responsibility of the host State is engaged. But if the private party pays and the public official accepts, bribery is consummated and the question of State responsibility becomes less certain.

Analytically, this asymmetry should first be considered within the terms of Article 2 of the ILC Articles: to ascertain whether an internationally wrongful act has occurred, the first element to consider is whether the act or omission "is attributable to the State under international law."[42] In turn, Article 7 of the ILC Articles articulates the principle of attribution for acts in excess of authority or in contravention of instructions, as discussed above.

Article 7 straightforwardly attributes the act of an "organ of a State" or a "person or entity empowered to exercise elements of the governmental authority" to the State itself, *even if* that organ, person, or entity "exceeds its authority or contravenes instructions." Translated into corruption, the fact that a public official was acting against international (or national) anti-corruption law in excess of his authority is no defense for the State—that act would be attributable to the State. That principle makes good sense: in many instances where the responsibility of a State is in question, the illegal act complained of is not formally or informally sanctioned by the State. And yet responsibility remains—as the *Commentary* to Article 7 observes, a State should not be able to take refuge behind the notion that its internal law, the actions of those public officials ought not to have occurred. An equally basic rule of State responsibility, codified in Article 3, is that internationally wrongful acts remain so under international law even if the same act is characterized as lawful under the national law of that State; "otherwise a State could rely on its internal law in order to argue that conduct, in fact carried out by its organs, was not attributable to it."[43]

Unsurprisingly, a number of investment tribunals have relied on Article 7 to attribute responsibility over illegal conduct of public officials against host States,

---

[42]International Law Commission, *Draft Articles on Responsibility of States for Internationally Wrongful Acts*, UN Doc. A/RES/56/83, 53rd Session of the International Law Commission, Supplement No. 10 (A/56/10) (November 2001) article 2(a). "There is an internationally wrongful act of a State when conduct consisting of an action or omission: (a) is attributable to the State under international law; and [. . .]".

[43]*Report of the International Law Commission on the work of its fifty-third session*, International Law Commission, 53rd Session, UN Doc A/56/10 (2001), 45 ¶2.

even when doing so was contrary to their responsibilities and mandate[44]—albeit not in instances of bribery or other forms of corruption.

Nonetheless, the asymmetries described in the prior section demonstrate that there are differences in treatment between *attempted* bribery instigated by public officials (in the form of corrupt solicitation or extortion) that *is* attributable to the host State, versus *consummated* bribery that is not attributable. This author had previously attempted to find a principled rule that would explain the reasons for that difference within the general logic of the ILC Article 7.[45] That effort focused on the bilateral nature of corruption. Bribery cannot be committed unilaterally—it "always involves two sides: those who bribe and those who take bribes", with the State having "participated in creating the situation" of corruption, in the words of the *Spentex* and *Metal-Tech* tribunals.[46] By contrast, other forms of illegality—fraud, misrepresentations, and violations of host State law (and indeed, most other violations of international law)—usually lack significant contribution or collusion on the counterparty's part, thus genuinely creating a victim of that illegal act.[47] In other words, those violations of international law can be unilaterally perpetrated by a State upon another or *erga omnes*. Article 7 makes good sense in such cases, as it would be too convenient for a State to dodge responsibility or arrogate it to individual public officials that lack the capacity to pay compensation or provide redress.

The logic of Article 7 does, in fact, apply straightforwardly for corrupt solicitations or extortion initiated by a public official without acceptance or participation from the claimant/investor, even if not articulated within the framework of the articles on State responsibility. In *F-W Oil v Trinidad and Tobago*,[48] for example,

---

[44]*See* e.g. *Noble Ventures, Inc. v. Romania*, ICSID Case No. ARB/01/11, Award ¶81 (12 October 2005). ("This is because of the generally recognized rule recorded in Art. 7 2001 ILC Draft according to which the conduct of an organ of a State or of a person or entity empowered to exercise elements of governmental authority shall be considered an act of the State under international law if the organ, person or entity acts in that capacity, even if it exceeds its authority or contravenes instructions. Since, from the Claimant's perspective, SOF and APAPS always acted as if they were entities entitled by the Respondent to do so, their acts would still have to be attributed to the Respondent, even if an excess of competence has been shown."); *Ioannis Kardassopoulos v. The Republic of Georgia*, ICSID Case No. ARB.05/18, Decision on Jurisdiction ¶190 (06 July 2007). ("It is [. . .] immaterial whether or not SakNavtobi and Transneft were authorized to grant the rights contemplated by the JVA and the Concession or whether or not they otherwise acted beyond their authority under Georgian law. Article 7 of the *Articles on State Responsibility* provides that even in cases where an entity empowered to exercise governmental authority acts *ultra vires* of it, the conduct in question is nevertheless attributable to the State.").

[45]Llamzon (2014), pp. 254–268.

[46]*Spentex Netherlands, B.V. v. Republic of Uzbekistan*, ICSID Case No. ARB/13/26, Award ¶973 (27 December 2016); *Metal-Tech Ltd. v. The Republic of Uzbekistan*, ICSID Case No. ARB/10/3, Award ¶422 (04 October 2013).

[47]For a comprehensive study of fraud and other violations of host State law, *see* Llamzon and Sinclair (2015).

[48]This needs to be compared against trading in influence (also known as "influence peddling"), whose full consummation does not require the public official's cooperation—*see* Llamzon (2019), p. 192.

the investor alleged that a $1.5 million bribe had been solicited by a public official of the host State as it was negotiating an oil and gas development project with the State-owned energy company. The investor said that it had reported the solicitation attempt to the then-Prime Minister on two occasions, without action. The investor eventually withdrew these allegations, having been unable to prove them; nonetheless, the Tribunal emphasized that had corruption been proven, it would have had "a most substantial effect on the view of the case taken by the Tribunal", particularly regarding the applicable investment treaty's standards of treatment for foreign investors.

Similarly, and as discussed earlier, in *EDF (Services) v. Romania* the investor alleged that bribe solicitations made by the Prime Minister of Romania were rebuffed by the investor, which then resulted in retaliatory acts by Romanian State-owned enterprises that were, in principle, attributable to the State itself. In the tribunal's analysis, the corrupt solicitation of a bribe by "a State agency" would be a "violation of the fair and equitable treatment obligation owed to the claimant pursuant to the BIT as well as a violation of international public policy." The tribunal also agreed with the claimant's submission that when the host State's discretion was exercised on the basis of corruption, a "fundamental breach of transparency and legitimate expectations" occurs.[49] Case law therefore provides a measure of clarity on State responsibility where the public official was engaged in bribe solicitation/extortion.

Unfortunately, the same clarity is not present in the case of consummated bribery, where the solicitation or offer of a bribe is met with agreement from the other side. That meeting of the minds (to put it in contractual terms) causes the investor's participation and potential culpability for corruption to form part of the factual matrix.[50] The key point here is not the knowledge of the public official's illegality—knowledge that the public official was acting outside his mandate and in contravention of law would not alone result in that act being attributable to the State.[51] Rather, in the case of consummated bribery, the investor not only knows that the public official is acting outside the scope of his power, but also that he/she

---

[49]*EDF (Services) Limited. v Romania*, ICSID Case No. ARB/05/13, Award (08 October 2009).

[50]This needs to be compared against trading in influence (also known as "influence peddling"), whose full consummation does not require the public official's cooperation—*see* Llamzon (2019), p. 192.

[51]*Yeager v. Iran (Kenneth P. Yeager v. The Islamic Republic of Iran) (*Award) (Iran-US Claims Tribunal, Award No. 324-10199-1, 02 November 1987). In this case, the foreign private party claimed that an employee of the State airline Iran Air forced the private party to make an "extra payment" for a plane ticket. The IUSCT did not attribute to Iran this corrupt act by the State employee: "[a]cts which an organ commits in a purely private capacity, even if it has used the means placed at its disposal by the state for the exercise of its functions, are not attributable to the state. . . . There is no indication in this case that the Iran Air agent was acting for any other reason than personal profit, or that he had passed on the payment to Iran Air. He evidently did not act on behalf or in the interests of Iran Air. The Tribunal finds, therefore, that this agent acted in a private capacity and not in his official capacity as an organ for Iran Air." Prof. Anne Peters finds this explanation unconvincing: "[t]his finding is defensible, but the reasoning is not persuasive. Rather, it was

participated in the corrupt act. Indeed, *World Duty Free v Kenya* itself concerned a corrupt solicitation initiated by the sitting Kenyan President at the time[52]—and yet the payment of that bribe led to the dismissal of the private investor's claims entirely. Professor Reisman criticizes *World Duty Free* for precisely this reason.[53]

Parsing out the text of Article 7 of the ILC Articles, the qualification "if the organ, person or entity *acts in that capacity*" *arguably* obviates State responsibility for consummated corruption, as the public official is visibly acting in excess of his authority and the other party, knowing that the public official is acting for private gain, freely participated in the corrupt act.[54] In other words, the investor knew the public official was engaged in an act manifestly not "in th[e] capacity" of a State organ, person, or entity, within the meaning of Article 7. This author did not consider the explanation fully satisfactory given the lack of any logical or policy-oriented reason for differentiating between attempted solicitation versus consummated bribery, and certainly not to the extent that it should override the logic of Article 7; nonetheless, it was posited as an attempt to harmonize the findings of the case law with the ILC Articles and rationalize why tribunals might be unwilling to attribute public official corruption, short of fashioning a special rule of attribution that would apply to corruption only.[55] And indeed, most commentators who view the issue continue to consider, to varying degrees, that as a matter of international law, corrupt acts of public officials should be attributable and States should in principle be responsible for bribery committed by their public officials.[56]

---

significant that the employee did not pretend to be demanding the extra payment on behalf of the state." *See* Peters (2018), p. 1251.

[52] *World Duty Free Company Limited v. The Republic of Kenya*, ICSID Case No. ARB/00/7, Award ¶180 (04 October 2006). ("Moreover, on the evidence before this Tribunal, the bribe was apparently solicited by the Kenyan President and not wholly initiated by the Claimant.").

[53] Bonucci and Reisman (2015), p. 245. ("*World Duty Free* is often celebrated because it clearly condemned an overt case of bribery, one that, moreover, was facilitated or, if you like, imposed on the tribunal by the admission against interest of the claimant himself. However, from the standpoint of implementation of a broad policy against bribery and corruption, it is fair to ask whether the outcome in that particular case was rather perverse. The claimant had made an investment, which he lost. The claimant had paid a substantial bribe, which he lost or he received, at least, an antique case full of corn. The Kenyan government received the benefit of the investment, had the opportunity to sell the concession a second time and double that benefit, and walked away with the bribe. If there was a shame sanction, a loss of face sanction imposed on the government or on the president, I must say I think that both were able to bear it very lightly.").

[54] *See* Llamzon (2014), p. 262 ("This *participation* even after full knowledge that the public official is acting with private enrichment in mind arguably negates the application of ordinary attribution rules, at least with respect to the bilateral relationship between investor and host State, as the investor would know that the public official was not 'act[ing] in that capacity' (see Article 7) and could thus not be engaging in an act of State. Corruption that would ordinarily have been subject to the attribution-for-*ultra vires*-acts doctrine would thus be precluded in the case of the investor.").

[55] *See* Llamzon (2014) p. 279 (concluding that "the logic supporting the attribution asymmetry does not fully cohere.").

[56] *See* Kreindler (2013), pp. 286–293. ("Bribery may or may not raise issues of attribution. And the question of the tainting of a contract or investment may or may not require an analysis applying the

Professor Crawford and Mr. Mertenskötter present a distinct view on State responsibility for corruption, and correctly so to a significant extent. They disagree with this author's attempt to explain why States might not be held responsible for the corruption of their public officials within the framework of Article 7. They consider that under Article 7, what matters is the *exercise* of State authority, not its propriety. Thus, the use of that authority as part of a corrupt transaction would ordinarily operate to attribute corruption of a public official to the State, because the alternative would be to allow a State to always find a way to absolve itself of responsibility by simply saying that the official was not acting in a public capacity.[57]

Crawford and Mertenskötter give a vivid example that illustrates their view on attribution: a head of State (a President or Prime Minister for example) can say: "for you to get the concession you have to pay me a facilitation fee of $1 million." Both sides know the President is acting illegally in soliciting a bribe, and if paid, the investor is complicit. In that case, would the illegal act be attributable? Yes, because of the President's position as an organ of the State. Even if the president explicitly

---

ILC Draft Articles. Manifest corruption may be equally manifestly 'attributable.'"); Spalding (2015), p. 494. (calling for the attribution of corruption to the State through the application of Article 7 of the ILC Articles, and concluding that "A holding that provides an absolute defense to the state's solicitation and acceptance of bribes [. . .] reinforces and exacerbates deep structural imbalances that now exist in anti-bribery enforcement, whereby select capital-exporters enforce prohibitions against those companies subject to their jurisdiction, while corrupt officials continue to demand bribes without penalty and companies from non-enforcing home countries do the same. *Duty Free* represents a zero-tolerance approach to the supply of bribes, but facilitates the demand side."); Donoghue (2015), p. 761. (" The modest deterrent effect of the corruption trump comes at a price, because respondent States are left unaccountable either for corruption that they may have endorsed or for the measures that gave rise to the investor's claim."); Klaw (2015), p. 62.

Similar arguments in favor of recognizing the responsibility of States for corruption outside the regime of ILC Articles also exist. *See, e.g.,* Raeschke-Kessler and Gottwald (2008), pp. 15–16.

For a contrary view, *see* Wood (2018) ("Whereas the standard has been conceived of as a liberal one, which will normally result in state responsibility for the conduct of corrupt officials (especially of high rank), this note argues for a more stringent approach. In general, and by virtue of states' international anti-corruption obligations, it is suggested that a foreign investor cannot reasonably assume an official (no matter how high-ranking) to be authorized to engage in and act upon corruption. Consequently, the conduct of a corrupt official should seldom, if ever, be attributable to the state.").

[57]Notably, Crawford and Mertenskötter seem to give very little consideration to host State attribution and responsibility for breaches of investment treaties when bribe solicitations and extortion are made by public officials—their analysis seems to be that such acts would result in attributability and responsibility because of temporality, *i.e.,* attribution and responsibility can occur for post-investment acts of solicitation and bribery so long as the investment itself was made without corruption. Crawford and Mertenskötter (2016), p. 38. ("But circumstances could be envisaged where issues of attribution would arise, for example under the fair and equitable treatment clause with respect to contracts procured by corruption in the course of giving effect to a pre-existing investment.").

For reasons discussed by inter alia Prof. Zachary Douglas, that temporal-based analysis has serious difficulties of principle. *See* Douglas (2014), p. 175. ("This temporal dividing line between pleas of illegality that go to jurisdiction and to the merits has no sound basis in principle."). *See also* Llamzon (2015), p. 322.

came out and said: "by the way, I'm only acting in my private capacity," that violation of international anti-corruption law would still be attributable in a situation where the conduct of the State, through its organs and representatives, makes it reasonable to assume that the President's words have the backing of the State. This should be true whether authoritarian regimes or functioning democracies are involved. However, if a local traffic policeman sought a bribe, promising to obtain the concession for the bribe-payer if paid a thousand dollars (or a million, for that matter), that, according to Crawford and Mertenskötter, would not be attributable to the State—the traffic policeman does not have a position where it would be reasonable to presume that his actions were cloaked with authority by the State.[58] Thus, the more powerful the official is under that State's internal structure, the higher international law's expectation for the State to control that official's conduct will be. And the less able the State should be to dodge responsibility.[59]

All that said, neither Article 7 of the ILC Articles nor the position articulated above on how that rule on apparent authority might ordinarily apply in cases of bribery—at least in the absence of a primary rule that is unique to corruption cases (a key point of difference with this author, discussed in Sect. 3 *infra*)—have been explicitly adopted in the case law. Indeed, even by inference, the case record mostly cuts against the application of Article 7—tribunals that have found the existence of bribery have *not* held States responsible for the public official's role in the bribe. As explained earlier, the *Spentex* tribunal considered that Uzbekistan's public officials had done a variety of acts exhibiting their complicity with the bribery that had occurred, and saw a fundamental unfairness in apportioning all the negative consequences of bribery to the investor by dismissing its claims for lack of jurisdiction, concluding that "for the time being, arbitration tribunals (which apply the law and do not create it) are somewhat helpless to 'sanction' respondent States that have engaged in corruption, since tribunals primarily possess tools to deny remedies to claimants that have engaged in corruption."[60]

The same postulate is found in *World Duty Free*—although that tribunal did not employ international law, it held that host States cannot be responsible for corrupt acts of a public official, no matter how high (in that case, it was the sitting President of the country himself), because such corruption amounted to purely private conduct *and* was known to be so by the investor, and thus cannot be attributed to the host State.[61]

---

[58]Crawford and Mertenskotter (2016), p. 41.

[59]Crawford and Mertenskotter (2016), pp. 41–42.

[60]*Spentex Netherlands, B.V. v. Republic of Uzbekistan*, ICSID Case No. ARB/13/26, Award ¶975 (27 December 2016).

[61]*World Duty Free Company Limited v. The Republic of Kenya*, ICSID Case No. ARB/00/7, Award ¶185 (04 October 2006. ("Moreover, there can be no affirmation or waiver in this case based on the knowledge of the Kenyan President attributable to Kenya. The President was here acting corruptly, to the detriment of Kenya and in violation of Kenyan law (including the 1956 Act). There is no warrant at English or Kenyan law for attributing knowledge to the state (as the otherwise innocent principal) of a state officer engaged as its agent in bribery.").

Finally, in *Metal-Tech v. Uzbekistan*, the Tribunal expressed that States bear a degree of culpability for bribery committed by their public officials: "[t]that does not mean, however, that the State has not participated in creating the situation that leads to the dismissal of the claims."[62] That tribunal's finding that the State had "participated in creating the situation" of corruption is a tacit acceptance of the basic logic of State responsibility for the illegal acts of its officials. However, the extent of liability extended to Uzbekistan for that corrupt act was limited to the sharing of the costs of the case: "[b]ecause of this participation, which is implicit in the very nature of corruption, it appears fair that the Parties share in the costs."[63] As with the later *Spentex* case, the *Metal-Tech v. Uzbekistan* tribunal was constrained from doing more because of the presence of a "legality clause" in the applicable investment treaty that deprived the tribunal of jurisdiction over the dispute: "[t]he law is clear – and rightly so – that in such a situation [of an investment tainted by corruption] the investor is deprived of protection and, consequently, the host State avoids any potential liability."[64]

Thus, tribunals acknowledge that an asymmetry exists in the legal consequences that attach to bribery and are clearly uncomfortable with its implications. In terms of the ordinary 'secondary' rules of State responsibility, this case law is difficult to reconcile with Article 7, which plays a surprisingly invisible role in the tribunals' analyses. Could those findings (and the absence of a sustained engagement with Article 7) be ascribed to the existence of a unique "primary rule" that governs corruption issues in international law, overriding the attribution of responsibility that would otherwise have had occurred through the application of ILC Article 7?

3 Does a Relevant Primary Rule Exist on the Consequences of Corruption, Whether Grounded in National Law, Transnational Public Policy, or International Law?

As the prior section discusses, an asymmetry exists that cannot be explained by the ordinary application of Article 7 of the ILC Articles. When the investor is the victim of bribe solicitations and extortions, the case law seems to have no doubt that international responsibility for the public official's conduct can attach. And it seems that following ordinary rules on attribution, the conduct of public officials when bribery is consummated, is attributable to the State. But attribution is only one element of the two-part test under Article 2 of the Articles on State responsibility:

---

[62]*Metal-Tech Ltd. v. The Republic of Uzbekistan*, ICSID Case No ARB/10/3, Award, ¶422 (04 October 2013) (emphasis supplied).

[63]*Metal-Tech Ltd. v. The Republic of Uzbekistan*, ICSID Case No ARB/10/3, Award, ¶422 (04 October 2013).

[64]*Metal-Tech Ltd. v. The Republic of Uzbekistan*, ICSID Case No ARB/10/3, Award, ¶422 (04 October 2013).

even if conduct might be attributable, would it nonetheless *not* be considered a breach of an international obligation of the State? Crawford and Mertenskötter believe that a primary rule does exist on the consequences of corruption that precludes holding States responsible for consummated corruption. And there lies the primary disagreement with this author (as well as others).[65]

To arrive at their conclusion that anti-corruption principles in international law operate to insulate host States from responsibility for corruption, Crawford and Mertenskötter's analysis begins with a recollection of the *World Duty Free* case. They correctly note that this was not a case on attribution in the international legal sense, "and the tribunal was not suggesting otherwise;"[66] the case rested on the application of Kenyan and English law. In their view, the issue in the case

> was rather one of the enforceability of a corrupt transaction in a situation where the parties were, or to be treated as, in pari delicto. An equally well-established principle holds that significant corruption inducing an investment transaction invalidates it, and that in such cases the loss lies where it falls. The party corruptly inducing the transaction cannot rely on the law of State responsibility to reallocate its losses; the act of entering into the transaction is nonetheless attributable to the State.[67]

Crawford and Mertenskötter take issue with this author's consideration of State responsibility as a means to bring balance to the apportionment of economic and moral costs of corruption—"[t]his argument assumes that it is the law of State responsibility that creates the imbalance, but in our view it is rather the relevant substantive primary rule that does so (if imbalance there is)."[68]

Articulating this supposed "relevant substantive primary rule" further, Crawford and Mertenskötter then make two sets of conclusions. The *first* and most significant conclusion they make concerns the consequences of corruption supposedly demanded by law. In relation to investment contracts, they rely on *World Duty Free* to articulate the principle that corruption not only affects the validity of the contract (which becomes either void or voidable), but also the "lets the loss of the parties lie where it falls – *in pari delicto melior est conditio possidentis.*"[69] They add that "the source of that rule will (as in *World Duty Free v Kenya*) usually be national

---

[65] *See* Drude (2018), p. 695. ("Yet, to this present day, the *World Duty Free* tribunal's excruciating and, considering the logic of its reasoning, entirely unwarranted reference to the *ex turpi causa* maxim prompts even the most learned and distinguished scholars to maintain 'that . . . corruption inducing an investment transaction invalidates it, and that in such cases the loss lies where it falls.' (*citing* Crawford and Mertenskotter 2016, p. 37). As demonstrated above, this is clearly not the case in contract-based investment arbitration. Constantine Partasides, counsel for Kenya in the *World Duty Free* case, recently acknowledged that corrupt investors could bring restitutionary claims under the respectively applicable law. What is more, he rightly observed that answers in the contractual context 'can translate into investment treaty arbitration.'"). *See also* Partasides (2017), p. 745.

[66] Crawford and Mertenskotter (2016), p. 37.

[67] Crawford and Mertenskotter (2016), p. 37.

[68] Crawford and Mertenskotter (2016), p. 38.

[69] Crawford and Mertenskotter (2016), p. 38.

law and the relevant international law will make a *renvoi* to it, although international public policy may also be invoked."[70]

Second, they extend this principle to investment treaty arbitration, concluding that "this substantive rule" (*i.e.,* the rule on voidness or voidability plus the *pari delicto* rule) "will usually have the distributive effect of favouring the State, whether or not its officials are themselves prosecuted or made to disgorge." They then explore why, normatively, such a rule may be acceptable, employing a logic that the *World Duty Free* tribunal found compelling:

> [t]he normative justification of the rule is rooted elsewhere, namely in the conviction that socially harmful and manifestly unlawful activity should not be protected by the law in any of its facets or repercussions. The justification is not rooted in a normative assessment that the State is somehow more deserving of the proceeds from corruption than the investor is to get its money back. The pro-State distributive effect occurs in spite of, and not because of, the principle's normative justification. This distributive effect is solely due to the primary rule, for which a cogent normative justification exists, and wholly independent of international law's rules on attribution as stated in ILC Articles 4–11. To the extent that Llamzon focuses on the rules of attribution to explain the empirical situation of States not paying for corruption, he is looking in the wrong place.[71]

Crawford and Mertenskötter are undoubtedly right to find the proper rule first in any rule specific to corruption that might hold primacy over the general, 'secondary' rules on attribution.[72] But their core conclusion—that a primary rule exists on corruption that require not only the voidness (or voidability) of a contract, but also the absence of jurisdiction or inadmissibility of claims[73] based on a contract tainted by corruption, whether in contract or investment treaty based arbitration—is largely incorrect.[74] Undoubtedly, a durable consensus exists proscribing corruption generally (and bribery, in particular). But no similar consensus exists on what the proper *consequences* attendant to a finding of corruption are or should be. That is true whether the law applied is national law, international law, or any principle of transnational public policy; or whether the modality of dispute resolution is contract or investment treaty-based.

---

[70]Crawford and Mertenskotter (2016), p. 38.

[71]Crawford and Mertenskotter (2016), pp. 38–39.

[72]This is an intellectual task this author undertook as well: for an analysis of the absence of a "primary" substantive rule on international anti-corruption law—which does not punish host State corruption—*see* Llamzon (2014), pp. 264–268.

[73]*See* Llamzon and Sinclair (2015), p. 524. ("In this context, jurisdiction is a "plea that the tribunal itself is incompetent to give any ruling at all whether as to the merits or as to the admissibility of the claim," while admissibility is "a plea that the tribunal should rule the claim to be inadmissible on some ground other than its ultimate merits". While jurisdiction and admissibility have different legal effects, particularly as to the res judicata effect of the decision rendered by the investment tribunal, the immediate effect is the same, for practical purposes. Investor wrongdoing acts as a complete defense, a "trump" with preclusive effect vis-à-vis any investor claim for expropriation, etc. From the perspective of the host State, no liability attaches; for the investor, no relief is possible in investment arbitration (and often, in any fora at all).").

[74]*See also* Drude (2018), pp. 695–696.

3.1 The Consequences of Corruption in National Law

At the level of contract invalidity, corruption is usually treated in civil and common law jurisdictions alike as a taint on a party's consent to a contract, which would under the laws of most States result in a voidable contract. This is to be distinguished from when corruption is the actual object of the contract, as for example in the case of a simulated consultancy agreement that was merely meant to legitimize the use of an intermediary to facilitate bribery—in those case, the contract would be void *ab initio*.[75] In *World Duty Free,* the tribunal's primary finding under English and Kenyan law was to confirm the host State's avoidance of the investment agreement due to corruption, dismissing the case on the merits. The tribunal also arguably considered the investor's claims inadmissible.[76] In so doing, the investor's claims of contractual breach and allegations of expropriation were not discussed at all. Conversely, in *Niko Resources v. Bangladesh,* the tribunal refused to uphold the host State's submission that the tribunal was without jurisdiction, whilst also noting that the State-owned enterprises that entered into the contract did not seek to avoid the contract in question.[77]

However, the key contractual consequence of corruption that engages the issue of attribution is less contract validity than it is the admissibility of claims. The position that consummated corruption is a *pari delicto* that would lead to the inadmissibility of claims—Crawford and Mertenskötter's core basis for relying upon a supposed primary rule on corruption that insulates the State[78]—would only be correct *if* the

---

[75]In civil and common law jurisdictions, there is a key distinction between contracts that provide for corruption (void ab initio) and contracts that are procured by corruption (voidable at the instance of the innocent party). *See* Gearing and Kwong (2015), p. 159; Arnesto (2015), p. 169; *Niko Resources (Bangladesh) Ltd. v. Bangladesh Petroleum Exploration ("Bapex") and Bangladesh Oil Gas and Mineral Corporation ("Petrobangla"),* ICSID Case Nos. ARB/10/11 and ARB/10/18, Decision on Jurisdiction, ¶¶434–464 (19 August 2013).

[76]*World Duty Free Company Limited v. The Republic of Kenya,* ICSID Case No. ARB/00/7, Award ¶188 (04 October 2006): "The Claimant is not legally entitled to maintain any of its pleaded claims in these proceedings as a matter of *ordre public international* and public policy under the contract's applicable laws." Interpreting the phrase "not legally entitled to maintain", A. Newcombe states "the claim was inadmissible because of a breach of international public policy." Newcombe (2012), p. 197.

[77]*Niko Resources (Bangladesh) Ltd. v. Bangladesh Petroleum Exploration ("Bapex") and Bangladesh Oil Gas and Mineral Corporation ("Petrobangla"),* ICSID Case Nos. ARB/10/11 and ARB/10/18, Decision on Jurisdiction, ¶¶452 & 456 (19 August 2013).

[78]In *World Duty Free Company Limited v. The Republic of Kenya,* ICSID Case No. ARB/00/7, Award (04 October 2006). In *World Duty Free,* the tribunal considered that "as regards public policy under English law and Kenyan law (being materially identical" and on the specific facts of this case, the Tribunal concludes that the Claimant is not legally entitled to maintain any of its pleaded claims in these proceedings on the ground of *ex turpi causa non oritur action.* These claims all sound or depend upon the Agreement of 27 April 1989 (as amended); and no other claim is pleaded, including any non-contractual proprietary or restitutionary claim.").

applicable national law actually contains such a rule, which is *not* generally true.[79] Even under English law, the rule was never clear-cut, and the UK Supreme Court in 2016—about a decade after *World Duty Free*—put the issue to rest by ruling that illegality does not necessarily (or even mostly) give rise to unenforceable or inadmissible contracts. In *Patel v. Mirza*,[80] the UK Supreme Court reviewed the 250-year jurisprudence of English courts (as well as Commonwealth and US case law) on the illegality defense and expressly overturned the *in pari delicto potior est conditio defendentis* principle that animated *World Duty Free*. Instead of an automatic inadmissibility of claims when the Claimant had engaged in wrongdoing, a more flexible test was applied wherein the courts would now consider—among other factors—whether denying a claimant's claim would be a proportionate response to the nature and seriousness of the Claimant's wrongdoing.[81] Speaking for the Court's majority, Lord Toulson stated:

> one cannot judge whether allowing a claim which is in some way tainted by illegality would be contrary to the public interest, because it would be harmful to the integrity of the legal system, without a) considering the underlying purpose of the prohibition which has been transgressed, b) considering conversely any other relevant public policies which may be rendered ineffective or less effective by denial of the claim, and c) keeping in mind the possibility of overkill unless the law is applied with a due sense of proportionality.[82]

Moreover, most national laws incorporate principles of international law as part of their law. In these States, the presence of an important international element—such as the identity of a foreign investor—would lead under national law to a *renvoi* to, or at least a consideration of, international legal principles. To take the *World Duty Free* example, considering that the applicable English law (and presumably Kenyan law as well) incorporate international law as part of the its national law, principles of public international law can be applied directly (albeit with some conditions).[83] Thus, even if one assumes that the contractual choice of law would

---

[79]*See* Drude (2018), p. 707. (simply adducing *ex turpi causa* and similar Latin maxims as expressions of a purported general principle (of law) is unhelpful. Again, a rigorous comparative analysis of how the maxims have evolved over time and play out in practice across different legal systems would be imperative. There is indeed no one-size-fits-all.").

[80]Patel v. Mirza (2016) UK Supreme Court, UKSC 2014/0218. *Supreme Court UK* [Online]. Available at: https://www.supremecourt.uk/cases/docs/uksc-2014-0218-judgment.pdf (Accessed: 13 March 2021).

[81]Patel v. Mirza (2016) UK Supreme Court, UKSC 2014/0218, ¶ 101. *Supreme Court UK* [Online]. Available at: https://www.supremecourt.uk/cases/docs/uksc-2014-0218-judgment.pdf (Accessed: 13 March 2021). ("In considering whether it would be disproportionate to refuse relief to which the claimant would otherwise be entitled, as a matter of public policy, various factors may be relevant. Professor Burrows' list is helpful but I would not attempt to lay down a prescriptive or definitive list because of the infinite possible variety of cases. Potentially relevant factors include the seriousness of the conduct, its centrality to the contract, whether it was intentional and whether there was a marked disparity in the parties' respective culpability.").

[82]Patel v. Mirza (2016) UK Supreme Court, UKSC 2014/0218, ¶ 101.

[83]In their edition of *Oppenheim's International Law*, Sir Robert Jennings and Sir Arthur Watts stated that the law of nations is part of English law and has been repeatedly acted on by English

forestall the direct application of public international law, reference to customary international law might yet be mandated by the applicable national law.

3.2 The Consequences of Corruption in Transnational Public Policy

Serious forms of illegality such as corruption often trigger an analysis in terms of "transnational public policy" or "truly international public policy".[84] The English House of Lords defined the term "public policy" as early as 1853 as meaning "that principle of law which holds that no subject can lawfully do that which has a tendency to be injurious to the public, or against public good".[85] Modern "transnational public policy" tends to be traced back to Pierre Lalive, who spoke in 1986 of a "transnational (or truly international) public policy"[86] that could potentially "trump" applicable national law.

Arbitrators in international commercial and investment arbitration often consider themselves to be bound to respect an overarching set of principles of "transnational public policy", independent of specific national rules or interests. Whereas national public policy is used to refer to fundamental principles of one particular State, transnational public policy is a term "usually employed to refer to certain fundamental principles of law that are considered to be common among developed legal systems, and to have mandatory application, regardless of what the parties have agreed."[87] Such principles are said to reflect the values and fundamental interests of

---

courts. Jennings and Watts (2008), pp. 56–57. That said, English courts have recently expressed caution regarding the use of customary international law as a direct source of rights and obligations under English law: R Al-Saadoon & Others v. Secretary of State for Defence (2015) High Court of Justice, Queen's Bench Division, Case Nos: CO/5608/2008; CO/8695/2009; CO/6345/2008; CO/9925/2008; CO/11858/2009; CO/11442/2008; CO/953/2009; CO/9719/2009; CO/12803/2009; CO/1684/2010; CO/2631/2010, C8620/2010, *Judiciary UK* [Online]. Available at: https://www.judiciary.uk/wp-content/uploads/2015/12/r-al-saadoon-v-secretary-of-state-for-defence-2015-ewhc-715-admin.pdf (Accessed: 13 March 2021) (the 'proposition that a customary rule may be sued on as a cause of action in the English courts is perhaps not so clear cut').

[84]Although often used interchangeably in the cases, some scholars would define "international public policy" as a forum state's public policies applicable in an international context, while "transnational public policy" points to an autonomous and generally applicable group of international policies derived from international sources and national practices. *See* Born (2009), pp. 2621–2623; Lalive (1986b), pp. 258–316.

[85]Egerton v. Earl Brownlow (1853), IV HLC 1, 196.

[86]Lalive (1986a), p. 329.

[87]Born (2009), pp. 2194–2195 (citing prohibitions against agreements to perform criminal acts, slavery and similar abuses, supplying arms to terrorist groups, and comparable acts within the concept of international public policy).

the international community.[88] The notion of "transnational public policy" has been recognized by courts of several jurisdictions, both civil and common law based, as well as in arbitral practice. This fairly consistent practice has led commentators to announce the end of any debate as to the existence of transnational public policy.[89]

The bribing of public officials to achieve particular ends has been singled out, especially in arbitral practice and by some scholarly commentary, as well as in some treaties, as being contrary to universally accepted principles of transnational public policy. In the 1960s, three decades prior to the first major multilateral instruments regulating corruption, Judge Lagergren as sole arbitrator in ICC Case No. 1110 famously declared: "[w]hether one is taking the point of view of good government or that of commercial ethics it is impossible to close one's eyes to the probable destination of amounts of this magnitude, and to the destructive effect thereof on the business pattern with the consequent impairment of industrial progress. Such corruption is an international evil; it is contrary to good morals and to international public policy common to the community of nations."[90] Corruption of state officials is generally considered as incompatible with fundamental moral and social values and thus is said to constitute both a clear violation of "international public policy" or "transnational public policy", and also the national public policy of most States. This has been recognized by a large number of judicial decisions and by international arbitrators alike in commercial arbitrations, applying different national laws.[91]

---

[88]Kessedijan (2007), pp. 861–862. ("Transnational public policy is composed of mandatory norms which may be imposed on actors in the market either because they have been created by those actors themselves or by civil society at large, or because they have been widely accepted by different societies around the world. These norms aim at being universal. They are the sign of the maturity of the international communities (that of merchants and that of the civil societies) who know very well that there are limits to their activities.").

[89]Gaillard and Savage (1999), p. 864. ("Although it may not be part of the substantive law of every sovereign state, genuinely international public policy is nevertheless a reality, and it is perfectly able to operate so as to override the law which would otherwise apply, just as the local conception of international public policy would operate in a national court.").

[90]ICC Award No. 1110 of 1963 by Gunnar Lagergren (Award) (ICC, Case No. 1110, 15 January 1963).

[91]See ICC Award No. 1110 of 1963 by Gunnar Lagergren (Award) (ICC, Case No. 1110, 15 January 1963); Westacre Investments Inc. v. Jugoimport-SDRP Holding Co. Ltd. (1999) England and Wales, Court of Appeal, QBCMI 1998/0485/3. New York Convention 1958 [Online]. Available at: https://newyorkconvention1958.org/index.php?lvl=notice_display&id=546 (Accessed: 13 March 2021); Omnium de Traitement et de Valorisation SA v. Hilmarton Ltd. (1999) England and Wales High Court, 1998 Folio No 1003. New York Convention 1958 [Online]. Available at: https://newyorkconvention1958.org/index.php?lvl=notice_display&id=885 (Accessed: 13 March 2021); Société European Gas Turbines SA v. Société Westman International Ltd. (1993) Paris Court of Appeals (1Ch.C); National Power Corp. v. Westinghouse, Swiss Federal Tribunal, Decision of 02 September 1993, ASA BULLETIN 244, 247 (1994); ICC Case No. 3913 of 1981, cited in Derains (1985), p. 989; Frontier AG & Brunner Sociedade v. Thomson CSF (Award) (ICC, ICC Case No. 7664, 31 July 1996) cited in Sayed (2004), p. 307; ICC Case No. 8891 of 1998 cited in, Journal du droit International (Clunet) (2000).

Similarly, multilateral instruments on the subject, notably the OECD Anti-Bribery Convention, point to a "consensus... within and outside the international arbitration community"[92] condemning such practices, and have arguably "contributed to, or confirmed, the development of certain national and transnational concepts of public policy in abhorrence of illegality of contracts".[93]

The existence of a transnational public policy condemning corruption has been confirmed and applied in certain commercial and primarily contract-based investment arbitrations, most notably *World Duty Free*. There, the Tribunal was faced with a question of whether a transnational public policy against bribery existed and how this principle should affect the proceedings. The Tribunal used the term "international public policy" to signify "an international consensus as to universal standards and accepted norms of conduct that must be applied in all fora"; *i.e.,* what is more frequently referred to as *transnational* public policy.[94] It noted the wide acceptance of anti-bribery and anti-corruption policies in the national law of many countries,[95] the significant number of international conventions addressing corruption and bribery (including the OECD Anti-Bribery Convention, the UN Convention Against Corruption, and other multilateral anti-corruption treaties),[96] and a line of arbitral decisions holding that proof of corruption mandated a tribunal to refrain from applying the contract on transnational public policy grounds.[97] Specifically, the international *ordre public* was found through the corpus of English and Kenyan national law: "[a]lthough this name ["international public policy ('ordre public international')"] suggests that it is in some way a supra-national principle, it is in fact no more than domestic public policy applied to foreign awards and its content and application remains subjective to each State."[98]

The tribunal proceeded to review the concept of 'transnational public policy', and concluded after a review of national laws, international anti-corruption conventions, and court and arbitral tribunal decisions, "that bribery [was] contrary to international public policy of most, if not all, States or, to use another formula, to transnational

---

[92]Beale and Esposito (2009), p. 368.

[93]Kreindler (2003), p. 210. ("[O]ver the last several years a number of states have acceded to multilateral conventions condemning illegal contracts, corruption, bribery of public officials, etc. These accessions have arguably contributed to, or confirmed, the development of certain national and transnational concepts of public policy in abhorrence of illegality of contracts".).

[94]*World Duty Free Company Limited v. The Republic of Kenya*, ICSID Case No. ARB/00/7, Award ¶139 (04 October 2006).

[95]*World Duty Free Company Limited v. The Republic of Kenya*, ICSID Case No. ARB/00/7, Award ¶142 (04 October 2006).

[96]*World Duty Free Company Limited v. The Republic of Kenya*, ICSID Case No. ARB/00/7, Award ¶143–144 (04 October 2006).

[97]*World Duty Free Company Limited v. The Republic of Kenya*, ICSID Case No. ARB/00/7, Award ¶148 (04 October 2006).

[98]*World Duty Free Company Limited v. The Republic of Kenya*, ICSID Case No. ARB/00/7, Award ¶138 (04 October 2006).

public policy".[99] As a consequence, the *World Duty Free* Tribunal concluded that "claims based on contracts of corruption or on contracts obtained by corruption cannot be upheld by this Arbitral Tribunal."[100]

From the foregoing, there seems to be sufficient authority to conclude that a transnational public policy exists proscribing bribery and corruption. In many ways, however, this conclusion only states the obvious: States invariably prohibit corruption in their national laws, and international law contains similar proscriptions. Thus, whatever the parties choose as the applicable law, invoking a transnational principle affirming the existence of a proscription on corruption may be unnecessary.[101] Resort to transnational public policy may also be unnecessary when the applicable national law incorporates international law,[102] and the public policies sought to be invoked are actually part of international law. Commentators have noted that the transnational public policy against corruption forms part of international law, relying on the strong conventional and customary international law status among the vast majority of States that receive investments. At best, transnational public policy produces no better guidance for arbitral decision-makers than the OECD Convention or other very general statements of policy, and is certainly much less specific than national law.[103]

Nonetheless, for adherents, reference to transnational public policy in cases of corruption "is not entirely obsolete" since the multilateral conventions that do exist are emphatic in the criminalization of such conduct but do not address the civil consequences of corruption in such prescriptive terms.[104] *World Duty Free* has been held up, including by Crawford and Mertenskötter, as a case that identifies a transnational public policy that not only proscribes corruption, but also a supposedly universally-upheld consequence for corruption—the inadmissibility of claims. If true, this may for some justify a tribunal's finding that an investment tainted by corruption or fraud is inadmissible, notwithstanding any provision under national law that allows contracts tainted by corruption to obtain relief. Moreover, in the investment treaty context, transnational public policy has also been referenced in

---

[99]*World Duty Free Company Limited v. The Republic of Kenya*, ICSID Case No. ARB/00/7, Award ¶157 (04 October 2006).

[100]*World Duty Free Company Limited v. The Republic of Kenya*, ICSID Case No. ARB/00/7, Award ¶157 (04 October 2006). (tribunal considered whether the fact that a contract was concluded further to actions constituting corruption might justify its invalidation, not only by virtue of contract law principles with respect to fraud, but also by the invocation of public order, in either the municipal or international context. The tribunal declined to allow the Claimant to rely on the legal rights contained in the contract due to its "breach of public order.").

[101]*See* Donovan (2007), p. 215; Richardson v. Mellish, 2 Bing 229, 303 (1824) *cited in* Reisman (2007), p. 849. ("Public Policy; – it is an unruly horse, and when once you get astride it, you never know where it will carry you. It may lead you from the sound law. It is never argued at all but when other points fail").

[102]*See* Lamm and Moloo (2010), p. 716.

[103]*See* Redfern (2007), p. 874.

[104]*See* Kessedijan (2007), p. 861.

sustaining the inadmissibility of claims despite the absence of an "in accordance with host State law" provision. However, commentators adhering to this point of view proceed from incorrect premises: *World Duty Free* by its own terms does not stand for the inadmissibility of claims when contracts are declared void because of corruption—indeed, by its own terms, *World Duty Free* held out the possibility of restitution for the investor even after the contract was avoided, with the tribunal left open the possibility of "legal consequences following the avoidance of the Agreement".[105] More recent scholarship also casts a critical eye on the notion that transnational public policy exists mandating a certain consequence for corrupt acts. Joachim Drude's comparative study in 2018 asks "whether it is appropriate in the investment arbitration context to deny contracts or investments produced by corruption any form of protection as the tribunals in *World Duty Free, Metal-Tech* and *Spentex* have done, relying considerations of international (transnational) public policy." After a "comparative analysis of how several jurisdictions deal with the issue", Drude concludes that, subject to certain limitations, it is not against international (transnational) public policy to accord protection to contracts and investments tainted by corruption."[106] If neither national law nor transnational public policy support the assertion that claim inadmissibility and/or a lack of jurisdiction are the proper civil consequences of a finding of corruption, does international law mandate a different rule?

3.3   The Consequences of Corruption in International Law and Investment Arbitration

The importance of ascertaining the actual content of international law in anti-corruption decisionmaking cannot be understated. Crawford and Mertenskötter maintain that States might not ultimately be responsible for the corruption of public officials under the framework of the ILC Articles because of the supposed existence of a primary rule that mandates an outcome having the practical effect of insulating host States from responsibility, at least for consummated corruption. The matter of State responsibility for corruption is thus intimately tied with what kind of corruption is being invoked, and the consequences attendant to proven corruption: when a tribunal determines that contracts or investments tainted by corruption during the

---

[105] *World Duty Free Company Limited v. The Republic of Kenya*, ICSID Case No. ARB/00/7, Award ¶186 (04 October 2006). ("there may be legal consequences following the avoidance of the Agreement, although restitutio in integrum cannot include the return of the bribe to the Claimant: see Logic Rose v. Southend United (1988), per Mr. Justice Millett, pp. 1263–1264. These legal consequences are not pleaded claims by the Claimant in this proceeding and they do not form part of this Award."). *See also* Drude (2018), pp. 695–696; Llamzon and Sinclair (2015), p. 529.

[106] *See* Drude (2018), pp. 665–718. ("This article analyses whether it is appropriate in the investment arbitration context to deny contracts or investments procured by corruption any form of protection as the tribunals in World Duty Free, Metal-Tech and Spentex have done, relying on.

time the investment leads to a lack of jurisdiction or the inadmissibility of claims, the State is effectively not held responsible for the corrupt acts its public official freely facilitated or participated in. The consequences of corruption in that case are shifted to the investor alone, who will not be able to pursue its claims. Thus, whether State responsibility attaches to proven instances of corruption requires an inquiry into the *content* of the international law against corruption itself. In that sense, any "primary rule" that might exist necessitating a lack of jurisdiction or inadmissibility is dispositive.

3.3.1 "Corruption" Is Not Monolithic: Distinguishing Bribery from Influence Peddling and Their Consequences

There is no doubt whatsoever that corruption—particularly in its paradigmatic form in international trade and investment, transnational bribery—is proscribed under international law. Beginning in the late 1990s, multiple multilateral conventions have been dedicated to combating foreign bribery and other corrupt practices, and all contemporary States' formal laws prohibit corruption in its different forms. It does bear recalling that this consensus in itself is an achievement: the long history of transnational corruption with little adverse consequence is well documented, and states such as Germany continued well into the 1990s allowed their companies operating abroad to claim bribe payments as legitimate tax-deductible expenses.

The content of the proscription is less precise, however. Much of international anti-corruption law consists of *lex lata* proscriptions whose consequences are left to States to enact and implement. States have continued to leave the enforcement of international anti-corruption norms to national authorities, refusing to create any effective international control mechanisms for combating transnational corruption—a somewhat disturbing indication that for all the rhetoric about the desire to punish and eradicate corruption, States remain unserious about doing anything concrete to add coercive teeth to the prohibitions, at least at the international level.[107] As to the persons whose actions are proscribed, the 1997 OECD Anti-Bribery Convention, one of the pillars of international anti-corruption norms, is focused exclusively on the criminalization of the offer or payment of a bribe to foreign public officials by the foreign private entity,[108] and does not deal with the "demand" side of the corruption equation—the acceptance or solicitation of that bribe by the public official.

---

[107]Llamzon (2014), pp. 66–67 and 74–77.

[108]OECD Convention on Combating Bribery of Foreign Public Officials in International Business Transactions, Article 1(1), *signed on* 17 December 1997, S. Treaty Doc. O. 10-43 ("[e]ach Party shall take such measures as may be necessary to establish that it is a criminal offence under its law for any person intentionally to offer, promise or give any undue pecuniary or other advantage, whether directly or through intermediaries, to a foreign public official, for that official or for a third party, in order that the official act or refrain from acting in relation to the performance of official duties, in order to obtain or retain business or other improper advantage in the conduct of international business.").

This focus on only the 'supply' side of bribery was subsequently rectified by the 2003 U.N. Convention Against Corruption, the most universally accepted and comprehensive anti-corruption framework for the international community.[109] As to both national and transnational bribery, at least, the United Nations Convention against Corruption (UNCAC) requires States to criminalize *both* the "promise, offering or giving, to a public official, directly or indirectly" (the supply side) *and* importantly, "the solicitation and acceptance by a public official, directly or indirectly, of an undue advantage"[110] (the demand side). UNCAC also requires the State Party to enact laws and other measures to prevent "embezzlement, misappropriation or other diversion of property by a public official."[111]

However, other forms of corruption identified by UNCAC are not deemed by the treaty (and therefore by the States parties) to be mandatory in nature: trading in influence ("influence peddling"), abuse of functions, illicit enrichment, concealment, and bribery (as well as embezzlement) in the private sector[112] are all offenses that UNCAC identifies but does not mandate criminalization: States are only asked to "consider adopting such legislative and other measures as may be necessary" to create these offenses under each State party's domestic legislation.[113] In *Kim v. Uzbekistan*, the tribunal considered the dichotomy between the prohibitive treatment of transnational bribery and the optional treatment accorded to trading in influence and private bribery, and concluded that unlike bribery, 'trading in influence' as well as 'bribery in the private sector' did not fall within the scope of the international public policy against corruption.[114]

---

[109] As of December 2020, the UN Convention Against Corruption had 187 States Party, making it by far the most widely accepted of the international anti-corruption treaties. *See* United Nations Office on Drugs and Crime (2020) Signature and Ratification, https://www.unodc.org/unodc/en/corruption/ratification-status.html (last accessed 13 March 2021). Indeed UNCAC is among the most widely accepted multilateral treaties.

[110] UN General Assembly, *United Nations Convention Against Corruption*, A/RES/58/4, 58th Session (31 October 2003) Articles 15–16.

[111] UN General Assembly, *United Nations Convention Against Corruption*, A/RES/58/4, 58th Session (31 October 2003) Article 17. ("*Article 17. Embezzlement, misappropriation or other diversion of property by a public official.* Each State Party shall adopt such legislative and other measures as may be necessary to establish as criminal offences, when committed intentionally, the embezzlement, misappropriation or other diversion by a public official for his or her benefit or for the benefit of another person or entity, of any property, public or private funds or securities or any other thing of value entrusted to the public official by virtue of his or her position.")

[112] U UN General Assembly, *United Nations Convention Against Corruption*, A/RES/58/4, 58th Session (31 October 2003) Articles 18–22 & 24.

[113] For example, transnational bribery under UNCAC Article 16 states that "[e]ach State Party shall adopt such legislative and other measures . . .", whereas trading in influence under Article 18 states that "[e]ach State Party shall consider adopting such legislative and other measures. . ."

[114] *Vladislav Kim and others v. Republic of Uzbekistan*, ICSID Case No. ARB/13/6, Decision on Jurisdiction (08 March 2017), ¶¶ 595–596. (". . .the OECD Convention, which Respondent cites as indicative of international public policy, takes as its focus the bribery of government officials. Thus, the titular concern of the OECD Convention is 'Combating Bribery of Foreign Public Officials in International Business Transactions' and the substantive provisions of the Convention bear out this

In this sense, the case law's blanket identification of "corruption" as a violation of transnational public policy and international law lacks nuance. In *World Duty Free*, for example, the tribunal noted "that bribery or influence peddling, as well as both active and passive corruption, are sanctioned by criminal law in most, if not all, countries."[115] As seen above, the UN Convention supports this statement for national and transnational bribery as well as embezzlement by a public official, but not for trading in influence, abuse of functions, illicit enrichment, and bribery (and embezzlement) in the private sector. This remains true despite the fact that trading in influence is a species of corruption adjudicated by investment tribunals with increasing frequency.[116] Thus, however seemingly self-evident the international consensus

---

conclusion. The UN Convention, which Respondent also cites, also has this focus. Simultaneously, the Tribunal acknowledges that the effort to combat corruption is an evolving area. Insofar as the UN Convention makes broader reference to "Trading in Influence", or "Bribery in the Private Sector", the relevant articles of the Convention use the language "consider making". This language matches the evolving and serious effort to combat corruption. It also suggests a lower level of consensus amongst the parties to the Convention as to corruption within the private sector, a sector governed by a broad range of criminal statutes. In that sense, the language employed, if anything, supports the conclusion that the scope of international public policy is focused on the corruption.

[115]*World Duty Free Company Limited v. The Republic of Kenya*, ICSID Case No. ARB/00/7, Award ¶142 (04 October 2006). *See also World Duty Free Company Limited v. The Republic of Kenya*, ICSID Case No. ARB/00/7, Award ¶144 (04 October 2006 "[t]he same trend can be observed in Africa: on 11 July 2003, in Maputo, Mozambique, the Heads of States and Governments of the African Union approved a Convention on Preventing and Combating Corruption, which has been signed by 39 African States (including Kenya) and has already been ratified by 11 of these 39 States. In this Convention, the Member States of the African Union declare themselves 'concerned about the negative effects of corruption and impunity on the political, economic, social and cultural stability of African States and its devastating effects on the economic and social development of the African peoples'. They 'acknowledge that corruption undermines accountability and transparency in the management of public affairs as well as socio-economic development in the continent'. Article 4 of the Convention lists the acts of corruption to which it applies and covers in particular '*the solicitation or acceptance, directly or indirectly, by a public official or any other person, of any goods of monetary value or other benefit, such as a gift, favour, promise or advantage for himself or herself or for another person or entity, in exchange of any act or omission in the performance of his or her public functions*'. Under Article 5 of the Convention, legislative and other measures must be taken to establish such acts as offences.") (emphasis supplied).

[116]In *Union Fenosa Gas v. Egypt*, for example, the host State made serious allegations about the supposed use of a local partner to exert influence over the Egyptian Minister of Energy in negotiations over a long-term gas sale and purchase agreement; these allegations of influence peddling were ultimately dismissed by the Tribunal's majority for insufficient evidence. *Unión Fenosa Gas, S.A. v. Arab Republic of Egypt*, ICSID Case No. ARB/14/4, Award ¶7.6 (31 August 2018). ("The Respondent contends that the Damietta Project "was the result of influence peddling and corrupt practices as the then-Minister of Petroleum, Mr Sameh Fahmy, steered the Damietta LNG Project to UFG at the behest of a personal friend, Mr Yehia El Komy, based on their personal relationship and to enrich Mr El Komy."); 7.14 ("According to the Respondent, 'Mr El Komy's 'contribution' was nothing more than money funneled to him by Claimant in exchange for his personal connections and back-channel influence.'"); and para. 7.109 ("Mr El Komy and EATCO were not passive or secretive participants in the Damietta Project. He openly identified himself (with EATCO) and was publicly identified with UFACEX from the outset of his involvement in the Project with UFACEX. He did not act as a covert peddler of influence, with his principal's identity

is against corruption, the depth of that consensus starts to fray the more specific one goes into the kind of corruption that is at issue.

Simply put, international law recognizes differences in the various species of the genus corruption—the elements comprising the offenses of bribery, influence peddling, private corruption, and other modalities of corruption are not the same, nor are their consequences. When "corruption" is stated in the case law as being universally proscribed, what is actually being discussed is usually *bribery* (to be more specific, transnational bribery), in both its consummated and attempted forms (including solicitation and extortion). But this universal proscription does not, for now, extend to trading in influence, given the very real differences States have in differentiating between the use of influence in a non-offensive manner (such as lobbying) as opposed to the use of influence improperly, in order to obtain an advantage.[117]

The intention behind establishing the offense of 'trading in influence' codified in Article 18 of UNCAC was

> to meet a timeless need: to fill the gaps by targeting not only the specific quid pro quo of bribery, but also the various uses of influence to gain improper advantage from public officials, thus 'improv[ing] the battery of criminal law measures against corruption'.

> However, trading in influence's broadness of purpose is also arguably the source of its principal weakness: in order to act as a 'catch-all' offence, trading in influence lacks the precision found in other species of corruption under UNCAC, and can encompass conduct widely considered to be legal. Distinguishing between permitted lobbying, where the use of influence by an intermediary (who might also be called the 'peddler') to persuade public officials to act in ways favourable to a client, as opposed to improper influence that amounts to influence peddling, is sometimes a very fine line. Thus, unlike bribery, the elements of which are largely a matter of international consensus, trading in influence is a concept where uncertainty lingers as to its precise scope, which leads to its non-adoption as a mandatory offence under UNCAC, and continuing hesitance on the part of many states parties to embrace the offence fully.[118]

The difficulties of distinguishing between permitted lobbying and impermissible trading in influence lead to considerable variation in defining what precisely "influence peddling" is and where to draw the line when foreign investors in new markets employ intermediaries to secure concessions, licenses, or contracts.[119] Most

---

kept hidden from the Respondent's decision-makers. To this extent, the Tribunal accepts the Claimant's submission that no evidence exists, in this arbitration, of any "back-channel influence." However, the Tribunal does not accept that there was no "influence." It concludes that there was influence exercised by Mr El Komy over senior decisionmakers at the Ministry of Petroleum and EGPC over the SPA; but that it was not corrupt."). (Note: In full disclosure, the author was a member of the counsel team for the claimant in this case.) (Note: In full disclosure, the author was a member of the counsel team for the claimant in this case.)

[117]Llamzon (2019), pp. 192–209.

[118]Llamzon (2019), p. 193 *citing* Council of Europe, *Explanatory Report to the Criminal Law Convention on Corruption* para. 64 ("The purpose of the [Criminal Law Convention on Corruption] being to improve the battery of criminal law measures against corruption it appeared essential to introduce this offence of trading in influence, which would be relatively new to some States.")

[119]Llamzon (2019), pp. 197–199.

importantly for this essay, the consequences of influence peddling is usually at least an order of magnitude less draconian than for bribery. In Egypt, for example, influence peddling is a misdemeanour for a private party, carrying a penalty of detention of no more than 3 years with a fine of no less than two hundred nor more than five hundred Egyptian Pounds (about US$15 and US$30),[120] criminal consequences that are hardly the same as those attendant to bribery. In the same vein, the civil consequences of a finding of influence peddling would not necessarily be the same as that of bribery—if bribery does not lead to an automatic lack of jurisdiction or inadmissibility of claims (as discussed in the next section), then *a fortiori* the civil consequences of trading in influence would be significantly milder.

Finally, it should be noted that while the OECD Anti-Bribery Convention and the UNCAC oblige signatories to enact penal legislation in their States criminalizing certain forms of corruption such as transnational bribery, the act of making corruption an international crime subject to individual criminal responsibility would not negate State responsibility. The law on State responsibility does not differentiate between 'civil' and 'criminal' responsibility; in that sense, it is an undifferentiated regime. In a similar vein, Article 26 of UNCAC ascribes liability for corruption to legal persons in addition to natural persons, and requires States Parties to "ensure that legal persons held liable [. . .] are subject to effective, proportionate and dissuasive criminal or non-criminal sanctions, including monetary sanctions."

3.3.2 The Consequences of Bribery in International Law Are Not Binary, and Are Affected by the Unique Circumstances of Each Case

Crucially for the issue of State responsibility for corruption, the lack of consensus surrounding the substantive content of international anti-corruption law extends to the *consequences* of corruption, including the consequences of a finding that bribery occurred. The issue can be considered in two parts: *first*, whether any international legal principle exists concerning the consequences of corruption that would justify the lack of jurisdiction or inadmissibility of claims outcomes found in many cases; and *second*, whether a discernible rule limiting attributability of public official corruption upon the host State exists as a matter of international anti-corruption law.

International Anti-Corruption Treaties Contain No Rule Apportioning the Consequences of Corruption Solely to the Private Party or Investor
Under the UNCAC, there is no provision calling for contracts tainted by corruption to be unenforceable or void *ab initio*, nor for claims under such contracts to be automatically inadmissible or for courts to be deprived of jurisdiction.[121] Instead,

---

[120]Llamzon (2019), p. 199 *citing* Chazly (2005), pp. 191–193.

[121]*See* UN General Assembly, *United Nations Convention Against Corruption*, A/RES/58/4, 58th Session (31 October 2003) Article 34. (corruption is only a "relevant factor in legal proceedings to annul or rescind a contract").

Article 34 of that Convention leaves the question of consequences largely within the discretion of individual States:

Article 34. Consequences of acts of corruption

With due regard to the rights of third parties acquired in good faith, each State Party shall take measures, in accordance with the fundamental principles of its domestic law, to address consequences of corruption. In this context, States Parties may consider corruption a relevant factor in legal proceedings to annul or rescind a contract, withdraw a concession or other similar instrument or take any other remedial action.[122]

UNCAC thus does *not* require the automatic nullification of investment contracts or concessions as a consequence, much less provide for a lack of jurisdiction over, or the inadmissibility of, claims derived from those contracts. Rather, such issues are left for individual assessment by State Parties or arbitral tribunals.[123] Indeed, if anything, the weight of the international community rests firmly on maintaining that a contract tainted by corruption is *not* void *ab initio,* much less are claims relating to contracts that suffer such a taint *per se* inadmissible or without jurisdiction. In these cases, the court or tribunal can take "remedial action" (in the words of Article 34)— such contracts are considered voidable and can only be avoided by going through an annulment process through a court or tribunal, thus negating the idea of automatic inadmissibility.

The 1999 Council of Europe Civil Law Convention on Corruption ("Civil Law Convention") is the treaty that most directly addresses the question of what the civil consequences for corruption should be. The Civil Law Convention distinguishes between contracts "providing for corruption" (such as intermediary agreements through which the parties intended that bribes be paid), which must be considered null and void, and contracts "whose consent has been undermined by an act of corruption," which are voidable contracts that may be declared void by a proper court:[124]

Article 8.

Validity of contracts

---

[122]UN General Assembly, *United Nations Convention Against Corruption,* A/RES/58/4, 58th Session (31 October 2003) Article 34.

[123]Notably, the status of Article 34 of the Convention Against Corruption as a general principle of law and of public international law was confirmed in *Niko Resources (Bangladesh) Ltd. v. Bangladesh Petroleum Exploration ("Bapex") and Bangladesh Oil Gas and Mineral Corporation ("Petrobangla"),* ICSID Case Nos. ARB/10/11 and ARB/10/18, Decision on Jurisdiction, ¶446 (19 August 2013).

[124]Council of Europe Civil Convention on Corruption, Article 8, *signed on* 04 November 1999, ETS No. 174.

(1) Each Party shall provide in its internal law for any contract or clause of a contract providing for corruption to be null and void.

(2) Each Party shall provide in its internal law for the possibility of all parties to a contract whose consent has been undermined by an act of corruption to be able to apply to the court for the contract to be declared void, notwithstanding their right to claim for damages.

(1) Each party shall provide in its internal law for any contract or clause of a contract providing for corruption to be null and void.

(2) Each party shall provide in its internal law for the possibility for all parties to a contract whose consent has been undermined by an act of corruption to be able to apply to the court for the contract to be declared void, notwithstanding their right to claim for damages.[125]

Thus, whether or not a contract in the latter category (Article 8(2))—which is the type of contract that forms the source of claims in most treaty arbitrations—is ultimately found to be void, the consequence of corruption would not be a lack of jurisdiction over claims to which that contract is relevant.[126] This reflects the reality that, as discussed above, the civil consequences of a contract tainted by corruption under civil and common law systems alike do *not* deprive a tribunal of jurisdiction over a dispute but do include the potential voidability of that contract; and in turn, the voidability of the contract means that it is valid until avoided, and thus is subject to various legal defenses, such as principles of waiver, acquiescence, estoppel, and unjust enrichment.

In a similar vein, the principle of proportionality, which animates so much of international law,[127] also finds its way into the 1997 OECD Convention, which considered the proper consequences of a finding of bribery:

Article 3

Sanctions

- The bribery of a foreign public official shall be punishable by effective, proportionate and dissuasive criminal penalties. The range of penalties shall be comparable to that applicable to the bribery of the Party's own public officials and shall, in the case of natural persons, include deprivation of liberty sufficient to enable effective mutual legal assistance and extradition.

---

[125]Council of Europe Civil Convention on Corruption, Article 8, *signed on* 04 November 1999, ETS No. 174.

[126]In this regard, it should be noted that Judge Lagergren's influential decision in Case No. 1110, where he declined jurisdiction (or considered the claims inadmissible) on grounds of corruption, concerned a contract that had as its very object a corrupt purpose: that case involved an agency agreement between a company and a "consultant" to obtain Argentinian energy contracts on a 10% commission basis. In other words, this was an instance covered more by Article 8(1) of the Civil Law Convention than Article 8(2). Council of Europe Civil Convention on Corruption, Article 8, *signed on* 04 November 1999, ETS No. 174.

[127]On proportionality, within the context of treaty law, "the remedy must have some degree of equivalence with the alleged breach" (Greig 1993, p. 342) before withholding of performance of a reciprocal obligation is allowed. See also Art 60, Vienna Convention on the Law of Treaties (termination of a treaty for material breach). In that sense, proportionality also bears real similarities to the principles of reciprocity and counter-measures. On reciprocity, Judge Simma has observed that "a State basing a claim on a particular norm of international law must accept that rule as also binding upon itself." Simma, Reciprocity, MPEI para 15 (2008). As to counter-measures, "a State whose wrongful act has provoked or contributed to illegal (or what would normally be illegal) action by another, [retains] its right of complaint if such action was out of reasonable proportion or relation to the provocation or contributory acts." Fitzmaurice (1957) (Hague Academy of International Law 1957).

- In the event that, under the legal system of a Party, criminal responsibility is not applicable to legal persons, that Party shall ensure that legal persons shall be subject to effective, proportionate and dissuasive non-criminal sanctions, including monetary sanctions, for bribery of foreign public officials.

  [...][128]

Thus, as to the civil penalties envisaged for both natural and legal persons who engage in transnational bribery, the range of criminal as well as civil penalties must not only be effective and dissuasive, but also proportionate. As observed by Professor Reisman, decisionmakers must consider in light of Article 3 whether a finding of lack of jurisdiction or inadmissibility of claims due to bribery might not be a proportional response that dissuades such conduct on the part of the State: "Article 3 of the OCED [Anti-Bribery] Convention says...that sanctions, among other things, should be proportionate. One of the questions [...] will be: How do arbitration tribunals encountering these complex issues accommodate the general policy expressed in the OECD and many of the other anti-bribery conventions with the need for proportionality so that this problematic behaviour is disincentivized and not incentivized?"[129]

The Legality Doctrine and the Clean Hands Doctrine: **The Case Law on the Consequences of Corruption Is Evolving Away from Treating Corruption as a Binary Issue of Jurisdiction or Admissibility**

Given the above, specific rules on the consequences of corruption are more likely to arise from case law, not from multilateral anti-corruption treaties. As seen in the discussion of the *World Duty Free* and *Spentex* cases in Sect. 2 above, the case law in instances where findings of corruption are made tend to point towards the lack of jurisdiction or inadmissibility of claims. And in investment *treaty* arbitration, especially, accusations of investor wrongdoing have led increasingly to a set of binary outcomes:[130] if unproven, no results attach. But if proven, tribunals treat corruption as a complete defense, either due to (1) a lack of jurisdiction[131] or (2) the

---

[128]OECD Convention on Combating Bribery of Foreign Public Officials in International Business Transactions, Article 3, *signed on* 17 December 1997, S. Treaty Doc. O. 10-43.

[129]Bonucci and Reisman (2015), p. 245.

[130]Douglas (2014), p. 15. ("The answer to a jurisdictional objection must be to affirm or to deny, and yet the responses to an illegality in national law are not that straightforward and cannot be forced into a binary scheme. This suggests that respect for the integrity of the law of the host State as an argument for characterizing a plea of illegality as a jurisdictional objection must be rejected."); Llamzon (2014), pp. 1–2 ("arbitrators are routinely required by the law to decide in binary fashion, thereby taking overt or implied sides in favour of one party in cases where most, if not all, actors are tainted by corruption.").

[131]*Metal-Tech Ltd. v. The Republic of Uzbekistan*, ICSID Case No. ARB/10/3, Award, ¶422 (04 October 2013); *Fraport AG Frankfurt Airport Services Worldwide v. The Republic of the Philippines*, ICSID Case No. ARB/03/25, Award (16 August, 2007); *Inceysa Vallisoletana S.L. v. Republic of El Salvador*, ICSID Case No. ARB/03/26, Award (02 August2006); *TSA Spectrum de Argentina S.A. v. Argentine Republic*, ICSID Case No. ARB/05/5, Award (December 19, 2008).

inadmissibility of claims,[132] either of which stops the claimant's case dead in its tracks for all practical purposes, without any further evaluation of the respondent State's conduct. This limited range of consequences for illegal conduct has been described by Professor Zachary Douglas as "draconian,"[133] at least from the investor's perspective. By contrast, the consequences of illegality and corruption in *contract*-based investment arbitration tend to be decided together with the tribunal's overall decision on the merits, or at most, relate to the admissibility of the private party's claims.

The orthodox view is that the range of consequences that apply to instances of investor illegality apply even in the case of bribery. However, as discussed previously, bribery is uniquely bilateral in nature among the forms of illegality, because it by definition requires the active participation of public officials in order to succeed (the bilateral nature of corruption is discussed in Sect. 2 above). As the other forms of illegality are unilaterally committed by the investor against the host State, without the investor's participation, questions of State responsibility are not implicated in the way they are in the case of corruption.

The Legality Doctrine
In investment treaty arbitration, the prism through which investor wrongdoing is typically addressed is the "legality" (or "in accordance with law") clause found in many investment treaties (although expressed in varying ways), according to which investments are considered as such only when made "in accordance with" the laws of the host State.[134] Considerable case law and commentary view these clauses as a limit on a host State's consent to refer disputes to arbitration and thus, the formation of the agreement to arbitrate. Under this view, the 'legality' of an investment, including its compliance with anti-corruption laws, operates as a condition for jurisdiction,[135] with the "in accordance with law" provisions being considered as relating to "the validity of the investment and not its definition."[136]

---

[132]*See Plama Consortium Limited v. Republic of Bulgaria,* ICSID Case No. ARB/03/24, Award, August 27, 2008); *World Duty Free Company Limited v. The Republic of Kenya,* ICSID Case No. ARB/00/7, Award (04 October 2006).

[133]Douglas (2014), p. 22. ("It would appear that the category of violations that do not provoke a jurisdictional infirmity is expanding in the jurisprudence to avoid the draconian effects of the approach to the plea of illegality under consideration.") Douglas (2014), p. 27. ("Tribunals must exercise care in their recognition of grounds of international public policy given the draconian consequences that follow the application of this doctrine.").

[134]Schill (2012), pp. 281–323. (Differentiates between (1) the "in accordance with host State law" sub-clause found in many treaty definitions of investment; (2) clauses governing the admission of new investments; and (3) clauses defining temporal scope of application, which confirm that a treaty applies *inter alia* to investments lawfully made prior to its entry into force.).

[135]*See* Knahr (2007), p. 5; Bottini (2010), p. 297; Kriebaum (2010), p. 307; Moloo and Khachaturian (2011), p. 1473; Schill (2012); Newcombe (2012), p. 187; Miles (2012), p. 18.

[136]*Salini Costruttori S.p.A. and Italstrade S.p.A. v. Kingdom of Morocco,* ICSID Case No. ARB/00/4, Decision on Jurisdiction ¶46 (July 23, 2001); *Tokios Tokeles v. Ukraine,* ICSID Case No. ARB/02/18, Decision on Jurisdiction ¶84 (April 29, 2004); *Railroad Development Corporation v. Republic of Guatemala,* ICSID Case No. ARB/07/23, Second Decision on Objections to

Metal-Tech v Uzbekistan was the first instance where an investment tribunal concluded that corruption had occurred was considered to have impacted upon the tribunal's very jurisdiction. That tribunal found that there was a lack of consent to arbitrate disputes tainted by investor illegality by virtue of the legality clause contained in the underlying investment treaty: "the Contracting Parties to an investment treaty may limit the protections of the treaty to investments made in accordance with the laws and regulations of the host State. Depending on the wording of the investment treaty, this limitation may be a bar to jurisdiction, *i.e.* to the procedural protections under the BIT, or a defense on the merits, i.e. to the application of the substantive treaty guarantees."[137]

Metal-Tech's lack of jurisdiction finding is consistent with the manner by which issues of fraud and other illegalities have resulted in positive findings of investor wrongdoing in other cases, the majority of which concluded that the tribunal had no jurisdiction, whether for violation of the legality clause in an investment treaty,[138] on the basis of failure to prove that the claimant is a covered "investor",[139] or broader still, because fraudulent conduct as a violation of "transnational public policy" should result in a denial of jurisdiction.[140]

However, strong arguments exist that legality clauses have been misunderstood and misapplied. In *Fraport v Philippines*, arbitrator Bernardo Cremades dissented from the majority stating that such clauses only concern whether "assets", which would otherwise qualify as investments", could in the context of that case be owned by foreigners.[141] Professor Douglas endorses Dr. Cremades' dissent and adds that legality clauses are more properly interpreted as having imposed only the conditions upon which a beneficial interest in an asset (an investment) may be formally acquired under host State law, *i.e.*, the formal conditions under host State law by which an investor might acquire title to an asset.[142] Treaty protection will arise upon the

---

Jurisdiction ¶140 (May 18, 2004);*Ioannis Kardassopoulos v. The Republic of Georgia,* ICSID Case No. ARB/05/18, Decision on Jurisdiction ¶182 (July 6, 2007).

[137]*Metal-Tech Ltd. v. The Republic of Uzbekistan,* ICSID Case No ARB/10/3, Award, 127 (04 October 2013).

[138]*See Fraport AG Frankfurt Airport Services Worldwide v. The Republic of the Philippines,* ICSID Case No. ARB/03/25, Award (16 August, 2007).

[139]*See, e.g. Cementownia "Nowa Huta" S.A. v. Republic of Turkey,* ICSID Case No. ARB(AF)/06/2, Award (September 17, 2009); *Europe Cement Investment & Trade S.A. v. Republic of Turkey,* ICSID Case No. ARB(AF)/07/2, Award (August 13, 2009); *Libananco Holdings Co. Limited v. Republic of Turkey,* ICSID Case No. ARB/06/8, Award (September 2, 2011).

[140]*See e.g. Inceysa Vallisoletana S.L. v. Republic of El Salvador,* ICSID Case No. ARB/03/26, Award (02 August 2006).

[141]*Fraport AG Frankfurt Airport Services Worldwide v. The Republic of the Philippines,* ICSID Case No. ARB/03/25, Dissenting Opinion of Bernardo M. Cremades ¶¶ 12–14 (16 August 2007).

[142]Douglas (2014), p. 159. Douglas' thesis begins from the premise that treaty protection will arise merely upon the acquisition of an asset falling within the scope of the definition of "investment" in an applicable treaty. From this, he concludes that a breach of host State law will only exceptionally vitiate the agreement to arbitrate disputes, which commercial arbitral tribunals, by analogy, widely consider to be "separable" from the "main" contract in which they are embedded. Douglas does not

acquisition of an asset falling within the scope of the treaty's definition of "investment", provided those formal conditions are met. Prof. Douglas observes that illegality will seldom, if ever, impinge upon the formation of the agreement to arbitrate disputes. He considers that a breach of host State law will almost never prevent the formation of an agreement to refer investment disputes to arbitration, which he believes are matters of separability and *competence-competence*. It would in his view be wrong to deny a remedy for such investments outright, as the consequences of such wrongdoing are seldom so severe under host State law.

The logic of that view is compelling. Legality clauses are essentially a *renvoi* to national law—and so the *entirety* of national law, including how corruption issues would be treated under that national law before national courts, should be considered in the calculus. As discussed in Sect. 3.1 above, in most cases, national courts are not barred from deciding upon disputes where the underlying contract suffers a taint of corruption (as discussed in Sect. 3.1 above)—as with other forms of fraud and illegality, corruption is usually not considered a jurisdictional issue, nor an issue that automatically bars the admissibility of claims. Indeed, when properly read, even *World Duty Free* stands for this proposition, as the case left open the possibility of non-contractual relief being accorded to the company.[143]

This less binary approach to corruption as a jurisdictional issue finds support from other leading scholars, who have considered treating corruption (as well as other forms of illegality) as an automatic jurisdictional issue to be fundamentally unlawful and unfair. John Crook, for example, argues that the all-or-nothing approach of the corruption defense as posing a jurisdictional bar is inequitable, allows for unjust enrichment, and has negative effects on the arbitration system: "[t]he binary rule makes an investor bear a heavy price for the actions of the State's agents or representatives, while the State potentially typically bears no consequences for misconduct of its agents."[144] Viewing the issue from a policy-oriented perspective, Professor W Michael Reisman states:

---

directly address, however, the arbitral practice holding that "in accordance with law" clauses qualify the scope of the host State's offer to arbitrate disputes (and, in extension, to also make contingent the offer of substantive treaty protection) and thereby directly impinge upon the formation of an agreement to arbitrate.

[143]In their edition of Oppenheim's International Law, Sir Robert Jennings and Sir Arthur Watts stated that the law of nations is part of English law and has been repeatedly acted on by English courts. Jennings and Watts (2008), pp. 56–57. That said, English courts have recently expressed caution regarding the use of customary international law as a direct source of rights and obligations under English law: R Al-Saadoon & Others v. Secretary of State for Defence (2015) High Court of Justice, Queen's Bench Division, Case Nos: CO/5608/2008; CO/8695/2009; CO/6345/2008; CO/9925/2008; CO/11858/2009; CO/11442/2008; CO/953/2009; CO/9719/2009; CO/12803/2009; CO/1684/2010; CO/2631/2010, C8620/2010, Judiciary UK [Online]. Available at: https://www.judiciary.uk/wp-content/uploads/2015/12/r-al-saadoon-v-secretary-of-state-for-defence-2015-ewhc-715-admin.pdf (Accessed: 13 March 2021) (the 'proposition that a customary rule may be sued on as a cause of action in the English courts is perhaps not so clear cut').

[144]Crook (2015), p. 311.

Now, it does not seem to me that this is a model that provides a proper incentive for host State officials who participate in the bribery process to comply with the general policy. If you are willing to contemplate this dimension, then a series of very awkward questions are presented of the international arbitrators who decide these cases. Article 3 of the OCED [Anti-Bribery] Convention says. . .that sanctions, among other things, should be proportionate. One of the questions. . .will be: How do arbitration tribunals encountering these complex issues accommodate the general policy expressed in the OECD and many of the other anti-bribery conventions with the need for proportionality so that this problematic behavior is disincentivized and not incentivized? . . . When we talk about sanctions, we ought to make a distinction between sanctions that are effective and actually tend to disincentivize subsequent behavior and sanctions that are ceremonial taps on the wrist.

Similarly, ICJ Judge Joan Donoghue has weighed the question of potential corruption deterrence on the part of investors vis-à-vis host States in the case law and observes that the "contemporary focus is the role of the investor, not that of the host state" and expresses doubts about the deterrent effect of "impos[ing] the costs of corruption entirely on the investor"—in her view, "it is hard to see how that knowledge would dissuade [public officials] from taking bribes. Ironically, their acts of personal greed may actually insulate the host State from investor claims." Ultimately, "respondent States are left unaccountable either for corruption that they may have endorsed or for the measures that gave rise to the investor's claim."[145]

In contrast to the relative rigidity of *Metal-Tech v Uzbekistan* in requiring that findings of corruption deprive the tribunal of jurisdiction, more recent case law has tended to take policy considerations more seriously, and emphasizing the need to take proportionality and host State accountability for enforcing anti-corruption norms more seriously, and not simply give States a free pass for corrupt acts done by public officials in an abuse of their public power (if not the State's tacit *imprimatur*). As explained in *Kim v. Uzbekistan*, when assessing the legality requirement found in an investment treaty, tribunals should not focus solely on the "gravity of the law" but also review the "particulars of the investor's violation."[146] *Kim* rejected the binary approach to "legality clause" analysis by explicitly taking proportionality analysis into account: it stated that in considering corruption allegations it would be "guided by the principle of proportionality."[147] The *Kim* tribunal found that it was required to "balance the object of promoting economic relations by providing a stable investment framework with the harsh consequence of denying the application of the [treaty] in total:"[148] Specifically, a

[t]ribunal must balance the object[ive] of promoting economic relations by providing a stable investment framework with the harsh consequence of denying the application of the BIT in total when the investment is not made in compliance with legislation. The denial of

---

[145]Donoghue (2015), pp. 760–761.

[146]*Vladislav Kim and others v. Republic of Uzbekistan*, ICSID Case No. ARB/13/6, Decision on Jurisdiction (08 March 2017), ¶ 398.

[147]*Vladislav Kim and others v. Republic of Uzbekistan*, ICSID Case No. ARB/13/6, Decision on Jurisdiction (08 March 2017), ¶ 413.

[148]*Vladislav Kim and others v. Republic of Uzbekistan*, ICSID Case No. ARB/13/6, Decision on Jurisdiction (08 March 2017), ¶ 396.

the protections of the BIT is a harsh consequence that is a proportional response only when its application is triggered by noncompliance with a law that results in a compromise of a correspondingly significant interest of the Host State.[149]

The *Kim v. Uzbekistan* tribunal went on to explain that the phrase "noncompliance with a law that results in a compromise of a correspondingly significant interest of the Host State" was chosen "so as to focus more sharply on the substantive scope of the legality requirement not on whether the law is fundamental but rather on the significance of the violation."[150] On this basis, it found that the focus should not solely be on the "gravity of the law," but should also include a review of the "particulars of the investor's violation."[151] Indeed, according to the tribunal, "*[s]eriousness to the Host State is to be determined by the overall outcome, which will depend on the seriousness of the law viewed in concert with the seriousness of the violation.*"[152] The tribunal concluded that the denial of the treaty protections "is a proportional response only" in the event of "noncompliance with a law that results in a compromise of a correspondingly significant interest of the Host State."[153]

Kim marks a significant watershed in the case law, as it directly challenges the view in *Metal-Tech* and its progeny that the existence of a legality clause found in a BIT makes the analysis of corruption straightforward and binary—even if bribery were proven (and it was ultimately not proven in that case), *Kim* rejects the idea that the automatic outcome in that situation would be a denial of jurisdiction because of a withholding of consent on the part of the State to arbitrate. What *Kim* focuses on instead is to interpret the "bare bones language" of legality clauses through the "application of a principle. The use of principle-based reasoning rather than rule-based categorical divides is more appropriate when States themselves in drafting a treaty provide only objectives. [...] The Tribunal [...] aims to identify the underlying principle that can provide a more nuanced definition of the limits of

---

[149] *Vladislav Kim and others v. Republic of Uzbekistan*, ICSID Case No. ARB/13/6, Decision on Jurisdiction ¶20 (08 March 2017) (emphasis added). *See also Metalpar S.A. and Buenos Aire S.A. v. The Argentine* Republic, ICSID Case No. ARB/03/5, Decision on Jurisdiction ¶¶83–84 (April 27, 2006) (excerpts of English translation) [hereinafter "Metalpar"]. ("In the Tribunal's view, the lack of adequate registration could be sanctioned by refusing to register certain documents of the company, through a notice of warning, or by imposition of a fine on the company or its directors, but it would be disproportionate to punish this omission to register by denying the investor an essential protection such as access to ICSID tribunals.").

[150] *Vladislav Kim and others v. Republic of Uzbekistan*, ICSID Case No. ARB/13/6, Decision on Jurisdiction (08 March 2017), ¶ 398.

[151] *Vladislav Kim and others v. Republic of Uzbekistan*, ICSID Case No. ARB/13/6, Decision on Jurisdiction (08 March 2017), ¶ 398.

[152] *Vladislav Kim and others v. Republic of Uzbekistan*, ICSID Case No. ARB/13/6, Decision on Jurisdiction (08 March 2017), ¶ 398. (emphasis added)

[153] *Vladislav Kim and others v. Republic of Uzbekistan*, ICSID Case No. ARB/13/6, Decision on Jurisdiction (08 March 2017), ¶ 396.

the acts of noncompliance that would trigger the legality requirement."[154] The Tribunal then states:

> In the Tribunal's view, the interpretive task is guided by the principle of proportionality. The Tribunal must balance the object of promoting economic relations by providing a stable investment framework with the harsh consequence of denying the application of the BIT in total when the investment is not made in compliance with legislation. The denial of the protections of the BIT is a harsh consequence that is a proportional response only when its application is triggered by noncompliance with a law that results in a compromise of a correspondingly significant interest of the Host State.[155]

By engaging explicitly in principle-based proportionality analysis, *Kim* also goes a significant step further than the *Spentex v. Uzbekistan* tribunal, which predated the *Kim* award by a few months.[156] As discussed earlier, the host State raised allegations of bribery as a defense against host State claims, arguing that the investor had engaged consultants (including the daughter of a high government official) and paid them millions of dollars that were actually bribes given to Uzbek officials to win a bid for textile plant contracts. The tribunal found that bribery had occurred, but that Uzbekistan was not going to do anything about the corruption vis-à-vis its own officials, with no domestic law enforcement in the country regarding corruption officials forthcoming, and even a refusal to identify the officials who had participated in the bribery scheme.[157] The Tribunal expressed concern about the "perverse incentives for respondent States in the context of corruption. It would ask an investment tribunal to dismiss a claimant's claim, while granting impunity to a respondent State both in respect of the alleged corruption and the claimant's investment claims."[158] The tribunal voiced its disquiet that the claims would have to be dismissed following the legality doctrine despite the "implication of the finding of corruption is that not only the Claimant, but also the Respondent [State], engaged in or condoned illegal activities."[159] The tribunal stated that "an important policy dilemma" had now confronted international investment tribunals in view of the "approach of the tribunals in *Metal-Tech* and in *World Duty Free*":

> An investment procured by corruption always involves two sides: those who bribe and those who take bribes. Where corruption routinely leads to the dismissal of investment claims, respondent States with corrupt officials will always benefit from their own corruption by

---

[154]*Vladislav Kim and others v. Republic of Uzbekistan*, ICSID Case No. ARB/13/6, Decision on Jurisdiction (08 March 2017), ¶ 399.

[155]*Vladislav Kim and others v. Republic of Uzbekistan*, ICSID Case No. ARB/13/6, Decision on Jurisdiction (08 March 2017), ¶ 20.

[156]The *Spentex v Uzbekistan* Award is dated 27 December 2016; whereas the *Kim v Uzbekistan* Decision on Jurisdiction is dated March 8, 2017.

[157]Betz (2017), p. 134 *citing Spentex Netherlands, B.V. v. Republic of Uzbekistan*, ICSID Case No. ARB/13/26, Award ¶944 (27 December 2016).

[158]Betz (2017), p. 134 *citing Spentex Netherlands, B.V. v. Republic of Uzbekistan*, ICSID Case No. ARB/13/26, Award ¶940 (27 December 2016).

[159]*Spentex Netherlands, B.V. v. Republic of Uzbekistan*, ICSID Case No. ARB/13/26, Award ¶970 (27 December 2016).

preempting even otherwise legitimate claims that arise subsequently during the operation of an investment. Such a situation could even lead to a perverse inventive for States to attract foreign investments through corruption, thereby acquiring an "insurance policy" against investment claims.

Where a finding of corruption leads to the dismissal of investment claims, claimants are clearly "punished" for their misbehavior, whereas respondent States are "off the hook." To award them costs for such a "victory" would be wholly inappropriate. Likewise, making them simply pay their own costs (and share the costs of the proceedings) would be a "cheap way out," devoid of any negative consequences for the corrupt conduct itself (as distinct from the conduct that led to the claimant's claims and thus the costs of the proceeding).[160]

While the *Spentex* tribunal concluded that "for the time being, arbitral tribunals (which apply the law and do not create it) are somewhat helpless to 'sanction' respondent States that have engaged in corruption, since tribunals primarily possess tools to deny remedies to claimants that have engaged in corruption",[161] the *Kim* tribunal's Decision on Jurisdiction points to the possibility of employing the international legal principle of proportionality to allow tribunals the possibility of greater nuance in modulating the consequences of corruption notwithstanding the existence of a legality clause. Moreover, and as discussed further in Sect. 4 below, the default "secondary" rules found in the law on State responsibility, as codified in the ILC Articles—including principles of waiver, estoppel, and acquiescence—may provide further tools for arbitrators to arrive at outcomes that better comport with the anti-corruption goals set by international law itself.

One further point bears consideration. Cases such as *Metal-Tech, Spentex,* and *Kim* are all grounded on investment treaties where an explicit legality clause exists. In the absence of such an express clause, would the scope of the host State's consent to arbitration be construed differently? Some tribunals have concluded that a legality requirement can be found by inference, whether in the ICSID Convention or in an investment treaty.[162] Most tribunals, however, have rejected any reading of the ICSID Convention, at least, that would import a sweeping jurisdictional requirement of lawfulness by implication, even when considering that States may expressly condition access to treaty protection in this manner.[163]

---

[160]*Spentex Netherlands, B.V. v. Republic of Uzbekistan,* ICSID Case No. ARB/13/26, Award ¶¶973–974 (27 December 2016).

[161]*Phoenix Action, Ltd. v. The Czech Republic,* ICSID Case No. ARB/06/5, Award ¶¶136–143 (April 15, 2009).

[162]*Phoenix Action, Ltd. v. The Czech Republic,* ICSID Case No. ARB/06/5, Award ¶¶136–143 (April 15, 2009).

[163]*See, e.g., Saba Fakes v. Republic of Turkey,* ICSID Case No. ARB/07/20, Award ¶114 (July 14, 2010) ("As far as the legality of investments is concerned, this question does not relate to the definition of 'investment' provided in Article 25(1) of the ICSID Convention and in Article 1(b) of the BIT. In the Tribunal's opinion, while the ICSID Convention remains neutral on this issue, bilateral investment treaties are at liberty to condition their application and the whole protection they afford, including consent to arbitration, to a legality requirement of one form or another."); Luttrell (2019), pp. 139–140. The *Phoenix Action* tribunal arguably over-extended the principle that treaties must be interpreted in "good faith" (Vienna Convention, Article 31) by transforming it into

Overall, as with many issues on corruption decisionmaking, much discretion remains in the hands of arbitrators who can pick from a significant number of cases on both sides of the issue (although the more ascendant view is likely that breach of host State law whether at the inception of an investment or subsequently is not a jurisdictional matter). But assuming implicit (or even explicit) legality clauses do not necessarily lead to a lack of jurisdiction outcome, following the *Kim v Uzbekistan,* tribunals would still need to grapple with the possibility of another principle of international law being made to apply to issues of corruption—the clean hands doctrine and its cognates.

The Clean Hands Doctrine and Its Roman Law Cognates

In seeking to establish a primary rule under international anti-corruption law that would insulate host States from responsibility for corruption, Professor Crawford invoked the *in pari delicto melio est conditio possidentis* as the source.[164] The doctrine is frequently phrased as "he who has done iniquity shall not have equity",[165] or, "he who desires relief in equity must himself be free from fault".[166] These, plus a host of related Latin maxims derived from Roman law with the same general effect,[167] are variants of the doctrine "he who comes into equity must come with clean hands",[168] *i.e.,* the clean hands doctrine (sometime expressed as the "unclean" hands doctrine).[169] Whatever the manner of expression, the doctrine demands that a

---

an implicit substantive component of the term "investment". *See* Miles (2012), p. 35. (*"Phoenix Action* is best explained as juridical overreach").

[164]Crawford and Mertenskotter (2016), p. 38.

[165]*See, e.g., Reynolds v. Boland,* 202 Pa. 642, 52 Atl. 19 (1902).

[166]*See, e.g., Harms v. Stern,* 231 Fed. 645 (C.C.A. 2d, 1916).

[167]*See Inceysa Vallisoletana S.L. v. Republic of El Salvador,* ICSID Case No. ARB/03/26, Award ¶¶239–240 (002 August 2006), which links the principle *nemo auditur propriam turpitudinem allegans* and six related Latin maxims. *See also* Llamzon and Sinclair (2015), p. 508 ("The "clean hands" doctrine is sometimes termed the "unclean hands" or "dirty hands" doctrine. The clean hands doctrine is also closely related to several other Latin maxims, such as *ex delicto non oritur actio* ("an unlawful act cannot serve as the basis of an action at law", *nemo ex suo delicto meliorem suam conditionem facit* ("no can put himself in a better legal position by means of a delict"), *ex turpi causa non oritur* ("an action cannot arise from a dishonourable cause"), *inadimplenti non est adimplendum* ("one has no need to respect his obligation if the counter-party has not respected its own"), and *nullus commodum capere potest de in juria sua propria* ("no one can be allowed to take advantage of his own wrong").

[168]Precision Instrument Mfg Co v Automotive Co 324 US 806, 814 (1945). The US Supreme Court continued: "This maxim is far more than a mere banality. It is a self-imposed ordinance that closes the doors of a court of equity to one tainted with inequitableness or bad faith relative to the matter in which he seeks relief, however improper may have been the behavior of the defendant. That doctrine is rooted in the historical concept of court of equity as a vehicle for affirmatively enforcing the requirements of conscience and good faith. This presupposes a refusal on its part to be "the abetter of iniquity.""

[169]*See* Kreindler (2010), p. 319. ("Reliance on the maxim *ex turpi causa non oritur actio* can and should be considered as another application of the Unclean Hands Doctrine.").

claimant seeking equitable relief come into court having acted equitably in that matter for which he seeks a remedy.

The clean hands doctrine and its related principles have been used as a legal basis for barring a claimant's claims due to its illegal or improper conduct in relation to those claims.[170] Applying that rule, claims tainted by wrongdoing will not succeed, and the loss will lie where it falls. The principles that underpin the clean hands doctrine are said to be judicial integrity, justice, and the public interest.[171] The inequitable conduct which causes the clean hands doctrine to be invoked typically must be willful, and the claimant's alleged misconduct must have reference to the matters in controversy. The doctrine is invoked and applied to deny relief in three general circumstances, that is, where transactions are (1) fraudulent; (2) illegal; or (3) unconscionable.

The clean hands doctrine as found in national law has been discussed and applied by ICSID tribunals in contractual arbitrations where the investments in question were tainted by corruption. In *World Duty Free v. Kenya,* the tribunal decided that an investor that has engaged in bribery comes to arbitration with unclean hands in relation to its investment and should therefore not be entitled to pursue a claim to protect that investment, regardless of whether the host State has facilitated or participated in the wrongdoing.[172] Specifically, the Tribunal found that the claimant's pleaded claims were inadmissible because its investment had been tainted by bribery:

> In conclusion, as regards public policy both under English law and Kenyan law (being materially identical) and on the specific facts of this case, the Tribunal concludes that the Claimant is not legally entitled to maintain any of its pleaded claims in these proceedings on the ground of ex turpi causa non oritur actio.[173]

By upholding Kenya's *ex turpi causa* defence in this manner, the tribunal appears to have applied the clean hands doctrine as found to exist in municipal law as a standalone basis for dismissing claims. How about international law?

As investment treaty arbitration is created and sustained by international law, which therefore forms part of the applicable law in investment treaty arbitrations,[174]

---

[170]*See* Martin (1994) (describing the clean hands doctrine as follows: "a person who makes a claim in equity must be free from any taint of fraud with respect to that claim. For example, a person seeking to enforce an agreement must not himself be in breach of it"); International News Service v. The Associated Press, 248 U.S. 215 (U.S. Supreme Court 1918) (stating that the court would "refuse to aid a complainant in protecting any right acquired or retained by inequitable conduct.").

[171]*Precision Instrument Mfg. Co. v. Automotive Maintenance Mach. Co.*, 324 U.S. at 815.

[172]*World Duty Free Company Limited v. The Republic of Kenya*, ICSID Case No. ARB/00/7, Award ¶¶180–181 (04 October 2006).

[173]*World Duty Free Company Limited v. The Republic of Kenya*, ICSID Case No. ARB/00/7, Award ¶179 (04 October 2006).

[174]*See, e.g.,* Convention on the Settlement of Investment Disputes between States and nationals of other States, Article 42(1), *entered into force* on 14 October 1966, 575 UNTS 159. ("The Tribunal shall decide a dispute in accordance with such rules of law as may be agreed by the parties. In the absence of such agreement, the Tribunal shall apply the law of the Contracting State party to the

it has been asserted that the clean hands doctrine can be applied by investment tribunals even in the absence of support from applicable national law. But the status of that doctrine in international law is far from settled.

Having been adopted in the domestic legal orders of many States, the clean hands doctrine is frequently asserted to qualify as a "general principle of law" pursuant to Article 38(1)(c) of the ICJ Statute.[175] Some tribunals have applied principles that may arguably be considered part of the clean hands doctrine in the nineteenth[176] and twentieth[177] centuries, finding claims inadmissible where claimants had engaged in wrongful conduct in relation to their claims. A number of individual opinions by judges of the Permanent Court of International Justice[178]

---

dispute (including its rules on the conflict of laws) *and such rules of international law as may be applicable*") (emphasis added).

[175]The application of the clean hands doctrine in international law also finds support in the writings of commentators, another source of international law pursuant to the Statute of the International Court of Justice, Article 38(1)(d), *signed on* 26 June 1945, 33 UNTS 993. *See, e.g.* Fitzmaurice (1957), p. 119. ("'He who comes to equity for relief must come with clean hands'. Thus a State which is guilty of illegal conduct may be deprived of the necessary *locus standi in judicio* for complaining of corresponding illegalities on the part of other States, especially if these were consequential on or were embarked upon in order to counter its own illegality – in short were provoked by it").

[176]In the *Medea* and *Good Return* cases, the Ecuador-United States Claims Commission found that the claimant had "committed depredations" against two nations, which disqualified him as a legitimate claimant on the basis that "[a] party who asks for redress must present himself with clean hands". Moore (1995), p. 2739.

[177]*Diversion of Water from the Meuse (Netherlands v. Belgium)*, Ser E (No 14) (PCIJ, 1937). The case concerned the interpretation of a treaty between Holland and Belgium regarding the regime of diversions of water from the River Meuse. Holland sought to prevent Belgium from making use of waters from the Meuse which it considered contrary to the applicable treaty, but Holland itself was making use of the waters in a similar manner. The PCIJ rejected Holland's claim, and in so doing applied the clean hands doctrine, as follows: "the Court finds it difficult to admit that the Netherlands are now warranted in complaining of the construction and operation of a lock of which they themselves set an example in the past". *See also Factory at Chorzow (Germany v. Poland) (Merits)*, Ser. A (No. 9) (PCIJ, 1927) 31 ("one party cannot avail himself of the fact that the other has not fulfilled some obligation ... if the former party has, by some illegal act, prevented the latter from fulfilling the obligation in question or from having recourse to the tribunal which would have been open to him.").

[178]In *Diversion of Water from the Meuse*, Judge Hudson noted that "[w]hat are widely known as principles of equity have long been considered to constitute part of international law, and as such they have often been applied by international tribunals". With reference to English law, Judge Hudson proceeded to apply the doctrine, "He who seeks equity must do equity", concluding:

> It would seem to be an important principle of equity that where two parties have assumed an identical or reciprocal obligation, one party which is engaged in a continuing non-performance of that obligation should not be permitted to take advantage of a similar non-performance of that obligation by the other party ... a tribunal bound by international law ought not to shrink from applying a principle of such obvious fairness. *Diversion of Water from the Meuse (Netherlands v. Belgium)*, Ser E (No 14) (PCIJ, 1937), Individual Opinion of Judge Hudson, 77.

In similar terms, Judge Anzilotti in his Dissenting Opinion held:

and the ICJ[179] also identify clean hands as a principle of international law. The clean hands doctrine has also been invoked by States in other ICJ proceedings, namely, by the United States in *Oil Platforms*,[180] *La Grand*,[181] and *Avena*,[182] by the NATO respondents in the *Legality of Use of Force* cases,[183] and by Israel in the advisory proceedings on *Legal Consequences of the Construction of a Wall in the Occupied Palestinian Territory*.[184]

Notwithstanding these cases, there remains serious debate as to the scope of application of the clean hands doctrine in international law. This is due partly to the fact that the ICJ is yet to uphold the clean hands doctrine in a majority opinion, despite having had the aforementioned opportunities to do so. The *Guyana v. Suriname* inter-State arbitral tribunal was similarly hesitant to recognize the doctrine.[185] Indeed, according to Professor Crawford himself, even the utilization of the clean hands doctrine in most of the early claims commission cases resulted from violations of laws on slavery and neutrality, and also arose within the context of diplomatic protection:

> it appears that these cases are all characterized by the fact that the breach of international law by the victim was the sole cause of the damage claimed, [and] that the cause-and-effect relationship between the damage and the victim's conduct was pure, involving no wrongful

"I am convinced that the principle underlying this submission (*inadimplenti non est adimplendum*) is so just, so equitable, so universally recognised, that it must be applied in international relations also. In any case, it is one of these "general principles of law recognised by civilised nations" which the Court applies in virtue of Article 38 of its Statute". Dissenting Opinion of Judge Anzilotti, 50. Judge Anzilotti reached a similar conclusion in his Dissenting Opinion in *Legal Status of Eastern Greenland*, where he held that "[t]his claim should, in my view, be rejected, for an unlawful act cannot serve as the basis of an action at law": *Denmark v. Norway*, Ser. A/B (No 53) (PCIJ, 1933), Dissenting Opinion of Judge Anzilotti, 95.

[179] See *Military and Paramilitary Activities in and against Nicaragua (Nicaragua v. United States)*, Merits, ICJ REPORTS 14 (1986), Dissenting Opinion of Judge Schwebel. Nicaragua had brought claims against the United States for various alleged military and paramilitary acts conducted in and against Nicaragua. The ICJ, both at the provisional measures and merits stages, gave no weight to considerations of clean hands, for the reason that it (controversially) found the hands of Nicaragua to be clean. Judge Schwebel disagreed with the majority decision, finding that the United States' acts were in response to what was tantamount to an armed attack by Nicaragua against El Salvador.

[180] *Oil Platforms (Iran v. United States)*, Merits, ICJ REPORTS 161, 176–78 (2003).

[181] *LaGrand (Germany v. United States)*, Merits, ICJ REPORTS 466, 488–89 (2001).

[182] *Avena (Mexico v. United States)*, Merits, ICJ REPORTS 12, 38 (2004).

[183] Schwebel (1999), p. 31.

[184] International Law Commission, Sixth Report on Diplomatic Protection, by Special Rapporteur Mr. John R. Dugard, A/CN.4/546 (57th Session, 2005), ¶5.

[185] See *Guyana v. Suriname (Award)* (Permanent Court of Arbitration, PCA Case No. 200405, 17 September 2007) ¶¶418. ("use of the clean hands doctrine has been sparse, and its application in the instances in which it has been invoked have been inconsistent").

act by the respondent State. When, on the contrary, the latter has in turn violated international law in taking repressive action against the applicant, the arbitrators have never declared the claim inadmissible.[186]

Professor Crawford concluded in his report as Special Rapporteur on State Responsibility to the UN International Law Commission that: "it is not possible to consider the 'clean hands' theory as an institution of general customary law."[187] Similarly, ILC Special Rapporteur on diplomatic protection John Dugard stated that:

> evidence in favour of the clean hands doctrine is inconclusive. . . . In these circumstances the Special Rapporteur sees no reason to include a provision in the draft articles dealing with the clean hands doctrine. Such a provision would clearly not be an exercise in codification and is unwarranted as an exercise in progressive development in the light of the uncertainty relating to the very existence of the doctrine and its applicability to diplomatic protection.[188]

Notwithstanding the unsettled status of the clean hands doctrine as a principle of public international law and in inter-State adjudication and arbitration, the doctrine has been repeatedly argued in respect of claims made by investors against States in investment treaty cases.[189] Arbitral practice there is also mixed, with some tribunals determined to utilize the principle and others firmly unpersuaded that the principle exists, at least as a matter of automatic inadmissibility of claims. This author's position is broadly supportive of the *Yukos* tribunal's conclusion, which stated categorically (as discussed further below) that the clean hands doctrine has not achieved the status of a principle of international law.[190] But the path to that position by international investment arbitration tribunals was not straightforward, and may yet have further complications given more recent cases and commentaries,[191] and thus merits further elaboration.

As a threshold point, some tribunals and commentators have argued that the clean hands doctrine informs and helps explain the legality clause in investment

---

[186]International Law Commission, Second Report on State Responsibility by Special Rapporteur Mr. James Crawford, UN Doc A/CN.4/498/Add.2 (51st Session, 1999) *citing* Salmon (1964), p. 259.

[187]International Law Commission, Second Report on State Responsibility by Special Rapporteur Mr. James Crawford, UN Doc A/CN.4/498/Add.2 (51st Session, 1999).

[188]International Law Commission, Sixth Report on Diplomatic Protection, by Special Rapporteur Mr. John R. Dugard, A/CN.4/546 (57th Session, 2005), ¶18.

[189]*See* Kreindler (2010), p. 309; Lamm and Moloo (2010), pp. 723–726; Moloo (2011); Moloo and Khachaturian (2011), pp. 1485–1486; Dumberry and Dumas-Aubin (2013).

[190]Llamzon (2015), p. 315.

[191]*See, e.g. Churchill Mining PLC and Planet Mining Pty. Ltd. v. Republic of Indonesia*, ICSID Case No. ARB/12/14 and 12/40, Award ¶493 (06 December 2016) (referring to the "common law doctrine of unclean hands" as having its "exact contours [as] subject to debate" while still finding the claimant's claims inadmissible) vis-à-vis *Hesham TM Al Warraq v. Republic of Indonesia*, UNCITRAL, Final Award ¶646 (December 15, 2014) ("[T]he Tribunal is of the view that the doctrine of 'clean hands' renders the Claimant's claims inadmissible"). For a scholarly view that supports the position that the clean hands principle is a general principle of international law, *see* Dumberry (2020), p. 489.

treaties.[192] The view that only investors with clean hands are entitled to protection under such treaties was posited in *Inceysa v. El Salvador*, a case which concerned the interpretation and application of such a clause.[193] The investor in that case procured a concession contract for vehicle inspection services in El Salvador through fraud in the public bidding process. The Tribunal found that the claimant's investment did not meet the applicable treaty's requirements of legality,[194] and declined jurisdiction on grounds that the investment fell outside the scope of conditional consent expressed by the Contracting Parties to the treaty.[195] But the tribunal also analyzed the claimant's investment in light of the general principles of law, which it found formed "part of Salvadoran law",[196] including the maxim *nemo auditor propriam turpitudinem allegans* ("no one is heard when alleging one's own wrong"),[197] said to be a manifestation of the "clean hands" doctrine, which the tribunal understood as prohibiting an investor from "benefit[ting] from an investment effectuated by means of one or several illegal acts".[198] The tribunal found that the claimant's violation of this principle meant that the investment was not within the scope of the offer to arbitrate disputes (arguably deciding that such claims are inadmissible).[199] Notably, *Inceysa* was not decided on grounds of corruption—lack of jurisdiction and inadmissibility of claims was the consequence of a finding of fraud. As discussed in Sect. 2 above, bribery is unlike fraud in that it is bilateral in nature and requires the participation of public officials acting with real or apparent authority in order to be

---

[192]*See, e.g.* Agreement between the Federal Republic of Germany and the Republic of the Philippines for the Promotion and Reciprocal Protection of Investments, Germany and Philippines, Article 1(1), *signed on* July 24, 1998.

[193]*Inceysa Vallisoletana S.L. v. Republic of El Salvador*, ICSID Case No. ARB/03/26, Award (02 August 2006) ("the term 'investment' shall mean any kind of asset accepted in accordance with the respective laws and regulations of either Contracting State").

[194]*Inceysa Vallisoletana S.L. v. Republic of El Salvador*, ICSID Case No. ARB/03/26, Award ¶¶249–252 (02 August 2006) The applicable BIT in that case stated that "[e]ach Contracting Party shall protect in its territory the investments made, *in accordance with its legislation*", by investors from the other Contracting Party: Spain-El Salvador BIT, Art. III (emphasis added).

[195]*Inceysa Vallisoletana S.L. v. Republic of El Salvador*, ICSID Case No. ARB/03/26, Award ¶257 (02 August 2006) ("because Inceysa's investment was made in a manner that was clearly illegal, it is not included within the scope of consent expressed by Spain and the Republic of El Salvador in the BIT and, consequently, the disputes arising from it are not subject to the jurisdiction of the Centre").

[196]*Inceysa Vallisoletana S.L. v. Republic of El Salvador*, ICSID Case No. ARB/03/26, Award ¶243 (02 August 2006).

[197]*Inceysa Vallisoletana S.L. v. Republic of El Salvador*, ICSID Case No. ARB/03/26, Award Part VI(A)(viii)(b) (02 August 2006).

[198]*Inceysa Vallisoletana S.L. v. Republic of El Salvador*, ICSID Case No. ARB/03/26, Award ¶¶240–242 (02 August 2006).

[199]*Inceysa Vallisoletana S.L. v. Republic of El Salvador*, ICSID Case No. ARB/03/26, Award ¶243 (02 August 2006) ("Inceysa acted improperly in order to be awarded the bid that made its investment possible and, therefore, it cannot be given the protection granted by the BIT. Sustaining the contrary would be to violate the aforementioned general principles of law which, as indicated, are part of Salvadoran law").

consummated; whereas fraud can be committed by a private investor against public officials of the State unilaterally.

In another contract-based ICSID arbitration that does concern corruption, *Niko Resources v. Bangladesh*, the tribunal found that "[t]he question whether the [clean hands] principle forms part of international law remains controversial and its precise content is ill defined".[200] Adopting a narrow view of the doctrine, the tribunal set a legal test for the application of the clean hands doctrine composed of three elements: (1) the claimant's conduct said to give rise to "unclean hands" must amount to a continuing violation, (2) the remedy sought by the claimant in the proceedings must be "protection against continuance of that violation in the future", not damages for past violations, and (3) there must be a relationship of reciprocity between the obligations considered.[201] In other words, corruption that is unrelated to the claims before the arbitral tribunal ought not, on a strict application of the principle, trigger the clean hands doctrine. Thus, on the facts of that case, the tribunal found that the Respondents' objection in respect of the investor's alleged "unclean hands" did not meet the articulated criteria for the application of the clean hands doctrine in international law.[202] As to crucial third criterion concerning reciprocity of obligations, the tribunal found that in a situation where corruption occurred after the joint venture agreement which was the subject of the investment had already been concluded, "there is no relation of reciprocity between the relief which the Claimant now seeks in this arbitration and the acts in the past which the Respondents characterize as involving unclean hands."[203] By emphasizing the requirement that a direct *and* reciprocal relationship exist between the corruption complained of by the host State and the claimant's cause of action,[204] the *Niko* tribunal was echoing

---

[200]*Niko Resources (Bangladesh) Ltd. v. Bangladesh Petroleum Exploration ("Bapex") and Bangladesh Oil Gas and Mineral Corporation ("Petrobangla")*, ICSID Case Nos. ARB/10/11 and ARB/10/18, Decision on Jurisdiction, ¶477 (19 August 2013).

[201]*Niko Resources (Bangladesh) Ltd. v. Bangladesh Petroleum Exploration ("Bapex") and Bangladesh Oil Gas and Mineral Corporation ("Petrobangla")*, ICSID Case Nos. ARB/10/11 and ARB/10/18, Decision on Jurisdiction, ¶481 (19 August 2013). (applying the three criteria identified by the UNCLOS arbitral tribunal in *Guyana v. Suriname (Award)* (Permanent Court of Arbitration, PCA Case No. 200405, 17 September 2007) ¶¶420–421.

[202]*Niko Resources (Bangladesh) Ltd. v. Bangladesh Petroleum Exploration ("Bapex") and Bangladesh Oil Gas and Mineral Corporation ("Petrobangla")*, ICSID Case Nos. ARB/10/11 and ARB/10/18, Decision on Jurisdiction, ¶¶483–485 (19 August 2013).

[203]*Niko Resources (Bangladesh) Ltd. v. Bangladesh Petroleum Exploration ("Bapex") and Bangladesh Oil Gas and Mineral Corporation ("Petrobangla")*, ICSID Case Nos. ARB/10/11 and ARB/10/18, Decision on Jurisdiction, ¶¶483–485 (19 August 2013).

[204]*See* Cheng (1953), pp. 157–158. (the *ex turpi causa* principle "does not apply to cases where, although the claimant may be guilty of an unlawful act, such act is judicially extraneous to the cause of action.").

the purer form of the clean hands doctrine seen in inter-State claims commissions dating back over a century.[205] In a similar (though not identical) vein, the *Yukos* tribunals emphasized that the illegalities complained of against the Claimants were not related to the *making* of the investment, largely concerned post-investment illegalities, and thus could not deprive the Tribunal of jurisdiction or render the entirety of the Claimants' claims inadmissible.

The most closely considered expression of the status of the clean hands doctrine in investment arbitration case law thus far is found in the *Yukos* arbitrations.[206] Following a detailed review of the authorities, the Tribunal concluded that:

> [t]he Tribunal is not persuaded that there exists a "general principle of law recognized by civilized nations' within the meaning of Article 38(1)(c) of the ICJ Statute that would bar an investor from making a claim before an arbitral tribunal under an investment treaty because it has so-called "unclean hands." General principles of law require a certain level of recognition and consensus. However, on the basis of the cases cited by the Parties, the Tribunal has formed the view that there is a significant amount of controversy as to the existence of an "unclean hands" principle in international law.[207]

Thus, significant doubt exists on the status of the clean hands doctrine as a general principle of international law. Indeed, the *Yukos* cases are emphatic in closing the door on the application of this principle.[208] That uncertainty continues to be expressed in more recent cases investment treaty such as *Churchill Mining v. Indonesia,* a case that expressed uncertainty about the scope and contours of the clean hands doctrine,[209] or *South American Silver v. Bolivia,* which—much like *Yukos*—did not find sufficient evidence that the clean hands doctrine had achieved the necessary consensus in the international community to be considered a binding principle of international law.[210] By contrast, a few investment treaty cases either

---

[205] *Frierdich and Company*, French-Venezuela Mixed Claims Commission (31 July 1905) 10 RIAA 45, 54: "Here may be applied with a certain degree of propriety one of the most important maxims of equity, viz, 'He who comes into equity must come with clean hands'."

[206] *Hulley Enterprises (Cyprus) Limited, Yukos Universal Limited (Isle of Man) and Veteran Petroleum Limited (Cyprus) v. Russian Federation* (Final Award) (Permanent Court of Arbitration, PCA Case Nos. AA226-28, 18 July 2014).

[207] *Hulley Enterprises (Cyprus) Limited, Yukos Universal Limited (Isle of Man) and Veteran Petroleum Limited (Cyprus) v. Russian Federation* (Final Award) (Permanent Court of Arbitration, PCA Case Nos. AA226-28, 18 July 2014) ¶¶ 1358–1359.

[208] *Hulley Enterprises (Cyprus) Limited, Yukos Universal Limited (Isle of Man) and Veteran Petroleum Limited (Cyprus) v. Russian Federation* (Final Award) (Permanent Court of Arbitration, PCA Case Nos. AA226-28, 18 July 2014) ¶ 1363. ("The Tribunal therefore concludes that "unclean hands" does not exist as a general principle of international law which would bar a claim by an investor, such as the Claimants in this case".)

[209] *Churchill Mining PLC and Planet Mining Pty. Ltd. v. Republic of Indonesia*, ICSID Case No. ARB/12/14 and 12/40, Award ¶493 (06 December 2016) ("The common law doctrine of unclean hands barring claims based on illegal conduct has also found expression at the international level, although its status and exact contours are subject to debate and have been approached differently by international tribunals.").

[210] *South American Silver Limited v. Plurinational State of Bolivia* (Award) (Permanent Court of Arbitration, PCA Case No. 2013-15, 30 August 2018) ¶¶ 444–445.

explicitly or implicitly seem to support the application of the clean hands doctrine, but in an entirely unreasoned manner and without taking account of *Yukos'* reasoning.[211]

But even if the clean hands doctrine were to be considered a binding principle of international law, or even a rule of transnational public policy, that *still* would not necessarily lead to the lack of jurisdiction or inadmissibility outcome. In national as well as international legal systems, claimants are not required to be pure as snow before being able to bring forth a claim; otherwise, few States, individuals, or corporations would be able to raise claims. In relation to the clean hands doctrine in the common law, Professor Herstein observes that "[t]he law generally does not deny access to established legal recourse to a victim of legally recognized wrong-doing even if the victim's past is marred with moral, legal, or ethical blemishes". Legal claims could therefore should be assessed based on their substantive and procedural merits *unless* they are "among the operative or material facts on which the legal merits of the claim turn."[212] For its part, While "equity does not demand that its suitors shall have lead blameless lives . . . it does require that they shall have acted fairly and without fraud or deceit as to the controversy in issue."[213] This requirement is thus broadly similar to the reciprocity criterion in *Niko* discussed earlier, a requirement not straightforwardly met in many cases involving corruption.

Moreover, the clean hands doctrine is more grounded in prudential and circumstantial considerations than the legality doctrine, and may in that sense be a healthier lens from which corruption (and indeed other forms of investor wrongdoing) might be considered.[214] Three *meta*-principles animate the clean hands doctrine in the common law: court integrity, retribution, and *to quoque* ("you too!" or "you also").[215] Of these, court integrity is the principal justification for the clean hands doctrine in investment treaty arbitration: *World Duty Free,* for example, suggests that protecting courts (and by extension, arbitral tribunals) from being used to pursue claims from persons guilty of illegal conduct justifies the *ex turpi causa* defense.[216] By not granting relief to claimants, the policy intent is to keep the court's own hands

---

[211]*See Rusoro Mining Ltd. v. Bolivarian Republic of Venezuela*, ICSID Case No. ARB(AF)/12/5, Award ¶492 (22 August 2016); *Copper Mesa Mining Corp. v. Republic of Ecuador* (Award) (Permanent Court of Arbitration, PCA Case No. 2012-2, 14 March 2016) ¶¶ 5.60–5.66; *Hesham TM Al Warraq v. Republic of Indonesia*, UNCITRAL, Final Award ¶646 (15 December 2014).

[212]Herstein (2011), p. 171.

[213]Precision Instrument Mfg. Co. v. Automotive Maintenance Mach. Co., 324 U.S. at 814.

[214]*For an extended discussion of the clean hands doctrines, see* Llamzon (2015).

[215]Herstein (2011), p. 171.

[216]*See World Duty Free Company Limited v. The Republic of Kenya*, ICSID Case No. ARB/00/7, Award ¶161 (04 October 2006) citing *Chitty on Contracts*, which in turn cited *Euro-Diam v. Balhurst*, 1990 Q.B. 1 (Kerr, L.J.) (The *ex turpi causa* defense "rests on a principle of public policy that the courts will not assist a plaintiff who has been guilty of illegal (or immoral) conduct . . . It applies if in all the circumstances it would be an affront to public conscience to grant the plaintiff the relief which he seeks because the court would thereby appear to assist or encourage the plaintiff in his illegal conduct or to encourage others in similar acts".) to assist or encourage the plaintiff in his illegal conduct or to encourage others in similar acts".).

clean by protecting itself from perceptions of hypocrisy in allowing 'dirty' plaintiffs relief, thereby diluting the public's perception of courts as temples of fairness. Keen to show that it does not tolerate any malfeasance on the part of private parties, the idea of keeping the mechanism investment arbitration 'clean' has special resonance, as the system is sensitive to criticism stemming from its very nature as a supranational system whose key decisionmakers are appointed *ad hoc* and yet have the power to check on the sovereign prerogatives of States.

But should the conception of the clean hands doctrine as the *embodiment* of the norm of court or arbitral integrity[217] be the dominant concern of international decisionmaking with respect to corruption? The issue with problem with treating clean hands as if it required only one result—the inadmissibility of all investor claims—is that it potentially allows clear injustices that might have been perpetrated by the respondent State to remain entirely without redress. Even setting aside the question of host State culpability and State responsibility for public official corruption, States have been shown on occasion to have violated basic standards of fair treatment found in investment treaties, going even beyond property and into the improper arrest and incarceration of the investor.[218] These are also clear instances of injustice, and if a clean hands doctrine is used to relieve the host State from any liability for these treaty violations because of prior bribery commitment, concerns about court integrity—this time on the other side—may yet be felt. Injustice can indeed swing both ways through an unbending application of the unclean hands doctrine:[219] while it is true that investors can sometimes act so illicitly as to not be entitled to any arbitral redress, host States can and historically have engaged in arbitrary and egregious conduct as well.

This is where the other, equally important moral underpinnings of the clean hands doctrine—retribution and *tu quoque*—must be considered. Fairness in the form of retributive consequences and tu quoque ("you too!") bear close resemblance in international law to the principles of *proportionality* and *reciprocity* that were discussed earlier in respect of the legality doctrine.[220] In his recent study on the

---

[217]*See* Herstein (2011), p. 179.

[218]*See, e.g., Mohamed Abdel Raouf Bahgat v. Egypt* (Final Award) (Permanent Court of Arbitration, PCA Case No. 2012-07, 23 December 2019) ¶252. ("The review of the process by Egypt's Supreme State Security Court reveals that Claimant's arrest, prosecution, and incarceration lacked any probable cause, and were an irregular prosecutorial proceeding, performed arbitrarily, in bad faith, with a wilful disregard of any obligation to provide reasonable due diligence in the application of due process of law. All these acts or omissions by the prosecution constitute elements of denial of justice. Respondent has not advanced any reason to doubt the objectivity of the factual assessment of that court and its reasoning.").

[219]Herstein (2011), p. 179 ("[w]hile abetting, tolerating, or assisting plaintiffs who are guilty of iniquity, hypocrisy, and wrongdoing may certainly cut against the court's integrity as a court of justice, allowing a legally recognized injustice or wrong to go unchallenged and not remedies *also* cuts against the grain of the court's nature as a court of justice. This is especially true where but for her unclean hands the claimant would have been, for all practical matters, entitled to a remedy.").

[220]In *Yukos*, the Claimants argued that the clean hands doctrine, even if opposable, would not confer upon States the right to violate investors' rights, and argued, based on an analogy with counter-

clean hands doctrine, Professor Dumberry maintains that the clean hands doctrine exists as a rule of international law, but also does not see the doctrine as one of automatic inadmissibility; instead, proportionality is sees the value in factoring proportionality into the analysis "whenever violations have been committed by both the investors and the host States."[221]

Thus, there seems to be no principled basis to derive from the body of case law a binding clean hands doctrine under international law; and even if there was, the content of the clean hands doctrine does not contain any binary rule requiring the inadmissibility of claims without reference to other important principles, including proportionality.

In sum, this section has taken a close look at the claim that a primary rule on the consequences of corruption exists, overriding the general rules on Sate responsibility and requiring the dismissal of all private investor claims for lack of jurisdiction or inadmissibility. National law, transnational public policy, and international law (including the clean hands doctrine and the legality doctrine) were all considered in detail. The upshot is that while *corruption is universally condemned, it would be wrong to conflate the international consensus prohibiting corruption—which certainly exists—with an alleged universal agreement about the civil and criminal consequences of corruption, which does not exist.*

---

measures, that principles of proportionality require the Tribunal to consider the investor's illegality vis-à-vis the host State's original breach. *Yukos,* at ¶¶ 1340 and 1341. The Tribunal did not engage with this argument, but may have effectively conducted such an analysis through its findings on contributory fault, apportioning a part of the responsibility due to the Claimants' own willful and negligent acts that contributed to the destruction of Yukos. *Yukos,* at ¶1599. *Hulley Enterprises (Cyprus) Limited, Yukos Universal Limited (Isle of Man) and Veteran Petroleum Limited (Cyprus) v. Russian Federation* (Final Award) (Permanent Court of Arbitration, PCA Case Nos. AA226-28, 18 July 2014).

[221]Dumberry (2020), p. 489. ("It may sometimes be more appropriate to take into account the conduct of the investor in the context of a broader proportionality analysis rather than to simply flatly reject its claims on grounds of inadmissibility. This could be the case whenever violations have been committed by both the investors and the host State. The rejection of an investor's claim on the basis of its 'unclean' hands could result in not addressing at all BIT breaches committed by the host State (for instance, acts of expropriation). Violations committed by the host State should not go unpunished. In such circumstances, it would seem more appropriate to take into account all violations committed by all sides as part of a global proportionality analysis. In fact, more recent cases have shown that even an explicit legality requirement contained in a BIT can be applied in a flexible manner taking into account matters of proportionality.").

4 A Return to Ordinary Order: Circumstantial Responsibility for Corruption Grounded on the Draft Articles

The expansion of corruption as an issue in international arbitration is triumph of intentionality, in some ways: often forgotten is the fact that the ICSID system was created in the 1960s partly as a mechanism to curtail corruption, which was perceived as prevalent in developing States and an impediment to greater foreign investment.[222] The last 15 years have seen a significant variation of that original purpose in the practice of international arbitration: while some cases involve private investors seeking to hold States to account for the capture of their investment through corrupt solicitations and extortion by public officials, far more cases involve States invoking corruption as a defense *against* foreign investor claims.[223] This is a positive development, to a large extent—*any* exposure of corrupt practices to juridical scrutiny furthers the international rule of law and pushes back against the impunity and lack of accountability that has allowed corruption to flourish in governing palaces and boardrooms alike. But as detailed in Sect. 3 above, the manner by which the jurisprudence of corruption in treaty and contract-based arbitration had been developing from the time of *World Duty Free* and *Metal-Tech* was causing disquiet among some arbitrators and in scholarly commentators. Despite the fact most corruption involves a willing public official participating in the bribe (whether in passive acceptance, active solicitation, or somewhere in between), two outcome-determinative characteristics were nonetheless ascribed to it: first, corruption acted as a "trump" that overrode all other claims and counter-claims; and second, all th e adverse consequences of a finding of corruption were, as a practical matter, allocated upon the investor alone.

Thus, despite the participation of public officials in the corrupt act in question, States invoking corruption as a defense largely bore no consequence—and no accountability—for the abuse of public power that necessarily occurred. This is no small matter: there is a large gulf in outcomes between cases where a tribunal majority finds insufficient evidence of corruption, allowing for a decision on the merits that finds violations of investment treaty protections or contractual breaches amounting to damages that run into the many hundreds of millions of dollars, and cases where a majority finds that corruption attended the original securing of the contract and thus affords the claimant no relief at all (and the State, no responsibility); that gulf is sometimes separated by a single vote.[224] With such binary, all-or-nothing decision outcomes, corruption becomes an existential issue in every case.

---

[222] *See* Llamzon (2014), p. 288.

[223] *See* Llamzon (2014), pp. 198–199.

[224] *See Unión Fenosa Gas, S.A. v. Arab Republic of Egypt*, ICSID Case No. ARB/14/4, Award (31 August 2018), where a majority of the Tribunal found insufficient evidence of corruption and proceeded to find serious treaty violations resulting in over US$2 billion in damages; the dissenting

The only uncontroverted exception to the all-or-nothing corruption trump was the case of corrupt solicitations by public officials that remained unconsummated (as payment of the bribe by the private party would bring the corrupt transaction back to the general rule). In that minority of cases, accountability and responsibility did redound to the State, whether in the form of treaty breaches (usually, for violation of the fair and equitable treatment protection) or breach of contract. That exception led to observations on the asymmetry in State responsibility discussed in Sect. 2 above.

But how State responsibility operates and does or does not attach in particular forms of corruption remains undertheorized, a decade and a half after *World Duty Free* and almost a decade following *Metal-Tech*—indeed, case law to date is entirely silent on these issues. Some scholarly attention has been put to these issues, but they mostly center on consummated acts of bribery and whether the ordinary, secondary rules on State responsibility should apply or whether the severe consequences discussed above can be explained by reference to "primary" rules that are unique to international anti-corruption law. Expressing one view on State responsibility for corruption, Crawford and Mertenskötter maintain that the law on State responsibility ordinarily attributes public official corruption to the State, but that the absence of State responsibility stems from the nature of international (and national) anti-corruption law itself. In other words, and to use the nomenclature of Article 2 of the ILC Articles, because an internationally wrongful act would *not* occur even if conduct was attributable to the State, so long as the conduct in question does not "constitute[] a breach of an international obligation of the State."

Section 3 interrogated these premises in detail and found that neither the legality doctrine nor the Clean Hands and cognate doctrines necessitated an all-or-nothing corruption trump. The principles of law that supposedly forestall the possibility of holding States responsible for corruption are the legality doctrine and the clean hands doctrine (and its *nemo auditor, ex turpi causa*, and *in pari delicto* cognates). Without sufficient nuance, these legal doctrines categorize transnational bribery and other forms of corruption as *species* within the *genus* of fraud and illegality, and—at least as used by some tribunals—ascribe to corruption, fraud, and illegality the same lack of jurisdiction and inadmissibility outcome.

But when international treaties, transnational public policy, and national laws that specifically relate to the consequences of corruption are studied closely, none of them require outcomes that sustain a rigid absence of jurisdiction or inadmissibility (or even render contracts void *ab initio*) outcome.[225] Instead, national law looks into whether corruption was the very subject matter or purpose of the contract (in cases of

---

arbitrator, looking at the same facts, found sufficient evidence of corruption and would have dismissed the case entirely on lack of jurisdiction under the Legality Clause of the Egypt-Spain BIT.

[225] *See also* Drude (2018), p. 704. ("Now, corruption perforce requires the host state's complicity. The actions of its corrupt officials are attributable to the host state pursuant to ARSIWA, Articles 2, 3, 4 and 7. Hence, it is arguable that the host state cannot question its consent to arbitrate: objectively, it has itself frustrated the condition purportedly implied in its unilateral offer to arbitrate.").

corrupt agency or consultancy, for example), or whether corruption tainted the State's consent to a contract that has a valid subject matter and purpose (sale and purchase agreements, concessions, etc.). And in either case, the matter is decided as part of the overall merits, and even a situation where a contract is invalidated for corruption may yet lead to potential damages on a non-contractual, *quantum meruit* or unjust enrichment basis. The diversity of potential outcomes demonstrates the absence of anything resembling a durable *jurisprudence constante,* much less a principle of transnational public policy or international law, concerning the consequences of corruption. As Kalicki, Silberman, and McAsey observe, the "dual complicity scenario" found in corruption cases have led to a lack of consensus on what the proper consequences a finding of corruption should yield:

> It remains to be seen how tribunals in the future will deal with the apparent tension that the dual complicity scenario creates between (1) the notion that an investor cannot assert a cause of action when it has acted illegally; and (2) the notion that the State cannot use the illegality to defeat jurisdiction when it has participated in the illegality (for example, on the basis of the unclean hands doctrine or estoppel). To date, there is no clear consensus on how to handle this tension, although the principle that public policy considerations should dominate appears emergent. In light of the historically scarce findings by tribunals of corruption, further jurisprudential development may take some time.[226]

Thus, properly considered, the absence of any consensus on the civil consequences of corruption, coupled with the views of most commentators that corrupt acts of public officials of a State should be attributable to that State by virtue of ILC Article 7, leads to the conclusion that neither the legality doctrine nor the clean hands doctrine and its cognates (nor indeed any principles of transnational public policy) form any kind of special 'primary' rule that is preclusive of State responsibility for the corruption of public officials. The presence of corruption should not necessarily relieve the host State of its obligation to adhere to its treaty commitments to treat foreign investors with fairness and due process, and without discrimination—the investor's malfeasance should provide license for the host State to act illegally as well without repercussion.[227]

And if States can, in principle, be held responsible for the corruption of their public officials, the jurisprudential threads found to be increasingly troubling in cases ranging from *World Duty Free,* to *Metal-Tech,* to *Spentex,* to *Kim,* need not linger further. A return to the regular order, where principles codified in the ILC Articles on State Responsibility should apply, could occur. Without intending to be comprehensive in this essay, such a return would include the following:

---

[226]Kalicki et al. (2017), p. 729.

[227]Drude (2018), p. 714. ("However, in so doing, the host state must adhere to standards of due process and act on a non-discriminatory basis. The investor's malfeasance does not provide a license for the host state to act illegally in its turn. The principle that the investor may rely on the unbiased, non-discriminatory administration of the host state's laws and regulations remains intact. It is only the corruptly procured element of its expectations that the investor cannot place any reliance on.").

(i) Ending the Corruption "Trump" Under a regime where public official corruption is attributable to the State and no preclusive rule exists that would shift all the adverse consequences of corruption to the investor alone, corruption would cease to be an inflexible trump—that is to say, international arbitral tribunals should not automatically dismiss an entire case for lack of jurisdiction or inadmissibility when a finding of corruption occurs.

Ending the corruption trump would stop making corruption an unintended benefit to host States—far from becoming an object of State responsibility, the corruption trump actually became a preventer of responsibility and result in the unjust enrichment of States. As observed by ICJ Judge Joan Donoghue, the "corruption trump [. . .] imposes the costs of corruption entirely on the investor, has much potential to deter corruption in foreign investment. . . . Ironically, [State officials'] acts of personal greed may actually insulate the host State from investor claims." Similarly, Professor Reisman questioned the fairness and potential for moral hazard of the corruption trump, with the risk it poses of actually incentivizing corruption instead of combatting it: "[a]s a constitutive matter, should the international policy guiding investment tribunals be one of zero tolerance? If it is, the only question for the tribunal confronting allegations of bribery is whether it occurred. If it has, none of the other, post-factual questions would even be admissible. The apparent moral clarity and simple ability to implement such a constitutive principle generates its own problems: it punishes only one party while rewarding the other in a bilateral transaction in which both parties are *in pari delicto*; in so doing it may actually incentivize official demands for bribes."[228] While these observations were made in the context of investment arbitration, their basic logic to applies equally to contract-based arbitrations. As Judge Lagergren admonished in ICC Case 1110:

> [b]efore invoking good morals and public policy as barring parties from recourse to judicial or arbitral instances in settling their disputes care must be taken to see that one party is not thereby enabled to reap the fruits of his own dishonest conduct by enriching himself at the expense of the other.[229]

With the end of the corruption trump, arbitrators would regain the capacity to make more nuanced and fact-sensitive assessments based on principles regularly applicable to State responsibility analyses, such as proportionality, estoppel, acquiescence, and waiver, which have long been posited as important correctives in the case law as well as by numerous commentators (including this author).[230] Moreover, international (as well as national) anti-corruption law would gain richer dimension,

---

[228]W W. Michael Reisman, Foreword in Llamzon (2014), pp. xi–xii.

[229]ICC Award No. 1110 of 1963 by Gunnar Lagergren (Award) (ICC, Case No. 1110, 15 January 1963) ¶21.

[230]For a discussion of the critical role the principles of estoppel, waiver, and acquiesce have in corruption decision-making, *see* Llamzon (2014), pp. 2268–2275. *See also* Tams (2010), p. 1035. Notably, Article 45 of the ILC Articles employs principles of waiver and acquiescence by conduct to ascertain whether responsibility for internationally unlawful conduct can no longer be invoked against the counterparty.

as tribunals would be able to recognize and give effect to the obligations imposed upon States to take effective steps to ensure compliance with international anti-corruption norms.[231]

(ii) Fact-Specific Decisionmaking A proper regard for the possibility of State responsibility for corruption would also lead to deeper engagement with the facts surrounding that corrupt conduct and its implications on the overall assessment of

---

[231]Regional anti-corruption treaties, as well as the OECD Anti-Bribery Convention and the U.N. Convention Against Corruption, require legislation and the taking of active measures to curb corruption, including by criminal prosecution of suspected public officials. *See* UN General Assembly, *United Nations Convention Against Corruption*, A/RES/58/4, 58th Session (31 October 2003) Articles 15(b), 18, 19; Convention drawn up on the basis of Article K.3 (2) (c) of the Treaty on European Union on the fight against corruption involving officials of the European Communities or officials of Member States of the European Union [2005] OJ C195/2 Article 2; Inter-American Convention Against Corruption articles 6–7, 29 March 1996, S. Treaty Doc No. 105-39, 35 ILM 724. *See also* Llamzon (2014), Ch. 4, paras. 4.06–4.73, particularly 4.57–4.65.

For an investor seeking to minimize risk, two purposes might animate corrupt activity: first, there is the *economic* reason—bribery of public officials will make a risky investment worth the risk and push an investor towards committing to invest when the profit potential exceeding that of market returns (even after the bribe payment is taken into account) is offered by the counterparty State or State-controlled corporation. Indeed, the rate of return would usually be so high (or the quality required of the investor's construction project so low) that it could only be accepted by a State when its public officials have been bribed. This can often be distinguished from a second reason for engaging in corruption: to secure leave from unfair, inequitable, or outright oppressive acts perpetrated by public officials of the host State in the form of legislation, regulations, or discretionary conduct that would adversely affect the investment; in other words, to protect the potential or already existing investment from *political* risk.

    [. . .]

[A] policy orientation that looks to good governance as a key aspect of economic development might begin with an analysis of corruption-related issues from the perspective of risk: *precisely what form of government action or inaction did the bribe purchase? Was it protection from commercial risks, or from non-commercial, governmental risk?* This distinction may serve as a useful analytical tool to distinguish what type of treatment should be given by investment arbitrators to specific issues relating to corruption such as standards of proof, burdens of proof, jurisdiction and admissibility, and consequences or sanctions.

If corruption is employed to insulate oneself from *political* uncertainty, this kind of corruption, while still illegal and subject to sanction, may in appropriate instances be subject to less onerous treatment (e.g. a mitigated sanctions regime) because it bears some consistency with precisely the same forms of political and non-commercial risks that investment treaties themselves were designed to protect foreign investors against. In other words, mitigation can occur to the extent that corruption was employed to purchase conduct broadly consistent with fair and equitable treatment, or freedom from arbitrary and discriminatory treatment, principles that are not coincidentally the subject of investment treaty protections. This class of corruption is also not necessarily destructive of fair competition, one of the other principal policy goals of anti-corruption norms.

However, if corruption occurred as a means to hedge against *economic* uncertainty by virtually guaranteeing a return, thereby insulating the investment from market forces, no mitigation whatsoever should occur (e.g. a sanctions regime that is more onerous). Indeed, linking this concept once again to investment treaties, the attempt through corruption to insulate the investment from economic risks would place that investment outside the class of treaty-defined 'investments' that merit protection by international investment arbitration, as subjecting capital to *risk* is an essential and legally recognized element of protected 'investments' under international investment law.

dispute. Tribunals would be permitted to consider the specific circumstances of that case when rendering a decision on what the consequences of corruption should be. Account would be taken of what kind of corruptly procured gains and advantages were obtained by the private investor or extorted by public officials (or both). Monetary damages that take account of the degree to which the bribes paid allowed for the investor to receive an above-market level of return (vis-à-vis bribes paid in order to be treated neutrally), how the underlying project benefitted of the host State's economy, and other factors.[232]

Equally important, the current asymmetry that holds States responsible for corrupt solicitations and extortions by public officials, but not for consummated corruption (even if initiated by the public official), would no longer be valid. The public official's role in and complicity the corrupt act would become a more important factor in assessing the State's level of responsibility, particularly if no steps are taken to investigate and prosecute those officials known to be corrupt. (See discussion in criterion (iv) below)

Context is key, as ever, and tribunals should not shy away from the difficult task of weighing not only whether sufficient proof of bribery exists, but what to do *next* once bribery has been admitted or proven. A salutary example of this kind of decisionmaking is found in the ICSID contract-based case of *Niko Resources v Bangladesh, BAPEX, and Petrobangla.*[233] In *Niko*, the respondents objected to the tribunal's jurisdiction by pointing to the admitted bribe paid to the Minister for the purpose of securing the contract. They alleged violations of "principles of good faith," "international public policy," "fundamental principles of law," and "fraudulent conduct." The respondents maintained that bribery occurred when the payment was given to the public official with the intent of influencing that official; it was immaterial in its view whether the bribe actually caused the official to act in the way desired. The respondents argued that jurisdiction should be declined because the bribe was made "in a manner intimately linked to the alleged investment" and that the tribunal was "empowered to protect the integrity of the ICSID dispute settlement mechanism" by dismissing claims not brought in good faith or with clean hands, "whether or not, on the facts, the bribery achieved its admitted purpose."[234] The tribunal rejected the respondent's jurisdictional objection and allowed the case to proceed to the merits, notwithstanding the plea agreement where claimant admitted bribery.

For the Niko tribunal, the core question was "whether any instance of bribery and corruption in which the Claimant has been or may have been involved deprives the

---

[232]Llamzon (2014), Ch. 11, especially paras. 11.38–11.52.

[233]*Niko Resources (Bangladesh) Ltd. v. Bangladesh Petroleum Exploration ("Bapex") and Bangladesh Oil Gas and Mineral Corporation ("Petrobangla")*, ICSID Case Nos. ARB/10/11 and ARB/10/18, Decision on Jurisdiction (19 August 2013).

[234]*Niko Resources (Bangladesh) Ltd. v. Bangladesh Petroleum Exploration ("Bapex") and Bangladesh Oil Gas and Mineral Corporation ("Petrobangla")*, ICSID Case Nos. ARB/10/11 and ARB/10/18, Decision on Jurisdiction, ¶376 (19 August 2013).

Claimant from having its claims considered and ruled upon".[235] The tribunal found that it had jurisdiction over the dispute and could proceed to the merits. Among the factors it looked to were that it was unproven that the relevant contract was secured as a result of the benefits given to the Minister who was bribed;[236] and the fact that Bangladesh entered into the contract despite knowing about the bribe paid to the Minister. Under these circumstances, the tribunal did not think that respondents could rely on the clean hands doctrine, as "the Respondents disregarded this situation. They may not now rely on these events to deny jurisdiction under an arbitration agreement which they then accepted."[237]

(iii) Proportionality Analysis In the real world of corruption decisionmaking, it is not uncommon for an investor to have little more invested in a project than a project procured through bribe payments, In those instances, there may be little reason to afford an investor any kind of relief at all; proportionality might still not grant any reprieve to the investor, as little tangible benefit to the State has occurred, and the principles that animate the protection of foreign investment are not truly met. But it is at least equally common to have cases where an investor has sunk tens of millions of dollars (sometimes many times more than that) and has been operating a going concern in the State for years. Similarly, in an international trade and commerce context, it is not unusual for bribes to have attended the entry into a high-value contract involving a foreign State as counterparty (for example a military arms deal or the procurement of high-value equipment for a State-owned and operated oil and gas or mining concern), but for the goods and equipment purchased to then have been utilized over the course of many years by that State. These scenarios all raise difficult issues concerning liability and responsibility, even (or perhaps because) the contract may be the proper subject of avoidance, making non-contractual relief necessary.

So far, international investment arbitration case law has provided almost no guidance on how to properly assess the proper consequences of corruption in such situations. The most ambitious apportionment of the consequences of consensual bribery occurred in *Spentex,* where the tribunal came up with a novel costs decision in an attempt to prevent the respondent State from being left "off the hook" and

---

[235]*Niko Resources (Bangladesh) Ltd. v. Bangladesh Petroleum Exploration ("Bapex") and Bangladesh Oil Gas and Mineral Corporation ("Petrobangla"),* ICSID Case Nos. ARB/10/11 and ARB/10/18, Decision on Jurisdiction, ¶380 (19 August 2013).

[236]In *Niko v. Bangladesh,* the tribunal ruled that if the payments confessed to did not have the effect of actually influencing the conclusion or content of the purchase agreements (especially price), then the admission of corruption may not invalidate the agreement or serve as a basis for the inadmissibility of claims due to a break in the chain of causation. *Niko Resources (Bangladesh) Ltd. v. Bangladesh Petroleum Exploration ("Bapex") and Bangladesh Oil Gas and Mineral Corporation ("Petrobangla"),* ICSID Case Nos. ARB/10/11 and ARB/10/18, Decision on Jurisdiction, ¶¶453–455 (19 August 2013).

[237]*Niko Resources (Bangladesh) Ltd. v. Bangladesh Petroleum Exploration ("Bapex") and Bangladesh Oil Gas and Mineral Corporation ("Petrobangla"),* ICSID Case Nos. ARB/10/11 and ARB/10/18, Decision on Jurisdiction, ¶484 (19 August 2013).

creating a moral hazard.[238] It suggested that future BITs should provide specifically for this issue, providing for the following: (a) that claimants cannot have their claims entertained; but then also (b) that a "but for" scenario be considered, where the claim is decided on the merits without first considering corruption and that the entire amount then be transferred not to claimant but to an appropriate body such as the UN or OECD, in order to fight corruption. The *Spentex* tribunal then used its discretionary costs powers and decided that costs should be allocated more against the State— in this case, in the amount of $8 million to the UNDP to fight corruption (equivalent to the legal fees; the bribe was $6 million). But if Uzbekistan decided not to pay that amount to the UN within 90 days, it should pay the costs of the claimant's reasonable costs.

This form of creative cost allocation is helpful in shifting some of the adverse consequences of corruption towards the host State. But as a matter of proportionality analysis, this is not nearly satisfactory as a solution, as it remains bound to the legality doctrine, which prevents any form of analysis of the merits of the case.

Kim v Uzbekistan provides a better solution. Extrapolating a "new test in *Kim*" that should apply to issues of illegality (including corruption), one commentator identifies a three-prong test for tribunals to consider:

The tribunal opined that 'the proper test must be applied on a case-by-case basis taking into account all relevant factors,' which involves three steps:

> *'First the Tribunal must assess the significance of the obligation with which the investor is alleged to not comply'* – the considerations that are relevant in this first step include: (i) the level of sanction provided in the law, including whether the violation is curable; (ii) whether there is general non-enforcement of the obligation by the host State; (iii) whether the host State has specifically decided not to investigate or prosecute the particular alleged act of noncompliance; and (iv) whether there is widespread noncompliance with the obligation;

> *'Second, the Tribunal must assess the seriousness of the investor's conduct'* – the relevant considerations in this step include: (i) whether the investor's conduct violates the obligation as alleged; (ii) the investor's intent; (iii) whether the law is unclear, evolving or incoherent; (iv) the investor's due diligence and efforts to understand and comply with the law; (v) whether the State has failed to investigate or prosecute the alleged particular act of noncompliance; and (vi) the investor's subsequent conduct; and

> *'Third, the Tribunal must evaluate whether the combination of the investor's conduct and the law involved results in a compromise of a significant interest of the Host State to such an extent that the harshness of the sanction of placing the investment outside of the protections of the BIT is a proportionate consequence for the violation examined'.*[239]

While some of the foregoing factors may not be as salient—for example, generally the lack of compliance with an obligation should not necessarily affect its authoritative nature (otherwise, bribery would often fall with the classification of "widespread noncompliance"), the test identified in *Kim* would be a very helpful step

---

[238]*Spentex Netherlands, B.V. v. Republic of Uzbekistan*, ICSID Case No. ARB/13/26, Award ¶974 (27 December 2016).

[239]Luttrell (2019), pp. 139–140 (citations omitted).

forward. And indeed, some of this analysis can already be found in more recent cases such as *Union Fenosa Gas v Egypt*. More importantly, as helpful as *Kim* is, it focuses mostly on the circumstances surrounding the corruption being alleged; an analysis of the overall nature of the investment made, how much that has contributed to the economy of the host State (or not), and the degree to which the host State committed violations of investment treaty protections or breaches of the investment or sales contract (depending on the nature of the case), should also be taken into account.

(iv) Focus on Prosecution   The host State's duty to prosecute the public officials said to have participated in the bribery has increasingly been recognized by arbitrators as a condition to being permitted to invoke the corruption defense.[240] While much of the reason for proposing that prosecution of corrupt public officials is animated by the law on State responsibility concerning principles of waiver, acquiescence, and estoppel,[241] it is also prompted by positive obligations under international anti-corruption law to ensure effective enforcement of anti-corruption law: a State's unwillingness to prosecute *in circumstances that would have required action* puts that State in potential breach of international anti-corruption law.[242]

In *Spentex,* part of the tribunal's decision to apportion some \$8 million dollars of costs against the host State appears to have been animated by the fact that the State refused to investigate or prosecute—or even identify—those persons said to be corrupt. The *Spentex* tribunal's findings in that regard echoed this author's focus on ensuring that States prosecute corrupt public officials:

> The host State being let 'off the hook' has real and adverse implications for the fight against corruption. [...] If good governance is an important step towards development, States ought to have an incentive under the system of investment arbitration to actually prosecute their own officials who engage in corruption. Allowing them to have it both ways – to resist

---

[240] *See Unión Fenosa Gas, S.A. v. Arab Republic of Egypt*, ICSID Case No. ARB/14/4, Award, ¶7.53 (31 August 2018) ("Whilst the lapse of time provides, by itself, no complete answer to the Respondent's allegations under international law, it raises doubts as to why such allegations were not raised and investigated by the Respondent's criminal authorities long before 2015; and why criminal prosecutions have still not been brought against certain individuals in Egypt."), 7.111 ("Although Mr El Komy was prosecuted and convicted for other crimes in Egypt, it is significant that he has never been prosecuted by the Respondent for criminal conduct in regard to the SPA. Nor has any senior decision-maker at EGPC or the Ministry of Petroleum (including Minister Fahmy) been prosecuted in regard to the SPA."); *Southern Pacific Properties (Middle East) Limited v. Arab Republic of Egypt*, ICSID Case No. ARB/84/3, Award ¶127 (20 May 1992) highlighting the State's refusal to implicate particular officials to the alleged corrupt acts as a reason for not entertaining its 'repeated allusions' to corruption); *Wena Hotels Ltd v. Arab Republic of Egypt*, ICSID Case No. ARB/98/4, Award, ¶116 (08 December 2000) (State's failure to prosecute alleged corrupt officials made the tribunal "reluctant to immunize Egypt from liability"). *See also* Llamzon (2014), pp. 275 and 280–281.

[241] *See* Llamzon (2014), pp. 268–275.

[242] *See* Llamzon (2014), p. 275, *citing* Tams (2010), p. 1044.

arbitration while simultaneously letting corrupt public officials go free – is often unfair, impolitic, and more importantly, creates exactly the wrong incentives, exacerbating instead of punishing corruption in the national sphere.).[243]

5 Conclusion

International anti-corruption law's incorporation into the corpus of international investment and commercial arbitration is undergoing significant development. Initially, corruption's strong sense of moral clarity translated into a regime of bright lines and clear condemnation/approbation, where the burdens of upholding anti-corruption norms were placed almost solely on the shoulders of the private investor and the State bore no responsibility for the corruption of its public officials. Recent case law and the weight of commentary have started to call that prior détente into question, insisting that States be held accountable for the role they play in perpetuating transnational bribery. The ordinary rules of State responsibility have a significant role to play in the development of a more holistic jurisprudence of corruption, one that does not shy away from the complexities corruption brings by virtue of its bilateral nature, and forces all parties to be accountable to each other and to international public order.

References

Arnesto J (2015) The effects of a positive finding of corruption in addressing. In: Baizeau D, Kreindler R (eds). Addressing issues of corruption in commercial and investment arbitration. International Chamber of Commerce, pp 167–174

Beale K, Esposito P (2009) Emergent international attitudes towards bribery. Arbitration 75 (3):360–373

Betz K (2017) Proving bribery, fraud, and money laundering in international arbitration, Cambridge

Bonucci N, Reisman M (2015) Keynote address, 125th annual ITA-ASIL conference: corruption in international arbitration, evidence and remedies. World Arbitr Mediation Rev 9(3):239–248

Born G (2009) International commercial arbitration. Walters Kluwer

Bottini G (2010) Legality of investments under ICSID jurisprudence. In: Waibel M et al (eds) The backlash against international arbitration. Kluwer Law International, p 297

Chazly F (2005) The explanation of the criminal code

Cheng B (1953) General principles of law as applies by international courts and tribunals

Crawford J, Mertenskotter P (2016) The use of the ILC's attribution rules in investment arbitration. In: Kinnear M et al (eds) Building international investment law: the first 50 years of ICSID, pp 27–42

Crook J (2015) Remedies for corruption. World Arbitr Mediation Rev 9(3):311–325

Derains Y (1985) Chronique of Arbitral Awards of the ICC. Journal du droit international (Clunet): 985–989

---

[243]*Spentex Netherlands, B.V. v. Republic of Uzbekistan*, ICSID Case No. ARB/13/26, Award ¶974 (27 December 2016) *citing* Llamzon (2014), p. 290.

Donoghue J (2015) The corruption Trump in investment arbitration. ICSID Rev – Foreign Invest Law J 30(3):756–761

Donovan D (2007) The relevance (or lack thereof) of the notion of "mandatory laws". Am Rev Int Arbitr 18(1-2):205–215

Douglas Z (2014) The plea of illegality in investment treaty arbitration. ICSID Rev – Foreign Invest Law J 29(1):155–186

Drude J (2018) Fiat Iustitia, Ne Pereat Mundus: a novel approach to corruption and investment arbitration. J Int Arbitr 35(1):665–718

Dumberry P (2020) The Unclean Hands doctrine as a general principle of international law. J World Invest Trade 21:489–527

Dumberry P, Dumas-Aubin G (2013) The doctrine of 'Clean Hands' and the inadmissibility of claims by investors breaching international human rights law. Transnatl Dispute Manag 10:1–10

Fitzmaurice G (1957) The general principles of international law considered from the standpoint of the rule of law. Recueil des Cours 9:1–227

Gailard E, Savage J (1999) Fouchard Gaillard Goldman on international commercial arbitration. Kluwer Law International

Gearing M, Kwong R (2015) The common law consequences and effects of allegations of a positive finding of corruption. In: Baizeau D, Kreindler R (eds) Addressing issues of corruption in commercial and investment arbitration. International Chamber of Commerce, pp 158–166

Greig D (1993) Reciprocity, proportionality, and the law of treaties. Virginia J Int Law 34 (2):295–342

Herstein O (2011) A normative theory of the Clean Hands doctrine. Leg Theory 17:1–38

Higgins R (1994) Problems and process: international law and how we use it. Citing Meron T (1957) International Responsibility of States for Unauthorized acts of their Officials. Br Yearb Int Law 33:85–113

Jennings R, Watts A (2008) Oppenheim's international law, 9th edn, vol 1: Peace. Oxford

Kalicki J, Silberman M, McAsey B (2017) What are appropriate remedies for findings of illegality in investment arbitration? In: Menaker A (ed) International arbitration and the rule of law: contribution and conformity, ICCA Congress Series, Vol, vol 19, pp 721–729

Kessedjian C (2007) Transnational public policy. In: van de Berg A (eds) International Arbitration 2006: back to basics? ICCA International arbitration congress series no. 13. Kluwer Law International, pp 857–870

Klaw B (2015) State responsibility for bribe solicitation and extortion: obligations, obstacles, and opportunities. Berkeley J Int Law 3:60–104

Knahr C (2007) Investments in accordance with host state law. Transnatl Dispute Manag 4(1):5

Kreindler R (2003) Aspects of illegality in the formation and performance of contracts. ICCA Congress Series No. 11:209–260

Kreindler R (2010) Corruption in international investment arbitration: jurisdiction and the Unclean Hands Doctrine. In: Hober K et al (eds) Between east and west: essays in honour of Ulf Franke. New York, pp 309–328

Kreindler R (2013) Competence-competence in the face of illegality in contracts and arbitration agreements. Recueil des Cours: Collected Courses on the Hague Academy of International Law 361:292–293

Kriebaum U (2010) Chapter V: Investment arbitration – illegal investments. In: Klausegger C et al (eds) Austrian yearbook on international arbitration 2010, pp 307–335

Lalive P (1986a) Ordre Public Transnational (ou réellement international) et Arbitrage International. Revue de l'arbitrage 3(3):329–374

Lalive P (1986b) Transnational (or truly international) public policy and international arbitration. ICCA Congress Series 3:258–318

Lamm C and Moloo R (2010) Fraud and corruption in international arbitration. In: Fernandez-Ballesteros M, Arias D (eds) Liber Amicorum Bernardo Cremades, p 716

Llamzon A (2013) State responsibility for corruption: the attribution asymmetry in international investment arbitration. Transnational Dispute Management 3

Llamzon A (2014) Corruption in international investment arbitration, Oxford

Llamzon A (2015) Yukos Universal Limited (Isle of Man) v the Russian Federation: the state of the 'Unclean Hands' doctrine in international investment law: Yukos as both omega and alpha. ICSID Rev Foreign Invest Law J 30(2):315–325

Llamzon A (2019) Trading in influence. In: Rose C et al (eds) The United Nations Convention against corruption: a commentary, pp 192–209

Llamzon A, Sinclair A (2015) Investor wrongdoing in investment arbitration: standards governing issues of corruption, fraud, misrepresentation, and other investor misconduct. In: van de Burg A (eds) Legitimacy: myths, realities, challenges. ICCA Congress Series No. 18, pp 451–530

Low L (2019) Dealing with allegations of corruption in international arbitration. Am J Int Law 113:341–345

Luttrell S (2019) Fall of the phoenix: a new approach to illegality objections in investment treaty arbitration. Univ Western Aust Law Rev 44(2):120–142

Martin E (1994) A dictionary of law. In: Martin E (eds)

Miles C (2012) Corruption, jurisdiction and admissibility in international investment claims. J Int Dispute Settlement 3(2):329–369

Moloo R (2011) A comment on the Clean Hands doctrine in international law. Transnatl Dispute Manag 8(1):1

Moloo R, Khachaturian A (2011) The compliance with the law requirement in international investment law. Fordham Int Law J 34:1473

Moore J (1995) History and digest of the international arbitrations to which the United States has been a party

Newcombe A (2012) Investor misconduct: jurisdiction, admissibility or Merits. In: Brown C, Miles K (eds) Evolution in investment treaty law and arbitration, pp 187–200

Partasides C (2017) Remedies for findings of illegality in investment arbitration. In: Menaker A (eds) International arbitration and the rule of law: contribution and conformity, pp 740–745

Peters A (2018) Corruption as a violation of international human rights. Eur J Int Law 29 (4):1251–1287

Raeschke-Kessler H, Gottwald D (2008) Corruption in foreign investment – contracts and dispute settlement between investors, states, and agents. J World Invest Trade 9:1–40

Redfern A (2007) Comments on commercial arbitration and transnational public policy. In: van de Berg A (eds) International Arbitration 2006: back to basics? ICCA International arbitration congress series no. 13. Kluwer Law International, pp 849–856.

Reisman M (1979) Folded lies: bribery, crusades and reforms

Reisman M (2000) The regime for Lacunae in the ICSID choice of law provision and the question of its threshold. ICSID Rev – Foreign Invest Law J 15(2):362–381

Reisman M (2007) Transnational public policy. In: van de Berg A (eds) International Arbitration 2006: back to basics? ICCA International arbitration congress series no. 13. Kluwer Law International, pp 849–856

Salmon J (1964) Des 'Mains Propres' Comme Condition de Recevabilite des Reclamations Internationales. Annuaire Fraincais de Droit International 10:225–266

Sayed A (2004) Corruption in international trade and commercial arbitration. Kluwer Law International

Schill S (2012) Illegal investments in international arbitration. Law Pract Int Courts Tribunals 11 (2):281–323

Schwebel S (1999) Clean Hands in the court. Stud Transnatl Leg Policy 31:74–78

Spalding A (2015) Deconstructing duty-free: Investor-State Arbitration as private anti-bribery enforcement. UC Davis Law Rev 49:443–495

Tams C (2010) Waiver, acquiescence, and extinctive prescription. In: Crawford J et al (eds) The law of international responsibility. Oxford, pp 1035–1049

Wood T (2018) State responsibility for the acts of corrupt officials: applying the 'Reasonable Foreign Investor' standard. J Int Arbitr 35(1):103–117

Aloysius P. Llamzon is a partner in the International Arbitration Group of King & Spalding LLP (Washington, D.C. and New York) and a Research Professor of Law at the Ateneo de Manila University School of Law (Philippines). Dr. Llamzon received his LL.M. and J.S.D. degrees from Yale Law School, and his book "Corruption in International Investment Arbitration" (OUP, 2014) was adapted from his dissertation. Louie has practiced and taught at leading institutions in Manila, Hong Kong, and The Hague, and was formerly Senior Legal Counsel at the Permanent Court of Arbitration, where his work included acting as Registrar and Tribunal Secretary in numerous public international law and treaty-based disputes. He is counsel and advocate for corporate, individual, and sovereign clients in commercial, investment, and inter-State arbitrations across the globe.

Human Rights in International Investment Law

Barnali Choudhury

Contents

Abstract Covid has highlighted the pre-existing weaknesses in the social structure that leave vulnerable members of society at risk. This has reinforced the importance of states being able to protect their nationals' human rights. A state's role in this regard has been recognized not only by society but by business as well. Yet while progress is being made in these areas, international investment law remains bereft of increased attention to matters of human rights. Indeed, reforms in this area remain primarily procedural in nature.

This essay argues that issues of human rights must be given greater consideration in international investment treaties. Businesses are being asked to give greater attention to human rights matters in almost every area apart from international investment treaties. To ensure international investment law aligns with progress in other areas of the law, international investment law must delineate a role for human

B. Choudhury (✉)
University College London, London, UK
e-mail: b.choudhury@ucl.ac.uk

© Springer Nature Switzerland AG 2021   175
M. Bungenberg et al. (eds.), *European Yearbook of International Economic Law 2020*,
European Yearbook of International Economic Law (2022) 11: 175–194,
https://doi.org/10.1007/8165_2021_65, Published online: 23 July 2021

rights. This can be achieved, among other ways, through independent provisions on human rights, investor obligations, and carve-outs.

1 Introduction

The events of 2020 have precipitated a profound change in society's mood. Living with a global pandemic, which at the time of writing has already resulted in over one million deaths, and caused untold harms on, in particular, already vulnerable members of society has underlined the importance of a state's duty to protect, respect, and fulfil its nationals' human rights. The need for states to be able to flexibly regulate as well as to protect human rights has also been highlighted by the Black Lives Matter Movement which has also found a voice more listened to by society in 2020.

Against the backdrop of the growing recognition of the importance for states to protect human rights, there has also been a societal shift in the role business plays in this arena. In part, the swing in society's perception of the role of business has been a reflection of business itself which has increasingly been declaring the importance of issues beyond profit. Between the Business Roundtable Statement signed by 181 American Chief Executive Officers (CEOs),[1] the Davos Manifesto promulgated by business leaders at the World Economic Forum,[2] or declarations by numerous CEOs in a multi-jurisdiction longitudinal study,[3] it is become apparent that businesses, themselves, recognize their role in promoting social welfare.

2020 has thus heralded a profound awareness by both society and business of the importance and the need for the protection of human rights. Yet, while society and business move forward by working to better incorporate human rights ideals in their dealings, recognition of the importance of human rights has made less headway in the area of international investment law. Certainly, for proponents of investment arbitration, this is not surprising as international investment law has traditionally been viewed—by commentators and arbitrators alike—as a matter of private law and

---

[1]Business Roundtable (2019) Business Roundtable Redefines the Purpose of a Corporation to Promote 'An Economy That Serves All Americans', https://www.businessroundtable.org/business-roundtable-redefines-the-purpose-of-a-corporation-to-promote-an-economy-that-serves-all-americans (last accessed 17 November 2020).

[2]World Economic Forum (2020) Davos Manifesto 2020: The Universal Purpose of a Company in the Fourth Industrial Revolution, https://www.weforum.org/agenda/2019/12/davos-manifesto-2020-the-universal-purpose-of-a-company-in-the-fourth-industrial-revolution/ (last accessed 17 November 2020).

[3]Leaders on Purpose (2019) Purpose-Driven Leadership For The 21st Century: How Corporate Purpose Is Fundamental To Reimagining Capitalism, 2017–2019 Global Multi-Year CEO Study, https://www.thegeniusworks.com/wp-content/uploads/2019/10/Leaders-on-Purpose.pdf (last accessed 17 November 2020).

thus an area of law not relevant to human rights.[4] Indeed, the issue of human rights for these proponents may only be relevant insofar as it forms part of the rights foreign investors seek to protect.[5]

However, what is more surprising is that organizations, such as the United Nations Conference on Trade and Development (UNCTAD), which have been working to reform international investment law for quite some time now, have chosen to focus only on procedural reforms, leaving little room for the consideration of human rights.[6] This limited mandate for reform is even more astonishing given that UNCTAD, itself, has recognized that a failure to reform both the substantive and procedural elements of international investment law risks achieving only "piecemeal change".[7]

Yet, there is good reason to consider issues of human rights within international investment law. Not least because foreign investment and human rights can be thought of as 'two sides of the same coin', given their common origin of arising in an effort to protect individuals from the state's overriding power and their vulnerability to that power when used to adversely affect their rights. The main difference between the two areas is that foreign investors can access a powerful tool in the form of investment arbitration to hold states accountable for violations of their rights while human rights victims lack a similar accountability mechanism.

This essay makes the argument that human rights should be considered within the ambit of international investment law in particular because society now demands that corporations, including foreign investors, consider the social implications of their activities. It begins by looking at the human rights responsibilities that both law and society have established for business. It then moves to explore the relationship between international investment law and human rights, finding that these areas of law are disconnected and that both investment arbitration and investor-state contracts pose risks to human rights. The essay then explores specific human rights provisions found in investment treaties and investor-state contracts and discusses their treatment by investment arbitral panels. Finally, it examines the utility of including human rights provisions in investment treaties and investor-state contracts.

---

[4]Hirsch (2009), pp. 112 f.

[5]See e.g. *Al-Warraq v. Indonesia* in which the investor relied on numerous arguments relating to human rights to protect his interests as a foreign investor, *Al-Warraq v. Indonesia*, UNCITRAL, Final Award, 15 December 2014, para. 177–184, 202–204, 240–246.

[6]UNCTAD, Report of Working Group III (Investor-State Dispute Settlement Reform) on the work of its thirty-fifth session, UN Doc A/CN.9/935, 14 May 2018, https://undocs.org/en/A/CN.9/935 (last accessed 17 November 2020), para. 18.

[7]UNCTAD, Improving Investment Dispute Settlement: UNCTAD Policy Tools, IIA Issues Note (Nov. 2017), https://investmentpolicy.unctad.org/publications/182/iia-issues-note-improving-investment-dispute-settlement-unctad-s-policy-tools (last accessed 17 November 2020), p. 12.

2 Law and Society's Demands on Business vis-à-vis Human Rights

Human rights are entitlements that belong to every person by virtue of being human.[8] They are derived from the concept of human dignity and justified by references to equality.[9] While states retain primary responsibility for the protection of human rights, both law and society have carved out a role for business vis-à-vis human rights as well.

From society's viewpoint, businesses must take into account issues of human rights. The relationship between business and society can be described as symbiotic in that each entity is reliant on the other for survival. Accordingly, business should consider human rights issues on account of the 'licence' given by society to them to engage in business activities. The notion that businesses holds a licence from society arises from social contract theory. In the same way that the government's role in relation to its citizenry is justified by its respect of the terms of the social contract with the people, a corporation's existence is similarly justified by its respect of the terms of the social contract; that is, the indirect obligations it has with the people.[10] Therefore, businesses need to consider issues of human rights as a condition of their licence granted by society to business to operate.

From a legal standpoint, businesses should respect human rights. This view arises from a long history of international initiatives which have shaped global norms for business responsibility for human rights, culminating most recently in the United Nations' *Protect, Respect and Remedy* Framework[11] and resulting in the *UN Guiding Principles for Business and Human Rights* (UNGPs).[12] These require corporations to refrain from harming human rights as well as preventing and mitigating operations-related adverse human rights impacts by engaging in human rights due diligence.[13] Moreover, although the corporate responsibility to respect human rights

---

[8]Randall (2013), p. 3.

[9]Besson (2014), pp. 44–46.

[10]Donaldson (1982), p. 37.

[11]UN Human Rights Council, Protect, Respect and Remedy: a Framework for Business and Human Rights. Report of the Special Representative of the Secretary-General on the issue of human rights and transnational corporations and other business enterprises, John Ruggie. UN Doc. A/HRC/8/5, 7 April 2008, https://www.undocs.org/A/HRC/8/5 (last accessed 17 November 2020).

[12]UN Human Rights Council, Guiding Principles on Business and Human Rights: Implementing the United Nations "Protect, Respect and Remedy" Framework, UN Doc. HR/PUB/11/04, 2011, https://www.ohchr.org/documents/publications/guidingprinciplesbusinesshr_en.pdf (last accessed 17 November 2020), Guiding Principle 11.

[13]UN Human Rights Council, Guiding Principles on Business and Human Rights: Implementing the United Nations "Protect, Respect and Remedy" Framework, 2011, UN Doc. HR/PUB/11/04, 2011, https://www.ohchr.org/documents/publications/guidingprinciplesbusinesshr_en.pdf (last accessed 17 November 2020), Guiding Principle 13.

is not binding, it is viewed as 'a global expectation of all companies' and one that is not optional.[14]

The corporate responsibility to respect human rights is also gradually moving from an expectation to a binding legal norm. Laws that hold corporations accountable for failing to ensure that they have been duly diligent in preventing human rights harms have emerged in France and are expected to be enacted throughout the European Union shortly.[15] Switzerland has proposed similar legislation which is due to be pushed through by support from its citizens.[16] In the Netherlands, corporations are being held liable for failing to identify and prevent child labour in their supply chains,[17] while the Supreme Court of Canada has recently confirmed that Canadian corporations can be held liable for jus cogens violations.[18] Finally, state parties continue to negotiate a legally binding instrument on business and human rights.[19]

3   Links Between International Investment Law and Human Rights

While the corporate responsibility to respect human rights has become a global norm in public international law, for the most part, it has failed to penetrate the world of international investment law. International investment law therefore continues to fail to attend to issues of human rights.

One reason for this failure is because international law views human rights as being the primary purview of states. As human rights obligations are mainly directed at states, states bear the obligation to respect, protect, and fulfil these human rights

---

[14]UN Human Rights Office of the High Commissioner, Frequently Asked Questions about The Guiding Principles on Business and Human Rights, 2014, https://www.ohchr.org/documents/publications/faq_principlesbussineshr.pdf (last accessed 17 November 2020), p. 10.

[15]Assemblee Nationale, Proposition De Loi Relative Au Devoir De Vigilance Des Sociétés Mères Et Des Entreprises Donneuses D'ordre (adopted 21 February 2017); European Coalition for Corporate Justice, Commissioner Reynders announces EU corporate due diligence legislation, 30 April 2020, https://corporatejustice.org/news/16806-commissioner-reynders-announces-eu-corporate-due-diligence-legislation (last accessed 17 November 2020).

[16]Reuters Staff, Swiss to vote on companies' global liability for rights abuses, 4 June 2020, https://cn.reuters.com/article/instant-article/idUKKBN23B2B7 (last accessed 17 November 2020).

[17]Wet Zorgplicht Kinderarbeid (Child Labor Duty of Care Act) (adopted 24 October 2019).

[18]Supreme Court of Canada, *Nevsun Resources Ltd v Araya*, 2020 SCC 5 (2020).

[19]Open-ended intergovernmental working group on transnational corporations and other business enterprises with respect to human rights, Legally Binding Instrument To Regulate, In International Human Rights Law, The Activities Of Transnational Corporations And Other Business Enterprises, Second Revised Draft, 6 Aug 2020, https://www.ohchr.org/Documents/HRBodies/HRCouncil/WGTransCorp/Session6/OEIGWG_Chair-Rapporteur_second_revised_draft_LBI_on_TNCs_and_OBEs_with_respect_to_Human_Rights.pdf (last accessed 17 November 2020).

obligations[20] and foreign investors or corporations are not thought to be directly responsible for human rights. Since international law fails to impose direct responsibility on foreign investors, international investment law has tended to view issues of human rights as beyond its purview.

The lack of attention to human rights issues in international investment law may also be a result of the tendency, by commentators and arbitrators, to view international investment and international human rights law as separate areas of the law.[21] The isolation of international investment law from other areas of public international law has even enabled it to develop as a self-contained regime. International investment law therefore relies on its own *lex specialis* to ensure the application of its norms and, consequently, negates or downplays other international law norms—such as human rights—that belong to the general international legal order.[22]

Arbitrators are also reluctant to engage in human rights issues.[23] This may be because they see their jurisdiction as being limited to disputes that arise out of the protection of the foreign investment and human rights issues are seen as too far removed from this subject. Alternatively, it may be because they lack expertise in broader areas of public international law.[24]

Yet, while international investment law downplays or negates human rights issues, it continues to affect issues of human rights. Principally, it does this by constraining state sovereignty in areas related to human rights. For instance, foreign investors have used investment arbitration to challenge state regulations aimed at improving human rights or environmental issues. They have challenged regulations aimed at addressing racial discrimination,[25] regulations enacted to protect public health[26] and regulations addressed at improving the environment, among others.[27] Even though some arbitral tribunals have recognized that human rights regulations, which are non-discriminatory and enacted with due process, can affect a foreign

---

[20]De Schutter (2014), p. 280.

[21]Dupuy (2009), p. 46.

[22]UN GA, Report of the International Law Commission, UN Doc. A/61/10, 2006, https://legal.un.org/ilc/documentation/english/reports/a_61_10.pdf (last accessed 17 November 2020), para. 233–251.

[23]Choudhury (2020), p. 1.

[24]Saldarriaga and Magraw (2015), pp. 125–146.

[25]*Piero Foresti, Laura de Carli & Others v. The Republic of South Africa,* ICSID Case No ARB (AF)/07/01, Award (4 August 2010).

[26]See e.g. *Urbaser S.A. and Consorcio de Aguas Bilbao Bizkaia, Bilbao Biskaia Ur Partzuergoa v. The Argentine Republic,* ICSID Case No. ARB/07/26, Award (8 December 2016); *Philip Morris Brands Sàrl, et al. v. Uruguay,* ICSID Case No. ARB/10/7, Award (8 July 2016); *Methanex Corporation v. United States of America,* UNCITRAL, Final Award of the Tribunal on Jurisdiction and Merits (3 August 2005).

[27]See e.g. *Bilcon of Delaware et al v. Government of Canada,* PCA Case No. 2009-04, Award (17 March 2015); *Crystallex International Corporation v. Venezuela,* ICSID Case No. ARB(AF)/11/2, Award (4 April 2016); *Vattenfall AB, Vattenfall Europe AG, Vattenfall Europe Generation AG v. Federal Republic of Germany,* ICSID Case No. ARB/09/6 (2009), Award (11 March 2011).

investment without triggering compensation,[28] more tribunals have found that a state's human rights commitments do not supersede its investment treaty commitments.[29] As a result, state regulations aimed at human rights or related areas that affect foreign investments often continue to trigger compensation.[30] Both the actual or potential costs of investment arbitration may then force states to choose between their investment treaty commitments or their human rights or environmental commitments. The potential costs of investment arbitration by an aggrieved foreign investor may also thwart states from enacting these types of regulation at all, a practice known as 'regulatory chill'.[31]

4 Human Rights Provisions in Investment Treaties and Investor-State Contracts

Despite the fact that international investment law poses considerable risks to human rights, investor treaty provisions or investor-state contract clauses typically do not make any reference to human rights. In fact, human rights provisions in investment treaties are a relatively recent phenomenon. Until the twenty-first century, most investment treaties typically did not contain any reference to human rights. Since then, however, there has been an attempt by some states to include issues of human rights within investment treaties and investor-state contracts. These include references to human rights and human rights-based exemptions, investor obligations, human rights-related provisions, specific provisions in investor-state contracts, and other sources.

4.1 References and Exemptions

One of the most common approaches to including human rights in investment treaties is to refer to them, for instance in the preamble or objectives, but refrain from including independent provisions creating any legally binding obligations. For

---

[28]*Methanex Corporation v. United States of America*, UNCITRAL, Final Award of the Tribunal on Jurisdiction and Merits (3 August 2005), pt. IV, ch. D, para. 7.

[29]*Suez, Sociedad General de Aguas de Barcelona S.A. v. Argentina*, ICSID Case No. ARB/03/17, Decision on Liability (30 July 2010), para. 232; *Suez, Sociedad General de Aguas de Barcelona S.A. and Interagua Servicios Integrales de Agua S.A. v. Argentina*, ICSID Case No. ARB/03/19, Decision on Liability (30 July 2010), para. 252.

[30]See e.g. *Bilcon of Delaware et al v. Government of Canada*, PCA Case No. 2009-04, Award (17 March 2015); *Gold Reserve Inc. v. Venezuela*, ICSID Case No. ARB(AF)/09/1, Award (22 September 2014); *Copper Mesa Mining Corp. v. Ecuador*, PCA No. 2012-2, Award (15 March 2016).

[31]Van Harten (2020), ch. 6.

instance, the preamble of the agreement of the Cape Verde-Hungary Bilateral Investment Treaty (BIT) stipulates that the agreement seeks "to ensure that investment is consistent with. . . the promotion and protection of internationally and domestically recognised human rights".[32] Other treaties refer to human rights by committing not to lower human rights standards to encourage investment[33] while still others dictate the state's right to regulate measures relating to investments to meet policy or public welfare objectives.[34]

While these treaty provisions refer to human rights, they do not give rise to any human rights obligations, per se. Nevertheless, their utility stems from guiding interpretations of other provisions of the treaty. The Vienna Convention on the Law of Treaties (VCLT) notes, for instance, that the context and purpose of a treaty can be derived from its preamble.[35] Since the standards of treatment found in investment treaties are often vague, references to human rights in other provisions of the treaty can provide context when interpreting these standards.

Another common approach states use to include human rights references in treaties is by way of exception clauses. For example, most modern Canadian investment treaties exempt the host state from some of its investment treaty obligations in order to protect human, animal or plant life or health or to protect public security, public morals or to maintain public order.[36] This borrows from the language found in the General Agreement on Tariffs and Trade (GATT)[37] and is designed to provide the host state with a defence to arbitral claims involving bona fide human rights and human rights-related regulations. Conversely, other states refrain from relying on GATT language and create a straightforward exception to protect human rights issues. Thus, the Egypt-Mauritius BIT provides, under the heading 'Security Exceptions', that nothing in this Agreement shall be construed to prevent either Contracting Party from taking measures to fulfil its obligations with respect to. . . the protection of public health.[38]

Some states are being more diligent in using human rights as exceptions to host states obligations by carving out human rights regulation entirely from certain standards of treatment. Thus, the ASEAN—India Investment Agreement provides that "financial assistance or measures taken by a Party . . . in pursuit of legitimate public purpose including the protection of health, safety, the environment" will not be considered as a violation of national treatment obligations.[39] This provision

---

[32]Cape Verde-Hungary BIT (2019), Pmbl. See also Belarus-Hungary BIT (2019), Pmbl.

[33]See e.g. Azerbaijan-Hungary BIT (2007), Art. 2; Cambodia-Japan BIT (2007), Pmbl.

[34]Nigeria-Morocco BIT (2016), Pmbl.; Argentina-Qatar BIT (2016), Art. 10.

[35]Vienna Convention on the Law of Treaties, Art. 31(2).

[36]See e.g. Canada-European Union: Comprehensive Economic and Trade Agreement (2017), Art. 28.3; Canada-China BIT (2012), Art. 33.

[37]Marrakesh Agreement Establishing the World Trade Organization (15 April 1994), Art. XX, U.N.T.S. Vol. 1867, pp. 154 ff.

[38]Egypt-Mauritius BIT (2014), Art. 13.

[39]ASEAN-India Investment Agreement (2014), Art. 3(5).

would, for instance, remove a state's bona fide health regulation entirely from the scope of its national treatment obligations under an investment treaty. Other states have adopted a similar approach for expropriation claims, by including provisions that exempt state measures designed to protect public welfare objectives, such as health, safety and the environment, from being considered indirect expropriation.[40] The China-Australia FTA goes even further by removing all measures for legitimate public welfare objectives—including public health, public morals, and the environment—from the scope of investment arbitration altogether.[41] This type of provision ensures that specified human rights issues will never become arbitrable.

4.2 Investor Obligations

International human rights law not only requires states to protect individual's human rights but also to protect third parties, including corporations and other private actors from violating individuals' human rights. Some states have translated this second obligation by creating human rights responsibilities for foreign investors in investment treaties. However, the approach to doing so varies. In some treaties, the responsibility imposed on foreign investors is decidedly soft. These treaties only *recommend* that states *encourage* foreign investors to voluntarily incorporate international standards of corporate social responsibility such as human rights.[42] Consequently, these treaty provisions do not oblige state parties to impose human rights regulations upon foreign investors and foreign investors are also not mandated to respect human rights.

Other investment treaties have introduced more stringent investor obligations. These entail, for example, requiring foreign investors to develop 'best efforts' to "respect the human rights of those involved in the companies' activities".[43] The draft Pan African Investment Code similarly takes such an approach by prescribing principles that should govern foreign investor conduct, including by respecting human rights and not being complicit in human abuses.[44] These treaties confirm that foreign investors have human rights responsibilities but enable investors to self-regulate how they and their investments will comply with such responsibilities.

A third set of treaties rely on actual binding legal obligations for foreign investors. For instance, the Morocco-Nigeria BIT specifies that investors shall uphold human rights in the host state, act in accordance with core labour standards, and not manage

---

[40]See e.g. Austria-Kyrgyzstan BIT (2016), Art. 7(4).

[41]Australia-China FTA (2015), Art. 9.11(4).

[42]See e.g. Agreement between the United States of America, the United Mexican States, and Canada (USMCA) (2018), Art. 14.17; Belarus-India BIT (2018), Art. 12; Nigeria-Singapore BIT (2016), Art. 11.

[43]Brazil-Malawi BIT (2015), Art. 9. See also Brazil-Mozambique BIT (2010), Art. 10.

[44]African Union Commission, Draft Pan African Investment Code (2016), Art. 24(a) and (b).

or operate investments in "a manner that circumvents international environmental, labour and human rights obligations".[45] Similarly, the Economic Community of Western African States (ECOWAS) Supplementary Act on Common Investment Rules for the Community stipulates that investors shall uphold human rights in the workplace and in the community and shall manage and operate their investments without breaching or circumventing human rights.[46] It also requires foreign investors to refrain from, either complicity or with the assistance of others, violating human rights in times of peace or during socio-political upheaval.[47] The Southern African Development Community (SADC) Model BIT adopts similar language to the ECOWAS rules in requiring foreign investors to refrain from assisting or being complicit in the violation of human rights and further stipulates that investors have a 'duty' to respect human rights.[48]

Some states have ensured their obligations for foreign investors are legally binding by delineating consequences for a failure to act. For instance, the Bangladesh-Denmark BIT provides that if the host state 'suffers from a loss, destruction of damages with regard to its public health or life or the environment, including natural resources by the investor' then the investor is obliged to accord the host state adequate and effective compensation under domestic or international law.[49] Other treaties stipulate that home states can hold investors civilly liable for any acts relating to their investment in the host state that causes significant damage, injuries or loss of life.[50] Finally, a third set of treaties enforce foreign investor's human rights-related conduct by denying them access to arbitration in case of a violation or incorporate the human rights violation in calculating damages for any arbitral claims made by the investor.[51]

4.3 Human Rights-Related Provisions in Investment Treaties

Apart from direct provisions on human rights, several investment treaties contain references or provisions to issues closely related to human rights. Several investment

---

[45]Morocco-Nigeria BIT (2016), Art. 18.

[46]Supplementary Act A/SA.3/12/08 Adopting Community Rules on Investment and the Modalities for their Implementation with ECOWAS (2008), Art. 14(2).

[47]Supplementary Act A/SA.3/12/08 Adopting Community Rules on Investment and the Modalities for their Implementation with ECOWAS (2008), Art. 14(3).

[48]Southern African Development Community, SADC Model Bilateral Investment Treaty Template with Commentary (2012), Art. 15.

[49]Bangladesh-Denmark BIT (2009), Art. 2(2).

[50]Morocco-Nigeria BIT (2016), Art. 20; Indian Model BIT (2016), Art. 13.

[51]Supplementary Act A/SA.3/12/08 Adopting Community Rules on Investment and the Modalities for their Implementation with ECOWAS (2008), Art. 18(2) and (3); Netherlands Model Investment Agreement (2018), Art. 23; Southern African Development Community, SADC Model Bilateral Investment Treaty Template with Commentary (2012), Art. 19.1.

treaties, for instance, contain references or provisions relating to sustainable development. As with human rights provisions, references to sustainable development may be confined to treaty preambles or they may entail independent responsibilities for foreign investors in this regard.[52]

An increasing number of treaties are relying on corporate social responsibility (CSR) provisions as a catch-all for a number of social issues including human rights. Typically, these provisions only specify soft standards for foreign investors.[53] The wording of the India-Belarus BIT's CSR provision is typical of such a standard, specifying that foreign investors "shall endeavour to voluntarily incorporate internationally recognized standards of corporate social responsibility in their practices and internal policies".[54]

Other treaties have chosen to define CSR in terms of international instruments such as the OECD Guidelines on Multinational Enterprises (OECD Guidelines) or the UN Global Compact (UNGC)[55] or to reference international CSR initiatives such as the ILO Tripartite Declaration,[56] or the UN Guiding Principles on Business and Human Rights.[57] Regardless of the CSR definition chosen, each of the international CSR initiatives contain non-binding recommendations for corporations to respect human rights.

A number of other treaties also make references to labour, environmental, or anti-corruption issues. For example, treaties specify that investors shall act in accordance with labour standards and not operate investments in a way that circumvents labour standards;[58] should protect the environment and remediate environmental damage;[59] or refrain from engaging in corruption or being complicit in corrupt acts.[60]

4.4 Human Rights Provisions in Investor-State Contracts

Apart from investment treaties, human rights provisions are also, at times, included in investor-state contracts. Likely the most well-known example of such a provision in an investor-state contract are those associated with the Baku-Tbilisi-Ceyhan

---

[52]See e.g. China-Switzerland FTA (2013), Pmbl; CARIFORUM-UK Economic Partnership Agreement (2019), Art. 3.

[53]See e.g. China-Switzerland FTA (2013), Pmbl; EU-Moldova BIT (2014), Art. 35.

[54]India-Belarus BIT (2018), Art. 12. See also Argentina-Japan BIT (2018), Art. 17; Australia-Hong Kong FTA (2019), Art. 16.

[55]Brazil-Chile BIT (2015), Art. 15; Austria-Nigeria BIT (2013), Pmbl.

[56]See eg. EU-Ukraine BIT, Art. 422; EU-Moldova BIT (2014), Art. 35.

[57]See e.g. Netherlands Model Investment Agreement (2018), Art. 7.

[58]Morocco-Nigeria BIT (2016), Art. 18 (3) and (4); Southern African Development Community, SADC Model Bilateral Investment Treaty Template with Commentary (2012), Art. 15.2.

[59]African Union Commission, Draft Pan African Investment Code (2016), Art. 37(3).

[60]See e.g. Belarus-India BIT (2018), Art. 11(ii); Morocco-Nigeria BIT, Art. 17 (2) and (3).

(BTC) oil pipeline project. After protests by Amnesty International, the project partners adopted a Human Rights Undertaking in connection with the project which made a number of warranties. For instance, they guaranteed not to challenge any host state regulation enacted to protect human rights or the health, safety or environmental aspects of the project, stipulating that human rights victims would be able to seek remedy for human rights violations in the domestic courts. Further they warranted not to seek compensation under the economic equilibrium clause in connection with state action or inaction reasonably required to fulfil human rights obligations.[61]

In other investor-state contracts, states have chosen to narrow economic equilibrium clauses or stabilization clauses even further than the BTC project approach. While still others have removed them entirely.[62]

Some contracts are even more direct in terms of the investor's human rights obligations. An Iraqi product-sharing agreement, for instance, specifies that both the investor and the state commit to promoting respect for and complying with human rights principles and a failure to do so is considered a force majeure event.[63] Other contracts can require investors to employ locals, build schools, develop training programs for local employees, prevent and remediate any environmental damage.[64]

4.5 Other Sources of Human Rights and Human Rights-Related Issues

Besides specific human rights provisions in investment treaties or investor-state contracts, human rights can infiltrate the world of international investment law from other sources as well.[65] For instance, in *Urbaser v. Argentina*, the tribunal found that international law in general could govern matters in the dispute.[66] As a

---

[61] Baku-Tbilisi-Ceyhan Pipeline Company, BTC Human Rights Undertaking (22 September 2003), https://subsites.bp.com/caspian/Human%20Rights%20Undertaking.pdf (last accessed 17 November 2020), Art. 2.

[62] See e.g. Exploration and Production Concession Contract between the Government of the Republic of Mozambique and ENI East Africa S.p.A and Empresa Nacional di Hidrocarbonetos, E.P. for Area 4 Offshore of the Rovuma Block Republic of Mozambique 2006, Art. 27.13; Kaul R (2009) Getting a Better Deal from the Extractive Sector Concession Negotiation in Liberia, 2006–2008: A report to the Liberian Reconstruction and Development Committee Office of the President, Republic of Liberia. Revenue Watch Institute, https://resourcegovernance.org/sites/default/files/RWI-Getting-a-Better-Deal-final0226.pdf (last accessed 17 November 2020).

[63] Product Sharing Contract, Topkhana Block, Kurdistan Region between Kurdistan Regional Government of Iraq and Talisman (Block K39) B.V (2011), Art. 43.11.

[64] Herat Cement Contract between Majd Industrial Pishgaman Company and Ministry of Mines, Islamic Republic of Afghanistan (2011), Art. 13 and 14.

[65] For a good overview of arguments in this area see generally Krajewski (2020), p. 105.

[66] *Urbaser S.A. and Consorcio de Aguas Bilbao Bizkaia, Bilbao Biskaia Ur Partzuergoa v. The Argentine Republic*, ICSID Case No. ARB/07/26, Award (8 December 2016), para. 1191–1192.

result, the tribunal relied on a number of different international human rights treaties, including the Universal Declaration of Human Rights (UDHR) and the International Covenant on Economic, Social and Cultural Rights (ICESCR), to determine whether the investor had an obligation to guarantee the human right to water. Indeed, the tribunal specifically observed that where there was "an obligation to abstain, like a prohibition to commit acts violating human rights", international law would support a finding that a foreign investor had specific obligations in this regard.[67] Accordingly, foreign investors could have human rights obligations that are recognized by international law as *jus cogens* or *erga omnes*.[68]

Human rights and related issues may also enter international investment law through domestic law. Thus, in *Burlington Resources Inc. v. Ecuador*[69] and *Perenco v. Ecuador*,[70] Ecuador counterclaimed against the foreign investor, alleging that he had breached domestic environmental law. Finding that the foreign investor had not acted as "a responsible environmental steward," the tribunal concluded that he had breached Ecuador's environmental laws and awarded damages to Ecuador for its counterclaims.[71]

States may also be able to allege that other provisions in either the investment treaty or the investor-state contract have given rise to human rights responsibilities for the foreign investor. In *Aven v. Costa Rica*, the tribunal concluded that the investor had an obligation not to cause environmental damage, in part, because of the numerous references to the importance of environmental protection found in other provisions of the treaty.[72]

---

[67] *Urbaser S.A. and Consorcio de Aguas Bilbao Bizkaia, Bilbao Biskaia Ur Partzuergoa v. The Argentine Republic*, ICSID Case No. ARB/07/26, Award (8 December 2016), para. 1196–1198.

[68] *David R. Aven and Others v. Republic of Costa Rica*, Award, ICSID Case No. UNCT/15/3, Award (18 September 2018), para. 738.

[69] *Burlington Resources Inc. v. Republic of Ecuador*, ICSID Case No. ARB/08/5, Decision On Counterclaims (7 February 2017).

[70] *Perenco Ecuador Ltd. v. The Republic of Ecuador and Empresa Estatal Petróleos del Ecuador (Petroecuador)*, ICSID Case No. ARB/08/6, Interim Decision on The Environmental Counterclaim (11 August 2015).

[71] *Burlington Resources Inc. v. Republic of Ecuador*, ICSID Case No. ARB/08/5, Decision On Counterclaims (7 February 2017), para. 889; *Perenco Ecuador Ltd. v. The Republic of Ecuador and Empresa Estatal Petróleos del Ecuador (Petroecuador)*, ICSID Case No. ARB/08/6, Interim Decision on The Environmental Counterclaim (11 August 2015), para. 447; *Perenco Ecuador Ltd. v. The Republic of Ecuador and Empresa Estatal Petróleos del Ecuador (Petroecuador)*, ICSID Case No. ARB/08/6, Damages Award (27 September 2019), para. 899.

[72] *David R. Aven and Others v. Republic of Costa Rica*, ICSID Case No. UNCT/15/3, Award (18 September 2018), para. 737–739.

5   The Utility of Human Rights Provisions in International Investment Treaties and Investor State-Contracts

The relationship between international investment law and human rights parallels the UN Special Rapporteur on Business and Human Rights' Protect, Respect, and Remedy Framework. As the Special Rapporteur notes, the root of the business and human rights predicament lies in the governance gaps created and/or perpetuated by globalization. Because individual actions, whether by states or corporations, to close these gaps are constrained, a multi-pillared approach is needed to address these issues.[73] For that reason, the Special Rapporteur advocated in favour of *both* a state duty to protect and a corporate responsibility to respect human rights.

The international investment law and human rights relationship is also shaped by multiple actors. On the one hand, states must have ample regulatory sovereignty to protect human rights and international investment law—whether through the operation of the wording of treaties or through the use of stabilization clauses in investor-state contracts—may constrain this use of regulatory sovereignty. There is, therefore, a need to ensure that international investment law does not impinge on state regulatory space.

On the other hand, human rights impacts of foreign investments could be minimized or mitigated by the acts of individual foreign investors. Corporations or foreign investors are often best placed—even better than states—to determine how to ensure their corporate activities minimize human rights impacts. As a result, foreign investors may be particularly well suited to bear responsibilities to respect human rights.

From an international investment law standpoint, the need to protect a state's regulatory sovereignty for human rights issues thus supports the inclusion of human rights provisions in treaties and investor-state contracts in two ways. First, to ensure regulatory sovereignty for human rights issues and second, to justify state regulatory actions. There is also a need to have foreign investors bear an onus to respect human rights, because states alone may not be able to protect human rights. This would warrant investor obligations for human rights.

---

[73]UN Human Rights Council (2008) Protect, Respect and Remedy: a Framework for Business and Human Rights. Report of the Special Representative of the Secretary-General on the issue of human rights and transnational corporations and other business enterprises, John Ruggie. UN Doc. A/HRC/8/5, 7 April 2008, https://www.undocs.org/A/HRC/8/5 (last accessed 17 November 2020), para. 17.

5.1 The Utility of Human Rights Provisions for State Regulatory Sovereignty

Curiously, most of the extant human rights provisions in investment treaties and investor-state contracts do little to specifically ensure that states will continue to maintain sufficient regulatory space for human rights. One notable exception to this practice are the narrowed down stabilization clauses found in the examined investor-state contracts. The BTC Human Rights Undertaking, for instance, reinforces the notion that states can, in either treaties or contracts, specifically stipulate that the treaty or contract does not limit or constrain the promulgation of laws in the state which are in the interest of human rights. This type of clause can help ensure that human rights regulations that impinge on foreign investments are excluded from the ambit of the contract.

Some investment treaties have adopted similar language as the narrowed down stabilization clause even though they are not human rights provisions *per se*. Thus, the Argentina-Qatar BIT specifies that nothing in the BIT shall affect the right of state parties to regulate "through measures necessary to achieve legitimate policy objectives."[74] Other treaties proclaim that they will not relax human rights standards to meet investment objectives.[75] However, in investment treaties, these types of provisions neither create legally enforceable rights or obligations nor regulatory space.[76] Rather, they perform "auxiliary functions" by denoting the weight to be accorded to specific public interests, offer a presumption that state regulatory interest will be taken into account, or confirm that investor protection obligations are not absolute.[77] Thus, although they may be useful in the overall interpretation of the investment treaty, on their own, they are unlikely to guarantee human rights regulatory space.

A second provision in investment treaties that attempts to ensure state regulatory space are exception provisions. These are the provisions that may borrow from GATT language to denote that measures that are necessary to protect human life, for instance, are exempted from investment treaties with the aim of creating a defence for states against investment claims that target human rights and related legislation. The utility of these types of human rights provisions depends on their wording. States that draft their exception provisions using GATT language must pass a "necessity" test to rely on such a provision. This requires the state to prove the necessity of its measure as well as to demonstrate that its measure is not arbitrary, discriminatory, or a disguised restriction on trade.[78] In several arbitrations arising out of the Argentine financial crisis, tribunals have interpreted the necessity test in a

---

[74] Argentina-Qatar BIT (2016), Art. 10.

[75] See e.g. Azerbaijan-Hungary BIT (2007), Art. 2; Cambodia-Japan BIT (2007), Pmbl.

[76] Titi (2014), p. 104.

[77] Korzun (2017), p. 374; Titi (2014), pp. 104–105.

[78] Appleton (1997), p. 136; Du (2016), p. 817.

variety of ways suggesting that state reliance on such a provision is far from certain.[79]

Reliance on this type of provision may further be problematic if the list of enumerated exceptions is treated as exhaustive. In *Bear Creek v. Peru*, Peru attempted to argue that its actions were justified by the police powers exception despite this not being listed in the treaty's GATT-style exceptions provision.[80] The tribunal ruled that the general exceptions provision was exhaustive, thereby preventing Peru from relying on the police powers exception unless specifically provided for in the list of general exceptions.[81]

Exception provisions that do not use the term 'necessary' or more closely tie their exception to human rights may be more useful than GATT-style language as they limit the role of arbitrators in interpreting such provisions. Similarly, ensuring that the state parties are given sole authority to determine whether a state may rely on a particular exception provision may also better preserve state regulatory power as this again limits arbitral review power.[82]

However, a more apt way of ensuring that states regulatory powers in this area are preserved would be to exempt human rights regulations from states' investment treaty obligations. The ASEAN-India BIT exempts human rights measures from both the state parties' national treatment and expropriation obligations.[83] Other states have focused on issue areas, for instance, denying investors the ability to bring tobacco control measure claims, as these measures are designed to protect public health with respect to tobacco consumption.[84] Even more radically, the Australia-China FTA exempts all public welfare regulations from investor-state arbitration, subject to investor challenges to the nature of the regulation settled through joint-treaty party control.[85] Of all the human rights provisions examined, these are likely to be the most useful for preserving state regulatory space for human rights measures.

---

[79]Choudhury (2011), p. 697.

[80]*Bear Creek Mining Corp. v. Peru*, ICSID Case No. ARB/14/2, Award (30 November 2017), para. 451–452.

[81]*Bear Creek Mining Corp. v. Peru*, ICSID Case No. ARB/14/2, Award (30 November 2017), para. 473–474.

[82]See e.g. China-Australia FTA (2015), Art. 9.11.4–9.11.6.

[83]ASEAN-India BIT (2014), Art. 3(5) and 8(9).

[84]Singapore-Kazakhstan BIT (2018), Art. 11(2); Singapore-Australia FTA (2017), Art. 22.

[85]China-Australia FTA (2015), Art. 9.11.4–9.11.16.

5.2 The Utility of Human Rights Provisions for Investor Obligations

Human rights provisions in investment treaties and investor-state contracts that establish obligations for investors help to establish the norms being established by the UN Guiding Principles on Business and Human Rights on the corporate responsibility to respect human rights. By introducing investor obligations for human rights, international investment law begins to better conform with public international law which now views the corporate responsibility to respect as, at the very least, a global expectation, and, at best, as a global norm.

Investor-related human rights obligations also help to counter the asymmetric nature of international investment law that offers investors rights but not obligations. Including human rights obligations for investors may also influence investor behaviour, improve the quality of the investments being made, and help promote sustainable development.[86] Use of investor obligations for human rights may also work towards promoting the development aspects of international investment agreements (IIAs), which possess cogent elements of economic and sustainable development alongside investor protection.

In this regard, the investor obligations found in investment treaties and investor-state obligations that amount to binding obligations are particularly helpful. Non-mandatory CSR provisions, such as those that 'encourage' states to have investors voluntarily incorporate CSR, do not achieve to the standards espoused in the UN Guiding Principles on Business and Human Rights. The UN Guiding Principles require corporations both to refrain from harming human rights and to engage in human rights due diligence. Investment treaties and investor-state contracts therefore should, at a minimum, prescribe this negative obligation, a practice that only a few of the treaties and investor-state contracts explored earlier have adopted. To a lesser extent, investment treaties that take into account investor failure to respect human rights in determining the compensation for an award may also implicitly conform to the UN Guiding Principles' requirement to 'do no harm'.

However, the UN Guiding Principles make clear that the corporate responsibility to respect also entails human rights due diligence obligations. This involves assessing actual and potential human rights impacts, integrating and acting upon the findings, tracking responses, and communicating how impacts are addressed. With some exceptions, most of the investment treaties do not contain comparable obligations.

However, some investor-state contracts do contain due diligence-like obligations and the practices of investor-state contracts, in general, are useful in determining how best to move forward in incorporating human rights due diligence elements in

---

[86]International Institut for Sustainable Development (2018) Harnessing Investment for Sustainable Development: Inclusion of investor obligations and corporate accountability provisions in trade and investment agreements, https://www.iisd.org/system/files/meterial/harnessing-investment-sustainable-development.pdf (last accessed 17 November 2020), p. 6.

investment treaties. The UN Special Rapporteur for Business and Human Rights has formulated principles for incorporating human rights into investor-state contracts and these can be relied on for incorporating human rights provisions into investment treaties.[87] Two of the principles require that human rights considerations form part of the contract negotiation process and that responsibilities for the prevention and mitigation of human rights risks for the project are clarified and agreed before finalization of the contract. For foreign investors, this entails human rights considerations being integrated into the investment from the outset and being reflected in the contract's negotiation and throughout the life-cycle of the investment[88] as well as assessing human rights risks of the investment as early as possible in the context of a new activity.[89] In keeping with these principles, investment treaties could similarly require foreign investors to integrate human rights considerations from inception of the investment throughout its life-cycle. This could be done, for example, by requiring foreign investors to complete a human rights impact assessment before the investment is established and engaging in periodic human rights impact assessments throughout the course of the investment.

6 Conclusion

If we have learned anything from 2020 it is that the status quo is no longer acceptable. As society and the law gradually move to better incorporate human rights into business activities, international investment law's failure to do the same risks leaving it an outlier. Reforms of international investment law that focus only on procedural rules and do not consider the role for human rights are therefore inadequate.

Including human rights provisions in investment treaties and investor-state contracts is therefore a prudent approach by states. Not only does this ensure states' regulatory powers for human rights but it can also be useful for working to delineate human rights obligations for foreign investors. These types of provisions may also play a role in the interpretation of other provisions of investment treaties. More

---

[87]UN Human Rights Office of the High Commissioner, Principles For Responsible Contracts Integrating The Management Of Human Rights Risks Into State-Investor Contract Negotiations, UN Doc. HR/PUB/15/1, 2015, https://www.ohchr.org/Documents/Publications/Principles_ResponsibleContracts_HR_PUB_15_1_EN.pdf (last accessed 17 November 2020).

[88]UN Human Rights Office of the High Commissioner, Principles For Responsible Contracts Integrating The Management Of Human Rights Risks Into State-Investor Contract Negotiations, UN Doc. HR/PUB/15/1, 2015, https://www.ohchr.org/Documents/Publications/Principles_ResponsibleContracts_HR_PUB_15_1_EN.pdf (last accessed 17 November 2020), p. 8.

[89]UN Human Rights Office of the High Commissioner, Principles For Responsible Contracts Integrating The Management Of Human Rights Risks Into State-Investor Contract Negotiations, UN Doc. HR/PUB/15/1, 2015, https://www.ohchr.org/Documents/Publications/Principles_ResponsibleContracts_HR_PUB_15_1_EN.pdf (last accessed 17 November 2020), p. 10.

importantly, including human rights provisions in investment treaties and investor-state contracts is an important step to ensuring that investor-friendly interpretations of investment treaties stay firmly in the past and protection of human rights in the investment context paves a way forward in the future.

References

Appleton A (1997) GATT Article XX's chapeau: a disguised 'necessary' test? The WTO Appellate Body's ruling in United States – standards for reformulated and conventional gasoline. Rev Eur Community Int Environ Law 6(2):131–138

Besson S (2014) Justifications. In: Moeckli D, Shah S, Sivakumaran S (eds) International human rights law. Oxford University Press, Oxford, pp 34–52

Choudhury B (2011) Exception provisions as a gateway to incorporating human rights issues into international investment agreements. Columbia J Transnational Law 49(3):670–716

Choudhury B (2020) International economic law and non-economic issues. Vanderbilt J Transnational Law 53(1):1–77

De Schutter O (2014) International human rights law: cases, materials, commentary. Cambridge University Press, Cambridge

Donaldson T (1982) Corporations and morality. Prentice-Hall, Englewood Cliffs

Du M (2016) The necessity test in world trade law: what now? Chinese J Int Law 15(4):817–847

Dupuy PM (2009) Unification rather than fragmentation of international law? The case of international investment law and human rights law. In: Dupuy PM, Petersmann EU, Francioni F (eds) Human rights in international investment law and arbitration. Oxford University Press, Oxford, pp 45–62

Hirsch M (2009) Investment tribunals and human rights: divergent paths. In: Dupuy PM, Petersmann EU, Francioni F (eds) Human rights in international investment law and arbitration. Oxford University Press, Oxford, pp 97–114

Korzun V (2017) The right to regulate in investor-state arbitration: slicing and dicing regulatory carve-outs. Vanderbilt J Transnational Law 50:355–414

Krajewski M (2020) A nightmare or a noble dream? Establishing investor obligations through treaty-making and treaty-application. Bus Hum Rights J 5(1):105–129

Randall MH (2013) The history of international human rights law. In: Kolb R, Gaggioli G (eds) Research handbook on human rights and humanitarian law. Edward Elgar, Cheltenham, pp 3–24

Saldarriaga A, Magraw K (2015) UNCTAD's effort to foster the relationship between international investment law and sustainable development. In: Schill SW, Tams CJ, Hofmann R (eds) International investment law and development: bridging the gap. Edward Elgar, Cheltenham, pp 125–146

Titi C (2014) The right to regulate in international investment law. Nomos/Hart, Baden-Baden

Van Harten G (2020) The trouble with foreign investor protection. Oxford University Press, Oxford

Barnali Choudhury is Professor of Law at University College London. She is the author of numerous books and articles and is currently editing a commentary on the United Nations Guiding Principles on Business and Human Rights for Edward Elgar. She has been invited to give talks on her research around the globe and her research has been cited by the United Nations, the House of Commons and the House of Lords EU Select Committee, among others. Prior to joining academia, Barnali worked as a corporate and international investment lawyer.

Rights of Action of Business Entities in Regional Economic Systems

Patricia Wiater

Contents

Abstract Direct and state-independent rights of action of private business entities are still exceptional in international economic law and are limited to a small number of regional economic systems. Based on the examples of the European Union (EU), the European Economic Area (EEA), the East African Community (EAC), the Southern African Development Community (SADC), the Economic Community of West African States (ECOWAS) and the Caribbean Community (CARICOM), this article examines the status quo of the procedural empowerment of business entities on regional integration levels. It reveals that both the contracting states and the regional economic courts engaged in interpreting individual rights of action attribute different functions to the role of business entities as litigants: Understood as instruments of economic and legal participation and control, individual rights of action give companies the opportunity to actively contribute to shaping the effectiveness of law enforcement in the integration process by means of court proceedings. This functional understanding has to be complemented by a rule of law approach. In this approach, states and courts perceive business entities' rights of action to the regional courts primarily as defensive instruments, guaranteeing

P. Wiater (✉)
Friedrich–Alexander University Erlangen–Nürnberg, Erlangen, Germany
e-mail: patricia.wiater@fau.de

© Springer Nature Switzerland AG 2020   195
M. Bungenberg et al. (eds.), *European Yearbook of International Economic Law 2020*,
European Yearbook of International Economic Law (2022) 11: 195–236,
https://doi.org/10.1007/8165_2020_55, Published online: 26 November 2020

freedom from burdensome state or Community law interventions in the legal or economic positions of a company. The understanding as defensive instruments prevails (with the exception of the historical European Court of Justice (ECJ) in interpreting the Treaty establishing the European Coal and Steel Community (ECSC Treaty)) in the European systems of individual legal protection and, in some regards, in the ECOWAS legal system. By contrast, a functional understanding can be found in the rest of the African systems and in the Caribbean Community.

1 Introduction

The end of the bipolar world order had various vitalising effects on international law in general, as well as on international economic law and on the power of private economic actors to participate in the progress of international economic law in particular. One effect declared as the "most important development"[1] of international law at the turn of the Millennium was that the number of newly established or revived permanent international courts had increased significantly. A characteristic feature of many of the courts established after 1989 is that they were set up in the framework of regional integration projects and reflect classical liberal state interests, above all the liberalisation of trade and economic relations. Against this background, most of the so-called "new-style"[2] international courts continue a tradition that was established by the European Court of Justice in the 1950s. From the very beginning of the European integration project, the founders of the ECJ had opened its doors for private companies.[3]

After the end of the "Cold War", this approach to empower private business entities with state-independent regional rights of action as experienced in Europe spread all over the world. The failure of the communist alternative to the Western model of a liberal and democratic order oriented towards capitalism and the "triumph"[4] of the market-economy paradigm explain the willingness of some states to become increasingly involved in regional economic integration agreements, in which a permanent court—open for private litigants—monitors compliance with treaty obligations. Today, rights of action of private business entities exist in

---

[1] Romano (1998–1999), p. 709.

[2] Alter (2006), pp. 25 et seq. On the "export" of the "European Model" Baudenbacher (2004), pp. 382 et seq.

[3] This right was, however, limited to companies of the coal and steel industry: Article 33(2) of the Treaty establishing the European Coal and Steel Community (ECSC Treaty) allowed "undertakings or the associations referred to in Article 48" to access the ECJ. Article 80 of the ECSC Treaty provided a legal definition of undertakings and restricted them to an "undertaking engaged in production in the coal or the steel industry". Article 48 of the ECSC Treaty provided for the right of undertakings to form associations.

[4] Romano (1998–1999), pp. 709 and 729.

different regional integration systems all over the world: On the European continent, we can look at rights of action in the European Union, in the European Economic Area, and in the Eurasian Economic Union (EAEU).[5] In Africa, we can assess access to justice for business entities inter alia in the East African Community, as originally foreseen in the Southern African Development Community[6] and in the Economic Community of West African States.[7] On the American continent,[8] rights of action for business entities are in place in the Caribbean Community, in the Andean Community (CAN) and in the Central American Integration System (SICA).

The trend towards establishing permanent international courts and expanding the procedural power of companies on the international level was—and is—by no means uniform. From the 1990s onwards, the number of bilateral and multilateral trade agreements notified to the World Trade Organization (WTO) also increased significantly.[9] With regard to the modes of dispute settlement, the vast majority of these agreements only empower states and show, thereby, a trend which does *not* allow direct access to justice for the private business entities concerned.[10] The willingness of the states involved to rely on a purely political and diplomatic mode of dispute settlement seems to be stagnating.[11] By contrast, quasi-judicial dispute settlement, based on a two-stage process of negotiation and subsequent referral to an

---

[5]Since the analysis presented in this contribution is limited to judicial decisions published in English or French, the Court of Justice of the EAEU is not covered by it.

[6]See on the *de facto* abolishment of the right of action for natural or legal persons below, footnote 174.

[7]The following analysis of African regional economic integration is of exemplary nature. For instance, it does not take into account access to justice in the system of the Common Market for Eastern and Southern Africa (COMESA) or in the Organisation for the Harmonisation of Commercial Law in Africa (OHADA).

[8]For linguistic reasons, as official judicial decisions of the Andean Tribunal of Justice and the Central American Court of Justice are not published in English, the analysis focuses on CARICOM as an example of a regional economic community in the Americas.

[9]See the list of regional trade agreements notified to the WTO (available online at http://rtais.wto. org/UI/PublicAllRTAList.aspx, last accessed on 14 August 2020).

[10]This is the conclusion of a study published in June 2013 by Claude Chase, Alan Yanovich, Jo-Ann Crawford and Pamela Ugaz, in which they compared the dispute settlement mechanisms in the 226 regional trade agreements notified to the WTO by the end of 2012, see Chase C, Yanovich A, Crawford, JA, Ugaz P, Mapping of Dispute Settlement Mechanisms in Regional Trade Agreements – Innovative or Variations on a Theme?. WTO, Staff Working Paper ERSD-2013-07, 10 June 2013, https://www.oecd-ilibrary.org/docserver/93a8fc27-en.pdf? expires =1602851272&id =id&accname =guest& checksum=D7C882C82AF7C619E61007D4CF8C9B9B (last accessed 14 August 2020).

[11]Chase et al. include under this category regional trade agreements (RTAs) that (1) either do not regulate a dispute settlement mechanism at all, (2) provide for dispute settlement by negotiation and/or by a purely political body and (3) transfer dispute settlement to an external body (third-party adjudication) but grant one of the parties to the dispute a right of veto. Of the 226 RTAs examined, 69 (30%) had this mode of dispute resolution Chase C, Yanovich A, Crawford, JA, Ugaz P, Mapping of Dispute Settlement Mechanisms in Regional Trade Agreements – Innovative or Variations on a Theme?. WTO, Staff Working Paper ERSD-2013-07, 10 June 2013, https:// www.oecd-ilibrary.org/docserver/93a8fc27-en.pdf?expires=1602851272&id=id&

ad hoc panel (arbitration tribunals or commissions),[12] has experienced a remarkable increase since the 1990s.[13] As in the WTO model, states reserve for themselves the "right to act as a political filter"[14] in order to decide whether proceedings in trade matters are initiated—or not. The international enforcement of individual rights is carried out in the traditional manner through diplomatic protection by the home state of the aggrieved private party.

Moreover, as the integration systems mentioned above demonstrate, the procedural empowerment experienced by business entities is regionally concentrated and limited to integration projects on the European, African and American continents. Comparable processes of judicialisation are foreign to Asian and Arab regional alliances.[15] Also, within the institutional framework of the North American Free Trade Agreement (NAFTA) or that of the Common Market of South America (MERCOSUR), the right of business entities to decide "whether" and "how" their individual rights are enforced is decisively limited and mediatised in various forms by the states concerned.[16]

The questions of whether states establish a dispute settlement body as a permanent court with obligatory jurisdiction and whether private parties are given comprehensive, direct and state-independent access to court prove to be crucial regulatory issues. This holds true not only for the phase of "new regionalism",[17] initiated in the early 1990s, but also for integration projects launched before the end of the Cold War. Direct and state-independent rights of action of private business entities are still exceptional in international economic law. They are noteworthy precisely for this regulatory reason. Against this background, this article aims to examine the status quo of the procedural empowerment of business entities in regional economic integration systems.[18] Its main part is divided into two subsections: In assessing and systematising the existing rights of actions, we not only

---

accname=guest&checksum=D7C882C82AF7C619E61007D4CF8C9B9B   (last   accessed 14 August 2020), pp. 11 and 13.

[12]De Mestral (2013), p. 779.

[13]This mechanism was used in 147 of the 226 agreements examined (65%); for this and for the increasing number since 1990 Chase C, Yanovich A, Crawford, JA, Ugaz P, Mapping of Dispute Settlement Mechanisms in Regional Trade Agreements – Innovative or Variations on a Theme?. WTO, Staff Working Paper ERSD-2013-07, 10 June 2013, https://www.oecd-ilibrary.org/docserver/93a8fc27-en.pdf?expires=1602851272&id=id&accname=guest&checksum=D7C882C82AF7C619E61007D4CF8C9B9B (last accessed 14 August 2020), p. 13.

[14]Sykes (2005), p. 631.

[15]Alter and Hooghe (2016), p. 538.

[16]On NAFTA's and MERCOSUR's dispute settlement mechanism Krapohl S, Dinkel J, Faude B, Judicial Integration in the Americas? – A Comparison of Dispute Settlement in NAFTA and MERCOSUR. Bamberger Online Papers on Integration Research No. 4, 2009, http://www.ssoar.info/ssoar/bitstream/handle/document/13055/ssoar-2009-krapohl_et_al-judicial_integration_in_the_americas.pdf?sequence=1 (last accessed 14 August 2020).

[17]On the different phases of regionalism Fawcett (2008), pp. 15 et seq.

[18]This analysis is one part of a comprehensive analysis of the procedural status of private litigants in international economic law (Wiater 2020).

ask why[19] states decided to go for "the uncommon" by opening access to international courts for the non-state actor "private company" and how they laid down this procedural empowerment in concrete rights of action (Sect. 2). We also analyse how the regional courts open for private business entities interpret these rights of action in their case-law and, thereby, further develop and expand the procedural status of business entities (Sect. 3). Some concluding remarks systematise counterpoints of the possible procedural empowerment of companies in regional economic systems (Sect. 4).

A definitional preliminary note has to be made: In most integration systems,[20] the procedural empowerment of business entities is subsumed under the broader procedural law category "natural and legal persons". The notion of "private litigants" and of "individual access to court",[21] used in the following, is an expression for this comprehensive procedural law category and includes the procedural status of business entities.

2 Member States' Motivation to Introduce Rights of Action and Their Procedural Details

We can abstract two basic reasons that have motivated states to establish individual access to regional economic courts: In integration systems belonging to a first model, states consider the introduction of direct rights of action as the necessary consequence of a bundling of decision-making power and sovereignty at the regional level. The power of private parties to bring actions is explained by the direct, possibly onerous effects that this sovereignty has on the (economic) position of the business entity. An example of this model are the rights of action before the ECJ and the EFTA Court. A second model, on the other hand, sees the opening of direct access to regional courts as an instrument to mobilise the private sector to take economic or legal action and to accept co-responsibility for the integration process. The Economic Community of West African States, the East African Community, the Southern African Development Community, and the Caribbean Community can be assigned to this second model.

What is indicated by the different motives for the introduction of rights of action is perpetuated in the procedural design of individual access to courts: Rights of

---

[19] As far as possible, the motivation of states to introduce individual rights of action is based on an evaluation of the travaux préparatoires and national ratification materials for the various treaties or publicly available political opinions. See in detail on the respective integration systems Wiater (2020), pp. 25 et seq.

[20] Only the right of action that was existent in the ECSC (see footnote 3) relates to "undertakings" and "associations".

[21] Consequently, the notions "individual" and "private" do not primarily relate to the human being as litigant, but serve as an umbrella term for economic non-state actors primarily including companies.

action of the first model tend to be narrow and privileged. By contrast, states that understand the introduction of individual rights of action as a functional contribution to pursuing economic or community goals more effectively, generally develop them broadly. Thereby, the procedural status of states, on the one hand, and of private business entities, on the other hand, are brought closer together.

2.1 The Rule of Law Model: Rights of Action as Defence Instruments

2.1.1 Historical Will

The rights of action to the ECJ as originally developed in the European Coal and Steel Community (1952)[22] and further continued[23] in the European Economic Community (EEC, 1958) as well as in the European Union (2009) are paradigmatic for the first model of state motivation to open access to justice for private business entities. From the very beginning of the European integration project onwards, the concept of judicial protection of individual rights was considered to interdependently relate to the specific subject and institutional design of the integration project. In the eyes of the founding fathers, the concept of "supranationality",[24] as already laid down in the Schuman Plan, created a "novelty in the field of international organisational law":[25] In an unprecedented manner, the High Authority of the ECSC (predecessor of the EU Commission) was empowered to exercise legislative and executive powers over companies in the coal and steel industry. The member states agreed to transfer powers in the field of coal and steel administration to the High Authority while at the same time eliminating the competence of the member states. In its capacity as the main legislative body, the High Authority was empowered to adopt legally binding "decisions" (décision) and "recommendations" (recommendation) in the areas regulated conclusively and enumeratively in the ECSC Treaty after consultation with or approval by the Council. The ECSC Treaty was the law (traité loi). In this sense, the High Authority of the ECSC, designed as a largely independent body, acted as the executive body of the partial integration of the coal and steel industries, as specified by the participating states in the Treaty.

The direct and considerable burdensome effects that this competence would have on the economic activities of the coal and steel companies of the participating states

---

[22]The ECSC Treaty applied from 1952, it was valid for 50 years and expired in 2002.

[23]The admissibility requirements of the individual action for annulment (which has proved to be the fundamental right of action for private business entities under EU law), were only modified in the course of these three integration steps. The wording of this right of action remained unaffected, in particular, by the fundamental changes the judicial architecture experienced with the progressive integration by the Treaties of Maastricht (1992), Amsterdam (1997) and Nice (2001).

[24]Mosler (1966), pp. 366 et seq. with further references.

[25]Jaenicke (1951), p. 730.

finally motivated the founding states to open access to the ECJ for the companies concerned. In the eyes of the founders, the design of the European integration project differed to such an extent from classic intergovernmental international agreements that a radical departure from "the usual" diplomatic protection model was considered inevitable for the protection of individual rights. Particularly the German negotiators were in favour of clarifying the relationship between those private companies concerned and the High Authority by introducing direct rights of action:[26] The central argument was based on a recent achievement of the Bonn Basic Law— Article 19(4)[27]—which had created a "general clause for complaints against administrative interventions".[28] If burdening measures of the High Authority against individual enterprises were permitted, these enterprises would inevitably also have to be granted a direct right of action to the European Court of Justice.

This premise was maintained in the process of founding the European Economic Community and the resulting change towards the regulatory concept of the EEC Treaty as *traité cadre* or *traité de procédure* (as opposed to the ECSC Treaty as *traité loi* or *traité de règles*).[29] The extension of the Community's sphere of activity to *all* sectors of the economy inevitably had the consequence that Community law could no longer be implemented solely by the EU Commission under its own administration in a manner comparable to the task of its predecessor, the High Authority, in the European Coal and Steel Community. Consequently, the point of reference for the private entities' need for legal protection shifted to the burdensome effects of secondary legislation, for which the Council of Ministers was initially largely responsible. However, the postulate that independent rights of action of private litigants necessarily derive from burdensome effects of the supranational character of European integration remained unchanged in the EEC[30] and is still valid in the EU as framed by the Lisbon Treaty of 2009. The negotiating parties of the (failed) constitutional reform process of the early 2000s and of the Lisbon Treaty deliberately affirmed the rule of law rationale of direct rights of action of private litigants.[31]

The rule of law model also applies to business entities' rights of action to the Court of the European Free Trade Association (EFTA Court). The EFTA Court, nowadays[32] also located in Luxembourg, has jurisdiction with regard to the EFTA States Iceland, Liechtenstein and Norway which are parties to the Agreement on the

---

[26]Mosler (1966), p. 369.

[27]Article 19(4) Basic Law reads: "(4) Should any person's rights be violated by public authority, he may have recourse to the courts. If no other jurisdiction has been established, recourse shall be to the ordinary courts."

[28]Mosler (1966), p. 369 ("Generalklausel für jegliche Art von Beschwerde durch behördliches Vorgehen").

[29]On this linguistic differentiation Reuter (1965), pp. 174 et seq.

[30]Daig (1958), p. 168.

[31]On the reform process and the revision of the individual action for annulment see below (footnote 48).

[32]In 1996, the EFTA Court moved from its founding seat in Geneva to Luxembourg.

European Economic Area (EEA Agreement),[33] concluded in Porto on 2 May 1992. The EEA Agreement is formally an association agreement within the meaning of Article 217 of the Treaty on the Functioning of the European Union (TFEU). However, the agreement differs categorically from other types of EU association agreements in that its basic idea is to accomplish equal treatment and non-discrimination of economic operators of the EFTA States and to realise, thereby, a widening of the EU internal market.[34] From the very beginning, the founders of the EFTA Court aimed at creating an "ECJ-like" judicial mechanism to avoid the risk of a legal imbalance[35] to the detriment of individuals and economic operators in the EFTA States. In various aspects, the right of natural or legal persons to initiate actions for annulment under the Agreement between the EFTA States on the Establishment of a Surveillance Authority and a Court of Justice[36] (Surveillance and Court Agreement, SCA) complies with the pertinent EU provision. This parallelism in the design of the judicial and procedural architecture[37] corresponds to a parallel design of the surveillance mechanism: The EFTA States also entrusted an independent administrative body, the EFTA Surveillance Authority (ESA), to adopt binding measures on undertakings and individuals when implementing state aid and competition law. As in the case of the ECSC, the founders of the EFTA Court were convinced that the impact the surveillance mechanism would have on private economic operators would necessarily have to be supplemented by a corresponding right to directly access the regional Court of Justice.[38]

2.1.2 Procedural Details: Subordinating Business Entities Procedurally

The procedural consequence of this rule of law postulate is a restrictive design of individual access to court. The rights of action before the ECJ and the EFTA Court are mainly designed as defensive instruments and focus on legal protection against the burdensome effects of Community law. Natural and legal persons are excluded from purely abstract-objective proceedings aiming at a judicial clarification of the interpretation and application of integration treaties in general. Thus, they cannot initiate proceedings addressed at the uniform enforcement of the respective programme of rights and obligations under the integration treaty. In this model, the procedural function of private entities is primarily reduced to seeking legal

---

[33]OJ L 1, 3.1.1994, p. 3. Switzerland is a member of EFTA but does not take part in the EEA.

[34]Fredriksen and Franklin (2015), p. 630 contrast the relative absence of political and academic interest in the Agreement with the fact that Norway alone is the EU's fifth most important trading partner and the high number (in 2015 about 200,000) of EU citizens currently exercising their EEA-based rights to take up employment in Norway.

[35]Norberg and Johansson (2016), p. 20.

[36]Agreement between the EFTA States on the Establishment of a Surveillance Authority and a Court of Justice, OJ L 344, 31.1.1994, p. 3.

[37]Sevón (1992), pp. 331 et seq.

[38]Norberg and Johansson (2016), p. 83.

protection, only subordinate to that of a co-responsible party for the efficient functioning of the regional legal order. Abstract proceedings are reserved for the member states and the respective international supervisory body (High Authority/ Commission, ESA).

Accessing the ECJ

The system of legal protection under EU law derives from the principle that private litigants cannot participate in proceedings with an exclusively objective legal focus. Within the legal protection system, there is a judgmental gradation between procedural rights of natural and legal persons on the one hand and member states or the EU Commission on the other. Since the introduction of the infringement procedure, which is objective in nature and serves the enforcement of EU law,[39] only member states and the EU Commission have had the status of active parties.[40] Moreover, since the action for annulment has been established in the system of the European Coal and Steel Community,[41] the legal protection system has distinguished between litigants with unlimited rights and privileges (as an expression of their emphasised importance in the institutional setting), on the one hand, and private litigants with only limited procedural rights, on the other.[42] Despite this clear procedural subordination natural and legal persons still experience in the system of current EU law, the latter opens up a middle way: In the framework of actions for annulment, private litigants are in some regards involved in the objective control of the legality of secondary EU law if they overcome the high standard of *locus standi*. The circle of natural and legal persons who are entitled to participate in this control was, however, from the outset of the European integration project conceived as narrowly and as restrictively as possible. The uniform principle, which endured the Treaty establishing the European Coal and Steel Community (1952), the Treaties of Rome (1958) and the Treaty of Lisbon (2009), was to grant legal protection only to the extent that the litigant was burdened by the act of supranational sovereignty. Consequently, participation in the control of normative and administrative measures

---

[39]Lenaerts et al. (2015), p. 159, para. 5.01.

[40]Article 258 TFEU lays down the right of the Commission to initiate infringement proceedings against a member state. Article 259 TFEU regulates infringement proceedings of a member state against another.

[41]The following analysis focuses on the individual action for annulment as the right of action which is of paramount practical relevance. In addition, natural and legal persons have the right to initiate actions for failure to act (Article 265(3) TFEU), Article 268 TFEU lays down the right to bring an action for damages and under Article 277 TFEU, "any party" (this covers natural and legal persons) may raise an objection of illegality.

[42]The circle of privileged applicants gradually expanded: from the member states and the Council, as referred to in Article 33(1) ECSC Treaty, to the member states, the European Parliament, the Council or the Commission as foreseen in Article 263(2) TFEU.

was limited in equal manner. Inspired by the French administrative law,[43] in which *règlements* and *décisions* as *actes administratifs* can be challenged indiscriminately with an action for annulment, Article 33(2) ECSC Treaty equipped undertakings or associations of the coal and steel industry[44] with legal protection against individual and general decisions as well as against recommendations of the High Authority.[45] According to the historic will of the authors of the Coal and Steel Treaty, however, only such general decisions were to be reviewable which (although of a general nature in terms of *form*) in terms of their *content* actually concerned a company or association of companies. This restrictive intention was to be served by a differentiated regulation of the *locus standi* requirement: For companies, asserting a misuse of powers (*détournement de pouvoir*) was a precondition for challenging *general* decisions and recommendations of the High Authority. Thus, the litigant had to show that the High Authority had the intention to address the litigant individually despite the general external form of the decision.[46] By contrast, the entirety of possible grounds for invalidity (lack of competence, infringement of an essential procedural requirement, infringement of the Treaty or of any rule of law relating to its application, or misuse of powers) applied to *individual* acts of the High Authority.

This restrictive approach towards actions for annulment initiated by private litigants remained unchanged in the legal protection system of the Treaty of Rome. On the one hand, the authors of the EEC Treaty extended the reach of individual actions for annulment in various aspects: Article 173(2) of the EEC Treaty[47] allowed recourse to the four possible grounds for invalidity in *any* situation of challenge. Due to the aim of achieving total economic integration in the framework of the EEC, the exclusive circle of litigants (coal and steel companies and associations) was broadened to "natural and legal" persons. On the other hand, the authors shifted the restriction of the individual right of action to the legal nature of

---

[43]On the influence of French administrative law on the system of legal protection in the ECSC Reuter (1953), pp. 87 et seq.

[44]Private parties not belonging to the coal and steel industry were only allowed to access the ECJ on the basis of a few special provisions, for example in their capacity as buyers, Article 63 ECSC.

[45]Article 33(2) ECSC Treaty reads: "Undertakings or the associations referred to in Article 48 may, under the same conditions, institute proceedings against decisions or recommendations concerning them which are individual in character or against general decisions or recommendations which they consider to involve a misuse of powers affecting them."

[46]On the historic will, see AG Lagrange, Case C-3/54, Assider, ECLI:EU:C:1954:6, p. 87: "(..) (H)aving just included misuse of powers among the grounds for annulment, the authors of the Treaty thought of the situation where a decision which, while in fact individually affecting an undertaking, is 'disguised' (...) as, to all appearances, a general decision and is, in consequence, clearly invalidated as a misuse of powers." and Reuter (1953), p. 90.

[47]Article 173(2) EEC Treaty reads: "Any natural or legal person may, under the same conditions, institute proceedings against a decision addressed to that person or against a decision which, although in the form of a regulation or a decision addressed to another person, is of direct and individual concern to the former." This wording was maintained in Article 173 of the EC Treaty (Maastricht consolidated version) as well as in Article 230 Treaty establishing the European Community (Nice consolidated version).

the measure to be challenged and to its special relationship to the situation of the private litigant. The second paragraph of Article 173 of the EEC Treaty grants natural or legal persons an unlimited right to institute proceedings against a decision addressed to that person. By contrast, the right of action contesting decisions which "although in the form of a regulation or a decision addressed to another person" only existed if the decision concerned the litigant "directly and individually". The wording of the Coal and Steel Treaty "un recours contre les décisions et recommandations individuelle les concernant" was significantly tightened in the new wording of the EEC Treaty, as the French wording reads "la concernent directement et individuellement". While the requirement of individualisation of the Coal and Steel Treaty was related to the subject matter of the action, the EEC Treaty required an individualisation of the litigant's concern.

This restrictive approach was still not abandoned in the course of the reform of the legal protection system, as reflected in the Lisbon Treaty. In addition to the aforementioned types of action, Article 263 para. 4 alt. 3 TFEU[48] authorises natural and legal persons to bring an action against a regulatory act which is of direct concern to them and does not entail implementing measures. However, by abandoning the criterion of individual concern, the authors of the Lisbon Treaty merely pursued the goal of closing obvious gaps in legal protection. The extension of the right to institute proceedings should apply only to those problematical cases where otherwise the private party concerned would have had first to infringe the law in order to gain access to a court.[49] Thus, it was not the intention to give up the principle of procedural subordination of private litigants: Legislative acts adopted by legislative procedure (Article 289 para. 3 TFEU)—the result of political negotiations—should be excluded as suitable objects of an action brought by natural and legal persons. The overriding objective that was pursued with this consistently "restrictive approach"[50] was to place direct legal protection before the EU courts in relation to the increased democratic content of intra-Union decision-making, especially the increased importance of the European Parliament in the legislative procedure.[51] Since the European Parliament—as directly and democratically legitimised actor by the citizens of the Union—has been attributed more competences in the decision-making process in the

---

[48] Article 263(4) TFEU reads: "Any natural or legal person may, under the conditions laid down in the first and second paragraphs, institute proceedings against an act addressed to that person or which is of direct and individual concern to them, and against a regulatory act which is of direct concern to them and does not entail implementing measures."

[49] The reform of the legal protection system was initially part of the (failed) process of drafting a Constitution for Europe and finalised in the Lisbon Treaty. On maintaining the restrictive approach towards annulment proceedings of private litigants in the reform process see for example CONV 636/03 of 25 March 2003 CERCLE I 13, p. 7 para. 21.

[50] Quote from the transmission note of the Praesidium, CONV 734/03 of 12 May 2003, p. 20.

[51] On the particularly "high democratic legitimation of parliamentary legislation" as a reason for restriction see AG Kokott, Case C-583/11 P, Inuit Tapiriit Kanatami and Others, ECLI:EU: C:2013:21, para. 38.

course of the reform process, increasing the procedural power of private litigants at EU level was considered unnecessary.

Accessing the EFTA Court

Similar to the EU legal protection system, natural and legal persons accessing the EFTA Court also experience different forms of procedural subordination comparable to the rights of action of EU member states and of the EFTA Surveillance Authority (ESA): Abstract disputes concerning the interpretation or application of EEA law can only be settled in intergovernmental proceedings.[52] Moreover, companies are excluded from initiating treaty infringement proceedings against EFTA States. This right is reserved to the ESA.[53]

With regard to the action for annulment[54] (and the action for failure to act), the three EEA EFTA States took an even more restrictive approach than the EU contracting states in the framework of the Lisbon Treaty. Before the EFTA Court, the possible subject matter of annulment proceedings of companies is limited to a minimum since natural and legal persons are only allowed to challenge decisions in the field of competition and state aid taken by the EFTA Surveillance Authority[55] if they are addressees or "directly and individually concerned". Neither secondary legislation incorporated into the EEA Agreement nor upstream decisions of the EEA Joint Committee incorporating EU acts into the EEA Agreement constitute valid objects of action under Article 36(2) of the SCA. The EEA Joint Committee, bringing together "representatives of the Contracting Parties",[56] is the actual decision-making body of the EEA. The Committee continuously monitors EU legislative processes and determines which EU legal acts affecting the internal market are to be integrated into the EEA Agreement and become binding on the EFTA States.[57] EEA law is created by transferring EU law from the EU pillar to the EFTA pillar.[58]

This restrictive nature of the subject matter of the annulment procedure is based on the logic and purpose underlying the institutional framework of the European

---

[52] Article 32 SCA.

[53] Article 108(2) sub-para. 2 lit. a EEA Agreement, Article 31 SCA.

[54] Article 36(2) SCA: "Any natural or legal person may, under the same conditions, institute proceedings before the EFTA Court against a decision of the EFTA Surveillance Authority addressed to that person or against a decision addressed to another person, if it is of direct and individual concern to the former".

[55] Article 108(2) sub-para. 2 lit. b EEA Agreement limits the right of action to "decisions in the field of competition". Article 36(2) SCA, cited in footnote 54, is not limited to competition matters; the subject matter therefore includes state aide decisions of ESA.

[56] Article 93 EEA Agreement.

[57] Article 92(1) EEA Agreement, Article 102(1) EEA Agreement.

[58] More specifically, this is implemented by amending the Annexes and Protocols to the EEA Agreement, Article 98 EEA Agreement.

Economic Area. One institutional characteristic of the two-pillar structure (and a reaction to prior institutional objections of the ECJ in safeguarding the "autonomy of the Community legal order"[59]) is that the EU and EFTA each have their own institutions which are separately responsible for the proper functioning of the agreement. Its objective is to avoid an impairment of the EU's system of competences and thus also of the autonomy of EU law caused by the intervention of the EFTA Court. From the EU perspective, maintaining this autonomy is the exclusive and core responsibility of the ECJ. In this regard, the EFTA States do not have any rights of participation or decision-making powers to influence the outcome of EU legislation processes, nor should natural and legal persons acting as litigants before the EFTA Court be able to participate in the development of the substance of Community or subsequent EU law through judicial procedures. In order to take action against burdensome secondary EU law, the only means of choice are proceedings before the ECJ.[60]

2.2 The Functional Model: Rights of Action as Instruments of Control and Participation

2.2.1 Historical Will

In a second model, the state's motivation to give private business entities direct access to a regional economic court is primarily functional and not a postulate of the international rule of law. In the Eurasian, African and American systems of regional economic integration, in which this motivation predominated, the introduction of individual rights of action were the expression of a political turnaround. For the participating states, the process of empowering private business entities with procedural rights was one essential facet of a deliberately initiated, overarching push towards deepening economic integration by means of judicialisation. A purely intergovernmental concept of dispute settlement and law enforcement was to be overcome because it had largely proved to be ineffective. As a consequence, the participating states acknowledged the principal role private companies play as relevant economic stakeholders and as law enforcers. Particularly after the end of the Cold War, this group of states increasingly recognised the economic importance of the private sector in order to avoid the economic marginalisation of their respective region on the world market. Thus, in the early 1990s, introducing rights of action for private business entities was meant as an internal and external commitment (to foreign investors) to promote the agreed economic integration programme with full commitment for the future.

---

[59]ECJ, Case 1/91, Accord EEE—I, ECLI:EU:C:1991:490, para. 35.
[60]Baudenbacher (2016), p. 165.

Against this background, the Economic Community of West African States[61] is a special case. Here, the integration goals and institutional design of the Community also underwent a fundamental reform at the beginning of the 1990s. However, even in the course of revising the ECOWAS Treaty,[62] the contracting states did not initially abandon the restriction of jurisdiction to intergovernmental procedures which had already been laid down in the 1975 "Treaty of Lagos".[63] This came about despite the increasing number of substantive individual guarantees in ECOWAS law and the recommendation to the contrary by the "Committee of Eminent Persons" which had unequivocally spoken out in favour of guaranteeing direct rights of action for private actors (companies, individuals, and interest groups). Rather, the introduction of access to justice for "individuals and corporate bodies" took place later, in the 2000s, mainly as a reaction to a political campaign promoted by the ECOWAS Court itself.[64]

The East African Community[65] based in Arusha, Tanzania, by contrast, is a classic example for a process of judicialisation set in motion by the member states as a consequence of the end of the bipolar world order. The EAC reinvented itself in 1999 and, thereby, distanced itself from its predecessor institution, also named the "East African Community", which had been dissolved in 1984.[66] In the preamble of the EAC Treaty of 1999[67], the "lack of strong participation of the private sector and civil society in the co-operation activities" is cited as one of the main reasons contributing to the collapse of the previous EAC. The founding treaty of the old EAC had also provided for a "Common Market Tribunal" as judicial body, before which, however, only states were entitled to bring an action.[68] Facets of the "reinvention" of the EAC were not only the objective of creating a customs union, a common market, a monetary union and a political federation as integration pillars.

---

[61]https://www.ecowas.int/ (last accessed 14 August 2020). Member states of ECOWAS are Benin, Burkina Faso, Cabo Verde, Côte d'Ivoire, The Gambia, Ghana, Guinea, Guinea Bissau, Liberia, Mali, Niger, Nigeria, Senegal, Sierra Leone and Togo.

[62]Revised Treaty of the Economic Community of West African States (ECOWAS) of 24 July 1993, UNTS Vol. 2373, p. 233.

[63]Treaty of the Economic Community of West African States (ECOWAS) of 28 May 1975, UNTS Vol. 1010, p. 17.

[64]On this reform process Alter et al. (2013), pp. 745 et seq.

[65]https://www.eac.int/ (last accessed 14 August 2020). Today, the EAC includes the Republics of Burundi, Kenya, Rwanda, South Sudan, the United Republic of Tanzania, and the Republic of Uganda as Partner States.

[66]On the negotiation processes in the course of the dissolution of the old EAC, the conclusion of the mediation agreement and the refoundation of the EAC see Umbricht (1989), pp. 7 et seq.

[67]The Treaty for the Establishment of the East African Community (EAC Treaty) (UNTS Vol. 2144, p. 255, EAC Publication, No. 1) was signed on 30 November 1999 in Arusha, Tanzania, and entered into force on 7 July 2000.

[68]Treaty for East African cooperation of 6 June 1967, UNTS Vol. 1989, p. 3. See Chapter X, Article 36.

Rather, the member states also reformed the law enforcement mechanisms and, for the first time, introduced a right of action for natural and legal persons.[69]

A similar process took place in the Southern African Development Community,[70] located in Gaborone, Botswana. In the course of deepening the level of integration of its predecessor association, the Southern African Development Coordinating Conference (SADCC), which was founded in 1980 by the so-called "frontline states", the integration was extended in the early 1990s by the goal to establish a common market.[71] Moreover, as formulated in the Windhoek Declaration of 1992,[72] the member states made the success of their regional integration project closely dependent on the fact that the responsible community institutions had to be provided with sufficient competencies and financial resources to effectively advance the integration process. In this sense, the 1992 SADC Treaty[73] had already provided for the legalisation of dispute settlement with the establishment of a tribunal which, in SADCC, was still reserved on a purely political level for the heads of state and government meeting in the Summit. It was by means of the Protocol on the SADC Tribunal of 2000[74] that the member states further deepened the integration level by opening access to court for private litigants. The influence of external integration partners who saw the success of the integration project in close connection with a "credible and effective" dispute settlement body, may have been decisive for the SADC countries to grant individual access to the SADC Tribunal.[75]

In a similar way, in 1989, the heads of government of the Caribbean Community[76] also noted that the purely political nature of the dispute settlement

---

[69]On the East African Court of Justice (EACJ) Gathii (2016), pp. 38 et seq.

[70]https://www.sadc.int/ (last accessed 14 August 2020). Today's SADC has 16 member states, Angola, Botswana, the Democratic Republic of Congo, the Union of Comoros, Lesotho, Madagascar, Malawi, Mauritius, Mozambique, Namibia, the Seychelles, South Africa, Eswatini (Swaziland), Tanzania, Zambia and Zimbabwe.

[71]The Protocol on Trade, signed in 1996 and entered into force in 2001 provides for the establishment of a Free Trade Area in the SADC region and marks a first milestone on the path of SADC integration, which is to culminate in the establishment of a Customs Union, a Common Market, a Monetary Union and a Single Currency. On the historical development and the (partly deficient) realisation of the ambitious SADC integration scheme see Mapuva and Muyengwa-Mapuva (2014), pp. 24 et seq.

[72]Online available at https://www.sadc.int/files/8613/5292/8378/Declaration__Treaty_of_SADC.pdf (last accessed 14 August 2020).

[73]Treaty of the Southern African Development Community of 17 August 1992, 32 ILM 1993, p. 116.

[74]Protocol on the Tribunal in the Southern African Development Community of 7 August 2000 (2000 Protocol), entered into force on 14 August 2011, online available at https://www.sadc.int/documents-publications/show/Protocol%20on%20the%20Tribunal%20and%20Rules%20thereof%20(2000) (last accessed 14 August 2020).

[75]Lenz (2012), p. 166 with further references.

[76]https://caricom.org/ (last accessed 14 August 2020). CARICOM, which has its headquarters in Georgetown (Guyana), currently comprises of a community of 15 small and micro-states, which, with the exception of Belize, Guyana and Suriname, consists of islands and extends over North, Central and South America.

mechanisms provided for in the 1973 "Treaty of Chaguaramas"[77] had had a negative impact on the Community's economic successes. That was mainly due to member states' negligence in implementing Community measures.[78] Notwithstanding this relatively negative balance on previous integration successes, the 1989 "Grand Anse Declaration" declared the creation of a single market to be a CARICOM objective. Based on the reform agenda proposed to the member states by the West Indian Commission,[79] the Treaty of Chaguaramas was revised in 2001[80] and, at the same time, the member states adopted an agreement establishing the Caribbean Court of Justice (CCJ)[81] which is open to private business entities. Thereby, the CARICOM States approved the West Indian Commission's assumption that there is an indissoluble link between the success of the integration project and its constitutionality under the rule of law, the existence of rights and obligations under Community law and their effective judicial enforcement—by no less than "any CARICOM citizen (individual or corporate)".[82]

2.2.2 Procedural Details: Approximating the Procedural Status of Business Entities and States

In this second model of empowering business entities by providing them with direct rights of action before a regional court, one central common feature prevails: The introduction of the rights of action resulted in the company's authorisation to initiate proceedings against states in order to subject state measures to judicial review by the regional courts. In such proceedings, private litigants (in their function as applicants) and states (in their role as defendants) are placed on an equal footing with the effect that the classic dogma of sovereignty is relaxed. To varying degrees, the member states of the different integration systems were prepared to grant even further reaching procedural equality between the state and business entities. Compared to

---

[77]The Treaty was signed in Chaguaramas, Trinidad and Tobago, on 4 July 1973 and entered into force on 1 August 1973. It consists of two separate parts: the Treaty establishing the Caribbean Community, UNTS Vol. 946, p. 17, and the Agreement establishing a Common Market, UNTS Vol. 946, p. 28.

[78]Miskelley (1990), pp. 192 et seq.

[79]On the deficiencies of the implementation mechanisms see The West Indian Commission (1993), pp. 462 et seq., p. 463.

[80]The Revised Treaty of Chaguaramas Establishing the Caribbean Community, including the CARICOM Single Market and Economy (RTC), UNTS Vol. 2259, p. 293, was signed at the 22nd Summit of Heads of Government in July 2001 and finally came into force on 1 January 2006. The Court has "hybrid" jurisdiction, that is "original jurisdiction" in its function as a regional economic court as well as "appellate jurisdiction".

[81]Agreement establishing the Caribbean Court of Justice of 14 February 2001, UNTS Vol. 2255, p. 319. On the establishment of the CCJ and its double function as a CARICOM Court and a shared regional appellate court see Kocken and van Roozendaal (2012), pp. 96 et seq.

[82]The West Indian Commission (1993), p. 500.

the rule of law model, in this second model the member states agreed to opening access to court on a broader scale.

The "Minimum Model" of Broad Access to Court: Companies Before the ECOWAS Court of Justice

In ECOWAS law (reformed by a Supplementary Protocol of 2005),[83] the subjective dimension of legal protection is the dominant feature of the rights of action of private litigants. Subjective dimension refers to the fact that the rights of action mainly serve the litigant's personal need for legal protection. This subjective focus is opposed to an objective nature of judicial proceedings initiated in the overall interest of the economic community. The procedural consequence of this "minimum model" is that the member states grant themselves a broader scope of proceedings than natural and legal persons.

In the English language version, ECOWAS law distinguishes between rights of action of "individuals or corporate bodies", on the one hand, and "individuals" on the other: Individuals *or* corporate bodies have the right to have determined that the action or inaction of a Community official has violated their rights (Article 10(c) 2005 Protocol). According to the wording of Article 10(d) 2005 Protocol,[84] only individuals can apply for relief for a violation of their human rights.[85] This latter procedure, which is directed against states, is subject to the fulfilment of the admissibility conditions that the application is lodged within 3 years of the harmful event, cannot be made anonymously and is not simultaneously pending before another international court for adjudication. Consequently, ECOWAS law, similar to private parties' rights of action before the ECJ or the EFTA Court, also excludes business entities from purely abstract proceedings aimed at objective legality control: It is not open to companies to initiate infringement proceedings in order to establish that a member state has not fulfilled its contractual obligations. These procedures, comparable to the restrictive approach of the first rule of law model, are reserved for the member states or the ECOWAS Commission[86] (Article 10(a) 2005

---

[83]Supplementary Protocol A/SP1/01/05 Amending the Preamble and Articles 1, 2, 9 and 30 of Protocol (A/P.1/7/91) Relating to the Community Court of Justice and Article 4 para. 1 of the English Version of the Said Protocol of 19 January 2005 (2005 Protocol), available at http://prod. courtecowas.org/wp-content/uploads/2018/11/Supplementary_Protocol_ASP.10105_ENG.pdf (last accessed 14 August 2020).

[84]The authentic French version of the Protocol, (authentic in addition to the English and Portuguese language versions), extends human rights procedures neutrally to "toute personne victim".

[85]Article 10(d) 2005 Protocol reads: "Individuals on application for relief for violation of their human rights; the submission of application for which shall: i. Not be anonymous; nor ii. Be made whilst the same matter has been instituted before another International Court for adjudication."

[86]The Executive Secretariat mentioned in Article 17 et seq. ECOWAS Treaty was renamed in ECOWAS Commission as of 1 January 2007. The legal basis was the "Supplementary Protocol Amending the Revised ECOWAS Treaty" of 14 June 2006, ECOWAS Doc. A/SP.1/06/06.

Protocol). Furthermore, according to the wording of Article 10(b) 2005 Protocol, natural and legal persons are not authorised to bring actions for annulment which can be brought by a member state, the Council of Ministers or the Commission alone.

The "Maximum Model" of Broad Access to Courts

The "maximum model" of broad access to courts, on the other hand, puts states and companies and, in some legal systems also the Community law enforcement body (Commission), on an equal footing in terms of the types of proceedings and the canon of suitable subjects of action. In varying degrees, the maximum model also allows natural and legal persons to act as actors of objective legality control. The legal protection system of the East African Community, the Southern African Development Community, and the Caribbean Community are examples of this model. Nevertheless, a complete levelling of the procedural status of state and private parties is not realised in this model either, since the participating states consistently restrict access to court for natural and legal persons by means of various admissibility criteria.

Within the maximum model, individual access to court in the CARICOM system is the most restrictive type due to the high demands placed on standing and because of the remaining right of intervention of the litigant's home state. The right of action of business entities constitutes, by a combination of the special provision governing the "locus standi of private entities",[87] the jurisdiction norm of the CCJ[88] and the provision differentiating the dispute settlement system into various interpretation

---

[87] Article 222 of the RTC reads: "Persons, natural or juridical, of a Contracting Party may, with the special leave of the Court, be allowed to appear as parties in proceedings before the Court where: (a) the Court has determined in any particular case that this Treaty intended that a right or benefit conferred by or under this Treaty on a Contracting Party shall ensure to the benefit of such persons directly; and (b) the persons concerned have established that such persons have been prejudiced in respect of the enjoyment of the right or benefit mentioned in paragraph (a) of this Article; and (c) the Contracting Party entitled to espouse the claim in proceedings before the Court has: (i) omitted or declined to espouse the claim, or (ii) expressly agreed that the persons concerned may espouse the claim instead of the Contracting Party so entitled; and (d) the Court has found that the interest of justice requires that the persons be allowed to espouse the claim."; The text of the parallel provision in the Agreement Establishing the Caribbean Court of Justice, Art. XXIV, differs in an essential detail from the provision of Art. 222 RTC: Art. 222 RTC replaces the wording "Nationals of a Contracting Party" by "Persons, natural or juridical, of a Contracting Party". However, the wording is otherwise identical.

[88] Art. 211(1) of the RTC reads: "Subject to this Treaty, the Court shall have compulsory and exclusive jurisdiction to hear and determine disputes concerning the interpretation and application of the Treaty, including: (a) disputes between the Member States parties to the Agreement; (b) disputes between the Member States parties to the Agreement and the Community; (c) referrals from national courts of the Member States parties to the Agreement; (d) applications by persons in accordance with Article 222, concerning the interpretation and application of this Treaty."

and application disputes.[89] From this systematic interplay of pertinent procedural norms, an all-encompassing right of individual action results: It includes, according to Article 187 Revised Treaty of Chaguaramas (RTC), allegations that an actual or proposed measure of another member state is, or would be, inconsistent with the objectives of the Community (Article 187 (a) RTC); allegations of injury, serious prejudice suffered or likely to be suffered, nullification or impairment of benefits expected from the establishment and operation of the Caribbean Single Market and Economy (CSME, Article 187 (b) RTC); allegations that an organ or body of the Community has acted ultra vires (Article 187 (c) RTC), as well as allegations that the purpose or object of the Treaty is being frustrated or prejudiced (Article 187 (d) RTC). In addition, private parties have a special right of action against determinations of the CARICOM Commission in competition matters.[90]

The restrictive nature of individual rights of action is revealed in requirements set in the so-called "special leave stage" and in the detailed requirements for the standing of private litigants.[91] In addition to belonging to the circle of applicants ("natural or juridical persons of a contracting party"), these requirements include the conviction of the Court that the applicant, in accordance with the intention of the Treaty, directly benefits from rights or benefits conferred by or under the RTC and that he or she has established to have been prejudiced in respect of the enjoyment of these rights. By means of the criteria of legal standing, the broad right of action in the CARICOM system approaches a subjective model of legal protection. Moreover, the contracting states restricted the procedural autonomy of private litigants substantially with a reminiscence of the mediatised enforcement of rights by way of diplomatic protection: Natural or juridical persons of a Contracting Party may, with the special leave of the Court, only be allowed to appear as parties in proceedings before the Court where the Contracting Party entitled to espouse the claim in proceedings before the Court has omitted or declined to espouse the claim, or expressly agreed that the persons concerned may espouse the claim instead of the Contracting Party so entitled.[92]

Business entities experience a more far-reaching procedural status in the legal protection system of the East African Community: According to its wording, Article 30 of the EAC Treaty, both in its version of 30 November 1999 and in its revised version of 2007, grants natural and legal persons domiciled in one of the EAC

---

[89] Article 211 regulates in general terms the "Jurisdiction of the Court in Contentious Proceedings" and, in para. 1(d), also includes in general and indefinitely "applications by persons in accordance with Article 222" among the CCJ's areas of competence. In the absence of a limitation of types of proceedings, defendants and subjects of action (in Article 211 or Article 222 RTC), the individual right of action systematically extends to all disputes of interpretation and application generally listed in Article 187 RTC.

[90] Article 175(12) RTC.

[91] Article 222(a)–(d) RTC.

[92] A further criterion is listed in (d): "the Court has found that the interest of justice requires that the persons be allowed to espouse the claim."

member states a broad, almost unconditional right of action.[93] The breadth of the right of action refers not only to the circle of litigants ("any person who is resident"[94]), but also to the lack of criteria of legal standing. The right to bring an action is based solely on the accusation that one of the possible subjects of action is unlawful or constitutes an infringement of the provisions of this Treaty. Valid subject matters constitute not only (in the style of an individual action for annulment) measures or secondary legislation of one of the Community institutions, but also decisions or measures of a member state ("any act, regulation, directive, decision or action of a Partner State or an institution of the Community").

However, the structure of the provision differs from the system of the right of action of member states in that the first paragraph of this right explicitly refers to infringement proceedings (against "another Partner State or an organ or institution of the Community")[95] and the second paragraph regulates annulment proceedings.[96] Member states may also base annulment proceedings on the accusation that the secondary Community law has been created *ultra vires* or that it constitutes an abuse or misuse of discretion. Despite this broader nature of states' rights of action, by also authorising private litigants to initiate proceedings against contracting states in which state measures are controlled by reference to the programme of treaty obligations, private litigants participate in an abstract-objective procedure addressed at legality control. In this respect, the right of individual action contains a sub-form of the infringement procedure and results in an approximation of the procedural significance of states, the Secretary General of the EAC[97] and natural and legal persons. In the course of a revision of the EAC Treaty in 2007, the state parties to the

---

[93] Article 30 EAC Treaty (2007) reads: (1) "Subject to the provisions of Article 27 of this Treaty, any person who is resident in a Partner State may refer for determination by the Court, the legality of any Act, regulation, directive, decision or action of a Partner State or an institution of the Community on the grounds that such Act, regulation, directive, decision or action is unlawful or is an infringement of the provisions of this Treaty." (2): "The proceedings provided for in this Article shall be instituted within two months of the enactment, publication, directive, decision or action complained of, or in the absence thereof, of the day in which it came to the knowledge of the complainant, as the case may be;" (3): "The Court shall have no jurisdiction under this Article where an Act, regulation, directive, decision or action has been reserved under this Treaty to an institution of a Partner State." The second and the third paragraph were introduced in the course of the revision.

[94] The concept of resident must be distinguished from that of national; while the latter is linked to the nationality of the litigant, the individual right of action under the EAC Treaty is directed at anyone who is domiciled in the geographical area.

[95] Article 28(1) EAC Treaty reads: "A Partner State which considers that another Partner State or an organ or institution of the Community has failed to fulfil an obligation under this Treaty or has infringed a provision of this Treaty, may refer the matter to the Court for adjudication."

[96] Article 28(1) EAC Treaty reads: "A Partner State may refer for determination by the Court, the legality of any Act, regulation, directive, decision or action on the ground that it is ultra vires or unlawful or an infringement of the provisions of this Treaty or any rule of law relating to its application or amounts to a misuse or abuse of power."

[97] Article 29 EAC Treaty lays down the multistage procedure for infringement proceedings initiated by the Secretary General against a Partner State.

EAC restricted the right of action of private litigants by introducing a 2-month period for bringing an action and by excluding the competence of the East African Court of Justice (EACJ) for measures reserved by the treaty for member state institutions.[98] However, since the revised law of the EAC did not introduce criteria of legal standing, and due to the breadth of the subject matter of the action, the model of legal protection continues to be an example of the participation of business entities in objective legality control and stands for maximum procedural autonomy.

Before its abolition by the Protocol on the Tribunal in the Southern African Development Community, which was adopted in August 2014,[99] the right of individual action granted to natural and legal persons in the SADC legal system was another example of far-reaching procedural equality between the state and private litigants. According to its broad wording, the right of individual action encompassed all disputes between the member states on the one hand and natural or legal persons on the other.[100] The only restriction of admissibility imposed on private litigants was that he or she had to exhaust all available remedies or was unable to proceed under the domestic jurisdiction before bringing an action.[101] Parallel to the corresponding state right of action, natural and legal persons were also authorised to conduct objective proceedings against the SADC dealing with the interpretation and application of primary and secondary law.[102]

3 Rights of Action of Business Entities in Practice: Comparison of "Legal Protection Models"

The motivation for introducing rights of action for business entities, as well as the procedural design of individual access to court, go back to the will of the participating states. This dominance of states as law-makers and decisive instances on how the procedural status of natural or legal persons should look corresponds to the traditional understanding of international law centring around states as core subjects. However, this dominance of states loses considerable importance in the context of judicial proceedings initiated by natural or legal persons: In this phase, the focus is mainly on the interaction between the private litigant and the regional economic court, more precisely between the litigant's request for legal protection and the judicial interpretation of the rules of admissibility and jurisdiction shaping the respective rights of action. In this phase of the proceedings, the state is actively

---

[98]In the course of the revision, para. 2 and para. 3 of Article 30 were added (see footnote 93 above).

[99]On the political backlash against the SADC Tribunal see below footnote 174.

[100]Article 15(1) of the 2000 Protocol does not make any distinction between states and private litigants with regard to possible subjects of proceedings: "The Tribunal shall have jurisdiction over disputes between Member States, and between natural or legal persons and Member States."

[101]Article 15(2) 2000 Protocol.

[102]Article 18 read in conjunction with Article 14 2000 Protocol.

involved, at most, as a defendant or intervener. If the judicial practice, concretising individual access to court in this way, is characterised as "legal protection models", we can abstract two basic models from our comparative analysis: A court's willingness to "expand" individual access to court by means of a broad interpretation of admissibility and jurisdictional criteria must be contrasted with the tendency to "restrict" it. Incidental thereto, the regional courts formulate fundamental structural decisions about the procedural status and function of business entities in the framework of the integration project.

Contrasting the states' motivation for introducing rights of action of companies and the affiliation to one of the two legal protection models, on the other hand, reveals a remarkable insight: The broad, functional model of introductory motivation (Sect. 2.2), which conceives rights of action as instruments of economic and legal participation of the private sector, predominantly promotes the judicial tendency to further extend the procedural power of private litigants. This is what happened, for example, in the case law of the East African Court of Justice and of the Caribbean Court of Justice. However, this does not apply without exception: Even the narrow concept of individual rights of action motivated by a rule of law approach (Sect. 2.1) can lead to the judicial tendency to expand individual access to court. A historic example of this is the case law of the ECJ in applying the individual action for annulment of the ECSC Treaty. The same applies vice versa: Not only the comparatively narrow, rule-of-law motivated procedural design of individual rights of action, but also the broad, functional procedural design can lead to its tendentious restriction of access to court in judicial practice. Thus, in addition to the ECJ (since the application of the EEC Treaty) and the EFTA Court as representatives of a narrow approach, the legal protection model of the restriction also includes, at least in part, the ECOWAS Court of Justice which applies functionally motivated rights of action.

The evaluation of the judicial practice thus confirms the assumption that the judicial interpretation of rules of jurisdiction and admissibility is far more than the application of value-neutral procedural law. It is the expression of an independent "policy"[103] consideration of the regional court on the role private (economic) stakeholders are supposed to play in the political, legal and economic integration scheme. While the methods of interpretation by means of which the courts extend or restrict individual access to the court differ fundamentally, the doctrinal determinants are the same: Concretising the possible cause of action as well as the criteria of legal standing are the crucial doctrinal points of reference allowing the judicial body to either expand or restrict individual access to justice.

---

[103]Shany (2014), pp. 88 et seq.

3.1 Judicial Extension of Individual Access to Court

An extension of individual access to justice was practiced, for example, by the early ECJ in interpreting and applying the individual action for annulment of the ECSC Treaty, the Court of Justice of the EAC, and by the Court of Justice of CARICOM. While the ECJ had to interpret a right of action that was motivated by a rule of law rationale and conceived comparatively restrictively by the ECSC member states, the other courts had to structure individual access to the courts on the basis of deliberately broad but often undefined procedural conditions. The doctrinal determinants by which the courts expand access to court or lower procedural hurdles are identical in various respects. By contrast, a dividing line runs on a methodological level. The European Court of Justice extended access to court for companies and business associations of the coal and steel sector by means of strict literal interpretation and only in a second step substantiated this interpretation in a value-laden *pro homine* manner. Those courts that have to deal with functionally motivated rights of action, on the other hand, have tended to extend the participation function of individual rights of action from the outset by means of teleological interpretation. Against this background, independent "policy" considerations on the procedural function of private litigants can be more easily found in the rulings of those courts than in the case law of the European Court of Justice in interpreting the ECSC Treaty.

3.1.1 Doctrinal Determinants for Expanding Individual Access to Court

The regional economic courts representing this legal protection model facilitate access to court for private litigants by broadly defining the possible cause of action, by lowering the criteria of legal standing and by marginalising the litigant's obligation to go through a domestic preliminary procedure. Thereby, these courts modify the "separation of procedural powers" between states, on the one hand, and natural and legal persons, on the other, as originally defined by the participating states.

Subject Matter

Permitting a broader cause of action to be subjected to judicial review other than as originally intended by the founders of the respective integration treaty, regional courts alter and expand the procedural power of natural and legal persons. The early ECJ made this possible by applying the action for annulment under the ECSC Treaty on the premise that general decisions in the literal sense also constitute contestable legal acts. In the ASSIDER and I.S.A. cases, the applicants, two Italian associations, challenged decisions of the High Authority which specified prohibited practices within the meaning of Article 60(1) of the ECSC Treaty and which laid down rules on the publication of price lists and conditions of sale for the steel market. The general nature of the decisions was not disputed between the parties. Rather, the question was under scrutiny as to what extent the additional requirement in Article 33(2) ECSC Treaty, according to which general measures of the High Authority had to constitute a misuse of powers vis-à-vis the litigant (*à leur égard*), at the same time constituted a restriction of the acts admissible to be brought before the Court. The High Authority had contested the admissibility of the application on the grounds that the "misuse of powers" criterion of Article 33(2) ECSC Treaty presupposed that the contested decision was general only in appearance and in reality referred individually to the applicant undertaking or undertakings (with the consequence that the High Authority had thus exercised its powers for a purpose other than that provided for by the Treaty).[104] The ECJ, by contrast, opposed the assumption that the additional requirement of Article 33(2) ECSC Treaty at the same time implies a restriction of the subject matter of an application for annulment.[105] Consequently, the Court of Justice involved natural and legal persons in the legality control of normative acts of the ECSC.

In addition, the East African Court of Justice opted for a broad understanding of the scope of supranational sovereignty which private litigants are entitled to challenge. The wording of the respective right of action limits the subjects of action to measures of a contracting state or a Community institution.[106] Article 9 EAC Treaty distinguishes between "organs", such as the Summit, the Council and the East African Legislative Assembly, and Community "institutions", such as the Development Bank or the EAC Fisheries Organisation. Notwithstanding this limitation in the wording, the EACJ allows individual actions against acts adopted by the totality of contracting states or a Community institution. For the EACJ, "(i)t is clear from the provision of Article 30 that the residents of the Partner States are vested with the right to access this Court for the purpose of challenging any form of infringement of provisions of the Treaty. Several provisions in the Treaty lend weight to the view that this was a deliberate provision to ensure that East Africans for whose benefit the Community was established participate in protecting the integrity of the Treaty."[107] The effects of this expansive understanding of the right of action on the institutional setting are considerable: The EACJ approximates the legal standing of companies (and individuals) resident in the EAC to the standing of states. Every possible issue, particularly political decisions of the member states, is a potential subject matter

---

[104]ECJ, Case C-3/54, Assider, ECLI:EU:C:1955:2, p. 66; ECJ, Case C-4/54, I.S.A, ECLI:EU:C:1955:3, p. 94.

[105]In the cases Assider and I.S.A., the ECJ upheld the admissibility without even problematising the issue raised by the High Authority ECJ, Case C-3/54, Assider, ECLI:EU:C:1955:2, p. 69; ECJ, Case C-4/54, I.S.A, ECLI:EU:C:1955:3, pp. 97 et seq. In the case Fédéchar, the Court finally made its opinion clear that "(. . .) Article 33 clearly states that associations and undertakings may contest not only individual decisions but also general decisions in the true sense of the term.", ECJ, Case C-8/55, Fédération Charbonnière de Belgique, ECLI:EU:C:1956:7, pp. 257 et seq.

[106]Article 30 EAC Treaty refers to "any Act, regulation, directive, decision or action of a Partner State or an institution of the Community".

[107]EACJ, East African Law Society and Others. The Attorney General of Kenya and Others, Ref. No. 3 of 2007, 31 August 2008, 14.

before the EACJ.[108] Thereby, the East African Court of Justice negates the systematic conclusion that could have been drawn from a comparison with the procedural design of the EAC member state's right of action. By contrast to private litigants, the latter are explicitly empowered to bring an action dealing with breaches of the EAC Treaty by other Partner States or by Community institutions or bodies.[109]

The Caribbean Court of Justice extends the canon of suitable subjects of action (and defendants) by allowing individual actions not only against foreign states, but also against measures of the company's home state. In the case of Trinidad Cement Limited, the CARICOM member state Guyana had contended the action brought by a company incorporated under Guyanese law claiming that Guyana had suspended the Common External Tariff ("the CET") on cement imported into that state from third states. Guyana referred to its own procedural rights as laid down in Article 222 (c) RTC.[110] According to Guyana, if a state was reserved a priority right of co-decision to bring an individual protection action before the CCJ (or not), it was excluded that this state of origin could be both litigant and defendant in the proceedings. Consequently, this provision had to be interpreted in such a way that a private entity could not bring an action against his home state.[111] The CCJ did not draw this restrictive conclusion. Instead, the Court reduced Article 222(c) RTC to such case constellations in which a state is exposed to concurrent actions by individuals and their home states and must be protected from a "duplication of suits".[112] Moreover, comparable to the EACJ, the Court of Justice of CARICOM also defines the subject matter of individual actions against the community in a broad manner. It understands the right of action, as mentioned in Article 211 and specified in Article 222 RTC, to be comprehensively applicable to "all manner of disputes concerning the interpretation and application of the Revised Treaty including

---

[108]This includes the question of whether the failure of an EAC Partner State to enter into more far reaching obligations under international treaties constitutes a violation of the principle of the rule of law guaranteed by the EAC Treaty. See e.g. EACJ (First Instance), Honorable Sitenda Sebalu. Secretary General of the East African Community and Attorney General of Uganda, Ref. No. 1 of 2010, 30 June 2011; EACJ (First Instance), Democratic Party. The Secretary General of the East African Community, Attorney General of Uganda, Attorney General of Kenya, Attorney General of Rwanda, Attorney General of Burundi, Ref. No. 2 of 2012, 29 November 2013.

[109]Article 28(1) EAC Treaty reads: "A Partner State which considers that another Partner State or an organ or institution of the Community has failed to fulfil an obligation under this Treaty or has infringed a provision of this Treaty, may refer the matter to the Court for adjudication."

[110]Article 222(c) RTC reads: "Persons, natural or juridical, of a Contracting Party may, with the special leave of the Court, be allowed to appear as parties in proceedings before the Court where: (...) the Contracting Party entitled to espouse the claim in proceedings before the Court has: (i) omitted or declined to espouse the claim, or (ii) expressly agreed that the persons concerned may espouse the claim instead of the Contracting Party so entitled".

[111]CCJ, Trinidad Cement Limited & TCL Guyana Incorporated. The State of the Co-operative Republic of Guyana, [2009] CCJ 1 (OJ), para. 37.

[112]CCJ, Trinidad Cement Limited & TCL Guyana Incorporated. The State of the Co-operative Republic of Guyana, [2009] CCJ 1 (OJ), para. 43.

allegations that a body or organ of the Community acted ultra vires."[113] As a consequence, the CCJ has consistently allowed actions to be brought against Community organs and bodies,[114] including the Secretary General and the Commission,[115] but has declined to bring an action against a Community institution within the meaning of Article 21 RTC.[116]

Locus Standi

The regional courts opting for expanding access to court also change the institutional balance of power between the relevant procedural actors by means of low-threshold requirements for the criteria of legal standing. This is the case when Community institutions and/or states are confronted with a larger group of possible private litigants as well as with an increased intensity and frequency of judicial proceedings. The Court of Justice of the European Coal and Steel Community applied low-threshold requirements when interpreting the requirements of Article 33 (2) ECSC Treaty. These provided that individual actions for annulment could only be directed against individual measures "concerning" an undertaking or association or against general measures constituting a misuse of power vis-à-vis the litigant. The Court rejected a restrictive interpretation according to which "concerning" was to be understood as "direct interest",[117] which would have meant that the private litigant was "the only, or almost the only party concerned by the decision".[118] Instead, the ECJ recognised sufficiently concrete effects on the financial situation as well as on the competitive relationships between companies in the coal and steel sector to justify the right to bring an action.[119] CARICOM's Court of Justice has a similarly broad understanding of the right of action under Article 222(a) and (b) RTC. The CCJ considers it sufficient that the state's violation of the treaty provision creating individual rights potentially causes damage to the market participants concerned. In

---

[113]CCJ, Trinidad Cement Limited. The Caribbean Community, [2009] CCJ 2 (OJ), para. 30.

[114]CCJ, Doreen Johnson. Caribbean Centre for Development Administration, [2009] CCJ 3 (OJ), para. 15: "It is clear that the Community can be sued for the conduct of its Organs and Bodies and that of the Secretary General."

[115]CCJ, Trinidad Cement Limited. The Competition Commission, [2012] CCJ 4 (OJ), para. 10 et seq.; para. 13.

[116]CCJ, Doreen Johnson. Caribbean Centre for Development Administration, [2009] CCJ 3 (OJ), para. 14.

[117]AG Lagrange, Case C-30/59, De Gezamenlijke Steenkolenmijnen in Limburg, ECLI:EU:C:1960:41, p. 37.

[118]ECJ, Case C-30/59, De Gezamenlijke Steenkolenmijnen in Limburg, ECLI:EU:C:1961:2, p. 17.

[119]Exemplary: ECJ, Joined Cases C-24/58 and C-34/58, Chambre syndicale de la sidérurgie de l'est de la France, ECLI:EU:C:1960:32, p. 292: "The applicants and the German undertakings benefiting from the contested tariff rates are in competition with each other, since they carry on the same productive activity in the Common Market, sell the same products and obtain their supplies of mineral fuels from the same mines."

order to bring an action before the CCJ, it is sufficient to be an operator in the relevant sector who claims to be adversely affected by a government measure and to have suffered damage as a result of the measure contrary to Community law.[120]

The ECJ of the European Coal and Steel Community had already been accused by the High Authority of opening the door to "actio popularis"[121] by making low demands on the criteria of legal standing. The Court of Justice of the East African Community explicitly recognises such "Public Interest Litigation" as a "category" of its jurisdictional activities.[122] Similar to the ECJ, it was called upon to restrict the right of individual action by means of unwritten admissibility criteria. The broad and indefinite wording of Article 30 EAC Treaty led defendant states to demand that the EACJ added the criterion that the litigant had to claim his rights or interests granted under the EAC Treaty (cause of action) had been infringed. The East African Court of Justice rejects such a teleological reduction, by which the circle of private litigants would have been considerably narrowed. It found that none of the treaty provisions defining the individual right of action required the litigant, directly or by implication, to show a right or an interest that had been infringed and/or damage that had been suffered as a consequence of the matter complained of in the reference.[123] As a consequence, in the framework of the EAC, private parties are entitled to demand compliance with the programme of obligations under the EAC Treaty in the public interest. One essential effect of this type of procedural equality of state and private litigants is that the Court of Justice proclaims that the latter are authorised to demand state compliance with the rule of law in the EAC.[124] While human rights advocates actively take up this broad procedural empowerment and repeatedly litigate human rights related cases before the EACJ, business actors have (with few exceptions) eschewed litigating before the Court so far. This occurs despite the fact that nontariff barriers impose high costs for business in the EAC.[125]

---

[120]See e.g. CCJ, Trinidad Cement Limited & TCL Guyana Incorporated. The State of the Co-operative Republic of Guyana, [2009] CCJ 1 (OJ), para. 35: "The Applicants have alleged, and it has not been contradicted, that they are engaged in the production, packaging, sale and distribution of cement throughout the Community and in particular in Guyana. They have also alleged that Guyana's unilateral suspension of the CET on cement for the period claimed by them (. . .) has caused and continues to cause them loss."

[121]ECJ, Case C-30/59, De Gezamenlijke Steenkolenmijnen in Limburg, ECLI:EU:C:1961:2, p. 5.

[122]See for example EACJ (First Instance), The East African Centre for Trade Policy and Law. The Secretary General of the East African Community, Ref. No. 9 of 2012, 9 May 2013. On the historical reasons for this approach Milej (2018), pp. 114 et seq.

[123]EACJ, Prof. Peter Anyang' Nyong'o and Others Vs Attorney General of Kenya and Others, Ref. No 1. of 2006, 30 March 2007, 16 f.

[124]EACJ, East African Law Society and Others. The Attorney General of Kenya and Others, Ref. No. 9 of 2007, 11 July 2007, 4.

[125]On possible reasons for this phenomenon see Gathii (2016), pp. 41 et seq.

3.1.2 Method

The Restrictive Model of Literal Interpretation

In expanding access to court for companies and associations, the European Court of Justice, in applying the ECSC Treaty, can be seen as a representative of a comparatively restrictive method of interpretation: It only argued *in dubio pro homine* in case of a clear corresponding wording of the Treaty. The decisive factor for the ECJ in extending access to justice for private litigants were the contractual requirements imposed on it by the wording of Article 33(2) ECSC Treaty. The Court considered this wording to be so "clear"[126] with regard to the legal acts which could be challenged that, in this regard, a litigant-friendly, broad interpretation was open to it. The ECJ only consistently saw the limit of a broad interpretation of provisions on legal protection reached where the extension of access to court would have violated the requirements of the ECSC Treaty and would have been based solely on judicial law-making.[127] This close orientation to the wording prompted the ECJ not to allow the historical will of the contracting states as derived from national ratification materials to be given any relevance in terms of interpretation.[128] The historic interpretation of the individual action for annulment would have argued against expanding access to court with regards to the subject matter and the locus standi criterion.

The Broad Model of Teleological Interpretation: Extending Access to Justice Beyond Wording and Systematics

The fact that the rights of action in the East African Community and in CARICOM were introduced as a state commitment to the key economic and legal role of the private sector continues to influence the choice of the dominant method of interpretation with which the courts of these communities facilitate access to justice. By means of a broad teleological interpretation, the representatives of this extension model take up the states' motivation for introducing the individual right of action and use it as a basis of legitimation for deepening the procedural autonomy of natural and legal persons as well as for expanding the control and participation function of private litigants.

Both the Court of Justice of the East African Community as well as the Caribbean Court of Justice of CARICOM justify the outlined extensions of the individual right

---

[126]ECJ, Case C-8/55, Fédération Charbonnière de Belgique, ECLI:EU:C:1956:7, pp. 257 et seq.

[127]This concerned, for example, an extension of the limited circle of litigants which, since the adoption of the Coal and Steel Treaty, had been limited to companies and business associations in the coal and steel sector (see ECJ, Case C-222/83, Commune de Differdange, ECLI:EU: C:1984:266, para. 8).

[128]On this historical will AG Lagrange, Fédération charbonnière de Belgique, Joined Opinion, Cases C-8/55, C-9/55, ECLI:EU:C:1956:6, p. 271 et seq.

of action primarily teleologically from the overriding purpose of assigning a leading role to the private sector and civil society in the economic and legal integration process. In doing so, the courts base their decision, inter alia, on statements in the preamble of the respective Community Treaty.[129] The Caribbean Court of Justice also places the core procedural role of natural and legal persons in the broader context of a change in legal theory that international law has undergone with regard to the status of individuals. Starting from a purely state-dependent object status, the original (albeit initially state-mediated) ownership of rights and the power to enforce rights of the individual is being increasingly recognised in international law. The CCJ believes that this change in understanding towards individuals as the authoritative entity under international law has also been implemented in the revised CARICOM Treaty: In the eyes of the Court, given the important role envisaged for private economic entities in achieving the objectives of the CARICOM Single Market and Economy, the contracting parties "clearly intended that such entities should be important actors in the regime created by the RTC; that they should have conferred upon them and be entitled to enjoy rights capable of being enforced directly on the international plane."[130]

In recourse to the superior telos, both courts, at times, transgress the limits of law which are set by the wording of the individual rights of action, on the one hand, and by a systematic comparison with the (broader) rights of action granted to states, on the other. Based on the premise that the East African Community has to serve the interests of the population, the EACJ assumes that the latter is also to be empowered to comprehensively monitor state compliance with the treaty programme of obligations. In the eyes of the Court, the procedural status of private litigants is on an equal footing with the contracting states and the Secretary General of the EAC. Thereby, the EACJ exercises judicial law-making *contra legem*. It legitimises such an approach by referring to the dynamic nature of the integration process to which the member states have committed themselves; this is associated with the ongoing necessity to subordinate state sovereignty objections to the success of the integration process.[131] Similarly, the Caribbean Court of Justice also rejects a strict literal interpretation *a priori* and relies on the pertinent danger of not sufficiently realizing the overarching purpose of the revised Treaty of Chaguaramas which is to transform a loose association of states into a rule-based system of regional integration.[132] The

---

[129]EACJ, East African Law Society and Others. The Attorney General of Kenya and Others, Ref. No. 3 of 2007, 31 August 2008, 14 et seq.; CCJ, Trinidad Cement Limited & TCL Guyana Incorporated. The State of the Co-operative Republic of Guyana, [2009] CCJ 1 (OJ), para. 13.

[130]CCJ, Trinidad Cement Limited & TCL Guyana Incorporated. The State of the Co-operative Republic of Guyana, [2009] CCJ 1 (OJ), para. 18.

[131]EACJ, East African Law Society and Others. The Attorney General of Kenya and Others, Ref. No. 3 of 2007, 31 August 2008, 15.

[132]CCJ, Trinidad Cement Limited. The Caribbean Community, [2009] CCJ 2 (OJ), para. 32. Confirmed in CCJ, Trinidad Cement Limited. The Competition Commission, [2012] CCJ 4 (OJ), para. 16.

CCJ also places this objective above restrictions on the legal standing of natural and legal persons which derive from a literal and systematic approach of interpretation.

3.2 Judicial Restriction of Individual Access to Court

The European Court of Justice, since applying the EEC Treaty, the EFTA Court and, in some cases, the ECOWAS Court have been advocating a tendency to restrict individual access to justice.[133] However, the members of this group of courts had to deal with different state motives for introducing individual rights of action: Within the framework of the EEC, the original state understanding of having to grant rights of direct action as instruments to fend off negative effects of supranationality, as already laid down in the European Coal and Steel Community, remained perpetuated. The right of action before the EFTA Court is also based on such an allocation of functions.[134] By contrast, the individual rights of action, which the ECOWAS Court of Justice has to interpret, have the double function of guaranteeing legal protection, on the one hand, and of empowering natural and legal persons to participate in the economic and legal integration progress, on the other.[135]

Remarkably, the doctrinal determinants by means of which these courts tend to restrict access to regional legal protection are consistent with those of the extension model described above: Particularly the canon of contestable legal acts (cause of action/subject matter) and the criteria of legal standing offer the community courts the opportunity to do so. The dividing line to the extension model runs on a methodical level and concerns the role the regional courts assign to the domestic system of legal protection. There is a consensus among the regional community courts that the restriction of individual access to international legal protection is accompanied by judicially strengthening the framework conditions for national enforcement of law and decentralised individual legal protection. This premise of empowering domestic courts to apply the community legal order is flanked by the assumption that the courts apply a "new" Community legal order which differs fundamentally from traditional international law features. However, the legal framework conditions for decentralised, national enforcement of law, which serves as the basis of legitimation for limiting access to international legal protection, are completely different for the representatives of the model—the ECJ, the EFTA Court and the ECOWAS Court.

---

[133]The restriction of individual access to court by the ECOWAS Court of Justice is only one tendency, which must be supplemented by expansionary tendencies, which particularly affect the individual right of action against human rights violations. On this Wiater (2020), pp. 303 et seq.

[134]See above at Sect. 2.1.

[135]See above at Sect. 2.2.

3.2.1 Doctrinal Determinants for Restricting Individual Access to Court

The representatives of the "restriction model" raise the bar for individual access to court by means of a narrow understanding of the canon of contestable legal acts and by placing high demands on locus standi. The separation of procedural powers between the key actors—states, international supervisory bodies (ESA, EU Commission) and private litigants—as originally intended by the participating states thus remains maintained.

Subject Matter

In its early years as a court of the EEC, in 1962, the European Court of Justice distanced itself from the broader approach in interpreting the ECSC Treaty and practiced a restrictive interpretation of the contestable legal acts under Article 173 (2) EEC Treaty. In interpreting "decisions (...) in the form of a regulation" as subject matter of annulment proceedings initiated by natural or legal persons, the ECJ limited the right of action to decisions that were only "apparently" in the form of regulations, but, in reality, did not have the character of a regulation.[136] Associations had challenged quantitative import restrictions and measures having equivalent effect, serving to progressively establish a common organisation of the market in fruit and vegetables. Thus, the Court interpreted the right of action conferred by the second paragraph of Article 173 of the EEC Treaty on natural or legal persons as *not* entitling them to bring actions for annulment of Council or Commission regulations.[137] By contrast to the ECSC, companies were not entitled to challenge normative measures of general application, but only provisions which affected them not only directly but also individually. In the early 1960s, when the ECJ took these landmark decisions, the comparison between the wording of the right of action under the EEC Treaty and the one laid down in the Coal and Steel Treaty was relevant to the decision. The authors of the EEC Treaty had amended—and deliberately restricted—the subject matter of individual actions for annulment.[138]

This comparison and the relative restriction of the procedural details seem to have lost their importance over the course of time. Without going into the change in its own case law, 30 years later, in 1994, the ECJ affirmed the admissibility of an action brought by a producer of quality sparkling wines. This occurred after and even though the Court had previously held that the contested provision was normative in

---

[136]Already in the Assider (Case 3/54) and I.S.A (Case 4/54) proceedings and in the framework of the ECSC Treaty, General Advocate Lagrange had argued to limit annulment proceedings initiated by private litigants in this regard.

[137]ECJ, Joined Cases 16/62 and 17/62, Confédération nationale des producteurs de fruits et légumes, ECLI:EU:C:1962:47, p. 478. ECJ, Case 19/62 to 22/62, Boucherie en gros, ECLI:EU:C:1962:48, p. 498.

[138]See the wording of Article 33(2) ECSC Treaty (footnote 45) and of Article 173(2) EEC Treaty (footnote 47) above.

nature, since it applied generally to the economic operators concerned.[139] In spite of that classification, the Court examined whether the contested regulation could affect the litigant individually (locus standi).[140]

In applying the Lisbon Treaty of 2009, the ECJ re-established its restrictive approach towards the subject matter of individual annulment proceedings when interpreting a "regulatory act which is of direct concern to them and does not entail implementing measures." This subject matter was introduced in Article 263(4) alternative 3 TFEU as a consequence of the reform of the system of individual legal protection in the EU. In contrast to the second alternative (proceedings against an act which is of direct *and* individual concern), the new third alternative abandons the criterion of *individual* concern and only requires the litigant's *direct* concern. The reason for this alteration was that the ECJ's interpretation of the criterion of "direct and individual concern" under the fourth paragraph of Article 230 Treaty Establishing the European Community (TEC; Plaumann formula) had resulted in certain gaps in the legal protection. This occurred in constellations in which private litigants would—without infringing the law—be denied access to the Community courts against an onerous act with general effect which does not contain any implementing provisions (which alone would have opened access to the national courts).[141]

The central issue in the leading case dealing with the interpretation of the new concept of "regulatory acts" was whether legislative acts could be the subject matter of individual annulment proceedings. A definition concretising the subjects of action covered by the new alternative of Article 263(4) TFEU is absent in the Treaty.[142] In concreto, the ECJ had to decide whether the litigants, the Inuit Tapiriit Kanatami, as a representative of the interests of the indigenous ethnic group Inuit as well as a number of other parties involved (above all producers or traders of seal products), were entitled to the facilitated right of action of the third alternative in order to attack a regulation which the European Parliament and the Council had jointly adopted and which brought into force a fundamental ban on the marketing of seal products on the European internal market. The Court of Justice of the EU (CJEU), like the General Court before, excludes natural and legal persons from challenging "legislative acts", that means acts adopted in accordance with a legislative procedure involving the Council and the European Parliament under the simplified conditions of standing. In positive terms, the term "regulatory act" is thus to be understood in such a way that,

---

[139]ECJ, Case C-309/89, Codorníu SA, ECLI:EU:C:1994:197, para. 17.

[140]ECJ, Case C-309/89, Codorníu SA, ECLI:EU:C:1994:197, para. 19: "Although it is true that according to the criteria in the second paragraph of Article 173 of the Treaty the contested provision is, by nature and by virtue of its sphere of application, of a legislative nature in that it applies to the traders concerned in general, that does not prevent it from being of individual concern to some of them."

[141]On the drafting process. in the framework of the European Convention CONV 636/03 of 25 March 2003 (CERCLE I 13), p. 7.

[142]EGC, Case T-18/10, Inuit Tapiriit Kanatami, ECLI:EU:T:2011:419, para. 39.

with the exception of legislative acts, it covers any act of general application.[143] This restriction excludes private business entities from being co-responsible for ensuring the correctness of political decision-making processes within the legislative procedure in the procedural framework of annulment proceedings.

Locus Standi

The central doctrinal determinant the ECJ, the EFTA Court and the ECOWAS Court refer to in restricting individual access to justice are the criteria of legal standing. At an early stage, the ECJ had considerably limited the circle of potential private litigants (and, linked to this, the circle of all those who could participate in an objective legality control in the course of annulment proceedings) by concretising "individual concern" by means of the "Plaumann formula". According to this formula, "(p)ersons other than those to whom a decision is addressed may only claim to be individually concerned if that decision affects them by reason of certain attributes which are peculiar to them or by reason of circumstances in which they are differentiated from all other persons and by virtue of these factors distinguishes them individually just as in the case of the person addressed."[144] In the Plaumann case, these criteria of legal standing were not fulfilled since the applicant was affected by the disputed Decision only in his capacity as an importer of clementines, a commercial activity which could have "at any time be practised by any person".[145] Despite the fact that only the wording of Article 36(2) SCA, which the EFTA Court has to interpret, takes up the criteria of "individual concern" as defined in the EU legal protection system, both the EFTA Court and the ECOWAS Court refer to the ECJ's Plaumann formula to specify the locus standi. It is, therefore, not sufficient that a private person or corporation is affected in his or her capacity as a competitor as long as he or she is not at the same time a member of a group of persons whose composition was already determined when the challenged legal act was adopted. The ECJ continuously upholds this premise in its interpretation of the individual action for annulment, most recently in the reformed legal protection system of the Lisbon Treaty.[146]

As an expression of the principle of "procedural homogeneity"[147] between EU law and EEA law, the EFTA Court also uses the strict standards of the Plaumann formula when interpreting the criterion of "individual concern" within the meaning

---

[143]EGC, Case T-18/10, Inuit Tapiriit Kanatami, ECLI:EU:T:2011:419, para. 56; CoJ, Case C-583/11 P, Inuit Tapiriit Kanatami, ECLI:EU:C:2013:625, para. 60.

[144]ECJ, Case C-25/62, Plaumann, ECLI:EU:C:1963:17, p. 107.

[145]ECJ, Case C-25/62, Plaumann, ECLI:EU:C:1963:17, p. 107.

[146]CoJ, Case C-583/11 P, Inuit Tapiriit Kanatami, ECLI:EU:C:2013:625, para. 71. Confirmed, inter alia, in CoJ, Case C-274/12 P, Telefónica, ECLI:EU:C:2013:852, para. 46; CoJ, Case C-384/16 P, European Union Copper Task Force, ECLI:EU:C:2018:176, para. 93.

[147]On this principle see EFTA Court, Aleris Ungplan AS, E-13/10, EFTA Ct. Rep. 2011, 3, 12 para. 24; EFTA Court, EFTA Surveillance Authority. The Kingdom of Norway, E-18/10, EFTA Ct. Rep.

of Article 36(2) SCA. Similar to the EU courts, what counts for standing giving access to the EFTA Court is not the intensity with which the decision of the EFTA Surveillance Authority affects the rights or interests of natural or legal persons. Rather, the highly formalistic question whether the measure affects him/her so much because of personal characteristics that he/she could also have been its addressee.[148]

The ECOWAS Court of Justice pursues a two-edged strategy: On the one hand, the Court broadly interpreted the right of action as laid down in Article 10(c) 2005 Protocol with regard to the possible cause of action and extended it to proceedings against the ECOWAS community, its institutions and officials. Article 10(c) 2005 Protocol opens access to court for "(i)ndividuals and corporate bodies in proceedings from the determination of an act or inaction of a *Community official* which violates the rights of the individuals or corporate bodies".[149] Despite the restriction to "Community officials", the ECOWAS Community Court of Justice (ECCJ) broadly interprets the question of who may be the author of the infringing measure and against whom the request for legal protection may be directed. In the leading Pinheiro case, the court interpreted the right of action as allowing "direct access to the Court, in particular, for actions against the Community, its Institutions or its employees."[150] On the other hand, however, the ECCJ restricts this right of action of individuals or corporate bodies to a considerable extent by the high standard it sets for the (unwritten criterion of) "interest" in the proceedings to be demonstrated. In the Court's view, such an interest can only be assumed if the Community measure under challenge directly, individually and immediately affects the litigant.[151] In this context, the ECCJ also takes up the interpretation of the criterion of individual concern, as established by the ECJ with the Plaumann formula in the 1960s.[152]

The ECJ was able to set up the restrictive standards it applies to the individual right to bring an action for annulment on the stricter requirements, as laid down in the EEC Treaty, in comparison with the ECSC Treaty. By contrast, both the EFTA Court and the ECOWAS Court execute an act of voluntary self-restriction in

---

2011, 202, 210 f., para. 26; EFTA Court, Norwegian Board of Appeal for Industrial Property Rights, E-5/16, EFTA Ct. Rep. 2017, 52, 70 para. 37.

[148]EFTA Court, Technologien Bau- und Wirtschaftsberatung GmbH and Bellona Foundation, E-2/02, EFTA Ct. Rep. 2003, 52, para 42; EFTA Court, Kimek Offshore AS, E-23/14, EFTA Ct. Rep. 2015, 414, 430 para. 61; EFTA Court, Míla ehf., E-7/16, Order of the Court, EFTA Ct. Rep. 2016, 904, 911 para. 27.

[149]Emphasis by the author.

[150]ECCJ, Kemi Pinheiro (San). Republic of Ghana, ECW/CCJ/JUD/11/12, 6 July 2012, para. 48.

[151]ECCJ, Odafe Oserada. ECOWAS Council of Ministers, ECW/CCJ/JUD/01/08, 16 May 2008, para. 27 f.

[152]ECCJ, Odafe Oserada. ECOWAS Council of Ministers, ECW/CCJ/JUD/01/08, 16 May 2008, para. 34 f., confirmed in ECCJ, Mrs. Oluwatosin Rinu Adewale v. Council of Ministers, ECOWAS & 3 ors, ECW/CCJ/JUD/07/12, 16 May 2012, in the framework of an Article 10(d) proceeding ECCJ, Rev. Fr. Solomon Mfa & 11 Ors. Federal Republic of Nigeria & 5 Ors, ECW/CCJ/JUD/06/19, 26 February 2019, 15 f.

applying the strict standards of the Plaumann formula: Article 3(1) SCA[153] does not necessarily extend the obligation of homogeneity incumbent on the EFTA Court to procedural rules. Rather, the reception of the Plaumann formula is based on the EFTA Court's consideration that, in the case of concurrent formulations in the Surveillance and Court Agreement and EU law, it should nevertheless be complied with in order to maintain systematic uniformity.[154] The right of action the ECOWAS Court of Justice must interpret can be addressed against an act or inaction of a Community official which violates the rights of the individuals or corporate bodies. In that, the wording suggests that the private litigant must be closely related to the object of the action in so far as he has to assert an infringement of individual rights. However, the criteria of direct, individual and immediate concern leading the ECOWAS Court of Justice to accept the Plaumann formula are not reflected in the wording of the right of action. In both contexts, the restriction of the circle of possible litigants is thus an expression of a policy decision of the respective community court.

3.2.2 Method

With regard to the transparency of the methodical approach, there are fundamental differences between the ECJ, on the one hand, and the EFTA Court and the ECOWAS Court on the other. The EFTA Court only uses the comparability of the wording of the respective rights of action under EU law and in the Surveillance and Court Agreement to justify the legal concept of "procedural homogeneity". Since the entry into force of the Lisbon Treaty and the associated reform of the EU's legal protection system, however, this logic no longer unquestionably applies. The ECOWAS Court of Justice does not disclose its method of interpretation at all.

---

[153]Article 3(1) SCA reads: "Without prejudice to future developments of case law, the provisions of Protocols 1 to 4 and the provisions of the acts corresponding to those listed in Annexes I and II to this Agreement, in so far as they are identical in substance to corresponding rules of the Treaty establishing the European Economic Community and the Treaty establishing the European Coal and Steel Community and to acts adopted in application of these two Treaties, shall in their implementation and application be interpreted in conformity with the relevant rulings of the Court of Justice of the European Communities given prior to the date of signature of the EEA Agreement."

[154]EFTA Court, Scottish Salmon Growers Association Ltd. EFTA Surveillance Authority, E-2/94, EFTA Ct. Rep. 1994/1995, 58, 63 f. para 1: "Although the EFTA Court is not required by Article 3 (1) of the Surveillance and Court Agreement to follow the reasoning of the EC Court of Justice when interpreting the main part of that Agreement, the reasoning which led the EC Court of Justice to its interpretations of expressions in Community law is relevant when those expressions are identical in substance to those which this Court has to interpret. The Court finds that this principle must also apply when considering interpretations of the same expressions in relation to issues such as what constitutes a decision of the EFTA Surveillance Authority, whether a measure is reviewable and who has locus standi to bring an action for annulment of a decision."

The ECJ, on the other hand, applies a strict literal interpretation of the action for annulment. Its initial exclusion of normative acts as suitable subjects of action and the restrictive interpretation of locus standi can be explained, in particular, by the systematic comparison between the regulatory details of the individual action for annulment of the ECSC Treaty and the narrower wording of the action for annulment of the EEC Treaty. In its early case-law under the EEC Treaty, the ECJ practiced a method of "historical concretisation".[155] This means that the Court and the Advocates General systematically compared the wording of the rights of action as laid down in the ECSC Treaty and in the EEC Treaty in order to explain and justify the restriction of access to the ECJ under the "new" regime of legal protection in the European Economic Community. In this sense, the ECJ considered it "reasonable to think that the authors of the Treaty signed in Rome on 25 March 1957 were aware of the ECSC Treaty, adopted 6 years previously, in particular of the content and scope of Article 33, and intentionally gave a different scope to the provisions of Article 173 of the EEC Treaty."[156] Most recently, in the reformed framework of the Lisbon Treaty, the ECJ excluded legislative acts as suitable subjects of action by referring to the historical will of the contracting parties.[157] In contrast to the *pro homine* approach applied by the group of courts extending individual access to justice (above, Sect. 2.2.1), the ECJ's literal interpretation as well as the historical method of interpretation are reminiscences of state sovereignty and state consensus as the basis and limit of international jurisprudence.

3.2.3 Decentralising Legal Protection of Business Entities Before Domestic Courts

As demonstrated, the ECJ, the EFTA Court and, at least in part, the ECOWAS Court of Justice, as representatives of the "restriction model", are reluctant to expand the procedural status of private business entities on the regional level. In contrast thereto, they are proactive in advocating decentralised law enforcement before national courts as the "second way" of protecting individual rights. What the three courts have in common is that they define two fundamental structural principles for the interaction between national and regional courts which serve as a normative basis for activating the national responsibility for the legal protection of business entities. Firstly, all courts characterise their respective legal order (irrespective of the very different depth of integration) as a *sui generis* legal order which has distanced itself from features of classical international law.[158] Secondly, in addition, all courts are

---

[155]Wendel (2008), p. 810 ("historische Konkretisierung").

[156]ECJ, Case C-75/02 P, Diputación Foral de Álava, ECLI:EU:C:2003:189, para. 27.

[157]ECJ, Case C-274/12 P, Telefónica, ECLI:EU:C:2013:852, para. 27.

[158]"The European Economic Community constitutes a new legal order of international law for the benefit of which the states have limited their sovereign rights, albeit within limited fields, and the subjects of which comprise not only the Member States but also their nationals." (ECJ, Case C-26/

committed to a cooperative relationship with the national legal protection bodies with which they interconnect by way of the preliminary ruling procedures.[159] Thus, they distance themselves from the premise of a general supremacy of international courts.

It is noteworthy that the ECJ and the EFTA Court have based their assessment of the *sui generis* character of the respective legal system on the decisive role which individuals and economic operators as legal subjects play for the success of the integration project.[160] Thus, these courts refer to the identical teleological considerations on which the judicial representatives of the "expansion model" base the extension of the procedural status of private litigants on the regional level. In doing so, the ECJ was able to rely on the concept of supranationality, on far-reaching restrictions of sovereign rights of the member states as well as on the fact that "nationals" constitute core legal subjects of EU law in order to describe the distinctiveness of the legal order Community law creates. By contrast, the EFTA Court can only refer to the latter aspect in order to draw the identical conclusion. The "distinctive feature" of the three legal orders thus applies irrespective of the significantly lower degree of supranationalisation to which the EFTA States as well as the member states of ECOWAS were prepared to adhere. The EFTA States had not only deliberately refrained from transferring competences to supranational institutions, but had also firmly excluded from the EEA and the SCA essential framework conditions which safeguard decentralised law enforcement at the level of EU law (e.g. direct effect and primacy).[161] Moreover, there is no binding obligation for courts of last instance to refer cases to the EFTA Court or to the ECOWAS Court of Justice. Also, in ECOWAS law, there is no direct applicability of primary and secondary Community law in the member states.[162] In both legal systems, crucial preconditions for activating national courts to grant the individual legal protection owed under Community law (as known from EU law) are absent.

To varying degrees, the courts are effectuating the legal conditions for decentralised Community law enforcement by means of judicial activism. As is

---

62, Van Gend en Loos, ECLI:EU:C:1963:1, syllabus 3); "(...) (T)he EEA Agreement is an international treaty sui generis which contains a distinct legal order of its own." (EFTA Court, Advisory Opinion, Erla Maria Sveinbjörnsdóttir. The Government of Iceland, Rs. E-9/97, EFTA Ct. Rep. 1998, 95, 112 para. 59); the ECCJ talks about a "distinctive feature of the Community legal order of ECOWAS" (ECCJ, Hon. Dr. Jerry Ugokwe. Federal Republic of Nigeria, ECW/CCJ/JUD/03/05, 7 October 2005, para. 32).

[159]See, e.g., ECJ, Case C-343/90, Manuel José Lourenço Dias, ECLI:EU:C:1992:327, para. 14 "instrument for cooperation"; EFTA Court, Irish Bank Resolution Corporation. Kaupthing Bank hf., E-18/11, EFTA Ct. Rep. 2012, 592, 610 para. 57; in the framework of an Article 10 (d) proceeding ECCJ, Hon. Dr. Jerry Ugokwe. Federal Republic of Nigeria, ECW/CCJ/JUD/03/05, 7 October 2005, para. 32; ECCJ, Kemi Pinheiro (San). Republic of Ghana, ECW/CCJ/JUD/11/12, 6 July 2012, para. 51 f.

[160]EFTA Court, Advisory Opinion, Erla Maria Sveinbjörnsdóttir. The Government of Iceland, Rs. E-9/97, EFTA Ct. Rep. 1998, 95, 112 para. 58–60.

[161]Fredriksen and Franklin (2015), pp. 660 et seq.

[162]Ukaigwe (2016), p. 213.

well known, the ECJ most comprehensively set the framework conditions for the decentralised enforcement of individual rights arising from EU law. The direct applicability of primary and secondary EU law and its supremacy effect in the national legal systems as well as the comprehensive state liability of the member states under Union law can be mentioned in brief.[163] The ECOWAS Court elevates the national courts to the status of Community courts with jurisdiction to apply ECOWAS law as an integral part of their national legal systems and calls for recognising and implementing decisions of the ECOWAS Court of Justice in the member state area. However, the doctrinal details of this duty remain as unclear as the Court's postulate of a "judicial monism"[164] integrating ECOWAS law automatically in the domestic legal systems.

Much more proactively and more in line with the ECJ, the EFTA Court ensures doctrinal preconditions for the effective enforcement of EEA law before domestic courts. It does so by means of a twofold argumentation: On the one hand, the Court acknowledges, entirely in the interests of the dualistic EFTA States, that the EFTA States have decided against the direct effect of non-implemented EEA law in the national legal system.[165] On the other hand, the Court derives an unwritten legal principle of state liability from the EEA[166] and imposes on the courts of the member states the obligation to interpret national law in conformity with EEA law.[167] By means of a teleological, human rights-based interpretation, the EFTA Court also limits the freedom of final instance courts to submit final decisions via preliminary proceedings.[168]

---

[163]On these principles De Búrca and Craig (2020), pp. 218 et seq. (direct effect), pp. 288 et seq. (state liability), pp. 303 et seq. (supremacy).

[164]ECCJ, Hon. Dr. Jerry Ugokwe. Federal Republic of Nigeria, ECW/CCJ/JUD/03/05, 7 October 2005, para. 32.

[165]EFTA Court, Karl K. Karlsson hf. The Icelandic State, E-4/01, EFTA Ct. Rep. 2002, 240, 249 para. 28: "It follows from Article 7 EEA and Protocol 35 to the EEA Agreement that EEA law does not entail a transfer of legislative powers. Therefore, EEA law does not require that individuals and economic operators can rely directly on nonimplemented EEA rules before national courts."

[166]EFTA Court, Advisory Opinion, Erla Maria Sveinbjörnsdóttir. The Government of Iceland, Rs. E-9/97, EFTA Ct. Rep. 1998, 95, 112 para. 62. Inter alia confirmed in EFTA Court, Irish Bank Resolution Corporation. Kaupthing Bank hf., E-18/11, EFTA Ct. Rep. 2012, 592, 629 para. 125; EFTA Court, EFTA Surveillance Authority. Iceland, Joined Cases E-2/17 and E-3/17, EFTA Ct. Rep. 2017, 725, 771 para. 113.

[167]EFTA Court, Irish Bank Resolution Corporation. Kaupthing Bank hf., E-18/11, EFTA Ct. Rep. 2012, 592, 629 para. 124.

[168]EFTA Court, Irish Bank Resolution Corporation. Kaupthing Bank hf., E-18/11, EFTA Ct. Rep. 2012, 592, 612 f. para. 63 et seq.; EFTA Court, Staten v/Arbeidsdepartementet. Stig Arne Jonsson, E-03/12, EFTA Ct. Rep. 2013, 136, 156 para. 60.

4 Conclusion

The overview of rights of action which business entities possess in regional economic systems allows us to summarise the overall spectrum of their procedural empowerment: At the one end of the spectrum is the maximum possible loss of state sovereignty and, associated with this, the procedural autonomy of business entities. This is achieved when natural and legal persons are empowered to initiate proceedings directly against states before the regional court without prior involvement of national legal protection bodies. The aim of these proceedings are to subject state measures in the general interest to judicial review—regardless of whether the proceedings serve to protect subjective rights or individual interests. In this model, a procedural equality of the power of states and companies to bring actions is realised. Understood in this way as *instruments of economic and legal participation and control*, individual rights of action open up the opportunity to actively contribute towards the shaping of the effectiveness of law enforcement in the integration process by means of court proceedings. With varying intensity, functionally motivated rights of action (Sect. 2.2) and regional economic courts expanding individual access to justice by broadly interpreting rights of action (Sect. 3.1) are approaching this counterpoint. The early ECJ in interpreting and applying the individual action for annulment of the ECSC Treaty, the Court of Justice of the EAC, and the Caribbean Court of Justice belong to this group of courts.

At the other end of the spectrum, the minimum possible procedural autonomy, is the business entity's power to access the regional economic court only for reasons of legal protection, because particular interests, individual freedoms or subjective rights are affected. National sovereignty is curtailed in the least possible way if court proceedings can only be directed against measures of supranational sovereignty as suitable subjects of action. Understood in this way as mere *defensive instruments*, rights of action guarantee freedom from burdensome state or Community law interventions in the legal or economic positions of a company. Rights of action introduced with this sort of rule of law rationale (Sect. 2.1) and regional economic courts that interpret these rights restrictively (Sect. 3.2) are approaching this counterpoint of procedural empowerment. The European Court of Justice (since applying the EEC Treaty), the EFTA Court and, in some regards, the ECOWAS Court can be mentioned by way of example as representatives of this group. These courts have the fact in common that they tend to restrict access to regional judicial protection, but effectuate decentralised individual protection in the domestic legal system.

The question of whether one or the other model more or less serves the effectiveness of the legal protection of companies and the enforcement of regional economic law can ultimately only be answered quantitatively and empirically.[169] It is certain, however, that the judicial restriction of individual access to regional courts did not provoke any kind of state counter-reaction in any of the systems

---

[169]As an example of an empirical research approach to the long-term effects of international court decisions see Leitão et al. (2019).

considered. By contrast, nearly all courts that expanded the *control and participation function* of individual rights of action were confronted with the resistance of the contracting states. This resistance took different forms: In the case of rights of action to the European Court of Justice, when drafting the Treaty of the European Economic Community, the member states re-formulated the individual action for annulment as introduced in the European Coal and Steel Community in order to refine and adapt the right of action to their original historical will; i.e., to the will to exclude measures of general nature as possible subject matters of the proceedings.[170] The litigant friendly, broad interpretation of the ECJ had provoked this state reaction. The expansive interpretation of the right of action opening access to the Court of Justice of the East African Community also incited the member states to restrict the admissibility criteria of the individual right of action in order to "put the court back on track". The states restricted the right of action by setting a 2-month time limit and by excluding the competence of the EACJ with regard to the protection of individual rights for community measures which the EAC Treaty reserves to member state institutions.[171] Despite the fact that the procedural power of natural and legal persons is curtailed as a consequence of this kind of state reaction,[172] the authority of the regional economic court—and thereby, the participation and/or rule of law function of rights of action for business entities—is not challenged as such.[173] The procedural status of business entities is the product of a dynamic process of "back and forth" in which the states, litigants and the regional courts are engaged. In the light of this finding, a real "backlash" against the regional court's activism to expand these functions of rights of action, as in the case of the Southern African Development Community,[174] remains an exception.

References

Alter K (2006) Private litigants and the new international courts. Comp Polit Stud 39(1):22–49
Alter K, Hooghe L (2016) Regional dispute settlement systems. In: Börzel T, Risse T (eds) Oxford handbook of comparative regionalism. Oxford University Press, Oxford, pp 538–558

---

[170]On the different wordings of the individual action for annulment see above, Sect. 2.1.1.

[171]See the wording of the revised right of action above (Sect. 2.2.2, footnote 93).

[172]In the case of the ECJ, this happened only in the "new" framework of the EEC Treaty since the ECJ upheld its interpretation of the individual action for annulment as laid down in the ECSC Treaty.

[173]In the words of Madsen et al. (2018), p. 202 one could characterise this kind of resistance as mere "pushbacks".

[174]The SADC Tribunal's expansive, human rights friendly interpretation in the case SADCT, Mike Campbell (PVT) Limited and Another. Republic of Zimbabwe, (2/07) [2007] SADCT 1 (13 December 2007) had provoked the *de facto* abolishment of the individual right of action by limiting the jurisdiction of the SADC Tribunal to the determination of interstate disputes. On this backlash Obonye (2013).

Alter K, Helfer L, McAllister J (2013) A new International Human Rights Court for West Africa: The ECOWAS Community Court of Justice. Am J Int Law 107:737–779

Baudenbacher C (2004) Judicialization: can the European model be exported to other parts of the world? Texas Int Law J 39:381–400

Baudenbacher C (2016) The EFTA Court: structure and tasks. In: Baudenbacher C (ed) The handbook of EEA law. Springer, Heidelberg, pp 139–178

Daig HW (1958) Die Gerichtsbarkeit in der Europäischen Wirtschaftsgemeinschaft und der Europäischen Atomgemeinschaft – mit vergleichenden Hinweisen auf die Europäische Gemeinschaft für Kohle und Stahl. Archiv des öffentlichen Rechts 44:132–208

De Búrca G, Craig P (2020) EU law: text, cases, and materials, 7th edn. Oxford University Press, Oxford

De Mestral A (2013) Dispute settlement under the WTO and RTAs: an uneasy relationship. J Int Econ Law 16:777–825

Fawcett L (2008) Regionalism in world politics: past and present. In: Kösler A, Zimmek M (eds) Elements of regional integration – a multidimensional approach. Nomos, Baden-Baden, pp 15–28

Fredriksen H, Franklin C (2015) Of pragmatism and principles: the EEA agreement 20 years on. Common Mark Law Rev 52:629–684

Gathii J (2016) Variation in the use of sub-regional integration courts between business and human rights actors: the case of the East African Court of Justice. Law Contemp Probl 79(1):37–62

Jaenicke G (1951) Die Europäische Gemeinschaft für Kohle und Stahl (Montanunion) – Struktur und Funktionen ihrer Organe. Zeitschrift für ausländisches öffentliches Recht und Völkerrecht 14:727–788

Kocken J, van Roozendaal G (2012) Constructing the Caribbean Court of Justice: how ideas inform institutional choices. Eur Rev Latin Am Caribbean Stud (93):95–112

Leitão J, Lehmann S, Palmer Olsen H (2019) Quantifying long-term impact of court decisions. Appl Netw Sci 4(3):1–15

Lenaerts K, Maselis I, Gutman K (2015) EU procedural law. Oxford University Press, Oxford

Lenz T (2012) Spurred emulation: the EU and regional integration in Mercosur and SADC. West Eur Polit 35:155–173

Madsen M, Cebulak P, Wiebusch M (2018) Backlash against international courts: explaining the forms and patterns of resistance to international courts. Int J Law Context 14:197–220

Mapuva J, Muyengwa-Mapuva L (2014) The SADC regional bloc: what challenges and prospects for regional integration? Law Democr Dev 18:22–36

Milej T (2018) Human rights protection by international courts – what role for the East African Court of Justice? Afr J Int Comp Law 26(1):108–129

Miskelley R (1990) Grand Anse Declaration: can the Caribbean Community realistically integrate intraregional trade and production within the confines of the CARICOM Treaty by 1993? Georgia J Int Comp Law 20:185–205

Mosler H (1966) Die Entstehung des Modells supranationaler und gewaltenteilender Staatenverbindungen in den Verhandlungen über den Schuman-Plan. In: von Caemmerer E, Schlochauer HJ, Steindorff E (eds) Probleme des Europäischen Rechts. Festschrift für Walter Hallstein. Klostermann, Frankfurt a.M., pp 355–386

Norberg S, Johansson M (2016) The history of the EEA agreement and the first twenty years of its existence. In: Baudenbacher C (ed) The handbook of EEA law. Springer, Heidelberg, pp 3–42

Obonye J (2013) Neutering the SADC tribunal by blocking individuals' access to the tribunal. Int Hum Rights Law Rev 2:294–321

Reuter P (1953) La Communauté Européenne du Charbon et de l'Acier. Librairie Générale de Droit et de Jurisprudence, Paris

Reuter P (1965) Organisations Européennes. Presses Universitaires de France, Paris

Romano C (1998–1999) The proliferation of international judicial bodies: the pieces of the puzzle. N Y J Int Law Polit 31:709–751

Sevón L (1992) The EEA judicial system and the supreme courts of the EFTA states. Eur J Int Law 3:329–340

Shany Y (2014) Assessing the effectiveness of international courts. Oxford University Press, Oxford

Sykes A (2005) Public vs. private enforcement of international economic law: of standing and remedy. J Leg Stud 34:631–666

The West Indian Commission (1993) Time for action. University Press of the West Indies, Kingston

Ukaigwe J (2016) ECOWAS law. Springer, Heidelberg

Umbricht V (1989) Multilateral mediation. Practical experiences and lessons. Martinus Nijhoff, Dordrecht

Wendel M (2008) Renaissance der historischen Auslegungsmethode im europäischen Verfassungsrecht? Überlegungen zur Tragweite der historischen Auslegungsmethode infolge des jüngsten EU-Reformprozesses. Zeitschrift für ausländisches öffentliches Recht und Völkerrecht 68:803–827

Wiater P (2020) Internationale Individualkläger. Ein Vergleich des Zugangs zu Gericht im Wirtschaftsvölkerrecht. Mohr Siebeck, Tübingen

Patricia Wiater (born 1982) studied law (First State Exam 2006), political science and modern German literature (M.A.) in Augsburg; 2008 binational doctorate in law at the Universities of Strasbourg and Leipzig (Dr. iur.); 2010 Second State Exam in Freiburg; 2011–2016 Councillor at the Bavarian Ministry of Science; 2012 doctorate in political science at the University of Freiburg (Dr. phil.); Academic (senior) councillor at the Institute for Politics and Public Law at the Ludwig-Maximilians-University Munich; since 2018 Tenure Track Professor at the University of Erlangen-Nuremberg; 2019 Habilitation (LMU Munich).

Can Current Regulation Effectively Manage PMC Conduct and Ensure Accountability?

Katerina Galai

Contents

Abstract There is no simple answer to how international law regulates private military companies (PMCs). The first challenge is to decipher what PMC regulation entails and who should be regulated. Today, PMCs dispose of vast resources, performing various security functions across the world, ranging from strategy and logistics to civilian detention and combat training. Treated differently under international law to states and individuals, these *a priori* legitimate companies often find themselves in close proximity to conflict or areas of heightened risk. PMCs are made up of individual contractors and directors; but, unlike mercenaries, they also exist as corporate structures. With the sole purpose of delivering a service on behalf of the client, PMCs perplex accountability mechanisms when gross violations occur. In that scenario who should be responsible and in what way: the contractor who fired the gun? The company that did not follow appropriate practices? Or the state that outsourced the support of military activities to a private entity? Although PMCs are regulated by the industry internationally and guided by performance standards, the

---

K. Galai (✉)
University of Cambridge, Cambridge, UK

© Springer Nature Switzerland AG 2021
M. Bungenberg et al. (eds.), *European Yearbook of International Economic Law 2020*,
European Yearbook of International Economic Law (2022) 11: 237–264,
https://doi.org/10.1007/8165_2021_66, Published online: 26 March 2021

effectiveness of PMC regulation is often questioned. This article examines the full landscape of PMC regulation, from setting the rules to its ability to enforce them and establish accountability in the event of misconduct. Based on identified challenges posed by PMCs and limitations of different bodies of law that attempt to regulate them, I propose possible ways in which the law could develop and be implemented at a level that is less likely to generate impunity.

1 Introduction

Private military contractors exist somewhere between civilians and combatants: they are perceived as mercenaries but form part of legitimate corporate structures; they operate internationally but are not recognised as actors under international law, in the way that states and international institutions are; and they carry out a variety of functions but are not codified. Unlike pirates, terrorists, freedom fighters, or militias, mercenaries and PMCs are typically hired to provide their services on behalf of a client, rather than waging a conflict to pursue their own political or ideological goals.[1] Under current provisions of international law, mercenaries cannot be considered direct perpetrators. Instead, only states can commit acts of aggression using mercenaries as their implements.[2] It follows, therefore, that private military activity is characterised by a *transactional* relationship between the supply and demand of private security which existed long before modern sovereign states, national armies, and arguments concerning the ethics and morality of private military resources.

Are private military companies thus simply a modern reincarnation of mercenaries, given the nature of their activities have substantial similarities and their motives and methods often overlap? While there are plenty of critics blurring the lines between PMCs and mercenaries,[3] it is important to distinguish the basic components of a PMC from a specifically *legal* rather than ethical or political standpoint. From a corporate legal perspective, PMCs arose from the juxtaposition of civilian corporations and the lack of any clear criminalisation of mercenaries by the instruments of international law (IL).[4] Like mercenary groups, PMCs are still formed and run exclusively by civilians, although the majority are former military personnel. However, PMCs acquired a corporate legal personality which distinguishes them from their legally dubious predecessors. The construct of incorporation turned a private business of mercenarism into a legitimate company. However, this essence is not

---

[1]Galai (2019), p. 17.

[2]Liu (2015), p. 181.

[3]See for example Scahill (2007), Armstrong (2008) and Young Pelton (2006).

[4]Liu (2015), p. 192.

captured in any of the existing PMC definitions and the terminology used to classify these actors varies.[5]

In addition to classification challenges, the nature of PMC activity has an impact on how well we understand the problem. While the growth of the private military industry can be observed in the media and through privatisation of various sectors and functions,[6] obtaining comprehensive and reliable data on PMC activity remains inherently problematic. There are several reasons for this: firstly, unlike national armies and government agencies, the activities of PMCs are more obscured due to them not being subject to legislation which requires corporate transparency. Secondly, government-led enquiries into the private military industry are limited, leading to little reporting on or regulation of the industry.[7] Thirdly, contracts between governments and PMCs are fraught with commercial- and security-related sensitivities, and are therefore not widely available for public scrutiny.[8] These factors together create a high level of secrecy veiled around private military companies, and collectively go towards explaining why these bodies are difficult to regulate.

Despite private armies dominating the security landscape at different periods throughout history, PMCs are often considered a new issue under the different bodies of international law.[9] PMCs, however, have not emerged overnight. As primary clients of PMCs, states have historically welcomed the integration of private violence into their government policy and were not prepared to outlaw it. This normalisation of private security came from every direction. Beginning in the 1980s, leading powers promoted neoliberal policies; states debilitated by decolonisation[10] and the new wars[11] lacked strong national military structures and the capacity to sustain local security; international organisations, such as the International Monetary Fund (IMF) and the World Bank, imposed impossible loan terms on developing nations while encouraging private military assistance.[12]

Furthermore, contemporary industry advocates promote the perception of PMCs only participating in the legitimate non-military aspects of security. Meanwhile, in reality, by the nature of their trade, PMCs often find themselves in close proximity to conflict, in areas of heightened risk (e.g. post-conflict reconstruction) and dealing with vulnerable communities (e.g. operating detention centres or providing interrogation services). While these conditions are common amongst private security

---

[5]The industry provides a variety of terms: private security company (PSC), private military company (PMC), private security and military companies (PMSC), private security companies and other private security service providers (PSCs).

[6]Cropley and Lewis (2015); Arduino (2015).

[7]McFate (2014), p. 9.

[8]Kinsey (2004), pp. 155–173.

[9]Liu (2015), p. 289.

[10]See Galai (2019), Chapter 3.

[11]See Kaldor (2002).

[12]Peet (2009), pp. 66–177.

providers, they are often overlooked and obscured by the more unproductive argument that states choose to use PMCs to avoid responsibility for their acts abroad. While this may be true for certain cases, companies, and countries, such claims do little to aid a more comprehensive regulation, diverting the attention away from a constructive debate. Perception of legitimacy is also driven by large reputable companies, like G4S, who take pride in upholding human right standards and ensure compliance in the course of providing their services.[13]

When thinking about PMC regulation, a number of up to date mechanisms come to mind: the International Code of Conduct (ICoC), the Montreux Document, relevant standards of the International Organization for Standardization (ISO) and the UN Guiding Principles on Business and Human Rights (UNGPs). However, upon closer examination, all these regulatory efforts fall under the framework of corporate social responsibility, predominantly originating from the industry rather than international law. Yet, the assumption exists that international law regulates PMCs—but from where does this assumption originate?

So why the assumption that international law regulates PMCs? International law was originally intended to solely apply to states and international organisations. As a result of post-Second World War tribunals individuals can also come under international legal scrutiny. Individual criminal responsibility has been solidified through international criminal law and continues to be ascribed through The Hague's ad hoc tribunals and the International Criminal Court (ICC). To date, companies have not been recognised as actors under international law and therefore cannot be held criminally liable for committing international crimes. International humanitarian law (IHL) regulates the conduct of war but has limited application to PMCs as companies and even their contractors, unless they are properly incorporated into the state forces and are therefore treated as combatants for the purposes of an armed conflict.

As a discipline, international law is naturally politicised. Designed to govern relationships between states, it requires state 'buy-in' for any practice or convention to be accepted and enacted effectively. The fact that it pertains only to states and individuals makes its application to any hybrid threats limited and highly problematic. Furthermore, as a relatively new discipline, it lacks the ability to take a broader historical view. As a result, many definitions and conventions are limited to the specific context under which they were produced and do not account for 'old wines in new bottles', which this writer considers PMCs to be. The above perhaps speaks more to the challenges inherent to international law, rather than the quality of PMC regulation. Nonetheless, it is important at the starting point of this discussion to recognise that many such problems are inherent to international law, that they are indicative of how PMCs are treated today, and the barriers to developing legal accountability mechanisms in the future.

---

[13]G4S representative, UK-Russia Security Dialogue—Private Military Companies, 9 December 2019, RUSI Whitehall, London.

This article attempts to cut through the noise which surrounds this controversial and legally ambiguous industry and provides a more fulsome view on how PMCs are regulated and held responsible for their actions.

Staying true to the title of this piece, I first assess various international efforts which attempt to regulate PMC use and conduct. I then take a broader view, looking beyond PMC regulation and considering available legally-binding mechanisms that could help address accountability gaps produced by the corporate status of PMCs and the voluntary nature of existing regulation. Then, I examine the different bodies of law at international, domestic and transnational level to identify the appropriate forum to invoke PMC responsibility. Finally, I conclude my analysis by suggesting possible avenues for the law to develop to ensure a more sound regulatory framework and consider barriers to successful realisation of these proposed solutions.

2 Regulation

The complexity of PMC regulation is reflective of the complexity of the phenomenon itself. Ever-present in the security supply chain, a PMC is a vehicle carrying out its client's agenda based on a contract. Its contractors are employees who, depending on the terms of that contract, could be considered either combatants or civilians in any given operation. Meanwhile the nature of PMC activity, now widespread and conventional, was frowned upon during the Cold War and unimaginable 50 years prior. Thus, it may be questioned if broad scope and specific application can be expected from attempts to regulate PMCs.

However, it would be inaccurate to suggest that PMCs exist in a legal vacuum. There are numerous regulatory bodies which make provisions for PMC regulation; some international, some domestic, some binding, and some self-regulating and voluntary. Inevitably, the result of such an active regulatory response concerning private military conduct is a conflicting network of laws and guidelines which all separately claim to regulate the private military space.

Under current international law, PMC regulation predominantly exists in the form of voluntary industry standards, such as the International Code of Conduct and the Montreux Document, or in the form of human rights-driven initiatives, such as the UN guidelines aimed at implementing the corporate responsibility of respecting human rights. All of these fall under the framework of corporate social responsibility.

The following sections describe and analyse various international efforts which attempt to regulate PMC use and conduct.

2.1 UN-Level Regulation

2.1.1 Guiding Principles

Approved in 2011, the UN Guiding Principles on Business and Human Rights address the responsibilities of states and corporations, and require them to respect, protect, and comply with all applicable laws to uphold human rights. Acknowledging the heightened risk of human rights violations in areas affected by conflict, the guidelines propose an increased state presence to identify and monitor the risks, denying access to public support and services for businesses which are found to have violated human rights and ensuring that adequate liability mechanisms are in place when violations occur.[14] However, the guidelines neglect to mention an adequate vetting process which ought to be undertaken by the state prior to engaging a PMC, nor do they stipulate that human rights provisions to be explicitly incorporated into the terms of any contracts between states and PMCs. The Principles also misleadingly point to the provisions of the Rome Statute of the ICC when discussing the sources of corporate criminal liability for companies, while in fact referring to national jurisdictions.[15]

2.1.2 Legally Binding Instrument

In response to the shortcomings of the Guiding Principles, the Human Rights Council established an "open-ended intergovernmental working group on transnational corporations and other business enterprises with respect to human rights."[16] The intergovernmental working group (IGWG) was created to consider the possibility of developing an international framework, including the option of drafting a legally binding instrument on the regulation, monitoring, and oversight of private military and security companies.[17] The purpose of such an instrument would be to increase corporate accountability and ensure access to remedy for victims of business-related human rights abuse.

While the overall strategy is yet to be defined, its current form appears to have some notable gaps. The treaty is limited to gross violations, therefore not encompassing all forms of corporate human rights abuses. With its main focus on transnational corporations, the resolution does not apply to national companies and

---

[14]Guiding Principles on Business and Human Rights. Implementing the United Nations 'Protect, Respect and Remedy' Framework, UN Human Rights Office of the High Commissioner, New York and Geneva, 2011, pp. 8–9.

[15]Guiding Principles on Business and Human Rights. Implementing the United Nations 'Protect, Respect and Remedy' Framework, UN Human Rights Office of the High Commissioner, New York and Geneva, 2011, pp. 25–26.

[16]Established at the 26th HRC session in June 2014, by adopting resolution 26/9, A/HRC/RES/26/9, p. 2.

[17]A/HRC/32/39, p. 10.

currently does not provide a definition of 'transnational organisation.'[18] It is also currently not clear whether the instrument would define available remedies and processes for accessing those remedies if states fail to act on obligations, if it would focus on establishing corporate liability, or both.[19]

2.1.3 UN Draft Convention

Before the mandate was granted to the IGWG to draft a legally-binding instrument, the UN Working Group on the use of mercenaries[20] had been working on a Draft Convention specifically aimed at private military and security companies (PMSCs).[21] The Draft Convention emerged as a legally binding response to the over-inclusive nature of the Montreux Document and the self-regulatory nature of the Code of Conduct.[22] Taking a highly conservative stance, influenced by the anti-mercenary views of its authors, the Draft Convention proposed not to allow for inherently governmental functions to be performed by anyone other than the state itself.[23] Striving for stricter regulation and greater accountability, it asks that "each State party bears responsibility for the military and security activities of PMSCs registered or operating in their jurisdiction, whether or not these entities are contracted by the State."[24] This fundamentally contradicts the basic principle that the state is only responsible for its own actions, nor is it consistent with the attribution clauses of the ILC Articles.[25] While, in theory, the Draft Convention was an effort to create a firmer legal position on state responsibility when using PMCs, in practice, it identified a vast discrepancy between existing public IL and an emerging treaty. A bold but ill-informed attempt at PMC regulation, it has not seen any further developments in recent years.

Even at the UN level there is a general polarisation between a softer, guidelines-based approach and a legally binding approach to PMC regulation. While the IGWG insists that a legally binding instrument will be designed to complement the Guiding Principles, there is a lack of coherence in the overall UN methodology.

---

[18] A/HRC/31/50, pp. 5 and 12.

[19] This concern was also raised during the session's panel on state obligations—Panel V. Obligations of States to guarantee the respect for human rights by transnational corporations and other business enterprises, including extraterritorial obligation, A/HRC/31/50, pp. 13–15.

[20] Working Group on the use of mercenaries as a means of violating human rights and impeding the exercise of the right of peoples to self-determination, https://www.ohchr.org/EN/Issues/Mercenaries/WGMercenaries/Pages/WGMercenariesIndex.aspx (last accessed 1 July 2020).

[21] Draft International Convention on the Regulation, Oversight and Monitoring of Private Military and Security Companies, 13 July 2009.

[22] On the criticism of the Montreux Document by the UN Working Group: White (2012), p. 17.

[23] Draft International Convention on the Regulation, Oversight and Monitoring of Private Military and Security Companies, 13 July 2009, Preamble, p. 3.

[24] Article 4 (1) on state responsibility towards PMCs.

[25] Described in more detail below, Sect. 3.2.1.

2.2 Industry Standards and Regulation

2.2.1 Montreux Doc

The Montreux Document[26] is another intergovernmental initiative intended to promote respect for international humanitarian law (IHL) and human rights law whenever PMCs are present in armed conflicts.[27] Largely state-centric in nature, it outlines: the obligations of a 'contracting state' entering into an agreement with PMCs; the 'home state' where the companies are registered; and the 'territorial state' where PMCs operate.[28] Yet, the Document does not create any new legal obligations for states or PMCs, and, while it does provide guidelines, it is not necessarily a step towards a new treaty.[29] States that sign up to the Montreux Process are not required to introduce any new standards or procedures in their use of PMCs. Equally, the companies are not bound by the Document, thereby rendering this regulation largely theoretical.

2.2.2 ISO Standards and Toolkit

The proliferation of private military activity has also triggered the need for international standardisation. Since 2015 PMCs can obtain ISO certification (ISO 18788:2015) to demonstrate their compliance with internationally-accepted standards for private security operations.[30] It provides PMCs and their clients with a business and risk management framework which is compliant with the law, human rights, and relevant voluntary regulatory measures the ISO is a part of.

More recently the International Committee of the Red Cross (ICRC) and the Geneva Centre for the Democratic Control of Armed Forces (DCAF) have collectively developed a Toolkit for Addressing Security and Human Rights Challenges in Complex Environments.[31] Designed to offer practical tools for PMCs, such as

---

[26]The Montreux Document on Pertinent International Legal Obligations and Good Practices for States related to Operations of Private Military and Security Companies during Armed Conflict (Montreux Document), 17 September 2008, https://www.icrc.org/en/publication/0996-montreux-document-private-military-and-security-companies (last accessed 1 July 2020).

[27]Montreux Document, p. 31.

[28]Montreux Document, p. 10; The International Code of Conduct for Private Security Service Providers, Geneva Academy, August 2013, https://www.icoca.ch/sites/all/themes/icoca/assets/icoc_english3.pdf (last accessed 1 July 2020), p. 5.

[29]A/HRC/32/39, p. 11.

[30]See ISO 18788:2015; Management system for private security operations. Requirements with guidance for use, www.iso.org/iso/home/store/catalogue_tc/catalogue_detail.htm?csnumber=63380 (last accessed 1 July 2020).

[31]Addressing Security and Human Rights Challenges in Complex Environments Toolkit, Third Edition, DCAF and ICRC, June 2016, http://www.securityhumanrightshub.org/content/toolkit (last accessed 1 July 2020).

checklists, templates, and case studies based on good practices, the Toolkit addresses real-life security and human rights challenges identified through consultation with various stakeholders.[32] While the Toolkit does not form part of a regulation, it demonstrates the extent of the issue and the aspiration of the international community to better regulate PMCs.

2.2.3 International Code of Conduct

The most prominent international example of PMC (self-)regulation is the International Code of Conduct. The code originated from a 2005 Swiss Federal Council report on private military and security companies which "recommended pursuing further dialogue and action in this area."[33] It stems from the Montreux Process, however, unlike the ICRC-endorsed initiative, it aims to regulate companies rather than the states themselves. It is also administered by the industry, thus making it a self-regulatory body. The stated purpose of the ICoC is to set out a range of industry-developed principles and standards to guide PMCs on matters of international human rights and humanitarian law. It currently lists over 700 companies and has an external oversight body (ICoCA[34]) which incorporates ISO standards into its certification procedures, forming a solid foundation for measures of quality.

There are however a number of challenges that undermine the effectiveness of ICoC in holding the conduct of PMCs to account. Primarily, the Code is currently lacking any means of enforcement. If a company is found to have committed a human rights offence, which under the ICoC is considered inadmissible, this company would have to undergo a self-imposed grievance procedure, and, as a result, establish the amount of a 'reasonable' financial damage, while not being legally bound to do so. While the Code states that "the procedures must allow complaints to be brought by personnel or third parties",[35] the only practical repercussions against violations of the Code are aimed at PMC personnel and could result in their dismissal.[36] The ICoC contains provisions concerning respect for human rights and mandates, stating that "Signatory Companies will adhere to the Code whether or not the Code is included in a contractual agreement with a Client."[37] However, according to contract law, the contracting party is obliged to follow only those provisions that are explicitly listed in the contract. In other words, if the human rights provisions are not stated in the contract, the client cannot expect them to be

---

[32]See Sect. 3 on Working with Private Security Providers.

[33]The International Code of Conduct for Private Security Service Providers, Geneva Academy (ICoC), August 2103, p. 5, https://www.geneva-academy.ch/joomlatools-files/docman-files/Publications/Academy%20Briefings/Icoc_web_final.pdf (last accessed 1 July 2020).

[34]International Code of Conduct Association, see https://www.icoca.ch (last accessed 1 July 2020).

[35]ICoC, para. 66, p. 51.

[36]ICoC, para. 67 (f), p. 52.

[37]ICoC, para. 19.

adhered to.[38] In fact, the concluding paragraph in the liability section reinforces this exact point, stating that the provisions listed in the Code cannot replace or override any contractual requirements or specific company policies or procedures concerning wrongdoing.[39]

The language used in the ICoC is of the utmost importance as it inflates the legal significance of the document. It references IHL and includes extracts from the Rome Statute on the definition of war crimes in the knowledge that PMCs fall outside the scope of IHL unless the company is incorporated into armed forces and the Rome Statute does not extend to corporate entities.[40]

Another way in which the ICoC is ineffective is by awarding its approval to companies who have previously misconducted themselves (e.g. Academi, formerly Xe, formerly Blackwater[41]) or were involved in major controversy (e.g. DynCorp[42]). ICoC certification hence legitimises these publicly contentious companies but also undermines itself as a potential serious regulator of the private military industry. As such, creating this false sense of legitimacy does not only leave a gap in PMC regulation, but it could also prevent other, more robust, enforcement mechanisms from emerging.

2.3 Challenges of Self-Regulation

Self-regulation raises another important issue in the context of shifting power and authority from a state to a corporation. PMCs as a phenomenon have been on the rise since the 1980s as the neoliberal trends in the West promoted deregulation, privatisation and outsourcing. As a result, states have been transferring services to the private sector, including certain defence and security functions, to PMCs. From early twentieth century[43] such functions have primarily been contained within the realm of the public sector and could be considered one of the key components of state monopoly on force. This tradition has also informed the building blocks of international law and, more specifically, the law of armed conflict. The stipulation that a private entity cannot wage war set a premise for all existing regulatory efforts with regards to PMCs.

---

[38]Liu (2015), p. 199.

[39]ICoC, para. 68, p. 53.

[40]Galai (2019), p. 145.

[41]On 16 September 2007, in Nisour Square in Iraq, Blackwater contractors opened fire and killed seventeen Iraqi civilians, while 24 were wounded.

[42]DynCorp contractors were allegedly involved in prostitution and human trafficking in Bosnia. See Isenberg (2011); Robson (2002); Diu (2012); SFOR Contractor Involvement, Human Rights Watch.

[43]Many earlier forms of governance had an explicit element of private security with mercenarism and privateering dominating the military landscape for centuries.

The fact that companies have taken over the functions formerly owned by states, such as logistics, organising security operations, training and, in some instances, detaining, interrogation and killing, signals a shift away from a form of governance in which the state has full control. Furthermore, parallel to the military power which these companies possess, PMCs also make claims to a form of legitimacy through establishing a self-governing body which is being recognised by the industry, but also by states and international organisations.

This consideration is important for PMC regulation for two reasons. First, all existing PMC regulation is based on an outdated perception of distribution of power and is therefore incapable of fully grasping the scope of the phenomenon. Second, if the realm of private security has transformed from illegitimate 'fortune-seekers' into a corporate establishment fulfilling government contracts through legitimate channels, as actors they ought to bear responsibility proportionate to their power.

3 Accountability: Mechanisms and Challenges

In addition to regulatory provisions for the sector, there are channels for invoking responsibility at different levels of the PMC supply chain. Given that all existing PMC regulation is voluntary in nature, it is important to examine the effectiveness of relevant accountability mechanisms.

What sets PMCs apart from other private actors is the exceptional nature of their activity. Although there exists a set of well-established international and domestic legal mechanisms to invoke individual criminal responsibility, exceptions and protections are often extended to PMC contractors, thereby altering the typical course of accountability pathways.

There are norms and treaties within international humanitarian law designed to ensure that a state cannot evade its responsibility by transferring its functions to a private entity. PMCs are service providers who operate on behalf of a client rather than independently. They do not pursue a political agenda or an ideology; instead, they lend support or carry out another party's desired actions on their behalf. This supply-and-demand relationship of security services is administered by two legal frameworks. The first is a contract which defines the terms of the agreement between a state institution and the PMC; and the second are criteria drawn from IHL which determine the responsible party (or the party that has directed and controlled the actor or activity).

The corporate legal status of PMCs complicates this picture further, as company law, contract law, and tort law are introduced into the mix. It is therefore crucial, for completeness of the picture, not only to understand what, if any, PMC-specific regulation exists and how it works, but also to shed light on the entire regulatory and legal landscape concerning private military conduct.

3.1 Individual Responsibility and PMC Immunity

There currently exist different immunity mechanisms which can prevent domestic extraterritorial jurisdictions and the international criminal law framework from treating PMC employees in the same way as all other civilians in the event of a human rights violation. For example, there have been international treaties, such as the Forces Agreement between the UK and Afghanistan,[44] and the Article 98 agreements[45] which shield UK and US military personnel from ICC investigations.

Customarily, if a non-combatant commits a crime abroad, the laws of the jurisdiction in which the crime was committed would be applicable. Historically, in the case of PMCs, a series of strategic exceptions have been made, which underline the extraordinary nature of private contractors. Hiring states can provide contractors with immunity which has the effect of shielding them from being charged and tried in the jurisdiction where the crime has been committed.[46] For example, during the Coalition Provisional Authority (CPA) administration in Iraq, the hiring state granted PMC contractors legal immunity from the local criminal legal system of the state where the services were performed.[47]

Similarly, exceptions were made in the case of CACI International[48] and Titan Corporation (now L-3 Services),[49] whose personnel was charged with human rights abuses during interrogations conducted at the Abu Ghraib prison in Iraq. By establishing that Titan employees "performed their duties under the direct command and exclusive operational control of the military,"[50] the US federal court had extended the government contractor immunity to Titan employees, thereby pre-empting any potential claims of the plaintiffs. While CACI employees were found to have operated under a dual chain of command, supervised by both military and company managers, the court found CACI employees to have been integrated into a military mission, and, therefore, also in possession of government contractor immunity. As a result, the District of Columbia Circuit Court of Appeals ruled in favour of the defendants in September 2009.

The ability to establish and invoke individual responsibility for private contractors is hamstrung, first of all, by several peculiarities of this group. Non-combatants who operate in close proximity to conflict, generally in a foreign country, under a

---

[44]As part of the International Security Assistance Force.

[45]See Rome Statute of the International Criminal Court, Art. 98, https://legal.un.org/icc/statute/99_corr/cstatute.htm (last accessed 1 July 2020); see also The Status of Bilateral Immunity Agreements, http://www.iccnow.org/documents/CICCFS_BIAstatus_current.pdf (last accessed 1 July 2020).

[46]Cameron and Chetail (2013), p. 623.

[47]Galai (2019), p. 24.

[48]Al Shemari et al. v. CACI et al.

[49]Saleh et al. v. Titan.

[50]Business and Human Rights Resource Centre, *Abu Ghraib lawsuits against CACI, Titan (now L-3)*, https://business-humanrights.org/en/abu-ghraib-lawsuits-against-caci-titan-now-l-3-0 (last accessed 1 July 2020).

valid contract, already raise many considerations. Any form of state immunity shielding private military contractors only undermines the legitimacy of using PMCs and prevents PMC personnel from being liable for their actions.

3.2 IHL and State Responsibility When Using PMCs

Given that states hire PMCs to provide security services predominantly abroad and often in close proximity to conflict, it is arguable that states themselves ought to carry a certain responsibility for PMC conduct. The below sections thus examine the ability of IHL to step in and invoke state responsibility either through command and control protocols or by invoking a set of International Law Commission Articles (ILC Articles), which outline the criteria for ascribing responsibility for private conduct to the acts of a state.

3.2.1 ILC Articles

In 2001, the International Law Commission (ILC) adopted a complete text of the Articles on Responsibility of States for Internationally Wrongful Acts that stipulate the conditions for attribution of private conduct to the state.[51] In other words, this framework provides accountability mechanisms under IHL which provide for cases where a state outsources parts of its functions to a private actor. These are based on the fundamental principle that every internationally wrongful act of a state entails the international responsibility of that state.

ILC Article 4 provides the basic rule of attributing the conduct of state organs to the state. This means that the conduct of state organs shall be considered as an act of the state itself.[52] While a state organ is considered to be any entity which carries out the function of a state, the absence of specific examples leaves this open to interpretation. This could, in theory, apply to situations where detention and correctional facilities have been outsourced to a private company.[53] It would be possible to argue that any PMC fulfilling a state security contract overseas is in fact carrying out a state function. However, none of the historic cases invoked this clause to establish state responsibility.[54]

---

[51]More specifically, Articles 4, 5, 8, 9, and 11 of the ILC cover the conditions for attribution of private conduct to the state.

[52]ILC "Report of the International Law Commission: Fifty-Third Session" (UNGA, 2001) A/56/10.

[53]Such as CACI International and Titan Corporation at Abu Graib prison in Iraq.

[54]Amongst the examples are companies such as Sandline and Executive Outcomes whose personnel were enrolled as "Special Constables" on an assignment to Papua New Guinea. See Singer (2003), p. 38.

ILC Article 5 applies to entities that are empowered by the state and are exercising elements of governmental authority. There is little clarity on what this empowerment should look like, aside from the fact that only entities that are empowered by internal law can exercise governmental authority.[55] While a contract between a state and a PMC could be considered such an instrument, without a specific empowerment clause a contract can be interpreted as a horizontal agreement between two equal parties.

Similarly, ILC Article 8 attributes responsibility to the state for conduct carried out under its direction or control. These examples may include auxiliaries and volunteers who do not necessarily form part of the armed forces but who are authorised by the state to carry out a particular mission.[56] However, the lack of specific parameters defining 'direction and control' makes it almost impossible to attribute PMC conduct to a state. In addition to the principles of state responsibility being extremely abstract, there is a lack of precedent in historically significant cases, such as like *Nicaragua*[57] and *Tadic,*[58] that reinforces states' and PMCs' impunity when irregular forces are used.

ILC Articles 9 and 11 prove to be even weaker mechanisms; Article 9 comes into play when the private entity is "in fact exercising elements of the governmental authority in the absence or default of the official authorities and in circumstances such as to call for the exercise of those elements of authority", and Article 11 requires a state to "acknowledge and adopt the conduct in question as its own."

3.2.2 Command and Control

The inefficacy of the ILC Articles can be explained by conflicting protocols governing command and control of PMCs in the armed conflict. Private military companies are usually bound to the state only through contracts between the contracting entities, meaning that "commanders do not have direct control over contractors or their employees; only contractors manage, supervise, and give directions to their employees".[59] Therefore, military commanders cannot give binding instructions to employees of contractors. This in turn means that since states do not exercise effective control, they also are not the ones charging these individuals or

---

[55]ILC "Report of the International Law Commission: Fifty-Third Session", p. 94.

[56]Liu (2015), p. 104.

[57]The Case concerning military and paramilitary activities in and against Nicaragua; International Court of Justice, Pleadings, oral arguments, documents, Vol. IV, https://www.icj-cij.org/files/case-related/70/9627.pdf (last accessed 1 July 2020).

[58]*The Prosecutor v. Duško Tadic*, Case No.: IT-94-1-T, Trial Chamber II, 7 May 1997.

[59]United States Headquarters Department of the Army, *Contractors on the Battlefield, Field Manual*, paras 1–22.

entities with functions that would constitute direct participation in hostilities, and, therefore, cannot be accountable for such action.[60]

Furthermore, this construct renders states unable to exercise their duty of due diligence under IHL as those obligations will most likely not be achievable if the commanders on-site have limited authority over PMC contractors. By the very nature of contract, the client (state) and the provider (PMC) enter into a 'horizontal' agreement, whereby both parties are equal under the contract and neither is subordinate to the other. This is further solidified in the US Field Manual, which stipulates that "the terms and conditions of the contract establish the relationship between the military (US Government) and the contractor; this relationship does not extend through the contractor supervisor to his employees. Only the contractor can directly supervise its employees. The military chain of command exercises management control through the contract"[61]

To ensure a state's authority over the means of private violence, the contract ought to explicitly state that the client, any entity recruiting a PMC, is superior and, therefore, assumes overall accountability for the PMC and the actions of the PMC's employees, who are the subordinates in terms of the contract. If such provisions are not included in the contract, then states and PMCs will continue to exist in a horizontal relationship, circumventing the ILC attribution framework and reinforcing PMCs' claims of power and legitimacy.

In sum, the UN Guiding Principles explicitly set out that the corporate responsibility to respect human rights exists independently of the state's responsibility to fulfil its human rights duties, and, most importantly, does not diminish those duties.[62] This is distinct from the question of legal liability, which remains largely defined by national law provisions in relevant jurisdictions.[63] Similarly, the ICoC does not "replace the control exercised by Competent Authorities, and does not limit or alter applicable international law or relevant national law."[64] This means that, while existing PMC regulation does not interfere with domestic and international law, it also does not complement or enable the ILC Articles. The two frameworks appear to be disconnected, with voluntary regulation not offering any enforcement mechanisms to hold companies to account and ILC attribution clauses failing to

---

[60]Kees (2011), p. 206.

[61]*United States Headquarters Department of the Army, Contractors on the Battlefield, Field Manual,* paras 1–25.

[62]Ruggie, J (2011) Report of the Special Representative of the Secretary-General on the issue of human rights and transnational corporations and other business enterprises, Guiding Principles for the Implementation of the United Nations "Protect, Respect and Remedy" Framework, 2011, Principle 12 The Corporate Responsibility to Respect Human Rights, Commentary, p. 12.

[63]Ruggie, J (2011) Report of the Special Representative of the Secretary-General on the issue of human rights and transnational corporations and other business enterprises, Guiding Principles for the Implementation of the United Nations "Protect, Respect and Remedy" Framework, p. 13.

[64]The International Code of Conduct for Private Security Service Providers, Geneva Academy, August 2103, para. 14, p. 23.

provide practical means and methods of implementation for state responsibility in the context of private company conduct.

3.3 Challenges Associated with the Corporate Status of PMCs

In addition to the aforementioned issues surrounding regulation and the specific nature of PMCs not lending itself easily to existing accountability mechanisms, there are also procedural and territorial obstacles which arise from their corporate status. The fact that PMCs are considered companies rather than mercenaries introduces another dimension as to how their conduct and misconduct is treated in legal terms, which shall now be considered.

3.3.1 Societas Delinquere Non Potest

First, the corporate status of the company poses a number of issues to its recognition and treatment under criminal law. There has been a long tradition of deeming that a company cannot be criminally responsible (*societas delinquere non potest*). In the *Ferguson v. Wilson* case from 1886, it was concluded that "a company cannot act in its own person for it has no person, it can only act through directors, who are the agents of the company."[65]

Viewed by many jurisdictions as "an abstraction,"[66] a corporation may only bear liability through its agent(s), who carry out its acting and directing will as it cannot do so itself.[67] This is derived from the notion that a company cannot physically kill a person nor can it physically stand in a criminal trial. Therefore, if corporations are understood as inanimate tools run by individuals, the responsibility will be placed on *natural* rather than *juridical* persons.[68]

However, a counter-argument, posited by Peter French, suggests that companies are more than just "organised crowds of people;" they have "metaphysical-logical identity that does not reduce to a mere sum of human members."[69] Such an approach, in my view, is applicable to PMCs as these companies undertake a consorted action on behalf of the client, often fulfilling multi-year government contracts.[70]

As businesses, PMCs operate in a high-risk domain. Due to the potentially lethal nature of PMC activity and their intrinsic proximity to hostile environments or

---

[65]*Ferguson v. Wilson*, 1866, Chamber of Appeals 77, p. 89.

[66]Described by Viscount Haldane L. C. in the judgement of the civil case of *Lennard's Carrying Co. Ltd v. Asiatic Petroleum Co. Ltd;* 1915, A. C., 705.

[67]1915, A. C., 713.

[68]Moore (2010), pp. 246–247 and 623.

[69]French (1984), p. 32.

[70]DynCorp has held multiyear contracts through the US government programme LOGCAP (the Logistics Civil Augmentation Program) from 1997 onwards.

vulnerable communities, it would be disproportionate to place all responsibility on the contractors. If a company is involved in systemic human rights violations or aiding and abetting war crimes, is it enough to charge individuals alone who were likely following the mission brief? The infamous Blackwater case is very much in point in this context. Here, the company committed indisputable crimes, yet its founder and former CEO moved on to a new endeavour in the same sector, while the company itself was renamed, sold, and then once again renamed. It continues to offer military and security services, and, rather ironically, is also a signatory company to the International Code of Conduct. Although at the time, the four contractors responsible for the Nisour Square atrocities were given custodial sentences, President Donald Trump pardoned then in December 2020.[71] Meanwhile, the company which facilitated the intelligence, arms, and other means of carrying out the events, continues to operate and prosper, albeit under a different name.[72]

3.3.2 Corporate Veil

As companies, PMCs benefit from the same corporate structure of shareholding and subsidiaries as any other corporation. Most jurisdictions recognise the company law doctrine of "separate corporate personality", whereby a parent company and its subsidiaries are considered to be separate legal entities, despite being linked by their shareholdings.[73] The doctrine was reinforced in *Prest v. Petrodel*,[74] as the UK Supreme Court asserted that the "courts may only 'pierce the corporate veil' in exceptionally limited circumstances."[75] This construct of legal separation and limited liability breeds impunity on the part of PMCs and removes the regulation of legal mechanisms which otherwise apply to corporations.

---

[71] https://www.theguardian.com/world/2020/dec/23/trump-pardons-blackwater-contractors-jailed-for-massacre-of-iraq-civilians.

[72] Galai (2019), p. 156.

[73] Schutter, OF (2006) Extraterritorial Jurisdiction as a Tool for Improving the Human Rights Accountability of Transnational Corporations, https://www.business-humanrights.org/en/pdf-extraterritorial-jurisdiction-as-a-tool-for-improving-the-human-rights-accountability-of-transnational-corporations (last accessed 1 July 2020), p. 36.

[74] *Prest v. Petrodel Resources Ltd & Others* (2013) UKSC 34.

[75] Davies and Worthington (2016), pp. 2–8.

4   Who Can Hold PMCs to Account and How Will the Law Develop?

The disparity in criminal corporate responsibility as a norm in domestic jurisdiction also explains why, on the international level, corporate liability developed in a different way to that of states or individuals. Unlike individuals and states, who can be tried at the ICC (and ad hoc Tribunals) and the International Court of Justice respectively, legal persons cannot be held criminally liable at an international level. Thus, another important question arises when thinking about the effectiveness of existing regulatory and accountability mechanisms: who is best placed to enforce these? In other words, what is the appropriate body of law that has the competence, means and authority to hold PMCs to account?

4.1   Finding the Appropriate Body of Law to Invoke Responsibility

4.1.1   Domestic Criminal Legal Systems

Criminal justice systems, at a domestic level, are often challenged by the extraterritorial nature of PMC activity. When the two components of criminal liability, *actus reus* (criminal act) and *mens rea* (criminal intent), are located in the same location, the question of applicable jurisdiction is straightforward.[76] However, when it comes to the corporate liability of PMCs, in most scenarios the criminal act would occur in a different country to that of the PMC headquarters or incorporation address—meaning that the criminal *intent* is formulated in a different location to that where the criminal *act* is ultimately carried out. In 1988 the Council of Europe urged its member states to support the practice of corporate criminal responsibility due to the limitations of individual criminal liability of corporate officers, which left a regulatory gap meaning that corporate criminal responsibility could fill.[77] Although today a number of member states allow for extraterritorial legislation concerning human rights, most of these laws do not extend to companies.[78]

---

[76]Pinto and Evans (2008), p. 91.

[77]Council of Europe, Recommendation no. R (88) 18 of the Committee of Ministers to Member States Concerning Liability of Enterprises Having Legal Personality for Offences Committed in the Exercise of Their Activities.

[78]Kirshner (2015), p. 19.

4.1.2 International Criminal Law

While domestic legal systems may be inconsistent and piecemeal concerning corporate responsibility and specific PMC provisions, the absence of a strong norm of international criminal liability for corporations creates an additional gap in accountability. Although inclusion of corporations has been discussed in the preparatory works of the Rome Statute of the International Criminal Court (ICC), in its current form it applies exclusively to natural persons. Also, even though PMCs operate internationally, the crimes they may commit will likely not fall under the definition of 'international crimes,' which exclusively concern genocide, crimes against humanity, crime of aggression, and war crimes, and must be systemic, rather than isolated, in nature.[79] Further, the question of corporate criminal responsibility was raised in the early discussions of the International Law Commission (ILC) on the creation of an international criminal legislative body.[80] However, this motion faced criticism and was rejected as novel and controversial.[81] In 2000, a reference to the liability of legal persons was made in Article 10 of the UN Convention against Transnational Organised Crime,[82] although this later removed in subsequent revisions.

Paradoxically, although private armies dominated the security landscape at many periods throughout history, PMCs are often considered a new issue by the different bodies of IL.[83] Even the most prominent and serious cases of corporate crime struggle to get traction with the ILC. In 2018, French cement giant Lafarge Holcim was placed under formal investigation on charges of terrorist financing and the aiding and abetting of crimes against humanity as the company continued their operations in the midst of Syrian civil war.[84] In November 2019, the crimes against humanity charges against the company were dropped. The lack of strong precedent and the rigidity of legal procedure would suggest that the ILC is not an appropriate body of law to invoke corporate responsibility, at least not in the short term.

---

[79] Art. 25 Statute of the International Criminal Court UN Doc./A.CONF.183.9*, 2187 UNTS 1998, p. 90.

[80] 1951/53 Reports of the Committee on International Criminal Jurisdiction of the ILC.

[81] Clapham (2000), pp. 171–172.

[82] United Nations Convention against Transnational Organized Crime, https://www.unodc.org/unodc/en/organized-crime/intro/UNTOC.html (last accessed 1 July 2020).

[83] Liu (2015), p. 289.

[84] Business and Human Rights Resource Centre, *Lafarge lawsuit (re complicity in crimes against humanity in Syria)*, https://www.business-humanrights.org/en/lafarge-lawsuit-re-complicity-in-crimes-against-humanity-in-syria (last accessed 1 July 2020).

4.1.3 Transnational Model: Alien Tort Statute

There are a number of cases that were brought specifically against PMCs under the Alien Tort Statute (ATS). These include DynCorp pesticide spraying in Ecuador,[85] KBR human trafficking in Iraq,[86] and Blackwater's extrajudicial killings in Iraq.[87] Despite its jurisdiction over trying corporate cases, the scope of the ATS has been restricted over the years[88] and, historically, judgments have swayed in favour of corporations.

However, recently there has been an important development regarding the ATS, resulting from Abu Ghraib lawsuits against CACI and Titan.[89] On 28 June 2017, a US court ruled[90] that claims for: torture; cruel, inhuman, and degrading treatment; and war crimes can be brought under the Alien Tort Statute against private actors.[91] Nearly 15 years after the abuses at the Abu Ghraib "hard site" prison in Iraq came to light, a Virginia federal judge ruled that the PMC can be held liable for its employees conspiring to commit and aiding and abetting these crimes, rejecting the company's decade-long claim it should be shielded from liability. Building a precedent, this ruling importantly concludes that a company may be held liable for crimes committed internationally.

Furthermore, the outcome of this case could determine the pathway for establishing international criminal responsibility for corporations—and PMCs in particular. Additionally, academic and legal commentary on these cases aids in creating a new historical narrative; an important first step towards formulating corporate responsibility and addressing impunity.[92]

---

[85] Arias v. DynCorp.

[86] Adhikari et al v. Daoud & Partners et al.

[87] Abtan, et al. v. Prince, et al. and Albazzaz, et al. v. Prince, et al.

[88] Following Sosa v. Alvarez-Machain (2004) it only reviews claims based on fundamental principles of customary IL and Kiobel v. Royal Dutch Petroleum has curtailed ATS applicability to corporations.

[89] Abu Graib lawsuits against CACI, Titan (now L-3).

[90] US District Court for the Eastern District of Virginia, Alexandria Division: Suhail Najim Abdullah Al Shimari, et al., v. CACI Premier Tech, Inc., 28 Jun 2017.

[91] Centre for Constitutional Rights: Private Corporation May be Sued for Role in Abu Ghraib Torture, Judge Rule, Judge Rules, 21 Feb 2018, https://ccrjustice.org/home/press-center/press-releases/private-corporation-may-be-sued-role-abu-ghraib-torture-judge-rules (last accessed 1 July 2020).

[92] Kaleck and Saage-Maasz: The Expressive Value of Corporate Prosecutions, 30 April 2015, http://jamesgstewart.com/author/wolfgang-kaleck/ (last accessed 1 July 2020).

4.2 How Is the Law Likely to Evolve?

Whether the actor in question is a PMC, a multinational cement business, or any other corporate actor that operates in close proximity to hostilities and uses lethal force, existing regulation and accountability mechanisms are unlikely to tackle their misconduct. At an international level, reliable human rights protection relies on voluntary, not legally-binding, norms and misconduct is unlikely to invoke corporate responsibility beyond the specific terms of the contract between the parties. Any prospective international codification of corporate criminal liability is rendered problematic by the inconsistencies across national legislation and numerous challenges posed by procedural, territorial and historic specificities of corporate actors. Existing legally-binding mechanisms, such as domestic criminal jurisdictions and the Alien Tort Statute, are insufficient (in their current form) to address the transnational extent of corporate criminal liability. Meanwhile, those states which actively use PMCs as part of their foreign policy and consider industry self-regulation sufficient enough, are also likely to obstruct the emergence of a legally-binding international treaty.

Conceptually, if we perceive regulation as "the intentional activity of attempting to control, order or influence the behaviour of others,"[93] it has a clear, normative purpose. This definition sets regulation apart from both the government enforcing domestic state laws, as well as market and social forces, by invoking an element of intentionality. While regulation can have multiple goals, most generally it aims to provide some sort of organisation. It can also aim to manage risk,[94] provide access to justice,[95] or strive to achieve justice.[96]

Given the special nature of PMC activity, the function these companies perform, the vulnerable environments they operate in, and the lethal force they possess, I believe an effective PMC regulatory framework would be one which that both respect for the guidelines and an efficient vetting procedure, but also provides enforcement mechanisms to invoke responsibility for non-compliance. This is because regulation without accountability would only create a semblance of legitimacy; leaving victims exposed, companies immune to misconduct, and human rights abuses unpunished.

Generally, the current regulatory landscape for corporations (and PMCs in particular) lacks reliable mechanisms which would enable ascribing responsibility directly to the company, proportionate to the degree of misconduct. More specifically, there are three distinct areas that, if advanced, could significantly reduce corporate impunity and contribute to the effectiveness of PMC regulation.

---

[93]Black (2002), p. 25.

[94]Black (2002), p. 10.

[95]Parker (1999).

[96]See Ayres and Braithwaite (1992), Chapter 3.

4.2.1 Consolidate Existing PMC Regulation

Firstly, the above assessment suggests there is a strong impetus for the development of systems for monitoring and operating which are not purely industry-driven and are capable of imposing proportionate sanctions for misconduct. Indeed, the ICoC took positive steps when, in 2013, the International Code of Conduct Association was established.[97] A Swiss non-profit association, the ICoCA currently lists 92 companies, 30 civil society organisations, and nine states,[98] with all members publicly identified on the ICoC Association website.[99] While the aim of this external governance and oversight mechanism was to improve accountability in the sector and provide a forum for third party complaints, currently the Association does not have the necessary resources to realise these stated aims.[100]

More importantly, a non-legally-binding industry body exercising social liability is not sufficient to address gross human rights violations, war crimes, nor crimes against humanity. While such actors may take concrete steps towards raising the standards of PMC services and spread human rights awareness, they simply do not have adequate tools and competence to tackle serious violations adequately or bring justice to victims.[101]

A potential remedy may consist of a hybrid approach, whereby an international industry oversight body (such as the ICoCA, for example) is supported by national regulators in the event of misconduct. For example, the UK Security Industry Authority was set up under the Private Security Industry Act 2001, which is "responsible for regulating the private security industry by, *inter alia*, operating a licensing regime for individual security operatives and a voluntary approvals scheme for security businesses."[102] Additionally, the Security in Complex Environments Group (SCEG) has been designated to develop and implement international standards for the private security sector and in 2014 the UK Accreditation Service accredited two certification bodies for PSC1 and three, for ISO 28007.[103]

Further, it could defer to domestic criminal jurisdictions if a PMC-committed transgression constitutes a human rights violation and cannot be resolved with a fine or another sanction. For example, national legislation in France, Canada, Norway,

---

[97]See https://www.icoca.ch/en/history (last accessed 1 July 2020).

[98]These include: Australia, Canada, Norway, Sweden, Switzerland, the UK, and the US.

[99]See https://www.icoca.ch/en/membership (last accessed 1 July 2020).

[100]A/HRC/32/39, p. 11.

[101]See Galai (2019), Chapter 6.

[102]A/HRC/30/47, Art. 23, p. 7.

[103]White, N (2015) The UK and the Regulation of PMSCs, United Nations Human Rights Office of the High Commissioner, https://www.ohchr.org/Documents/Issues/Mercenaries/WG/Event2015/NigelWhite.pdf (last accessed 1 July 2020).

and the US encompasses corporate criminal liability for businesses that operate abroad.[104]

4.2.2 Reinforce National Jurisdiction to Tackle Corporate Impunity

Secondly, changes should be implemented at a national level to enable national jurisdictions to step in when voluntary forms of regulation are unable or unwilling to invoke corporate responsibility. Such developments may include changes to corporate law and the criminal law as it relates to human rights violations, in line with the UN Guiding Principles.

Notionally, it is important to shift the focus of liability from individual guilt to identifying gross negligence in the way a corporation organises and conducts its activities. One such example of domestic legislation is the UK Corporate Manslaughter and Corporate Homicide Act (2007).[105] Under the Act, a company may be criminally liable if its conduct "causes a person's death, and amounts to a gross breach of a relevant duty of care owed by the organisation to the deceased."[106] However, to make such legislation watertight, it is important that it can deliver justice and/or adequate compensation to victims who fall outside of the contractual framework between the government and the company. Unless explicitly stipulated otherwise in the contract, only parties to a contract can seek damages as a result of a breach under contract law. It is, therefore, debatable whether or not a PMC would owe a relevant duty of care to third party individuals outside of company employees.

4.2.3 Adopt TCL/ILC Procedure

Thirdly, another way for domestic jurisdictions to aid in closing the corporate impunity gap and support the recognition of criminal corporate responsibility internationally is to support the ILC procedure for the most serious international crimes. For example, the UK can impose criminal liability on corporations acting both inside and outside of British territory by enacting the International Criminal Court Act of 2001.[107] Furthermore, the premise of corporate liability for international crimes exists in many jurisdictions.[108]

---

[104]Fafo Report (2005), Business and international crimes: assessing the liability of business entities for grave violations of international law, http://www.fafo.no/index.php?option=com_zoo& task=item&item_id=3742&Itemid=927&lang=en (last accessed 1 July 2020), p. 12.

[105]In 2015 New sentencing guidelines for corporate manslaughter were introduced.

[106]Corporate Manslaughter and Corporate Homicide Act 2007, Chapter 19, Art. 1 (1) (a), (b), p. 1.

[107]International Criminal Court Act, 2001, c. 17, § 4 (UK), http://www.legislation.gov.uk/ukpga/ 2001/17/2005-06-07 (last accessed 1 July 2020).

[108]See Fafo Report (2005), Business and international crimes: assessing the liability of business entities for grave violations of international law, http://www.fafo.no/index.php?option=com_zoo& task=item&item_id=3742&Itemid=927&lang=en (last accessed 1 July 2020).

Choosing a national legal system as the criminal liability forum for corporations could overcome the challenges which exist in the ICC and ad hoc tribunals.[109] If PMCs were charged and tried at an international level, consensus would have to be reached on a number of provisions, including definitions of types of crimes and enforcement measures, procedures, and fora. By giving national courts a relative freedom of interpretation over what constitutes an international crime, a 'domestic' solution could overcome the resistance of international law practitioners to the recognition of corporate legal personality without compromising the ability to cover the transnational realm of PMC operation. By adopting ILC language in domestic legal systems, corporate responsibility could bypass the limitation of complicity posed by corporate criminal procedure, and potentially expose corporations to a greater level of criminal responsibility in the event of misconduct.[110]

Another avenue that could be adopted is a hybrid model of looking to transnational criminal law (TCL) for content and to domestic courts for implementation. In its current form, TCL could be better suited to corporations than international law as it does not require adjustment to the same extent or recognition of international legal personality. Unlike international crimes that require state or individual responsibility-attribution, transnational crimes are those committed by private or non-state actors.[111] Such classification is thus more tailored to PMC conduct as it removes the necessity of establishing a link to state bodies in order for the crimes of PMCs to be recognised as international or as part of state conduct carried out in a different state.[112] Integrating transnational criminal law could be seen as loosely replicating the principle of the Alien Tort Statute, though only through criminal responsibility rather than purely corporate social responsibility.

Although consistently extending criminal responsibility to corporations would achieve a more proportionate accountability mechanism to the growing authority and reach of PMCs as corporations, this change will not develop overnight. In addition to the aforementioned challenges of ascribing criminal responsibility to corporations, this development will have to overcome a number of other barriers. Pushbacks may arise from very practical considerations of capacity and costs generated by any additional legal procedures, types and volume of new cases, equal opportunity considerations for victims, and various other factors. Moreover, it is very unlikely for national jurisdictions to develop at the same pace, especially without any overarching international directive to stimulate such change. This could, in turn, exacerbate the impunity gap for countries that have weaker legal systems and already struggle to regulate other human rights violations. At the same time, obtaining political buy-in will pose significant challenges for PMC-welcoming states

---

[109]ICTY and ICTR have limited jurisdictional reach, while the principle of the complementarity of the ICC tasks domestic courts with prosecuting international crimes. See Simpson (2007), p. 50.

[110]Galai (2019), p. 185, also see Stewart (2014).

[111]Bassiouni (1974), p. 421.

[112]Galai (2019), p. 187.

who subscribe to voluntary norms and do not necessarily want the private military space to become regulated to a greater extent.

5 Conclusion

Like many companies PMCs operate transnationally, but, unlike most, the nature of their activity takes them to areas of conflict, high-risk environments and vulnerable communities. As states and international organisations become more reliant on the private sector for the provision of security, regulations and norms ought to evolve and recognise the need for these companies to respect human rights and introduce certain standards into their conduct.

Yet, we should not think of PMCs as inherently problematic. They exist and operate legitimately under agreed contractual arrangements with governments, international institutions and other corporations. The problem arises from the lack of clarity in the regulation of PMC conduct and the inability of existing legal mechanisms to effectively ascribe responsibility in the event of PMC misconduct.

The industry has produced extensive regulation at the international level, urging companies to respect human rights and adhere to various voluntary guidelines. At the national level, some counties are incorporating ISO standards in PMC certification and enabling industry bodies to develop and implement international standards for the private security sector.[113]

Regulation is only effective if it is able to encourage the behaviour it sets out and to ensure adherence to rules it stipulates. Alternatively, a successful regulation could exist in tandem with other laws and policies which complement it and ensure any gaps and loopholes are covered. However, PMCs and their clients operate in a seemingly regulated environment where neither party is likely to be held accountable for any serious transgressions. Such perception of legality and regulation is boosted by corporate social responsibility rhetoric and availability of ILC articles which, in theory alone, provide a framework for attributing private misconduct to the state on behalf of which these acts were carried out.

The corporate status of PMCs introduces a number of challenges and proves to be incompatible with existing regulatory frameworks. First, the voluntary guidelines on PMC conduct and responsibility to uphold human rights are undermined by the contract between the client and the company. As a legally binding document, the contract alone stipulates the terms of PMC behaviour in the private sphere of their activity. Since corporations fall outside of the remit of IHL and attribution clauses are too vague to be practically applied, existing international legal instruments also do not seem fit to ensure accountability and deliver justice.

This article has considered a number of potential developments which could lead to a more robust regulatory framework for an industry that has been actively

---

[113]Such as Security in Complex Environments Group (SCEG) in the UK.

operating for the past four decades and, as it would appear, is here to stay. None of the proposed solutions, however, lie distinctly within the realm of public international law. This can be explained in part by the incompatibility of the discipline and the non-state nature of the issue at hand; but also, by the strong presence of domestic bodies of law that could provide a more tailored and timely solution.

How the law develops in the realm of PMC regulation will be determined first, by the outcome of ongoing and future cases involving corporate liability in serious crimes committed abroad, and second, by scholarly efforts in the field, successfully connecting the dots and putting forward compelling evidence for advancing corporate accountability mechanisms for private military companies one jurisdiction at a time.

References

Arduino A (2015) Security privatisation with Chinese characteristics. The role of Chinese private security corporations in protecting chinese outbound investments and citizens, policy report, s. rajaratnam school of international studies

Armstrong S (2008) War PLC: the rise of the new corporate mercenary. Faber & Faber Limited, London

Ayres I, Braithwaite J (1992) Responsive regulation: transcending the deregulation debate. OUP, Oxford

Bassiouni CM (1974) An appraisal of the growth and developing trends of international criminal law. Revue Internationale de Droit Penal 45:405–433

Black J (2002) Critical reflections on regulation. Aust J Leg Philos 27:1–36

Cameron L, Chetail V (2013) Privatizing war: private military and security companies under public international law. CUP, Cambridge

Cropley E, Lewis D (2015) Nigeria drafts in foreign mercenaries to take on Boko Haram, Reuters. Available at: http://uk.reuters.com/article/uk-nigeria-violence-mercenaries-idUKKBN0M80VT20150312

Clapham A (2000) The questions of jurisdiction under international criminal law over legal persons: lessons from the Rome conference on an International Criminal Court. In: Kamminga MT, Zia-Zarifi S (eds) Liability of multinational corporations under international law. Kluwer, The Hague

Davies PL, Worthington S (2016) Gower principles of modern company law: tenth edition. Sweet and Maxwell, London

Diu NL (2012) What the UN doesn't want you to know, The Telegraph. Available at: http://www.telegraph.co.uk/culture/film/9041974/What-the-UN-Doesnt-Want-You-to-Know.html

French P (1984) Collective and corporate responsibility. Columbia University Press, New York

Galai K (2019) Regulating private military companies: conflicts of law, history and governance. Routledge, Oxford

Isenberg D (2011) It's Déjà Vu for DynCorp all over again, Huffpost business, Available at: http://www.huffingtonpost.com/david-isenberg/its-dj-vu-for-dyncorpall_b_792394.html

Kaldor M (2002) New and old wars: organized violence in a global era. Polity Press, Cambridge

Kees A (2011) Regulation of private military companies. Goettingen J Int Law 3(1):199–216

Kinsey MA (2004) Transparency in government procurement: an international consensus? Public Contract Law J 34(1):155–173

Kirshner JA (2015) A call for the EU to assume jurisdiction over extraterritorial corporate human rights abuses. Northwest J Int Hum Rights 13(1):1–26

Liu HY (2015) Law's impunity: responsibility and the modern private military company. Hart Publishing, Oxford

McFate S (2014) The modern mercenary: private armies and what they mean for the world order. OUP, Oxford

Moore M (2010) Causation and responsibility: an essay in law, morals, and metaphysics. OUP, Oxford

Parker C (1999) Just lawyers: regulation and access to justice. OUP, Oxford

Peet R (2009) Unholy trinity: IMF, World Bank and WTO, 2nd edn. Zed Books, London

Pinto A, Evans M (2008) Corporate criminal liability, 2nd edn. Thompson, Sweet & Maxwell, London

Robson T (2002) Bosnia: The United Nations, human trafficking and prostitution. Available at: https://www.wsws.org/en/articles/2002/08/bosn-a21.html

Scahill J (2007) Blackwater: the rise of the world's most powerful mercenary army. Serpent's Tail, London

Simpson G (2007) Law, war and crime: war crimes trials and the reinvention of international law. Polity Press, Cambridge

Singer P (2003) Corporate warriors: the rise of the privatized military industry. Cornell University Press, New York

Stewart JG (2014) The turn to corporate criminal liability for international crimes: transcending the Alien Tort Statute. N Y Univ J Int Law Polit 47(1):121–206

White N (2012) Regulatory initiatives at the international level. In: Bakker C, Sossai M (eds) Multilevel regulation of military and security contractors: the interplay between international, European, and domestic norms. Hart Publishing, Oxford

Young Pelton R (2006) Licensed to kill: privatising the war on terror. Three Rivers Press, New York

Katerina Galai is a multidisciplinary scholar with research expertise in law, international security and historical sociology. She holds an LLM and a PhD from the University of Sussex. She is a UK expert on the use and regulation of private military companies and she recently published a monograph with Routledge on the topic.

As of August 2020, Katerina is associate Director for COVID-19 Genomics UK (COG-UK) Consortium, heading up communications, governance, strategic planning, legal and financial functions, based at the University of Cambridge.

Dual-Use Export Control: Security and Human Rights Challenges to Multilateralism

Machiko Kanetake

Contents

Abstract International standard-setting in the field of export control has been shaped by the presence of non-binding multilateral regimes. Central to international regulatory harmonisation is the Wassenaar Arrangement concerning export controls for conventional arms as well as for dual-use goods and technologies. Institutionalised regulatory coordination through multilateral regimes is essential, in part because the multilateral trade regime accommodates apologetic security exceptions that flexibly allow each member's own export control practices. Multilateralism in the context of dual-use export control has been subject to various political and normative challenges, however. Numerous attempts to circumvent the Wassenaar Arrangement have been based not only on national security narratives. The multilateral regime has also been fundamentally challenged by human rights

The research for this paper is supported by a grant (2020–2021) from Gerda Henkel Stiftung.

M. Kanetake (✉)
Utrecht University, Utrecht, The Netherlands
e-mail: m.kanetake@uu.nl

© Springer Nature Switzerland AG 2021
M. Bungenberg et al. (eds.), *European Yearbook of International Economic Law 2020*,
European Yearbook of International Economic Law (2022) 11: 265–290,
https://doi.org/10.1007/8165_2021_67, Published online: 11 March 2021

narratives. This paper sheds light on these dual challenges through the analysis of export controls over digital and so-called emerging technologies.

1 Introduction

Export control is one of the fields of law in which international standard-setting has been led by non-binding multilateral regimes. Central to international regulatory harmonisation is the Wassenaar Arrangement concerning export controls for conventional arms as well as for dual-use goods and technologies. The regime was established in 1996 in the Dutch town of Wassenaar and has 42 participating states as of October 2020. As its core product, the Wassenaar Arrangement furnishes the lengthy so-called "control lists",[1] which serve as the catalogue of military and dual-use items. According to the Wassenaar Arrangement, each participating state controls the export of all listed items therein for the sake of preventing the unauthorised cross-border transfer of such items.[2] The Wassenaar Arrangement is by no means a treaty regime. Instead, it is an international forum in which the diplomats of some 42 industrial states gather, exchange information on a confidential basis,[3] and update the list of sensitive items subject to export control. While it is ultimately up to each participating state to decide at the national level whether to allow the transfer of controlled items in specific instances,[4] the Wassenaar Arrangement has served, overall, as a well-recognised multilateral venue for setting standards for export control practices, exchanging information, and reducing regulatory gaps across participating states.

The presence of multilateral export control regimes is relevant, not merely for the sake of ensuring effective export control practices and procedures. The locus of the multilateral export control regimes should also be understood as contributing, simultaneously, to the normative stability of the multilateral trade system under the World Trade Organization (WTO) agreements. Export control over military and dual-use items is one of the fields of law that necessarily counterbalances the idea of removing trade barriers across WTO members. Despite this inherent tension, the WTO regime in itself does not furnish guidance on export control practices, as will be pointed out in Sect. 3 of this paper. The lack of foreseeability in the imposition of

---

[1]The Wassenaar Arrangement on Export Controls for Conventional Arms and Dual-Use Goods and Technologies, Control Lists, https://www.wassenaar.org/control-lists/ (last accessed 15 November 2020).

[2]The Wassenaar Arrangement on Export Controls for Conventional Arms and Dual-Use Goods and Technologies, Initial Elements, 11 July 1996, Section III.1.

[3]The Wassenaar Arrangement on Export Controls for Conventional Arms and Dual-Use Goods and Technologies, Initial Elements, 11 July 1996, Section IX (Confidentiality).

[4]The Wassenaar Arrangement on Export Controls for Conventional Arms and Dual-Use Goods and Technologies, Initial Elements, 11 July 1996, Section II.3.

trade restrictions has in part been remedied, instead, by the functioning of multilateral export control regimes.

Against this background, this paper analyses some of the challenges to multilateralism in the context of export control, and, more precisely, export control over dual-use items. While multilateralism is a multi-faceted concept, its significance should be more than the mere congregation of multiple actors. As Odermatt articulated, it pertains to "commitment to certain values, including the involvement of international institutions, the respect for certain global norms and international law".[5] Complexity arises when actors resort to a unilateral approach by claiming at the same time that it would, in substance, contribute to the realisation of the values or norms that a multilateral regime is expected to honour. Multilateralism in the field of dual-use export control is not immune to such an intricate relationship between, on the one hand, loyalty to multilateral regimes, and, on the other hand, adherence to values and norms.

The paper will begin with a brief explanation of the concept of dual-use export control (Sect. 2). While export control entails restrictions contrary to some of the principles of the WTO agreements, the WTO regime's apologetic "security exceptions" provide a flexible basis for each member to justify its own export control practices (Sect. 3). While the exceptions constitute "possibly a very big loophole"[6] in the multilateral trade regime, the Wassenaar Arrangement and other multilateral export control regimes have provided foreseeability in the possibly unpredictable field of trade control (Sect. 4). A type of multilateralism represented by the Wassenaar Arrangement is subject to various challenges, however. The initiatives to circumvent the Wassenaar Arrangement emanate, not only from the invocation of broad "national security" narratives which further stretch the security exceptions. The challenges have also been brought based on "human rights" narratives, from which the Wassenaar Arrangement has ostensibly distanced itself due to its military focus. This paper sheds light on these dual challenges based on security and human rights. It does so, in particular, by analysing legislative changes on export controls over digital and emerging technologies (Sect. 5).

2   Dual-Use Export Control: Concept and Frameworks

2.1   Concept of Dual-Use Items

Before discussing export controls through the lens of multilateralism, it is necessary to briefly explain the concept of "dual-use" export control, which is the focus of this

---

[5]Odermatt (2020), p. 50.

[6]Second Session of the Preparatory Committee of the UN Conference on Trade and Employment, Thirty-Third Meeting of Commission, UN Doc. E/PC/T/A/PV/33, 24 July 1947, p. 19 (Dr. Speekenbrink of the Netherlands).

paper. The concept of a dual-use item has been primarily understood through the duality of civilian and military purposes for which the item can serve. The basic concept is most clearly articulated by the EU's dual-use regulation adopted in 2009. According to Article 2(1) of Council Regulation (EC) No 428/2009, dual-use items are defined as items "which can be used for both civil and military purposes".[7]

Whether or not we are aware of it, a variety of materials that sustain our daily lives can be used for military purposes. To provide one specific example, sodium fluoride is one of such dual-use chemicals which have been prevalently used. The chemical material can serve for the production of toothpaste and, at the same time, as a precursor for the nerve agent sarin, a chemical weapon. This is why the export of sodium fluoride became controversial in connection to the use of sarin against civilians in the Ghouta area of Damascus on 21 August 2013.[8] After the incident, it was revealed that the UK government had granted licences in January 2012 to allow the export of sodium fluoride and another chemical to Syria.[9] In the media, the UK government met criticism for authorising the export of potentially harmful chemical materials to Syria[10]—despite the lack of credible evidence of a link between the particular use of the sarin in Syria and the exported materials. The controversy already revealed the inherently precarious nature of dual-use export control, both in terms of assessing risks in advance based upon available information, and tracing post-export misuse of the exported items by trading partners.

2.2   Legal Frameworks for Dual-Use Export Control

As illustrated by the definition of "dual-use" items, the field of law is an extension of the trade control of military items and it has been led by concerns over the military use of materials, goods, and technologies. At the international level, the international transfer of dual-use items is therefore intertwined with a set of international treaties concerning the non-proliferation of weapons of mass destruction (i.e. biological, chemical, and nuclear weapons): namely, the 1972 Biological and Toxin Weapons

---

[7]Council Regulation (EC) No 428/2009 of 5 May 2009 setting up a Community regime for the control of exports, transfer, brokering and transit of dual-use items, OJ 2009 L134/1, Article 2(1). On the concept of dual-use items, see Kanetake (2018).

[8]United Nations Mission to Investigate Allegations of the Use of Chemical Weapons in the Syrian Arab Republic: Final Report, UN Doc. A/68/663–S/2013/735, 13 December 2013, paras. 109–110.

[9]Letter to the Chair of the Committees from the Rt Hon Vince Cable MP, Secretary of State for Business, Innovation and Skills, 6 September 2012, in: UK House of Commons, Committees on Arms Export Controls, First Joint Report of the Business, Innovation and Skills, Defence, Foreign Affairs and International Development Committees of Session 2013–14, Vol III, 17 June 2013, p. 90.

[10]See, e.g., Milmo C, McSmith A, Kumar N, Revealed: UK Government Let British Company Export Nerve Gas Chemicals to Syria, Independent, 2 September 2013, http://www.independent.co.uk/news/uk/politics/revealed-uk-government-let-british-company-export-nerve-gas-chemicals-to-syria-8793642.html (last accessed 15 November 2020).

Convention (BTWC),[11] the 1993 Chemical Weapons Convention (CWC),[12] and the 1968 Treaty on the Non-Proliferation of Nuclear Weapons (NPT).[13]

These treaties have similar provisions concerning export control. Under Article III of the 1972 BTWC, for instance, states parties are prohibited from transferring "any of the agents, toxins, weapons, equipment or means of delivery" prohibited by the Convention. Cross-border transfer is forbidden to "any recipient whatsoever",[14] including not only to other states parties, but also to non-party states, international organisations, private entities, or individuals.[15] Likewise, the transfer of chemical materials is regulated by the 1993 CWC, whose implementation is monitored by the Organization for the Prohibition of Chemical Weapons (OPCW). Article VI(2) of the CWC serves as a general legal basis for chemical export control,[16] according to which states parties are required to ensure that toxic chemicals and their precursors are transferred only "for purposes not prohibited under this Convention". The CWC comes with the specific list of controlled toxic chemicals and their precursors, which are divided into three categories ("Schedules") depending on their applicability to chemical weapons and their commercial usage. The CWC prohibits the transfer of chemicals listed under Schedules 1 and 2 to non-parties[17] and limits the purposes for which these chemicals are transferred to another state party.[18] With regard to the chemicals listed under Schedule 3, the CWC requires end user certificates for exports to non-parties.[19] Finally, when it comes to nuclear export controls, Article III.2 of the 1968 NPT obliges states not to transfer non-nuclear-weapons states "equipment or material especially designed or prepared for the processing, use or production of special fissionable material" unless such material is subject to the safeguards of the International Atomic Energy Agency (IAEA).[20]

While the treaties on biological, chemical, and nuclear weapons respectively envisage export control on sensitive materials, these conventions, apart from the

---

[11]Convention on the Prohibition of the Development, Production and Stockpiling of Bacteriological (Biological) and Toxin Weapons and on Their Destruction, 10 April 1972, 1015 UNTS 163 (entered into force 26 March 1975).

[12]Convention on the Prohibition of the Development, Production, Stockpiling and Use of Chemical Weapons and on Their Destruction, 13 January 1993, 1974 UNTS 45 (entered into force 29 April 1997).

[13]Treaty on the Non-proliferation of Nuclear Weapons, 1 July 1968 (entered into force 5 March 1970), 729 UNTS 161.

[14]BTWC, Article III.

[15]Goldblat (1997), p. 255.

[16]Krutzsch et al. (2014), p. 190.

[17]CWC, Verification Annex, Part VI(A), (B) (Schedule 1 chemicals) and Part VII(C) (Schedule 2 chemicals).

[18]CWC, Verification Annex, Part VI(A), (B) (Schedule 1 chemicals) and Part VII(C) (Schedule 2 chemicals).

[19]CWC, Verification Annex, Part VIII(C) (Schedule 3 chemicals).

[20]NPT, Article III.2.

CWC, lack a catalogue of specific materials, products, or technologies subject to export control. The treaty regimes have thus been supplemented in greater detail by a series of non-treaty international regimes which furnish and update the "lists" of controlled items.[21] One of such regimes is the Australia Group, which was established in 1985 in view of harmonising export control measures on chemical and biological weapons and related dual-use items.[22] As for nuclear export controls, the Nuclear Suppliers Group (NSG), formed in 1975, maintains guidelines containing the list of nuclear-related dual-use items subject to export control by participating governments.[23] Since 1971, the Zangger Committee also provides the understandings and lists for nuclear export controls.[24] On top of these domain-specific regimes, the Wassenaar Arrangement was established in 1996 as a post-Cold War alternative to replace the Western bloc's export control regime, the Coordinating Committee for Multilateral Export Control (COCOM).[25] As noted in the introductory section of this paper, the Wassenaar Arrangement furnishes a lengthy list of items subject to export control, encompassing both conventional arms and dual-use goods and technologies.

On the basis of these treaties and international (non-treaty) regimes, each state formulates its own export control laws at the domestic level. Within the EU, dual-use export control forms the EU's Common Commercial Policy (CCP) and has been regulated foremost by Council regulations. Council Regulation (EC) No 428/2009 of 5 May 2009 has been the relevant framework since August 2009, which has direct effect in the EU.[26] As of November 2020, Council Regulation No 428/2009 remains the applicable legal framework in the EU. However, Council Regulation No 428/2009 has been reviewed since 2013, as will be discussed further in Sect. 5.2 of this paper. After several years of deliberation, on 9 November 2020, the Council and European Parliament finally reached a provisional political agreement on a revised dual-use regulation,[27] which should pave the way for the adoption of a new framework to replace Regulation No 428/2009.

What matters for the purpose of this paper is the fact that the EU's export control has been intertwined with international regimes. According to Council Regulation (EC) No 1334/2000 of 22 June 2000, a predecessor of Regulation No 428/2009, the list of dual-use items subject to export control "implements internationally agreed dual-use controls", including the Wassenaar Arrangement, the Missile Technology

---

[21] For an overview, see, e.g., Anthony and Zanders (1998); Achilleas (2017), pp. 11–13.

[22] Ali (2001), p. 50.

[23] Nuclear Supplies Group, Guidelines, https://www.nuclearsuppliersgroup.org/en/guidelines (last accessed 15 November 2020).

[24] Joyner (2009), pp. 27–30.

[25] Dursht (1997), p. 1098.

[26] Council Regulation (EC) No 428/2009 of 5 May 2009 setting up a Community regime for the control of exports, transfer, brokering and transit of dual-use items, OJ 2009 L134/1.

[27] Council of the EU, New rules on trade of dual-use items agreed, Press release, 9 November 2020, https://www.consilium.europa.eu/en/press/press-releases/2020/11/09/new-rules-on-trade-of-dual-use-items-agreed/ (last accessed 15 November 2020).

Control Regime (MTCR), the Nuclear Suppliers' Group, the Australia Group, and the CWC.[28] The same idea that the EU's export control "implements" internationally agreed controls is reiterated in Regulation No 428/2009.[29] While EU Member States can add their own national control lists, the EU's regional framework is based upon the assumption that the EU's legal framework should build upon multilateral export control regimes.

3   Unilateralism Within the Multilateral Trade Regime

3.1   The Security Exception

Export control, when applied, by definition imposes restrictions on international trade in goods and services. In this sense, as noted in the introduction of this paper, export control is one of the fields of law that counterbalance a core tenet of international trade agreements that reduce or eliminate trade barriers. Export controls can readily undermine the principle of most-favoured-nation treatment[30] and a general duty to minimise the incidence and complexity of import and export formalities[31] under the General Agreement on Tariffs and Trade (GATT) and the General Agreement on Trade in Services (GATS). It is reasonable to be wary of the fact that export controls can frustrate the basic tenet of the WTO regime, which, despite various setbacks,[32] has served as a key vehicle for facilitating international trade through a set of common rules.

The crux is, however, that the WTO agreements themselves have explicitly embraced the exceptions in such a manner that each member can flexibly justify its own export controls without the need for international coordination. This is most salient in the case of "security exceptions" under Article XXI of the GATT. While the GATT also accommodates a set of "general exceptions" under Article XX which can serve to justify trade-restrictive measures, security exceptions "afford greater discretion to governments than general exceptions".[33] This is also implied by the fact that the WTO panel appears to have treated GATT's security exception as a

---

[28]Council Regulation (EC) No 1334/2000 of 22 June 2000 setting up a Community regime for the control of exports of dual-use items and technology, OJ 2000 L159/1, Annex I.

[29]Council Regulation (EC) No 428/2009 of 5 May 2009 setting up a Community regime for the control of exports, transfer, brokering and transit of dual-use items, OJ 2009 L134/1, Annex I.

[30]Article I GATT; Article II GATS.

[31]Article VIII(1)(c) GATT; Achilleas (2017), p. 10.

[32]For instance, on the US government's non-cooperative stance towards WTO dispute settlement since 2016, see, e.g., Petersmann (2019).

[33]Henckels (2020), p. 561.

permission as opposed to a defence with which to preclude wrongfulness on the part of a member.[34]

Article XXI of the GATT envisages three groups of instances for invoking security exceptions.[35] A member may invoke such exceptions for denying information disclosure (Article XXI(a)) or implementing the obligations under the UN Charter (Article XXI(c)). The most expansive and controversial is however the reliance upon Article XXI(b), under which a member may take "*any* action which *it* considers necessary for the protection of *its* essential security interests" (emphasis added).

The flexible and expansive nature of the essential security exception is already evident from the wording of Article XXI(b). According to the provision quoted above, "nothing" in the agreement shall be construed to prevent any contracting party from taking "*any* action" which "*it*" (i.e. the party) considers necessary for protecting "*its*" essential security interests—as long as the action meets one of the broad conditions laid down in Article XXI(b) (emphasis added). It appears undeniable that the terms of Article XXI(b) are destined to allow ample space for each member's own self-serving interpretation without the need for regulatory harmonisation.

3.2 Deferential Review

Due to the aforementioned apologetic wording of Article XXI(b) of the GATT, it may be fair to observe that the WTO trade regime accommodated an element of unilateralism *within* its own multilateral legal framework from its outset. The characterisation of the security exception as an expression of unilateralism (as embraced by the multilateral framework) is connected to the long-standing debate[36] as to whether the security exception may be "unreviewable"[37] by adjudicators.

Since the inception of the GATT, the US government is one of several states that have continued to maintain the idea that the security exception is self-judging and non-justiciable beyond the scrutiny of the WTO's dispute settlement. At the stage of negotiating the provisions of the 1947 GATT provisions, concerns were understandably levelled regarding the impact of security exceptions on the effectiveness of the multilateral agreement. During the negotiation of July 1947, the Dutch delegation expressed its difficulty in defining the security exception and labelled it as "possibly

---

[34]Henckels (2020), p. 570; WTO Panel Report, *Russia – Measures Concerning Traffic in Transit*, WT/DS512/R, 5 April 2019, para. 7.108.

[35]See Swaak-Goldman (1996).

[36]Among voluminous literature, see, e.g., Hahn (1990), Swaak-Goldman (1996) and Alford (2011).

[37]Alford (2011), p. 698.

a very big loophole in the whole Charter".[38] The US' delegation argued in defence, that the relevant provisions were drafted in such a manner that they would limit the circumstances under which members could invoke the security exceptions.[39] At the same time, the US delegation made it clear that the treaty preserved a member's ability to "determine for itself . . . what its security interests are".[40] On various occasions, the US government indeed claimed that the security exceptions are self-judging *and* unreviewable. For instance, in June 2018, in the context of *US – Steel and Aluminium Products (EU)*, the US observed that issues of national security were "not susceptible to review or capable of resolution by WTO dispute settlement".[41] In the same vein, the United Arab Emirates argued that there was "clear language" in the WTO agreements that excludes national security matters from the WTO's adjudication.[42] The United Arab Emirates' position was endorsed by Bahrain, Saudi Arabia, and Egypt.[43]

The occasion to test the possibility for external scrutiny has arrived as part of the WTO panel's ruling in April 2019 on the *Russia – Measures Concerning Traffic in Transit* case.[44] This was the "first instance"[45] in which a WTO panel provided its interpretation of security exceptions under Article XXI of the GATT 1994. The case was brought by Ukraine to challenge the transit restrictions imposed by Russia between 2014 and 2018. The Ukrainian claim was responded to by the Russian reliance upon the security exception under Article XXI(b)(iii), which necessitated the panel to interpret its scope. Article XXI(b)(iii) allows a member to take any action for its essential security interests if the action is "(iii) taken in time of war or other emergency in international relations". Russia—accompanied by the US—has claimed that Article XXI(b)(iii) was "self-judging" and therefore not justiciable before the WTO panel.[46]

---

[38]Second Session of the Preparatory Committee of the UN Conference on Trade and Employment, Thirty-Third Meeting of Commission, UN Doc. E/PC/T/A/PV/33, 24 July 1947, p. 19 (Dr. Speekenbrink of the Netherlands).

[39]Second Session of the Preparatory Committee of the UN Conference on Trade and Employment, Thirty-Third Meeting of Commission, UN Doc. E/PC/T/A/PV/33, 24 July 1947, pp. 20–21 (Mr. J.-M. Leddy of the US).

[40]Second Session of the Preparatory Committee of the UN Conference on Trade and Employment, Thirty-Third Meeting of Commission, UN Doc. E/PC/T/A/PV/33, 24 July 1947, p. 20 (Mr. J.-M. Leddy of the US).

[41]*United States – Certain Measures on Steel and Aluminium Products*, Communication from the United States (dated 11 June 2018), WT/DS548/13, 6 July 2018.

[42]WTO, Dispute Settlement Body, *Minutes of Meeting Held in the Centre William Rappard on 23 October 2017*, WT/DSB/M/403, 20 February 2018, para. 4.4.

[43]WTO, Dispute Settlement Body, *Minutes of Meeting Held in the Centre William Rappard on 23 October 2017*, WT/DSB/M/403, 20 February 2018, paras. 4.5–4.7.

[44]Panel Report, *Russia – Measures Concerning Traffic in Transit*, WT/DS512/R, 5 April 2019. For analysis, see, e.g., Voon (2020).

[45]Hartmann (2019), p. 899.

[46]Panel Report, *Russia – Measures Concerning Traffic in Transit*, WT/DS512/R, 5 April 2019, paras. 7.57 (Russia), 7.51–7.52 (US).

In response to the claim of non-justiciability, the WTO panel, in its April 2019 report, managed to preserve its own role in scrutinising the WTO-compatibility of restrictive measures taken on the basis of a member's essential security. The WTO panel has done so by claiming the need for objectivity and external scrutiny concerning the interpretation of the requirements under the three subparagraphs of Article XXI(b) of the GATT.[47] As noted above, Russia invoked one of such conditions under Article XXI(b)(iii), according to which a member may take restrictive measures "in time of war or other emergency in international relations". The panel gave its interpretation of the requirement and observed that political or economic differences among WTO members would not in themselves constitute an "emergency in international relations" under subparagraph (iii).[48] According to the panel, the emergencies may not arise unless such political or economic differences give rise to "particular types of interests" for the member,[49] namely, "defence and military interests" or the "maintenance of law and public order interests".[50] The panel therefore made it clear that the wider political or economic conflicts cannot by themselves serve to justify the reliance upon an "emergency in international relations" under subparagraph (iii) of Article XXI(b).

At the same time, in its April 2019 report, the need for objectivity mentioned above was counterbalanced by the WTO panel's approach to the interpretation of the following two aspects of Article XXI: namely, to determine what constitutes a member's essential security interests, and to decide how such interests are connected to the restrictive measures. In short, the panel accepted the fact that it is left to each WTO member to define "its essential security interests".[51] What is still applicable is the general obligation of good faith, which means that members cannot use the exceptions in order to circumvent the obligation.[52] The obligation of good faith should also govern the determination of the connection between a member's security interests and the restrictive measures. According to the WTO panel, the measures must "meet a minimum requirement of plausibility" in connection to the claimed essential security interests.[53]

---

[47]Panel Report, *Russia – Measures Concerning Traffic in Transit*, WT/DS512/R, 5 April 2019, paras. 7.62–7.82, 7.100–7.101.

[48]Panel Report, *Russia – Measures Concerning Traffic in Transit*, WT/DS512/R, 5 April 2019, para. 7.75.

[49]Panel Report, *Russia – Measures Concerning Traffic in Transit*, WT/DS512/R, 5 April 2019, para. 7.76.

[50]Panel Report, *Russia – Measures Concerning Traffic in Transit*, WT/DS512/R, 5 April 2019, para. 7.75.

[51]Panel Report, *Russia – Measures Concerning Traffic in Transit*, WT/DS512/R, 5 April 2019, para. 7.131.

[52]Panel Report, *Russia – Measures Concerning Traffic in Transit*, WT/DS512/R, 5 April 2019, paras. 7.132–7.133.

[53]Panel Report, *Russia – Measures Concerning Traffic in Transit*, WT/DS512/R, 5 April 2019, para. 7.138.

Overall, in the *Russia – Traffic in Transit* case, the WTO panel, while retaining a possibility for review, ultimately permitted each member to exercise broad discretion. It is true that the interpretation of the emergency in international relations was subject to substantive scrutiny.[54] The panel's plausibility test (applied for the assessment of the connection between the restrictive measures and security interests) could be understood as one form of "reasonableness" review which is less deferential than a mere self-judging clause.[55] Nevertheless, as Lapa pointed out, the plausibility test was construed as a "very relaxed requirement".[56] In addition, the interpretation of essential security interests is left to each member (and is thus self-judging), which also reduces the practical relevance of the good faith principle. While the *Russia – Traffic in Transit* case is one of the few available instances in which the panel interpreted security exceptions, future jurisprudence cannot be separated from the fact that the security exception is a "highly sensitive"[57] dimension of the trade regime. While external scrutiny may prevent the possibility of members effectively circumventing WTO rules by invoking the security exception, the stringent scrutiny may invite political backlash from powerful states.[58]

4   Multilateralism Within Export Controls

Given the broad discretion states enjoy in the interpretation of the security exception, the Dutch delegation's aforementioned concern in 1947 appears convincing, in that the exception can potentially create a large loophole.[59] However, in practice, despite the broad permission given to states, according to Alford's analysis published in 2011, the exception "has worked reasonably well" inasmuch as states acted under the assumption that it should be used in good faith.[60] Needless to say, there must be a wide range of economic, political, and legal considerations that may have sustained prudence in the conduct of states. It is not the purpose of this paper to provide any comprehensive account regarding states' self-restraint in imposing trade restrictions.

As far as regularly applied export controls are concerned, however, one of the factors we should not overlook is the presence of multilateral export control regimes. Participating states are expected to work through the export control regimes that serve as a focal point for regulatory harmonisation and information exchange. The

---

[54]Lapa (2020), p. 25.

[55]See Lapa (2020), p. 25; Pauwelyn (2020), pp. 90, 106.

[56]Lapa (2020), p. 25.

[57]Voon (2019), p. 45.

[58]Chen (2017).

[59]Second Session of the Preparatory Committee of the UN Conference on Trade and Employment, Thirty-Third Meeting of Commission, UN Doc. E/PC/T/A/PV/33, 24 July 1947, p. 19 (Dr. Speekenbrink of the Netherlands).

[60]Alford (2011), p. 758.

presence of such regimes helps shape *national* security interests through the lens of *regional and international* security concerns, and arguably sustains the incentive to limit unilateral paths in imposing export controls. In fact, the US government has long advocated the international export control regimes and requested that other countries adopt the international lists at the domestic level.[61]

Among various export control regimes, an international focal point for dual-use export controls has been the Wassenaar Arrangement established in 1996, which aims at contributing to "regional and international security and stability".[62] It builds upon COCOM, an informal multilateral export control mechanism embedded in the climate of the Cold War. COCOM drew up the list of specific items subject to export controls as a method of facilitating regulatory harmonisation.[63] COCOM's control list was justified based on the military capabilities of certain technologies and other items.[64] The importance of COCOM was explicitly recognised in the 1979 Export Administration Act in the US. The 1979 Act required the US President to negotiate with COCOM participating governments in a view of maintaining the common list of controlled items.[65] The 1979 Act's reference to COCOM was in recognition of the need for greater multilateral cooperation,[66] reflecting, in turn, "the obsolescence of unilateral controls" in view of the diversification of suppliers in globalised economy.[67]

While COCOM was a Western bloc's cooperative regime embedded in the Cold War, its informal and "list-based" methods provided the model for the post-Cold War international export control regimes aimed at harmonising domestic export controls.[68] The control lists are indeed central to multilateral regulatory harmonisation. According to the "Initial Elements" of the Wassenaar Arrangement, which articulate its basic objectives and procedures, participating states "will control all items" set forth in the Arrangement's own control lists of dual-use items and munitions.[69] While licensing decisions are ultimately in the hands of each partici-pating state, Wassenaar members exchange information on their licensing deci-sions.[70] As the US Department of State's senior advisor observed in 2000, the

---

[61]Whang (2019), p. 579.

[62]The Wassenaar Arrangement on Export Controls for Conventional Arms and Dual-Use Goods and Technologies, Initial Elements, 11 July 1996, Section I.1.

[63]Whang (2019), pp. 585–586.

[64]Whang (2019), pp. 585–587.

[65]Export Administration Act of 1979, Public Law 96-72, 50 U.S.C. app. 2404, Sec. 5(i).

[66]Donovan (1981), p. 101.

[67]Donovan (1981), p. 101.

[68]Whang (2019), p. 584.

[69]The Wassenaar Arrangement on Export Controls for Conventional Arms and Dual-Use Goods and Technologies, Initial Elements, 11 July 1996, Section III.1.

[70]United States Senate, 106th Congress, Second Session, Hearing before the Committee on Governmental Affairs, Wassenaar Arrangement and the Future of Multilateral Export Controls, S. Hrg. 106-613 (12 April 2000), p. 6 (Hon. John D. Holum, Senior Advisor for Arms Control and International Security, US Department of State).

Wassenaar Arrangement provides a "venue in which governments can consider collectively the implications of various transfers of their international and regional security interests".[71] Through the formulation of the control lists and the exchange of information regarding license denials, the Wassenaar Arrangement and other multilateral export control regimes provide certain stability and foreseeability in decentralised export control practices.

5   Return of Unilateralism with a Universalistic Twist?

As discussed in previous sections, the security exception under the WTO's multilateral trade regime allows broad discretion to members to instigate trade-restrictive measures. Such an exception clearly serves as one of the primary legal bases for justifying export control policies.[72] Despite the possibility that the trade regime allows for a unilateral path, multilateral regulatory coordination has been achieved through the presence of export controls regimes, at least with regard to the types of materials and technologies subject to trade restrictions.

Needless to say, many challenges still persist for multilateral export control regimes. One of such challenges has arisen in the context of the export control of digital and other emerging technologies. Their speed of development casts doubt on the relevance of multilateral export control regimes. In fact, in the US and EU, attempts have been made to impose autonomous export controls on technological fronts—albeit, interestingly, through different narratives. In the US, since 2018, national security approaches have dominated its export control policies on emerging technologies (Sect. 5.1). By contrast, the EU has employed rather universalistic human rights languages in discussing whether the EU ought to impose an autonomous export control on digital surveillance technologies (Sect. 5.2).

5.1   US' Export Controls Act: Departure from Military-Based Rationale

5.1.1   Export Controls Act of 2018

During the US administration under President Trump, the country's export controls framework made an important turn by, in essence, altering a justification for applying export controls. In August 2018, President Trump signed a piece of

---

[71]United States Senate, 106th Congress, Second Session, Hearing before the Committee on Governmental Affairs, Wassenaar Arrangement and the Future of Multilateral Export Controls, S. Hrg. 106-613 (12 April 2000), p. 6 (Hon. John D. Holum, Senior Advisor for Arms Control and International Security, US Department of State).

[72]Achilleas (2017), pp. 10–11.

legislation, called the John S. McCain National Defense Authorization Act for Fiscal Year 2019,[73] which contains the Export Controls Reform Act of 2018 (ECRA).[74] For the sake of this paper, one of the relevant parts of the ECRA is the Export Controls Act of 2018.[75] The ECRA repealed the Export Administration Act of 1979[76] which had already expired in 1994 yet continued, in effect, under the International Emergency Economic Powers Act and relevant executive orders.[77]

In a nutshell, from the wording of the legislation, the ECRA could potentially frustrate the delicate interdependence between the WTO's trade regime and multilateral export control arrangements.[78] As Whang argued, the ECRA could have a "long-lasting influence" on international export regimes and the rationale of export controls.[79] This is because the ECRA explicitly integrated domestic economic policy considerations into national security-based export controls.[80] The crux is that this conceptual expansion simultaneously facilitates the possibilities for the US to apply unilateral export controls without seeking consensus at multilateral export control fora.[81]

Under the ECRA of 2018, export controls are characterised as a mechanism for the US to safeguard its "national security" and further its "foreign policy".[82] The concept of "national security" is inherently an elusive one, but it is important to highlight the fact that the concept has been linked to the *military* capabilities of other states. Under the ECRA, export controls can be applied if they are necessary to restrict the export of items that "would make a significant contribution" to other

---

[73]John S. McCain National Defense Authorization Act for Fiscal Year 2019, Public Law 115-232 (13 August 2018).

[74]Export Control Reform Act, Public Law 115-232, 50 U.S.C. 4801.

[75]Export Controls Act of 2018, Public Law 115-232, 50 U.S.C. 4801, 132 Stat. 2209, Section 1751 et seq.

[76]Export Controls Act of 2018, Section 1766(a); Export Administration Act of 1979, Public Law 96-72, 50 U.S.C. app. 2401.

[77]International Emergency Economic Powers Act, 50 U.S.C. 1701; US Presidential Executive Order 12929, 19 August 1994; An Act to Provide for Increased Penalties for Violations of the Export Administration Act of 1979, and for Other Purposes, Public Law 106-508, 13 November 2000 (for the reauthorisation of the 1979 Act until 20 August 2001); US Presidential Executive Order 13222, 17 August 2001.

[78]See, however, Sect. 5.2.1 below regarding the US' continuous engagement with the Wassenaar Arrangement.

[79]Whang (2019), p. 579.

[80]Whang (2019), pp. 579–599.

[81]Whang (2019), pp. 579–599.

[82]Export Controls Act of 2018, Section 1752(1). In general, the US export controls have rested broadly on three rationales: to prevent domestic shortage in commodities; to safeguard the US' national security; and to further its foreign policy: Donovan (1981), pp. 79–82; Fergusson IF, The Export Administration Act: evolution, provisions, and debate, Congressional Research Service (CRS) Report for Congress, 15 July 2009, p. 2. Among these rationales, national security and foreign policy controls have primarily guided the US' export controls.

countries' *"military* potential" which would prove "detrimental to the national security" of the US.[83]

The ECRA's military-based national security builds on the longstanding legislative development of US export controls, which aimed at limiting the presidential authority to invoke national security for the imposition of export controls. Under the Export Control Act of 1949,[84] one of the overall objectives of export controls was to "exercise the necessary vigilance over exports from the standpoint of their significance to the national security".[85] This broad formulation of national security was circumscribed by the 1962 amendment of the Export Control Act of 1949. Under the 1962 amendment, the invocation of such controls is based upon the president's determination that relevant export "makes a significant contribution to the *military or economic* potential" of other countries, "which would prove detrimental to the national security and welfare" of the US.[86] The Export Administration Act of 1969 marked one of the turning points in that the Act shifted its focus to liberalising US trade and restricting unwarranted restrictions on it.[87] The 1969 Act begins with its commitment to encourage international trade and justified national security controls on the basis that exports would "make a significant contribution to the *military* potential" of other countries in such a manner that it would be detrimental to US national security.[88] In other words, under the 1969 Act, national security controls were linked to *military* potentials.

The Export Administration Act of 1979 further deleted the "economic" part. According to the 1979 Act, national security-based export controls concern whether the exports of items would make a significant contribution to the *"military* potential" of other countries.[89] The 1979 Act also came with the provision that highlighted the importance of international cooperation. The 1979 Act made it explicit that the US must apply controls "to the maximum extent possible in cooperation with all nations" and facilitate "uniform export control policy" among states with which the US has defence treaty commitments.[90] The 1979 Act also placed a greater emphasis on controlling technologies or know-how, and not only on the controls on end-products.[91] One of national security controls under the 1979 Act pertained to

---

[83]Export Controls Act of 2018, Section 1752(1)(A) (emphasis added).

[84]Export Control Act of 1949, 63 Stat. 7.

[85]Export Control Act of 1949, 63 Stat. 7, Section 2(c).

[86]An Act to Provide for Continuation of Authority for Regulation of Exports, and for Other Purposes, Public Law 87-515, 1 July 1962, Section 4 (amending Sec. 3(a) of the Export Control Act of 1949) (emphasis added).

[87]Dvorin (1980), p. 183; Overly (1985), p. 429.

[88]Export Administration Act of 1969, Public Law 91-184, Section 3(1) (emphasis added).

[89]Export Administration Act of 1979, Public Law 96-72, 50 U.S.C. app. 2402, Section 3(2)(A) (emphasis added).

[90]Export Administration Act of 1979, Public Law 96-72, 50 U.S.C. app. 2402, Section 3(3).

[91]Donovan (1981), p. 97.

"critical technologies".[92] Yet such controls over technologies were still construed as "*military* critical technologies"[93] on the basis of a significant advantage that the technologies would accord to a military system of other countries.[94]

Overall, the series of legislative developments demonstrates that the US export controls have been situated as the "economic arm of the *military*-related national security strategy".[95] In principle, as noted above, the 2018 ECRA's definition of national security remains to be based on the 1979 Export Administration Act. Under the 2018 ECRA, export controls should be used where it is necessary to restrict the export of items "which would make a significant contribution to the *military* potential" of other countries.[96] At the same time, the 2018 ECRA marked a clear departure from its predecessor in terms of its apparently stretched construction of "national security". Under the 2018 ECRA, "national security" is understood as requiring the maintenance of the US' global-level "leadership in the science, technology, engineering, and manufacturing sectors" including, *inter alia*, "foundational technology that is essential to innovation".[97] By stretching the interpretation of national security, and by making it less connected to military risks, the ECRA appears to have provided a further justification for the US' unilateral paths and departure from international multilateral export control regimes.[98]

5.1.2 National Security-Based Controls on Emerging Technologies

The greater integration of domestic economic policy considerations into the US' national security controls is most visible with regard to the ECRA's regulation over so-called "emerging" technologies. Under Section 1758 of the ECRA, the US President is required to take steps to identify "emerging and foundational technologies" that are "essential to the national security" of the US.[99] The specification of such technologies is left to the Bureau of Industry and Security (BIS) of the US Department of Commerce, which, on 19 November 2018, published the list of the 14 broad categories of emerging technology.[100] The categories of technology range broadly from biotechnology to microprocessor technology, robotics, artificial intelligence (AI) and machine learning technology, and advanced surveillance technologies. Some of these technologies can be deeply prevalent in society, which

---

[92]Export Administration Act of 1979, Public Law 96-72, 50 U.S.C. app. 2404, Section 5(a)(3).

[93]Export Administration Act of 1979, Public Law 96-72, 50 U.S.C. app. 2404, Section 5(d).

[94]Export Administration Act of 1979, Public Law 96-72, 50 U.S.C. app. 2404, Section 5(d)(2).

[95]Whang (2019), p. 581 (emphasis added).

[96]Export Controls Act of 2018, 50 U.S.C. 4811, Section 1752(1)(A) (emphasis added).

[97]Export Controls Act of 2018, 50 U.S.C. 4811, Section 1752(3).

[98]Whang (2019).

[99]Export Controls Act of 2018, 50 U.S.C. 4817, Section 1758(a)(1).

[100]US Department of Commerce, Bureau of Industry and Security, 'Review of Controls for Certain Emerging Technologies' (Advance Notice of Proposed Rulemaking, ANPRM), 83 FR 58201, 19 November 2018.

complicates the discussions on precisely which technologies ought to be subject to export controls.[101] By publishing the list of these categories, the BIS sought public comment regarding the identification of much more specific emerging technologies subject to national security controls.

As of October 2020, the US introduced control over certain "emerging technologies", although the measures were not strictly under Section 1758 of the ECRA. For example, on 6 January 2020, the BIS issued the first interim rule to impose a license requirement for the export of a specific item: software specially designed to automate the analysis of geospatial imagery.[102] On 17 June 2020, the BIS designated the three additional items after the Australia Group, one of the multilateral export control regimes, had decided to add them to its control lists.[103] On 5 October 2020, the BIS further issued the final rule for the implementation of export controls on emerging technologies in order to add six emerging technologies that were deemed essential to the US' national security.[104] Included in the listed technologies were, for instance, digital forensics tools, which circumvent authentication or authorisation mechanisms and extract raw data from a computer or communication device, and surveillance software specifically designed for use by law enforcement to analyse the content of communications.[105]

In short, the ECRA allowed a wide range of technologies to be added to the catalogue of the US' export control under the broad and flexible category of "emerging technologies" that are essential to US national security. While the ECRA in principle paves the way for the US' unilateral paths, it is noteworthy that the US has, in practice, worked through existing multilateral export control regimes. The items added in June 2020 were precisely to "implement" the prior decisions made through the Australia Group. Likewise, the October 2020 addition was based on the changes agreed on at the meeting of the Wassenaar Arrangement in December 2019. The concept of "national security" under the ECRA is, in practice, presented as if it is diffused into the wider "regional and international security and stability" that the Wassenaar Arrangement is supposed to safeguard.[106] Therefore, these

---

[101]Dekker and Okano-Heijmans (2020), pp. 54–55.

[102]US Department of Commerce, Bureau of Industry and Security, Addition of Software Specially Designed To Automate the Analysis of Geospatial Imagery to the Export Control Classification Number 0Y521 Series, 85 FR 459, 6 January 2020.

[103]US Department of Commerce, Bureau of Industry and Security, Implementation of the February 2020 Australia Group Intersessional Decisions: Addition of Certain Rigid-Walled, Single-Use Cultivation Chambers and Precursor Chemicals to the Commerce Control List, 85 FR 36483, 17 June 2020.

[104]US Department of Commerce, Bureau of Industry and Security, Implementation of Certain New Controls on Emerging Technologies Agreed at Wassenaar Arrangement 2019 Plenary, 85 FR 62583, 5 October 2020.

[105]US Department of Commerce, Bureau of Industry and Security, Implementation of Certain New Controls on Emerging Technologies Agreed at Wassenaar Arrangement 2019 Plenary, 85 FR 62583, 5 October 2020.

[106]US Department of Commerce, Bureau of Industry and Security, Implementation of Certain New Controls on Emerging Technologies Agreed at Wassenaar Arrangement 2019 Plenary, 85 FR 62583, 5 October 2020.

developments seem to suggest the US government's continued willingness to act *through* multilateral regimes—instead of opting for unilateral control without multilateral consensus.

5.2 Revising the EU's Dual-Use Regulation: Human Rights Perspectives

5.2.1 The Proposed Autonomous Export Control on Cyber Surveillance

As noted above, the US has stretched its national security controls under the ECRA and created a possibility for unilateral export controls—although the US has, in practice, continued to work through multilateral export control regimes. On the other side of the Atlantic, the EU has also engaged in debates about whether and to what extent it should impose autonomous export control. It is noteworthy, however, that the debates within the EU have been generated, not necessarily from the security perspectives, but from human rights narratives with which to regulate technological exports.[107]

While there is nothing novel in the EU employing human rights as a normative ground for restricting the export of sensitive items,[108] a fresh political momentum was built in response to the use of surveillance technologies during and in the aftermath of the Arab Spring (2010–2012). Political controversies pertained to a series of allegations that EU-based companies sold surveillance technologies and provided technical assistance to the governments which experienced the popular uprising and monitored dissidents during and in the aftermath of the Arab Spring movement.[109] The controversies invited responses from the European Parliament which, in the resolution of September 2015, observed that the EU's standards, particularly the EU Charter of Fundamental Rights (CFR), "should prevail" in the assessment of dual-use technologies used in ways that may restrict human rights.[110] The parliamentary calls have been translated into a concrete proposal in the pursuit of the so-called "modernization"[111] of the EU's export control. In September 2016, the European Commission submitted a proposal to recast and replace Council

---

[107]See further Kanetake (2019, 2020).

[108]Kanetake (2019), pp. 5–6.

[109]Wagner (2012); Privacy International, Open Season: Building Syria's Surveillance State, December 2016.

[110]European Parliament, Human rights and technology: the impact of intrusion and surveillance systems on human rights in third countries (2014/2232(INI)), P8_TA(2015)0288, 8 September 2015, para. 39.

[111]European Commission, Communication from the Commission to the Council and the European Parliament: the review of export control policy: ensuring security and competitiveness in a changing world, COM (2014) 244 final, 24 April 2014, p. 2.

Regulation No 428/2009,[112] aiming, at least in part, to provide an "effective response to threats for human rights resulting from their uncontrolled export".[113] Particular emphasis was placed on respect for the right to privacy, freedom of expression and freedom of association.[114]

The September 2016 proposal gives rise to a wide range of discussion points.[115] What is most relevant for the sake of this paper is the proposal to introduce the EU's "autonomous list"[116] to be added to a catalogue of items subject to export control. Under Annex I of Council Regulation No 428/2009, dual-use items have been categorised into ten groups, from "Category 0" to "Category 9". The Commission's September 2016 proposal launched a new group of controlled items as "Category 10" in order to regulate certain "cyber surveillance technology".[117] Under this new autonomous category, the proposal listed items which had, at the time of the proposal, not yet been regulated by the Wassenaar Arrangement. The creation of the new category is intertwined with the Commission's suggestion to "revise the definition of dual-use items".[118] The September 2016 proposal therefore went beyond the military-focused understanding of dual-use items and proposed to include, within the stretched concept of dual-use items, "cyber-surveillance technology which can be used for the commission of serious violations of human rights or international humanitarian law".[119]

The greater integration of human rights considerations into the EU's dual-use regulation is part of the EU's overall constitutional mandate to be pursued in its external relations. Given that the EU's dual-use regulation forms an integral part of the EU's CCP, the EU's law and policies on dual-use export control ought to be carried out "in the context of the principles and objectives of the Union's external action", as envisaged by Article 207 TFEU.[120] One of these principles, referred to in Article 21(1) TEU, pertains to "the universality and indivisibility of human rights and fundamental freedoms".

---

[112]European Commission, Proposal for a Regulation of the European Parliament and of the Council Setting up a Union regime for the control of exports, transfer, brokering, technical assistance and transit of dual-use items (recast), COM(2016) 616 final, 28 September 2016, Article 2(1).

[113]European Commission Proposal of 28 September 2016, p. 6.

[114]European Commission Proposal of 28 September 2016, p. 6.

[115]See further Kanetake (2019, 2020).

[116]European Commission Proposal of 28 September 2016, p. 9.

[117]European Commission, Annexes to the Proposal for a Regulation of the European Parliament and of the Council Setting up a Union regime for the control of exports, transfer, brokering, technical assistance and transit of dual-use items (recast), COM(2016) 616 final, Annexes 1–6, 28 September 2016, pp. 243–244, Annex I, Category 10.

[118]European Commission, Proposal for a Regulation of the European Parliament and of the Council Setting up a Union regime for the control of exports, transfer, brokering, technical assistance and transit of dual-use items (recast), COM(2016) 616 final, 28 September 2016, p. 12, recital para 6.

[119]European Commission Proposal of 28 September 2016, Article 2(1)(b).

[120]On these general external objectives, see, e.g., Cremona (2017), pp. 10–15.

Not surprisingly, the Commission's September 2016 proposal was welcomed by several leading human rights non-governmental organisations (NGOs) in that the proposal gave an important recognition to the human rights responsibilities of states and businesses.[121] Yet, the EU's autonomous approach invited a great deal of resistance from some of the industry associations as well as many EU Member States. One of the frequently raised concerns was the need for multilateral coordination through existing export control regimes. For example, DIGITALEUROPE, which represents the digital technology industry in Europe, made it clear in February 2017 that a "unilateral viewpoint must be avoided" and that the newly proposed "category 10 should not [be] added without being aligned with Wassenaar".[122] Likewise, in its December 2019 statement, the European Semiconductor Industry Association (ESIA), reiterated that it favours an "internationally aligned approach" which "contributes to strengthening the global level playing field". On this basis, ESIA recommended the "elimination of the unilateral EU listing".[123]

Contestations also came from EU Member States' authorities. In their leaked working paper dated 29 January 2018, eleven EU Member States expressed their clear dissent from the Commission's proposal.[124] The working paper, drafted primarily by Germany and France, stressed the fact that the EU "does not work in isolation" in dual-use controls. The EU should instead continue working through international export control regimes as a global "level-playing field".[125] Likewise, in another working paper dated 15 May 2018, nine EU Member States opposed the introduction of the EU's "unilateral measures"[126] and favoured working through

---

[121]Shared Statement on the Update of the EU Dual-Use Regulation, May 2017, https://www.accessnow.org/cms/assets/uploads/2017/05/NGO_Sharedstatement_dualuse_May2017.pdf (last accessed 15 November 2020), p. 2.

[122]DIGITALEUROPE, European Commission Proposed Recast of the European Export Control Regime: Making the Rules Fit for the Digital World, 24 February 2017, https://www.digitaleurope.org/resources/european-commission-proposed-recast-of-the-european-export-control-regime/ (last accessed 15 November 2020), pp. 5, 8.

[123]European Semiconductor Industry Association, Comments in Support of the Trilogue Negotiations on the Recast of the Dual-Use Regulation, 10 December 2019, https://www.eusemiconductors.eu/sites/default/files/191210_ESIAComments_Dual-UseRegRecast.pdf (last visited 15 November 2020), p. 4.

[124]Working paper: EU export control—recast of Regulation 428/2009, WK 1019/2018 INIT, 29 January 2018, https://www.euractiv.com/wp-content/uploads/sites/2/2018/02/11_member_states_dual-use.pdf (last accessed 15 November 2020). The document was prepared on behalf of the Croatian, Czech, French, German, Italian, Polish, Portuguese, Romanian, Slovak, Slovenian, and Spanish delegations.

[125]Working paper: EU export control—recast of Regulation 428/2009, WK 1019/2018 INIT, 29 January 2018, https://www.euractiv.com/wp-content/uploads/sites/2/2018/02/11_member_states_dual-use.pdf (last accessed 15 November 2020), p. 1.

[126]Working paper: paper for discussion—for adoption of an improved EU export control regulation 428/2009 and for cyber surveillance controls promoting human rights and international humanitarian law globally, WK 5755/2018 INIT, 15 May 2018, https://www.euractiv.com/wp-content/uploads/sites/2/2018/06/nine-countries-paper-on-dual-use.pdf (last accessed 15 November 2020),

international export control regimes.[127] The Council's negotiating mandate released in June 2019 further reiterated the importance of regulatory harmonisation with international regimes.[128]

5.2.2 November 2020 Draft Text

After several years of deliberation, on 9 November 2020, a provisional political agreement was reached between the Council and European Parliament.[129] An informal version of the text of the regulation which would repeal Council Regulation No 428/ 2009 was published on 18 November 2020.[130] While the text gives rise to a number of issues to be discussed, it is important to note, for the sake of the present analysis, that the text clearly places a greater emphasis upon multilateralism in this field.

In line with the political deliberation surrounding the recast process, the informal draft text of November 2020 explicitly acknowledged human rights risks associated with the export of cyber surveillance items. One of the most relevant provisions is Article 4a of the draft text regarding a so-called "catch-all" control. It is a residual mechanism to allow authorities to exert export control over items which are not specifically listed in Annex I of the EU's dual-use regulation. According to Article 4a(2), for instance, if an exporter is "aware" according to its "due diligence findings" that non-listed cyber-surveillance items are "intended, in their entirety or in part" for use in connection with internal repression or the commission of serious violations of international human rights and international humanitarian law, the exporter "shall notify the competent authority" which "shall decide whether or not to make the export concerned subject to authorisation". The draft regulation therefore anticipates that exporters themselves will conduct human rights due diligence.[131]

---

pp. 1–2. The Working Paper was prepared on behalf of the Czech Republic, Cyprus, Estonia, Finland, Ireland, Italy, Poland, Sweden, and the United Kingdom.

[127] Working paper: paper for discussion—for adoption of an improved EU export control regulation 428/2009 and for cyber surveillance controls promoting human rights and international humanitarian law globally, WK 5755/2018 INIT, 15 May 2018, https://www.euractiv.com/wp-content/uploads/sites/2/2018/06/nine-countries-paper-on-dual-use.pdf (last accessed 15 November 2020), pp. 2–4.

[128] Council of the European Union, Proposal for a Regulation of the European Parliament and of the Council Setting up a Union regime for the control of exports, brokering, technical assistance, transit and transfer of dual-use items (recast): mandate for negotiations with the European Parliament, 5 June 2019.

[129] Council of the EU, New rules on trade of dual-use items agreed, Press release, 9 November 2020, https://www.consilium.europa.eu/en/press/press-releases/2020/11/09/new-rules-on-trade-of-dual-use-items-agreed/ (last accessed 15 November 2020).

[130] Council of the EU, Proposal for a Regulation of the European Parliament and of the Council setting up a Union regime for the control of exports, brokering, technical assistance, transit and transfer of dual-use items (recast), Confirmation of the final compromise text with a view to agreement, 13 November 2020.

[131] On human rights due diligence and export controls, see further Kanetake (2020), pp. 70–76.

At the same time, the explicit reference to cyber surveillance items in the catch-all control does not necessarily mean that the draft endorsed the EU's unilateral approach when it comes to the identification of controlled items. According to the draft text of November 2020, in responding to "serious misuse of existing technologies, or to new risks associated with emerging technologies", Member States' coordinated responses should be followed by "initiatives to introduce equivalent controls at the multilateral level".[132] The list of controlled items "should be in conformity with the obligations and commitments" under treaties and multilateral export control regimes.[133] The draft text reiterated the point that Member States and the Commission "should enhance their contribution to the activities of multilateral export control regimes" so that these arrangements, as a multilateral level playing field, would serve "as a model for international best practice and a global basis".[134] The draft text for the regulation thus obliges the Commission and EU Member States to maintain dialogues with third countries "with a view to promoting the global convergence of controls".[135]

Overall, it is fair to say that the processes of revising the EU's dual-use regulation has resulted in the explicit commitment to multilateralism in this field, while acknowledging, at the same time, the unique role of the EU in proactively altering international export control regimes. Regardless of the final outcomes of the EU's legislative process, the process of revising the EU's regulation provided a crucial opportunity for the EU to decide precisely how it takes part in multilateral regimes while pursuing the materialisation of its principles and objectives in external relations.

While this paper focused on particular aspects of the US and EU's export controls, it is by no means the intention of this paper to reduce the US's approach to national security narratives, in comparison to the EU's emphasis on human rights narratives. For instance, the US has taken one of the first steps in developing guidance for applying human rights due diligence to export control. On 30 September 2020, the US Department of State released its human rights due diligence guidance to assist US companies that export products or services with surveillance capabilities. In the guidance, the US government made it clear that US businesses were "encouraged to integrate human rights due diligence into compliance programs, including *export compliance programs*",[136] in line with the UN's

---

[132]Council of the EU, Confirmation of the final compromise text with a view to agreement, 13 November 2020, Recital para. 6 (original emphasis omitted).

[133]Council of the EU, Confirmation of the final compromise text with a view to agreement, 13 November 2020, Recital para. 18 (original emphasis omitted).

[134]Council of the EU, Confirmation of the final compromise text with a view to agreement, 13 November 2020, Recital para. 29 (original emphasis omitted).

[135]Council of the EU, Confirmation of the final compromise text with a view to agreement, 13 November 2020, Article 27(1) (original emphasis omitted).

[136]US Department of State, Guidance on Implementing the *UN Guiding Principles* for Transactions Linked to Foreign Government End-Users for Products or Services with Surveillance Capabilities, 30 September 2020, https://www.state.gov/release-of-u-s-department-of-state-guidance-on-

Guiding Principles on Business and Human Rights (UNGPs).[137] It remains to be seen how the underlying narratives that shape the framework of dual-use export control would converge across both sides of the Atlantic, especially with regard to their technological export control policies.

6 Conclusion

International trade law and export control laws can be mutually interdependent when it comes to the preservation and development of multilateralism. This is paradoxical, given the fact that export control can, almost by definition, go against some of the basic principles of the WTO trade agreements. Even though export control could frustrate some of the tenets of the multilateral trade regime, the WTO agreements accommodate broad discretion on the part of governments to impose export controls for the sake of each member's essential security. While the WTO panel in the *Russia – Traffic in Transit* case in 2019 made it clear that the invocation of the security exception would not be immune from the panel's scrutiny, the panel left it up to each member's good faith in deciding what constitutes its essential security interests.

Certain regulatory harmonisation has still been achieved, however, outside the WTO regime, through the presence of multilateral export control regimes. They devise the catalogues of materials, products, and technologies subject to export control and, more importantly, serve as a forum through which regulatory officials exchange their licensing practices. Needless to say, the level of regulatory harmonisation arranged through the Wassenaar Arrangement and other export control regimes is limited in nature. Ultimately, it is for each participating state to decide whether to allow the transfer of controlled items in specific circumstances. Moreover, while the Wassenaar Arrangement provides the lengthy list of controlled items, the arrangement is not meant to designate specific destinations or entities that should be considered sensitive and thus require export authorisation. Despite various limitations, however, the Wassenaar Arrangement and other export control regimes create the expectation that participating states should act through these regimes in order for export control to be effective.

The incentives to act through multilateral regimes have not been lost in the US and the EU, despite various attempts that paved the way for unilateral or autonomous export control. In the US, the national security-based export controls have been applied for emerging and foundational technologies, but the US continued working

---

implementing-the-un-guiding-principles-for-transactions-linked-to-foreign-government-end-users-for-products-or-services-with-surveillance-capabilities/ (last accessed 15 November 2020), p. 1 (emphasis added).

[137]United Nations, Guiding Principles on Business and Human Rights: Implementing the UN "Protect, Respect and Remedy" Framework, HR/PUB/11/04, 2011.

through the Australia Group and the Wassenaar Arrangement. In the EU, the review of Council Regulation No 428/2009 since 2013 has led, in September 2016, to the Commission's proposal, which marked the watershed in strengthening human rights considerations in the framework of the EU's dual-use regulation, apparently at the expense of multilateral regulatory harmonisation. In the end, the November 2020 draft, based upon the provisional political agreement between the Council and the European Parliament, created the possibility for the EU's autonomous controls but stressed, at the same time, the importance of multilateral export control regimes as a path through which the EU should promote its export control priorities.

Despite various indications to support multilateralism in export controls, international export control regimes have long been subject to criticisms, precisely because of a particular type of multilateralism that they represent. As noted at the beginning of this paper, multilateralism should entail more than the mere aggregation of multiple states and involve commitment to certain values. In this sense, the rationale of the Wassenaar Arrangement discussed in this paper lies in the reduction of military risks that undermine regional and international security and stability. This remains to be a "laudable and necessary objective",[138] as David Kaye, the Human Rights Council's Special Rapporteur on the freedom of opinion and expression, rather cynically stated. At the same time, the Special Rapporteur was critical of the role of the Wassenaar Arrangement, in that, despite the important role that export control can play in regulating surveillance trade, the Wassenaar Arrangement is "ill-suited" to addressing human rights violations caused by the cross-border transfer of surveillance tools.[139] Should the EU pursue its human rights considerations in its external action, including dual-use export control, the EU cannot avoid engaging with Wassenaar members in altering its narrative, potentially, in the long run, towards more rights-based approaches to the construction of regional and international security.

References

Achilleas P (2017) Introduction export control. In: Tamada D, Achilleas P (eds) Theory and practice of export control: balancing international security and international economic relations. Springer, Singapore, pp 3–16

Alford RP (2011) The self-judging WTO security exception. Utah Law Rev 2011:697–760

Ali J (2001) Chemical weapons and the Iran-Iraq war: a case study in noncompliance. Nonproliferation Rev 8:43–58

---

[138] UN Human Rights Council, Report of the Special Rapporteur on the Promotion and Protection of the Right to Freedom of Opinion and Expression, Surveillance and Human Rights, UN Doc. A/HRC/41/35, 28 May 2019, para. 34.

[139] UN Human Rights Council, Report of the Special Rapporteur on the Promotion and Protection of the Right to Freedom of Opinion and Expression, Surveillance and Human Rights, UN Doc. A/HRC/41/35, 28 May 2019, para. 34.

Anthony I, Zanders JP (1998) Multilateral security-related export controls. SIPRI Yearbook 1998: Armaments, Disarmament and International Security 394–395

Chen T (2017) To judge the self-judging security exception under the GATT 1994 - a systematic approach. Asian J WTO Int Health Law Policy 12:311–356

Cremona M (2017) Distinguished essay: a quiet revolution—the changing nature of the EU's Common Commercial Policy. In: European yearbook of international economic law 2017. Springer, Heidelberg, pp 3–34

Dekker B, Okano-Heijmans M (2020) Emerging technologies and competition in the fourth industrial revolution: the need for new approaches to export control. Strateg Trade Rev 6:53–68

Donovan CJ (1981) The Export Administration Act of 1979: refining United States export control machinery. Boston College Int Comp Law Rev 4:77–114

Dursht KA (1997) From containment to cooperation: collective action and the Wassenaar Arrangement. Cardozo Law Rev 19:1079–1123

Dvorin SM (1980) The Export Administration Act of 1979: an examination of foreign availability of controlled goods and technologies. Northwest J Int Law Bus 2:179–199

Goldblat J (1997) The Biological Weapons Convention: an overview. Int Rev Red Cross Arch 37:251–265

Hahn MJ (1990) Vital interests and the law of GATT: an analysis of GATT's security exception. Mich J Int Law 12:558–620

Hartmann S (2019) Introductory note to Russia – measures concerning traffic in transit (WTO). Int Leg Mater 58:899–1027

Henckels C (2020) Permission to act: the legal character of general and security exceptions in international trade and investment law. Int Comp Law Q 69:557–584

Joyner D (2009) International law and the proliferation of weapons of mass destruction. Oxford University Press, Oxford

Kanetake M (2018) Balancing innovation, development, and security: dual-use concepts in export control laws. In: Craik N, Jefferies CS, Seck SL, Stephens T (eds) Global environmental change and innovation in international law. Cambridge University Press, Cambridge, pp 180–200

Kanetake M (2019) The EU's dual-use export control and human rights risks: the case of cyber surveillance technology. Europe and the World: A Law Review

Kanetake M (2020) Converging dual-use export control with human rights norms: the EU's responses to digital surveillance exports. In: Fahey E (ed) Framing convergence with the global legal order: the EU and the world. Hart Publishing, Bloomsbury Publishing Plc, Oxford, pp 65–81

Krutzsch W, Myjer E, Trapp R, Herbach J (2014) The chemical weapons convention: a commentary. Oxford University Press, Oxford

Lapa V (2020) The WTO panel report in Russia – traffic in transit: cutting the Gordian knot of the GATT security exception? Quest Int Law Zoom-In 69:5–27

Odermatt J (2020) Convergence through EU unilateralism. In: Fahey E (ed) Framing convergence with the global legal order: the EU and the world. Hart Publishing, Bloomsbury Publishing Plc, Oxford, pp 49–63

Overly SD (1985) Regulation of critical technologies under the Export Administration Act of 1979 and the proposed Export Administration Amendments of 1983: American business versus national security. NCJ Int Law Com Regul 10:423–462

Pauwelyn J (2020) Defences and the burden of proof in international law. In: Bartels L, Federica P (eds) Exceptions in international law. Oxford University Press, Oxford, pp 88–107

Petersmann EU (2019) How should WTO members react to their WTO crises? World Trade Rev 18:503–525

Swaak-Goldman OQ (1996) Who defines members' security interest in the WTO? Leiden J Int Law 9:361–372

Voon T (2019) Can international trade law recover? The security exception in WTO law: entering a new era. AJIL Unbound 113:45–50

Voon T (2020) Russia—measures concerning traffic in transit. Am J Int Law 114:96–103

Wagner B (2012) Exporting censorship and surveillance technology. Humanist Institute for Cooperation with Developing Countries (Hivos), The Hague

Whang C (2019) Undermining the consensus-building and list-based standards in export controls: what the US export controls act means to the global export control regime. J Int Econ Law 22:579–599

Machiko Kanetake is Assistant Professor of International Law at Utrecht University, where she coordinates the Law School's LLM in public international law. She is an Editorial Board member of the Leiden Journal of International Law and a Board Member of the Utrecht Centre for Regulation and Enforcement in Europe. She has received Ph.D. from Kyoto University and LLM at the London School of Economics (LSE). Previously, she has been appointed as a postdoctoral researcher at the University of Amsterdam. She has also been appointed, among others, as: a Hauser Visiting Doctoral Researcher of the Global Fellows Program at New York University (NYU) School of Law; a Visiting Fellow at the Human Rights Program, Harvard Law School; and a Visiting Fellow at the Transnational Law Institute, the Dickson Poon School of Law, King's College London.

Part II
Current Challenges, Development and Events in European and International Economic Law

The New European Parliament and Its Role in EU Trade Policy: Reset or Repeat?

Gijs Berends

Contents

Abstract In May 2019, elections took place to elect Members of the European Parliament (MEP) for the ninth legislature (2019–2024). The elections produced a Parliament with new features. Against a turnout of more than 50%, voters elected a record number of politicians new to the European Parliament and a record number of female MEPs. The elections also marked the first time in the European Parliament's electoral history that the European People's Party (EPP) and the Progressive Alliance of Socialists and Democrats (S&D) did not win enough votes to form a majority

I would like to thank Bruno Arce Baigorri, Martti Kalaus, Myriam Martins Gistelinck, Peter Sandler, Frauke Sommer, Jorge Vitorino, and Martina Vukusic for their help and for making this a better chapter. The views expressed in this chapter do not necessarily correspond to those of the European Commission.

G. Berends (✉)
European Commission, Brussels, Belgium
e-mail: Gijs.berends@ec.europa.eu

© Springer Nature Switzerland AG 2021
M. Bungenberg et al. (eds.), *European Yearbook of International Economic Law 2020*,
European Yearbook of International Economic Law (2022) 11: 293–320,
https://doi.org/10.1007/8165_2020_54, Published online: 22 November 2020

and an obvious new ruling coalition has not yet revealed itself. This chapter will consider whether this new Parliament with these novel features will promote a revised trade policy or whether it will remain as supportive of trade policy as the eighth legislature. This chapter will first look at the formal and informal powers of the European Parliament for each of the instruments that together constitute EU trade policy. It then looks at whether the new legislature is likely to change trade policy by examining three questions: (a) has the new European Parliament gained institutional strength?; (b) has the numerical strength of a trade-friendly coalition changed?; (c) is it likely that new political ideas or priorities within the political groups lead to a revision of their views on trade policy?

1 The Newly Elected European Parliament

In May 2019, elections took place to elect Members of the European Parliament (MEP) for the 2019–2024 legislature. The most conspicuous result was that both the European People's Party (EPP) and the Progressive Alliance of Socialists and Democrats (S&D) lost a large number of seats. For the first time, the two groups are not able to form a majority coalition in the European Parliament. It is true that this "Grand Coalition", as it used to be called, was already in retreat from late 2016 onwards, and the S&D, led by the Italian MEP Gianni Pitella, subsequently declared its demise in December of that year. This announcement was said to be the result of disagreements between the two groups on austerity policy and the allocation of senior posts. The election results now mean that the Grand Coalition, already considered politically unworkable, has also become numerically impossible. This was considered one of the main conclusions of the election and therefore widely picked up in the press.

The liberals, who used to be united in the Alliance for Liberals and Democrats for Europe (ALDE), substantially increased their number of seats. They managed this, partly because the candidates from *La République en marche*, the party of French President Macron, together with some allies like the *Mouvement démocrate*, joined forces with ALDE. The partnership was agreed on the condition that the term *liberal* would no longer feature in the group's name, given its unpalatable economic connotation in France. The group was renamed *Renew Europe*. The Greens and the nationalists/populists also made considerable gains. The nationalists/populists of ten Member States bonded in a new political group called *Identity and Democracy* (ID) and are now established as the fourth largest group in Parliament.

The elections undeniably produced a landscape of distinct winners and losers. But the end result did not point to an obvious coalition that could dominate Parliament. A first attempt to build a new coalition was made in early June by four political groups: the EPP, the S&D, Renew Europe and the Greens. Their ambition was to draft a work plan for the next legislative period, "to which we expect the upcoming President of the European Commission to commit in order to enjoy a broad and stable majority in the European Parliament."[1] Because the European Parliament approves any new Commission President, producing such a work plan was a wise strategy to translate leverage into genuine influence over new Commission's policies. This work plan, however, never materialised and the effort was quietly abandoned only a few weeks later. It was testimony, not only to the intricacies of decision-making across EU institutions and Member States,[2] but also to the view that a stable new majority was difficult to construe. Some observers started to take the view that each new policy initiative by the Commission would require a re-assessment of what coalition could emerge to give a favourable opinion—an important conclusion of the election all by itself.

Another much noticed outcome of the elections was the fact that turnout topped 50%. This was a decent percentage in itself, but, more importantly, it stopped a trend of declining turnout that had gotten underway right after the first elections in 1979. In another first, the number of female Members of the European Parliament (MEP) crossed the 40% threshold. And never before had such a large number of elected MEPs been new to the European Parliament (more than 60% when calculated early June 2019). The elections then, it can be said, produced a new Parliament with distinct features.

The new European Parliament also had to face the consequences of Brexit. Its initial consequence was that the political strength of each political group was slightly distorted right after the election. The United Kingdom (UK), after all, ended up taking part in elections for the European Parliament against earlier expectations. In the UK, both the Conservative Party and Labour fared badly and were punished by voters who did not think that the Brexit process was well managed by either party. The Liberal Democrats and the Green Party benefited, which temporarily increased the political weight of Renew Europe and the European Greens respectively. The Brexit Party became the biggest national delegation in the European Parliament and chose not to join any political group. The British MEPs who had been elected could naturally not be considered second-class Members in anticipation of Brexit. They were treated as full-fledged members despite the pending withdrawal of the UK from the European Union (EU). This meant that many were appointed as rapporteurs for ongoing legislative files or for the drafting of parliamentary resolutions. Two British MEPs were elected as committee chair. This was all fair and reasonable but it also meant that once the UK officially withdrew from the EU, all these responsibilities had to be reassigned.

One more complication concerned the rebalancing of the number of MEPs per Member State. In anticipation of Brexit, the Parliament had agreed (after approval by the European Council, which brings together the Heads of State or Government) to

---

[1] Joint Statement of the main political groups of the European Parliament on a new programme for the European Commission, retrieved from https://www.eppgroup.eu/newsroom/news/ep-main-political-groups-on-new-programme-for-the-commission (last accessed 7 April 2020).

[2] In addition, negotiations over key posts complicated the discussions.

re-allocate 27 of the 73 seats that the UK would vacate upon Brexit.[3] These 27 seats were to be distributed amongst 14 Member States that were considered somewhat underrepresented in the Parliament in terms of population. The new seats were in competition during the May election and it was foreseen that the successful MEPs would take them up right after. The delay in the UK's withdrawal, however, also delayed this re-allocation and kept 27 MEPs in the waiting room until 31 January 2020, the day that the UK left the EU.

All of this meant that what emerged from the electoral season was a Parliament that was not ruled by the Grand Coalition; that did not reveal a natural new majority coalition; that contained a membership of distinct features in terms of gender and experience; and for which the picture of the exact size of the political groups, the names of MEPs, the names of committee chairs and vice-chairs and so on, was not stabilised until the actual withdrawal of the UK in January 2020.

2   What Is EU Trade Policy?

This chapter of the yearbook will consider the role of the European Parliament in trade policy and will reflect especially on whether the new Parliament of the 2019–2024 (the ninth legislature) will be any different from the 2014–2019 legislature (the eighth legislature). Any writing on the role of the European Parliament in EU trade policy will need to start by considering what constitutes trade policy. At times, the impression of outside observers seems to be that EU trade policy concerns itself mainly with the negotiation of trade agreements that may either be generally welcome (for instance the Economic Partnership Agreement with Japan) or more controversial (such as the Transatlantic Trade and Investment Partnership (TTIP) negotiations with the US). Whilst trade agreements are indeed core business, trade policy consists rather of many different policy initiatives that inform, shape or determine EU trade policy. The European Parliament, this chapter will hopefully show, will have more influence on some of these initiatives than others. This is an important point that requires some explanation and this is why a classification of initiatives can be useful here. The European Commission can take three kinds of initiatives in trade policy: (a) non-legislative initiatives; (b) legislative initiatives; or (c) initiatives with outside trading partners.[4]

---

[3]The remaining 46 seats are kept available for possible EU enlargements.

[4]This list is not exhaustive but represents the tools commonly used in EU trade policy. For an exhaustive, and legally more accurate overview of the EU's legal instruments, see for example EU Monitor at https://www.eumonitor.eu/9353000/1/j9vvik7m1c3gyxp/vh75mdhkg4s0 (last accessed 7 April 2020).

2.1 Non-Legislative Initiatives

A first example of a non-legislative initiative is a *Communication*. Communications are adopted by the College of Commissioners and they usually set out an action plan, which may include concrete proposals for legislation. It is a forward-looking document that wishes to reveal the Commission's thinking on the direction of policy. One example is the Communication *Trade for All,* published in 2015. Then Commissioner Malmström presented it at the beginning of her term to set out the objectives she wanted to achieve during her mandate as Commissioner and how she wished to respond to the "intense debate about trade across the European Union".[5]

The second of these initiatives is the *Staff Working Document* (SWD). SWDs are factual documents produced by the Directorate-General for Trade (DG Trade). They do not have any legal effect, they normally do not set out new policy priorities, and they do not commit the European Commission because they are not adopted by the College of Commissioners. Despite all this, they can be informative and revealing. The SWD on *Foreign Direct Investment in the EU*, for instance, presents a detailed analysis of the nature and the origin of the ultimate owner that makes an acquisition in the EU. Amongst other things, it concludes that "foreign ownership is remarkably high in a number of sectors that are at the heart of the economy".[6] One can imagine that such facts will inform the EU's investment policy in some shape or form, despite the fact that SWDs are not prescriptive.

A third example of a non-legislative initiative is a so-called *Report*. A Report fulfils a reporting obligation under existing legislation. An example can for instance be found in the Generalised Scheme of Preferences (GSP) Regulation, which removes import duties from products coming into the EU market from vulnerable developing countries. The Regulation requires the Commission to submit once every 2 years a report on how the scheme is functioning, the latest of which was published in February 2020.[7] Because the Regulation is scheduled to expire on 31 December 2023, these biannual reports will undoubtedly shape the decision whether and how the Commission will revise the legislation.

---

[5]Commission Communication, Trade for all; Towards a more responsible trade and investment policy, October 2015, Foreword, https://trade.ec.europa.eu/doclib/docs/2015/october/tradoc_153846.pdf (last accessed 7 April 2020).

[6]Commission Staff Working Document on Foreign Direct Investment in the EU, 13 March 2019, SWD(2019) 108 final, p. 2.

[7]Commission Report on the Generalised Scheme of Preferences covering the period 2018–2019, JOIN(2020) 3 final.

2.2 Legislative Initiatives

As for legislative initiatives, the *ordinary legislative procedure* (OLP) is the procedure by which regulations and directives are adopted and is laid down in Article 294 of the Treaty on the Functioning of the European Union (TFEU). Even if DG Trade is not considered a Directorate-General that mass-produces legislation, it contributes its fair share. The EU's trade defence legislation, the above-mentioned GSP Regulation, the Enforcement Regulation, the Conflict Minerals Legislation and the EU's Export Control Regime Regulation are all examples, amongst others, of trade legislation that is produced via the ordinary legislative procedure.

The Council and the European Parliament, as co-legislators, can decide to delegate to the Commission the power to adopt legal acts to supplement or amend certain non-essential elements of a legislative act (Article 290(1) TFEU). In such case, the Commission legislates through a so-called *Delegated Act*. In trade policy, Delegated Acts are regularly produced and 35 Delegated Acts were considered in the eighth legislature. They are used, for instance, to amend the annexes of the EU's Export Control Regime Regulation to add or remove goods that will need authorisation before export. The Delegated Act therefore amends the Regulation but does not change the "essential elements" of the basic act. Complementary to Delegated Acts, the Commission can exercise an implementing power through the adoption of *Implementing Acts* "where uniform conditions for implementing legally binding Union acts are needed" (Article 291(2) TFEU). Contrary to a Delegated Act, Implementing Acts cannot supplement or amend elements of the basic legislation. In DG Trade, they are predominantly used in the area of trade defence. Anti-dumping measures, for instance, are imposed through Implementing Acts.

Finally, there are *Internal Commission Decisions* that produce legal effects only within the institution. A typical case for EU trade policy is an Internal Commission Decision to decide on next steps when the EU resorts to WTO Dispute Settlement. When the EU requests consultations with a WTO Member in case of a dispute, or when the EU request the establishment of a panel, such requests are preceded by the adoption of an Internal Commission Decision.

2.3 Initiatives with Trading Partners Outside the EU

In this category of initiatives with trading partners, the most obvious instrument is the negotiation of a trade agreement with one or more countries outside the European Union.[8] Trade agreements can be sub-divided in a number of ways. One could look at how widely trade is covered by the agreement (Deep and Comprehensive Free Trade Agreements versus Investment Protection Agreements versus goods-only Agreements etc.). One could also distinguish agreements by considering their legal

---

[8]Procedures to adopt trade agreements are laid down in Articles 207 and 218 TFEU.

basis (Association Agreements versus Trade Agreements). Alternatively, one could consider whether the agreement covers exclusive, shared or Member State competences (mixed versus EU-only agreements). Each of these agreements is likely to contain provisions that set up 'bodies' to manage the agreement after it has entered into force (or into provisional application). Such a body is likely to be called *Joint Ministerial Committee* or a *Joint Council* or a name along those lines. They are often entitled to adopt acts having legal effect.[9] Typically, this concerns measures to ensure the smooth operation of the agreement. Such body can, for instance, adopt the Rules of Procedure for the committees under the agreement. Finally, the EU and its partner could also agree to a *Non-Binding Instrument* (NBI). An NBI is a document, like a Memorandum of Understanding, that records an understanding between the EU and a third country without giving rise to obligations that are legally binding. One example of this is the recommendation on climate change of the Joint Committee under the trade agreement between the EU and Canada (CETA), which calls for joint actions to tackle climate change.[10]

3   The Role of the European Parliament in Trade Policy

This listing of the numerous policy initiatives that together constitute EU Trade Policy may be lengthy, but it is central to understand the role of the European Parliament in EU trade policy. This is because the European Parliament has a stronger role in the case of some of these initiatives than in others. This is mainly a function of the kind of powers the Treaty on the Functioning of the European Union accords to the European Parliament. One can identify three categories of institutional strength. First, the TFEU gives considerable powers in the case of (a) the ordinary legislative procedure; (b) delegated acts; and (c) agreements with third countries. Secondly, the Treaty accords a limited role to the European Parliament in case of Implementing Acts and grants only a narrow role for the European Parliament when it comes to the Right of Initiative. Thirdly, for all other trade initiatives, like the three non-legislative initiatives, the Internal Commission Decision, the decisions adopted by a Body under a trade agreement, or any non-binding instrument with a third country, the European Parliament will have no institutionalised role and it has to generate influence through other means. The following paragraphs will consider these three categories.

---

[9]Its procedure can be read in Article 218(9) TFEU.

[10]Recommendation of the CETA Joint Committee on trade, climate action, and the Paris Agreement, 2018. https://trade.ec.europa.eu/doclib/docs/2018/september/tradoc_157415.pdf (last accessed 7 April 2020).

3.1   The OLP, Delegated Acts and Trade Agreements

For the ordinary legislative procedure, no Commission proposal can be adopted without the approval of the European Parliament. Article 294 TFEU stipulates that the adoption procedure can consist of maximum three readings. Each reading has distinct procedural features that determine the voting procedure used by the European Parliament and the kind of amendments it can propose. For instance, the European Parliament normally votes by simple majority but in the second reading, it can reject the position or amendments by the Council only by absolute majority. These days, upon a Commission proposal, the Council and European Parliament, as soon as they are mandated to do so, start discussions with each other in so-called *trilogues* (by custom in the presence of the European Commission). The two co-legislators tend to proceed to closing the first reading only once the trilogues have produced a successful outcome. As a result, most legislative files are nowadays concluded in first reading. The European Parliament therefore often votes on OLP files on the basis of a simple majority.

The role of the European Parliament in the case of a Delegated Act differs from its role in the OLP in three ways. First, Article 290 TFEU does not say that the European Parliament needs to approve the proposal of the European Commission. Rather, it allows the European Parliament to revoke or object to the Delegated Act. If the European Parliament takes no action, the Delegated Act will be adopted (provided the Council does not object to the Delegated Act either). Secondly, the European Parliament, when it wishes to object to the Delegated Act, must do so on the basis of absolute majority voting.[11] The third of these differences is that the European Parliament does not have the right to put forward amendments to the Delegated Act.

In case of trade agreements, an agreement can only be concluded after consent of the European Parliament (Article 218(6)(a) TFEU). The European Parliament will vote on the basis of a simple majority and, just like for Delegated Acts, it cannot propose amendments to the agreement that the Commission has negotiated on behalf of the European Union.

These powers of the European Parliament are considerable. Of course, the European Parliament can deploy its voting powers to reject a Commission proposal. After all, it voted against the Anti-Counterfeiting Trade Agreement (ACTA) in 2012. Still, its influence rests more in the *possibility* of a negative vote. And the European Parliament is skilled and experienced in leveraging this. Two examples can illustrate this point. First, in regard of the ordinary legislative procedure, the European Commission proposed in 2014 legislation on conflict minerals. Its aim was to stem the trade in four minerals—tin, tantalum, tungsten and gold—because such trade may finance armed conflict. Amongst other ideas, the Commission proposed that EU companies would undertake voluntary due diligence checks on their suppliers. Due

---

[11]Article 290 (2) TFEU: "the European Parliament shall act by a majority of its component members."

to pressure from the European Parliament, this voluntary due diligence was turned into mandatory due diligence requirements (with exceptions for the smallest operators).

Secondly, in regard of the consent procedure, the European Parliament, through its Resolution on the TTIP negotiations, expressed its wish to do away with the old system for resolving disputes between investors and states (which is called Investor-State Dispute Settlement or ISDS) and replace it with something new. This new system, the European Parliament demanded, was to be "subject to democratic principles and scrutiny, where potential cases are treated in a transparent manner by publicly appointed, independent professional judges in public hearings and which includes an appellate mechanism, where consistency of judicial decisions is ensured, the jurisdiction of courts of the EU and of the Member States is respected, and where private interests cannot undermine public policy objectives."[12] As one of the officials in the office of the International Trade Committee's (INTA) Chair Mr. Lange later wrote, "it was particularly the sentence on ISDS that changed the direction of the TTIP negotiations."[13] Indeed, this paragraph, combined with existing pressure from Member States, fuelled a fundamental reform of the EU's investment protection policy, because it signalled that the European Parliament would no longer contemplate giving consent to any agreement with the US or, as it spilled over into the consent procedure for CETA, with Canada, should such changes not be realised. The Commission proceeded to create an independent investment court system (ICS) that became a system with a permanent tribunal and an appeal tribunal competent to review decisions of the tribunal. Dispute settlement proceedings were to be conducted in a transparent and impartial manner, whereby strict rules of ethical behaviour were imposed on the members of the tribunal.

3.2 Implementing Acts and the Right of Initiative

Whereas the Treaty on the Functioning of the European Union accords considerable powers to the European Parliament for the OLP, Delegated Acts and trade agreements, it offers much more limited provisions in regard of Implementing Acts and the Right of Initiative. For one thing, once the European Parliament in the ordinary legislative procedure has agreed on an empowerment via an Implementing Act, its opinion will not be sought once such act will be adopted.[14] Instead, the Member States (and not the Council) control the European Commission in a process that is

---

[12]Paragraph 2(d)(xv), European Parliament resolution of 8 July 2015 containing the European Parliament's recommendations to the European Commission on the negotiations for the Transatlantic Trade and Investment Partnership (TTIP) (2014/2228(INI)).

[13]Martins Gistelinck (2020).

[14]Precisely because the TFEU accords such a different power between a Delegated Act and an Implementing Act, the three institutions agreed in 2019 on general principles regarding the delineation between the two. See Interinstitutional Agreement, Non-Binding Criteria for the

called *comitology*. Member States representatives take part in committees that enable EU countries to oversee the Commission's work. However, the European Parliament can indicate if it feels that the Implementing Act exceeds the Commission's powers compared to how it is defined in the original act. The committee responsible may table a motion for a resolution stating that a draft implementing act goes beyond the powers conferred in the basic legislative act and the resolution "may incorporate a request to the Commission to withdraw the draft implementing act or measure, to amend it in keeping with the objections raised by Parliament, or to submit a new legislative proposal."[15] If such an objection is put forward, the Commission is then under an obligation to review its proposal and decide whether to maintain, amend or withdraw it, taking into consideration the views of the European Parliament.

In trade policy, implementing acts are mainly used in the area of trade defence.[16] The European Parliament is not in the habit of raising the above-mentioned objections in this area.[17] In the case of authorisations of chemicals or GM-food (subject matters that are trade-related but not under trade competence), however, the European Parliament routinely questions the implementing acts put forward by the Commission. A recently granted authorisation of a genetically modified maize, for instance, triggered a resolution from the European Parliament that considered that "the draft Commission implementing decision exceeds the implementing powers provided for in Regulation (EC) No 1829/2003" and "calls on the Commission to withdraw its draft implementing decision."[18]

As for the Right of Initiative, the TFEU reserves this right essentially for the European Commission: "Union legislative acts may only be adopted on the basis of a Commission proposal, except where the Treaties provide otherwise."[19] This is different from Member States where this right is often shared between national governments and the national parliaments. Yet, the European Parliament is not entirely without sway. Article 225 TFEU says that "the European Parliament may, acting by a majority of its component Members, request the Commission to submit

---

application of Articles 290 and 291 of the Treaty on the Functioning of the European Union—18 June 2019 (2019/C 223/01).

[15]European Parliament Rule of Procedure Rule 106 (3) on Implementing acts and measures.

[16]At the time of writing, the Commission adopted an Implementing Act on the export authorisation of scarce Personal Protective Equipment in light of the COVID19 crisis. Given its sensitivity, it was followed closely by the European Parliament. INTA expressed support but also exerted political influence by publishing a letter from all group coordinators: https://www.europarl.europa.eu/committees/en/inta-supports-export-authorisation-for-p/product-details/20200402CAN54285 (last accessed 20 April 2020).

[17]Of course, the instruments mentioned under paragraph 3.3 can and will be deployed by interested MEPs.

[18]European Parliament resolution of 24 October 2018 on the draft Commission implementing decision renewing the authorisation for the placing on the market of products containing, consisting of or produced from genetically modified maize NK603 × MON 810 (MON-ØØ6Ø3-6 × MON-ØØ81Ø-6) pursuant to Regulation (EC) No 1829/2003 of the European Parliament and of the Council (D058360/01—2018/2872(RSP)).

[19]Article 17(2) TEU.

any appropriate proposal on matters on which it considers that a Union act is required for the purpose of implementing the Treaties. If the Commission does not submit a proposal, it shall inform the European Parliament of the reasons." The request will be drafted in the form of a legislative own-initiative report.[20] Article 225 TFEU contains a number of noticeable instructions. The European Parliament can invoke the article only by an absolute majority. The Commission is not required to respond positively to the request, but there is an obligation to react. If it does not agree with the European Parliament, it has to explain why it takes the course it has decided on. Inter-institutional agreements have further clarified that this explanation needs to be detailed, needs to discuss the alternatives and needs to answer questions from the European Parliament on the cost of "non-Europe." [21] Should the Commission decide to respond positively, it has promised to "come forward with a legislative proposal at the latest after one year or shall include the proposal in its next year's Work Programme."[22]

All in all, one can conclude there is an explicit legal base for the European Parliament to put pressure on the Commission to start legislating and that the institutions have developed clear rules and guidelines on how Article 225 TFEU can be invoked. But in reality, there has been little appetite to use this article in the area of trade policy. There is only one exception to this. In March 2017, ten Members of the European Parliament of the EPP submitted a proposal to ask the Commission to draft legislation on foreign direct investment. It asked for a law that would allow for Member States to intervene when an "envisaged direct investment by [a] third country does not comply with market rules or is facilitated by state subsidies resulting in a likely market disturbance."[23] Normally, the President of the European Parliament would have needed to present this proposal to the plenary after which it would have been allocated to the appropriate committee to draft a legislative initiative report. In the end, all of these procedural steps did not materialise, because the Commission President at the time, Mr Juncker, decided, also after consultations with large Member States like Germany, France and Italy, to already start drafting what later became the FDI Screening Regulation.[24] The proposal by the MEPs was noteworthy all the same, not only because it was the first time Article 225 TFEU was considered in the area of trade but also because it could have been successful given that it came at a time when the political climate was favourable.

---

[20]European Parliament Research Service, Parliament's right of legislative initiative, 2020, https://www.europarl.europa.eu/thinktank/en/document.html?reference=EPRS_BRI(2020)646174 (last accessed 7 April 2020).

[21]Inter-institutional agreement between the European Parliament, the Council of the European Union and the European Commission on Better Law-making, OJ L 123, 12.5.2016.

[22]Framework Agreement on relations between the European Parliament and the European Commission, OJ L304/47, 20.11.2010.

[23]This proposal has been retrieved from https://www.politico.eu/wp-content/uploads/2017/03/2017-03-20-Draft-Union-Act-on-Foreign-Investment.pdf (last accessed 7 April 2020).

[24]Regulation (EU) 2019/452 of the European Parliament and of the Council on establishing a framework for the screening of foreign direct investments into the Union, OJ 2019 L 79 I/1.

3.3   European Parliament's Own Instruments and the Right to be Informed

For all other trade initiatives identified above (to recall: the three non-legislative initiatives, the Internal Commission Decision, the decisions adopted by a Body under a trade agreement, or any non-binding instrument with a third country), the European Parliament would need to resort to instruments outside the Treaty to influence their content.[25] The European Parliament has many tools it can deploy to make its views known. Most MEPs submit written questions to the Commission or the Council on the subjects they or their constituents find important. MEPs can send letters, either individually or jointly with other MEPs, to the Commissioner(s) of their choice. Committees can try to get an Oral Question or Commission Statement on the agenda of the plenary as this will require the Commission to explain itself on the matter in a public debate. INTA and its members use these instruments frequently. In the entire eighth parliamentary term (2014–2019), for instance, MEPs submitted over 1300 written questions to DG Trade and sent over 200 letters to the Commissioner for Trade, while INTA presented 23 Oral Questions, 21 of which led to a debate in Plenary. DG Trade managed close to 4% of all Parliament's written questions submitted to the Commission in that period.[26] The Parliament can also schedule plenary or committee debates to make its views known or to pressure the Commission into publicly discussing what they are planning to do. Groups or committees can draft resolutions to reveal what the European Parliament is thinking. For instance, in deciding on the opening of the negotiations of a trade agreement, the European Parliament has no official role to play. It is up to the Council to authorise the opening of negotiations based on a recommendation of the European Commission (Article 207(3) TFEU). The European Parliament, however, started to proactively adopt resolutions on the opening of negotiations. This practice has become so rooted that in recent years one can detect a willingness by the Council to wait for the European Parliament to make its views known.[27]

The European Parliament also possesses the Treaty-based right to be informed: "The European Parliament shall be immediately and fully informed at all stages of the procedure."[28] This right was implemented in an interinstitutional agreement between the Commission and the European Parliament, which sets out in great detail

---

[25]It is true that for the non-legislative initiative of a *Report*, the European Parliament can of course in the process of drafting legislation under the ordinary legislative procedure co-decide on what and how often the Commission has to report.

[26]Internal calculations.

[27]Bart Kerremans, Johan Adriaensen, Francesca Colli, Evelyn Coremans, Parliamentary scrutiny of trade policies across the western world, Directorate-General for External Policies, Policy Department, European Parliament, March 2019. https://www.europarl.europa.eu/RegData/etudes/STUD/2019/603477/EXPO_STU(2019)603477_EN.pdf (last accessed 7 April 2020).

[28]Article 218 (10) TFEU.

the arrangements on information-sharing.[29] It particularly contains provisions to ensure that the European Parliament is informed at *the same time* as the Council of the various steps in the negotiations and that the European Parliament is informed of *the same information* as the Council. Over time, this right of information of the European Parliament, propelled by the TTIP negotiations, morphed into more and more transparency initiatives by the European Commission. The Commission now makes publicly available the draft negotiating directives it transmits to the Council to seek its authorisation to start a new negotiation.[30] It publishes the EU's initial proposal for legal texts during the negotiations and reports on the progress made after each round of talks. It seeks public views on the impact assessment and the sustainability impact assessment it undertakes. And it has committed to make available each year an FTA Implementation report that highlights the success and shortcomings in the implementation of trade agreements. The European Parliament will therefore be able to develop its views on the basis of this information and is also in the position to react publicly to all these instances of transparency.

4 The 2019–2024 European Parliament: What's New?

Will the ninth legislature lead to new dynamics in the area of trade policy? There are three ways to look at this question. First, has the new European Parliament somehow gained institutional strength? Secondly, in terms of numbers, is it more or less difficult for a 'trade-friendly' coalition to emerge in plenary or in INTA? And, thirdly, are the political groups changing their views on trade? For example, is there a risk that traditionally trade-friendly groups lose their appetite for trade policy or are there chances that the habitually trade-sceptical groups become more supportive?

4.1 Is the New European Parliament Institutionally Stronger?

The European Parliament has the right to elect the President of the European Commission, which it does on the basis of an absolute majority. It will need to give consent to the entire College of Commissioners on the basis of a simple majority (Art 17(7) TEU). The different political groups try to play their cards well in this process of parliamentary approval, by demanding as many commitments

---

[29]Framework Agreement on relations between the European Parliament and the European Commission, OJ L304/47, 20.11.2010, Annex III.

[30]The decision to publish the final version belongs to the Council and in some instances (for example for the agreement with Japan), the Council has decided to make it publicly available.

from the candidate for President and the individual Commissioners-designate as the political context allows. Getting approval is a delicate exercise for the candidates, as each electoral cycle demonstrates. This time, three Commissioner-candidates were rejected by the European Parliament. To convince the European Parliament of the merits of her possible Presidency, then President-candidate Ms Von Der Leyen, just as the previous Commission President Mr Juncker had done at the time, published "Political Guidelines" on 16 July 2019. The guidelines were made available just ahead of the vote on her election and they sketched out the policies she would be pursuing if elected. And this document contains three commitments that reinforce the institutional role of the European Parliament in trade policy.

The first of these concerns the Right of Initiative. As mentioned above, the Right of Initiative lies with the Commission and even if Article 225 TFEU allows for the Parliament to up the political pressure by asking the Commission to propose legislation, the Commission is under no obligation to react positively, even if it has to argue its case. President-candidate Von Der Leyen, however, declared her support for a Right of Initiative for the European Parliament and wrote that "when Parliament, acting by a majority of its members, adopts resolutions requesting that the Commission submit legislative proposals, I commit to responding with a legislative act in full respect of the proportionality, subsidiarity and better law making principles."[31] President Von Der Leyen suggests she will react and to do so in the form of a legislative proposal (unless for reasons of proportionality, subsidiarity and better law making, another response is required). The Treaty obligation for the Commission to explain its actions (which may include not taking any action) would then be replaced with a commitment to propose a legal act (that may of course differ from what the European Parliament had in mind). This has not been put to practice just yet, but the European Parliament has surely taken good note and is preparing various legislative initiative reports precisely to test the meaning.[32] In the area relevant to trade policy, a number of committees in the European Parliament (including INTA) are considering legislative initiative reports on how it can be ensured that the processing of goods the EU imports has not been detrimental to the environment, factory safety or forests.

President Von Der Leyen, secondly, has also made a modification in the decision-making process of trade agreements. Successive Trade Commissioners, Karel De Gucht and Cecilia Malmström, have promised the European Parliament that they will not ask the Council for provisional application of a trade agreement before the

---

[31] A Union that strives for more—My agenda for Europe, https://ec.europa.eu/commission/sites/beta-political/files/political-guidelines-next-commission_en.pdf. Page 20. She reiterates her "support for a right of initiative for the Parliament" in the Mission Letter from her to Trade Commissioner Hogan, https://ec.europa.eu/commission/sites/beta-political/files/mission-letter-phil-hogan-2019_en.pdf, page 3 (both pages last accessed 7 April 2020).

[32] There is some concern amongst MEPs that the Commission is already backtracking on its proposal. See https://www.spiegel.de/politik/deutschland/ursula-von-der-leyen-eu-parlamentarier-werfen-kommissionschefin-wortbruch-vor-a-42af6d54-568d-47b6-a6d8-8c835bdfde4d?sara_ecid=soci_upd_KsBF0AFjflf0DZCxpPYDCQgO1dEMph (last accessed 7 April 2020).

European Parliament has given its consent. Ms Malmström wrote that she was ready "when proposing decisions to sign politically important trade agreements which fall under my responsibility, to ask Council to delay provisional application until the European Parliament has given its consent. However, we need certain flexibility in applying such a practice as there will always be occasions where the urgency of a particular file, or its technical character, mean that it is unwarranted to delay its application pending the EP's consent."[33] This commitment has always been a strong political signal (and not a *legal* signal as the TFEU does not prescribe that parliamentary consent is required for provisional application) that the Trade Commissioner takes the European Parliament very seriously. And this is why trade agreements since the FTA with Korea have not been provisionally applied before consent of the European Parliament.

President Von Der Leyen has now gone a step further by saying that "my Commission will always propose that provisional application of trade agreements take place only once the European Parliament has given its consent."[34] It reveals three differences with the commitment by Trade Commissioner Malmström. First, President Von Der Leyen seems to have made a commitment that applies across the College of Commissioners and not just those that fall under the responsibility of the Trade Commissioner. Some agreements are legally considered *trade agreements* but fall under the competence of Commissioners responsible for, for instance, agriculture or for customs policy. Secondly, her commitment does not seem limited to "politically important trade agreements". And thirdly, the new commitment does not cater to exemptions for reasons of urgency or the technical character of the agreement. The European Parliament has therefore gained some institutional strength that INTA will surely enforce. The committee has always been much aware that the past political commitments of the Trade Commissioner did not spill over into the portfolios of other Commissioners.

The third commitment of President Von Der Leyen concerned transparency. In her Political Guidelines she declared: "I will ensure my Commissioners brief the European Parliament at all stages of all international negotiations, following the mould set by the Brexit negotiations. I will also ensure more appearances in Committee meetings and Commissioner presence in trilogue discussions between the European Parliament and the Council."[35] In her mission letter to the, at the time, Commissioner-designate Phil Hogan, she also instructed him to "ensure regular briefings are provided to the European Parliament before and after each round of talks."[36] What is new here is not so much that the European Parliament needs to be briefed before and after each round, because the Commission is already bound to

---

[33] Answers to the European Parliament—Questionnaire to the Commissioner-designate Cecilia MALMSTRÖM, https://www.europarl.europa.eu/hearings-2014/resources/questions-answers/Hearings2014_Malmstr%C3%B6m_Questionnaire_en.pdf (last accessed 7 April 2020).

[34] Political Guidelines page 17.

[35] Political Guidelines page 20.

[36] Mission letter, page 6.

provide information at all stages of the negotiations. It is more that the responsibility to do so is put more squarely on the shoulders of the Commissioner rather than that of the negotiating team. In practice, this may turn out to produce a similar outcome, but it elevates the obligation to ensure transparency to a higher level.

4.2 Is There a Trade-Friendly Coalition in the New Plenary?

In times of the Grand Coalition, a first step in seeking solid support for trade agreements was to look for the EPP and the S&D. As long as the two groups would agree, a trade agreement could pass through the European Parliament and some other groups could then be expected to join that backing. They after all occupied 54% of the seats in the eighth legislature (and more than 60% in the seventh). But when the Grand Coalition started to weaken, support amongst S&D MEPs also started to become more erratic, as Fig. 1 shows.

The reasons for the wavering of S&D support can be found in the characteristics of the individual agreements, debates about globalisation and austerity, the rising intensity of the debate on free trade and more. But the faltering Grand Coalition also released the S&D in certain ways from sticking to more traditional voting patterns. As a result, the EPP/S&D coalition did not muster enough votes for trade agreements such as with Canada, Southern Africa, Ghana and the agreements with Singapore (EPP/S&D support for these agreements amounted, respectively, to 41.7%; 40.9%; 37%; 42%; and 43.5% of the total votes cast). An alternative route to consent was through a coalition of groups that had proved to be supportive of trade agreements over time: EPP, the European Conservatives and Reformists Group (ECR) and ALDE. Their voting record in the eighth legislature, as shown in Table 1, shows a consistent and high degree of support for trade agreements. Only on rare occasions did the percentage of the voting MEPs in these three groups that supported trade agreement drop under the 90%.

Together, these three parties had a little less than 48% of the votes in the eighth legislature. When these three groups combined their votes and stuck to their historical record of trade-friendly voting behaviour, a trade agreement was already getting close to a majority for consent. The S&D all the same remained central to the vote. First because the EPP/ALDE/ECR coalition fell short of 50% of the seats.[37] Second, in order to ensure the public legitimacy of trade agreements, it was helpful to have as large a majority in the European Parliament as possible. The S&D was the only political group that could deliver a sufficient number of additional votes to the EPP/ALDE/ECR coalition.

---

[37]Because the consent vote is based on simple majority voting, who among the MEPs exactly shows up at voting time can make a big difference in the voting result.

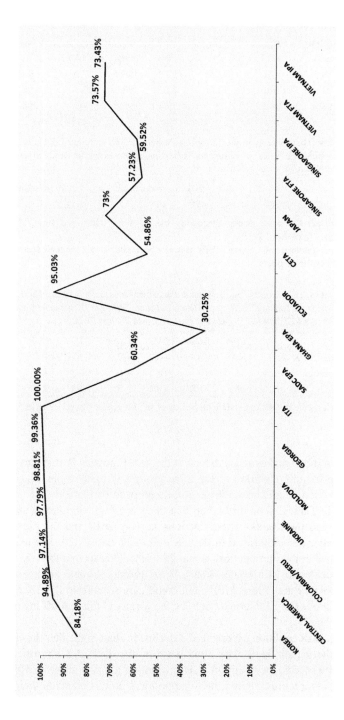

Fig. 1 Share of 'YES'-Votes for Trade Agreements in % of Total Votes Cast amongst S&D Members (February 2011–February 2020) [Calculated on the basis of the European Parliament voting records. See also https://www.europarl.europa.eu/plenary/en/votes.html?tab=votes (last accessed 20 July 2020)]

Table 1 Share of 'YES'-votes for trade agreements in % of total votes cast [www.votewatch.eu (last accessed 7 April 2020)]

	ITA (%)	SADC EPA (%)	Ghana EPA (%)	Ecuador (%)	CETA (%)	Japan (%)	Singapore FTA (%)	Singapore IPA (%)
EPP	100	88.5	99.5	99.5	94.2	96.4	97.2	97.9
ALDE	96.9	92	100	100	87.5	98.3	95.3	96.9
ECR	96.7	98.5	98.5	100	79.1	95.6	98.4	98.4

Table 2 Share of number of seats in the European Parliament (%) [Internal calculations, based amongst others on various editions of European Parliamentary Research Service, *European Parliament: Facts and Figures*]

	2014–2019[a] (%)	2019 post-elections[b] (%)	2019 post-Brexit (%)
EPP+ALDE/RE+ECR	47.8	47	49.2

[a]MEPs move from party to party so this percentage has not been stable over time. The figure presented here comes from April 2019
[b]Since the elections, a number of Catalan MEPs have not been able to take up their seats and that marginally influences the numbers

Table 3 Re-allocation of UK seats [See European Parliament Research Service, *The European Parliament after Brexit*, 14 January 2020, https://www.europarl.europa.eu/RegData/etudes/ATAG/2020/642259/EPRS_ATA(2020)642259_EN.pdf (last accessed 20 July 2020)]

	EPP	S&D	RE	Greens	ID	ECR	GUE[a]
Loss from 73 vacated UK seats	NA	−14	−17	−7	NA	−4	−1
Gains from reallocation 27 seats	+5	+4	+6	+4	+3	+4	NA
Total	+5	−10	−11	−3	+3	0	−1

[a]GUE is the French acronym for the Confederal Group of the European United Left/Nordic Green Left

With this in mind, it makes sense to look at the new European Parliament and see whether a trade-friendly coalition of the three groups, in light of the winners and losers of the election, maintains its share in the European Parliament.

The figures in Table 2 show first of all that there is a fairly significant statistical difference between the results of the elections in May 2019 and the picture that emerged right after the withdrawal of the UK end of January 2020. The reason for this, as mentioned in the introduction, is that 27 of the 73 seats that the UK vacated had to be reallocated to 14 Member States. Upon Brexit, political groups stood to lose the seats held by the British MEPs, but could gain seats from the 27 seats that were up for election. The EPP turned out to be the winner of this reshuffling of seats, as Table 3 displays.

The EPP/RE/ECR coalition experienced a decline in share right after the elections compared to the eighth legislature, but because the EPP did so well in the re-allocation of 27 seats, the coalition's share went up again to close to 50% right after Brexit. In other words, should the three political groups maintain their voting behaviour from the last term, this coalition, purely in numerical terms, could again constitute the core of a majority in the new European Parliament in favour of new trade agreements.

4.3   Is There a Trade-Friendly Coalition in the New INTA?

The Committee on International Trade is the committee of the European Parliament responsible for the Union's common commercial policy and its external economic relations and as such gets to express itself before the plenary decides on a trade agreement.[38] INTA votes on the basis of a simple majority, which means that also in committee votes one more 'YES'-vote than the number of 'NO'-votes is required for an agreement to pass. In the previous legislature, INTA had 41 seats. With all 41 MEPs present (at times, the number of INTA members who vote falls a few votes short of the maximum number of votes) and with no abstentions (this rarely occurs), 21 MEPs are needed to cast a 'YES'-vote for an agreement to pass. In the last months of the 2014–2019 legislature, at a time when the three trade agreements were passing through the European Parliament (the Investment Protection Agreement with Singapore, the Free Trade Agreement with Singapore, and the Economic Partnership Agreement with Japan), the EPP, ALDE, and ECR occupied 21 of the 41 seats. In other words, if these three groups would vote in line with their customary voting behaviour, passage through INTA was all but assured. The coalition was indeed slightly overrepresented. The strength of the political groups in committees normally needs to reflect their overall political strength in plenary,[39] but numerically this is difficult to guarantee and groups may prefer to round down the numbers in one committee in order to round them up in another. In addition, MEPs at times change political group.[40] The distribution of the political weight of the respective groups is therefore a little skewed on occasion.

In the new Parliament, INTA was one of three committees that experienced an increase in membership after Brexit. The number of seats went up from 41 to 43. Today, 22 MEPs would need to cast a 'YES'-vote for an agreement to pass. As Table 4 shows, the three groups today have 21 seats and therefore fall one short of a direct majority in INTA.

In conclusion then, the 'trade-friendly' coalition is slightly worse off compared to the situation just before the elections, but the three groups are well placed to form,

---

[38]This chapter will only consider INTA, even if it is acknowledged that the foreign affairs committee (AFET) will be officially in charge of Association Agreements, which have provisions that go much beyond trade policy.

[39]European Parliament Rule of Procedure 209 on composition of committees: "The composition of the committees shall, as far as possible, reflect the composition of Parliament" (209(2)).

[40]European Parliament Rule of Procedure 209 (4): "Where a Member's change of political group has the effect of disturbing the proportional distribution of committee seats as defined in paragraph 2, and there is no agreement among political groups to ensure compliance with the principles set out therein, the Conference of Presidents shall take the necessary decisions."

Table 4 Number of seats in INTA [INTA Members can be found at https://www.europarl.europa.eu/committees/en/inta/home/members (last accessed 20 July 2020)]

EPP	S&D	RE	ID	ECR	Greens	GUE	NI
11	9	6	5	4	4	2	2

purely in numerical terms, the core of a majority in the new INTA for trade agreements.

4.4 Do the Political Groups Have New Trade Priorities?

For supporters of trade policy, the numbers in plenary and in INTA may sound reassuring. But numerical analysis only goes so far. Because who is to say that the trade-friendly groups remain supportive of trade policy? And what about the sceptical political groups and their views; surely not everything just stays the same? One would have to march through all 5 years of the ninth legislature to be sure of the answer to these questions, but two matters are worth considering now. What are the risks that trade-friendly groups experience a softening of their enthusiasm? And what are the chances that the traditionally more trade-sceptical parties increase their appreciation?

4.4.1 The Risk of Waning Enthusiasm

The EPP manifesto was unambiguous in its support of free trade and argued that "we will negotiate new and additional free and fair-trade agreements."[41] But the EPP, like the other groups, has realised that many of the MEPs are new and many have not been involved in trade policy. It is therefore very likely that despite the pro-trade voting record over many years, many MEPs would first need to be convinced of the benefits of trade policy. Also, farmers have by tradition been amongst the core constituents of national parties that belong to the EPP family and they have often been sceptical of expanding the network of trade agreements. While most of the agreements that have been concluded in recent years may well have had a relatively mild impact on the farming sector and while studies have shown that EU's agricultural sector is one of the beneficiary sectors of EU trade agreements, some interest groups insist that trade is the altar on which the agricultural sector is being sacrificed. Another risk is that if *Fidesz*, the ruling party in Hungary, leaves the EPP, they may

---

[41]EPP Manifesto "Let's open the next chapter for Europe together" https://www.epp.eu/files/uploads/2019/04/EPP-MANIFESTO-2019-002.pdf (last accessed 7 April 2020).

join or start building a political group that will be more nationalist in nature than the EPP is today.[42]

ALDE, as a former liberal bulwark, was a consistent supporter of trade agreements in the previous legislature, even if sustainability and the human rights situation in third countries was a constant source of concern. In newly renamed Renew Europe, which, to recall, no longer carries the term liberal in their name, the French delegation is by far the largest national contingent. A number of French politicians have been unequivocal about changing trade policy to realign it with climate policy. Jean-Baptiste Lemoyne, President Macron's junior foreign minister, said in 2019 about the elections that "if you look at the results of the vote, you see a wish of Europeans to be protected, a wish that climate change is taken into account and France will continue aggressively to push certain issues to adapt our trade policy."[43] Another example is Mr Canfin, the chair of the Environment, Public Health, and Food Safety (ENVI) committee of the European Parliament, who has said that his task within Renew Europe will be to reconcile climate and trade policy. He wishes to investigate how trade agreements can actively contribute to solving the climate crisis and how they can be used as leverage to force other countries to do the same. In an interview, he was quoted as saying that "I want to have it recorded I am not against trade deals and France is not against trade deals. But we need to take into account there is a massive change in expectations."[44]

The ECR campaigned on a manifesto that was explicitly in favour of rules-based trade and trade agreements. Its website today also states that "more open trade means more jobs, increased business opportunities, and cheaper goods for the consumer. That is why the ECR Group has been the driving force within the European Parliament on putting in place a number of important international agreements."[45] But Brexit has changed the dynamic in the group. The British conservatives used to be the biggest group in the ECR and were steady supporters of trade agreements. The withdrawal of the UK means that the Polish MEPs now constitute the largest delegation in the ECR and their nationalist appeals combined with wining 70% of the farmers' vote in the election for the European Parliament may sit uncomfortably with liberalisation of trade.[46] The Italian and Spanish delegations of the ECR may feel similar pressure to defend agricultural constituents.

---

[42]Fidesz may leave voluntarily or involuntarily. In April 2020, in a letter to EPP President Mr Tusk, political leaders of 13 national member parties of the EPP called for asked the expulsion of Fidesz from the EPP.

[43]"European trade policy seen going greener after EU parliament vote", Reuters, 27 May 2019.

[44]"EU trade deals must not contradict climate goals, says MEP", the Guardian, 9 December 2019, https://www.theguardian.com/world/2019/dec/09/eu-trade-deals-must-not-contradict-climate-goals-says-mep (last accessed 7 April 2020).

[45]ECR website, A Global Approach, https://ecrgroup.eu/vision/a_global_approach (last accessed 7 April 2020).

[46]Poland's farmers switch loyalties to boost ruling party, Politico, 31 May 2019, https://www.politico.eu/article/polands-farmers-switch-loyalties-to-boost-ruling-party-pis-law-and-justice/ (last accessed 7 April 2020).

4.4.2 The Chances of Growing Appreciation

Contrary to other policy areas, trade has always been too thorny a topic for the S&D to unite around. Group coherence has been uneven, with 30% of S&D MEPs voting in favour of a trade agreement with Ghana despite the fact that the group position of the S&D was to vote against.[47] Similarly, despite an official recommendation to vote in favour of the agreements with Singapore, more than 40% of the S&D membership voted against or abstained. How to square this? In 2018, the S&D published a paper to present a progressive model of trade policy. This paper recognised that international trade has "played an important role in promoting economic growth, job creation and better living standards at the global level" but at the same time argued that "the traditional approach, which argues that 'trade is good, but we need to work on the side effects,' is outdated." [48] It therefore calls for trade agreements that do not merely liberalise but regulate trade; that deliver for the many and not the few; that evenly distribute the positive effects of trade; and that promote global and binding standards to ensure fiscal fairness, consumer protection, labour rights, and measures against climate change. MEPs may well differ in their views whether the EU's trade agreements live up to these demands and a degree of unevenness is therefore likely to remain.

The Greens, in the run-up to the election, seemed to adopt a moderate position on trade. They published a paper in 2018 that, although critical of trade policy, asserted that "Greens are open to the world; indeed our political stage is the world and the planet. International trade is not our enemy." [49] They argued that the Greens could consider voting in favour of trade agreements if they would be redesigned to fit "a vision of socio-ecological justice of economic policies." Amongst other suggestions, they proposed: (a) constant monitoring of Greenhouse gas emissions during implementation phase; (b) a climate veto in FTAs, that allows for suspending or limiting intellectual property rights if necessary to combat climate change; (c) economic consequences and financial sanctions to be imposed on the trading partner in case of violation of the FTA chapter on trade and sustainable development; and (d) ratification of core International Labour Organisation (ILO) standards as a condition prior to parliamentary consent. It remains doubtful Green MEPs will be satisfied that these suggestions are met.

GUE has been consistent in arguing that trade liberalisation has led to social and ecological destruction and that trade deals are designed in the interests of big business and multinationals. In a recent post on their website, GUE has argued

---

[47]The opposition to the agreement with Ghana rested in part on the belief that the agreement could damage the regional integration process in West-Africa.

[48]Global Progressive Forum, For the Many; not the Few. A progressive model for international trade and investment, December 2018, https://www.socialistsanddemocrats.eu/sites/default/files/international%20trade%20and%20investment_181205_en.pdf (last accessed 7 April 2020), p. 6.

[49]The Greens/European Free Alliance, Green Trade for All, A Greens/EFA paper adopted on 12 June 2018, http://extranet.greens-efa-service.eu/public/media/file/1/5646, p. 1 (last accessed 7 April 2020).

that recent agreements with Vietnam and Singapore contain provisions that have "deep implications for citizens' rights, the environment, and even democracy."[50] GUE is not expected to change its views in the next years.[51]

Finally, Identity and Democracy is at heart a nationalist group that is not likely to warm to trade liberalisation. They profess that "the opposition to any transfer of national sovereignty to [. . .] European institutions is one of the fundamental principles uniting members of the ID party" [52] and this principle sits uncomfortably with trade policy which is an exclusive policy of the EU. Having said this, German members have argued in INTA in favour of trade agreements with some countries and Italian Lega Nord MEPs have voted in favour of the trade agreement with Japan in December 2018, when Lega Nord was part of the Government. The coherence within the group against trade policy may therefore be more patchy than anticipated.

5 Results so Far in This European Parliament

At the time of writing, the ninth legislature has voted on consent for three trade agreements and has considered six Delegated Acts. Objection to a Delegated Act is rare. Across all policy areas, the Council has in its history so far blocked two Delegated Acts, whereas the European Parliament has rejected seven. None of these concerned trade policy. It does not follow that individual political groups have not tried to seek the rejection of trade-related Delegated Acts. The political group GUE, for instance, asked for a plenary vote in April of 2017 to reject a Delegated Act that concerned the amount of unilateral market access Sri Lanka was entitled to under the GSP Regulation. They were not successful. Between 2014 and 2019, DG Trade produced 35 Delegated Acts for adoption by the Commission and the European Parliament objected to none of them. The new European Parliament continues in this vein. INTA has not voted on any of the six Delegated Acts it has so far considered and absence of action means non-objection. Most of the Delegated Acts were routine, with the exception of a Delegated Act through which the Commission proposed to partially withdraw Cambodia's preferential access to the EU market. As a least developed country, Cambodia benefits from duty-free, quota-free access to the EU market under the EU's Everything But Arms' (EBA) trade scheme, which is part of the GSP Regulation. The Commission decided on partial withdrawal due "to the serious and systematic violations of the human rights

---

[50]GUE, The EU-Vietnam Free Trade Agreement—an explainer, https://www.guengl.eu/issues/explainers/the-eu-vietnam-free-trade-agreement-an-explainer/, 11 February 2020 (last accessed 7 April 2020).

[51]Exceptionally, for the Accession of Ecuador to the Colombia/Peru Agreement, 22 out of 46 voted in favour or abstained. This was largely due to the fact that the rapporteur, Mr Scholz, was a Member of GUE. The group position, nonetheless, was to vote against the agreement.

[52]ID, Sovereignty, https://www.id-party.eu/ (last accessed 7 April 2020).

principles enshrined in the International Covenant on Civil and Political Rights."[53] This was the first time the Commission decided on partial withdrawal of preferences. Yet INTA group coordinators decided not to raise objections to this far-reaching decision on 1 April 2020.

The European Parliament has voted on three trade agreements. In December 2019, the European Parliament overwhelmingly accepted the accession of the Solomon Islands to an already existing agreement—the Pacific Economic Partnership Agreement (EPA)—with 534 votes in favour, 145 against and 13 abstentions. Given that the Pacific EPA was already in force and given the small size of the economy of the Solomon Islands, the first real test-case for how the new European Parliament positions itself on trade came in February 2020, when it voted on the Free Trade Agreement (FTA) as well as the Investment Protection Agreement (IPA) with Vietnam. In total, 62.8% of the MEPs who cast a vote, voted in favour of the FTA and 63.4% did so for the IPA. What conclusion can be drawn from this vote? First of all, one needs to be aware that the European Parliament's vote did not come without strings attached. INTA, its Chairman Mr Lange (S&D), and the rapporteur Mr Bourgeois (ECR) demanded progress from Vietnam on human rights, the adoption of the reform of the Labour code, clear timelines for the ratification of core ILO Conventions, and a work plan for the implementation of the FTA's chapter on trade and sustainable development. Only when the European Parliament was satisfied that Vietnam had made sufficient headway did the vote go ahead. The European Parliament took ownership of the file and acted independently in deciding what it wanted before it proceeded to vote. This may well be the model they envisage for other trade agreements too. Secondly, the number of MEPs supporting the agreement was higher than most observers had expected. In Fig. 2, one can see how this vote compares to previously adopted agreements. The agreements fared better than the CETA and the EPAs with southern Africa and with Ghana, but just fell short of the percentages accorded to the agreements with Singapore and Japan.

Thirdly, the data for the individual groups are also worth considering. The percentage of S&D MEPs voting in favour was respectively 73.6% and 73.4% (see again Fig. 1). These percentages were higher than for any other bilateral trade agreement in the eighth legislature, with the exception of the agreement with Ecuador. The French MEPs from Renew Europe predominantly backed the agreements, but the fact that 91.1% of Renew Europe MEPs voted in favour of the FTA should not hide that the MEPs debated long and hard about the merits of the two agreements.[54] And 21% of the MEPs of the ECR cast a vote abstaining or voting against the FTA. This resulted in a percentage of ECR members voting in favour that

---

[53]Commission decides to partially withdraw Cambodia's preferential access to the EU market, 12 February 2020, https://trade.ec.europa.eu/doclib/press/index.cfm?id=2113 (last accessed 7 April 2020).

[54]For a good summary of such deliberations, see the personal explanation of his vote by Mr Canfin, "Pourquoi je ne voterai pas contre l'accord commercial avec le Vietnam": https://www.linkedin.com/pulse/pourquoi-je-ne-voterai-pas-contre-laccord-commercial-avec-canfin (last accessed 7 April 2020).

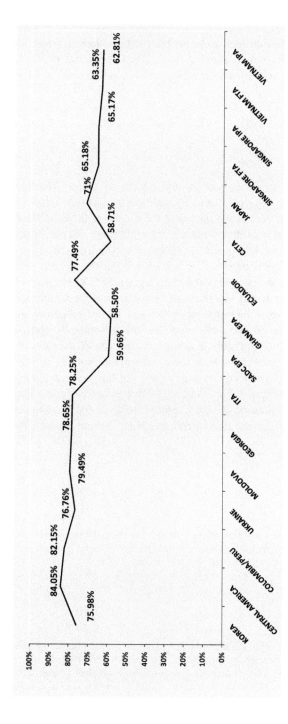

Fig. 2 Share of 'YES'-Votes for Trade Agreements in % of Total Votes Cast in the EP (February 2011–February 2020) [Calculated on the basis of the European Parliament voting records. See also https://www.europarl.europa.eu/plenary/en/votes.html?tab=votes (last accessed 20 July 2020)]

was lower than for any trade agreement in the eight legislature (see Table 1). One explanation for this is that Italian and Spanish members of the ECR voted against the FTA arguing that they needed to protect agricultural interests like the rice sector which, in their view, would stand to lose. The Greens and GUE voted in large numbers against the agreements but a handful of ID politicians from Germany voted in favour.

6 Conclusion

The European Parliament has been through a turbulent period from May 2019 until summer 2020. During this time, it had to manage the outcome of the elections, face the consequences of Brexit, and deal with the impact of the COVID-19 crisis. The European Parliament is probably not yet set in its ways and the positioning of the political groups can still be expected to evolve, something that the matter of recovery from the pandemic crisis may further influence.[55] All the same, a few conclusions can be drawn from the first year of the ninth legislature. The European Parliament is institutionally stronger than before given the support of the Commission President for a right of initiative of the European Parliament, her unambiguous commitment to seeking the European Parliament's views before provisionally applying any trade agreement, and her calls for more transparency. In terms of numbers and strength of the political groups, there have been clear winners and losers after the election, but the equation to get to a majority on trade agreement can continue to have at its core a coalition of EPP, Renew Europe and ECR. But to ensure a safe majority and to ensure the broad legitimacy, the S&D group's support (partial or not) will remain imperative. The vote on the two agreements with Vietnam bears testimony to this conclusion.

Reference

Martins Gistelinck M (2020) Multilevel party politics and trade: the case of the social democrats in the European Parliament and the German Social Democratic Party. In: Broscheck J, Goff P (eds) The multilevel politics of trade. University of Toronto Press

---

[55]Due to the COVID19 crisis, the Members of Parliament are, for instance, weighing up again the need for screening of predatory foreign investment, the need for a multilateral rules-based order, the resilience of supply chains, the wisdom of relying on a limited number of countries for the supply of critical goods, and more. This in turn is leading to a debate about how to ensure the availability of such critical goods and subsequently about the pros and cons of diversification, reshoring, near-shoring, strategic autonomy and in some cases even self-sufficiency.

Gijs Berends is deputy Head of Unit in the unit for inter-institutional relations in DG Trade. His most recent publication appeared in the *South African Journal of International Affairs* in 2017 under the title "What does the EU-SADC EPA really say? An analysis of the economic partnership agreement between the European Union and Southern Africa." He previously co-edited the volume *After the Great East Japan Earthquake: Political and Policy Change in Post-Fukushima Japan* (NIAS Press). Other publications have appeared in the *Journal of World Trade*, the *European Law Review*, and the *Food and Drug Law Journal*. He holds degrees from the universities of Rotterdam and Cambridge.

The WTO's Crisis: Between a Rock and a Hard Place

Jelena Bäumler

Contents

Abstract The perception of the World Trade Organization (WTO) is currently one of an organization in crisis. Yet, appraisal varies regarding its extent and seriousness: Is it merely a rough time or are we standing on the edge of destruction? The article will trace developments inside as well as outside of the WTO in order to assess the magnitude of the crisis. It will be argued that while certain developments inside the Organization, when seen in accumulation would already warrant serious attention, only together with developments taking place outside of the WTO, the two strands of developments unfold their full potential for the crisis. The overall situation renders

J. Bäumler (✉)
Leuphana University Lüneburg, Lüneburg, Germany
e-mail: jelena.baeumler@leuphana.de

© Springer Nature Switzerland AG 2020   321
M. Bungenberg et al. (eds.), *European Yearbook of International Economic Law 2020*,
European Yearbook of International Economic Law (2022) 11: 321–358,
https://doi.org/10.1007/8165_2020_60, Published online: 23 January 2021

the WTO in a difficult position, as it is currently unable to adapt to these challenges, while keeping calm and carrying on might similarly lead to its dissolution. While States might improve and further develop their trade relations in bi- and plurilateral agreements, it is only the WTO that reflects and stands for the multilateral post (cold) war order, which may be gradually fading in the years to come.

1 Introduction

The WTO is not just any international organization. In many ways, it may serve as proof for the development of the post-Cold War era towards an international rule of law, setting regulations for a globalized market order as well as pursuing an unrestrained multilateral approach with an international organization potentially accessible for all States. It bears some of its defining features exactly from its creation during a very special time in history at the end of the Cold War, overcoming some elements that have played out as perceived weaknesses of other international organizations, including its precise and binding rules, a common framework without much room for reservations[1] and a compulsory dispute settlement system including an oversight mechanism for its implementation. And indeed, in the years following its creation, the WTO appeared well-designed, efficient and robust. It attracted ever more members, spanning an almost universal net of economic relations around the globe,[2] its rules being broadly accepted and observed. In case a dispute arose, relatively fast proceedings would settle the dispute peacefully and in the majority of cases, the rulings were actually implemented.[3] One could even go as far as claiming that the WTO overcame the 'compliance trilemma'[4] of international law by providing for widespread participation, ambitious legal norms and high

---

[1]Generally, reservations are not allowed according to Article XVI:5 of the Agreement Establishing the World Trade Agreement (WTO Agreement) 1994, 1867 UNTS 154, except if provided in the respective agreement (e.g. Articles 15.1. Technical Barriers to Trade Agreement (TBT Agreement), 18.2. Anti-Dumping Agreement (ADA), 32.2. of the WTO Agreement on Subsidies and Countervailing Measures 1994, 1867 UNTS 14 (SCM), 72 of the WTO Agreement on Trade-Related Aspects of Intellectual Property Rights 1994 UNTS 299 (TRIPS), Annex III 2–4 Custom Valuation Agreement for developing countries, approval is required by the other members. Nevertheless, there is little actual relevance as can be inferred from the list of members' reservations, Doc G/VAL/W/311.

[2]Currently 164 members, see https://www.wto.org/english/thewto_e/whatis_e/tif_e/org6_e.htm (last accessed 10 June 2020).

[3]DG Azevêdo mentioned in his statement on occasion of the 25th anniversary of the conclusion of the Uruguay Round on 12 September 2019; that "To date, the WTO has dealt with almost 600 trade disputes. Many disputes are resolved before they reach the litigation stage, but when they do proceed to that stage compliance with rulings is very high, at around 90 per cent." See https://www.wto.org/english/news_e/spra_e/spra280_e.htm (last accessed 4 June 2020).

[4]Dunoff (2019), p. 198.

compliance rates all at the same time. Criticism, albeit sometimes fierce and loud, rather appeared as a mandate to improve and further develop the organization, than calling into question its general functionality or its very right of existence. Overall, one may say, at least when viewed in isolation, that the WTO was a success story in theory and practice.

These glorious days seem to be over. The WTO has slipped into a deep crisis. The challenges are posed by developments inside as well as outside the WTO and have squeezed the organization into a position that leaves it with little room for manoeuvre. Inside the WTO, the members interact with a changed tone and attitude towards each other and the organization itself. Critique on the design of the rules, both procedural and substantive, constant and undisguised violations, accusations of overreach of the Dispute Settlement Body (DSB)'s mandate leading ultimately to the destruction of the Appellate Body (AB) as well as the inability to reform existing or to conclude new agreements due to incompatible and uncompromising positions of its members have weakened and undermined the WTO. At the same time, developments outside the WTO backfire negatively onto the multilateral institution and increasingly relegate it to the side-lines. First, and foremost, the proliferation of preferential trade agreements, in a quantitative as well as in qualitative dimension, have eroded one of its main principles, namely non-discrimination and have brought about the renationalisation of products. Second, this increasingly leads to negotiations and the actual standard setting for international trade outside the WTO. Multilateralism, a global approach and perception of the WTO as the main negotiation forum is thereby considerably put in question.

Has thus, we may wonder, the WTO reached peak-law and will crumble in the years to come? Of course, wise scholars remind us that this is not the first time that serious turbulences and trade wars in the international economic order albeit extremely worrying at the time, did, in the end, not translate into destruction, but eventually even into the next step of integration and a strengthening of the global institution.[5] A prudent mindset might especially be important in order not to create damage by overemphasizing the 'crises-narrative'. Yet, at the same time, on the edge of disruptive developments sleep wandering by just believing in the resilience of an institution when it is already on the glimpse of collapsing would similarly prevent from comprehending the seriousness of the current state of affairs as well as analysing realistically proposals for a way out of the crisis. For the WTO at least, the accumulation of recent developments warrants a careful assessment.

The analysis will depart from analysing core developments taking place inside (Sect. 2), as well as outside the WTO (Sect. 3) that led to the current crisis. Against this background, it will be explored whether International Economic Law in general and the WTO in particular rather straddle on the rise or decline side (or both) of current international law life and discusses reasons for and ways out of the crisis (Sect. 4), before offering some concluding remarks.

---

[5]Kurtz (2019), see https://papers.ssrn.com/sol3/papers.cfm?abstract_id=3469496 (last accessed 4 June 2020), p. 3.

2 Developments Inside the WTO

Former Director General Roberto Azevêdo conflated that: "[. . .] the global economic order is under severe strain. Powerful voices claim that national well-being is hurt, not helped, by international rules."[6] The reasons for this assessment will be traced along four main developments: First, it is now—at the latest—more probable than not that the so-called Doha Development Agenda (DDA)[7] may never be concluded and consequently, some of the initial promises made during the Uruguay Round towards especially developing countries will not be honoured. At the same time, the failure also diminishes hope for the general 'reformability' of the WTO, rendering the Organization with the set of rules as they currently stand, which are regularly perceived by a wide variety of members as unsatisfactory (Sect. 2.1). Second, obvious and systemic violations in open disregard of the rules and agreements are unfolding their damaging effects on the ability of the WTO to effectively guarantee fair and open markets and the perception that most members observe most rules most of the time[8] (Sect. 2.2). Third, in the peaceful years, the WTO has failed to clarify its role in situations of increased tensions between its members, rendering security exceptions and countermeasures as two open flanks in the current escalating trade wars (Sect. 2.3). Fourth, the destruction of the Appellate Body by one member, paired with the inability of all others to unite against the rioter leave one of its main organs with amputated power that will have negative effects over and above the dispute settlement system, but for the Organization as a whole (Sect. 2.4).

2.1 *No Progress in the DDA and the Forecast of an Everlasting 'Reformstau'*

In 2001, when the DDA was launched, the decision appeared timely: not only did it reflect a uniting moment after 9/11, but it was also a strong signal to developing country members that the promises made during the Uruguay Round had an actual chance of being kept. The Doha Declaration expressly stated that "[t]he majority of WTO members are developing countries. We seek to place needs and interests at the heart of the Work Programme adopted in this Declaration."[9]

---

[6]WTO, DG Azevêdo: We're in danger of forgetting the lessons from Bretton Woods, 17 October 2019, https://www.wto.org/english/news_e/spra_e/spra287_e.htm (last accessed 4 June 2020).

[7]World Trade Organization, Ministerial Declaration of 14 November 2001, WTO Doc. WT/MIN (01)/DEC/1. (Doha Declaration).

[8]Borrowed from the famous statement by Louis Henkin that "[a]lmost all nations observe almost all principles of international law and almost all of their obligations almost all of the time", Henkin (1979), p. 47.

[9]Doha Declaration, para 2.

The beginning of the Round was indeed sanguine: Members expressed priority for improving the situation of developing countries and everyone showed strong motivation to reach compromise.[10] The initial positive atmosphere became soon overshadowed by disputes over the so-called Singapore issues[11] and the high expectations met with little actual proposals by developed countries, especially the EU and the US, in core sensitive areas such as subsidies and sectors, in particular agriculture.[12] As the years went by, the situation turned grimmer. The only agreement that could be achieved ever since the Uruguay Round[13] is the Trade Facilitation Agreement (TFA) that was concluded in Bali in 2013,[14] eventually entering into force on 22 February 2017.[15] The agreement requires accessibility and transparency of information regarding import and export and aims at smoothing and easing all processes related to cross-border trade.[16] Albeit it features an entire section on special and differential treatment,[17] it does not tackle or resolve any of the hard questions of the DDA for the developing countries.

Concerning the important systemic topics of the DDA, by now at the latest, it appears more probable than not that a compromise for those topics will not be reached any time soon.[18] For the ongoing every day import and export of goods and services, this might not be overly problematic. The real problem lies in the failure of having delivered on the Round: developing members felt that not even in a

---

[10]Id., e.g. Subsidies in agriculture (para. 13); market-access for non-agriculture products (para 16); interaction between trade and competition policy (para. 24); trade facilitation (para. 27); trade and transfer of technology (para. 37); technical cooperation and capacity building (paras 38–41); least-developed countries (paras. 42–43); special and differential treatment (para. 44); see also para 4 for the commitment to the WTO "as the unique forum for global trade rule-making".

[11]ICTSD, The Singapore Issues: Investment, Competition Policy, Transparency in Government Procurement and Trade Facilitation. 1 Doha Round Briefing Series 6, February 2003, https://www.iisd.org/sites/default/files/publications/wto_doha_singapore_issues.pdf   (last   accessed 1 October 2020).

[12]Especially export subsidies are a major part of the broader package in the agriculture negotiations. Yet, the draft text for ministers to agree in Bali (that ended with the 2013 Bali Ministerial Declaration on Export Competition) stops short of making legal commitments. See https://www.wto.org/english/thewto_e/minist_e/mc9_e/brief_agneg_e.htm#generalservices   (last   accessed 10 June 2020) and https://www.wto.org/english/news_e/news13_e/agng_23may13_e.htm#export (last accessed 5 June 2020).

[13]WTO, The WTO at Twenty: Challenges and achievements, September 2015, https://www.wto.org/english/res_e/booksp_e/wto_at_twenty_e.pdf (last accessed 1 October 2020), concludes that the WTO has achieved much over its first 20 years but the success of the WTO has inevitably given rise to new challenges.

[14]Final Text in Decision of 27 November 2014, WT/L/940, the TFA is a Protocol to WTO Agreement.

[15]After obtaining the two-thirds acceptance of the Agreement from its 164 Members.

[16]See especially Articles 1 and 5 (Publication and availability of information) and Article 10 (Formalities connected with importation, exportation on transit) of the TFA.

[17]Articles 13–22 Section II of the TFA.

[18]See Lester (2016), p. 64 and Cho S, Is the WTO Passé? Exploring the Meaning of the Doha Debacle. 1 May 2009, http://ssrn.com/abstract=1403464 (last accessed 1 October 2020), p. 7.

negotiation round that had their interest at the heart of the agenda and not even with regard to specific commodities or sectors was there enough determination of developed members to enter into binding commitments that would bring about actual changes to the situation of developing and least-developed members.[19] In fact, the single commodity cotton—for which the DSB had even confirmed the incompatibility of US subsidies with current WTO agreements[20]—was often perceived as a litmus test, that had however failed, and with it the entire Round.[21] The last Ministerial Conference in Buenos Aires in 2017 ended without a common Ministerial declaration and produced only a small number of Ministerial Decisions on five issues[22] as well as several joint statements supported by a varying subgroup of members.[23]

In a more general way, the unwillingness and inability to conclude the Round almost 20 years after its initiation casts serious doubt on the general 'reformability' of the WTO by consensus among the currently 164 members.[24] Important areas in which little or no progress could be made in the last decade include digital trade, e-commerce and related aspects of data flows, which are often perceived as some of the most pressing issues for the future development of global trade.[25] The General

---

[19]See Matthews A, Food Security and WTO Domestic Support Disciplines post-Bali, ICTSD Programme on Agricultural Trade and Sustainable Development. ICTSD, 2014, http://ageconsearch.umn.edu/record/160370/files/01-Matthews%20-%20EAAE%20135.pdf (last accessed 1 October 2020), p. 4.

[20]WTO, *United States — Subsidies on Upland Cotton*, WT/DS267.

[21]The Cotton-4 (Benin, Burkina Faso, Chad and Mali). Anderson K and Valenzuela E, The World Trade Organization's Doha Cotton Initiative: A Tale of Two Issues. World Bank, Policy Research Working Paper No. 3918, May 2006, http://documents.worldbank.org/curated/en/247241468010473451/pdf/wps3918.pdf (last accessed 1 October 2020); Ministerial Decision of Bali on Cotton (2013), reiterates members' commitment to "on-going dialogue and engagement" to make progress in the negotiations on cotton according to the 2005 objectives of the Hong Kong Ministerial Conference (WT/MIN(13)/41 WT/L/916).

[22]Work programmes on Fisheries (WT/MIN(17)/64), e-commerce (WT/MIN(17)65) and Small Economies (WT/MIN(17)/63) and a decision on the prolongation of TRIPS and non-violation complaints (WT/MIN(17)/66).

[23]WT/MIN(17)/61 Joint Ministerial statement on services domestic regulation; WT/MIN(17)/60 Joint statement on Electronic Commerce WT/MIN(17)/59; Joint ministerial statement on Investment Facilitation for Development WT/MIN(17)/58; Joint Ministerial statement—Declaration on the establishment of a WTO informal work programme for MSMES.

[24]See https://www.wto.org/english/thewto_e/whatis_e/tif_e/org6_e.htm (last accessed 31 May 2020).

[25]See https://www.wto.org/english/tratop_e/ecom_e/ecom_e.htm (last accessed 31 May 2020) and also Meltzer J P, WTO reform agenda. Data flows and international regulatory cooperation. Brookings Institute, Working Paper No. 130, September 2019, https://www.brookings.edu/wp-content/uploads/2019/09/WTO-ReformAgenda_final.pdf (last accessed 1 October 2020) this stands in stark contrast to FTAs having regularly incorporated e-commerce chapters into their coverage; see e.g. Wu M, Digital trade-related provisions in regional trade agreements: existing models and lessons for the multilateral trade system. RTA Exchange, Overview Paper, November 2017, https://rtaexchange.org/pdf/Digital%20Trade%20Related%20Provisions%20in%20RTA_%20WU.pdf (last accessed 1 October 2020), p. 6.

Agreement on Trade in Services (GATS) is still to a certain extent opaque and much less powerful than the General Agreement on Tariffs and Trade (GATT).[26] Any positive effects out of the Trade in Services Agreement (TISA) negotiations cannot be expected since the abrupt end of this process.[27] The same holds true for rules on currencies, competition and investment. In the same vein, so-called 'trade and' issues have not progressed. The initiative on an Environmental Goods Agreements (EGA) has not been further developed since 2015.[28] No reactivation of the former 'green box' subsidies under the Subsidies and Countervailing Measures Agreement (SCM) has taken place that would enable members to support green energy or environmentally friendly industries on a clear legal basis.[29] Similarly, the conclusion of an agreement on fishery subsidies planned for the end of 2019 was again postponed for another year.[30] Human rights and labour rights remain issues outside standing WTO agreements and the relationship is still disputed.[31] In short, hardly any visible progress was made in any significant core area of future trade challenges in the last decade. All those topics further the perception that the WTO is to a certain extent incomplete, especially when those areas have the potential of undermining or calling into question the legitimacy of other existing WTO commitments.[32]

The perception of incompleteness of the WTO agreements has recently been openly instrumentalised as a core defence argument in the US written statement in the so-called Section 301 dispute with China.[33] Besides its rather confusing construction of the relationship between domestic and international law, the US argues that the incompleteness renders the WTO partially illegitimate.[34] Consequently, in view of the US, the Panel should allow justification of the measures taken against China under the public morals exception of Article XX(a) GATT, based on the assumption that,

---

[26]General Agreement on Tariffs and Trade (GATT) 1994, 1867 UNTS 187; General Agreement on Trade in Services (GATS) 1994, 1869 UNTS 183.

[27]In themselves problematic due to their open relationship with WTO. Yet, the negotiations on TISA are now on hold, see https://ec.europa.eu/trade/policy/in-focus/tisa/ (last accessed 2 June 2020).

[28]See https://www.wto.org/english/tratop_e/envir_e/ega_e.htm (last accessed 5 June 2020).

[29]Genest (2014), p. 10.

[30]Negotiations on fisheries subsidies were launched in 2001 at the Doha Ministerial Conference, and at the eleventh Ministerial Conference held in Buenos Aires in 2017, WTO members agreed to conclude the agreement on fisheries subsidies which delivers on Sustainable Development Goal 14.6 by the end of 2019 (now postponed to be agreed in 2021 in Nur-Sultan).

[31]See on this discussion Petersmann (2000), pp. 19–25.

[32]Relation of currency and competition with trade; see further below US argument in WTO, *United States — Tariff Measures on Certain Goods from China*, WT/DS543, 27 August 2019.

[33]WTO, *United States — Tariff Measures on Certain Goods from China*, WT/DS543, see https://www.wto.org/english/ratop_e/dispu_e/cases_e/ds543_e.htm (last accessed 10 June 2020).

[34]"China's policy and practice of state-sanctioned theft [. . .] violates prevailing U.S. 'standards of right and wrong' as reflected in the state and federal laws of the United States, under which the act of 'theft' is universally deemed a criminal offense.", US Written statement in WT/DS543, para. 74, see https://ustr.gov/sites/default/files/enforcement/DS/US.Sub1.%28DS543%29.fin.%28public%29.pdf (last accessed 1 October 2020).

China's morally wrong behaviour further threatens to undermine U.S. society's belief in the fairness and utility of the WTO trading system, if that system creates the conditions for, and fails to address, a fundamentally uneven playing field.[35]

Although the argument might stand little chance of success, it reflects a deep discontent of a central WTO member about what it perceives as inchoateness and deficient functioning of the WTO rules regarding unfair trade policies not covered by current WTO agreements. Although the WTO never claimed to provide coverage of all aspects relevant for the economic relations among its members, the US position leaves the Panel in a dire situation and tone and arguments by the US certainly hung a Damocles sword over the Panel's head.

On a more general note, an organisation that functions on rules that are locked-in in history without an actual chance of adaptation to prevailing challenges in an area that is constantly posing new questions and challenges by a vivid global market and under close scrutiny by national societies might stand an imminent risk of becoming of ever lesser interest to its members over time.[36]

2.2   Broken Windows in the WTO House: Systemic Violations and Their Effects on the Functioning of the WTO

According to the broken windows theory,

> if a window in a building is broken and left unrepaired, all the rest of the windows will soon be broken [because] one unrepaired broken window is a signal that no one cares, and so breaking more windows costs nothing.[37]

This section does not focus on violations of particular rules, it will rather aim to identify violations that are signs for broken windows that no one is willing or able to repair in the WTO legal order. In fact, in the last decade and even before trade tensions escalated into full-fledged trade wars, smashing ever more windows of the trade rules house, were worrying signs of systematic violations of agreements by an increasing number of members against each other.

One of the evergreens of WTO law in this regard is dumping and the corresponding anti-dumping measures.[38] Regulating dumping is at the heart of a liberal market order, prohibiting members to introduce products into foreign markets

---

[35]Ibid., para. 76.

[36]Increasingly covering those issues in bi- and plurilateral agreements, see Sect. 2.3.

[37]Kelling and Wilson (1982): "Window-breaking does not necessarily occur on a large scale because some areas are inhabited by determined window-breakers whereas others are populated by window-lovers; rather, one unrepaired broken window is a signal that no one cares, and so breaking more windows costs nothing."

[38]See on the ADA in general https://www.wto.org/english/tratop_e/adp_e/adp_e.htm (last accessed 10 June 2020).

below the market value.[39] In the background of the very technical regulatory framework around the determination of the market value of a product, two main issues keep reappearing in WTO disputes on a more systemic level. First, how can the framework be applied fairly and equally when some members provide for strong state-driven elements in their economy,[40] especially but not restricted to China? Second, what is the allowed response, including in terms of the obligation and extent of investigations and the fixing of the dumping margin especially with regard to the technique of so-called "zeroing"?

The Anti-Dumping Agreement (ADA) stands as a reflection face and fault line for the harmonious coexistence of fundamentally different economic models under one common economic legal framework as well as the good faith of the members to observe and abide by the rules of that framework. The ADA is one of the most frequently cited agreements in WTO disputes[41] and the usage of its instruments has sparked over the last decade. While formerly dumping allegations and imposing of anti-dumping measures occurred among the usual suspects,[42] since a number of years it appears like an all-time favourite instrument by any member against any other member.[43] An increasing number of products is targeted by anti-dumping measures, often correlating exactly with a domestic market under pressure in the respective member State.[44] Until 2016 the system at least concerning China[45] was more or less stable, with its special status according to the accession protocol.[46] With the expiration of the respective clause, a dispute arose between China and several members as to the applicable proceeding for anti-dumping measures against Chinese

---

[39]See Article VI GATT and ADA https://www.wto.org/english/tratop_e/adp_e/adp_info_e.htm (last accessed 10 June 2020).

[40]"Market Economy": Economy in which fundamentals of supply and demand provide signals regarding resource utilization, see Gregory and Stuart (2004), p. 538. On the contrary, a "state-driven or directed economy" can be defined as a model whereby the State is instrumental in guiding economic development, based on the rule of the market, see Che (2019).

[41]A list of disputes citing the ADA can be found here: https://www.wto.org/english/tratop_e/dispu_e/dispu_agreements_index_e.htm?id=A6#selected_agreement (last accessed 1 October 2020).

[42]Usually of developed countries against certain developing countries. See https://docs.wto.org/dol2fe/Pages/FE_Search/FE_S_S006.aspx?Query=(%20@Symbol=%20g/adp/d*)andLanguage=ENGLISHandContext=FomerScriptedSearchandlanguageUIChanged=true# (last accessed 9 June 2020).

[43]See the database on https://www.wto.org/english/tratop_e/adp_e/adp_e.htm; https://www.wto.org/english/tratop_e/adp_e/AD_InitiationsByExpCty.pdf (last accessed 1 October 2020).

[44]By mid-2019 a total of 5725 anti-dumping initiations since 1995 have been surveyed with an increasing tendency https://www.wto.org/english/tratop_e/adp_e/AD_InitiationsByExpCty.pdf (1 last accessed 1 October 2020).

[45]In fact, 90% of products from China were subjected to anti-dumping or countervailing measures before 2019, see Bown C P, The 2018 US-China Trade Conflict After 40 Years of Special Protection. Peterson Institute for International Economics, Working Paper, April 2019, https://www.piie.com/system/files/documents/wp19-7.pdf (last accessed 1 October 2020), p. 16.

[46]WT/L/432, *Accession of the People's Republic of China*, Decision of 10 November 2001.

allegedly dumped products.[47] Yet, a WTO dispute that could have provided clarity was suspended by China just before the report came out, leaving this important and systemic question unresolved.[48] With regard to calculating the actual dumping margin, the practice of so-called zeroing has been constantly ruled out by panels and the Appellate Body. The by now more than 30 disputes that have dealt with this particular technique of calculating the dumping margin[49] and the constant refusal by the US to ultimately adjust its practice of zeroing can by now be categorized as a systemic challenge for the WTO. In fact, violations of the ADA by both exporting and importing members can thus be categorised as one of the broken windows that appears as not receiving reparation.

A similar observation holds true for subsidies and countervailing measures. China is also in the focus for its interwoven economic structure and the constant accusation of subsidies in all kinds of areas.[50] Yet, systemic challenges with regard to subsidies is not all restricted to China. In several disputes the DSB has confirmed that subsidies even in the agricultural sector can be reviewed and be found illegal under the SCM, at least if they cause injury to another member.[51] The EU and the US, nonetheless, by and large, subsidize their agricultural sector in open and blatant disregard of the rules and findings of the DSB.[52] The agreement between the US and Brazil following the Upland Cotton dispute[53] to the detriment of third States, has additionally increased the perception that the DSB is unable to ensure adherence to agreements in general but rather operates as a mechanism to resolve bilateral disputes at which end a bilateral agreement may even worsen the WTO-inconsistent situation for other members.[54] It left behind another broken window unrepaired.

A third example of violations with a systemic implication is related to intellectual property rights leading to the impression that some members are constantly not playing by the rules to establish a fair market order which values intellectual

---

[47]Huo (2002), p. 197.

[48]There can only be speculation about the reasons for China's suspension https://www.reuters.com/article/us-usa-china-wto-eu/china-pulls-wto-suit-over-claim-to-be-a-market-economy-idUSKCN1TI10A (last accessed 9 June 2020).

[49]See Mavroidis and Prusa (2018), pp. 239–264.

[50]Eckhaus (2006), pp. 1–13.

[51]Except there are in conformity with the Agriculture Agreement or do not fulfil the requirements of either Articles 3 or 5 SCM.

[52]Powell and Schmitz (2005), p. 289.

[53]WTO, *United States – Subsidies on Uplan Cotton*, WT/DS267.

[54]The text of the Memorandum of Understanding can be found here: https://ustr.gov/sites/default/files/20141001201606893.pdf (last accessed 15 October 2020); for an analysis see Guitchons (2015), Seventh Multi-year Expert Meeting on Commodities and Development, 15–16 April 2015, https://unctad.org/meetings/en/Presentation/SUC%20MYEM2015%20Andrei%20Guitchounts.pdf (last accessed 15 October 2020).

property rights as agreed upon in the WTO.[55] Numerous disputes against China have confirmed various Chinese practices to constitute violations of WTO agreements, especially but not limited to the Agreement on Trade-Related Aspects of Intellectual Property Rights (TRIPS).[56] And, while this is nothing uncommon, since especially the policies of important market powers are more often under review,[57] the piece-meal approach by China to rectify those shortcomings[58] has led to disappointment over its market-economy commitments, questioning its constructive role for world trade law and the WTO, at least in this particular field.

The steep increase of WTO-inconsistent measures as well as the spark in disputes, but also of countermeasures taken without prior reference to the DSB[59] may, as has been observed by former Appellate Body Member Sacerdoti, rather not be

> an indication of a healthy dispute settlement system. On the contrary, it hints at a looming crisis of the system, and manifests a widespread disrespect of substantive and procedural rules, such as resort to unilateral measures and countermeasures without following the DSU[60] procedures first.[61]

2.3 Two Pandora's Boxes: Trade Wars & Security Exceptions—And an Unhealthy Commonality of the Two

Resorting to measures and countermeasures has especially led to an escalation of tensions between members in clear violation of WTO rules and agreements in what is now regularly labelled as trade wars, first and foremost between the US

---

[55]Bacchus et al., Disciplining China's Trade Practices at the WTO: How WTO Complaints Can Help Make China More Market-Oriented. CATO Institute, Policy Analysis No. 856, 15 November 2018, https://www.cato.org/publications/policy-analysis/disciplining-chinas-trade-practices-wto-how-wto-complaints-can-help (last accessed 2 June 2020).

[56]See China TRIPS Cases: WTO, *China — Measures Affecting the Protection and Enforcement of Intellectual Property Rights*, WT/DS362; WTO, *China — Measures Affecting Financial Informa-tion Services and Foreign Financial Information Suppliers*, WT/DS372; WTO, *China — Measures Affecting the Protection of Intellectual Property Rights*, WT/DS542; and WTO, *China — Certain measures on the transfer of technology*, WT/DS549.

[57]The EC/EU stood as respondent in 96 cases and the US in 156 cases.

[58]China has in fact quite a good record of implementing WTO reports for the 41 disputes that had been brought between 2004–2018, of which 27 had found WTO inconsistent measures, see Bacchus et al. Disciplining China's Trade Practices at the WTO: How WTO Complaints Can Help Make China More Market-Oriented. CATO Institute, Policy Analysis No. 856, 15 November 2018, https://www.cato.org/publications/policy-analysis/disciplining-chinas-trade-practices-wto-how-wto-complaints-can-help (last accessed 2 June 2020); Zhou (2019).

[59]See especially Sect. 2.3.

[60]Understanding on Rules and Procedures Governing the Settlement of Disputes (DSU) 1994, 1869 UNTS 40.

[61]Sacerdoti (2019), pp. 6–7.

and China,[62] but also e.g. between Japan and South Korea[63] and UAE et al. and Qatar.[64] The initial measures, but also the resort to countermeasures have disrespected and violated the rules and procedure provided in the Dispute Settlement Understanding (DSU).[65]

At the heart of those developments lay two different, but interconnected sets of questions, namely the role of the security exceptions clause and Article XXI GATT more generally for the wider WTO system and the relationship between WTO law and general international law when it comes to countermeasures.[66] Both dimensions share the commonality of providing for "a source of new and unexpected problems"[67] as with regard to both, WTO members have failed to develop in more harmonious times clear guidelines for the robustness of WTO law for serious tensions and trade wars, in which WTO members resort to measures and countermeasures that may or may not be covered by the WTO agreements.

2.3.1   How Securely Designed Is the Security Exception Clause?

Article XXI GATT has long been—depending on the perspective—a sleeping beauty or buried landmine in the GATT. It had been included right at the beginning,

---

[62]So-called Section 301 dispute between US and China, WTO, *United States — Tariff Measures on Certain Goods from China*, WT/DS543.

[63]Since 2015, latest development is a request for consultation by Korea, see WTO, *Japan — Measures related to the Exportation of Products and Technology to Korea*, WT/DS590 https://www.wto.org/english/tratop_e/dispu_e/cases_e/ds590_e.htm.

[64]See WTO, *United Arab Emirates — Measures Relating to Trade in Goods and Services, and Trade-Related Aspects of Intellectual Property Rights*, WT/DS526.

[65]Especially in the so called Steel and Aluminium cases, that have also been brought to the attention of the WTO in altogether 12 disputes: WTO, *United States — Certain Measures on Steel and Aluminium Products;* WT/DS544; WTO, *United States — Certain Measures on Steel and Aluminium Products*, WT/DS548; WTO, *United States — Certain Measures on Steel and Aluminium Products*, WT/DS550; WTO, *United States — Certain Measures on Steel and Aluminium Products*, WT/DS551; WTO, *United States — Certain Measures on Steel and Aluminium Products*, WT/DS552; WTO, *United States — Certain Measures on Steel and Aluminium Products*, WT/DS554; WTO, *United States — Certain Measures on Steel and Aluminium Products*, WT/DS556; WTO, *United States — Certain Measures on Steel and Aluminium Products*, WT/DS564; WTO, *United States — Certain Measures on Steel and Aluminium Products*, WT/DS547; WTO, *United States — Certain Measures on Steel and Aluminium Products*, WT/DS556; WTO, *Canada — Additional Duties on Certain Products from the United States*, WT/DS557; WTO, *European Union — Additional Duties on Certain Products from the United States*, WT/DS559.

[66]Please note that the defence by Japan for its measures is not yet, available and not yet predictable.

[67]Cambridge Dictionary, "Pandora's Box".

but for almost 70 years of GATT's life it played no decisive role in any dispute.[68] Yet, the failure to have a clear understanding of the role and meaning of Article XXI GATT is especially frivolous against the background that even at the time of negotiations of the GATT, it was warned, "the atmosphere inside [the organization[69]] will be the only efficient guarantee against abuse."[70] Even back then—and it is not without a certain cynical turn in history—the US delegate brought forward that

> [...] we cannot make it too tight, because we cannot prohibit measures which are needed purely for security reasons. On the other hand, we cannot make it so broad that, under the guise of security, countries will put on measures which really have a commercial focus.[71]

It appears now as if the actual design of Article XXI GATT has not efficiently prevented the anticipated risks. A deteriorated atmosphere and increasing invocation of Article XXI GATT to guise commercial interests seem to have both realized at the same time.

In its first invocation in 2017 by Russia, the 'security measures' actually related to a dispute that was more to the heart of the initial conceptualization of Article XXI GATT, as the Russian measures were indeed imposed at a time of serious dispute over Eastern Ukraine and Crimea between the two members, arguably qualifying as a 'time of war or other emergency in international relations' as stipulated by Article XXI (b) (iii) GATT. Russia prohibited traffic in transit through its territory for Ukrainian products to reach other States.[72] Russia prevailed in the case based on the fulfilment of the preconditions for this subparagraph. The Panel applied an objective-subjective-objective test, in which it examined the objective circumstances for invoking Article XXI GATT, i.e. whether the situation was one of "war or other emergency in international relations" and more on a subjective level whether the member presented arguments for the measures to be taken in order to respond to the security threat and again more objectively whether these arguments were not implausible.[73]

However, the more problematic issue related to Russia's primary line of reasoning in that Russia had argued that the panel lacked jurisdiction for even determining the preconditions of Article XXI GATT, as this provision, in the eyes of Russia was

---

[68]Under the GATT 47 Article XXI (b) (3) became relevant in five disputes, see Analytical Index on Article XXI, pp. 602–605; under GATT 94 only in one panel report, namely *Russia – Traffic in transit*, the provision received broader discussion and was decisive for the outcome of the dispute, see Analytical Index GATT 1994—Article XXI (Jurisprudence), paras 10–14.

[69]International Trade Organization at the time.

[70]Second Session of the Preparatory Committee of the United Nations Conference on Trade and Employment, Verbatim Report, E/PC/T/A/PV/33 (July 24, 1947), 21 (US-41).

[71]EPCT/A/PV/33, 20-1 and Corr.3.

[72]WTO, *Russia — Traffic in Transit*, WT/DS512/R, para 2.1.

[73]Ibid., para 7.56.

a self-judging clause.[74] In view of the wording "nothing in this Agreement shall prevent" in Article XXI GATT, a member may only provide information on the measures it had imposed for security reasons, while any determination

> what essential security interests of a Member are, what actions are necessary for protection of such essential security interests, disclosure of what information may be contrary to the essential security interests of a Member, what constitutes an emergency in international relations, and whether such emergency exists in a particular case [. . .] all [. . .] are outside the scope of the WTO.[75]

The only member that openly supported Russia's view at the time was the USA, now following the same line of argumentation as the defendant in the steel and aluminium cases[76] and in other cases as a third party.[77] Following the panel report in *Russia – Traffic in Transit*, the US has argued that the panel had totally misconstrued Article XXI GATT in that it is upon the member invoking that clause—and that member alone—to apply this provision rendering the dispute outside the scope of jurisdiction of any panel.[78] In comparison to Russia, the US in its defence statements in the steel and aluminium disputes[79] did not even argue the cases further in substance.[80] The US, similarly relies strongly on the wording (especially the word '*considers*') and the negotiating history as well as on a disputed subsequent agreement that in their view confirmed the status of the self-judging character of Article

---

[74]WTO, *Russia — Traffic in Transit, First Executive Summary of the Arguments of the Russian Federation*, WT/DS512/R/Add.1, para 47: "The Russian Federation is of the view that Article XXI (a) and (b) of the GATT is of a self-judging nature. Each of the WTO Members individually and without any external involvement determines what its essential security interests are and how to protect them. Other reading of this Article will result in interference in internal and external affairs of a sovereign state".

[75]WTO, *Russia –Traffic in Transit – First Executive Summary of the Arguments of the Russian Federation*, WT/DS512/R/Add.1, para 60.

[76]WTO, *United States — Certain Measures on Steel and Aluminium Products;* WT/DS544; WTO, *United States — Certain Measures on Steel and Aluminium Products*, WT/DS548; WTO, *United States — Certain Measures on Steel and Aluminium Products*, WT/DS550; WTO, *United States — Certain Measures on Steel and Aluminium Products*, WT/DS551; WTO, *United States — Certain Measures on Steel and Aluminium Products*, WT/DS552; WTO, *United States — Certain Measures on Steel and Aluminium Products*, WT/DS554; WTO, *United States — Certain Measures on Steel and Aluminium Products*, WT/DS556; WTO, *United States — Certain Measures on Steel and Aluminium Products*, WT/DS564; WTO, *United States — Certain Measures on Steel and Aluminium Products*, WT/DS547; WTO, *United States — Certain Measures on Steel and Aluminium Products*, WT/DS556; WTO, *Canada — Additional Duties on Certain Products from the United States*, WT/DS557; WTO, *European Union — Additional Duties on Certain Products from the United States*, WT/DS559.

[77]WTO, *United Arab Emirates — Measures Relating to Trade in Goods and Services, and Trade-Related Aspects of Intellectual Property Rights*, WT/DS526.

[78]WTO, *United States — Certain Measures on Steel and Aluminium* Products, WT/DS552, US Written Statement, paras. 129–179.

[79]Please see fn. 76.

[80]WTO, *United States — Certain Measures on Steel and Aluminium Products, US Written Statement*, WT/DS552.

XXI GATT.[81] The panel in *Russia – Traffic in Transit,* in turn, relied mainly on the object and purpose of the GATT and the DSU of providing security and predictability in international trade relations. Indeed, if all members were allowed to invoke a provision to their own gusto, without any option of jurisdictional oversight that would be a Trojan Horse for any (trade) agreement. Additionally, the Panel considered that any subparagraphs would indeed be superfluous if the only requirement was a declaration of the respective member of having taken the measure for alleged security reasons.[82]

While both arguments have stronger and weaker points, the established instruments of interpretation reach their limits in terms of the underlying question of both views, namely the overall perception and role of the WTO and its agreements more generally. It is this underlying conceptualisation that renders the question so delicate: has the WTO come close to a legal trade order that was not and cannot be meant to have left room for a self-judging clause outside of the jurisdiction of panels and the AB? Or is it still merely an agreement between international sovereigns that finds its boundaries in the exercise of sovereignty of its members when it comes to their security interests? The Panel decided this aspect in the former way, relying on Article 3.2 DSU, the object and purpose of the WTO and the GATT in general and the limitation that follows from that for the interpretation of Article XXI GATT in particular. The US and to a lesser extent Russia openly question this understanding of the GATT and DSU. The US, similarly to its arguments with regard to the role of the DSU,[83] calls upon the members and the DSB to return to a more constrained interpretation on matters related to sovereignty and geopolitics.[84]

Three additional aspects require attention: first, the panel report has not been appealed and, there is not and—as will be seen shortly—there will most probably not be a final and authoritative decision by the AB on the issue any time soon. Of course it is possible that all panels concerned with the question may apply the same reasoning as the one in *Russia – Traffic in Transit.*[85] Yet, it can be expected that ultimately, other members will keep on pursuing the Russia/US-line of argumentation and portray the initial decision as a mere erroneous panel decision without any meaning for other disputes thereby constantly putting in question the legitimate exercise of jurisdiction by a panel in a GATT Article XXI-dispute.[86] Yet, even

---

[81] Namely Decision concerning Article XXI of the General Agreement, L/5426, see ibid, p. 6.

[82] WTO, *Russia — Traffic in Transit, Report of the Panel,* WT/DS512/R, 7.68.

[83] See Sect. 2.2.

[84] Statements Delivered to the General Council by Ambassador Dennis Shea U.S. Permanent Representative to the World Trade Organization, see https://geneva.usmission.gov/2019/10/15/statements-by-the-united-states-at-the-wto-general-council-meeting/ (last accessed 10 June 2020).

[85] The panel followed the *Russia — Traffic in Transit* interpretation with regard to Article 73 TRIPS, WTO, *Saudi Arabia — Measures concerning the Protection of Intellectual Property Rights, Report of the Panel,* WT/DS567/R.

[86] See WTO, *United States — Certain Measures on Steel and Aluminium Products, US Written Statement,* WT/DS552, https://ustr.gov/sites/default/files/enforcement/DS/US.Sub1.%28DS548%29.fin.%28public%29.pdf, paras. 129–179.

though quite unlikely for several reasons, due to the lack of an AB ruling, it is also not impossible that a panel might actually follow the line of reasoning of a defendant and denounce its jurisdiction, which would set a critical example.

Second, there are very few incidences in which the US and Russia have concurring views.[87] Most interestingly and maybe counter-intuitive, China in its third party submission did not share the view that the panel lacked jurisdiction to review Article XXI GATT and argued that indeed the preparatory work as well as the Decision on Article XXI taken on 30 November 1982[88] supported the general reviewability of this provision.[89] Yet, although China and other States agreed on the jurisdiction over Article XXI GATT,[90] it together with a number of other States indeed supported a restrained review of the panel due to the sensitive issues involved.[91] Indeed, it can be presumed that even more members will at least argue for a limited standard of review, once they have invoked Article XXI GATT for measures taken for alleged security reasons.[92]

Third, in comparison to the Russia/Ukraine state of affairs, invocation of the US argumentation in the relations between e.g. the US and the EU—a situation that not even *prima facie,* albeit those States had more harmonious times in their history, comes close to a situation of war or other emergency in their bilateral relations—warrants concern. The US reliance on Article XXI GATT for additional tariffs on steel and aluminium products by the US is thus, on its face, an attempt to justify these tariffs on specific products with regard to which the domestic industry came under pressure. Quite obviously, none of the alternatives of Article XXI (b) (i)–(iii) GATT is fulfilled.[93] Yet, with regard to the US position and despite non-fulfilment of the preconditions of Article XXI (b) GATT, it stands to reason that the US, having not even argued the case further, will not accept or implement a panel decision that confirms jurisdiction on Article XXI GATT and ultimately finds that its preconditions were not met.

However, if really Article XXI GATT was to be accepted as an all-out-option, either by lack of jurisdiction or by a very broad discretion upon its application, this

---

[87]See WTO, *Russia – Traffic in transit- US Third Party Statement,* WT/DS512/R/Add.1, 106.

[88]Decision concerning Article XXI of the General Agreement, L/5426.

[89]WTO, *Russia –Traffic in Transit – Report of the Panel,* WT/DS512/R/Add.1, 82.

[90]Ibid., e.g. Australia, 69; Brazil, 73; Canada, 76; EU, 84; Japan, 89; Singapore, 99.

[91]E.g. Australia, 72; Turkey, 103; to a lesser extent Brazil.

[92]The written Statement by the United Arab Emirates (UAE) is not yet available, but it can be expected that UAE will bring forward a similar argument, see WTO, *United Arab Emirates — Measures Relating to Trade in Goods and Services, and Trade-Related Aspects of Intellectual Property Rights,* WT/DS526.

[93]The text of Article XXI lit. b GATT reads: "(i) relating to fissionable materials or the materials from which they are derived; (ii) relating to the traffic in arms, ammunition and implements of war and to such traffic in other goods and materials as is carried on directly or indirectly for the purpose of supplying a military establishment; (iii) taken in time of war or other emergency in international relations".

would considerably weaken the WTO.[94] Invocation, as envisaged by the US, would allow any State, with regard to a particular economic sector and without the situation coming close to a serious disturbance in the international relations between two states, to impose protectionist measures by simply relying on some kind of security interests. The obvious way of overcoming these uncertainties related to Article XXI GATT at once would be a change of its wording or a general interpretation according to Article XI.2 WTO Agreement, both not very realistic options at present.

2.3.2 Countermeasures in Trade Wars

In the defence in its so-called *Section 301* dispute with China, the US did not ground its measure in a justification based on a particular GATT provision, but it rather argued that the US' measures were lawful countermeasures against what it perceives as "unfair trade practices" by China.[95] The US frankly construed the *US – China Section 301* dispute in essence as follows:

> Fundamentally, both the United States and China have recognized that this matter is not a WTO issue: China has taken the unilateral decision to adopt aggressive industrial policy measures to steal or otherwise unfairly acquire the technology of its trading partners; the United States has adopted tariff measures to try to obtain the elimination of China's unfair and distortive technology-transfer policies; and China has chosen to respond – not by addressing the legitimate concerns of the United States – but by adopting its own tariff measures in an attempt to pressure the United States to abandon its concerns, and thus in an effort to maintain its unfair policies indefinitely.[96]

Thus, according to the US:

> By taking actions in their own sovereign interests, both parties have recognized that this matter does not involve the WTO and have settled the matter themselves. Accordingly, there in fact is no live dispute involving WTO rights and obligations.[97]

The US argument requires attention in two ways: first, the US does not clearly establish that China has been violating international law, rendering a countermeasure argument without merit.[98] Second, and more relevant with regard to its actual perception of the role of the WTO, it argues that measures that by themselves are covered by the WTO agreements, namely a tariff increase on Chinese products, but

---

[94]Voon argues that "…the security exception lies at the center of multiple explosive disputes, posing a potential threat to the WTO's very existence." Voon (2019), p. 45.

[95]WTO, *United States — Tariff Measures on Certain Goods from China, US Written Statement,* WT/DS543.

[96]Ibid., para 9.

[97]Ibid., para. 10.

[98]It has been argued that forced technology transfer could be partially covered by Article 39 TRIPS, see Bacchus et al. Disciplining China's Trade Practices at the WTO: How WTO Complaints Can Help Make China More Market-Oriented. CATO Institute, Policy Analysis No. 856, 15 November 2018, https://www.cato.org/publications/policy-analysis/disciplining-chinas-trade-practices-wto-how-wto-complaints-can-help (last accessed 2 June 2020).

that responds to measures *outside* the scope of the WTO agreements, were also to fall outside the WTO *ratione materiae*.[99]

The underlying question of whether countermeasures are possible by resorting to general international law or whether the GATT is (still in this sense) a self-contained regime is contested.[100] The general possibility of imposing countermeasures has been rejected for a number of reasons.[101] Leaving aside the question whether the preconditions for countermeasures under general international law were actually fulfilled in the US-China relations or not, from the viewpoint of WTO-law, two arguments oppose this suggestion outright: first, according to the WTO rules members are required to follow a sequence of steps before imposing measures to counter WTO-inconsistent measures.[102] Yet, the direct resort to countermeasures would open a second path unforeseen by the rules in the WTO agreements. Second, if members were allowed to respond to violations that undoubtedly are outside the scope of current WTO agreements, by resorting to measures regulated within the WTO thereby violating their WTO commitments, this would open the economic toolbox despite having committed to certain e.g. tariffs with regard to a certain product towards all members.[103] The immediate question would be whether members could only react to measures related to economic aspects or whether they could also rely on other international law violations, such as violations of environmental obligations or the law of the sea. Yet, allowance of instrumentalisation of economic measures as response to any kind of international law violation or even measures not in breach of international law and ultimately for reaching geopolitical aims would exactly weaken a stable and predictable legal framework for international trade relations.

2.3.3 An Uncomfortable Commonality

Another dimension of the current trade conflicts signals a decrease in respect for the WTO framework, namely the reactions by those against which the measures were addressed, reacting WTO inconsistent themselves, albeit maybe less from a moral but from a legal point of view.

The WTO order is based on a strict sequence of steps to be followed in case of a WTO violation by a member before allowing resort to countermeasures.[104] After consultations, a panel is established, an appeal must be awaited and only after a

---

[99]WTO, *United States — Tariff Measures on Certain Goods from China, US Written Statement, WT/DS543*, paras. 9–10.

[100]Pauwelyn (2019a), p. 535.

[101]Ibid., p. 538.

[102]See Sect. 2.3.

[103]See the schedules of concessions of each member here: https://www.wto.org/english/tratop_e/schedules_e/goods_schedules_table_e.htm (last accessed 10 June 2020).

[104]According to the DSU included in Annex 2 of the WTO Agreement.

reasonable period of time and an actual determination as to the non-compliance, a member may request permission to react to violations by a suspension of concessions, while over the appropriate level once more an arbitrator has to decide.[105] In comparison to general international law,[106] a member may not take things into its own hands and react by immediately imposing countermeasures. Only after all the steps have been followed through a formal procedure and adoption of the reports by the DSB, may a member suspend concessions in the form of raising of tariffs or cross-retaliation in other sectors.[107] This process had for around 25 years, by and large, been accepted and followed by the members.[108] Even when members had fierce disputes over WTO-inconsistent measures, they would usually await panel proceedings before imposing retaliatory measures.[109]

Neither the US in its initial measures nor the EU[110] and China have followed this sequence of steps as outlined, but have reacted unilaterally by increasing duties on certain products to offset the tariffs imposed by the other side immediately.[111] Lamp argues with regard to the EU, that

> [t]he most plausible answer is that they [the responding members] perceived the US measures as an attempt to coerce them and saw immediate retaliation as necessary to deny the US any opportunity to use the measures as negotiating leverage.[112]

While the observation might hold true, it does not cure the problem, that also the EU and other members that like to portray themselves as adhering to the rule of law and proclaim to strengthen the multilateral order[113] similarly damage it by resorting to unilateral measures driven by a comparable logic of power play. Additionally, it

---

[105]Articles 4, 6, 12, and 22 (especially 22.2) DSU.

[106]Especially Article 49 Responsibility of States for internationally wrongful Acts, GA/RES 56/83, Annex.

[107]If, within 20 days after the expiry of the reasonable period of time, the parties have not agreed, the complainant may ask the DSB for permission to impose trade sanctions against the respondent that has failed to implement. Technically, this is called "suspending concessions or other obligations under the covered agreements" (Article 22.2 of the DSU). Concessions are, for example, tariff reduction commitments.

[108]Brewster (2019), pp. 62–63.

[109]For example, the US patiently awaited the required decisions in WTO, *European Communities — Measures Concerning Meat and Meat Products (Hormones)*, WT/DS26, to retaliate against the WTO-inconsistent import prohibition of hormone treated beef from the US. See Brewster (2019), pp. 62–63.

[110]The EU justifies these additional duties by relying on the Safeguards Agreement (Articles 8.2 and 8.3) while the USA has not itself officially qualified their measures as falling under the Safeguards Agreement, WT/DS559, EU written statement, see https://trade.ec.europa.eu/doclib/docs/2019/october/tradoc_158389.pdf.

[111]See reactions of EU and China, https://edition.cnn.com/2019/07/02/economy/us-tariffs-on-eu/index.html (last accessed 13 June 2020) and https://fortune.com/2019/10/08/trump-china-tariffs-trade-war-us-economy-impact/ (last accessed 13 June 2020).

[112]Lamp (2019), p. 7.

[113]See e.g. the Alliance for Multilateralism, https://new-york-un.diplo.de/un-en/news-corner/alliance-multilateralism/2250628 (last accessed 13 June 2020).

instigates other members to do the same, implying it to be a legitimate policy option in order to protect national interests.[114]

In a somewhat twisted logic, the US argued that China's resort to the DSB constitutes a misuse of the dispute settlement mechanism requesting the panel to make a finding that the parties found their own solution according to Article 12.7 DSU, basically by imposing measures and countermeasures,[115] including some covered by the WTO and some not. Under this perception, it would not anymore be the claimant who would be in a position to define the subject matter of the dispute, but the behaviour prior to the dispute that could render a dispute outside of the scope of jurisdiction. This stands in contradiction to the wording of Article 23.1 and Article 6.1 DSU, the latter one starting with: "[i]f the complaining party so requests [. . .]".[116] The position is overall not in line with the design of the WTO dispute settlement system, introduces an alien clean-hands argument and would ultimately mean a return to jungle law (or "might is right"), where parties act based on their strength and power without the ability to resort to the rule of law and the DSB.

2.4 Destruction of the AB: Sounding the Death Knell for the WTO?

A common introduction to the WTO dispute settlement system is a reference to it as the "crown jewel" of the WTO.[117] And due to its distinctive features, one tends to think that rightly so: it was compulsory, efficient and, in most cases, due to its strict adherence to the rule of law highly authoritative. Many panel and AB reports could, due to their fine and careful crafting and commendable examination of interpretation methods, serve as study cases in legal exercise books. In at least two major aspects, the WTO dispute settlement system is distinct from that of international law dispute settlement in general and the system during the GATT-time in particular: its compulsory nature and the effectively automatic adoption of reports as well as the increase in authority and coherence by a second instance.[118] These features enabled small and economically weak States to sue even much more powerful members[119] and reassured all members that despite imperfection of some of the rules and

---

[114]Brewster (2019), pp. 62–63.

[115]US Written statement in WT/DS543, p. 14 see https://ustr.gov/sites/default/files/enforcement/DS/US.Sub1.%28DS543%29.fin.%28public%29.pdf (last visited 15 October 2020).

[116]See also Bäumler (2019), marginal note 216.

[117]Reich (2019), p. 1.

[118]See on the functioning of the Dispute Settlement system, Van den Bossche and Zdouc (2017), p. 156.

[119]E.g. WTO, *United States — Measures Affecting the Cross-Border Supply of Gambling and Betting Services (Complainant Antigua and Barbuda)*, WT/DS285.

agreements, at least it could be trusted that the existing ones were enforceable. In 2009, after failure on finalizing the DDA, it was contested that "[...] one might suspect, the WTO's dispute settlement system would remain intact regardless of Doha's destiny."[120] This does not hold true as of 11 December 2019.

It is well known that the US has for quite some time criticised the AB and the reappointment blockage of particular judges in 2003, 2011 and 2016, especially when it concerned a non-US judge,[121] was regarded as a strong sign of increasing discontent.[122] In the latter case, open accusations of adopting reports in excess of rights and obligations of WTO members served as explanation for the US position.[123] Under the *Trump* administration, the level of systematic attack and criticism paired with actively allowing the running out of time for reappointment of new judges below the minimum amount of three judges finally led to the discontinuity of the AB on 11 December 2019. With only one judge left, no more cases can be appealed, with the mandate of the last judges to—and even that is disputed— allowing only to finish cases that had been appealed prior to the termination date.[124]

The most prominent arguments of the US were the overreach of the mandate and competencies of the AB and the DSB more generally, exceeding of timeframes as set out in the DSU, the characterization as precedence of AB decisions as well as the treatment of domestic law.[125] But the US has also raised even more systemic aspects, such as that an impasse at negotiations has led to "unchecked 'institutional creep' by the Appellate Body as members push to achieve through litigation what they haven't achieved or can't achieve at the negotiating table"; that in the US view the perception of the AB as an international court with judges that produces jurisprudence is a total misconception against the backdrop that panels and the AB were intended to act as agents of the parties directly involved in the dispute and that authoritative interpretation[126] can only be provided by the members and not the AB.[127] Moreover, it conceives the overreach of timeframes by panels and the AB as a sign for the agents (i.e. panels and the AB) of disobeying their masters, disregardful of the complexity of the facts and legal questions involved.

---

[120]Cho S, Is the WTO Passé? Exploring the Meaning of the Doha Debacle. 1 May 2009, http://ssrn. com/abstract=1403464 (last accessed 1 October 2020), p. 7.

[121]Fabry and Tate (2018), p. 6.

[122]Petersmann (2018), p. 2.

[123]Fabry and Tate (2018), p. 7.

[124]See Rule 15 Working Procedures for Appellate Review, WT/AB/WP/6.

[125]Statements by the United States at the WTO General Council Meeting on 15 October 2019 https://geneva.usmission.gov/2019/10/15/statements-by-the-united-states-at-the-wto-general-coun cil-meeting/ (last accessed 13 June 2020).

[126]Article 17 of the DSU.

[127]Statement by the United States at the WTO General Council Meeting on 15 October 2019.

Of course, the role of panels and the AB[128] and the development their reports have taken, is significant when seen over time. It was largely their achievement to resolve some of the open tensions e.g. with respect to environmental questions to, by way of interpretation and especially by an evolutive interpretation of e.g. Article XX GATT[129] or the SCM.[130] Yet, a comprehensive study recently accomplished, did not—except regarding the excess of timeframes—confirm any violation of provisions of the DSU by panels or the AB concerning their mandate.[131] This further warrants the impression that the decision to deconstruct the AB had more political than tangible legal reasons.[132]

Following the criticism of the US, a number of reform proposal were put on the table.[133] None of them has found enough supporters and the discussions reach in all kinds of directions. While some of the proposals might stand real potential to actually improve detected aberrations, the prompt option to have saved the AB immediately would have been uniting against the US and vote according to the majority voting option of Article X:1 WTO Agreement, when it was clear that consensus was blocked by the US.[134] Petersmann argues:

> The text of Article IX:1 ('where a decision cannot be arrived at by consensus, the matter at issue shall be decided by voting') confirms that WTO members are legally required ('shall') to overcome illegal 'blocking' of the filling of AB vacancies by such majority decisions in order to meet their collective legal duties to maintain the AB as prescribed in Article 17 DSU, similar to the existing WTO procedures for appointing the WTO Director-General through a majority decision 'where a decision cannot be arrived at by consensus'.[135]

---

[128]Pauwelyn J and Pelc K, Who Writes the Rulings of the World Trade Organization? A Critical Assessment of the Role of the Secretariat in WTO Dispute Settlement. 26 September 2019, https://ssrn.com/abstract=3458872 (last accessed 15 October 2020).

[129]See e.g. WTO, *United States — Measures Concerning the Importation, Marketing and Sale of Tuna and Tuna Products,* WT/DS381; WTO, *Canada — Measures Relating to the Feed-in Tariff Program,* WT/DS426; WTO, *European Communities — Measures Affecting Asbestos and Products Containing Asbestos,* WT/DS135; WTO, *United States — Import Prohibition of Certain Shrimp and Shrimp Products,* WT/DS58/DS61; GATT, *United States — Restrictions on Imports of Tuna,* (Not adopted, circulated on 3 September 1991) and GATT, *United States — Prohibition of Imports of Tuna and Tuna Products from Canada* (Panel finding adopted on 22 February 1982).

[130]WTO, *Canada – Measures Relating to the Feed-in tariff Program,* WT/DS426.

[131]Lehne (2019), 10 November 2019, https://ielp.worldtradelaw.net/2019/11/guest-post-is-the-blocking-of-appointments-to-the-wto-appellate-body-by-the-united-states-legally-ju.html   (last accessed 13 June 2020).

[132]Ibid.

[133]E.g. the European Union, China, Canada, India, Norway, New Zealand, Switzerland, Australia, Republic of Korea, Iceland, Singapore and Mexico raised concerns with the AB's approach to treat its own reports effectively as precedent that panels are to follow absent "cogent reasons" (WT/GC/W/752); see also Brewster (2011), p. 102.

[134]Petersmann (2018), p. 8.

[135]Petersmann (2018), p. 8.; of course, this suggestion is in light of the footnote to Article IX WTO Agreement, providing that the rule of Article 2 para 4 DSU requiring consensus regarding any decision taken by the DSB, not undisputed. Yet, Petersmann rightly points out that the obligation to maintain the AB might render a reference to majority voting possible. In support also Gao (2019),

This would have been a strong sign of all members that they would not allow one member to threaten and deconstruct the multilateral legal order. Yet, contrary to the usual perception of the US against the rest, a recent survey concluded that also other WTO members shared the US position that the AB had been going beyond its mandate at times.[136] Members used the opportunity and started to discuss reform options, thereby allowing the crisis to deepen and to unfold its full destructive potential. Following the impasse, individual members commenced concluding agreements to bilaterally resolve the appeals absence, providing for options for particular cases and particular members, but leaving unresolved the future of the AB as a systemic issue, falling into the trap of bilateralism instead of a strict upholding of multilateralism for the WTO in general and the AB in particular. Especially the EU, together with 16 other members, has been working towards establishing an interim appeals mechanism in order to ensure a two-step procedure.[137] The so called multi-party interim appeal arbitration agreement (MPIA) has been established on 30 April 2020 and is currently supported by 24 members.[138] It enables resort to arbitration according to Article 25 DSU instead of an appeal according to Article 16.4 and 17 DSU.[139] Aiming at keeping "the substantive and procedural aspects of the Appellate Body Review", the disputes[140] will be heard by three appeal arbitrators from a pool of 10 nominated arbitrators.[141] Whether the MPIA will attract more members and whether the decision will create similar authority as the Appellate Body decisions will only be seen in the future.

For other members, the danger of "appeals in the void"[142] describing the possibility of members to appeal a panel report that will never receive a report by the disabled AB, might even lead to a prevention tool for the adoption of a panel report

---

pp. 20–21; Hillman (2018) Institute of International Economic Law Georgetown University Law Center 12 October 2018, https://www.law.georgetown.edu/wp-content/uploads/2018/12/Hillman-Good-Bad-Ugly-Fix-to-WTO-AB.pdf (last accessed 15 October 2020), p. 11.

[136]Fiorini et al., WTO Dispute Settlement and the Appellate Body Crisis: Insider Perceptions and Members' Revealed Preferences. Bertelsmann Stiftung, Dispute Settlement Survey, 2019, https://www.bertelsmann-stiftung.de/fileadmin/files/BSt/Publikationen/GrauePublikationen/MT_WTO_Dispute_Settlement_and_the_Appellate_Body_Crisis_Survey.pdf (last visited 15 October 2020), p. 19ff.

[137]The declaration of the EU and 16 members can be found here: https://ec.europa.eu/commission/presscorner/detail/en/IP_20_113 (last accessed 13 June 2020).

[138]Benin was the last member to join on 29 June 2020, see WT Doc. JOB/DSB/1/Add.12/Suppl.

[139]See para. 1 and 2 of the MPIA Agreement, JOB/DSB/1/Add.1.

[140]So far in four disputes the new mechanism will be used, WTO, *Canada – Sale of Wine*, WT/DS537; WTO, *Costa Rica – Avocados*, WT/DS524; WTO, *Canada – Aircraft*, WT/DS522; WTO, *Colombia – AD Duties on French Fries*, WT/DS591.

[141]For the pool of arbitrators, see WT Doc. JOB/DSB/1/Add.12/Suppl.5.

[142]Pauwelyn (2019b), pp. 303–309.

and thus contains a real potential of providing members with a veto against a detrimental panel decision.[143] Thus, the dysfunctionality of the AB might also affect the functioning of the panel stage and eventually unravel the entire dispute settlement system.

3 Developments Outside of the WTO

The WTO is not only under pressure by the developments taking place on the inside, but also by activities at the outside. In fact, the two spheres interact: the less capable the WTO appears of regulating international trade relations effectively and comprehensively, the more members resort to other fora and negotiate agreements among a smaller group of like-minded States. This is exactly what has happened since 2006, when the US increased its efforts for bi- or plurilateral trade negotiations, with the EU soon to follow this approach. It is by now almost a commonplace to complain about the proliferation of preferential trade agreements (PTAs) that has led to the famous Spaghetti-Bowl image of *Baghwati*.[144] Yet, the problem is not only restricted to the sheer number of PTAs, but extends to their content in a qualitative sense, regulating aspects beyond and differently than the WTO agreements. Additionally, to the legal problems arising with regard to WTO-plus, -minus and -extra obligations from the viewpoint of the WTO, another element warrants further consideration, namely that of standard setting taking place outside of the WTO and particularly according to the conception of the most powerful parties at the negotiating table.

Those backlashes from the outside shall be traced along the following three lines: First, the proliferation of bi- or plurilateral trade agreements marginalizes the WTO from a sheer quantitative point of view and questions its core pillar, namely the most-favoured-nation (MFN) principle (Sect. 3.1). Second, the undefined legal relationship between the WTO and deviating obligations in PTAs challenges WTO obligations also from a qualitative point of view (Sect. 3.2). Closely related and as a consequence, with large PTAs standard setting increasingly takes place outside the WTO, negotiated by a handful powerful States with carefully selected like-minded friends and to the detriment of concentrating negotiations in the WTO forum with a more participatory and equal negotiation setting (Sect. 3.3).

---

[143]The US has in fact notified the DSB of an appeal on 18 December 2019 of the panel report in WTO, *United States — Countervailing Duty Measure on Certain Hot-Rolled Carbon Steel Flat Products from India: Recourse to art 21.5 DSU by India*, WT/DS436/RW, see WT/DS436/21; that communication was followed by another joint communication by India and the US the legal meaning of which is however unclear, see WT/DS436/22.

[144]The term was first used by Bhagwati (1995).

3.1 Proliferation of Preferential Trade Agreements: Is Most-Favoured-Nation Turning from the Rule to the Exception?

The GATT has always operated against the background of PTAs between two or more of its members. Article XXIV GATT allows free trade agreements based on the perception that trade liberalisation first in smaller, often regional settings, will eventually lead to further trade liberalisation on the global level.[145] Yet, the inherent tension between the most-favoured-nation principle as enshrined in Article I GATT (requiring to treat like products from all members equally) and better treatment between two or more members only, already played a significant role during the negotiations at the International Trade Organization (ITO) conferences.[146] The outcome is a rather complex design of Article XXIV GATT with a number of preconditions that have to be met by PTAs in order to be compatible with the GATT.[147]

As of August 2020, 490 free trade agreements have been notified to the WTO and 303 are actually in force.[148] By now, Djibouti and Sao Tomé and Principe are the only two States not member to a notified RTA.[149] The high number of PTAs has led to only about 50% of goods still being traded under the WTO-MFN tariff.[150] Against the background that MFN is one of the core principles of the GATT, the steep increase in PTAs seriously erodes one of the founding pillars of the WTO and will eventually render MFN as the exception and not the rule in the future.

Despite efforts to increase transparency of PTAs under the WTO regime, the forest of PTAs gets thicker and opaquer by the year. The members as well as the DSB, similarly to having missed clarifying Article XXI GATT, have failed to set clear and straightforward preconditions for PTAs when the number was relatively manageable.[151] In fact, the WTO DSB has not, with regard to any PTA, ever made a

---

[145] Article XXIV: 4 GATT: "The contracting parties recognize the desirability of increasing freedom of trade by the development, through voluntary agreements, of closer integration between the economies of the countries parties to such agreements. They also recognize that the purpose of a customs union or of a free-trade area should be to facilitate trade between the constituent territories and not to raise barriers to the trade of other contracting parties with such territories".

[146] WTO discussion paper, "RTAs and the WTO: A troublesome relationship", p. 26. https://www.wto.org/english/res_e/booksp_e/discussion_papers12b_e.pdf (last accessed 15 October 2020).

[147] See on the interpretation of Article XXIV GATT, Analytical Index, Article XXI GATT https://www.wto.org/english/res_e/publications_e/ai17_e/gatt1994_art24_jur.pdf (last accessed 15 October 2020); see also Hilpold (2003); Mathis (2002), pp. 39 ff.

[148] WTO, Regional Trade Agreements https://www.wto.org/english/tratop_e/region_e/region_e.htm (last accessed 14 June 2020).

[149] See WTO database of RTAs http://rtais.wto.org/UI/publicPreDefRepByCountry.aspx (last accessed 14 June 2020).

[150] World Tariff Profiles, publication by WTO, ITC and UNCTAD (2019).

[151] On the disputed aspects of Article XXIV GATT see generally Van den Bossche and Zdouc (2017), pp. 648–672.

clear statement as to its compatibility with Article XXIV GATT or not.[152] For some reason or the other, members have rarely challenged other PTAs and appear to accept inconsistent PTAs, not willing to break the stalemate that prevails with regard to questions of compatibility of PTAs with the WTO agreements.

In former times, members at least complied with the requirement that substantially all the trade was required to be covered in order to be in line with Article XXIV:8 GATT.[153] Nowadays, some agreements not even on their face, comply with the requirements as laid out by Article XXIV GATT. For example the recent US-Japan deal that was just signed, covers a limited number of products and aims at ensuring better access for US agricultural products to the Japanese market only.[154] Similarly, the US-China deal has a very limited coverage and serves the purpose of securing quotas for US agricultural products to the Chinese market.[155] In the same vein, the agreement currently negotiated between the US and the EU to prevent the US from imposing additional tariffs on cars from Europe, sometimes embellished as Transatlantic Trade and Investment Partnership (TTIP)-light, does not even aim at covering "substantially all the trade" between the EU and the US.[156] These agreements will have detrimental effects for other States by altering fair competition, especially when granting certain quotas for products from one country, and are thus not in line with Article XXIV GATT requiring that third members are not negatively affected by a PTA.[157] Additionally, it can be expected that these agreements will encourage other members to foster agreements for certain sectors and products only, without having to undergo the complications of liberalizing "substantially all the trade" between the parties.

Another side effect comes with the proliferation of PTAs, namely that the application of different rules and tariffs for different products increasingly requires the determination of the origin of a particular product. Birth certificates of products thus become incrementally important. Under MFN, the origin of the product mainly revolved around the question whether the product derived from a WTO member or

---

[152]Not even in *Turkey – Restrictions on Imports of Textile and Clothing*, WT/DS34.

[153]Equivalent in Article V GATS.

[154]Lester (2019b), 7 October 2019, https://ielp.worldtradelaw.net/2019/10/the-us-japan-trade-deal-can-a-political-agreement-liberalize-trade-without-institutions.html (last accessed 14 June 2020).

[155]"'US-China trade deal totally done', Trump aide Lighthizer says". The Guardian, 15 December 2019, see https://www.theguardian.com/us-news/2019/dec/15/us-china-trade-deal-trump-lighthizer (last accessed 15 October 2020).

[156]See http://www.europarl.europa.eu/legislative-train/theme-a-balanced-and-progressive-trade-policy-to-harness-globalisation/file-eu-us-trade-talks (last accessed 14 June 2020).

[157]Especially an RTA shall not raise trade barriers for third parties, Article XXIV:4 GATT, see WTO, *Turkey — Restrictions on Imports of Textile and Clothing Products- Appellate Body Report*, WT/DS34/11, 25 February 2000, para 57.

not.[158] With the increase of PTAs, punitive tariffs and countermeasure duties requiring different treatment for those products at the border, the renationalisation of products features prominently. This creates an impediment for trade, especially since the Rules of Origin in the WTO are rudimentary and leave a wide margin of discretion to the members.[159] It is for those reasons that *Jagdish Bhagwati* contested, that the world, when infested with these PTA "termites" is prone to an interwar economic balkanization redux.[160]

3.2 WTO-Plus, -Minus, -Extra Obligations and How They Relate to the WTO

On the other side of the spectrum of product and sector specific PTAs sit comprehensive economic and trade agreements that regulate, in line with their title, a wide range of topics related to international economic relations between the parties. Some of these issues are covered by WTO agreements and some are not.[161] In relation to the WTO, they are usually referred to as WTO-plus, -minus and -extra obligations, depending on their respective design with regard to the corresponding WTO obligation.[162] What makes them tricky is their uncertain relationship with WTO obligations, especially concerning WTO-plus and -extra obligations, but also WTO-minus obligations. While WTO-minus obligations provide for less obligations than what parties had committed themselves to in the WTO, WTO-plus obligations go beyond commitments on the multilateral level.[163] WTO-extra obligations concern aspects currently not covered by the WTO and beyond its current mandate and therefore do not directly relate to WTO obligations.[164]

---

[158]Of course, for anti-dumping and anti-circumvailing measures the origin is similarly of concern, see e.g. the results of the Committee on Anti-Dumping Practices—Informal Group on Anti-Circumvention—Meeting of 25 October 2017, where some members raised concerns in specific anti-dumping actions listed in semi-annual notifications.

[159]See on rules of Origin https://www.wto.org/english/docs_e/legal_e/22-roo_e.htm (last accessed 14 June 2020).

[160]Bhagwati (2008), p. 32.

[161]See e.g. the table of contents of the Comprehensive and Economic Trade Agreement (CETA) https://ec.europa.eu/trade/policy/in-focus/ceta/ceta-chapter-by-chapter/ (last accessed 14 June 2020).

[162]On these terms: Qin (2010) and Ruta M, Preferential Trade Agreements and Global Value Chains Theory, Evidence, and Open Questions. World Bank, Policy Research Working Paper No. 8190, September 2017, http://documents.worldbank.org/curated/en/991871505132824059/Preferential-trade-agreements-and-global-value-chains-theory-evidence-and-open-questions (last visited 15 October 2020).

[163]Horn et al. (2009), p. 4.

[164]Ruta (2017).

In a number of disputes, the DSB had before it the question of the compatibility and effects of WTO-minus obligations, including the question whether Article 41 (1) Vienna Convention of the Law of Treaties (VCLT) was applicable,[165] but never came to a straight answer.[166] So-called voluntary export restraint agreements are an increasingly relevant example of WTO-minus agreements. Therein a member, more or less voluntarily, agrees to export less than the market would allow in order to spare another member's domestic market from competition.[167] While presumably not in conformity with WTO agreements, especially the safeguards agreement,[168] it is uncommon for a panel or the AB to get into a position of making a finding on a clause that is part of an agreement outside of the WTO. Those clauses and agreements will rarely reach dispute settlement, as neither party may have an interest in subjecting them to dispute settlement resolution. Yet, they have an effect on global trade in making trade less free and allowing geopolitics to re-enter economic relations in which market access and tariffs to a great extent depend on the relative power between the parties involved.

The same holds true for WTO-plus and -extra obligations in that they not only undercut the WTO agreements, but also change the members terms of trade in agreements outside the scope of jurisdiction of the WTO. They lead to a diversification of rules and render the field of international economic law unclear and convoluted.

Vidigal rightly observes

> WTO-extra provisions challenge the WTO not so much because they conflict with WTO rules as because they establish an alternative institutional setting for the development of new trade rules. Institutional competition and fragmented rules could end up making trade more difficult rather than easier.[169]

3.3 Standard Setting or Why Weaker States Will Suffer Mostly from Bi- and Plurilateral Trade Negotiation Settings

Very closely related to the last aspect and going hand in hand with comprehensive coverage and new approaches in economic agreements, new standards for international trade are increasingly set outside the WTO.[170] The WTO Sanitary and

---

[165]According to WTO, *Appellate Body Report, Peru–Agricultural Products*, WT/DS457, para 5.112, it does not seem to be the case.

[166]See especially WTO, *Mexico — Tax Measures on Soft Drinks and Other Beverages*, WT/DS308 and WTO, *Peru — Additional Duty on Imports of Certain Agricultural Products*, WT/DS457.

[167]Vidigal (2019), pp. 187–188.

[168]Especially Article 11.1(b) Safeguards Agreement, Vidigal (2019), pp. 196ff.

[169]Vidigal (2019), pp. 191–192.

[170]Especially argued with regard to TRIPS: Taubman (2019).

Phytosanitary Measures agreement (SPS Agreement) and Technical Barriers to Trade agreement (TBT) were main achievements because of their promotion of international standards.[171] WTO members are encouraged to follow international standards, although they may still set their own standards under certain conditions.

Yet, in the last decade, the four central actors in the WTO, generally referred to as the "quad" consisting of the US, Europe, Canada and Japan have started to push for new standards in their FTAs,[172] especially concerning "trade and"-issues, including sustainable development, environment, labour and human rights, but also e.g. rules on competition and currency manipulation.[173] The comprehensive agreements negotiated and agreed upon reflect the incorporation of many more topics and aspects and broaden the regulatory scope of trade agreements.[174] With the negotiations in more intimate settings, often between a limited number of States, power can be and in fact is exerted more directly and immediate, especially if one of the major powers, EU, China or the US is involved in the process. The three have different ways of pushing their will. While the EU follows a softer approach, yet insisting on including considerably more WTO-plus and -extra provisions, which are in turn not to the same extent enforceable; the US postulates less demands, yet more directly and it ensures their enforceability.[175] China, in turn, tends to have a rather subtle seductive way of negotiating and concluding agreements based on economic incentives provided to its partners.

Yet, all those strategies have in common to push their regulatory approaches and to ensure spheres of power and influence.[176] The other side is often in a weaker position. The negotiating forum of the WTO not only gave members such as the African-Caribbean-Pacific[177] group an opportunity to align their position and thereby support each other, but also to benefit from big power negotiations by way of MFN and the making of arrangements to the benefit of all members. In short, "as powerful countries 'devalue' the WTO's authority, smaller countries will be stripped

---

[171]Although many aspects are still left to the discretion of members.

[172]Condon B J, To Dystopia and Beyond: The WTO in a Warming Megaregional World. Paradise Lost or Found? The Post-WTO International Legal Order (Utopian & Dystopian Possibilities), Fletcher School, Tufts University, 7 May 2019, see https://ssrn.com/abstract=3384248 (last visited 15 October 2020).

[173]EU-Singapore and EU-Vietnam FTA (Sustainable development provisions), EU-Mexico Global Agreement (Environment provisions), EU-South Korea FTA (Labour provisions), EU-Chile FTA (Competition provision), United States-Mexico-Canada Agreement (Currency provisions).

[174]See e.g. CETA, the proposed chapters for the EU-Mercosur agreement or the negotiations on the Regional Comprehensive Economic Partnership.

[175]Jinnah (2011), p. 191.

[176]Explicitly for the US and EU: Horn et al. (2009), p. 2.

[177]Glossary Term WTO: "African, Caribbean and Pacific countries. Group of countries with preferential trading relations with the EU under the former Lomé Treaty now called the Cotonou Agreement".

of the rule of law protection under the WTO system."[178] Additionally, the power imbalance often leads to unequal negotiation settings and to less influence of the weaker power on the design of the rules and the topics included.[179] Overall, the approach of PTAs between smaller groups of States stands in stark contrast to the multilateral approach of the WTO.

4 Fixing the WTO: Why and How?

The developments inside and outside the WTO evoked the picture of the rock and the hard place, rendering the multilateral trade organization in its current uncomfortable position. Especially when seen in accumulation, the overall picture allows an assessment of the current path for the WTO and international economic law more generally (Sect. 4.1). Against this background, the question arises whether the WTO is still reflective of the current needs of the international legal order and ultimately whether it is actually worth saving (Sect. 4.2). In answering in the affirmative, it will be discussed whether the WTO could not again be at the forefront of international law, by reverting to majority voting in order to overcome the current crisis of the multilateral trade order (Sect. 4.3).

4.1 Is International Economic Law in General or Only the WTO in Particular in Decline?

What overall picture appears, when putting the pieces together? Relevant factors for a reflection about the course a subfield in international law is taking, might include "systematically relevant disregard for international law, structural and institutional developments, which challenge its integrity, as well as contestations or rejections of a value-based international law".[180] These indicators help to analyse whether ultimately "the contemporary 'type' of international law is being transformed into another type of international law."[181]

The analysis above has shown that inside the WTO all reform efforts have failed in the last years; members constantly and increasingly violate especially the agreements related to trade remedies to the extent of systemic disregard; trade tensions and violations of the WTO agreements have escalated into trade wars and exposed systemic open legal questions regarding the security exceptions clause and

---

[178]Cho S, Is the WTO Passé? Exploring the Meaning of the Doha Debacle, 1 May 2009, http://ssrn.com/abstract=1403464 (last accessed 1 October 2020), p. 32.

[179]See already Axelrod and Keohane (1985), p. 239.

[180]Krieger et al. (2019), p. 18.

[181]Krieger et al. (2019), p. 20.

countermeasures; and finally the destruction of the AB marks a significant shift in the functioning of the WTO dispute settlement mechanism. These developments are not merely isolated incidences but reflective of a systemically relevant disregard for the terms of the Organization by more than a few members, ultimately challenging the integrity of the Organization, accompanied by contestations and rejections of the values on which the WTO was founded, including the international rule of law. At the same time, members have turned away from the WTO and towards alternative agreements and fora, in which they pursue different aims with different strategies. The negative impact for the WTO results from the obvious disregard for MFN especially by agreements in obvious violation of the preconditions of PTAs set by WTO agreements, the diversion of interest and effort away from the WTO, the renationalisation of products and standard setting increasingly taking place outside of the WTO subject to the spheres of influence by major powers, especially the US, China and the EU. For the WTO the developments indicate a gradual return to the GATT-era in terms of disposing the compulsory dispute settlement system for a more power-based system in which an instrumentalisation of economic means for strategic aims is under way.

From a different angle though, it could also be argued that International Economic Law is in fact an area in which international law is flourishing. Every year, new comprehensive agreements are negotiated and agreed upon and indeed the recent trade agreements deepen economic cooperation and include topics such as environmental protection, labour rights and sustainable development in a way further developing the international economic legal framework and international law more generally.[182] These approaches appear timely and in many ways necessary for a contemporary economic order reflective of factors such as systematic human rights violations, a deteriorating environment or climate change. In fact, the subordination of economic objectives for other important aims can best be achieved if an agreement provides for these goals to be achieved simultaneously instead of having to resolve all those tensions by way of interpretation.[183] Seen from this angle, International Economic Law is further developing and shaping international law in a positive way.

4.2 Is the WTO Worth Saving?

If the WTO is outdated, "unreformable" and weakened, is then a world with refined and enhanced bi- and plurilateral agreements not the preferable scenario? Or is there more to the WTO than the mere perception of an outdated organisation that set rules and regulations for international trade?

---

[182]See e.g. Condon and Sinha (2014).

[183]See on systemic integration McLachlan (2019), pp. 279–320.

Of course, the WTO was never perfect. Its rules and regulations were also negotiated and agreed upon by a limited number of States, first at the ITO negotiations and later during the Uruguay Round.[184] The outcome was also always reflective of market power and political strength and the ability of the negotiators at the table to translate their interests into the actual outcome of the agreement. Especially the Uruguay Round and later the DDA were not able to overcome power imbalances and certain shortcomings of the design of the agreements, in particular for those areas that were of particular importance to developing members. At the same time, it holds true that much needed concepts especially for the better protection of human rights and the environment, that are increasingly incorporated into bi- and plurilateral agreements, systemically integrate different pillars of international law and have the potential to improve the conditions for both humans and the environment along the value chains.

Yet, and the fundamental shift for the international legal order is significant, those are agreements among different subgroups of States. It will ultimately lead to a world of friends and better friends on the one side and foes and enemies on the other side, with maybe a number of neutral relationships less cared about. The new agreements might reflect much needed concepts and developments, but they come at a high price in at least two regards. First, the WTO had a strict rule of law approach, including that all rules and regulations were equally enforceable under the dispute settlement mechanism. The more recent bi- and plurilateral agreements often provide for less stringent approaches in their formulation as well as with regard to the enforcement, especially in the "trade and"-sections and certainly will not have an oversight mechanism similarly bound to the rule of law and comparable to that of the AB overall weakening the rule of law in International Economic Law. Second, and even more important and despite all criticism of its actual design,[185] those agreements undermine the post-World War II and post-Cold War era that had a global legal framework at the heart of their agenda. The positive aspects of modern PTAs among a limited number of States might not outweigh the value the WTO has brought to the global order. Only the WTO provides for a global legal framework for trade relations even among those States that would not dare or care to conclude an agreement between each other, yielding the rule of law to international relationships that would otherwise be inimical or not relevant enough for conclusion of an agreement. The latter ones bear an inherent potential to deteriorate over time. The WTO is potentially open to all members of the international community with an appeasing and fencing effect especially for global and regional hegemonic powers and truly reflective of the multilateral approach. In sum, the WTO, as rightly summarised by Osakwe,

---

[184]Preeg (2012), p. 1978.

[185]For a very critical assessment of the global international economic law framework see Slobodian (2018), *passim.*

is one of the central pillars of the global order. The institution has delivered global public goods and welfare, which is more than economic: it has delivered the public goods of security, peace and stability.[186]

Yet, if it is not treated and cared for, it might turn into a "Zombie" organisation,[187] not really alive but also not entirely dead either. While it is important to considerably improve and reform the WTO, there is little chance that the world turn into a better, fairer and more just place if the WTO is simply abondened.

4.3   Majority Voting as a Way Out or a Further Step into the Crisis?

How than could the WTO be saved from further slipping into a comatose condition, inoperable and without ever reaching compromises on anything, eventually becoming of ever lesser importance over time? One of the most important proposals for overcoming the current crisis has been the suggestion to activate the majority voting mechanism.[188] It is not something alien to the WTO agreement that would need to be implemented, but it is already there: Article IX:1 WTO agreement especially foresees the option that "where a decision cannot be arrived at by consensus, the matter at issue shall be decided by voting".

The design and actual voting mechanism is a long-standing issue in international law especially regarding decision making in international organisations.[189] An organisation may operate well on consensus when composed of a limited number of parties thereby preserving the sovereignty of States to the greatest extent possible.[190] Yet, with destructive States acting in bad faith, the reliance on consensus appears preposterous and threatens the WTO as well as the sovereignty of all other members. The WTO provides for and even requires ("*shall*") majority voting in case consensus cannot be reached.[191] In the current crisis, it might be regarded as necessary to activate this mechanism in order to oppose those members taking the WTO hostage in their blockage position. For WTO members it requires yielding to two consequences: for one, it necessitates accepting the chance of being overruled by majority in votings to come. Yet, this might be the price to pay in further developing International Economic Law in a WTO with currently 164 member. Second, it might lead to fierce opposition by some members. Yet, at least for now, presumably no member can allow itself to withdraw[192] from the WTO, not even the most powerful

---

[186]Osakwe (2015), p. 5.

[187]Gray (2018), p. 2.

[188]See supra Sect. 2.4.

[189]Sohn (1975) and Zemora (1980).

[190]Zemora (1980), p. 574.

[191]Petersmann (2018), p. 8.

[192]Possible at any time with a 6 months' notice, Article XV WTO Agreement.

ones. That should strengthen the back of the WTO and the supporters of the Organization in overcoming blockages and by activating a mechanism that is provided for in the founding document of the WTO. The majority voting should first be used to revive the AB and should become the default option for any decision in order to positively reform the WTO.[193]

Would members of the WTO accept majority voting? Yet, quite defining for a position that is perceived as between a rock and hard place is that any way out might require having to refer to robust options. Of course, there is a high risk that members would not accept majority voting decisions, that societies would not want their governments to be outvoted in Geneva and that States would ultimately withdraw from the WTO. At the same time, the WTO members desiring to keep the WTO working, cannot further sit and wait while the WTO is gradually destructed and fades into irrelevance.

If the WTO became an organisation that reverts to majority voting in areas of concern to the organisation and the members as a whole, it could serve as an example for further developing and giving effect to international law also in other areas, in which States cling onto their sovereignty while constantly assuring that global problems can only be resolved by global approaches. In fact, majority voting appears as an effective solution for overcoming an impasse of finding consensus. In the past, International Economic Law has often been—similarly to international environmental law—at the forefront of developments later taken up in other areas of international law. International Economic Law then has the potential to play a leading role again and function as a stepping-stone for the international legal order more generally, emerging out of the crisis in a more robust way than before.

5 Conclusion

The 1st of January 2020 marked the WTO's 25th anniversary since the agreement for its establishment entered into force. The past year has however left the Organization not exactly in a great condition for celebrations. The WTO is not just any organisation, but also a symbol for a globalised world with global rules for a globalised market. If the WTO were to disappear, the global market would remain, only the global rules would have gone. They would be replaced by a complicated net of rules and agreements among friends and allies diverting trade along the lines of power and influence.

For some, the post-WTO might not look altogether grim, but rather bear great potential. Almost enthusiastically, it was suggested:

> If the WTO were to disappear, the simplest answer for what to do in a post-WTO world is to recreate the WTO. We have a model that works. Let's just replicate it. But as it is sometimes said, 'Why let a good crisis go to waste?' If the WTO disappears or is no longer functioning,

---

[193]If no other voting mechanism is provided for in the agreements, Article IX:1 2 WTO Agreement.

and we then have the opportunity to start fresh, let's aim high. Why not strive for perfection, or, at the least, excellence, rather than just muddling through as we usually do?[194]

It might be true that every crisis bears the potential for something new and better. Yet, the risk for a steep deepening of the crisis of global relations before we reach a point of return again, might be greatly underestimated. There might be little chance for developing a new and better WTO, when compromise is already difficult to be reached for particular rules and agreements. With regard to the WTO it might then feel as though you do not know what you had until you lost it.[195] Answers and solutions should thus be searched within and for the WTO. Hope and effort to save the WTO and develop it further, strengthening it to be better equipped for the challenges currently posed by its members and to the earth in its entirety, should thus prevail over ideas to establish relations based on power and influence or on recreating something that might prove very difficult to be rebuild.

References

Axelrod R, Keohane R (1985) Achieving cooperation under anarchy: strategies and institutions. World Polit 38(1):226–254

Bäumler J (2019) WTO. In: Krenzler G, Herrmann C, Niestedt M (eds) EU-Außenwirtschafts- und Zollrecht. C.H. Beck, München

Bhagwati J (1995) US trade policy: the infatuation with FTAs. Columbia University, Columbia

Bhagwati J (2008) Termites in the trading system: how preferential agreements undermine free trade. Oxford University Press, Oxford

Brewster R (2011) The remedy gap: institutional design, retaliation, and trade law enforcement. George Wash Law Rev 80(1):102–158

Brewster R (2019) WTO dispute settlement: can we go back again? Am J Int Law Unbound 113:61–66

Che L (2019) China's state-directed economy and the international order. Springer Singapore, Singapore

Condon B, Sinha T (2014) The role of international economic law in addressing climate change. In: Jansen M, Jallab MS, Smeets M (eds) Connecting to global markets. WTO Publications, Geneva, pp 117–128

Dunoff J (2019) Is compliance an indicator for the state of international law? - exploring the 'Compliance Trilemma'. In: Krieger H, Nolte G, Zimmermann A (eds) The international rule of law: rise or decline? Oxford University Press, Oxford

Eckhaus R (2006) China's exports, subsidies to state-owned enterprises and the WTO. China Econ Rev 17(1):1–13

Fabry E, Tate E (2018) Saving the WTO Appellate Body or returning to the wild west of trade? Jacques Delors Institute, Paris

Gao H (2019) Disruptive construction or constructive destruction? Reflections on the Appellate Body crisis. In: Lo C, Nakagawa J, Lin T (eds) The Appellate Body of the WTO and its reform. Springer, Heidelberg, pp 215–238

---

[194]Lester (2019a), 17 June 2019, https://ssrn.com/abstract=3405637 (last accessed 15 October 2020).

[195]Ral Donner—You Don't Know What You've Got (Until You Lose It) (1961).

Genest A (2014) The Canada—FIT Case and the WTO Subsidies Agreement: failed fact-finding, needless complexity, and missed judicial economy. McGill J Sustain Dev Law 10(2):239–258

Gray J (2018) Life, death, or zombie? The vitality of international organizations. Int Stud Q 62 (1):1–13

Gregory P, Stuart R (2004) Comparing economic systems in the twenty-first century. Houghton Mifflin, Boston

Guitchons A (2015) Cotton provisions in the United States of America 2014 Farm Bill: United States-Brazil cotton settlement and the post-Bali agenda for cotton producer developing countries. UNCTAD, New York

Henkin L (1979) How nations behave. Law and foreign policy, 2nd edn. Columbia University Press, Columbia

Hillman J (2018) Three approaches to fixing the World Trade Organization's Appellate Body: the good, the bad, and the ugly? Georgetown University, Washington

Hilpold P (2003) Regional integration according to Article XXIV GATT – between law and politics. In: von Bogdandy A, Wolfrum R (eds) Max Planck Yearbook of United Nations Law, vol 7. Koninklijke Brill N.V., Netherlands, pp 219–260

Horn H, Mavroidis P, Sapir A (2009) Beyond the WTO? An anatomy of EU and US preferential trade agreements. Bruegel, Brussels

Huo W (2002) Introduction and critical analysis of anti-dumping regime and practice in China pending entry of WTO: transition toward a WTO-modeled trade legal mechanism. Int Lawyer 36(1):197–214

Jinnah S (2011) Strategic linkages: the evolving role of trade agreements in global environmental governance. J Environ Dev 20(2):191–215

Kelling GL, Wilson JQ (1982) Broken windows: the police and neighborhood safety. Atlantic 249 (3):29–38

Krieger H, Nolte G, Zimmermann A (2019) The international rule of law: rise or decline? Oxford University Press, Oxford

Kurtz J (2019) Past as prologue? Historical parallels and discontinuities in modern trade wars. Paradise lost or found? The post-WTO International Legal Order (Utopian & Dystopian Possibilities). Kings College London Workshop (2020)

Lamp N (2019) At the vanishing point of law: rebalancing, non-violation claims, and the role of the multilateral trade regime in the trade wars. J Int Econ Law 22(4):721–742

Lester S (2016) Is the Doha Round over? The WTO's negotiating agenda for 2016 and beyond. Cato Institute Free Trade Bull 64:1–4

Lehne J (2019) Guest post: is the blocking of appointments to the WTO appellate body by the United States legally justified? International Economic Law and Policy Blog

Lester S (2019a) In search of the next Cordell Hull. Paradise lost and found? The post-WTO international legal order (utopian & dystopian possibilities). Fletcher School, Tufts University

Lester S (2019b) The U.S.-Japan trade deal: can a political agreement liberalize trade without institutions? International Economic Law and Policy Blog

Mathis J (2002) Regional trade agreements in the GATT/WTO: Article XXIV and the internal trade requirement. T.M.C. Asser Press, Den Haag

Mavroidis P, Prusa T (2018) Die another day: zeroing in on targeted dumping – did the AB hit the mark in US–washing machines? World Trade Rev 17(2):239–264

McLachlan C (2019) The principle of systemic integration and Article 31(3)(c) of the Vienna Convention. Int Comp Law Q 54(2):279–320

Osakwe C (2015) Future of the multilateral trading system: why the WTO remains indispensable? Asian J WTO Int Health Law Policy 10(1):1–25

Pauwelyn J (2019a) The role of public international law in the WTO: how far can we go? Am J Int Law 95(3):535–578

Pauwelyn J (2019b) WTO dispute settlement post 2019: what to expect? J Int Econ Law 22 (3):297–321

Petersmann E-U (2000) The WTO constitution and human rights. J Int Econ Law 3:19–25

Petersmann E-U (2018) The crown jewel of the WTO has been stolen by US trade diplomats: and they have no intention of giving it back. In: Prévost D, Alexovicova I, Hillebrand Pohl J (eds) Restoring trust in trade: liber amicorum in honour of Peter Van den Bossche. Hart, Oxford, pp 9–46

Powell SJ, Schmitz A (2005) The cotton and sugar subsidies decisions: WTO's dispute settlement system rebalances the agreement on agriculture. Drake J Int Law 10(2):287–330

Preeg E (2012) The Uruguay Round negotiations and the creation of the WTO. In: Narlikar A, Daunton M, Stern R (eds) The Oxford handbook on the World Trade Organization. Oxford University Press, Oxford

Qin J (2010) The challenge of interpreting 'WTO-Plus' provisions. J World Trade 44(1):127–172

Reich A (2019) The effectiveness of the WTO dispute settlement system: a statistical analysis. In: Kono T, Hiscock M, Reich A (eds) Transnational commercial and consumer law: current trends in international business law. Springer, Heidelberg, pp 1–44

Ruta M (2017) Preferential trade agreements and global value chains: theory, evidence, and open questions. Policy research working paper no 8190, World Bank, Washington

Sacerdoti G (2019) The WTO in 2018: systemic developments, disputes and review of the Appellate Body's reports. Italian Yearb Int Law Online 28(1):351–411

Slobodian Q (2018) Globalists. The end of empire and the birth of nationalism. Harvard University Press, Cambridge

Sohn L (1975) Voting procedures in United Nations conferences for the codification of international law. Am J Int Law 69(2):310–353

Taubman A (2019) The variable geometry of geography: multilateral rules and bilateral deals on geographical indications. In: de Werra J (ed) Geographical indications: global and local perspectives. Schulthess Éditions Romandes, Geneva

Van den Bossche P, Zdouc W (2017) The law and policy of the World Trade Organization. Text, cases and materials, 4th edn. Cambridge University Press, Cambridge

Vidigal G (2019) The return of voluntary export restraints? How WTO law regulates (and doesn't regulate) bilateral trade-restrictive agreements. J World Trade 53(2):187–210

Voon T (2019) The security exception in WTO law: entering a new era. Am J Int Law Unbound 113:45–50

Zemora S (1980) Voting in international economic organizations. Am J Int Law 74(3):556–608

Zhou W (2019) China's implementation of the rulings of the World Trade Organization. Hart, London

Jelena Bäumler   is Professor of Public and International Law with a special focus on sustainability at the Leuphana University Lüneburg. She is a fully qualified lawyer and holds an LL.M. from the University of the Western Cape, South Africa. She acts as Counsel and Advisor in ICJ proceedings and has been a visiting Professor in China, South Africa and New Zealand. Her research focuses on Public International Law, Trade Law and International Environmental Law.

PPM-Based Trade Measures to Promote Sustainable Farming Systems? What the EU/EFTA-Mercosur Agreements Can Learn from the EFTA-Indonesian Agreement

Elisabeth Bürgi Bonanomi and Theresa Tribaldos

Contents

Abstract More sustainable systems of food production are urgently needed. The global community and all involved actors must go beyond focusing narrowly on

With our warmest thanks to Anu Lannen, editor, and Franziska Orler, research associate, both at the Centre for Development and Environment (CDE), University of Bern, who provided valuable assistance and feedback.

E. B. Bonanomi (✉) and T. Tribaldos
Centre for Development and Environment (CDE), University of Bern, Bern, Switzerland
e-mail: elisabeth.buergi@cde.unibe.ch; theresa.tribaldos@cde.unibe.ch

© Springer Nature Switzerland AG 2020   359
M. Bungenberg et al. (eds.), *European Yearbook of International Economic Law 2020*,
European Yearbook of International Economic Law (2022) 11: 359–386,
https://doi.org/10.1007/8165_2020_64, Published online: 13 January 2021

quantities of food produced; they must simultaneously address interlinked issues of water scarcity, soil fertility loss, agrobiodiversity, climate impacts, equitable land access, labour standards, and other environmental and social issues. The farming systems of the global North and South are highly interdependent, and agricultural trade rules can significantly influence global structures of food production. In view of the increasingly apparent flaws of private sustainability-oriented certification schemes, there is a growing consensus that states can and should use trade-related policy levers to foster more sustainable food production. The present text explores ways of doing so. The approaches taken in the European Free Trade Association (EFTA)-Mercosur Trade Agreement are juxtaposed with those of the EFTA-Indonesian Trade Agreement. The latter agreement structure is argued for, based on its incorporation of tariff differentiation along the lines of *process and production methods (PPMs)*. Accordingly, some thoughts are presented on the conformity of PPM-related trade measures with trade law. The primary concern that emerges regarding PPMs is not whether, but *how* these can be designed to avoid impinging on fundamental principles of international law, but rather to respect those. Finally, based on a look at the current state of farming systems in Brazil and Argentina, some recommendations are provided as to the optimal design of nuanced, sustainability-oriented trade rules.

1 Introduction

The need for more sustainable systems of food production and consumption is an urgent matter of global concern. The UN Global Sustainable Development Report (GSDR) 2019, authored by an independent group of scientists appointed by the UN Secretary-General, emphasises that continuing "business as usual" farming systems puts us on a path to disaster.[1] According to the authors, "upscaling current food production practices to meet the projected food demand of the world's population in 2050 would be completely incompatible with meeting the Paris Agreement as well as many of the Sustainable Development Goals" of the UN 2030 Agenda.[2] The question is how we can chart a new course in the direction of more sustainable farming systems. Importantly, agricultural trade represents a key policy lever to this end, but much depends on how trade relations are legally shaped.

In order to enable transitions to food sustainability—as envisaged by the Sustainable Development Goals (SDGs) 2, on "zero hunger", and 12, on "responsible consumption and production"—the global community and all involved actors must

---

[1] Independent Group of Scientists appointed by the Secretary-General, Global Sustainable Development Report (GSDR) (2019), p. xxv [cited: GSDR (2019)]. The GSDR 2019 includes summaries of data relating to severe challenges such as biodiversity loss etc.

[2] GSDR (2019), p. 64.

go beyond focusing narrowly on quantities of food produced. They must simultaneously address interlinked issues of water scarcity, soil fertility loss, climate impacts, food waste, plant pests, and diseases, and more, which are all evolving rapidly in our globalised world. They must also tackle social issues linked to farming systems, such as land concentration, the need for equitable and secure access to land, and labour standards.[3] More sustainable, *agrobiodiverse* farming practices need to be encouraged.[4] Also, smallholder production needs to be strengthened, since small-scale farmers and family farmers produce a major share of the world's food and are vital to rural poverty-reduction strategies.[5] According to the GSDR 2019, "to ensure that no one is left behind, much of the increase in food production will have to come from the 750 million smallholder farmers that estimates show will be operating in 2030."[6]

The farming systems of the global North and South are highly interdependent. Food consumption patterns in Europe strongly influence commodity and food production practices not only in European countries, but also in countries of Africa, Asia, and the Americas. Farming system interrelationships shape ecosystems, landscapes, and rural livelihoods at home and abroad. Switzerland's domestic food production, for instance, is very resource intensive and generates significant negative environmental externalities.[7] Indeed, approximately 73% of Switzerland's total ecological footprint occurs or originates outside of its national territory.[8] Consequently, Switzerland must address domestic sustainability issues as well as extraterritorial sustainability issues related to its imports and exports.

The 2030 Agenda—reflecting fundamental principles and objectives enshrined in international treaties on the environment, human rights, and trade—calls upon a broad spectrum of actors with reference to the concept of *shared responsibility*. Concerning the transition towards more sustainable farming systems, responsibility is attributed to *private actors* engaged in food-system value chains—including input providers, food processors, intermediaries, farmers, citizens, and consumers—but also to *public actors* at various levels of governance.[9] The present text deals with the latter; it considers the role of governments in promoting food sustainability by shaping regional and international trade policy.

Trade rules can significantly influence global structures of food production, since trade builds a bridge between geographically distant farming systems. Food

---

[3]GSDR (2019), pp. 65–66.

[4]For the "art of doing agriculture", and what it entails, see Bürgi Bonanomi (2015), Chapter 7.3.3; Rist et al. (2020).

[5]Ricciardi et al. (2018) and Graeub et al. (2016).

[6]GSDR (2019), p. 65.

[7]For related data, see Bürgi Bonanomi et al. (2018), pp. 27–65. For information concerning Switzerland, see chapter "International Sustainable Law: A New Branch of Law".

[8]Bundesamt für Umwelt (2018), p. 39.

[9]The GSDR distinguishes between four levers relevant for transformation: governance, economy and finance, individual and collective action, and science and technology, see GSDR (2019), pp. 67 and 68.

production and wider value chains are greatly impacted by the manner in which tariffs are set, subsidies are granted, food standards and labelling schemes are harmonised (or not), intellectual property schemes are aligned (or not), and competition rules are applied to intermediaries (or not). Today, trade in agriculture is governed by the Agreement on Agriculture of the World Trade Organisation (WTO), various other WTO agreements,[10] and a range of regional trade agreements. Also, domestic states unilaterally make use of trade measures—or refrain from their use—when operating within their remaining policy space.

In view of increasingly apparent flaws in private certification schemes and the persistence of severe sustainability problems worldwide, there is a growing consensus that states can and should use trade-related policy levers to foster more sustainable food production. For instance, in a recent public referendum, the citizens of Switzerland approved the addition of Article 104a lit. d to the Swiss Constitution,[11] which obliges the Swiss government to provide for "cross-border trade relations that contribute to the sustainable development of the agriculture and food sector". To date, however, the provision has not been fully realised in policy or practice.

The present text will explore ways of promoting more sustainable farming systems via trade relations. Two categories of farming systems will be outlined, according to which legal distinctions may be made. The possible role of trade in fostering one of the two categories will be reflected upon, and the approaches taken in the European Free Trade Association[12] (EFTA)-Mercosur Agreement will be juxtaposed with those of the EFTA-Indonesian Agreement. It will be argued for the latter agreements' structure, based on its incorporation of tariff differentiation along the lines of *process and production methods* (PPMs).

With PPMs, the primary concern that emerges is not whether, but how they can be designed to avoid impinging on fundamental principles of international law—as enshrined in trade, human rights, and environmental law—and thus, rather to respect those. A number of questions arise, such as: How can governments differentiate between *sustainable* and *unsustainable* food imports in a fair, responsible and balanced manner that respects the sovereignty of partner countries? How can sustainability distinctions be drawn that are effective, proportionate, context-sensitive, non-discriminatory, and reliable, by not violating basic principles of trade law and—in the case of wealthy countries—avoid increasing their "protected space" but instead facilitate market access for sustainably produced goods from poorer countries? While the legal analysis in this chapter will necessarily be limited in scope, some thoughts regarding the conformity of PPM-related trade measures with WTO law will be presented. Finally, based on a look at the current state of

---

[10]The following WTO agreements are also playing an important role in governing trade in agriculture: WTO General Agreement on Tariffs and Trade of 1947 (GATT); the WTO Agreement on the Application of Sanitary and Phytosanitary Measures of 1994 (SPS Agreement); the WTO Agreement on Technical Barriers to Trade of 1994 (TBT Agreement); the WTO Agreement on Trade-Related Aspects of Intellectual Property Rights of 1994 (TRIPS).

[11]The provision has been in force since 24th September 2017.

[12]EFTA countries include Norway, Switzerland, Iceland and Liechtenstein.

farming systems in Brazil and Argentina, some recommendations as to the optimal design of nuanced, sustainability-oriented trade rules will be provided.

The emphasis of the present text is not on unilateral trade measures, but rather on trade concessions negotiated in *preferential trade agreements* (PTAs).[13] While PTAs should follow basic rules of international trade law, they are typically less scrutinised and less frequently subject to dispute settlement proceedings when compared with domestic measures, since all partners involved have initially agreed to the general terms. This enables PTAs to serve as an experimental framework for testing of new approaches.

Three different interdisciplinary research projects, investigating different aspects of sustainability in farming systems, contributed to the lines of argumentation presented below. The Just Food project explores how just transitions towards sustainable, fair, and healthy food systems can be achieved.[14] The research project "Towards Food Sustainability" seeks to assess and compare the sustainability of different types of food systems in Bolivia and Kenya, as well as to explore the influence of different policies on the systems.[15] The research project "Sustainable Trade Relations for Diversified Food Systems", finally, seeks to explicitly find ways of granting tariff preferences for sustainably produced food in a non-discriminatory and balanced way.[16]

---

[13]Some use the term "Free Trade Agreements FTA". The term PTAs encompasses both bilateral and plurilateral trade agreements; it is more appropriate than FTA since in general, trade is facilitated through those agreements but no free trade area is established.

[14]Transdisciplinary research project "Just transition: Tackling inequalities on the way to a sustainable, healthy and climate-neutral food system (JUST-FOOD)" of the Strategic Research Council of Finland, financed by the Academy of Finland and led by Dr. Minna Kaljonen, Finnish Environment Institute. The project includes a case study, which is implemented with research partners in Switzerland and Brazil: https://justfood.fi/.

[15]Interdisciplinary research project "Towards Food Sustainability" of the Swiss Programme for Research on Global Issues for Development (r4d programme), financed by the Swiss National Science Foundation (SNF) and led by Prof. Stephan Rist of the CDE, University of Bern. The project has been implemented in collaboration with research partners in Bolivia, Kenya and Switzerland: https://www.cde.unibe.ch/research/projects/towards_food_sustainability/index_eng.html.

[16]Interdisciplinary research project "Sustainable Trade Relations for Diversified Food Systems", financed by the Swiss National Science Foundation (SNF), as part of the National Research Programme 73 on "Sustainable Economy", and led by Dr. iur. Elisabeth Bürgi Bonanomi of CDE, University of Bern: http://www.nrp73.ch/en/projects/governance/sustainable-trade-relations-for-diversified-food-systems.

2 Diversified Farming Systems Versus Specialised, Monoculture-Based Agricultural Systems

If trade rules are to provide an enabling environment for more sustainable farming systems—while *dis*enabling less sustainable ones—lines must be drawn between "the more and the less sustainable", that is, between those farming systems that need more public support/intervention and those that need less. While a great variety of farming systems exist, law-making requires categorisation, as rules and regulations necessarily seek to structure societal processes in a relatively generalised manner.[17]

Accordingly, there is a need for both *simplification* and legal techniques that enable *context-sensitive solutions* within general rules.[18] In the following, two categories will be presented whose contours illustrate useful dividing lines for policy. Subsequently, Sects. 4 and 5 will make recommendations for context-sensitive solutions along those lines.

2.1 Two Main Categories of Farming Systems for Policy Purposes

Debates on food sustainability in the natural sciences, social sciences, and international policy circles reveal a wide range of concepts that embrace those ways of food production that—in this way or the other—are deemed to be more sustainable than others. Prominent concepts include "sustainable agriculture and food value chains", "sustainable intensification", "climate smart agriculture", "climate resilient agriculture", "community supported agriculture", "conservation agriculture", "agroforestry", "organic" (or "bio"), "fair trade", "permaculture", "agroecology", "agroforestry", "nutrition sensitive agriculture", "sustainable land management", "restoration agriculture", and "ecosystem based approaches".[19] By promoting these and similar concepts, experts and decision-makers seek to foster agricultural systems that cause fewer negative externalities. Depending on their emphasis, corresponding policy advocates seek to ensure that soil quality, agrobiodiversity, and natural habitats are maintained; that cultural diversity and traditional knowledge are protected; that resources are used efficiently and greenhouse gas emissions are reduced; and/or that farmers' livelihoods are strengthened while local markets are supplied with healthy food at affordable prices.

Dr. Claire Kremen, a professor of applied conservation biology at the University of British Columbia, has sought to identify what constitutes the "core" of that which

---

[17]Tension between crafting broadly applicable rules and doing justice to the diversity of individual cases has always been inherent in law-making and policymaking; see e.g. Ostrom (2005).

[18]Cf. e.g. Oberlack et al. (2019).

[19]The compilation stems from the workshop "agroecology works", organised by various Swiss NGOs on 29th August 2019 in Bern.

is considered "more sustainable" in farming system-related debates. Her work has given rise to a means of categorisation that is useful for differentiated law-making. She distinguishes between *diversified farming systems* and *specialised, monoculture-based agricultural systems*.[20] In her classification, diversified farming systems are understood as "complex social-ecological systems that enable ecological diversification through the social institutions, practices, and governance processes that collectively manage food production and biodiversity".[21] In contrast, specialised, monoculture-based agricultural systems are those that "simplify ecosystems and utilise highly specialised, technical information with the goal of maximising the profitability of a commodity crop or livestock on a given farm".[22]

According to Kremen, diversified farming systems tend to "reduce negative environmental externalities and decrease social costs". On the other side, monoculture-based systems tend to maximise production and reduce labour costs.[23] With respect to environmental externalities, Kremen emphasises that the latter systems have proven "inherently unsustainable [by] mining soils", "polluting waterways, [...] destroying biodiverse habitats, releasing toxins into food chains [...] and contributing to climate warming".[24] Though it may not be possible to draw a simple dividing line between these two categories of farming systems in every case—especially given existing hybrid production forms—they can provide a helpful starting point for governments seeking to adjust their corresponding incentive and disincentive frameworks.[25]

2.2 Weak Framework Conditions for Diversified Farming Systems

Food sustainability scientists have indicated that diversified farming systems and specialised, agro-industrial farming systems could justifiably co-exist.[26] However, they face different challenges from the perspective of sustainability. Concerning specialised, agro-industrial systems, the primary issue is that of incorporating more

---

[20]Kremen et al. (2012).

[21]Kremen et al. (2012), p. 5.

[22]Kremen et al.(2012), p. 2.

[23]Kremen et al. (2012), p. 2.

[24]Kremen et al. (2012), p. 1.

[25]Legally, the concept of "diversified food systems" relates to the idea of "diversity", which is a key principle in sustainability research. It is opposed to the idea of "uniformity" as guiding paradigm of the twentieth century [see e.g. International Panel of Experts on Sustainable Food systems IPES-Food (2016); High Level Panel of Experts (HLPE) (2019)]. Reference to diversity has been made, for instance, in Article 6 of the International Seed Treaty (International Treaty on Plant Genetic Resources for Food and Agriculture [ITPGRFA] of 2001), which requires member states to pursue agricultural policies that promote "diverse farming systems". Bürgi Bonanomi (2015), pp. 284–288.

[26]Eyhorn et al. (2019).

integral, agrobiodiverse ways of food production into their approach.[27] Diversified farming systems, by contrast, tend to be marginalised by these dominating agro-industrial systems. Indeed, expansion of large-scale industrialised, monoculture-based systems frequently occurs at the direct expense of more diversified farming systems.[28] In addition, specialised systems generally benefit from current policy frameworks, while diversified systems typically suffer from insufficiently supportive policy architecture. In addition to lower economies of scale and, in some cases, higher costs of production, diversified systems tend to lack governmental support. Even if countries have innovative legal frameworks in place intended to encourage diversified systems, they tend not to receive the same level of institutional, political, and scientific backing.[29]

Domestic framework conditions primarily need to be adjusted by producer countries themselves. However, they often fail to do so due to their dependency on food commodity exports based on specialised production.[30] Consumer countries can counteract such dynamics by opening promising new market channels for products stemming from diversified systems and leveraging them for commercial purposes.[31] It is here that trade—and the way it is shaped—can play an important enabling role.

3 Need for an Enabling Trade Framework to Promote Diversified Farming Systems

In order to ensure that diversified farming systems gain momentum and do not get displaced by specialised, monoculture-based systems, framework conditions need to be adjusted. In a governance system that would *internalise* external costs (e.g. environmental harms), unsustainable patterns of farming would be costlier or even illegal. In practice, this does not (yet) happen. However, a sustainability-oriented trade framework could be used as a lever to address this. If products stemming from diversified farming systems could benefit from easier access to markets of high purchasing power, more investment for such systems could be

---

[27]Eyhorn et al. (2019).

[28]Kremen et al. (2012); Messerli et al. (2014), pp. 449–459.

[29]See e.g. for Kenya: Kiriti Nganga et al. (2018). The work is i.a. based on evidence from the R4D project "Towards Food Sustainability" in which the authors have participated. The R4D research in Bolivia, Kenya and further contexts has shown how those farming systems which are particularly relevant from a sustainability perspective are often too weak to evolve, given that they compete with systems producing more negative externalities. For related publications, see https://www.cde.unibe.ch/research/projects/towards_food_sustainability/index_eng.html.

[30]De Schutter (2009a).

[31]Food and Agriculture Organization of the United Nations (FAO), Institut national de la recherche agronomique (INRA) (2016); Tschopp et al. (2018), pp. 402–427.

secured.[32] Thereby, for farmers, access to both local as well as international markets is relevant and eventually complementary. In UNCTAD's Trade and Environment Review 2013, the authors put it as follows: "More regionalised/localised food production networks should be encouraged by trade rules, without excluding the supplementary role trade will have to play".[33] This gives rise to the following question: *How can trade measures be redesigned to create an enabling environment for the promotion and re-emergence of diversified farming systems?* The current trade system, by not differentiating between production types, incentivises the cheapest or most subsidised types of production, not those that perform most sustainably. To enable sustainable farming systems, corresponding incentives should be set differently.

When evaluating whether a unilateral trade measure respectively a trade agreement effectively creates an enabling environment for food sustainability, assessments must go further than the "legal letter". Instead, *effective impacts* of any new rule must be considered, including economic dynamics that may be reinforced. While one trade measure alone may not sufficiently strengthen diversified farming systems, it may do so when included as one element in a wider, more comprehensive policy package.[34]

4 Sustainability Chapter Versus PPM-Related Trade Measures

Debates over "trade and food sustainability" mainly revolve around whether to pursue any of the following policies in trade regulation: increasing discipline of agricultural subsidies; strengthening transparency in food value chains by means of voluntary or compulsory labelling requirements; introducing more nuanced sustainability chapters in trade agreements; limiting protection of intellectual property as related to agricultural inputs; control the use of standards by intermediaries in order to ensure that inclusive frameworks are in place; strengthening competition rules to ensure fair market prices; promoting recognition of equivalence of food and production standards; or introducing tariff differentiation based on PPMs.

The present text cannot address all of these policy aspects but will focus on two of them. It will compare and contrast two distinct regulatory approaches—namely, (1) introduction of a more nuanced sustainability chapter, as included in the

---

[32]See e.g. Bürgi Bonanomi (2011), pp. 68–88.

[33]United Nations Conference on Trade and Development (UNCTAD) (2013), Chapter 5.

[34]Theory on sustainability impact assessments (SIA) of trade agreements begins with the assumption that trade agreements should be understood as but one element of a broader policy picture: "Systemic thinking requires that the dynamics the agreement might trigger be explored in the context of the overall trade policy in which the agreement is embedded" (Bürgi Bonanomi 2017, pp. 481–503). Policy impacts may be anticipated based on detailed knowledge of the contexts involved.

EU-Mercosur Trade Agreement as well as the EFTA-Mercosur Free Trade Agreement (henceforth: the EU/EFTA-Mercosur Agreements), versus (2) PPM-related trade measures, as included in the EFTA-Indonesian Comprehensive Economic Partnership Agreement (CEPA) of 2018. While the latter approach—here introduction of PPM-related trade measures in the case of palm oil—promises to be more effective, some thoughts will be given as to their compatibility with WTO law.

4.1 EU/EFTA-Mercosur Agreement: More Nuanced Sustainability Chapter

4.1.1 Market Concessions in Agriculture

The following section refers to the documents available at the time of writing: the final draft text of the EU-Mercosur Trade Agreement, the concluding note as regards the EFTA-Mercosur Free Trade Agreement,[35] and the final text of the CEPA.[36]

Particularly relevant—from a food sustainability perspective—are the market concessions for agricultural products which are granted once the Agreement is finally ratified. As regards EU-Mercosur trade relations, on 93% of tariff lines, duties for EU agri-food exports to Mercosur countries will be eliminated gradually. At the same time, the EU will liberalise 82% of agricultural imports, and will offer limited tariff-rate quotas for sensitive products such as beef, poultry, pork, sugar, ethanol, rice, honey, and sweetcorn. Finally, reciprocal tariff-rate quotas for cheese and milk will be implemented. The EU states approvingly that the agreement will offer EU industries "cheaper high-quality raw material by reducing or eliminating duties that Mercosur currently imposes on exports to the EU of products such as soybean products (feed for EU livestock)."[37]

The EFTA-Mercosur Free Trade Agreement includes similar market concessions. According to the EFTA Secretariat, "the Agreement provides for meaningful tariff concessions on both basic and processed agricultural products." Exports from the EFTA to the Mercosur countries will be facilitated for cheese, roasted coffee, and processed sugar products such as chocolate, while at the same time, Mercosur products will benefit from more generous import quotas for beef, poultry, pork, soy, wheat, and oil.[38]

---

[35]European Free Trade Association Secretariat (EFTA) (2019) [cited: EFTA (2019)]. Final draft of the Agreement not yet published at the time of writing.

[36]Signed at the 16th December 2018, but not yet ratified at the time of writing.

[37]European Union EU (2019), p. 3.

[38]See EFTA (2019).

4.1.2 Sustainability Chapter to Increase Diplomatic Pressure

Aware that the production of meat, soy, and other agricultural products, is associated with serious sustainability concerns (see Sect. 5), the negotiators were under pressure to take account thereof. As a result, they opted to indirectly link market concessions to sustainability criteria by means of a sustainability chapter featuring more nuanced language than in the past. In the case of the EU-Mercosur agreement, a new institutional architecture for implementation of the chapter has been added.

In the relevant chapters on "trade and sustainable development", the trading partners commit to taking environmental and human rights standards seriously, in particular those to which they are already bound based on their prior adoption of international treaties. While each party is permitted to define its own level of social and environmental protection, a "race to the bottom" between the partner countries shall ostensibly be avoided by adhering to minimum standards.[39]

As previous sustainability chapters in trade agreements have been criticised for unspecific wording or lack of implementation,[40] the new sustainability chapter of the EU-Mercosur agreement includes quite specific, nuanced wording. According to its Article 6 on "Trade and Climate Change", for instance, each party to the agreement shall "promote the positive contribution of trade to a pathway towards low greenhouse gas emissions and climate-resilient development [...] that does not threaten food production". According to Article 7 on "Trade and Biodiversity", each party shall "encourage trade in natural resource-based products obtained through a sustainable use of biological resources or which contribute to the conservation of biodiversity". And according to Article 8 on "Trade and Sustainable Management of Forests", the parties shall "encourage trade in products from sustainably managed forests harvested in accordance with the law of the country of harvest", "promote [...] the inclusion of forest-based local communities and indigenous peoples in sustainable supply chains of timber and non-timber forest products", and "combat illegal logging and related trade". The EFTA-Mercosur Free Trade Agreement includes similar provisions, while a specific article on "trade and sustainable agriculture and farming systems" stipulates the commitment of the parties "to promote sustainable agriculture and associated trade and conduct a dialogue to address related issues".[41]

Technically, the sustainability chapter is legally binding. However, in the case of violations, access to dispute settlement mechanisms has regularly been excluded in EU and EFTA agreements.[42] As a result, in case of violations of the sustainability chapter, trade concessions will not be suspended. This architecture reflects the view

---

[39]By maintaining the partners' "right to regulate" and "right to define level of protection" in those areas.

[40]See e.g. Swiss Federal Council (2017), for sustainability chapters as included in EFTA-Agreements.

[41]See EFTA (2019).

[42]Cf. Bartels (2014).

that a trade-related dispute settlement body is not suited to adjudicate on implementation of environmental and human rights standards in partner countries, since the commitments laid down in the sustainability chapter concern each country as a whole. In cases of severe disregard of the sustainability chapter, partner countries—instead of suspending trade concessions—are called for consultations to ensure its implementation.

In response to past accusations of little relevance to this approach, a new institutional architecture has been included in recent agreements, including the EU-Mercosur Agreement. Recourse to dispute settlement remains excluded in case of violations of the chapter (Article 15). A party may, however, request consultations with the other party "regarding the interpretation or application of this Chapter" (Article 16). If no resolution can be reached, "a Party may request the establishment of a Panel of Experts to examine the matter" (Article 17). The panel of experts may issue recommendations which the parties shall discuss (Article 17). This institutional structure could serve to increase diplomatic pressure. However, no further sanctions are envisaged. As regards the EFTA-Mercosur agreement, the form of the "consultation architecture" is not yet known.

From a sustainability perspective, the EU, EFTA, and Mercosur countries deserve credit for having introduced a sustainability chapter into their trade agreements. In theory, the sustainability chapter restricts all partner countries to trading products that have been produced in compliance with the stated criteria, enabling effective promotion of diversified farming systems. However, due to the lack of sanctions or the possibility to suspend trade concessions in case of violations, the effectiveness of the chapter will remain limited: There is a risk of waning interest in debating sustainability issues after the agreement enters into force. Further, consultations cannot be requested by interested stakeholders, but only by parties to the agreement. The latter may be reluctant to request compliance with the sustainability chapter as a result of issues of political economy. It remains to be seen whether the new institutional setup in the EU-Mercosur Agreement, requiring the creation of a panel of experts, will reinforce the effectiveness of the chapter. As a particularly powerful actor, the EU could have more leeway in this regard than the EFTA or the Mercosur countries. Significantly, Mercosur countries could equally reproach the EU and EFTA countries for not producing in a sustainable way.

Finally, the effectiveness of the sustainability chapter will remain limited because "human rights and sustainability impacts flow from all parts of the agreement".[43] The trade concessions granted in the agreement, explicit commitments to strengthen *intellectual property* (IP) regimes—but also issues parties missed to address—can directly impact the sustainability trajectory of each country. In order to ensure sustainable outcomes, it is often more relevant how related provisions are shaped than how the sustainability chapter is formulated.

Taken together, sustainability chapters can serve as an important entry point not only for diplomatic discussions, but also for technical cooperation, ideally in

---

[43]Dommen (2020), p. 39.

combination with private-sector initiatives. However, more targeted mechanisms are available to promote diversified farming systems. The EFTA-Indonesian agreement, for instance, has made market concessions in palm oil trade directly conditional on sustainability criteria, as shall be discussed in the next section.

4.2 EFTA-Indonesia Agreement: Market Concessions Conditional on Sustainability Criteria

One particularly direct trade mechanism for promotion of diversified farming systems is that of *tariff differentiation* (or equivalent measures) based on the quality of PPMs. According to this approach, a partner country may—upon agreement with its negotiating partner(s)—introduce preferential tariffs for sustainably produced food, reserve (a share of) import quotas for them, or require domestic food processors to source from them. Tariff differentiation has been chosen in the CEPA to support more sustainable ways of producing palm oil in Indonesia.

The CEPA includes in its Annex V tariff concessions granted by the EFTA countries to Indonesia.[44] As stated in the "Schedule on tariff commitments on goods, commitments of Switzerland", raw palm oil of a certain category A (no feed) may benefit from an import quota ranging between 1000 and 1250 tons as well as a tariff reduction ranging between 30% and 53%. The quota for palm oil of a certain category B is a bit larger, and there are specific concessions for oil of specific quality.[45] Furthermore and significantly, the annex includes the following specification in small print:

> *= Products of HS heading 15.11 und 15.13 imported into Switzerland under this Agreement shall meet the sustainability objectives as set out in Article 8.10 (Sustainable Management of the Vegetable Oils Sector and Associated Trade) of the Agreement.[46]

This refers to Article 8.10 of the sustainability chapter of the CEPA, which explicitly states under paragraph 2 that the parties must:

> effectively apply laws, policies and practices aiming at protecting primary forests, peatlands, and related ecosystems, halting deforestation, peat drainage and fire clearing in land preparation, reducing air and water pollution, and respecting rights of local and indigenous communities and workers; [...]

and further that the parties must

---

[44]The text of the agreement can be found here: https://www.efta.int/free-trade/Free-Trade-Agreement/indonesia.

[45]For more detailed explanations regarding those commitments, see Bürgi Bonanomi (2019).

[46]Harmonised system (HS) heading 15.11 refers to palm oil, HS 15.13 to oil from coconut, palm kernel and babassu.

(e) ensure that vegetable oils and their derivatives traded between the Parties are produced in accordance with the sustainability objectives referred to in subparagraph (a).[47]

As a consequence, palm oil imported from Indonesia to the EFTA countries must be produced in a sustainable way that ensures Indonesian primary forests and peatlands remain protected; ensures deforestation, peat drainage, and fire clearing are halted; ensures air and water pollution are reduced; and ensures the rights of both local and indigenous communities as well as workers are respected. The provision refers to existing laws and policies of Indonesia, implicitly suggesting that requisite laws are in place but that their implementation needs to be strengthened.[48]

In addition, to ensure traceability along the value chain, further requirements have been included, such as that the respective palm oil must be transported "in tanks of not more than 22 tons".[49] Of significance in this regard is the Cooperation Chapter 9 of the CEPA, according to which EFTA countries agree to intensify cooperation, inter alia to assist Indonesia in establishing inclusive and sustainable production and value chains in the palm oil sector.[50] Cooperation consists in knowledge transfer and financial support. However, the desired extent of such cooperation is not explicitly quantified.

Hence, in the face of harsh criticism in the EFTA countries concerning "unsustainable" Indonesian palm oil production,[51] the partner countries to the CEPA have opted to go a step further and directly link sustainability criteria to trade concessions. Actual implementation will reveal whether such mechanisms can truly foster sustainable and inclusive value chains in the palm oil sector. Much will depend on the returns that can be obtained for sustainable palm oil when benefitting from (limited) tariff reduction, and on the control mechanism that is put in place. Importing countries will need to further concretise the criteria set out in Article 8.10.2 of the CEPA and further specify key elements of a sustainable and inclusive palm oil production system, such as equitable inclusion of small-scale farmers. They could then maintain a positive list of credible sustainability certification schemes that cover all the cited aspects. Certified products would then benefit from preferential tariffs as long as no serious doubts arise as to the rigour of certification.

Research on palm oil production in Indonesia shows that existing certification schemes come with serious deficiencies, as does actual palm oil production itself.[52]

---

[47]An identic add-on is included in the versions relevant for the other EFTA countries Norway, Iceland and Liechtenstein.

[48]See Bürgi Bonanomi (2019).

[49]Annex II, lit. i of the CEPA.

[50]Article 9.2 of the CEPA reads as follows: "Cooperation and capacity building shall cover sectors affected by the process of liberalisation and restructuring of the Indonesian economy as well as sectors with the potential to benefit from this Agreement."

[51]For academic literature concerning the challenges of palm oil production in Indonesia, see e.g. Znoj (2016), Colchester and Chao (2013), Murray Li (2014, 2017a, b), McCarthy (2010), Beckert et al. (2014) and Manoli et al. (2018).

[52]See e.g. Znoj (2016), Colchester and Chao (2013), Murray Li (2014, 2017a, b), McCarthy (2010), Beckert et al. (2014) and Manoli et al. (2018).

Tariff incentives alone may not be sufficient to improve the quality of certification schemes or actual production systems. Instead, strong programmes promoting transformation of current palm oil production, equipped with the necessary financial and technical support, may be needed.

To conclude, if the obligation to ensure compliance with sustainability criteria is solely left to private palm oil importers, these companies may find it too risky and shift their import business to other producer countries. If, however, tariff incentives to produce sustainably are combined with effective financial support of importing countries, the innovative approach is much more likely to succeed since regarded as equitable and fair by involved stakeholders.

5   WTO-Conformity of Tariff Preferences Based on PPMs

Overall, tariff incentives related to product differentiation—based on inclusive PPMs and combined with financial support—appear promising to promote more inclusive and diversified agricultural systems and incentivise respective transformation processes. Though such approaches may be required from a human rights and environmental law perspective, the question arises as to whether they are in compliance with WTO law. While bilateral and plurilateral trade agreements tend to be less scrutinised, they should still strive to follow the basic rules of international trade law to which most bilateral trade agreements refer explicitly and implicitly. The basic principles of international trade law are enshrined in various WTO agreements. To a limited extent, they provide some scope for sustainability related incentives.

5.1   Main Lines of Argumentation

A range of WTO case law deals with sustainability-oriented import barriers and quotas, conditioning of preference systems, sanitary and phytosanitary standards related to sustainability concerns, and labelling rules.[53] Though WTO compatibility

---

[53]The following WTO cases are particularly worthy of note: *US-Restrictions on Imports of Tuna II* (1994); *US–Measures Concerning the Importation, Marketing and Sale of Tuna and Tuna Products* (Tuna III, 2012); *US–Import Prohibition of Certain Shrimps and Shrimp Products* (Shrimps Case, 1998); *EC–Measures Concerning Meat and Meat Products* (Hormones Case, 1998); *EC–Conditions for the Granting of Tariff Preferences to Developing Countries* (GSP-Case, 2004); *US–Measures Affecting the Cross Border Supply of Gambling and Betting Services* (Gambling Case, 2005); *EC–Measures Affecting the Approval and Marketing of Biotech Products* (GMO-Case, 2006); *Brazil–Measures Affecting the Imports of Retreaded Tyres* (2007); *China–Measures Related to the Exportation of Various Raw Materials* (2012); and *EC–Measures Prohibiting the Importation and Marketing of Seal Products* (Seals Case, 2014). The full cases may be found at https://www. wto.org/english/tratop_e/dispu_e/dispu_status_e.html or http://www.worldtradelaw.net/. For explanations and the relevance of the cases for sustainability concerns, refer to De Schutter

is best examined in connection with concrete measures subject to challenge, there are several general considerations relevant to PPM-related trade measures that can be derived from current general jurisprudence.[54] At the centre of debate is, on the one hand, the question of how to interpret the *most-favoured nation* (MFN) clause and the *national treatment* (NT) clause as codified by Article I and Article III GATT (especially in connection with Article XI GATT on the regulation of import quotas). Should a product be considered a "like product" when it has similar characteristics to another product, but has been produced in a different way? According to current WTO jurisprudence—based above all on Border Tax Adjustment criteria[55]—one may assume that a conventionally produced banana and a banana stemming from a diversified farming system will be treated as "like" by the dispute settlement body of the WTO, thus excluding differential tariff treatment. Much depends, however, on how interpretation of the criteria of "consumer tastes and habits" evolves in the coming years, that is, whether consumers increasingly (desire to) distinguish between sustainably produced goods and non-sustainably produced goods such that they are not considered interchangeable.[56]

Since interpretation of the above-mentioned provisions has been rather restrictive so far, the General Exceptions formulated in Article XX GATT assume a further key role in the current jurisprudence. These exceptions allow for suspension of trade concessions for the protection of certain public interests—especially environmental interests, but also specific social goods, if they are "connected" in some way to the country providing the trade measure. In several cases, the existence of justifiable public interests in accordance with Article XX GATT has been recognised, showing there is some scope for sustainability-oriented trade measures. The main challenge today lies in the conditions of the chapeau of Article XX GATT, which refers to principles of non-discrimination and proportionality. As Cottier states, many PPMs imposed by countries have so far "failed to pass these tests and had to go back to the drawing board, however without being excluded in principle".[57] States that have introduced corresponding measures have lost in most cases, with their actions foundering on the non-discrimination clause. The arbitrators argued that the controversial measures served to favour domestic production, in a protectionist manner, since foreign suppliers could not implement them as easily as domestic suppliers.[58]

(2015) or to Bürgi Bonanomi (2015), Chapter 3. For a sustainability related analysis of the seal case, refer to Cottier (2018), pp. 69–92.

[54]PPMs in trade and related tariff differentiation have been debated in literature on climate protection and trade. See e.g. Holzer (2014) and Cottier et al. (2014a).

[55]According to border tax adjustment criteria as developed by the WTO jurisprudence, products must be treated as "like" if they come with the same physical characteristics, if consumers' tastes and habits imply that the products are substitutable, if the products' end-uses in a given market are identic and if tariff classification is the same. See Cottier and Oesch (2005), p. 403.

[56]See De Schutter (2015), pp. 48 ff. See also Howse (2012), p. 446.

[57]Cottier (2015), p. 4.

[58]The 1998 shrimp case is generally referred to as a key precedent. It was decided that a country seeking to introduce a trade-hindering measure based on public interest grounds must demonstrate

However, if designed in a non-discriminatory and proportional way, PPMs could very well pass WTO scrutiny. It is also important to note that WTO jurisprudence is dynamic and continues to evolve. In view of the global sustainable development agenda, it is becoming increasingly supportive of measures that seek to internalise social and environmental concerns, and is gradually shifting from a trade-liberalisation paradigm to a more complex trade-regulation paradigm that embraces trade and stabilisation concerns.[59]

5.2 Non-Discriminatory and Proportional PPMs

In view of the principles of non-discrimination and proportionality enshrined in WTO law, PPM-based tariff preferences have the best chance of withstanding WTO scrutiny when the following aspects are kept in mind. First, sustainability criteria should be flexibly tailored to cover various socio-environmental contexts and production conditions, building in particular on promising transformation processes already underway on the ground.[60] Accordingly, a requirement to comply with the domestic standards of the *importing* country—for instance mandating foreign production according to Swiss domestic organic ("bio") standards—would not be acceptable. Second, sustainability criteria as required by external suppliers should be equally applied to domestic actors in order for the policy measure to be consistent. Also, the measure must be designed in a proportional way, that is, no more interventional than necessary to reach the targeted objective. Finally, PPM-based tariff preferences will follow the spirit of trade law if—through the preferences—market access for sustainably produced products is effectively *facilitated*. This may require implementation of a package of policy measures, including recognition of local standards and procedures of foreign contexts as being equivalent to domestic ones, as well as the warranting of adequate financial and technical support.[61]

New practices as integrated in the CEPA bring the PPM issue back to the forefront of the debate. In general, the trade landscape is increasingly shaped by PPM-based trade measures. This can be seen, for instance, in domestic timber,

---

that it is working towards a concerted approach at the international level. At the same time, the measures must be designed such that trading partners could also implement them; see: Bürgi Bonanomi (2015), pp. 111 ff. The jurisprudence on standards and technical rules such as labels directly or indirectly supported by the government similarly requires—based on the SPS and TBT agreements—that these be designed in a consistent and non-discriminatory manner. The SPS Agreement further requires that the standards withstand scientific scrutiny (which led the EU to lose, for example, in the hormone case). For a thorough analysis of the current legal situation and corresponding jurisprudence, refer to De Schutter (2015).

[59]Musselli (2017).

[60]Bürgi Bonanomi et al. (2018).

[61]Cottier (2015), pp. 6–7.

fisheries, and biofuel regulation.[62] At the same time, there has been an evident shift in the public discourse as regards the PPM issue. Today, the argument is less that PPMs are not compliant with trade law, but rather that much depends on their design.[63] The question is, hence, not whether, but *how* the standard setting can be made transparent, inclusive, non-discriminatory, and consistent vis-à-vis domestic actors, without imposing unfair costs on the most vulnerable—namely, small producers, developing countries, and poor consumers. Finally, strengthening the economic competitiveness of sustainably produced food and making it affordable to low- and middle-income consumers presents another important economic rationale for involving not only private actors, but also state actors.

6 The Example of Brazil: A Missed Opportunity in the EU/EFTA-Mercosur Agreement?

In the previous sections, it has been argued that trade concessions based on PPMs, if designed in a non-discriminatory and inclusive way, have the potential to effectively promote diversified farming systems. In order to get their design right, in concrete trade negotiations, recourse to context-based knowledge is indispensable.

With respect to the EU/EFTA-Mercosur agreements, all the partner countries involved could have deliberately tabled sustainability-related arguments concerning food systems. Not only European, but also Mercosur countries could have asked the partner countries to promote diversified farming systems through the established trade relations. Also in most European countries, a rather ambivalent set of agricultural policies remains in place: Sustainability-oriented support measures have been introduced alongside measures promoting intensification of agricultural production—with the latter often generating negative environmental and social effects.[64] Nevertheless, in the relevant trade negotiations, it has mainly been the European countries confronting Mercosur countries with sustainability concerns rather than the other way round. Accordingly, in the following, some current patterns of farming systems in Brazil and Argentina will be presented that enable reflection on the optimal design of product differentiation.

---

[62]Solar and Bürgi Bonanomi (forthcoming, 2021).

[63]This was the agreed narrative at the World Trade Forum (WTF) 2019, organised by the World Trade Institute WTI in Bern, Switzerland. For a prominent reference in the media, see e.g. Vonplon (2019).

[64]For Switzerland, for instance, compare with Rist et al. (2020). For example, cities like Nuremberg or Geneva, or even entire countries, like Brazil (see Inguaggiato 2014), have committed to purchasing mainly "sustainably produced food" when supplying hospitals or schools.

6.1   Diversity in Brazil's Landscape and Socio-Economic Disparities: Potential and Threats

Brazil is an interesting case when investigating the potential for co-existence of diversified and specialised agro-industrial farming systems. Brazil is the fifth largest country in the world, encompassing an area of 236 million ha of which almost 30% is under agricultural production.[65] Its local biomes range from tropical rainforest to semi-arid savannah, presenting a wealth of opportunities for different forms of agricultural production. Since the 1960s, large-scale, agricultural production has massively expanded in Brazil, bringing with it severe environmental and social consequences.[66]

Deforestation of biomes rich in biodiversity is a well-known problem associated with expansion of agro-industrial production. While the Amazonian tropical rainforest in Brazil is not an appropriate biome for intensive agricultural production, national and international market opportunities for commodities such as soy and beef have nonetheless driven growth of intensive production in these areas and accordingly deforestation.[67] Existing state protection schemes of the Amazon and other natural landscapes have proven weak and incapable of hindering deforestation in practice.[68] After declining for a time, deforestation rates in the Amazon have been on the rise again since 2014.[69] The Cerrado, a Brazil-specific biome adjacent to the Amazon, can be described as something between tropical rainforest and savannah. Though it has received less media attention, the Cerrado is home to other key agricultural frontiers associated with severe pressures of deforestation.[70]

Both biomes, the Amazon and the Cerrado, are rich in biodiversity and could provide a good basis for inclusive, small-scale, agrobiodiversity-based forms of agricultural production. They are particularly suited to ways of cultivation that sustain intact nutrient cycles, protect soils and water resources by avoiding or limiting use of chemical inputs, and support existing biodiversity by applying agricultural practices that are adapted to local conditions. Such forms of agricultural production can provide livelihoods for rural communities and support healthy, diverse diets.[71] In economic terms, they have the potential to create jobs in production and processing of local agricultural goods, provided that profitable markets can be established for staple food and processed products resulting from such food systems.

---

[65]FAOSTAT (access to food and agriculture data of the Food and Agriculture Organization of the United Nations (FAO)) (2020).

[66]Graesser et al. (2018).

[67]Bowman et al. (2012).

[68]Graesser et al. (2018).

[69]Escobar (2019).

[70]Graesser et al. (2018); Moffette and Gibbs (2018), p. 21.

[71]Chappell and LaValle (2011).

At present, however, local expansion of agro-industrial frontiers seriously endangers biodiversity in both the Amazon and the Cerrado, also undermining the potentials described for local communities. Research evidence shows that this agro-industrial expansion is often associated with displacement of communities, sometimes including severe violations of human rights.[72] Under these conditions, co-existence of small-scale, diversified agricultural production and large-scale, agro-industrial production has proven to be too challenging.

The dynamics are exacerbated by socio-economic disparities. Brazil is characterised by extreme income and wealth inequality[73] as well as literacy problems among rural populations. Though inequality fell somewhat in Brazil between 2001 and 2014, owing to a combination of economic growth and social reforms,[74] the country still ranks among the most unequal in the world[75] in terms of income and wealth distribution. Inequality is also high in the states currently experiencing the greatest expansion of agricultural frontiers, including Amazonas, Para, Maranhão, Tocantins, Piaui, and Bahia. Among other issues, high illiteracy rates[76] complicate efforts to defend people against human rights violations and displacement in Brazil's poorest states.

6.2   Effective Policy Framework in Place, But Now Weakening

In order to cope with such challenges, an elaborate policy framework was developed in recent decades aimed both at reducing poverty and inequality and at supporting rural farming families. Based on the "zero hunger" strategy, the government of the Partido dos Trabalhadores (PT) introduced a widely praised programme in 2002 seeking to fight hunger, ensure social welfare, and stimulate jobs and income growth through well targeted economic measures. Introduced in a period of national economic growth, the strategy successfully lifted millions of Brazilians out of poverty.[77] Two of the most-influential parts of the strategy have been the family-farming food acquisition programme, known as Bolsa Familia, and the National School Feeding Programme, which effectively link family income and diets of poor people to small-scale agricultural production and family farming.[78] Bolsa Familia arranges cash

---

[72]Celentano et al. (2017), p. 694.

[73]International Social Science Council (ISSC), Institute of Development Studies (IDS), United Nations Educational, Scientific and Cultural Organization (UNESCO) (2016).

[74]Góes and Karpowicz (2017), p. 4.

[75]The World Bank (2020) World Development Indicators. http://datatopics.worldbank.org/world-development-indicators/ (last accessed 16 January 2020).

[76]Kempner and Loureiro (2002), p. 336.

[77]De Schutter (2009b), p. 19.

[78]For an analysis of the impact of the policies, see e.g. Inguaggiato (2014) and De Schutter (2009b).

transfers to poor families, which are linked to participation in specific health care programmes. The food acquisition programme guarantees that a proportion of the food procured for public schools, canteens, food baskets, etc. comes from family farmers.[79] Similarly, the National School Feeding Programme guarantees free meals for schoolchildren partly sourced from family farming, drawing on a well-established family-farming certificate.[80]

These programmes were lauded for effectively supporting a dual farming system in which more diversified small-scale farming systems could co-exist alongside large-scale, agro-industrial systems.[81] Though still in place, the programmes are under increasing pressure from Brazil's current government who is continuously cutting their funds. The government's publicly declared objective is neither to protect the natural environment in the Amazon and Cerrado nor to protect local communities,[82] but rather to promote the expansion of large-scale agro-industrial production and extraction. Overall, power structures have shifted significantly and political support has weakened for the successful programmes outlined above. Effective protection of diversified farming systems appears elusive in Brazil's current political climate. Against this backdrop, the question arises as to whether Brazil's existing, but threatened, framework to promote family farming should have served as an entry point for stronger negotiation of sustainability-related trade concessions with Brazil during EU/EFTA-Mercosur talks.

Similar patterns can be observed in Argentina. There are different laws and policies in place aimed at fostering more integrated, diversified ways of farming. These include the National Forest Law, concretised by provincial forest laws, the law on family agriculture, and policies to promote agroforestry-oriented ways of production where livestock farming and forest management are combined synergistically, known as "manejo de bosque con ganaderia interna" or MBGI.[83] However, research in Argentina has shown that, in practice, pressures of agro-industrial expansion often trump implementation of more integrated policy frameworks.[84]

---

[79]Veiga Aranha (2010), p. 96.

[80]Sanches Peraci and Alceu Bittencourt (2010), pp. 193ff.

[81]De Schutter (2009b).

[82]Diele-Viegas and Rocha (2020).

[83]See Ley 26.331 de Presupuestos Minimos de Proteccion Ambiental de los Bosques Nativos; Ley 27.118 de Agricultura Familiar, https://www.agro.unlp.edu.ar/novedad/argentina-tiene-una-ley-de-agricultura-familiar; and the Plan Nacional de Manejo de Bosques con Ganadería Integrada (PNMBGI), https://www.argentina.gob.ar/ambiente/tierra/bosques-suelos/manejo-sustentable-bosques/ganaderia-integrada.

[84]The EU funded Include project assesses the impacts of these policies: https://includeproject.wordpress.com/; see e.g. Inguaggiato (forthcoming, 2021).

6.3   Trade as a Lever to Promote Sustainable Development in Mercosur Countries and Europe

As these patterns suggest, enabling small-scale, diversified farming systems to co-exist alongside large-scale, specialised systems requires stronger protection for the former in such settings. Since protection of key (e.g. highly biodiverse) biomes and related human rights are increasingly considered vital matters of *common concern*,[85] international trade could and should be more deliberately shaped to avoid undesired dynamics like those noted above. Instead of merely opening up and liberalising markets in an undifferentiated manner as was criticised by Porto et al. (2019) in a critical response to the EU-Mercosur trade agreement.[86]

In the EU/EFTA-Mercosur negotiations, for instance, part of the conceded tariff rate quota for Brazil could have been reserved for soy, meat, and other agricultural products stemming explicitly from family-farming. These could have been combined with additional sustainability-oriented criteria. The reserved proportion of the tariff rate quota could have been increased over the years in order to incentivise expansion of more sustainable systems. Another option could have been to reserve a ratio of the conceded quota for products stemming from regions where—here in the case of Argentina—the forest law and MBGI policies are properly complied with, and/or where land tenure is effectively secured in line with the FAO Guidelines on Land Tenure.[87] A variety of tariff differentiations are conceivable in support of diversified, sustainable farming systems. Institutional frameworks to ensure sound implementation would need to be developed.

Such incentives would have to be combined with market concessions for *processed* products stemming from the promoted farming systems.[88] Enabling trade of value-added sustainable agricultural products would not only serve greater North–South equity, but also follow the recommendation by experts to transition towards farming systems that operate on the basis of closed nutrient cycles. Notably, this would also require more willingness in European countries to shift towards closed nutrient cycles in their own domestic farming systems and—as a consequence—to shift towards less intensive-livestock production, for example. Finally, European countries would need to reduce or dismantle certain policy mechanisms that serve to protect their domestic food-processing industry.[89]

Of course, it cannot be assumed that Mercosur countries would easily agree to such proposals, even if embedded in explicit reciprocal terms. If such trade

---

[85]For the emerging concept of common concern, see e.g. Cottier et al. (2014b).

[86]Porto et al. (2019).

[87]Food and Agriculture Organization (FAO) (2012).

[88]While, from a sustainability perspective, farming systems of closed nutrient cycles are to be promoted, there is a complementary need for a trading system encouraging not so much commodity trade but rather trade in value-added products. See e.g. a related World Bank report: Mattoo et al. (2013).

[89]See Bürgi Bonanomi et al. (2018), Chapter 3.

incentives, however, were combined with effective financial support and reliable prospects of increased access to European markets for high quality value-added products, the picture might look different.

7 Conclusion

Given the persistence of severe sustainability problems in food production world-wide—as illustrated by the Brazilian example—states should seize the opportunity offered by trade agreements to foster more sustainable farming systems. They can do so by incorporating innovative trade rules along the lines of carefully designed, non-discriminatory PPMs that comply with fundamental principles of international law, in combination with the provision of technical and financial support. Trade partners should strive to overcome their reluctance towards PPMs, recognising the reciprocal benefits they can provide. The EFTA-Indonesian Comprehensive Economic Partnership Agreement (CEPA) could serve as a good example going forward, provided its implementation is consistent with the text of the agreement. Nevertheless, the approach chosen in the CEPA has limitations. Merely market concessions for palm oil were made contingent on compliance with sustainability criteria, rather narrowly focusing on challenges related to palm oil production in Indonesia. A variety of other—likely acute—environmental and social problems of food production in EFTA countries were not considered in the negotiations. The chosen approach would gain recognition if the trade agreement was used as a lever to promote sustainable transformation of farming systems in *all* the partner countries involved.

In order to increase the sustainability impacts of this and other such agreements, effective market concessions are needed that cover not just a few, but rather a range of agricultural products—including high-value processed goods—stemming from diversified farming systems, especially for partner countries more in need of such concessions. Further, additional substantive provisions of the trade agreement—e.g. those concerning non-tariff barriers or the protection of intellectual property in seed production—would need to be shaped in view of the envisaged sustainability goals. In this way, the innovative approach presented and discussed in this paper is only part of a broader picture. It can and should be refined in future agreements to come.

References

Bartels L (2014) A model human rights clause for the EU's international trade agreements. German Institute for Human Rights and Misereor

Beckert B, Dittrich C, Adiwibowo S (2014) Contested land: an analysis of multi-layered conflicts in Jambi province, Sumatra, Indonesia. ASEAS. Aust J South-East Asian Stud 7(1):75–92

Bowman MS, Soares-Filho BS, Merry FD, Nepstad DC, Rodrigues H, Almeida OT (2012) Persistence of cattle ranching in the Brazilian Amazon: a spatial analysis of the rationale for beef production. Land Use Policy 29:558–568

Bundesamt für Umwelt (2018) Umwelt-Fussabdrücke der Schweiz. Zeitlicher Verlauf 1996 – 2015. BAFU, Bern

Bürgi Bonanomi E (2011) Trade law and responsible investment. In: International Land Coalition (ILC), Oxfam, Somo, WTI, International instruments influencing the rights of people facing investment in agricultural lands, pp 68–88

Bürgi Bonanomi E (2015) Sustainable development in international law making and trade, international food governance and trade in agriculture. Edward Elgar, Cheltenham, Chapter 7.3.3

Bürgi Bonanomi E (2017) Measuring human rights impacts of trade agreements: ideas for improving the methodology, comparing the EU's sustainability impact assessment practice and methodology with human rights impact assessment methodology. J Hum Rights Pract (Oxford University Press) 9:481–503

Bürgi Bonanomi E (2019) Die Nachhaltigkeit im Handelsabkommen mit Indonesien, mit besonderem Fokus auf die Regulierung des Palmöl-Imports. Studie im Auftrag der Agrarallianz, CDE

Bürgi Bonanomi E, Jacobi J, Scharrer B (2018) Food sustainability in Bolivia through fair food in Switzerland? How to improve food sustainability in both the north and the south through sustainable trade relations. Latin Am J Int Trade Law 6(2):27–65

Celentano D, Rousseau GX, Muniz FH, van Deursen Varga I, Martinez C, Carneiro MS, Miranda MVC, Barros MNR, Freitas L, da Silva Narvaes I, Adami M, Rodrigues Gomes A, Rodrigues JC, Martins MB (2017) Towards zero deforestation and forest restoration in the Amazon region of Maranhão state, Brazil. Land Use Policy 68:692–698. https://doi.org/10.1016/j.landusepol.2017.07.041

Chappell MJ, LaValle LA (2011) Food security and biodiversity: can we have both? An agroecological analysis. Agric Hum Values 28:3–26. https://doi.org/10.1007/s10460-009-9251-4

Colchester M, Chao S (eds) (2013) Conflict or consent? The oil palm sector at a crossroads. FPP, Sawit Watch, Tuk Indonesia

Cottier T (2015) Renewable energy and process and production methods (E15Initiative). International Centre for Trade and Sustainable Development (ICTSD) and World Economic Forum, Geneva

Cottier T (2018) The implications of EC – Seal products for the protection of core labour standards in WTO law. In: Gött H (ed) Labour standards in international economic law. Springer, pp 69–92

Cottier T, Oesch M (2005) International trade regulation. Staempfli, Bern

Cottier T, Nortova O, Shingal A (2014a) The potential of tariff policy for climate change mitigation: legal and economic analysis. J World Trade 48(5):1007–1037

Cottier T, Aerni P, Karapinar K, Matteotti S, de Sépibus J, Shingal A (2014b) The principle of common concern and climate change. Archiv des Völkerrechts 52(3):293–325

De Schutter O (2009a) Report of the special rapporteur on the right to food. Mission to the World Trade Organization, A/HRC/10/5/Add.2

De Schutter O (2009b) Mission to Brazil. Report of the special rapporteur on the right to food. A/HRC/13/33/Add.6

De Schutter O (2015) Trade in the service of sustainable development. Linking trade to labour rights and environmental standards. Hart, Oxford

Diele-Viegas LM, Rocha CFD (2020) Why releasing mining on Amazonian indigenous lands and the advance of agrobusiness is extremely harmful for the mitigation of world's climate change? Comment on Pereira et al. (Environmental Science & Policy 100 (2019) 8–12). Environ Sci Policy 103:30–31

Dommen C (2020) Blueprint for a human rights impact assessment of the planned comprehensive free trade agreement between EFTA and Mercosur. Study commissioned by Alliance Sud

Escobar H (2019) Amazon fires clearly linked to deforestation, scientists say. Science 365 (6456):853. https://doi.org/10.1126/science.365.6456.853

European Free Trade Association Secretariat (EFTA) (2019) EFTA-Mercosur free trade negotiation - Conclusion in substance of the EFTA-Mercosur free trade negotiations, 23 August 2019

European Union (EU) (2019) New EU-Mercosur trade agreement, The agreement in principle. 1st July 2019, Brussels, pp 1–17

Eyhorn F, Muller A, Reganold JP, Frison E, Herren HR, Luttikholt L, Mueller A, Sanders J, Scialabba NEH, Seufert V, Smith P (2019) Sustainability in global agriculture driven by organic farming. Nat Sustain 2:253–255

FAOSTAT (access to food and agriculture data of the Food and Agriculture Organization of the United Nations (FAO)) (2020) Data for the year 2017. http://www.fao.org/faostat/en/#data. Last accessed 15 Jan 2020

Food and Agriculture Organization of the United Nations (FAO) (2012) Voluntary guidelines on the responsible governance of tenure of land, fisheries and forests in the context of national food security. http://www.fao.org/3/a-i2801e.pdf

Food and Agriculture Organization of the United Nations (FAO), Institut national de la recherche agronomique (INRA) (2016) In: Loconto A, Poisot AS, Santacoloma P (eds) Innovative markets for sustainable agriculture. How innovations in market institutions encourage sustainable agriculture in developing countries. Rome

Góes C, Karpowicz I (2017) Inequality in Brazil: a regional perspective. International Monetary Fund

Graesser J, Ramankutty N, Coomes OT (2018) Increasing expansion of large-scale crop production onto deforested land in sub-Andean South America. Environ Res Lett 13(8):084021. https://doi.org/10.1088/1748-9326/aad5bf

Graeub BE, Jahi Chappell M, Wittman H, Ledermann S, Bezner Kerr R, Gemmill-Herren B (2016) The state of family farms in the world. World Dev 87:1–15

High Level Panel of Experts (HLPE) (2019) Agroecological and other innovative approaches for sustainable agriculture and food systems that enhance food security and nutrition. A report by the high level panel of experts on Food Security and Nutrition of the Committee on World Food Security, Rome

Holzer K (2014) Carbon-related border adjustment and WTO law. Edward Elgar, Cheltenham

Howse R (2012) Regulatory measures. In: Daunton M, Narlikar A, Stern RM (eds) The Oxford handbook on the World Trade Organization. Oxford University Press, Oxford

Independent Group of Scientists appointed by the Secretary-General (2019) The future is now – science for achieving sustainable development, Global Sustainable Development Report (GSDR), United Nations, New York

Inguaggiato C (2014) Agrarian reform, social movements and community based organization: the emergence of new organizational forms? A case study in Northeast Brazil. PhD dissertation, University of Trento

Inguaggiato C (forthcoming, 2021) Governance structures and competing forest policy preferences: a policy network study of forest law in Northwest of Argentina

International Social Science Council (ISSC), Institute of Development Studies (IDS), United Nations Educational, Scientific and Cultural Organization (UNESCO) (2016) World Social Science Report 2016. Challenging inequalities: pathways to a just world. UNESCO Publishing, Paris

IPES-Food (2016) From uniformity to diversity: a paradigm shift from industrial agriculture to diversified agroecological systems. International Panel of Experts on Sustainable Food systems

Kempner K, Loureiro A (2002) The global politics of education: Brazil and the World Bank. Higher Educ 43:331–354

Kiriti Nganga T, Mugo MG, Bürgi E, Kiteme B (2018) Impact of economic regimes on food systems in Kenya. R4D food sustainability, working paper no. 7

Kremen C, Iles A, Bacon C (2012) Diversified farming systems: an agroecological, systems-based alternative to modern industrial agriculture. Ecol Soc 17(4):44

Manoli G, Meijide A, Huth N, Knohl A, Kosugi Y, Burlando P, Ghazoul J, Fatichi S (2018) Ecohydrological changes after tropical forest conversion to oil palm. Environ Res Lett 13:064035

Mattoo A, Whang Z, Wei SJ (eds) (2013) Trade in value added, developing new measures of cross-border trade. The International Bank for Reconstruction and Development/The World Bank

McCarthy JF (2010) Processes of inclusion and adverse incorporation: oil palm and agrarian change in Sumatra. Indonesia J Peasant Stud 37(4):821–850

Messerli P, Giger M, Dwyer MB, Breu T, Eckert S (2014) The geography of large-scale land acquisitions: analysing socio-ecological patterns of target contexts in the global South. Appl Geogr 53:449–459

Moffette F, Gibbs H (2018) Agricultural displacement and deforestation leakage in the Brazilian legal Amazon. Retrieved from Semantic Scholar, 16 January 2020

Murray Li T (2014) The gendered dynamics of Indonesia's oil palm labour regime. Asia Research Institute, Working paper no. 225

Murray Li T (2017a) The price of un/freedom: Indonesia's colonial and contemporary plantation labor regimes. Comp Stud Soc Hist 59(2):245–276

Murray Li T (2017b) Intergenerational displacement in Indonesia's oil palm plantation zone. J Peasant Stud 44(6)

Musselli I (2017) Agriculture, price stabilisation and trade rules: a principled approach. Brill Nijhoff, Leiden

Oberlack C, Sietz D, Bürgi Bonanomi E, de Brémond A, Dell'Angelo J, Eisenack K, Ellis EC, Epstein G, Giger M, Heinimann A, Kimmich C, Kok MTJ, Manuel-Navarrete D, Messerli P, Meyfroidt P, Václavík T, Villamayor-Tomas S (2019) Archetype analysis in sustainability research: meanings, motivations, and evidence-based policy making. Ecol Soc 24(2):26

Ostrom E (2005) Understanding institutional diversity. Princeton University Press, Princeton

Porto S, Cintrão RP, Maluf R (2019) Trade agreement between European Union and the Mercosur: some critical points on agrifood matters. https://www.cde.unibe.ch/e65013/e542846/e542016/e837263/e837264/AgreementEU-Mercosur_eng.pdf

Ricciardi V, Ramankutty N, Mehrabi Z, Jarvis L, Chookolingo B (2018) How much of the world's food do smallholders produce? Glob Food Secur 17:64–72

Rist S, Bürgi Bonanomi E, Giger M, Hett C, Scharrer B, Jacobi J, Lannen A (2020) Variety is the source of life: agrobiodiversity benefits, challenges, and needs. Swiss Academies Factsheet 15 (1). Swiss Academies of Arts and Sciences. Bern

Sanches Peraci A, Alceu Bittencourt G (2010) Family farming and price guarantee programs in Brazil: the food acquisition program (PAA). In: da Silva JG, del Grossi M, de França CG (eds) The fome zero (zero hunger) program: the Brazilian experience

Solar J, Bürgi Bonanomi E (forthcoming, 2021) PPMs in European trade practice, comparative legal analysis

Swiss Federal Council (2017) Auswirkungen von Freihandelsabkommen, Bericht der GPK-N vom 4. Juli 2017, Stellungnahme des Bundesrates vom 22. September 2017

The World Bank (2020) World development indicators. http://datatopics.worldbank.org/world-development-indicators/. Last accessed 16 Jan 2020

Tschopp M, Bieri S, Rist S (2018) Quinoa and production rules: how are cooperatives contributing to governance of natural resources? Int J Commons 12(1):402–427

United Nations Conference on Trade and Development (UNCTAD) (2013) Trade and environment review 2013 - wake up before it is too late: make agriculture truly sustainable now for food security in a changing climate

Veiga Aranha A (2010) Zero hunger: a project turned into a government strategy. In: da Silva JG, del Grossi M, de França CG (eds) The fome zero (zero hunger) program: the Brazilian experience

Vonplon D (2019) Freihandel und Nachhaltigkeit passen zusammen. Neue Zürcher Zeitung NZZ, 17. Oktober 2019

Znoj H (2016) Korruption im und um das indonesische Verteidigungsministerium. Expertise. Institut für Sozialanthropologie, Universität Bern

Elisabeth Bürgi Bonanomi, attorney at law, is senior lecturer and research scientist at the CDE and the law faculty of the University of Bern. Her teaching, interdisciplinary research and legal consulting focuses on Sustainable Development Law and Governance, Sustainable Trade in Agriculture, International Tax Regulation and Development, Commodity Trade Governance as well as legal issues as related to Business Responsibility. She has field experience in Sierra Leone, Kenya, Bolivia, Laos, Ghana, Switzerland, Germany, Europe, and others.

Theresa Tribaldos is a geographer and political scientist by training and works as a senior research scientist at the CDE of the University of Bern. Her research focuses on the sustainability of food systems and interventions to make these systems more sustainable, transdisciplinary research approaches for sustainable development, and the contributions science can make to support sustainability transformations. She has field experience in various countries of South America, and others.

The Mercosur-EU FTA and the Obligation to Implement the Paris Agreement: An Analysis from the Brazilian Perspective

Alberto do Amaral Jr and Marina Martins Martes

Contents

Abstract Nowadays, the relation between trade and environment is widely recognized. Several trade agreements address environmental issues—including World Trade Organization (WTO) agreements, and there are extensive studies in this field as well as relevant international cases which have acknowledged the need to consider the environmental aspects of trade measures. The Free Trade Agreement (FTA) concluded between Mercosur and the European Union (EU) follows this tendency. It contains a Chapter on Trade and Sustainable Development, which comprises a provision establishing that the Parties shall effectively implement the United Nations Framework on Climate Change (UNFCC) and the Paris Agreement. In view of that, this paper explains the link between trade and climate change, analyses the obligations assumed by the Parties (particularly Brazil) under the Paris Agreement, and finally shows the consequences the inclusion of a provision on the implementation of an environmental commitment under a free trade

A. do Amaral Jr (✉) and M. M. Martes
Faculty of Law, University of São Paulo, São Paulo, Brazil

© Springer Nature Switzerland AG 2021
M. Bungenberg et al. (eds.), *European Yearbook of International Economic Law 2020*,
European Yearbook of International Economic Law (2022) 11: 387–410,
https://doi.org/10.1007/8165_2021_68, Published online: 6 March 2021

agreement brings about. Based on that, this paper concludes that, although there may be no legal or trade consequences in case of an eventual breach of environmental obligations, this would certainly have serious political effects, which may impair the implementation of the FTA.

1 Introduction

On June 28, 2019, Mercosur and the European Union (EU) concluded negotiations on the Free Trade Agreement (FTA). The FTA was highly celebrated, having seen that its negotiations extended for nearly two decades.

The FTA is far from a simple preferential tariff agreement. It addresses several non-tariff and non-trade issues, and contains a Chapter solely dedicated to Trade and Sustainable Development. Within such Chapter, there is a specific provision determining that Parties shall effectively implement the United Nations Framework on Climate Change and the Paris Agreement.

The incorporation of a Chapter exclusively concerned with trade and sustainable development is not an innovation brought by the Mercosur-EU FTA—there are other recent trade agreements which have done the same. Moreover, there are several other trade agreements that have already addressed environment related issues.

Nevertheless, the inclusion of a provision establishing that Parties shall "effectively implement" the UNFCC and the Paris Agreement here has an interesting political context. The provision seems to have been a demand by the French Government, after threats made by the Brazilian President to withdraw from the Paris Agreement. Therefore, implementation of the Paris Agreement is an important aspect of the FTA that will be likely monitored by the Parties—and Brazil seems to be in the spotlight.

In view of that, the purpose of this paper is to understand, firstly, how trade and climate change are connected. Secondly, to explain what the obligations assumed by Brazil under the Paris Agreement are.[1] Based on these two analyses, this paper intends to show the actual consequences of including such a provision in the Mercosur-EU FTA and how it may impact Brazil.

---

[1]The Mercosur-EU FTA provides that Parties shall effectively implement their obligations both under the UNFCC and the Paris Agreement. This paper focuses solely on the Paris Agreement, since it is the most recent agreement concluded under the UNFCC.

2 The Mercosur-EU FTA and Climate Change

The FTA is expected to progressively eliminate tariffs on several products exchanged between the two blocs, in a period of 15 years. Such products include agricultural goods, such as orange juice, meat, sugar, and ethanol—products of great value to Brazil.

According to estimates made by the Brazilian Ministry of the Economy, the FTA will represent earnings of 87.5 billion dollars in Brazil's GDP, over 15 years of tariff reduction. Investments are also expected to increase in 113 billion dollars and the Brazilian exports to the EU in 100 billion dollars.[2]

The FTA, therefore, represents a great opportunity for Brazil to expand its presence on the international market, especially when it comes to the export of agricultural and livestock products. Notwithstanding that, the Agreement is not a simple preferential treatment agreement. As part of the new generation of trade agreements, it encompasses clauses on services, government procurement, trade facilitation, technical barriers, sanitary and phytosanitary measures, intellectual property, and sustainable development.

The analysis hereby proposed is concerned specifically with Article 6.2 of the Sustainable Development Chapter, which deals with the issue of Trade and Climate Change and establishes that Parties shall implement the Paris Agreement.

As it will be seen below, the discussions on trade and climate change are not an innovation of the Mercosur-EU FTA. However, given the context in which this clause was included, special attention should be drawn to it.

2.1 Why Trade and Climate Change?

The connection between trade and environment protection is not a novelty brought about by recent trade agreements.

Several of the WTO Agreements, concluded as a result of the Uruguay Round back in 1994, have referred to the need to protect the environment and to foster sustainable development.

---

[2]Brazilian Ministry of Foreign Affairs, Conclusion of the Negotiations of the Agreement between Mercosur and the European Union: Joint Press Release of the Ministries of Foreign Affairs, of Economy and of Agriculture, Livestock and Food Supply. June 2019, http://www.itamaraty.gov.br/pt-BR/notas-a-imprensa/20560-conclusao-das-negociacoes-do-acordo-entre-o-mercosul-e-a-uniao-europeia-nota-conjunta-dos-ministerios-das-relacoes-exteriores-da-economia-e-da-agricultura-pecuaria-e-abastecimento-bruxelas-27-e-28-de-junho-de-2019 (last accessed 28 February 2020).

These include the Marrakesh Agreement Establishing the WTO,[3] the General Agreement on Tariffs and Trade (GATT),[4] the Subsidies and Countervailing Measures Agreement (SCM),[5] the Sanitary and Phytosanitary Measures (SPS) and the Technical Barriers to Trade (TBT) Agreement,[6] the Agreement on Agriculture (AoA)[7] and the Agreement on Trade Related Aspects of Intellectual Property Rights (TRIPS).[8]

In the very same year of its creation, the WTO has also instituted the Committee on Trade and Environment (CTE), which is responsible for understanding and making recommendations on how to better regulate the relationship between trade and environment.[9]

---

[3]The Preamble of the Agreement establishes that "*Recognizing that field of trade and economic endeavor should be conducted with a view to raising standards of living, ensuring full employment and a large and steadily growing volume of real income and effective demand, and expanding the production of and trade in goods and services, while allowing for the optimal use of the world's resources in accordance with the objective of sustainable development, seeking both to protect and preserve the environment and to enhance the means for doing so in a manner consistent with their respective needs and concerns at different levels of economic development*", https://www.wto.org/english/docs_e/legal_e/04-wto.pdf (last accessed 29 February 2020).

[4]Article XX(g), GATT, refers to measures "relating to the conservation of exhaustible natural resources". Additionally, Article XX(b) of GATT indicates the need to protect human, animal and plant life or health, https://www.wto.org/english/docs_e/legal_e/gatt47.pdf (last accessed 29 February 2020).

[5]One of the "non-actionable" subsidies provided by the Agreement (i.e. subsidies that do not entitle other Members to make claims at the WTO) are those that aim to provide "assistance to promote adaptation of existing facilities to new environmental requirements imposed by law and/or regulations which result in greater constraints and financial burden on firms". There are, of course, several additional conditions for such subsidies to be "non-actionable" to prevent disguised protectionism. Full Agreement available at: https://www.wto.org/english/docs_e/legal_e/24-scm.pdf (last accessed 29 February 2020).

[6]The SPS and TBT Agreements allow the imposition of barriers to trade to protect the environment, provided that these measures are duly justified and proportionate to the protection aimed. The requirements for a WTO Member to impose non-tariff barriers to trade under such Agreements are quite strict, so that Members are prevented from adopting disguised protectionist measures. SPS Full Agreement is available at: https://www.wto.org/English/tratop_e/sps_e/spsagr_e.htm (last accessed 29 February 2020). TBT Full Agreement available at: https://www.wto.org/english/docs_e/legal_e/17-tbt_e.htm (last accessed 29 February 2020).

[7]The preamble of the Agricultural Agreement establishes that the program to reform trade in agriculture should take into account non-trade concerns, including the need to protect the environment. Full Agreement is available at: https://www.wto.org/english/docs_e/legal_e/14-ag_01_e.htm (last accessed 29 February 2020).

[8]With respect to the TRIPS, it allows Members to exclude inventions from patentability in order to avoid serious prejudice to the environment. Full Agreement available at: https://www.wto.org/english/docs_e/legal_e/27-trips.pdf (last accessed 29 February 2020).

[9]More information available at: https://www.wto.org/english/tratop_e/envir_e/wrk_committee_e.htm (last accessed 29 February 2020).

Therefore, despite the resistance of many to recognize the linkage between trade and environment,[10] such connection has always been there, and it has already been addressed in relatively old trade agreements.

It is undeniable, though, that this new generation of trade agreements has been more concerned with environmental issues and has started to dedicate entire chapters to address them. To focus on the problem in a more effective manner, such agreements are dealing with more specific issues on trade and environment protection, including the relationship between trade and climate change.

In this regard, in 2009, the WTO, jointly with the United Nations Environment Program (UNEP), released a detailed report on trade and climate change,[11] which analyses the problem from three different perspectives: (1) the effects of trade on climate change; (2) the contribution of trade to mitigation and adaptation efforts to address climate change; and (3) the effects of climate change on trade.

With respect to the first perspective, the study concludes that trade is likely to increase gas emissions, mostly due to the consequent increase in production and transportation[12] caused by trade liberalization.[13]

Nonetheless, the report also indicates that international trade may contribute to mitigation and adaptation actions.[14] This is because trade usually enhances technology and know-how transfer, which may assist countries to develop new technologies to mitigate and adapt to climate change. Further, trade may facilitate the adaption to climate change by making products (especially food) available in areas where they have been extinguished or made scarce.[15]

Finally, the study concludes that there are likely two effects of climate change on trade: the modification of the parties' comparative advantage, given that climate change may seriously harm agriculture in certain regions, and the increase in the vulnerability of supply (chains), since extreme weather conditions (which, as we are

---

[10]This was the mindset reflected in the Tuna-Dolphin Case of 1991, when the Panel considered that the GATT did not authorize Members to adopt trade measures with the intention of enforcing its own domestic laws in other Members' countries, even if such measures were to protect animal health or exhaustible natural resources.
According to Howse, "these rulings were without a textual basis in GATT law but based, instead, on some intuitive notion that allowing trade measures to address global environmental externalities was somehow countenancing a slippery slope towards unconstrained green protection". Howse (2016), p. 37.

[11]UNEP, WTO (2009).

[12]The problem of high emissions of aviation and shipping has inflated in the last years. As highlighted in a study made in the Wuppertal Institute for Climate, Environment and Energy, "emissions from international aviation and shipping activities account for an ever larger share of greenhouse gas emissions globally. If they were a country, they would rank amongst the world's top 10 emitters and have in recent years grown twice as fast as emissions in general, with projected increases of 250–300 per cent until 2050". Obergassel et al. (2015).

[13]UNEP, WTO (2009), pp. 53–60.

[14]UNEP, WTO (2009), pp. 61–63.

[15]This is also the opinion of Alberto do Amaral Jr. in his book "International Trade and Environment Protection" (free translation). Amaral Jr (2011), p. 275.

already witnessing by 2020, are becoming more frequent due to the temperature increase) may close ports and damage transport routes as well as infrastructure necessary for trade.

Thus, the relation between trade and climate change is very close. That is why several trade agreements, such as the Mercosur-EU FTA, have been carefully addressing the matter.

2.2 Trade and Climate Change in the Mercosur-EU FTA

The climate change provision in the Mercosur-EU FTA is contained within the Sustainable Development Chapter and provides that:

Trade and Climate Change

1. The Parties recognise the importance of pursuing the ultimate objective of the United Nations Framework Convention on Climate Change (UNFCCC) in order to address the urgent threat of climate change and the role of trade to this end.

2. Pursuant to paragraph 1, each Party shall:

(a) effectively implement the UNFCCC and the Paris Agreement established thereunder;

(b) consistent with Article 2 of the Paris Agreement, promote the positive contribution of trade to a pathway towards low greenhouse gas emissions and climate-resilient development and to increasing the ability to adapt to the adverse impacts of climate change in a manner that does not threaten food production.

3. The Parties shall also cooperate, as appropriate, on trade-related climate change issues bilaterally, regionally and in international fora, particularly in the UNFCCC.[16]

Although not yet present in other agreements concluded by Mercosur,[17] this is not the first time that the EU has concluded free trade agreements containing clauses on climate change. The Agreements with Singapore[18] and Canada[19] comprise such provisions as well. The one with Singapore, concluded in 2018, encompasses a very similar clause to that of the EU-Mercosur FTA. It establishes that Parties will

---

[16]Article 6, Chapter Trade and Sustainable Development. Mercosur-EU FTA.

[17]The Mercosur-EU FTA is the first one which contains a clause exclusively dedicated to climate change. Recently Brazil and Chile have concluded a free trade agreement, which contains provisions on the environment. Such text of this Agreement, however, has not been yet released. More information is available at the Brazilian Ministry of Economy's website: http://www.mdic.gov.br/index.php/ultimas-noticias/3695-brasil-e-chile-assinam-acordo-de-livre-comercio (last accessed 29 February 2020).

[18]Free Trade Agreement between the European Union and the Republic of Singapore (EU-Singapore FTA), OJ 2019 L 294/3, https://eur-lex.europa.eu/legal-content/EN/TXT/PDF/?uri=CELEX:22019A1114(01)&from=EN (last accessed 29 February 2020).

[19]Comprehensive Economic and Free Trade Agreement (CETA) between Canada and the European Union, OJ 2017 L 11/23, https://eur-lex.europa.eu/legal-content/EN/TXT/PDF/?uri=CELEX:22017A0114(01)&from=EN (last accessed 29 February 2020).

implement the multilateral environmental agreements to which they are parties to and reinforces their commitments to the UNFCC and Paris Agreement.

In fact, the aspect of the Mercosur-EU FTA that calls more attention is the context in which the clause on climate change was included. At the beginning of 2019, Brazil's then newly elected president, Jair Bolsonaro, threatened to withdraw from the Paris' Agreement. Such threat has echoed in the international sphere and a few months later, in June 2019, during the 2019 G20 meeting, France's President, Emmanuel Macron, pressured Brazil to accept the inclusion of a strong reference to the Paris Agreement in the FTA.

In the very same week, the Agreement was concluded with a clause providing that the Parties shall effectively implement the UNFCC and the Paris Agreement established thereunder. The strong language of the clause, particularly the use of the term *shall*, shows that Parties have a binding obligation to implement and naturally not to withdraw from the Paris Agreement. It is also a clear response to the threats made by the Brazilian President.

In a factsheet on the Trade and Sustainable Development Chapter published by the European Commission right after the negotiations of the FTA were concluded, it is stated that:

> The EU and Mercosur commit to effectively implement the Paris Climate Agreement and agree to cooperate on the climate aspects of trade between the two sides. The Paris Agreement includes, for example:
>
> – a pledge by Brazil to reduce by 2025 its net greenhouse gas emissions by 37% compared to 2005 levels
> – action to stop illegal deforestation including in the Brazilian Amazon
> – a pledge by the EU to reduce its domestic emissions by at least 40% by 2030[20]

As seen, although Mercosur is composed of four countries, the EU seems to be particularly concerned with Brazil's implementation of the Paris Agreement. The question now is what this implies in practice and what are the trade effects (if there are any) of the inclusion of such a provision in the FTA.

3 The Paris Agreement and Brazil

In 2015, 197 Parties concluded the Paris Agreement to the UNFCC.[21] The Agreement is considered a landmark in international environmental law, given that it was the first time that all countries in the world achieved a (legally-binding) compromise on climate change.

---

[20]European Commission, EU-Mercosur Trade Agreement: Trade and Sustainable Development (2019), https://trade.ec.europa.eu/doclib/press/index.cfm?id=2038 (last accessed 01 March 2020).

[21]As informed by the UNFCC, until the present moment, 187 Parties have ratified the Agreement. UNFCC, Paris Agreement—Status of Ratification, https://unfccc.int/process/the-paris-agreement/status-of-ratification (last accessed 16 February 2020).

Despite some complications that arose after the Agreement was concluded, including the withdrawal from the United States of America,[22] the Paris Agreement is already in force[23] and is still very ambitious.

3.1 The Paris Agreement's Objectives

The Paris Agreement has the purpose of strengthening "the global response to the threat of climate change, in the context of sustainable development and efforts to eradicate poverty".[24] In order to make this strengthening possible, the Agreement establishes three main pillars.

The first one is *mitigation*, which consists in the general objective to hold the increase in the global average temperature to well below 2 °C pre-industrial levels and to pursue efforts to limit the temperature increase to 1.5 °C above pre-industrial levels.[25]

Different from the Kyoto Protocol, the Paris Agreement does not establish targets to be fulfilled by each country, but rather determines that each Party shall "prepare, communicate and maintain successive nationally determined contributions that it intends to achieve".[26]

The second main objective is *adaptation*, which is the aim to increase the ability of countries to adapt to the adverse impacts of climate change, and to foster climate resilience and the development of low greenhouse gas emissions, without threatening food production.[27]

Finally, the Agreement also has a *finance* goal, which refers to making finance flows consistent with a pathway towards low greenhouse gas emissions and climate-resilient development.[28]

Embedded in these three main pillars are two fundamental obligations: technology transfer and transparency.

---

[22]According to the UN's website, on 4 November 2019, the Government of the USA notified the United Nations Secretary-General of its decision to withdraw from the Paris Agreement. The withdrawal shall take effect on 4 November 2020. UNTC, https://treaties.un.org/Pages/ViewDetails.aspx?src=TREATY&mtdsg_no=XXVII-7-d&chapter=27&clang=_en#4 (last accessed 16 February 2020).

[23]The Paris Agreement entered into force on 04th November 2016. UNFCC, Paris Agreement—Status of Ratification, https://unfccc.int/process/the-paris-agreement/status-of-ratification (last accessed 16 February 2020).

[24]Paris Agreement, Article 2.1.

[25]Paris Agreement, Article 2.1 a).

[26]Paris Agreement, Article 4.2.

[27]Paris Agreement, Article 2.1 b).

[28]Paris Agreement, Article 2.1 c).

Technology transfer refers to providing support (including financial support)[29] to least developed and developing countries, in order to allow them to implement their nationally determined contributions and to adapt to climate change.[30]

The obligation of *transparency* aims at building mutual trust and confidence and promoting effective implementation.[31] The transparency framework is divided into two areas: transparency of action, which invokes the obligation of Parties' to report all actions taken to achieve their nationally determined contributions and adaptation actions;[32] and transparency of support, consisting in the obligation of all Parties' that have provided or received support, including financial and technology transfer, to report these.

As seen, the Paris Agreement has a very specific and hybrid structure, since it mixes a bottom-up with a top-down approach.[33] While Parties may determine their gas reduction emission targets by means of their nationally determined contributions (a bottom-up obligation), they have the obligation to duly report all measures taken as well as to comply with the transparency provisions (top-down obligation).

Another very interesting aspect of the Paris Agreement is that it is designed under the notion of sustainable development. Article 2.1, establishing the objective of the Agreement, provides that the global response to the threat of climate change should be given in the context of sustainable development.

Further, Article 2.2 establishes that the Agreement "will be implemented to reflect equity and the principle of common but differentiated responsibilities and respective capabilities, in the light of different national circumstances".[34] This is a clear reflection of the principle of sustainable development, given that it seeks to balance social, economic and environment protection aspects.[35]

That is why the Paris Agreement is concerned not only with mitigation measures, but also with adaption measures and, more importantly, with the obligation of developed countries to provide financial and technological support to least developed and developing countries.

---

[29]Paris Agreement, Article 10.6.

[30]Paris Agreement, Article 10.2.

[31]Paris Agreement, Article 13.1.

[32]Paris Agreement, Article 13.5.

[33]Rajamani (2016), p. 502.

[34]Paris Agreement, Article 2.2.

[35]It is important to bear in mind that the three pillars from sustainable development (economic growth, social development and environment protection) are interdependent and reinforcing pillars. In this regard, Jeffrey Sachs asserts that there are four objectives linked to sustainable development: "economic prosperity; social inclusion and cohesion; environmental sustainability; and good governance by major social actors, including governments and business". Sachs (2015), p. 23.

3.2   Brazil's Intended National Determined Contributions

Brazil's Intended Nationally Determined Contributions (iNDC)[36] are quite ambitious and include measures on mitigation, adaptation, and implementation.

With respect to *mitigation*, Brazil's primary commitment is to reduce greenhouse gas emissions by 37% below 2005 levels in 2025. Further, Brazil's subsequent indicative contribution is to reduce greenhouse gas emissions by 43% below 2005 levels in 2030.

The coverage of this commitment is 100% of the territory, economy-wide, and includes CO_2, CH_4, N_2O, perfluorocarbons, hydrofluorocarbons and SF_6.

As for *adaptation*, in the iNDC, Brazil commits to work on new public policies, by means of the National Adaptation Plan (NAP), aiming "to implement knowledge management systems, to promote research and technology development for adaptation, to develop processes and tools in support of adaptation actions and strategies, at different levels of government".[37]

In May 2016, Brazil's Federal Government published Ordinance n° 150 (Portaria n° 150), instituting the NAP. The NAP establishes three different objectives:[38] (1) expansion of scientific, technical, and traditional knowledge, including production, management, and dissemination of knowledge on climate risk; (2) coordination and cooperation between public bodies and civil society; and (3) identification and proposal of measures to promote the adaptation to climate risk. Each of these general objectives have specific goals established along with the designation of the respective responsible bodies.

In 2017, the Brazilian Ministry of the Environment published the first report on the activities of NAP. The report indicates that 96% of the established adaptation goals had already been achieved in the period of one year.[39] Since then, however, Brazil's NAP has not been further developed.

Attached to the iNDC, Brazil has reported additional information for clarification purposes. In this attachment, Brazil proposes "further measures" consistent with the 2 °C goal. Such measures are:

> increasing the share of sustainable biofuels in the Brazilian energy mix to approximately 18% by 2030, by expanding biofuel consumption, increasing ethanol supply, including by

---

[36]Brazilian Ministry of Foreign Affairs, Intended Nationally Determined Contribution. 2015, http://www.itamaraty.gov.br/images/ed_desenvsust/BRAZIL-iNDC-english.pdf   (last   accessed 01 March 2020).

[37]Brazilian Ministry of Foreign Affairs, Intended Nationally Determined Contribution. 2015, http://www.itamaraty.gov.br/images/ed_desenvsust/BRAZIL-iNDC-english.pdf (last accessed 01 March 2020), p. 3.

[38]Brazilian Ministry of Environment (2016). https://www.mma.gov.br/images/arquivo/80182/LIVRO_PNA_Resumo%20Executivo_.pdf (last accessed 01 March 2020).

[39]Brazilian Ministry of Environment (2017) 1° Relatório de Monitoramento e Avaliação (2016/2017) https://www.mma.gov.br/images/arquivo/80182/GTTm/RelatorioMonitoramento.pdf (last accessed 01 March 2020), p. 10.

increasing the share of advanced biofuels (second generation), and increasing the share of biodiesel in the diesel mix; in land use change and forests:

- strengthening and enforcing the implementation of the Forest Code, at federal, state and municipal levels;
- strengthening policies and measures with a view to achieve, in the Brazilian Amazonia, zero illegal deforestation by 2030 and compensating for greenhouse gas emissions from legal suppression of vegetation by 2030;
- restoring and reforesting 12 million ha of forests by 2030, for multiple purposes;
- enhancing sustainable native forest management systems, through georeferencing and tracking systems applicable to native forest management, with a view to curbing illegal and unsustainable practices;
- in the energy sector, achieving 45% of renewables in the energy mix by 2030, including:
- expanding the use of renewable energy sources other than hydropower in the total energy mix to between 28% and 33% by 2030;
- expanding the use of non-fossil fuel energy sources domestically, increasing the share of renewables (other than hydropower) in the power supply to at least 23% by 2030, including by raising the share of wind, biomass and solar;
- achieving 10% efficiency gains in the electricity sector by 2030.[40]

These specific intents are quite ambitious and would greatly contribute to achieving the Paris Agreement's goals. It is important to bear in mind, however, that they were established only for clarification purposes and, therefore, are not directly part of Brazil's iNDC.

3.3   Which Measures Has Brazil Already Adopted to Implement Its iNDCs?

Brazil has already endeavoured considerable efforts to implement the goals established in its iNDCs. When Brazil made its commitments back in 2015, the country had reasonable expectations that it would meet its 2025 goals.

This is because, even before the conclusion of the Paris Agreement, Brazil had already been implementing significant measures to reduce greenhouse emissions and fight climate change.

In 2009, Brazil enacted the National Policy on Climate Change (*Política Nacional sobre Mudança do Clima—PNMC*), by means of Law n° 12.187, from 19th December 2009. The PNMC established different objectives on mitigation and adaptation. Among them, it aims to reconcile economic and social development with the protection of the climate system,[41] reduce emissions of greenhouse gases,[42]

---

[40]Brazilian Ministry of Foreign Affairs, Intended Nationally Determined Contribution. 2015, http://www.itamaraty.gov.br/images/ed_desenvsust/BRAZIL-iNDC-english.pdf (last accessed 01 March 2020), p. 3.

[41]Article 4°, I, Law n° 12.187/2009.

[42]Art 4°, II, Law n° 12.187/2009.

preserve natural resources,[43] expand legally protected areas and encourage reforestation.[44]

Brazil has developed different action and sectoral plans to implement the objectives of the PNMC, including: (1) the Action Plan for the Prevention and Control of Deforestation in the Legal Amazon (PPCDAm),[45] (2) the Action Plan for the Prevention and Control of Deforestation in the Savanna Region—*Cerrado* (PPCerrado), (3) the Ten-Year Energy Expansion Plan, (4) the Sectoral Plan for the Mitigation and Adaptation to Climate Change for a Low-Carbon Emission Agriculture (ABC Plan), and (5) the Sustainable Steel Industry Plan (Charcoal).[46]

As a result of all these efforts, Brazil has achieved positive results in the last decades.

Since the creation of the PPCDAm and PPCerrado, Brazil managed to considerably reduce deforestation both in the Amazon and *Cerrado* regions in realisation of the *Action Plan on Control and Prevention of Deforestation*. According to the Brazilian Institute of Applied Economic Research (*Instituto de Pesquisa Econômica Aplicada—IPEA*), the average deforestation rate in Legal Amazon between 1996 and 2005 was of approximately 19.6 thousand square kilometres. In the period from 2015 to 2018, such rate fell to 7.2 thousand square kilometres. In *Cerrado*, the average deforestation rate from 2013 to 2017 was around 9.9 thousand square kilometers. In 2018, such rate declined to 6.6 thousand square kilometres.[47]

Concerning the Amazon in particular, it is interesting to note that the deforestation rates in Legal Amazon have started to significantly decrease in 2004—the same year when PPCDAm was created.

According to the information provided by the Brazilian National Institute on Space Research (*Instituto Nacional de Pesquisas Espaciais—INPE*), the deforestation rate in the Legal Amazon fell by 82% from 2004 to 2014. This is demonstrated in the chart below, which is available at INPE's website[48] and is constantly updated:

---

[43]Article 4°, VI, Law n° 12.187/2009.

[44]Article 4°, VII, Law n° 12.187/2009.

[45]PPCDAM was in fact developed in 2004, prior to the institution of the PNMC.

[46]These action plans are all described in Article 14, Decree n° 9.578/2018, which consolidated the normative acts on the National Fund for Climate Change and the PNMC.

[47]Brazilian Ministry of Economy, Brazilian Institute of Applied Economic Research (2019), p. 39.

[48]This was the chart extracted from INPE's website on 21 March 2020. The data from 2019 is still estimated and that is why 2019 is still marked in red. Information is frequently updated and made available at: http://terrabrasilis.dpi.inpe.br/app/dashboard/deforestation/biomes/legal_amazon/rates (last accessed 21 March 2020).

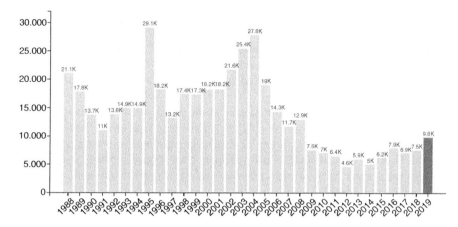

Deforestation Rates—Legal Amazon (km²) [Source: Brazilian National Institute on Space Research (National Institute on Space Research (Instituto Nacional de Pesquisas Espaciais – INPE). Deforestation Rates in Legal Amazon. http://terrabrasilis.dpi.inpe.br/app/dashboard/deforestation/biomes/legal_amazon/rates (last accessed on 21 March 2020))]

As observed, after the implementation of the Action Plans on Prevention and Control of Deforestation, Brazil has been succeeding in reducing deforestation. Notwithstanding that, there is still a lot of work to be done by Brazil to achieve the iNDCs goals, especially the aim to attain "zero illegal deforestation by 2030".[49]

As for *Brazil's Action Plan on Energy Expansion*, Brazil has been issuing Ten-Year Action Plans since 2015.[50] In 2018, the Brazilian Energy Research Office published the 2027 report, indicating that by the end of 2027, it is expected that 85% of Brazilian energy supply will come from renewable resources (including hydroelectric energy).[51]

Although a considerable part of Brazil's renewable energy supply comes from hydroelectric power, the use of other sources, particularly wind power and bioenergy, has been increasing in the last years.

---

[49] Brazilian Ministry of Foreign Affairs, Intended Nationally Determined Contribution. 2015, http://www.itamaraty.gov.br/images/ed_desenvsust/BRAZIL-iNDC-english.pdf (last accessed 01 March 2020), p. 3.

[50] All of them are available at Brazilian Energy Research Office (*Empresa de Pesquisa Energética*) website, http://www.epe.gov.br/pt/publicacoes-dados-abertos/publicacoes/plano-decenal-de-expansao-de-energia-pde (last accessed 21 March 2020).

[51] Brazilian Ministry of Mines and Energy (2017) Ten-year energy expansion plan 2027, http://www.epe.gov.br/sites-pt/publicacoes-dados-abertos/publicacoes/Documents/PDE%202027_aprovado_OFICIAL.pdf (last accessed 21 March 2020), p. 9.

In January 2010, wind energy capacity represented less than 1% of Brazil's total energy capacity.[52] By January 2020, this number increased to 8.9%.[53] Further, in December 2019, wind power represented 10.7% of Brazil's energy production.[54]

With respect to bioenergy (derived from sugar cane), in January 2010, it represented only 5.82% of the installed capacity.[55] In January 2020, this number increased to 8.7%.[56]

Certainly, there is still room for expanding the employment of other renewable energy sources. Yet, Brazil has been showing considerable advances in this area.

Furthermore, Brazil is a country that already employs renewable energy in general. In 2017, 43% of Brazil's energy supply came from renewable resources,[57] whereas the average of the world's renewable energy supply was of approximately 13% in the same year.[58]

Concerning *agriculture*, since the creation of the ABC Plan in 2012,[59] Brazil has been investing in the programs comprised by the Plan, which include measures on recovery of damaged pasture, integration of plantation, livestock and forest, and adaptation to climate change.[60]

---

[52]Brazilian Ministry of Mines and Energy, Monitoring of the Brazilian Electric System. 2010, http://www.mme.gov.br/web/guest/secretarias/energia-eletrica/publicacoes/boletim-de-monitoramento-do-sistema-eletrico (last accessed 21 March 2020), p. 15.

[53]Brazilian Ministry of Mines and Energy, Monitoring of the Brazilian Electric System. 2020, http://www.mme.gov.br/web/guest/secretarias/energia-eletrica/publicacoes/boletim-de-monitoramento-do-sistema-eletrico (last accessed 21 March 2020), p. 15.

[54]Brazilian Ministry of Mines and Energy, Monitoring of the Brazilian Electric System. 2020, http://www.mme.gov.br/web/guest/secretarias/energia-eletrica/publicacoes/boletim-de-monitoramento-do-sistema-eletrico (last accessed 21 March 2020), p. 25.

[55]Brazilian Ministry of Mines and Energy, Monitoring of the Brazilian Electric System. 2020, http://www.mme.gov.br/web/guest/secretarias/energia-eletrica/publicacoes/boletim-de-monitoramento-do-sistema-eletrico (last accessed 21 March 2020), p. 20.

[56]Brazilian Ministry of Mines and Energy, Monitoring of the Brazilian Electric System. 2020, http://www.mme.gov.br/web/guest/secretarias/energia-eletrica/publicacoes/boletim-de-monitoramento-do-sistema-eletrico (last accessed 21 March 2020), p. 25.

[57]Brazilian Ministry of Mines and Energy (2017) Ten-year energy expansion plan 2027, http://www.epe.gov.br/sites-pt/publicacoes-dados-abertos/publicacoes/Documents/PDE%202027_aprovado_OFICIAL.pdf (last accessed 21 March 2020), p. 238.

[58]OECD, Renewable Energy Data, https://data.oecd.org/energy/renewable-energy.htm#indicator-chart (last accessed 22 March 2020).

[59]Brazilian Ministry of Agriculture, Livestock and Food Supply, Sectoral Plan for the Mitigation and Adaptation to Climate Change for a Low-Carbon Emission Agriculture. 2012, http://www.agricultura.gov.br/assuntos/sustentabilidade/plano-abc/arquivo-publicacoes-plano-abc/download.pdf (last accessed 22 March 2020).

[60]The seven Programs comprised by ABC Plan are: (1) Damaged Pasture Recovery; (2) Plantation-Livestock-Forest Integration and Agroforestry Systems; (3) No-till systems; (4) Biological Fixation of Nitrogen; (5) Planted Forests; (6) Treatment of Animal Waste; and (7) Adaptation to Climate Change (free translation). Brazilian Ministry of Agriculture, Plano ABC – Agricultura de Baixa Emissão de Carbono (2016), http://www.agricultura.gov.br/assuntos/sustentabilidade/plano-abc/plano-abc-agricultura-de-baixa-emissao-de-carbono (last accessed 22 March 2020).

In a study published in 2018, the Brazilian Ministry of Agriculture, Livestock and Food Supply informed that until that moment, the ABC Plan had already resulted in a reduction from 100.21 to 154.38 million Mg CO2eq. This represents an achievement from 68% to 105% of the mitigation measures on greenhouse emissions established by the ABC Plan.[61]

This report does not provide for a precise number on greenhouse gas reduction, because such data varies considerably depending on the technical coefficient used. The study points out that, if the technical coefficient used is the one established in the ABC Plan, contribution is lower. On the other hand, if other technical coefficients developed by national scientific literature is applied, contribution increases.[62]

Hence, the 2018 report concludes that, even though numbers indicate that the goals of the ABC Plan will be achieved by 2020 and that Brazil has potential to meet its iNDCs by 2030, there is an urgent need to collect more accurate data, develop an efficient communication with all actors in the agriculture sector and in research centres, and to engage all relevant governmental organs.[63]

Finally, with respect to the *Sustainable Steel Industry*, in 2010, Brazil launched the *Emissions Reduction Plan for the Charcoal Steel Industry*. The program has the purpose of ensuring compliance with the sector's Nationally Appropriate Mitigation Actions (NAMA),[64] and of modernizing the production of charcoal to promote sustainability in the steel industry.

According to the information provided by the Brazilian Ministry of the Environment, the action plan has two main objectives: (1) increasing the stock value of planted forests in order to supply the steel industry with renewable and sustainable biomass; and (2) improving the production process of coal to reduce emissions and expand efficiency of biomass use.[65]

Nevertheless, there is no updated data on the effects of such plan. According to Brazil's Third Biennial Report sent to the UNFCC, a Measuring, Recording and Verifying Platform (MRV Platform) is being developed to "assist in the identification and quantification of the emission reduction of GHG associated with a given

---

[61]Brazilian Ministry of Agriculture, Livestock and Food Supply, Adoção e Mitigação de Gases de Efeitos Estufa pelas Tecnologias do Plano Setorial de Mitigação e Adaptação às Mudanças Climáticas (Plano ABC). (2018) https://www.gov.br/agricultura/pt-br/ assuntos/sustentabilidade/plano-abc/plano-abc-em-numeros/arquivos/ ResumodaadooemitigaodegasesdeefeitosestufapelastecnologiasdoPlanoABCPerodo2010a2018n ov.pdf (last accessed 22 March 2020).

[62]Ibid.

[63]Ibid.

[64]The NAMA for the steel sector in Brazil is to reduce 8–10 million tons of CO2e by 2020. Brazilian Ministry of Environment, Brazil's Nationally Appropriate Mitigation Actions, https:// unfccc.int/files/focus/mitigation/application/pdf/brazil_namas_and_mrv.pdf (last accessed 22 March 2020), p. 3.

[65]Brazilian Ministry of Environment, Siderurgia Sustentável: Ações, https://www.mma.gov.br/ clima/politica-nacional-sobre-mudanca-do-clima/siderurgia-sustentavel/acoes.html (last accessed 22 March 2020).

industrial process and/or technology for the production and use of charcoal as a thermal-reducer agent".[66]

Therefore, it is still not possible to verify the effects of the Sustainable Steel Plan, and this seems to be the least developed action plan until the present moment.

The adoption of all measures described above have resulted in a drop of greenhouse gas emissions. From 2005 to 2015, Brazil verified a decrease of approximately 36%.[67] Based on this data from 2005 to 2015, IPEA published a study in 2019 affirming that "Brazil finds itself in a very favourable position to meet the 2025 goal".[68]

3.4 Is Brazil Close to Implementing Its iNDCs?

Despite all the advances described in the foregoing topic, Brazil seems to have lately stopped investing in some initiatives, and even adopted certain measures which may put the efforts already endeavoured at risk.

There is no official data on greenhouse gas emissions published by the Brazilian Government after 2015.[69] However, it is possible to observe that certain policies which directly affect the implementation of the iNCDs are either paralyzed or relapsing.

From 2015 to 2019, *deforestation* rates in the Legal Amazon have increased in 58%. Albeit the (estimated) numbers of 2019 are still 65% lower than those of 2004 (when the PPCDAm was created), if Brazil wants to achieve the goals set in its iNDCs, it needs to endeavour better efforts in the next years and to continue investing in the Action Plans which have already been developed.

Moreover, Brazil still has a relevant challenge when it comes to deforestation. It needs to develop mechanisms and collect more accurate data in order to be able to distinguish illegal from legal deforestation. This is fundamental for Brazil to achieve its intention to reach a zero illegal deforestation rate by 2030.[70]

The implementation of deforestation goals is of great importance to Brazil, not only because of the Paris Agreement commitments, but also for political and economic reasons. Brazil, containing the largest part of the Amazon forest, has been in the spotlight of the international community lately. After news on the fires

---

[66]UNFCC, Brazil's Third Update Biennial Update Report (2019), https://unfccc.int/sites/default/files/resource/2018-02-28_BRA-BUR3_ENG_FINAL.pdf (last accessed 22 March 2020), p. 50.

[67]Brazilian Ministry of Economy, Brazilian Institute of Applied Economic Research (2019), p 39.

[68]Brazilian Ministry of Economy, Brazilian Institute of Applied Economic Research (2019), p. 39.

[69]Data presented in Annex I of the Third Biennial Report sent by Brazil to the UNFCC comprises the period from 1990–2015, https://unfccc.int/sites/default/files/resource/2018-02-28_BRA-BUR3_ENG_FINAL.pdf (last accessed 22 March 2019).

[70]UNFCC, Brazil's Third Update Biennial Update Report (2019), https://unfccc.int/sites/default/files/resource/2018-02-28_BRA-BUR3_ENG_FINAL.pdf, p. 39.

in the Amazon in 2019, Germany and Norway suspended donations to the Amazon Fund, a fund dedicated to financing the fight against deforestation in the region.[71]

Thus, aside from the implementation of its iNDCs, the achievement of deforestation goals seems to be important for Brazil to maintain stable relationships with foreign countries as well.

Brazil also needs to continue investing in other sources of *renewable energy*, other than hydroelectricity. Hydroelectric power, although sustainable, is limited and cost consuming. Therefore, having seen the raise in energy demand in the last decade,[72] for Brazil to be able implement its Action Plans on Energy Expansion, it needs to further develop and invest in other sorts of renewable energy.[73]

In this regard, Brazil has a substantial potential to develop other sorts of renewable energy, such as solar energy.[74] In December 2019, solar energy represented only 1% of energy supply in the country.[75] There is certainly space to further develop it.

As for *agriculture*, notwithstanding all the progress brought by the ABC Plan, Brazil still needs to develop better mechanisms for collecting data on greenhouse gases emissions. Communication with all sectors involved in the agriculture production is also fundamental.

Even though the biggest producers in Brazil are already highly technically qualified and have efficient managements, the smaller producers—which do not represent the biggest portion of production but are the majority in terms of numbers of producers, are still under qualified. Thus, investing in smaller producers, especially in their formation and awareness on sustainable practices, is fundamental for Brazil to continue developing its agricultural policies.[76]

In fact, Brazil should be concerned with making its agriculture more sustainable and adapted to climate change not only because of the Paris Agreement, but also because agricultural production is extremely sensitive to climate change. As highlighted by the Brazilian Agricultural Research Corporation (*Empresa Brasileira de Pesquisa Agropecuária—EMBRAPA*), "agriculture occupies two roles in the

---

[71]Boffey D, Norway halts Amazon fund donation in dispute with Brazil, The Guardian, 16 August 2019, https://www.theguardian.com/world/2019/aug/16/norway-halts-amazon-fund-donation-dispute-brazil-deforestation-jair-bolsonaro (last accessed 05 April 2020).

[72]The consumption of electric energy in Brazil has increased in 16% in the last decade, according to the data provided by the Brazilian Energy Research Office. Brazilian Ministry of Mines and Energy, Consumo Anual de Energia Elétrica por Classe (Nacional). http://www.epe.gov.br/pt/publicacoes-dados-abertos/publicacoes/consumo-de-energia-eletrica/consumo-anual-de-energia-eletrica-por-classe-(nacional) (last accessed 22 March 2020).

[73]See Losekann L and Hallack M (2018), Novas Energias Renováveis no Brasil: Desafios e Oportunidades. http://repositorio.ipea.gov.br/handle/11058/8446 (last accessed 22 March 2020).

[74]Brazilian Institute of Applied Economic Research (2019), p. 37.

[75]Brazilian Ministry of Mines and Energy, Monitoring of the Brazilian Electric System. 2020, http://www.mme.gov.br/web/guest/secretarias/energia-eletrica/publicacoes/boletim-de-monitoramento-do-sistema-eletrico (last accessed 21 March 2020), p. 25.

[76]Sacarro Jr and Vieira Filho (2018), p. 24.

climate change scenario. It is an activity that emits greenhouse gases, which contributes to global warming, and it is an activity highly sensitive to climate change".[77]

Additionally, it is expected that demand for agricultural products increases in the next years. As informed by the OECD and the Food and Agriculture Organization of the United Nations (FAO) in the Agricultural Outlook 2019–2028, demand for agricultural products will grow by 15% over the coming decade.[78] This expected rise makes it even more important to develop a sustainable and adapted agriculture.

Aside from the mitigation measures, Brazil should be concerned as well with improving and implementing its adaptation plans. As mentioned above, although Brazil has advanced in this field until 2017 (when the first report informed that 96% of the adaptation goals had been accomplished), since then, no further development has taken place.

As observed, in the first years following the Paris Agreement, Brazil has advanced both in terms of mitigation and adaptation. However, the lack of further investment in the last years and some of the new policies adopted by the newly elected Government raise some concern.

This is what IPEA indicated in a study published in 2019:

> With respect to environmental politics and the fight against climate change, Brazil has been achieving positive results, which are internationally recognized. For this reason, some of the measures recently announced by the Federal Government raise concern; for instance, the new structure of the MMA [Ministry of the Environment], which has not maintained the Secretariat on Climate Change and Forests, and the country's decision to give up hosting COP 25 of the UNFCC, in 2019, which will take place in December this year, now in Chile.

> In addition to these issues, other governmental proposals need to be better analysed, in order to verify whether they compromise progress already made. Among these, one should highlight: the normative and managing changes in the inspection on the fight against deforestation, the low execution and the undefinition on the destination of the financing funds of the area, such as the Climate Fund and Amazon Fund, and the change in the composition and acting of the National Council on Environment (CONAMA).[79] [free translation]

Brazil has already an established path to meet its commitments under the Paris Agreement. There is no reason for going backwards and establishing policies that compromise all efforts that have already been made.

As a final note and without prejudice to the above, it should be highlighted that Brazil (as well as almost all other countries in the world, including EU countries) will certainly have to review their climate change policies after the crisis caused by the coronavirus disease (COVID-19).

At the present moment, it is still very difficult to predict how this crisis will affect the world, both in economic and environmental terms. The UN Secretary General

---

[77]Brazilian Agricultural Research Corporation (EMBRAPA), Mudança do Clima https://www.embrapa.br/visao/mudanca-do-clima (last accessed 22 March 2020).

[78]OECD/FAO, Agricultural Outlook 2019–2029 (2019), http://www.fao.org/3/ca4076en/ca4076en.pdf (last accessed 22 March 2020), p. 3.

[79]Brazilian Institute of Applied Economic Research (2019), p. 39.

has also declared that this is an "unprecedented situation and the normal rules no longer apply".[80]

There is already evidence showing that the current crises will have considerable effects on the environment and the economy. On the one hand, NASA satellite images are demonstrating a remarkable reduction in nitrogen dioxide emissions in China in January and February (the period when China was in lockdown due to COVID-19).[81] On the other hand, the crisis caused by COVID-19 is expected to generate dramatic economic losses, especially for less developed and developing countries, such as Brazil.[82]

Therefore, COVID-19 may, at the same time, reduce greenhouse gas emissions and jeopardize the economy in a manner that impairs countries from further developing their environmental policies and technologies necessary for fighting climate change. It is still early to predict its effects, but the crisis that the world is facing right now will without doubts produce severe impacts.

4 What Is the Impact of a Climate Change Provision in the Mercosur-EU FTA?

As seen above, both the Mercosur-EU FTA and the Paris Agreement are very ambitious agreements and reflect the notion of sustainable development. The FTA addresses several non-tariff and non-trade issues and dedicates a separate chapter to the issue of sustainable development. The Paris Agreement, by its turn, aims to fight climate change, without threatening food production and by creating commitments considering different national circumstances.

Thus, both Agreements are designed in a manner that tries to balance social, economic and environmental concerns.

Notwithstanding that, it is a challenge to understand what the real impacts are of including an environmental provision—and, more specifically, a climate change provision—in a trade agreement. What does it mean to determine, within a trade agreement, that the Parties will implement a non-trade commitment? What are the consequences in case this commitment is not respected?

---

[80]UN News, 'Solidarity, hope' and coordinates global response needed to tackle COVID-19 pandemic, says UN chief, 19 march 2020, https://news.un.org/en/story/2020/03/1059752 (last accessed 22 March 2020).

[81]Wright R, There's an unlikely beneficiary of coronavirus: The planet, CNN Hong Kong, 17 march 2020, https://edition.cnn.com/2020/03/16/asia/china-pollution-coronavirus-hnk-intl/index.html (last accessed 22 March 2020).

[82]In Brazil, in less than one month after the first COVID-19 was detected, economic growth forecast in 2020 has already been reduced to nearly zero. See Rapoza K, In Brazil, The Crisis Begins Again, Forbes, 19 March 2020, https://www.forbes.com/sites/kenrapoza/2020/03/19/in-brazil-the-crisis-begins-again/#63bc128f36af (last accessed 22 March 2020).

4.1 What Does "Shall Effectively Implement" in Fact Mean?

As indicated above, Article 6 of the Chapter on Sustainable Development of the Mercosur-EU FTA determines that the Parties shall effectively implement the Paris Agreement.

Aside from the obvious implication that Parties cannot withdraw from the Paris Agreement, it is not easy to determine what *effectively implementing* in fact means here.

Not many provisions of the Paris Agreement contain a binding language and/or allow for an easy implementation test. Except for the provisions on transparency, which have a clear binding language and detailly indicate which information shall be reported by Parties,[83] all other fundamental obligations (mitigation, adaptation, finance and technology) are reflected in provisions whose language may hinder an accurate evaluation on whether they have been implemented or not.

With respect to the iNDCs, Article 3.2 of the Paris Agreement establishes that "[e] ach Party shall *prepare, communicate and maintain* successive nationally determined contributions that it intends to achieve. Parties *shall pursue domestic mitigation measures*, with the aim of achieving the objectives of such contributions."

As seen, when it comes to iNDCs, the obligation is to maintain and report these, and to pursue mitigation measures therein indicated. Hence, one may say that obligations assumed under the iNDCs consist in obligations of means rather than of result.

Implementation of obligations on finance and technology support is also hard to verify. Provisions establishing that least developed and developing countries shall receive support in order to implement the Agreement are rather in passive voice[84] or generally directed to all Parties of the Agreement.[85] This hinders the possibility of claiming that a specific developed country is not complying with its support obligations—unless this country has made commitments on this matter in its iNDC and has not been taking measures to ensure compliance with it.

In light of this, one may say that there are only three obligations that arise out of the inclusion of a clause establishing that Parties shall implement the Paris Agreement.

First, that Parties may not withdraw from the Agreement. Secondly, that Parties shall comply with their transparency obligation under the Paris Agreement and duly report all measures (mitigation, adaptation and support) taken. Thirdly, that Parties have at least an obligation of conduct to take measures to ensure compliance with the Agreement, which refers not only to taking mitigation and adaptation measures, but

---

[83]Paris Agreement, Article 13.7.

[84]Paris Agreement, Article 11.1.

[85]Paris Agreement, Article 11.3.

also to providing financial and technical support to ensure an effective implementation of the Agreement by less developed and developing countries.[86]

It is also important to note that the Mercosur-EU FTA determines that Parties shall *effectively* implement the Paris Agreement. The use of the term *effectively* indicate that this is a matter of importance to the Parties.

However, it is difficult to say that the use of such word allows for interpretations actually strengthening the Parties obligations, and even making certain obligations of conduct to be regarded as obligations of result. This is because Article 31.4 of the Vienna Convention on the Law of Treaties (VCLT) provides that "[a] special meaning shall be given to a term if it is established that the parties so intended". There is no evidence that the Parties, by including such provision in the EU-Mercosur Agreement, intended to turn the Paris Agreement's commitments into obligations of results. Hence, the most adequate interpretation of the term "effectively implement" is most likely that Parties shall take measures towards implementing their iNDCs.

Finally, as already indicated above, it is important to bear in mind that the implementation of the Paris Agreement in the next years will certainly be affected by the current COVID-19 crisis. Although greenhouse gas emissions may decrease in 2020 due to the lockdown in different regions (including in EU and Mercosur countries), the impacts of this crisis in the world economy is still unknown and will probably be enormous. It is possible that less developed and developing countries will need more support from developed countries to be able to implement their objectives under the Paris Agreement.

4.2 What Are the Consequences of an Eventual Violation of the Climate Change Provision?

Now, the remaining question is to understand the impacts of an eventual violation of the Paris Agreement to the Mercosur-EU FTA.

The first aspect that needs to be considered when answering this question is that the climate change provision is inserted in the Trade and Sustainable Development Chapter.

This means that the Dispute Settlement mechanism of the FTA is not applicable to solve any disputes that arise out of climate change issues.[87] According to the FTA,

---

[86]In this regard, it is important to note that Brazil's iNDCs establishes that although the implementation of the iNDC is not contingent upon international support, support from developed countries is welcome to "generate global benefits". Brazilian Ministry of Foreign Affairs, Intended Nationally Determined Contribution. 2015, http://www.itamaraty.gov.br/images/ed_desenvsust/BRAZIL-iNDC-english.pdf (last accessed 01 March 2020), p. 3.

[87]Mercosur-EU FTA. Chapter on Trade and Sustainable Development, Article 15.5.

if any disputes on this matter arise, Parties shall "make all efforts through dialogue, consultation, exchange of information and cooperation"[88] to try to solve it.

Additionally, there are no provisions in the FTA allowing for the imposition of any trade barrier in response to an eventual violation of the Paris Agreement. In fact, Article 2.6 of the Trade and Sustainable Development Chapter determines that no labour or environment legislation shall be applied in a manner that "would constitute a disguised restriction on trade or an unjustifiable or arbitrary discrimination".[89]

Therefore, an eventual violation of the Paris Agreement would have no legal consequences under the Mercosur-EU FTA. No trade measures are allowed in response to environment infringements.

Notwithstanding that, a breach of the Paris Agreement may have serious political effects, including non-ratification threats—which have already taken place by some European countries after the fires in the Amazon forest in 2019. Regardless of whether such threats are trade or environmentally driven, they should (and certainly can) be avoided by Brazil.

5 Conclusion

The Mercosur-EU FTA is a very important trade agreement not only because of the size of the two blocs involved and the expectation of large commercial exchange between them, but also because it goes beyond tariff issues. In addition to giving preferential tariff treatment to the Parties, the FTA aims at balancing economic interests with social and environmental concerns.

The Paris Agreement, by its turn, is one of the most important multilateral environmental agreements of the last decade and, if implemented, may enormously contribute to the fight against climate change. It encompasses obligations on mitigation and adaptation to climate change and creates obligations on financial and technical support, which is fundamental for ensuring implementation by less developed and developing countries.

The Paris Agreement is meaningful because it addresses the issue of climate change from a sustainable development perspective, by considering different national circumstances and, hence, trying to balance social, economic and environmental interests.

Therefore, the obligation of Parties' to effectively implement the Paris Agreement inserted in the Mercosur/FTA is certainly of great importance for recognizing the linkage between trade and climate change and reinforces the environmental commitments of Parties.

Notwithstanding that, the effects of the inclusion of this provision are not easy to determine. Implementation of the Paris Agreement may be difficult to verify and

---

[88]Mercosur-EU FTA. Chapter on Trade and Sustainable Development, Article 15.1.

[89]Mercosur-EU FTA. Chapter on Trade and Sustainable Development, Article 2.6.

there are no legal and/or trade measures to be taken under the FTA in response to an eventual breach.

This of course does not mean that Brazil should not use its best efforts to pursue the implementation of its iNDCs. It is probably the only way to avoid any political effects that an apparent or actual non-implementation of the Paris Agreement may have. Non-ratification threats have already occurred, and regardless of whether they are motivated by trade or environmental interests, they may have a negative effect for Brazil.

Finally, although it is still not possible to predict the effects of the current COVID-19 crisis, it will surely affect the world economy and environment. It may facilitate the implementation of greenhouse gas reduction commitments, but, at the same time, dramatically harm the economy of the world, including EU countries and, especially, Mercosur countries. Thus, the crisis may impact the implementation of the Paris Agreement and of the Mercosur-EU FTA. It will also make international cooperation even more important. The actual effects are, however, still to be seen.

References

Amaral A Jr (2011) Comércio Internacional e a Proteção do Meio Ambiente. Editora Atlas, São Paulo

Brazilian Ministry of Agriculture, Livestock and Food Supply (2016) Plano ABC – Agricultura de Baixa Emissão de Carbono. http://www.agricultura.gov.br/assuntos/sustentabilidade/plano-abc/plano-abc-agricultura-de-baixa-emissao-de-carbono. Accessed 22 Mar 2020

Brazilian Ministry of Economy, Brazilian Institute of Applied Economic Research (Instituto de Pesquisa Econômica Aplicada – IPEA) (2019) ODS 13: Tomar Medidas Urgentes Para Combater a Mudança do Clima e Seus Impactos: O Que Mostra o Retrato do Brasil? Cadernos ODS, Brasília

Brazilian Ministry of Environment (2016) Plano Nacional de Adaptação à Mudança Climática – Sumário Executivo (2016). https://www.mma.gov.br/images/arquivo/80182/LIVRO_PNA_Resumo%20Executivo_.pdf. Accessed 01 Mar 2020

Brazilian Ministry of Environment (2017) 1° Relatório de Monitoramento e Avaliação (2016/2017). Brasília, 2017. https://www.mma.gov.br/images/arquivo/80182/GTTm/RelatorioMonitoramento.pdf. Accessed 01 Mar 2020

Brazilian Ministry of Mines and Energy (2017) Ten-year energy expansion plan. http://www.epe.gov.br/pt/publicacoes-dados-abertos/publicacoes/plano-decenal-de-expansao-de-energia-pde. Accessed 21 Mar 2020

Howse R (2016) The World Trade Organization 20 years on: global governance by judiciary. Eur J Int Law 27(1):9–77

Obergassel W, Arens C, Hermwille L, Kreibich N, Mersmann F, Ott H, Wang-Helmreich H (2015) Phoenix from the ashes: an analysis of the Paris Agreement to the United Nations Framework Convention on Climate Change – Part I. Wuppertal Institute for Climate, Environment and Energy, Germany

Rajamani L (2016) Ambition and differentiation in the 2015 Paris Agreement: interpretative possibilities and underlying politics. Int Comp Law Q 65:493–514

Sacarro NL Jr, Vieira Filho JER (2018) Agricultura e Sustentabilidade: Esforços Brasileiros para Mitigação dos Problemas Climáticos. IPEA, Brasília

Sachs J (2015) The age of sustainable development. Columbia University Press, New York

United Nations Environment Programme, World Trade Organization (2009) Trade and climate
    change: a report by the United Nations Programme, Switzerland

Alberto do Amaral Jr is a full professor of International Law at the University of São Paulo
(USP), where he holds both a Bachelor and a PhD degree. He has extensive experience and
publications on International Trade Law, Human Rights and International Environmental Law.

Marina Martins Martes is a lawyer in São Paulo, holds a bachelor's degree in Law at the
Pontifical Catholic University of São Paulo (PUC/SP) and is currently a Masters' Candidate in
International Law at University of São Paulo (USP).

Part III
Book Reviews

Rodrigo Polanco, The Return of the Home State to Investor-State Disputes: Bringing Back Diplomatic Protection?

Cambridge University Press, 2019, ISBN 9781108628983

Andreas Kulick

Contents

1 Introduction: Back to the Future?

Is the past of investor-state dispute settlement ('ISDS') also its future? This is the question at the heart of Rodrigo Polanco's new monograph *The Return of the Home State to Investor-State Disputes: Bringing Back Diplomatic Protection?* (Cambridge University Press 2019). The current dispute settlement regime, providing access for investors to institutional arbitral proceedings before an international tribunal based on international treaty norms, is a fairly recent phenomenon. The International Centre for Settlement of Investment Disputes (ICSID) Convention, providing the main procedural framework, entered into force in 1966, whereas the first investment treaty award was only decided in 1990,[1] and ISDS only took off in the late 1990s or

---

[1] Cf. *Asian Agricultural Products Ltd. v. Republic of Sri Lanka*, ICSID Case No. ARB/87/3, Final Award of 27 June 1990.

A. Kulick (✉)
University of Tübingen, Tübingen, Germany

University of Göttingen, Göttingen, Germany
e-mail: andreas.kulick@uni-tuebingen.de

© Springer Nature Switzerland AG 2020   413
M. Bungenberg et al. (eds.), *European Yearbook of International Economic Law 2020*,
European Yearbook of International Economic Law (2022) 11: 413–420,
https://doi.org/10.1007/8165_2020_59, Published online: 25 November 2020

early 2000s.[2] Before this, the protection of investments abroad was a matter for the investor's home state, with diplomatic protection as the adequate legal mechanism for such intervention with the host state.[3] Under the Vattelian[4] paradigm the investor's dispute with the host state, under international law, constituted actually a dispute between the home and the host state: violating the interest of investors of the home state meant violating the home state's rights. Conversely, as its own rights were at issue (and not the investor's), it was within the home state's exclusive discretion whether or not to take up the matter with the host state.[5] This is what ISDS fundamentally changed: The dispute became a matter between the investor and the host state, with the investor enjoying authority over the decision whether or not to pursue its (international treaty) rights on the international level before an international tribunal—and with the home state mostly out of the picture, not at least due to Article 27 of the ICSID Convention.[6] Polanco's book confronts us with the question whether we are about to enter an age—or have already reached it—in which diplomatic protection and the home state's influence on the investment dispute again play a more prominent role.

2 Premise: Back with a Vengeance?

There is currently a backlash against investment arbitration.[7] The system that was created to counter the (perceived and actual) flaws of diplomatic protection is increasingly seen as flawed itself.[8] Fierce criticism has not only addressed shortcomings such as lack of transparency[9] and costs.[10] The entire regime itself, the privilege granted to foreign investors to bypass the domestic court system and sue the host state directly before an international tribunal based on international treaty rules, has come under attack.[11] Rodrigo Polanco thus asks the question whether and

---

[2] See UNCTAD World Investment Report 2019, p. 103, figure III.9.

[3] See Kulick (2018), pp. 41 et seq.

[4] Cf. de Vattel (1758), pp. 295 et seq.

[5] Cf. Kulick (2018).

[6] Article 27 ICSID Convention reads:

(1) No Contracting State shall give diplomatic protection, or bring an international claim, in respect of a dispute which one of its nationals and another Contracting State shall have consented to submit or shall have submitted to arbitration under this Convention, unless such other Contracting State shall have failed to abide by and comply with the award rendered in such dispute.

(2) Diplomatic protection, for the purposes of paragraph (1), shall not include informal diplomatic exchanges for the sole purpose of facilitating a settlement of the dispute.

[7] Cf. Waibel et al. (2010).

[8] See Miles (2013), pp. 123 et seq.

[9] Cf. Euler et al. (2015).

[10] Cf. Franck (2019).

[11] Cf. e.g. Kumm (2015), www.esil-sedi.eu/node/944 (last accessed 19 February 2020), p. 3.

to what extent this means "The Return of the Home State to Investor-State Disputes" and if such return "Bring[s] back Diplomatic Protection" (pp. 4 et seq.).

At four different stages of the investor-state dispute settlement process, so he argues, the home state increasingly thrusts itself into proceedings that primarily were intended as an exclusive relationship between the investor and the host state: (1) prior to arbitration by way of dispute prevention mechanisms; (2) during arbitration via various techniques such as joint interpretations or influencing the work of arbitrators; (3) in the enforcement or annulment phase; (4) through state-to-state arbitration alternatively to investor-state arbitration (p. 5 and Ch. III–V).

Polanco thus turns the tables: usually, when issues of backlash are addressed, the focus is rather on the host state than on the home state.[12] Such focus seems intuitive given that it is the host state that is faced with potential or actual investment claims. However, as the author correctly observes, given the dense web of international investment agreements (IIAs), home states may become host states in other proceedings (p. 311). Even more so at the current state of the world economy where many of the main players have become both major capital exporters *and* capital importers.[13] Such change in perspective, focusing on the home state, promises to be instructive. But it also requires more elaboration: How may this new trend that Polanco contends "bring[] back diplomatic protection" under a regime that mostly seeks to shut out this classical instrument of home state involvement via Article 27 ICSID Convention (see pp. 215–217)? And most of all: Is home state involvement rather a corollary of a general trend of the contracting parties to the IIAs attempting to take back control[14] over the application and interpretation of their treaty and the investor-state arbitration process instead of a primarily home state-driven effort to influence the proceedings and revive diplomatic protection (see pp. 6, 308 et seq.)?

3　Methodology, Structure, Take-Away

In order to tackle this normative premise, Polanco engages in a historical analysis and employs considerable empirical evidence (cf. pp. 7–9, Ch. I–II and III–V). The historical study involves delving into the evolution of diplomatic protection and its relationship to the Calvo doctrine (pp. 11–22), the precursors of investor-state arbitration, particularly mixed-claims-commissions (pp. 22–28), the origins of the ICSID Convention (pp. 29–35) and the reasons for which the current system has been established (pp. 35–45). Empirically, the book relies on data based on reviewing and coding all IIAs negotiated between 2004 and 2018 (1088 agreements), with a focus on those 568 treaties that include provisions on home state participation in investor-state disputes (cf. p. 8).

---

[12]Cf. Alvarez (2011), pp. 223 et seq; Hindelang and Krajewski (2016).

[13]See UNCTAD World Investment Report 2019, pp. 4, 5 and 7. See also Kulick (2017b), pp. 3, 14.

[14]Cf. Kulick (2017a).

Built around the premise of home state involvement in investor-state disputes and the potential revival of diplomatic protection, the book starts with an analysis of the historical origins and operation of diplomatic protection as well as the recent criticism of ISDS (Ch. I and II). This is followed by an exploration of the various forms of home state involvement (Ch. III–V). It concludes with discussing the current and future role of diplomatic protection (techniques) in ISDS and explaining why such role is limited (Ch. VI and VII). Chapters III to V (pp. 53–211) form the central part of the analysis. Chapters III (pp. 53–88) and V (pp. 167–211) primarily deal with mechanisms that the home state may employ on its own, looking at ISDS prevention tools that involve home states, including in current IIA policy (pp. 56–65) or through corporate social responsibility efforts (pp. 74–82), and non-disputing party interventions (pp. 167–195) or enforcement of ISDS awards (pp. 196–211). Chapter IV (pp. 89–166) analyses at length such control mechanisms over ISDS that the home state pursues jointly with the host state, *inter alia* the joint interpretation of IIA provisions (pp. 103–138) or regulating the dispute settlement regime as a whole—such as the selection of arbitrators or the current efforts to establish a standing investment court (pp. 151–166).

In the final chapters, the book's main take-away crystallises: The present and future of diplomatic protection is rather bleak. This is not only, as Polanco convincingly argues, due to the possibility of investment restructuring that makes it sometimes rather difficult to determine which state is the actual home state (pp. 275–284), but also owes much to the fact that the home state's interests often diverge from those of the investor (pp. 284–289). Indeed, Polanco concludes, "home states tend to advance arguments along the same lines as or closer to the position of the host state, and not of its national investor." (p. 307) As a result, "more than a return to diplomatic protection in investor-state disputes, we are witnessing a return of inter-state protection, restricting the space of arbitral tribunals to interpret investment agreements, or directly replacing this system for another one with larger state space and control [. . .]." (p. 311) Hence, Polanco acknowledges that the current backlash against investment arbitration is a "return of the state".[15] But it is not a return of the home state within the classical paradigm of diplomatic protection. Instead, it is a return of the states: Home state and host state have similar interests, i.e. to take back control over a regime they perceive to have run wild (cf. p. 308[16]).

---

[15] Alvarez (2011).

[16] Citing Kulick (2017b).

4 Critique: Why Only the Home State? Answering Unasked Questions

This is a rather sobering—albeit not very surprising—result considering the premise from which the book started. As noted at the beginning, changing perspective may prove to be instructive. And indeed, in the many discussions of the current and potential future state of ISDS published in recent years, the perspective of the home state has rarely been taken. However, it seems this has been for good reason: The role for diplomatic protection is, and is likely to remain, limited; joint efforts of home and host states to reassert control over IIAs and ISDS against the investment arbitration tribunal and the investor[17] are instead much more prominent than individual home state interventions.

The reasons for this are apparent: As Rodrigo Polanco acknowledges, "one of the main factors for the reassertion of control by states is that 'old' home states are now becoming 'new' respondent states in ISDS and some 'old' host states have experienced a change in position and will increasingly find themselves being 'new' home states." (p. 311) Just take the most obvious examples of the U.S. and China: The U.S. had been primarily a capital exporter, which was reflected in its early Model BIT policy.[18] China's role in the 1980s and 1990s as mainly a capital importer translated into a hesitancy to include ISDS provisions in its early IIAs.[19] At the start of the third decade of this new millennium, the global economy has become more complex and intertwined, with the U.S. importing tremendous amounts of capital while still investing abroad, and with China, alongside its continuing importance as capital importer, undertaking enormous capital exporting efforts due to its Belt and Road Initiative (BRI)[20] and beyond.[21] This has influenced the IIA practice of both countries[22] and is representative of changes to the IIA and ISDS regime as a whole: If the old capital exporters are also more likely to be hit by ISDS claims in the future, they are more careful in how they design treaties, and more likely to reign in investment arbitration's sometimes wide-ranging influence on domestic regulatory

---

[17]Cf. Kulick (2017b).

[18]Cf. US Model BITs 1984 and 2004, see https://www.law.nyu.edu/sites/default/files/ECM_PRO_066871.pdf (last accessed 19 February 2020).

[19]Cf. Shan and Gallagher (2009), pp. 109 et seq.

[20]Cf. People's Republic of China, State Council Website, http://english.www.gov.cn/beltAndRoad/ (last accessed 19 February 2020).

[21]See UNCTAD World Investment Report 2019, p. 4, figure I.3, pp. 5 and 7, figure I.6, with 2018 marking the U.S. as the largest capital importer (US$252 billion, far ahead of second place China with US$139 billion) and a sharp decline of its capital exports (US$ −200 billion).

[22]Cf. US Model BIT 2012, https://ustr.gov/sites/default/files/BIT%20text%20for%20ACIEP%20Meeting.pdf (last accessed 19 February 2020). On the recent Chinese BIT policy see Moynihan (2017), https://www.chathamhouse.org/publication/chinas-evolving-approach-international-dispute-settlement (last accessed 19 February 2020), p. 8. Recently concluded Chinese BITs with OBOR states and beyond contain robust investor-state dispute settlement clauses, see e.g. Article 12 of the China-Uzbekistan BIT of 2011 and Article 13 of the China-Tanzania BIT of 2014.

policy. In short, joint efforts of home and host states are becoming increasingly prominent, while it is rather unlikely that home states pursue matters on their own. As Polanco observes, the current debate about the investment court system, including the Multilateral Investment Court initiative under the auspices of UNCITRAL,[23] is emblematic of such a development (pp. 154–163).

Therefore, it appears that the book's central questions—are we witnessing a return of the home state/diplomatic protection?—clearly and rather unsurprisingly must be answered in the negative. Polanco does so in the end: "This book submits the idea that the changes introduced in the treaty-making of IIAs in recent years [. . .] are not a 'return' to diplomatic protection, but a return of the states in order to regain control as 'masters' of the investment treaty [. . .]." (p. 6, see also pp. 307, 308) answering questions that are rarely asked—and it seems for a reason. This is particularly regrettable considering that this is a well-written, well-researched study that has a lot of gems to offer, especially in its first two historical chapters, in the sharp analysis of states' joint reassertion efforts (Ch. IV) and of the intricacies and (limited) potential of state-to-state investment arbitration (pp. 246–273). Moreover, the book corroborates its exploration of normative claims with valuable empirical evidence (e.g. Table 4.1. on filtering claims and Table 4.2. on joint interpretation mechanism), which other studies on the states' reassertion of control over the investment treaty regime mostly lack.[24]

5   Conclusion: A Road Not Taken—And for Good Reason

It is a strength of this book that it is honest in providing a clearly negative answer to the question posed at the outset (pp. 6, 308 et seq.): It explains well why a return to diplomatic protection is a road not taken by home states in international investment law and policy (Ch. VII). This is because the interests of home and host states are converging while the interests of home states and investors are diverging. Therefore, the main avenue through which the home state "returns" to ISDS is by joint efforts with the host state (cf. Ch. IV). It is a central achievement of this work to add to this picture the side roads through which the home state may pursue control efforts vis-à-vis ISDS individually (cf. Ch. III and V and to some extent also Ch. VI). Polanco has written a valuable and well-researched study, supported by a lot of empirical evidence. However, considering the eventual outcome and the fact that such outcome was hardly surprising, one wonders whether the book may have benefitted from a different focus, either concentrating on diplomatic protection *tout court* or targeting joint state efforts.

---

[23]See UNCITRAL Working Group III: Investor-State Dispute Settlement Reform, https://uncitral.un.org/en/working_groups/3/investor-state (last accessed 19 February 2020).

[24]E.g. Kulick (2017a) and Hindelang and Krajewski (2016).

References

Alvarez JE (2011) The return of the state. Minn J Int Law 20(2):223–264

de Vattel E (1758) Le droit des gens ou principes de la loi naturelle appliqués à la conduite et aux affaires des nations et des souverains. First published 1758, Carnegie Institution of Washington tr/ed, 1916, vol II

Euler D, Gehring M, Scherer M (2015) Transparency in International Investment Arbitration: a guide to the UNCITRAL rules on transparency in treaty-based investor-state arbitration. Cambridge University Press, Cambridge

Franck SD (2019) Arbitration costs: myths and realities in investment treaty arbitration. Oxford University Press, Oxford

Hindelang S, Krajewski M (2016) Shifting paradigms in international investment law: more balanced, less isolated, increasingly diversified. Oxford University Press, Oxford

Kulick A (2017a) Reassertion of control over the investment treaty regime. Cambridge University Press, Cambridge

Kulick A (2017b) Reassertion of control – an introduction. In: Kulick (ed) Reassertion of control over the investment treaty regime. Cambridge University Press, Cambridge

Kulick A (2018) Narrating narratives of international investment law – history and epistemic forces. In: Hofmann R, Schill SW, Tams C (eds) International investment law and history. Edward Elgar, Cheltenham

Kumm M (2015) An empire of capital? Transatlantic investment protection as the institutionalization of unjustified privilege. ESIL Reflect 4(3):3

Miles K (2013) The origins of international investment law: empire, environment and the safeguarding of capital. Cambridge University Press, Cambridge

Moynihan H (2017) China's evolving approach to international dispute settlement. Chatham House

Shan W, Gallagher N (2009) Chinese investment treaties: policies and practice. Oxford University Press, Oxford

Waibel M, Kaushal A, Chung KH, Balchin C (2010) The backlash against investment arbitration: perceptions and reality. Wolters Kluwer, Alphen aan den Rijn

Andreas Kulick is visiting professor of International Law at the University of Heidelberg (winter semester 2020–2021). Having studied in Freiburg i. Br., Berlin (HU), Geneva (HEID) and New York (NYU), he is a German lawyer (qualified in 2012) and holds an LLM from NYU School of Law and a PhD from the University of Tübingen, where he is also a Privatdozent (veni legendi: Public Law, Public International Law and European Law; Habilitation in 2019). He is Member of the ILA Study Group on "Content and Evolution of the Rules of Interpretation in International Law" and has represented and advised states in proceedings before international courts and tribunals.

Constantinos Yiallourides, Maritime Disputes and International Law – Disputed Waters and Seabed Resources in Asia and Europe

Routledge, 2019, ISBN 9780815375203

Joanna Dingwall

Unresolved maritime boundaries pose one of the major causes of disputes between States. Less than half of the world's maritime boundaries have been delimited formally. Tensions between adjacent or opposite States may arise due to overlapping entitlements to territorial seas, exclusive economic zones (EEZs) or continental shelves. These disputes may include competing historical claims to maritime features, like islands, rocks and low-tide elevations. Frequently, a dispute will be intensified by the discovery of natural resources in contested maritime areas, such as oil and natural gas. Other factors compounding a dispute may include the presence of valuable fisheries or perceived strategic and defence benefits of particular maritime entitlements. Many maritime boundary disputes are well-entrenched and difficult to resolve by political or legal channels.

International law has a significant role to play in the resolution of maritime boundary disputes. The applicable international legal rules vary depending on whether the delimitation also raises issues of sovereignty over land or maritime features and whether the area to be delimited is part of the territorial sea between States or relates to the EEZ or continental shelf.[1] In practice, the case law of international courts and tribunals has been instrumental in developing this area of

---

The views expressed herein are those of the author alone and do not necessarily represent the views of the Scottish Government or the University of Glasgow.

---

[1] See, e.g., United Nations Convention on the Law of the Sea (adopted and opened for signature 10 December 1982, entered into force 16 November 1994) 1833 UNTS 3 (English language version at p. 397) Arts. 15 (territorial sea delimitation), 74 (EEZ delimitation) and 83 (continental shelf delimitation).

J. Dingwall (✉)
University of Glasgow, Glasgow, UK

Scottish Government, Edinburgh, UK
e-mail: Joanna.Dingwall@gov.scot

© Springer Nature Switzerland AG 2020
M. Bungenberg et al. (eds.), *European Yearbook of International Economic Law 2020*,
European Yearbook of International Economic Law (2022) 11: 421–426,
https://doi.org/10.1007/8165_2020_58, Published online: 6 December 2020

the law and devising a legal process for maritime delimitations, taking into account the complex and varying circumstances of specific disputes. Indeed, the caseload of the International Court of Justice (ICJ) has comprised more maritime boundary disputes than any other single topic. Such disputes have also been raised before various *ad hoc* tribunals, arbitral tribunals and the International Tribunal for the Law of the Sea (ITLOS).

Yet, despite the "emergence of a more uniform delimitation methodology in the jurisprudence of the ICJ and the other relevant international decision-making bodies" (as this book acknowledges at p. 245), there remains a need for pragmatic, results-driven solutions allowing for inter-State cooperation over contested maritime territories. This is especially so in intractable cases, where formal settlement of maritime boundaries is not achievable. In this context, Dr Constantinos Yiallourides's insightful assessment of the possibility for practical solutions to the settlement of certain resource-driven boundary disputes in the East China Sea and the Aegean Sea is a highly valuable and timely contribution to the field.

The author's study forms four parts. First, Yiallourides considers the "legal substance" of the East China Sea and Aegean maritime disputes, to determine the likelihood of achieving maritime boundary delimitation in these regions in "the near future" (p. 3). Second, he appraises the extent of State rights or obligations in relation to resource-related activities within disputed maritime areas and the impact of such disputes on exploitation activities. Third, he determines the practical benefits that inter-State cooperation may yield in disputed maritime territories, in circumstances where a final maritime delimitation is difficult to achieve. Finally and crucially, the author puts his findings into practice by evaluating whether joint development may constitute a viable approach with regard to resource exploitation in the East China Sea and the Aegean while the maritime boundaries in these areas remain unresolved.

The author's clear and compelling analysis is well-structured across eight easily-digestible chapters (including an introduction and conclusion). Following the introduction, Chapter 2 provides a helpful primer on the international law of maritime boundary delimitation, with a focus on the role of offshore seabed activities, such as oil and gas exploitation, in relation to the delimitation of maritime zones. It "reveals the role that offshore seabed activities have played in the progressive development of the law of the sea" (p. 6). For any general reader with an interest in the law of the sea, this chapter provides an excellent standalone snapshot of the historical development and current status of the international law of maritime boundary delimitation, including thorough engagement with case law and State practice (which is, indeed, a prominent positive feature throughout the book).

In Chapters 3 and 4, Yiallourides applies this analysis to the maritime boundary disputes in the Aegean Sea and the East China Sea, respectively, assessing whether maritime boundary delimitation is likely to be achieved in either of these cases in the near future (concluding in both cases that it is not). Out of the wide array of ongoing maritime boundary disputes, one may query why the author has selected these particular case studies. However, as Yiallourides demonstrates, there are compelling reasons why the Aegean and the East China Sea are worthy of sustained attention. Both of these areas are "locations of such intractable boundary disagreements, where the traditional legal approaches appear far less attractive to some of the actors involved than unilateralism, escalation and the threat or use of force" (p. 1). In addition, both of these case studies expose what to some extent could be construed as the outer limits of the United Nations Convention on the Law of the Sea 1982 (UNCLOS) regime for maritime boundary delimitations: "to the extent that it does not contain a clear delimitation method and to the extent that it fails to provide for any truly compulsory dispute settlement mechanisms entailing binding decisions" (p. 1).

Accordingly, both case studies are prime candidates for some form of pragmatic interim solution pending formal delimitation, such as joint development. Yiallourides also identifies "why now" is an appropriate juncture to undertake this study (p. 2). As he explains, these disputes have been "ongoing for the past several decades", but they have intensified in recent years due to the increasing desire for exploitation of offshore oil and gas deposits by the States concerned, leading to an "urgent need for a meaningful discussion on finding a practical way forward" before "one of the not infrequent confrontations spirals out of control" (p. 2).

Another reason why the focus on these case studies works well and holds the reader's attention is because both cases present interesting complexities in terms of the international law of maritime delimitation. The Aegean Sea dispute (between Greece and Turkey) primarily concerns the role and effect of islands on maritime delimitation. This is a matter which the author treats to a careful examination in Chapter 3, skillfully extrapolating relevant lessons from existing case law (see e.g., pp. 66–86).

Together with issues concerning the legal status of certain maritime features and their effect on delimitation, the East China Sea dispute (between China, Japan, Taiwan and South Korea) also concerns the legal significance of geology and geomorphology for the delimitation of the continental shelf and the EEZ. Therefore, considering this dispute allows Chapter 4 to engage with the comparatively unusual challenge posed by a maritime delimitation in which the area to be delimited measures less than 400 nautical miles (nm) from the coasts of opposite States, in circumstances where one of those States has a continental shelf extending beyond 200 nm from its coast (see e.g., pp. 109–129).

The discussion of both case studies is aided by the author's use of informative maps. In addition, the case studies are situated firmly within their economic context, due to the author's helpful overview of the extent of seabed resources which both areas may potentially yield (Aegean, pp. 86–91; East China Sea, pp. 138–142).

Having established that settlement of the Aegean and East China Sea maritime disputes is likely to prove elusive, Chapter 5 moves to consider coastal State rights and obligations in relation to resource-related activities within disputed maritime areas and the impact of such disputes on exploitation activities. Chapter 5 focusses on the basic rules in relation to unilateral seabed activities in disputed waters. Especially noteworthy is the author's distillation of key "lessons to be learned" from existing practice and case law in this area (pp. 159–169). As he recognises, in determining whether unilateral seabed activities violate international law, much will depend on "the overall context and the particular circumstances of the case" (p. 159).

However, a common factor is that such unilateral activities can pose "high risks" for international oil companies due to the absence of legal certainty (p. 171).

Thereafter, in Chapter 6, Yiallourides shifts his focus to examine the key legal aspects of joint development of seabed resources in disputed maritime areas. He extols joint development as a potential pragmatic path to enable "the peaceful and coordinated economic utilisation of disputed maritime areas while removing, even temporarily, the disruptive element of contested jurisdiction from the disputing States' agendas" (p. 172). Yiallourides conducts a comprehensive appraisal of the concept of joint development of offshore seabed resources, addressing: the key elements of the concept, including definitional issues (pp. 171–178); the functional character of joint development (pp. 179–184); and the legal foundations of the concept (pp. 184–193). Again, he draws together an illuminating evaluation of the increasing State practice in relation to the joint development of seabed resources (pp. 193–209), distinguishing between three basic operative models for joint development which are not mutually exclusive (namely, single State authority, joint authority and compulsory joint venture). In the course of this examination, he identifies the "growing trend among States involved in maritime boundary disputes towards concluding joint development agreements with a view to carrying out jointly seabed activities in the overlapping claims areas" (p. 209). Such an approach can be beneficial in allowing economic exploitation activities to proceed in the interim, even in the absence of settled maritime boundaries.

In the final substantive chapter (Chapter 7), Yiallourides applies his analysis concerning joint development agreements to the Aegean and East China Sea maritime disputes, thereby moving "beyond delimitation questions" (p. 211). In undertaking this valuable and original enquiry, he addresses the potential limitations which may impede the realisation of successful joint development arrangements. In doing so, he critiques existing precedents for joint development, and he considers whether these precedents could be used as models for the Aegean and the East China Sea.

Of key practical value, Chapter 7 includes an assessment of likely challenges to negotiating and constructing joint development arrangements in the Aegean and the East China Sea and evaluates, in practical terms, the type of joint development regime which may be most suitable for application to these disputes. The author recognises that this "is not an easy task" (p. 213). In order to work towards a joint development regime, the relevant States would need to make a number of compromises, including recognising the *prima facie* validity of their competing claims (pp. 213–214), mustering the necessary degree of political will (pp. 214–216), agreeing on the geographical location of a zone of cooperation (pp. 216–217) and choosing a legal framework to apply to the joint development zone (pp. 220 *et seq*). He conducts a thorough review of the most appropriate choice of mechanism for a joint development regime in respect of the case studies. After concluding that "a comprehensive joint development model, based, for example, on a joint venture or joint authority structure" would be most likely to be feasible, in political terms (p. 223), he then considers the key features which this should include (pp. 223–243). In conducting this evaluation, he engages in a comparative analysis of the domestic petroleum laws of Greece/Turkey and China/Japan (pp. 226–230), concluding that due to differing regulatory approaches, a "divide and manage" approach would be most suitable (as elaborated at p. 231). He then proposes key elements for institutional set-up under this "divide and manage" approach, including the need for some form of joint commission (p. 233), with certain strategic functions, such as commercial elements and marine environmental protection safeguards (pp. 233–243).

The author completes his study by setting out his key conclusions in Chapter 8. He argues persuasively that joint development agreements could be an attractive interim solution for the maritime disputes in the Aegean and East China Sea. As he concludes, inter-State cooperation in developing a joint zone could be "the best possible alternative to 'no action', thus no access to resources, or worse, unilateralism, escalated tensions and armed conflict" (p. 247). Such "pragmatic approach" tends to be "the consequence of strong socioeconomic and energy motives" (p. 247). While joint development agreements have led to unlikely alliances between otherwise unfriendly States, on occasion this has the additional benefit of improving relations between such States, increasing regional stability and cooperation.

Overall, this book delivers on its goals of assessing the Aegean and East China Sea maritime disputes against the rules and principles of international law, critically evaluating the potential models for inter-State cooperation over seabed activities in disputed maritime areas, and making recommendations for the potential use of joint development regimes for resource exploitation in the Aegean and East China Sea. I would recommend this book to readers interested in law of the sea and maritime disputes, and it would be of value to practitioners and academics alike. It will be especially relevant for those engaged with the pragmatic possibilities for resolution of complex boundary disputes, as it looks beyond the traditional focus on treaty-based boundary settlement or third party adjudication, to explore interim possibilities for resource exploitation without boundary settlement. In this regard, the author's focus on the role of joint development agreements in maritime boundary disputes is particularly welcome, given that it has been relatively under-considered in the literature despite the significant role that such agreements can play in practical terms in otherwise intractable disputes.

Joanna Dingwall is a public international lawyer admitted to practice law in Scotland, New York, and England and Wales. She lectures on international law at the University of Glasgow, School of Law, and she is a lawyer to the Scottish Government concerning legal aspects of Scotland's offshore renewable energy industry and the marine environment. Previously, she worked as a London-based public international law and international dispute resolution practitioner for several years. She holds a first class honours degree in law from the University of Glasgow (LL.B. Hons), an LL.M. in international law from New York University and a PhD from the University of Glasgow on law of the sea issues.

Martin Jarrett, Contributory Fault and Investor Misconduct in Investment Arbitration

Cambridge University Press, 2019, ISBN 9781108630511

Markus P. Beham

Contributory Fault and Investor Misconduct in Investment Arbitration is the outcome of a doctoral thesis defended at the University of Mannheim. The book consists of six chapters amounting to a total of 164 pages, not including tables of cases and materials, a bibliography, and an index. Chester Brown of the University of Sydney's Law School contributed a foreword.

Jarrett seeks to analyse how investment tribunals have dealt with the issue of investor misconduct. In particular, he calls the respective case law "disorganised and underdeveloped" (p. 2). He does so against the background of a supposed "asymmetry" (p. 1) of rights contained in investment treaties, and with a view to "[r]estoring some balance to international investment law" (p. 2). With his contribution, Jarrett hopes to bolster "the legitimacy of investment arbitration and international investment law" (p. 164).

The first chapter, "A Schematic of International Investment Law", starts off with an all too short introduction to the book's main research question before attempting a categorisation of the rules of international investment law into jurisdiction, admissibility, liability, and remedies. While the first two issues relate to preliminary questions in proceedings, liability relates to the merits phase (Jarrett does not fully explain why he uses "liability" as opposed to "responsibility"), the third issue—remedies—refer to reparations in the sense of the International Law Commission Articles on State Responsibility (ILC ARS). A roadmap beyond this brief introduction would have been helpful in navigating the following chapters.

The book proceeds to define the concept of a "defence". The chapter is theoretically and methodologically dense, drawing strongly from common law writing on defences in criminal and tort law. The core takeaway is that "if a legal element forms part of a defence, then the respondent assumes the burden of proof in respect of that

M. P. Beham (✉)
University of Passau, Passau, Germany
e-mail: markus.beham@uni-passau.de

© Springer Nature Switzerland AG 2020
M. Bungenberg et al. (eds.), *European Yearbook of International Economic Law 2020*,
European Yearbook of International Economic Law (2022) 11: 427–430,
https://doi.org/10.1007/8165_2020_57, Published online: 25 November 2020

legal element" (p. 19), an approach taken by arbitral tribunals with regard to contributory fault and investor misconduct, as Jarrett demonstrates later in his book.

In a similar fashion, the third chapter deals with the question of "causation". Jarrett provides an account and critique of different theories applied in domestic law, to develop his "new theory on causation for international investment law" (p. 53). Besides common law references, Jarrett claims to draw on German law (p. 44), though references seem restricted to a small number of general observations from comparative publications (see, for example, p. 46, ns. 22 and 26) and textbooks (p. 56, n. 84). Following a patchwork of partial aspects and examples from different layers of society, the gist of the new theory seems to be that "[f]or an antecedent to be counted as a cause of a consequence, it must be a member of that consequence's causal constellation" (p. 78).

In chapters four and five, Jarrett finally arrives at his main research question, the issue of contributory fault and investor misconduct, which he categorises according to three different constellations: "mismanagement", "investment reprisals", and "post-establishment illegality". Chapter four deals with the first, whereas chapter five deals with the latter two scenarios. The actual arbitral practice of interest to any academic or practitioner is regrettably—considering the promising table of cases—tucked between the lines. As Jarrett moves back and forth between his concepts and arguments, one must almost engage in a hermeneutical exegesis of the conclusions of each chapter to bring the various constellations into context: "Mismanagement" concerns the issue in which the investor invests against better knowledge; "investment reprisals" concern outrageous conduct by the investor provoking violations of investment treaty standards by the host State; "post-establishment illegality" concerns illegal conduct by the investor following the establishment of the investment. How arbitral tribunals have dealt with such cases is not addressed systematically, as Jarrett appears to only pick out instances where they fit into the respective argument he is making.

The book does not end with a conclusion but, perhaps somewhat unusually, with a "restatement" of the law. Read in the context of the commentary provided by Jarrett, it is unclear how far his propositions result from analysis or offer suggestions *de lege ferenda* for future application by arbitral tribunals. Formulations as "[i]t is a defence to any breach of an investment treaty by [...] the host state if the investor directly caused its main investment loss" (p. 162) or "conduct of the investor that amounts to an affront to the host state's sovereignty" (p. 163) are so broad that they add little to the existing argumentative framework.

The book is written to a highly specialised audience and clearly informed by an education in domestic common law. Without a profound understanding of international investment law and its context, it may appear difficult to follow the many allusions to conceptual debates. Considering the absence of roadmaps and author's guidance as to how one argument leads to another, Jarrett's analysis appears unnecessarily complex at times. Through the wordiness of each chapter, some aspects of his model only become fully clear at later stages in the book, for instance, when he straightforwardly professes "that causality is binary: it exists or it does not" (p. 133).

Some of the cross-references between chapters could have been replaced by brief elaborations for the sake of readability. Supposedly necessary "to satisfy the various regulations that apply to the publication of German doctorates" (p. xiv), the quite extensive methodological parts that take up almost the entire first half of the book could have been shortened for the publication as a monograph.

The book shows some of the familiar vanities of a debut, both in referencing and in style, for example, when framing even the most minute steps of the analysis as a grand endeavour (see, for example, pp. 16–17, in finding a definition for "defence", or p. 43, discussing the issue of causality). Metaphors would have benefitted from a little more explanatory effort to let the reader in on the author's imagination (see, for example, at pp. 8–9, where the author attempts to explain admissibility by reference to Merlot wine, an approach that only becomes comprehensible a few paragraphs later; or on p. 17, where he refers, without further explanation, to the "liability walnut"). Where such *bonmots* do not confuse, they make the book a more enjoyable read than any dry analysis. Other interdisciplinary references and pieces of information, however, seem odd and displaced in a book about investment law (take the author's claim on p. 63, that "[a]t the time of writing, gene therapy was still in its infancy", or his reference to a medical paper on the fact that the risk of HIV infection through contaminated blood is "very low").

The topicality of the issue and timeliness of the publication are highlighted by the increasingly reciprocal regulation of rights and duties between the host state and investors found in free trade agreements with investment chapters or in the new Dutch Model BIT, conferring rights on the host state while also imposing specific duties upon the investor. Jarrett shows that investment tribunals already take into account, implicitly at least, the question of investor misconduct.

For the comparative lawyer, much of the analysis presents an interesting look at the concepts applied by arbitral tribunals in relation to their domestic counterparts, but it lacks a clear delineation between individual legal systems and traditions. For users of international investment arbitration, the book should perhaps have been written differently, taking more the perspective of international law, as opposed to domestic common law. For those engaged in the debate about investor-state dispute settlement reform, chapters four and five have the potential to provide some argumentative fodder against the current critique of the system as "asymmetrical", but need to be distilled.

Irrespective of some of its shortcomings, the book remains a creative inspiration for anyone thinking broadly and conceptually about contributory fault and investor misconduct in investment arbitration. Thereby, Jarrett offers more than the descriptive analysis suggested by the title.

Markus P. Beham is Assistant Professor at the Chair of Constitutional and Administrative Law, Public International Law, European and International Economic Law of the University of Passau, Germany, and an adjunct lecturer in international law at the University of Vienna, Austria. He holds a joint doctoral degree from the Université Paris Nanterre and the University of Vienna and a doctoral degree in history from the latter as well as an LL.M. degree from Columbia Law School in New York. He has acted in cases before ICSID, ICC, DIS, and *ad hoc* tribunals as well as before the Austrian Supreme Court.

Margaretha Wewerinke-Singh, State Responsibility, Climate Change and Human Rights Under International Law

Hart Publishing, 2019, ISBN 9781509918447

Julian Scheu

On 20 December 2019, the Dutch Supreme Court ordered the country's government to take action against climate change by reducing Dutch greenhouse gas emissions by 25% by the end of 2020.[1] Based on the European Convention on Human Rights (ECHR) and in view of a real and immediate risk to people's lives and welfare, the Court concluded that The Netherlands were obliged to take suitable measures against the expected consequences of climate change. André Nollkaemper and Laura Burgers characterized the judgment in the *Urgenda* case as a landmark and a new classic in climate change litigation.[2] Outside legal circles, the decision provoked worldwide news coverage and was inter alia described as "Strongest' Climate Ruling Yet".[3] The ruling is indeed spectacular and illustrates that the need to take immediate and effective action against climate change is not only a matter of responsible policy, but also relevant to international human rights law.

In light of this relationship, the book by Margaretha Wewerinke-Singh entitled "State Responsibility, Climate Change and Human Rights under International Law" published in 2019 is in many ways remarkable.

---

[1] Dutch Supreme Court, 19/00135, *Climate case Urgenda*, 20.12.2019, ECLI:NL:HR:2019:2007, para. 8.3.4. The unofficial English translation is available at http://blogs2.law.columbia.edu/climate-change-litigation/wp-content/uploads/sites/16/non-us-case-documents/2020/20200113_2015-HAZA-C0900456689_judgment.pdf (last accessed 12 February 2020).

[2] André Nollkaemper and Laura Burgers, A New Classic in Climate Change Litigation: The Dutch Supreme Court Decision in the Urgenda Case, EJIL: Talk!, 6.01.2020, https://www.ejiltalk.org/a-new-classic-in-climate-change-litigation-the-dutch-supreme-court-decision-in-the-urgenda-case/ (last accessed 12 February 2020).

[3] John Schwartz, In 'Strongest' Climate Ruling Yet, Dutch Court Orders Leaders to Take Action, New York Times, 20 December 2019, https://www.nytimes.com/2019/12/20/climate/netherlands-climate-lawsuit.html (last accessed 12 February 2020).

J. Scheu (✉)
International Investment Law Centre Cologne, University of Cologne, Cologne, Germany
e-mail: Julian.scheu@uni-koeln.de

© Springer Nature Switzerland AG 2020   431
M. Bungenberg et al. (eds.), *European Yearbook of International Economic Law 2020*,
European Yearbook of International Economic Law (2022) 11: 431–438,
https://doi.org/10.1007/8165_2020_56, Published online: 4 February 2021

The first noteworthy aspect concerns the importance, complexity and timeliness of the topic which one can hardly overstate. The resonant voice of civil society and alarming news from representatives of the global scientific community such as the Intergovernmental Panel on Climate Change (IPCC) have placed climate change mitigation at the top of the political agenda.[4] As States across the globe seem to struggle with setting up effective and socially responsible policies, the legal perspective on anthropogenic climate change becomes more and more relevant. Far from being settled in theory or practice, viewing climate change as a human rights issue seems to be key, and it is exactly this perspective which lies at the heart of the book.

The second remarkable aspect concerns the way in which the author has chosen to address the topic. As recognized by Wewerinke-Singh, an assistant professor at Leiden University, the book does not seek to present something entirely new. Instead, its purpose is "to fill the gaps in our understanding of the role of international human rights law in enhancing accountability for actions related to climate change" by capturing "the emerging international trend of linking climate change with human rights from the perspective of the general law of State responsibility" (p. 165). Throughout the 168 pages of the book, the author manages to meet these high standards by addressing this complex relationship in a concise and comprehensible way. Its clear structure enables the reader to constantly know where to situate a chapter within the overall concept of the study. The first part introduces the different pieces of the puzzle (pp. 1–84), which are then assembled and put into context in part two (pp. 85–168).

Before even reaching the title, the very first impression of the book is marked by the cover picture showing a barefooted girl on a shore, facing a flooded piece of land. It seems certain that the palm trees in front of her will soon disappear in the encroaching ocean. The picture illustrates what the author recalls at the very outset of her introduction: that climate change is a human rights issue with multiple facets, such as the risks of death, injury, disrupted livelihoods, food insecurity, water scarcity, breakdown of infrastructure, and the loss of rural and costal ecosystems (pp. 16–17). Despite its alarming content, the author's *treatment of the subject* remains unagitated and analytical. As a result, the book's first pages are likely to capture the attention of any reader by making the seriousness and urgency of the topic abundantly clear. In this delicate situation, "human rights standards and principles can inform debates on equity and fair distribution of mitigation and adaptation burdens" (p. 6).[5]

The short introductory chapters dedicated to international human rights law (pp. 22–40), international climate change law (pp. 41–59) and the law of state responsibility (pp. 60–69) reveal that this book was not primarily written for those who have carefully studied and contributed to the ever growing and specialized legal

---

[4]Reports of the IPCC, available at https://www.ipcc.ch/reports/ (last accessed 12 February 2020).

[5]Citing Report of the Office of the United Nations High Commissioner for Human Rights on the relationship between climate change and human rights, 15 January 2009, A/HRC/10/61, para. 88.

scholarship on the relationship between human rights and climate change.[6] However, for readers not overly familiar with international human rights and climate change law, these introductions may serve as a helpful recap. Wewerinke-Singh makes sure that all readers, once they have reached Part 2 (starting at p. 85), have completed a veritable tour d'horizon and are (not only literally) *on the same page*. This educational approach makes the book an excellent introduction to its complex and relevant subject and at the same time particularly interesting for readers of this Yearbook.

As a useful reminder, in view of a truly globalized and multifactorial process such as anthropogenic climate change, the author recalls that the Draft Articles on Responsibility of States for Internationally Wrongful Acts adopted by the International Law Commission (ILC ARS)

> make it clear that wrongful conduct can be established even when no-one has been injured as a result of the wrongful act, [meaning that] even in the context of a complex global problem involving both public and private actors, establishing State responsibility still turns on the simple question of whether or not a particular State has acted in accordance with its international obligations. The simplicity of this question is no coincidence: it was specifically designed to address classic bilateral issues as well as issues of concern to humanity as a whole. (p. 63).

From the lack of any specific secondary rules Wewerinke-Singh concludes that the ILC ARS are applicable to breaches of the United Nations Framework Convention on Climate Change (UNFCCC), the Kyoto Protocol and the Paris Agreement (pp. 67–69).

In a conceptually relevant chapter, which synthesises the previous parts, Wewerinke-Singh offers thoughts on "Integrating Legal Frameworks in a Context of Fragmentation" (pp. 70–84). Here, the author suggests that "the lex specialis of human rights law may technically limit States' discretion in the interpretation of norms that are contained in the climate change regime or otherwise aid in the interpretation of the provisions of the UNCFCCC, especially where those provisions are vague" (p. 72). She concludes that the special characteristics of human rights law lay in "embodying norms that constitute intransgressible principles of customary law" forming a central part of a holistic legal framework (pp. 72–75). In addition, and referring to the principle of systemic integration enshrined in Article 31(3)(c) of the Vienna Convention on the Law of Treaties (VCLT), the author recalls that "human rights norms can also be applied as 'horizontal' norms that influence the interpretation of other treaties" (p. 73). Conversely, human rights law could be enriched by importing international environmental and climate change law concepts such as the precautionary principle. In view of scientific research concerning the causes and consequences of climate change, she concludes that "the precautionary principle creates a fairly high threshold that States must overcome to justify their actions when their compliance with international human rights obligations is assessed" (p. 76). Applied in conjunction with the relevant human rights norms,

---

[6]See for example recently Burger and Wentz (2019); Mapp and Gabel (2019); Lewis (2018).

"the [precautionary] principle could accordingly ease the evidential burden on claimants in international human rights litigation" (p. 76).

Climate change treaties are thus concretised by human rights and vice-versa, while obligations under both regimes may give rise to State responsibility under general international law. The reasoning is compelling and puts the three pieces of the puzzle together. As a follow-up question, which could inspire further research, one might ask whether the relationship as depicted by the author provides guidance on the unsolved problem of identifying erga omnes obligations in the sense of intransgressible principles of customary law.[7]

Part II of the book is dedicated to "State Responsibility and Remedies for Violations". It starts by addressing the topic of "Attributing Climate Change-Related Conduct to States" (pp. 85–96), which could be characterized as the elephant in the room in the context of climate change litigation. From the very beginning, Wewerinke-Singh clarifies that "specific attention is placed on the rules of causation and joint liability, given that virtually all States are involved in conduct leading to climate change while the resulting damage is remote and indivisible" (p. 85). What seems to lead into a legal dilemma is right away debunked as the mere illusion of a problem, given that the ILC ARS do not provide for a strict causal requirement (p. 86). Wewerinke-Singh considers attributing private carbon emissions directly to States under provisions such as Articles 8 and 11 of the ILC ARS to be too far-fetched. Instead, she argues in favour of attributing a State's omission to comply with positive human rights obligations associated with climate change pursuant to Article 4 (p. 88). She points to "an important practical consequence of this general rule of attribution, namely that where a wrongful act consists of an omission, the question of attribution may become evidentially indistinguishable from the question whether the State has complied with the substantive obligation" (p. 89). At the same time however, she considers the levelling of the distinction between attribution and breach to be potentially problematic because "the generality of the rule of attribution reflected in Article 4 means that an extremely broad range of conduct linked with climate change may be attributable to States" (p. 90). To reconcile these conflicting positions she suggests a contextual analysis of the State's climate change mitigation policy based on multiple sources—such as emission data reported under climate change treaties, national legislation and regulatory framework, energy subsidies, and trade policies—in order to assess whether the State complied with its climate change related human rights obligations (p. 92). With regard to joint liability, she recalls Article 47 of the ILC ARS, which sets out the basic principle according to which States are individually and independently responsible for any breach of their international obligations (p. 92). As a consequence, the responsibility of other States does not diminish or reduce the responsibility of individual States and hence, "the direct

---

[7]See Tams (2005), pp. 118–119 (pointing to the fact that neither State practice nor jurisprudence has shed much light on the process of identifying obligations erga omnes and "[g]iven this absence of guidance, it is not surprising that commentators express widely diverging views on the scope of the concept").

or indirect involvement of multiple States in the activities that cause climate change does not pose an obstacle to redress either, as under general international law each State is responsible for its own conduct" (p. 95).

The chapter dedicated to the establishment of violations of human rights affected by climate change (pp. 97–133) starts by noting that "State's human rights obligations to respond to climate change are not yet well understood". Therefore, Wewerinke-Singh analyses how climate change affects the enjoyment of group rights, civil and political rights, cultural rights, and economic and social rights. The reader's awareness is raised for a wide range of issues such as the impact of territories becoming gradually uninhabitable on local communities' right of self-determination (pp. 98–104) or the fact that the increasing mortality risk associated with rising temperatures affects the right to life (pp. 105–110). She also recalls that people forced to seek refuge abroad from the effects of climate change meet the definition of 'minorities' in the sense of the right to enjoy one's culture (pp. 110–118). With regard to the right to health she considers that States might be obliged to regulate private carbon emissions (pp. 118–124). The last subsection considers the conflict between human rights-based climate change mitigation policies on the one hand and the human rights of those affected by those policies on the other (pp. 124–129). This conflict raises a number of tricky legal and political questions such as "to what extent other States may need to restrict the enjoyment of selected rights within their own territory to prevent the violation of rights in the States whose populations are most severely affected by climate change" (p. 129). In this situation the Common but Differentiated Responsibilities and Respective Capabilities (CBDRRC) principle within the UNFCCC "could function as an application of the human rights principle of non-discrimination in inter-State relations, making it a form of affirmative action to correct historical inequities to ensure the equal enjoyment of rights at the global level" (p. 129). Together with the precautionary principle mentioned above, this example clearly illustrates the potential for systemic integration of legal concepts developed within the climate change regime into international human rights law.

The following chapters of the book are dedicated to remedies for climate change-related human rights violations (pp. 134–145) and climate change litigation before human rights bodies, courts and tribunals (pp. 146–164). In the context of remedies, Wewerinke-Singh recalls the close link between the duty to make reparation and the question of causation. However, the precise effect of the causality requirement may depend on the right in question. In addition, progress in climate impact research could lead adjudicators to characterise climate change-related harm as a reasonably foreseeable consequence (p. 137)—and thus to affirm causality.

In view of the author, the continuing debate around liability and compensation at international climate change negotiations is unlikely to yield meaningful results (p. 139). If States start to bring claims against each other this could lead to a chain of legal actions triggering "a 'race to the top', where States' respective obligations relating to climate change and human rights are clarified and progressively start influencing State conduct" (p. 140). In view of the massive potential for climate change related disputes, the author justifiably asks whether alternative methods of dispute resolution might be preferable to rights-based litigation (p. 146). The book ends with a presentation of different dispute resolution fora, which is characterized by strategic considerations in the fight for 'climate justice', such as pointing out that litigation before a domestic court offers "tremendous opportunities for involving civil society, the private sector, academia and the local media in the legal action" (p. 150).

At the end of a stimulating read it becomes apparent that the title suitably sums up Wewerinke-Singh's aim, which is to provide "an integrated analysis of three legal regimes – climate change, human rights and State responsibility – to explain the potential of innovative rights-based climate litigation that could shape climate and energy policies around the world" (p. 164). The book not only identifies the important legal issues within each of these regimes, but also provides a comprehensive overview of the relevant connections between the three fields of law. In doing so, Wewerinke-Singh skilfully managed to keep the right balance between taking account of complexity without oversimplifying.

Finally, the book is also remarkable for its gaps. In view of the fundamental changes that lie ahead for industrialized economies, international economic law has an essential role to play. And yet the book barely acknowledges trade and investment law. The author cannot be faulted for that: as is clear from the title, her focus is another one. However, for readers approaching the book from the perspective of international economic law, numerous questions will arise throughout the text, mainly in relation to whether an argument made in the context of human rights would also be valid in the context of international trade and investment law.

When the author for example illustrates the potential for systemic integration by arguing that the precautionary principle could shift the burden of proof in climate change litigation (pp. 95–96), readers of this Yearbook might wonder whether this principle could also be applied to the application of substantive investment protection standards such as fair and equitable treatment or full protection and security.

Certainly not all conclusions are transferrable to the relationship between international economic law and climate change. Being mindful of the robust protection of foreign private property under international investment treaties, one might for example be reluctant to share the author's view that conflicts involving private property can be resolved easily because the latter is subject to far-reaching limitations (p. 126). To what extent the author's suggestions that economic rights have the potential to hamper climate change action applies to international investment law is subject of ongoing academic and political debates.[8]

---

[8]See in this sense the report published by the Non-Governmental Organizations Corporate Europe Observatory (CEO) and the Transnational Institute (TNI): One Treaty to rule them all—The Energy Charter Treaty and the power it gives corporations to halt the energy transition (2018), https://corporateeurope.org/sites/default/files/attachments/one_treaty_to_rule_them_all.pdf (last accessed 1 February 2020). In contrast, emphasizing that international investment law is potentially helpful to a climate change-related energy transition: Baetens (2019); Elrifai et al. (2019); Boute (2015); Schill (2007), p. 477.

In this sense, Margaretha Wewerinke-Singh's book is an excellent introduction to an interdisciplinary topic that should inspire further exploration of the role of international economic law within the relationship of 'State Responsibility, Climate Change and Human Rights under International Law'. For future research, there are at least two additional takeaways. First, the book makes it clear that climate change mitigation faces unresolved legal complexities mainly caused by uncoordinated regime interaction within the international legal order. Second, Wewerinke-Singh rightfully recalls that future solutions must not only be legally coherent, but also inspired by a sense for global justice.

References

Baetens F (2019) Combating climate change through the promotion of green investment: from Kyoto to Paris without regime-specific dispute settlement. In: Miles K (ed) Research handbook on environment and investment law. Elgar, Cheltenham, pp 107–130

Boute A (2015) The potential contribution of international investment protection law to combat climate change. J Energy Nat Resour Law 27(3):333–376

Burger M, Wentz J (2019) Climate change and human rights. In: Faure M (ed) Elgar encyclopedia of environmental law. Edward Elgar, Cheltenham, pp 198–212

Elrifai SN, Sinsel SR, Hennerkes M, Rusinek H (2019) A model multilateral treaty for the encouragement of investment in climate change mitigation and adaptation. J Int Arbitr 36 (1):71–94

Lewis B (2018) Future directions for environmental human rights in a changing climate. Springer, Heidelberg

Mapp S, Gabel SG (2019) The climate crisis is a human rights emergency. J Hum Rights Soc Work 4(4):227–228

Schill SW (2007) Do investment treaties chill unilateral state regulation to mitigate climate change? J Int Arbitr 24(5):469–477

Tams CJ (2005) Enforcing obligations Erga Omnes in international law. Cambridge University Press, Cambridge

Julian Scheu is Junior Professor of Public Law, Public International Law, and International Investment Law at the University of Cologne and head of management at the International Investment Law Centre Cologne (IILCC). He studied law at the Universities of Cologne and Paris I (LL.M./maîtrise en droit, 2009; Dr. iur., 2016) and is qualified to practice law in Germany. Prior to joining the IILCC in 2018 he worked as legal assistant with the German Arbitration Institute (DIS). His practical experience includes acting as arbitral secretary and assistant to counsel, arbitrators, and legal experts in international commercial and investment arbitration proceedings.

Prabhash Ranjan, India and Bilateral Investment Treaties. Refusal, Acceptance, Backlash

Oxford University Press, 2019, ISBN 9780199493746

Silvia Steininger

Is international investment law international?[1] Prabhash Ranjan's excellent book "India and Bilateral Investment Treaties. Refusal, Acceptance, Backlash" makes a compelling argument for a nuanced reading of the evolution of the international investment regime. By closely tracing India's economic policy and treaty-making practices, Ranjan convincingly narrates how India's approach to the international investment treaty regime evolved from Nehru's pragmatic economic nationalism in 1947 to a period of booming engagement with bilateral treaty-making in the 1990s, and to a more critical approach nowadays, which ultimately was channeled in the 2016 Model BIT. His monograph on the Indian experience thus crucially complements insights on the historical evolution of international investment law[2] from a non-Western perspective.[3] Well-written and clearly structured, this book offers a comprehensive historical, ideological, doctrinal, and empirical overview of the Indian approach towards foreign direct investment. In the following, this book review will highlight and evaluate the four major perspectives in Ranjan's analysis: its historical approach, ideological argumentation, doctrinal mapping, and empirical insights.

The first, most obvious contribution of this monograph lies in its historical approach. In his historical narration of India's engagement with bilateral investment treaties, Ranjan distinguishes three specific periods: refusal, acceptance, and backlash. According to Ranjan, the *refusal* phase (phase I), ranging from 1947 to 1990, was characterized by India's unwillingness to sign any bilateral treaties. This changed in phase II, *acceptance*, when, starting from 1990, India was heavily

---

[1] See Roberts (2017).

[2] For recent historical research, see also Miles (2015), Schill and Tams (2018) and St John (2018).

[3] For similar case studies, see also Gallagher and Shan (2009) and Scharaw (2018).

S. Steininger (✉)
Max Planck Institute for Comparative Public Law and International Law, Heidelberg, Germany
e-mail: Steininger@mpil.de

© Springer Nature Switzerland AG 2020   439
M. Bungenberg et al. (eds.), *European Yearbook of International Economic Law 2020*,
European Yearbook of International Economic Law (2022) 11: 439–444,
https://doi.org/10.1007/8165_2020_62, Published online: 22 January 2021

engaged in negotiating bilateral investment treaties. However, in phase III, when India faced its first investor-state dispute settlement award in *White Industries v. India* in 2011, it engaged in *backlash* by terminating and renegotiating bilateral investment treaties.

Ranjan's historical analysis is most detailed in the first phase. He begins with an in-depth description of Nehruvian socialism in a newly independent India, which was reliant on foreign investment and thus developed a quite liberal and pragmatic stance towards foreign direct investment. Under the premise of economic nationalism, "foreign direct investment is welcome if it promotes the political goals of national independence and economic development."[4] Hence, in contrast to other socialist economies such as the Soviet Union and China, Nehru refrained from large-ruled nationalization and assured investors by rejecting the idea of nationalization without fair and equitable compensation. Moreover, the right to property was included as a fundamental right in the Indian constitution of 1950. Why Ranjan includes this period under the heading of *refusal* remains unclear, especially as the Nehru government signed investment guarantee agreements with the US and West Germany in 1957 and 1964.[5] Yet, starting with Indira Gandhi's government in 1966, the investment-critical attitude became more apparent. Under Indira Gandhi, nationalization of banks was pursued to redistribute income and the newly installed Foreign Investment Board vetted foreign direct investment carefully. In the 1960s and 1970s, India was actively involved in the New International Economic Order (NIEO) project and refused to sign the International Centre for Settlement of Investment Disputes (ICSID) Convention. However, Ranjan argues that the latter was not primarily caused by ideological debates on foreign direct investment, but due to certain, valid reservations. India had been concerned that the ICSID Convention would depart from international law by raising the status of investors vis-à-vis states and endowing investors with unspecified rights without imposing obligations. Moreover, the broad jurisdiction of ICSID tribunals would circumvent the scope of domestic policies and legislation, and the finality of the arbitral awards would contravene general principles of municipal law.[6] Economic nationalism turned to economic liberalism after the 1991 Indian economic crisis. During the 1980s, India built up an enormous fiscal deficit, which culminated in a massive debt crisis. The structural reforms implemented by P. B. Narasimha Rao's minority government aimed to attract foreign direct investment to boost economic growth. According to Ranjan, this paradigm shift was not imposed by Western institutions such as the International Monetary Fund (IMF) and the World Bank, but developed organically in domestic politics "independent of pressure from international institutions that played an important role in undertaking these reforms."[7]

---

[4]Ranjan (2019), p. 56.
[5]Ranjan (2019), p. 92.
[6]Ranjan (2019), pp. 88–92.
[7]Ranjan (2019), p. 107.

At this point, the ideological contribution of Ranjan's books becomes evident. Ranjan rejects the narrative promoted by critical scholars, and in particular those affiliated to the Third World Approaches to International Law (TWAIL), according to which investment treaties and foreign direct investment practices are imposed upon states such as India. He argues that India might have been a "rule taker" of international investment law in the past, but that it did so willingly and consciously during particular historical time periods to boost economic development. In particular, since India evolved from a capital-importing to a capital-exporting state, Ranjan analyzes how India developed a more nuanced engagement with foreign direct investment, for instance by ensuring the protection of Indian investment abroad,[8] and how it is now actively involved in re-calibrating investment law, especially investor-state dispute settlement.

This is an important contribution to the debate as Ranjan's historical insights offer valuable counter-arguments to influential TWAIL scholars from India such as BS Chimni. However, as he criticizes the TWAIL movement for oversimplification, one gets the impression that his engagement with the critique of investment law also remains one-sided. He almost exclusively argues against TWAIL scholars, accusing them of "ideological cherry picking"[9] and of employing "emotive terms [...] without offering any hard economic data or statistics",[10] while he neglects investment-critical voices from political economy and other areas of international law, such as human rights. Ranjan's critical stance towards TWAIL has already been extensively debated elsewhere.[11] In the monograph, Ranjan's anti-TWAIL position becomes visible in several parts of the book, which sometimes feels repetitive. It might have been useful to consolidate this ideological debate in a separate subchapter. Most importantly, it is difficult to claim that TWAILers have the "[t]he tendency to continuously keep imagining the presence of imperial ghosts",[12] when Ranjan himself limits his historical analysis to post-1947; thus remaining completely silent on the influence of the colonial time period on India's approach after gaining independence. By excluding a discussion on the influences of the colonial period on an independent India, he does not engage with the substantial arguments brought forward by TWAIL scholars. Moreover, this lack of engagement promotes a vision of newly independent states as being completely free from prior experiences and path dependencies developed in the colonial period, which is historically inaccurate. Hence, Ranjan's criticism of TWAIL scholars is based

---

[8]Ranjan (2019), p. 130.

[9]Ranjan (2019), p. 111.

[10]Ranjan (2019), p. 109.

[11]See Bagchi K, A BIT of resistance. A response to Prof. Prabhash Ranjan's plea for embedded liberalism, Völkerrechtsblog, 26 January 2019, https://voelkerrechtsblog.org/a-bit-of-resistance/ (last accessed 13 August 2020); Živković V, Of BITs and pieces, resistance and simplification, Völkerrechtsblog, 1 February 2019, https://voelkerrechtsblog.org/of-bits-and-pieces-resistance-and-simplification/ (last accessed 13 August 2020).

[12]Ranjan (2019), p. 107.

mainly on method and style, not on substance, thus undermining the force of his historical argument.

Ranjan's empirical and doctrinal contributions to the debate are to be found in the second part of his book. This part covers the historical period in which India had started to actively commit to international investment law. Specifically, Ranjan undertakes a comprehensive exercise in "mapping" both the *acceptance* and *backlash* of India vis-à-vis bilateral investment treaties. Following the 1991 economic reforms, Finance Minister Manmohan Singh demonstrated India's willingness to attract foreign capital by developing the first Indian Model BIT in 1993. One year later, India signed its very first bilateral agreement with the UK, which triggered "a BIT-signing spree".[13] Until the end of 2010, India had signed 79 bilateral investments treaties. Ranjan delves deep into the intricacies of those BIT and FTA investment chapters and uses those empirical insights to show how India embraced certain provisions in international investment law during this phase of *acceptance*. He compares their definition of investment, fair and equitable treatment, MFN clauses, and provisions on full protection and security in Chapter 4, as well as the regulation of expropriation, monetary transfer provisions, general exception clauses, and ISDS provisions in Chapter 5. While it is not quite clear why those empirical examinations are structured in two separate chapters, they clearly show Ranjan's deep understanding and in-depth empirical research on the intricacies of the Indian BITs. This is certainly a valuable contribution for practitioners, but also shifts the narrative of the monograph from a historical-analytical to a more descriptive and less engaging one.

Ranjan uses a similar approach for analyzing phase III, India's *backlash* against BITs. After India had refused to sign the ICSID convention in the 1960s due to concerns about investor-state dispute settlement, the first publicly known arbitral award against India in 2011 in the aforementioned *White Industries* case, marks another paradigm shift. In this new historical phase, India is not only reluctant to sign new BITs, but is also confronted with several ISDS cases brought against it in response to delays in domestic proceedings, the cancellation of licenses, and other state action impacting foreign investment. After investigating and categorizing the 13 known ISDS claims against India since 2011, Ranjan concludes that "none of the claims have been brought against India because India exercised its sovereign public power in good faith in order to attain an important public policy goal such as protection of the environment or promotion of public health."[14] Instead, he argues that Indian state organs themselves had caused the initiation of claims by foreign investors as they did not respect the legal obligations India had incurred towards foreign investors, e.g. by acting in bad faith, with excessive delays or not honoring assurances.

Still, the rise of ISDS proceedings changed public perception of BITs and many stakeholders felt the need to adapt the system to the benefit of India. In his ensuing

---

[13]Ranjan (2019), p. 121.
[14]Ranjan (2019), p. 265.

discussion, Ranjan again engages in "mapping" how this *backlash* unfolded. After several important stakeholders such as parliament, academia, civil society, and the Indian government itself demanded a better balancing of the rights of foreign investors with national sovereignty, the Indian government decided to review all existing BITs starting from 2012. This internal review identified in particular the threat posed by vague and broad provisions in the existing BITs, which resulted in the adoption of a new Model BIT, the termination of 58 BITs, and a request to 25 BIT partner states to issue joint interpretative statements to clarify the interpretation and application of particular provisions. Consequently, Ranjan zooms in on the 2016 Indian Model BIT, again describing the main procedural and substantive elements as identified in Chapters 4 and 5.

The book closes with a short and concise outlook, in which Ranjan sketches out his idea of a mutually beneficial new Indian policy on foreign investment protection and promotion, which gives authority to investment law and allows India to participate in ISDS, while protecting India's exercise of public power. He envisions India as a champion for a new model of embedded liberalism in investment law. The vision of embedded liberalism as depicted by John Ruggie in 1982[15] is certainly appealing, however, it is doubtful whether the political, economic, and institutional preconditions for establishing this economic model do actually exist today—both on the domestic and global sphere. Too often the pragmatic compromise of 'embedded liberalism' is an appealing narrative for neoliberal scholars as it avoids more substantive questions of power inequality and redistribution. Ranjan's appeal to "Throw the Bathwater, but Keep the Baby" might be true for India's approach towards BITs, however, in the context of the reform of investor-state arbitration, India is counted among the most critical states advocating paradigmatic reform.[16]

In sum, Ranjan's multi-perspective analysis makes for an accessible and informative reading even for the non-expert in investment law or Indian foreign and domestic policy. However, the lack of a clear and consistent methodology—Ranjan shortly touches upon the policy-oriented school of the New Haven School, but remains silent on the potentials and limitations of this approach[17]—makes it difficult to verify some of Ranjan's conclusions, for instance when he discusses the impact of foreign direct investment on India's economic reforms, development, and income inequality.[18] In particular the empirical insights gained from "mapping" would have benefited from a clearer methodological approach. Consequently, historical-analytical and empirical-descriptive elements of the monograph often seem disconnected. This eclectic approach might be explained by Ranjan's prolific publications on the topic in recent years, which mirror many elements of his book.[19]

---

[15]Ruggie (1982).

[16]Roberts (2018).

[17]Ranjan (2019), p. 42.

[18]Ranjan (2019), pp. 109ff.

[19]For his list of publications, see http://www.sau.int/faculty/faculty-profile.html?staff_id=65 (last accessed 22 January 2020).

Ultimately, Ranjan's book is an exemplary case study on a national perspective on foreign investment law. It puts forward a counter-narrative on the role of post-colonial states in engaging with international investment law, which, even when one might disagree in substance, is an insightful, accessible, and multi-faceted study very worth reading.

References

Gallagher N, Shan W (2009) Chinese investment treaties. Policies and practice. Oxford University Press, Oxford

Miles K (2015) The origins of international investment law. Cambridge University Press, Cambridge

Ranjan P (2019) India and bilateral investment treaties. Refusal, acceptance, backlash. Oxford University Press, Oxford

Roberts A (2017) Is international law international? Oxford University Press, Oxford

Roberts A (2018) Incremental, systemic, and paradigmatic reform of investor-state arbitration. Am J Int Law 112(3):410–432

Ruggie JG (1982) International regimes, transactions, and change: embedded liberalism in the postwar economic order. Int Organ 36(2):379–415

Scharaw B (2018) The protection of foreign direct investment in Mongolia. Springer, Heidelberg

Schill SW, Tams CJ (2018) International investment law and history. Edward Elgar, Cheltenham

St John T (2018) The rise of investor-state arbitration. Politics, law, and unintended consequences. Oxford University Press, Oxford

Silvia Steininger is a Research Fellow at the Max Planck Institute for Comparative Public of International Law in Heidelberg, Germany. She holds an M.A. in Political Science from the University of Heidelberg and an LL.M. in Public International Law (with distinction) from the University of Amsterdam. Her research interests lie in the interdisciplinary analysis of international institutions, in particular international courts and tribunals in the area of human rights and investment arbitration. Her latest publications in international economic law include an article on human rights references in investment article in the Leiden Journal of International Law (2018), an edited volume on "Democracy and Financial Order: Legal Perspectives" (with M. Goldmann, Springer, 2018), and a chapter on the role of human rights in investment law and arbitration forthcoming in the Cambridge Companion on Business and Human Rights.

Julien Fouret, Rémy Gerbay and Gloria M. Alvarez, The ICSID Convention, Regulations and Rules: A Practical Commentary

Edward Elgar, 2019, ISBN 9781786435231

Christian J. Tams

"In the beginning was the Word", an old German lawyers' adage has it, "but soon, it was followed by a Commentary". The German legal tradition is peculiar in its reliance on article-by-article commentaries as authoritative guides to the law, but international law is catching up fast: from the Charter of the United Nations via the United Nations Convention on the Law of the Sea, human rights treaties and the agreements of the World Trade Organisation to the Statute of the International Court of Justice, a fast-growing patchwork of commentaries covers an ever larger part of the discipline's major texts. This growth attracts new players. While dedicated series by Oxford University Press and Hart/Beck/Nomos have so far been dominant, Edward Elgar has entered the field: its *Practical Commentary* to *The ICSID Convention, Regulations and Rules*, edited by Julien Fouret, Rémy Gerbay and Gloria M Alvarez (with Denis Parchajev), adds a genuine international law title to the Elgar Commentaries series. By all accounts and standards, this is an impressive book. On circa 1300 pages of text, it offers detail on the meaning of the 74 provisions of the International Convention on the Settlement of Investment Disputes (ICSID Convention), as well as (in more summarised form) the Administrative and Financial Regulations, the Institution Rules and the Arbitration Rules. The result is a compact, one-stop guide to the most relevant arbitral framework of investment arbitration.

This guide is comprehensive and—as far as my background reading for this review suggests—very reliable. On dozens of issues, from the dramatic to the mundane, readers are provided with accessible information, and often with guidance as to the proper interpretation of controversial provisions. The following selection, while subjective rather than representative, illustrates some of the significant positions taken.

C. J. Tams (✉)
University of Glasgow, School of Law, Glasgow, UK
e-mail: Christian.Tams@glasgow.ac.uk

© Springer Nature Switzerland AG 2020
445
M. Bungenberg et al. (eds.), *European Yearbook of International Economic Law 2020*,
European Yearbook of International Economic Law (2022) 11: 445–448,
https://doi.org/10.1007/8165_2020_63, Published online: 15 December 2020

- In their discussion of Article 42 of the ICSID Convention, Andrea K. Bjorklund and Lukas Vanhonnaeker emphasise the importance of indirect choices of law: in their view, arbitral proceedings brought on the basis of treaties do not call into application the default rule contained in Article 42(1), *second sentence* (host State law plus applicable rules of international law). Instead, "by submitting a dispute under an investment treaty, the parties have made a choice of applicable law" (p. 354) in the sense of Article 42(1), *first sentence.*
- Discussing the scope of tribunals to entertain counterclaims, Eva Kalnina and Ankita Godbole take issue with the 'implied consent' approach. Prominently advocated in Michael Reisman's declaration in the *Roussalis case*, this approach views the election of ICSID proceedings as an implicit acceptance of certain counterclaims. Kalnina and Godbole are not convinced: they consider the approach to be "circular and inconsistent with the language of Article 46, which mentions consent as an independence pre-condition for exercising jurisdiction" (p. 423).
- With respect to corporate nationality, the late David D. Caron and Esmé Shirlow offer a robust defence of the double keyhole approach to jurisdiction: Article 25(2)(b) of the ICSID Convention sets out an independent, separate test, which needs to be met alongside nationality requirements in a Bilateral Investment Treaty (BIT) or other jurisdiction-conferring instrument. BITs thus do not control, at least not solely; and nor must the two tests be "conflated" (p. 186). The impact of this important conceptual clarification is limited by Caron's and Shirlow's understanding of the 'ICSID nationality test', which essentially is formal: the separate condition thus would mainly seem to impose an "objective", but wide "outer limit" to filter out instances of abuse (p. 190). But it remains an important clarification.
- In their discussion of arbitrator challenges, Simon Batifort and Chloe Baldwin welcome the ICSID Secretary-General's "recent efforts to clarify the applicable standard" based on an 'appearance' test (p. 776). While this standard reflects some degree of convergence with other arbitral frameworks (notably United Nations Commission on International Trade Law Arbitration Rules (UNCITRAL)), they argue that, despite agreement on "legal jargon", "it remains very difficult in practice to successfully challenge arbitrators in the ICSID system, perhaps more so than in cases conducted under other sets of arbitration rules" (p. 776).

While these are refreshingly clear (and helpful) statements that can be expected to shape the future debate, a significant number of other contributors prefer to hide their colours. Some in fact go to great lengths to present competing readings of a provision—but then opt to leave it at that. Such 'neutrality' deprives the *Commentary* of an important function: where it does not offer views, it will struggle to become a guide to the proper understanding of the ICSID framework. On some core issues, this limitation is a pity. To illustrate, it would have been interesting to learn the contributors' views on pressing questions such as: Can States, by denouncing the ICSID Convention, preclude future proceedings? Can standard MFN provisions, in the absence of explicit clarification, affect the interpretation of dispute settlement clauses? How does the *Achmea* judgment affect investment proceedings? On these and other issues, the *Commentary* informs, dissects, points to decisions, and relays arguments set out by others—but its contributors are careful not to be seen to have a view. Things depend, we learn; there are two prevailing approaches to this issue and three competing views on that question; and much requires a careful case-by-case analysis. Well, of course it does. And of course, especially in a work written with heavy practitioner input, there is room for the occasional argumentative *non liquet*. But a little less sitting on fences would have been beneficial.

Not all provisions governing ICSID proceedings invite grand interpretative argument. Most of them in fact do not; they are technical, sometimes mundane, but crucial to understanding how investment arbitration based on the ICSID Convention works. The *Commentary* is the first to cover, not only the ICSID Convention, but the Regulation, Institution Rules and Arbitration Rules as well. This sets it apart from existing works, notably Christoph Schreuer's pioneering *ICSID Commentary*, subsequently updated and expanded in collaboration with Loretta Malintoppi, August Reinisch and Anthony Sinclair. The editors' decision to include Regulations and Rules reflects the standardisation of ICSID arbitration. As with the Convention itself, the *Commentary* is a reliable compass. Contributors competently set out the meaning of Rules and Regulations, incl. where the task must have been quite thankless. And so, we learn about the life of ICSID and ICSID proceedings in its majestic mundanity: When filing pleadings, parties are required to include the original, plus a number of copies that exceed the number of tribunal members by two—but Rule 23(b) of the Arbitration Rules that says so does not apply to the filing of the original Request for Arbitration, for which Rule 4(1) of the Institution Rules fixes the number at five (see pp. 1072, 971). Notwithstanding her or his official function, a temporary presiding officer at meetings of the Administrative Council can cast a vote for the State that he or she represents (Regulation 4(2)). Regulation 14 and Article 60(1) permit the charging of an increased *per diem* subsistence allowance for work in certain 'high costs cities'; the ICSID Fees Schedule fixes it at \$\$135–185 instead of the regular \$115 (pp. 790, 933). The day on which a time-limit is announced to the parties does not count towards the calculation under Regulation 29 and Rule 26 of the Arbitration Rules: to meet this limit, documents need to be submitted before midnight, while "[i]n certain situations, Tribunals have admitted electronic submissions received by the Secretariat after midnight" (Fautos-Peterson and Umerov, p. 966). And so on and so forth.

No doubt, to distil and present such details in an accessible way stands an avowedly *Practical Commentary* in good stead. Thankfully, though, not everything in the Commentary is practical. Every now and then, readers will stance upon gems of decidedly "unpractical" information. My own selection of such surprise finds includes the following: It took an astonishing 4 years and 4 months to constitute the *Azurix* Tribunal (see Caicedo and Khayat, p. 291); Aron Broches signed the original text of the ICSID Convention (Taylor, p. 909); and finally, the use of Preambles can be traced back the Treaty of Kadesh of 1269 BC (Fouret and Saldanha Pena Costa,

p. 4). For readers who are afraid of drowning in the majestic mundanity of time limits and *per diems,* such bits of 'non-practical' information are lifelines.

"In the beginning was the Word, but soon, it was followed by a Commentary". It has taken quite a while for the Commentary genre to engage with the ICSID Convention. This work is not the first of its kind, but—at least for the time being—the most comprehensive, up-to-date and compact guide to the ICSID arbitration framework: it marks a significant achievement, on which the editors and the publisher are to be congratulated.

Christian J. Tams is Professor of International Law at the University of Glasgow, where he directs the Glasgow Centre for International Law and Security. He is a member of the Board of the European Society of International Law and of the Council of the German Society of International Law. An academic member of Matrix Chambers, he regularly advises States and other international actors on matters of international law, and has acted in cases before the International Court of Justice, the International Tribunal for the Law of the Sea, the Iran-United States Claims Tribunal, and arbitral tribunals.

Printed by Printforce, the Netherlands